1990 EDITION

Sunset

Road Atlas

UNITED STATES · CANADA · MEXICO

W9-AOV-149

Cover photo: Sunderland, Massachusetts, in the Pioneer Valley.
Photographer: Howard Karger/New England Stock Photo.

Cover design: Design Systems Group

Lane Publishing Co. · Menlo Park, California

Contents

4-5   U.S. Interstate Highway Map

6-7   Mileage Chart

8-9   Time & Distance Map

10-11   National Parks & Landmarks

12-13   Canada

14-15   Mexico

16   State Map Legend

17-98   State Maps (see listing)

99   United States Demographics

100   City Demographics

101-162   Vicinity Maps (see listing)

163-192   Index to U.S. Cities (listed alphabetically by state)

State Maps

Alabama 22
Alaska 17
Arizona 20-21
Arkansas 19
California 24-27
Colorado 28-29
Connecticut 30
Delaware 47
Florida 32-33
Georgia 23
Hawaii 18
Idaho 34-35
Illinois 36-37
Indiana 38
Iowa 39
Kansas 40-41
Kentucky 43
Louisiana 44
Maine 45
Maryland 46-47
Massachusetts 30-31
Michigan 48-49
Minnesota 50-51
Mississippi 56
Missouri 52-53
Montana 54-55
Nebraska 58-59
Nevada 60-61
New Hampshire 57
New Jersey 62-63

New Mexico 64-65
New York 66-69
North Carolina 70-71
North Dakota 72-73
Ohio 74-75
Oklahoma 76-77
Oregon 78-79
Pennsylvania 80-81
Rhode Island 31
South Carolina 70-71
South Dakota 82-83
Tennessee 42
Texas 94-98
Utah 84-85
Vermont 57
Virginia 86-87
Washington 88-89
West Virginia 86-87
Wisconsin 90-91
Wyoming 92-93

Vicinity Maps

Atlanta, GA 102-103
Baltimore, MD 101
Birmingham, AL 104
Boston, MA 106-107
Buffalo, NY 105
Chicago, IL 108-111
Cincinnati, OH 112
Cleveland, OH 113
Columbus, OH 116
Dallas, TX 115
Denver, CO 117
Detroit, MI 118-119
Ft. Worth, TX 114
Houston, TX 120-121
Indianapolis, IN 122
Jacksonville, FL 123
Kansas City, MO 124-125
Los Angeles, CA 126-129
Louisville, KY 130
Memphis, TN 131
Miami, FL 132
Milwaukee, WI 133
Minneapolis, MN 134
Nashville, TN 136
New Orleans, LA 137
New York City, NY 138-141
Norfolk, VA 142
Oakland, CA 156
Oklahoma City, OK 143
Omaha, NE 144

Orlando, FL 145
Philadelphia, PA 146-147
Phoenix, AZ 148
Pittsburgh, PA 149
Portland, OR 150
St. Louis, MO 152-153
St. Paul, MN 135
St. Petersburg, FL 160
Salt Lake City, UT 151
San Antonio, TX 154
San Diego, CA 155
San Francisco, CA 157
San Jose, CA 158
Seattle, WA 159
Tampa, FL 160
Tucson, AZ 161
Washington, DC 162

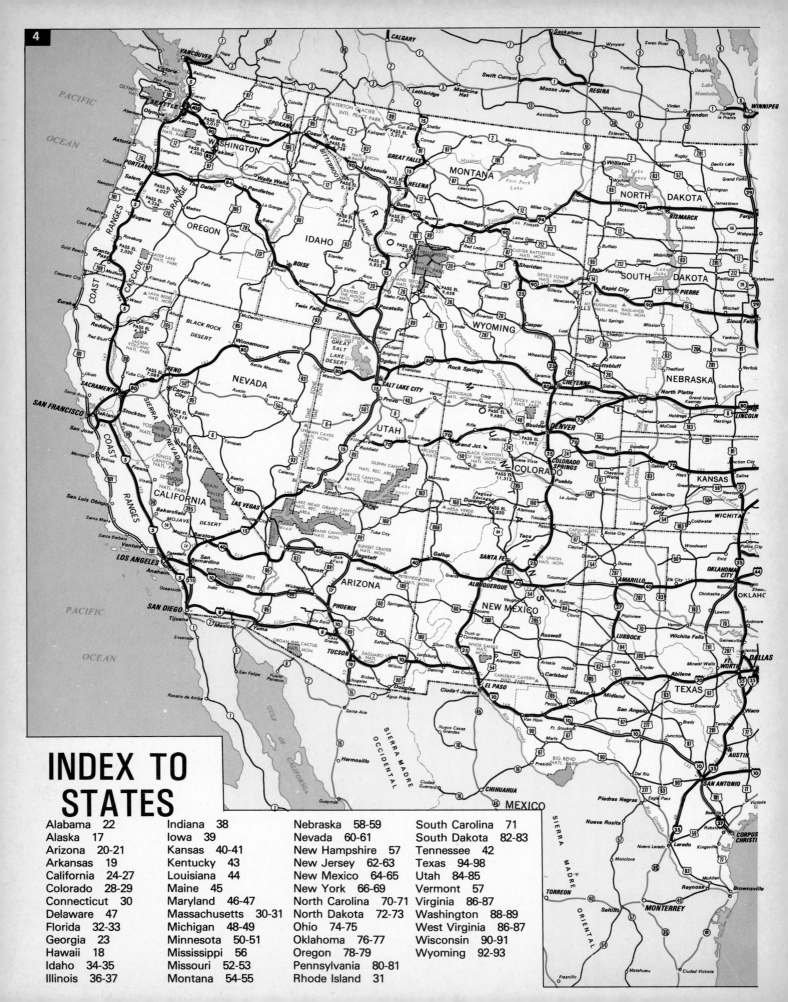

INDEX TO STATES

Alabama 22	Indiana 38	Nebraska 58-59	South Carolina 71
Alaska 17	Iowa 39	Nevada 60-61	South Dakota 82-83
Arizona 20-21	Kansas 40-41	New Hampshire 57	Tennessee 42
Arkansas 19	Kentucky 43	New Jersey 62-63	Texas 94-98
California 24-27	Louisiana 44	New Mexico 64-65	Utah 84-85
Colorado 28-29	Maine 45	New York 66-69	Vermont 57
Connecticut 30	Maryland 46-47	North Carolina 70-71	Virginia 86-87
Delaware 47	Massachusetts 30-31	North Dakota 72-73	Washington 88-89
Florida 32-33	Michigan 48-49	Ohio 74-75	West Virginia 86-87
Georgia 23	Minnesota 50-51	Oklahoma 76-77	Wisconsin 90-91
Hawaii 18	Mississippi 56	Oregon 78-79	Wyoming 92-93
Idaho 34-35	Missouri 52-53	Pennsylvania 80-81	
Illinois 36-37	Montana 54-55	Rhode Island 31	

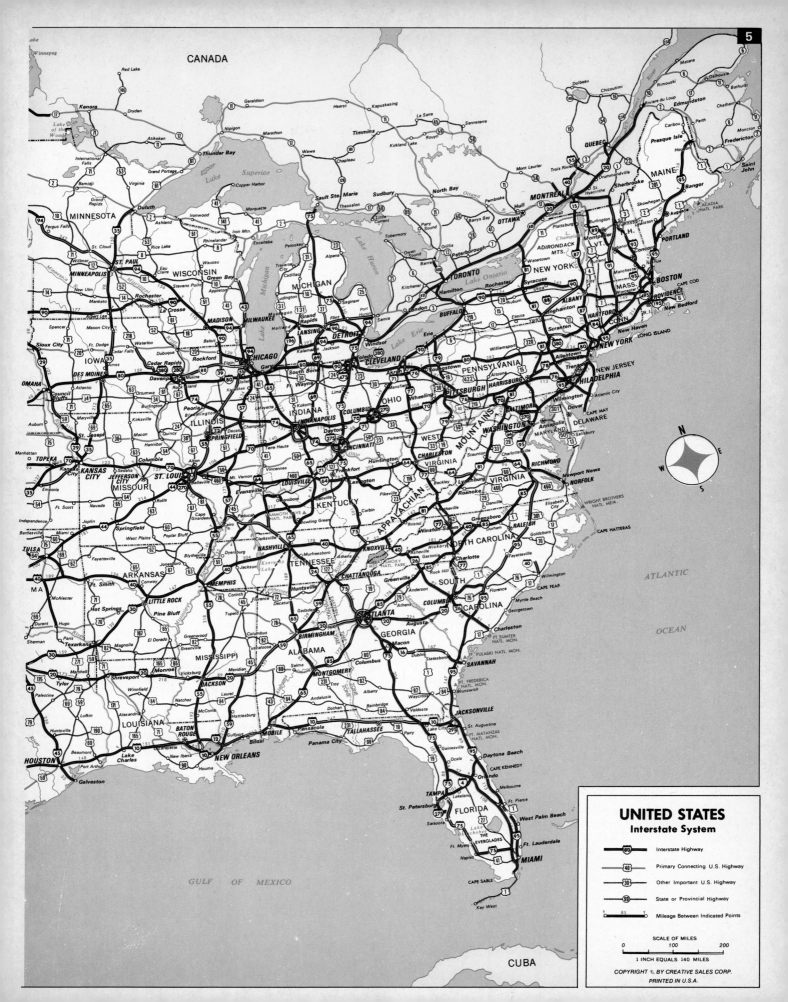

UNITED STATES
Interstate System

━━80━━	Interstate Highway
━━40━━	Primary Connecting U.S. Highway
━━30━━	Other Important U.S. Highway
━━99━━	State or Provincial Highway
85	Mileage Between Indicated Points

SCALE OF MILES

0   100   200

1 INCH EQUALS 140 MILES

Mileage Chart

	Albany, NY	Albuquerque, NM	Amarillo, TX	Atlanta, GA	Austin, TX	Baltimore, MD	Billings, MT	Birmingham, AL	Boise, ID	Boston, MA	Brownsville, TX	Buffalo, NY	Charleston, SC	Charleston, WV	Charlotte, NC	Chicago, IL	Cincinnati, OH	Cleveland, OH	Columbia, SC	Columbus, OH	Dallas, TX	Daytona Beach, FL	Denver, CO	Des Moines, IA	Detroit, MI	El Paso, TX	Fargo, ND	Fort Lauderdale, FL	Fort Wayne, IN	Fort Worth, TX	Grand Rapids, MI	Greensboro, NC	Hartford, CT	Houston, TX	Indianapolis, IN	Jackson, MS	Jacksonville, FL	Kansas City, MO	Knoxville, TN	Las Vegas, NV	Lincoln, NE	Little Rock, AK
Albany, NY	0	2125	1825	1007	1882	332	2073	1112	2601	170	2007	292	932	639	795	795	729	496	823	657	1679	1209	1853	1193	690	2327	1463	1403	705	1682	710	661	106	1825	836	1320	1111	1279	836	2609	1336	1370
Albuquerque, NM	2125	0	300	1387	716	1881	1022	1260	970	2214	988	1801	1695	1583	1628	1346	1394	1606	1598	1468	673	1716	446	1013	1537	267	1314	1953	1410	632	1491	1677	2084	870	1289	1087	1678	811	1407	576	837	883
Amarillo, TX	1825	300	0	1087	485	1581	1037	965	1235	1914	784	1501	1517	1304	1338	1046	1094	1306	1298	1168	363	1467	454	806	1289	508	999	1670	1109	344	1191	1377	1822	608	989	787	1378	552	1107	876	596	607
Atlanta, GA	1007	1387	1087	0	884	669	1804	160	2252	1068	1175	912	300	495	251	695	438	692	211	543	805	446	1401	924	726	1453	1364	681	612	837	749	348	969	816	543	397	329	810	204	1947	1013	540
Austin, TX	1882	716	485	884	0	1550	1449	793	1716	1930	331	1566	1247	1251	1237	1100	1127	1371	1095	1233	203	1158	1009	897	1330	583	1333	1326	1200	192	1288	1281	1867	162	1111	519	1057	680	1051	1297	851	520
Baltimore, MD	332	1881	1581	669	1550	0	1875	804	2416	409	1825	352	567	339	430	697	510	355	513	405	1347	876	1692	997	511	1997	1339	1036	550	1379	624	346	308	1409	584	1006	770	1078	503	2408	1192	1037
Billings, MT	2073	1022	1037	1804	1449	1875	0	1759	586	2232	1771	1857	2222	1762	2027	1214	1479	1662	2075	1654	1395	2173	579	959	1579	1284	625	2466	1405	1406	1396	1958	2169	1739	1400	1743	2227	1078	1723	1060	836	1439
Birmingham, AL	1112	1260	965	160	793	804	1759	0	2101	1267	1065	941	460	539	411	669	468	722	359	584	637	505	1370	838	721	1304	1311	764	610	702	739	493	1058	676	497	251	472	724	255	1822	953	394
Boise, ID	2601	970	1235	2252	1716	2416	586	2101	0	2794	1921	2271	2503	2246	2408	1777	1983	2058	2289	2069	1610	2576	870	1402	2020	1241	1245	2820	1871	1598	1917	2408	2652	1854	1890	2091	2579	1476	2022	662	1205	1781
Boston, MA	170	2214	1914	1068	1930	409	2232	1267	2794	0	2255	454	989	728	828	965	875	632	928	738	1727	1257	1953	1305	795	2376	1623	1492	847	1761	908	739	105	1878	933	1395	1167	1435	871	2765	1500	1472
Brownsville, TX	2007	988	784	1175	331	1825	1909	1065	1921	2255	0	1865	1500	1479	1426	1430	1426	1670	1360	1533	526	1353	1251	1184	1694	806	1601	1542	1455	518	1585	1480	2094	357	1427	791	1264	1008	1320	1573	1216	819
Buffalo, NY	292	1801	1501	912	1566	352	1857	941	2271	454	1865	0	947	430	666	543	438	195	822	333	1363	1069	1602	867	366	2011	1185	1400	381	1395	419	641	397	1492	512	1119	1068	1007	671	2254	1057	1046
Charleston, SC	932	1695	1517	300	1247	567	2222	460	2503	989	1500	947	0	479	203	912	628	750	113	670	1164	351	1743	1185	874	1729	1557	586	740	1116	959	271	867	1027	743	702	248	1135	368	2247	1287	814
Charleston, WV	639	1583	1304	495	1251	339	1762	539	2246	728	1479	430	479	0	276	469	178	284	376	156	1134	726	1377	761	371	1672	1126	1004	284	1056	457	227	662	1246	328	790	676	777	284	2119	960	707
Charlotte, NC	795	1628	1338	251	1237	430	2027	411	2408	828	1426	666	203	276	0	738	446	543	100	453	1054	469	1548	1029	607	1710	1414	721	602	1061	791	89	763	1053	551	640	413	940	219	2173	1151	743
Chicago, IL	795	1346	1046	695	1100	697	1214	669	1777	965	1430	543	912	469	738	0	291	348	794	340	932	1096	1037	357	284	1435	649	1348	159	945	178	729	875	1160	186	762	999	543	537	1749	527	675
Cincinnati, OH	729	1394	1094	438	1127	510	1479	468	1983	875	1426	438	628	178	446	291	0	249	502	105	924	861	1199	583	260	1472	940	1086	184	956	357	458	746	1053	105	680	786	591	246	1921	715	608
Cleveland, OH	496	1606	1306	692	1371	355	1662	722	2058	632	1670	195	750	284	543	348	249	0	627	138	1168	952	1407	672	171	1716	997	1232	211	1200	284	486	539	1297	317	924	908	803	489	2059	867	851
Columbia, SC	823	1598	1298	211	1095	513	2075	359	2289	928	1360	822	113	376	100	794	502	627	0	513	1032	381	1616	1126	745	1668	1446	622	671	1057	858	188	836	1066	625	610	290	1025	267	2162	1199	759
Columbus, OH	657	1469	1168	543	1233	405	1654	584	2069	738	1533	333	670	156	453	340	105	138	513	0	1030	901	1270	657	195	1540	989	1126	150	1062	311	381	641	1159	179	786	850	665	351	1995	776	713
Dallas, TX	1679	673	363	805	203	1347	1395	637	1610	1727	526	1363	1164	1134	1054	932	924	1168	1032	1030	0	1123	806	714	1203	648	1131	1097	1030	33	1110	1122	1664	243	908	422	1005	511	820	1249	648	317
Daytona Beach, FL	1209	1716	1467	446	1158	876	2173	505	2576	1257	1353	1069	351	726	469	1096	883	952	381	901	1123	0	1823	1329	1103	1728	1714	227	1006	1126	1143	551	1138	952	880	688	97	1209	603	2316	1401	904
Denver, CO	1853	446	454	1401	1009	1692	579	1370	870	1953	1251	1602	1743	1377	1548	1037	1199	1407	1616	1270	806	1823	0	695	1321	705	915	2067	1186	773	1201	1621	1988	1060	1091	1246	1779	608	1341	743	507	992
Des Moines, IA	1193	1013	806	924	897	997	959	838	1402	1305	1184	867	1185	761	1029	357	583	672	1126	657	714	1329	695	0	600	1114	475	1581	516	747	502	1028	1283	930	478	846	1270	203	821	1399	203	562
Detroit, MI	690	1537	1289	726	1330	511	1579	721	2020	795	1694	366	874	371	607	284	260	171	745	195	1203	1103	1321	600	0	1701	922	1346	170	1240	162	567	701	1304	293	923	1046	791	506	2011	819	850
El Paso, TX	2327	267	508	1453	583	1997	1274	1304	1241	2376	806	2011	1729	1672	1710	1435	1372	1716	1668	1540	648	1728	705	1114	1701	0	1460	1869	1573	609	1554	1783	2263	743	1460	1070	1626	915	1488	722	946	960
Fargo, ND	1463	1314	999	1364	1333	1339	625	1311	1245	1625	1601	1185	1557	1126	1414	649	940	997	1446	989	1131	1714	915	475	922	1460	0	2007	808	1072	827	1412	1531	1334	835	1335	1704	609	1195	1535	451	1091
Fort Lauderdale, FL	1435	1953	1670	681	1326	1036	2466	764	2820	1492	1542	1400	586	1004	721	1348	1086	1232	622	1126	1097	227	2067	1581	1346	1869	2007	0	1271	1129	1342	786	1403	1191	1232	883	332	1459	860	2530	1670	1184
Fort Wayne, IN	705	1410	1109	612	1200	550	1405	610	1871	847	1455	381	740	284	602	159	184	219	671	150	1030	1006	1186	516	170	1573	808	1271	0	1053	172	551	768	1176	122	784	929	648	430	1878	686	711
Fort Worth, TX	1682	632	344	837	192	1379	1406	702	1598	1761	518	1395	1116	1056	1061	945	956	1200	1057	1062	33	1126	773	747	1236	609	1072	1129	1053	0	1121	1154	1696	264	912	446	1037	513	853	1203	648	349
Grand Rapids, MI	710	1491	1191	749	1288	624	1396	739	1917	908	1585	419	959	457	791	178	357	284	858	311	1110	1143	1201	502	162	1554	827	1342	172	1121	0	707	794	1196	263	957	1071	638	573	1889	699	799
Greensboro, NC	661	1677	1377	348	1281	346	1958	493	2408	739	1480	641	271	227	89	729	458	486	188	381	1122	551	1621	1028	567	1783	1412	786	551	1154	707	0	650	1167	563	770	483	1013	283	2237	1202	778
Hartford	106	2084	1822	969	1867	308	2169	1058	2652	105	2044	397	867	662	763	875	746	339	836	641	1664	1138	1988	1283	701	2263	1531	1403	768	1696	794	650	0	1773	805	1306	1071	1297	841	2675	1378	1344
Houston, TX	1825	870	608	816	162	1409	1639	676	1854	1878	357	1492	1027	1246	1053	1160	1053	1297	1066	1159	243	952	1060	930	1304	743	1334	1191	1176	264	1196	1167	1773	0	1041	406	891	754	922	1468	892	446
Indianapolis, IN	836	1289	989	543	1111	584	1400	497	1890	933	1427	512	743	328	551	186	105	317	625	179	908	980	1091	478	293	1460	835	1232	122	912	263	563	805	1041	0	681	867	486	351	1816	673	608
Jackson, MS	1320	1087	787	397	519	1006	1743	251	2091	1395	991	1119	702	790	640	762	680	924	610	786	422	688	1246	846	923	1070	1335	883	784	446	957	770	1306	406	681	0	591	716	506	1650	874	251
Jacksonville, FL	1111	1678	1378	329	1057	770	2227	472	2579	1167	1264	1068	248	676	413	999	786	908	290	850	1005	97	1779	1270	1046	1626	1704	332	929	1037	1071	483	1071	891	867	591	0	1110	555	2238	1321	843
Kansas City, MO	1279	811	552	810	680	1078	1078	724	1476	1435	1008	1007	1135	777	940	543	591	803	1025	665	511	1209	608	203	791	916	609	1459	648	513	638	1013	1297	754	486	716	1110	0	752	1345	211	409
Knoxville, TN	836	1407	1107	204	1051	503	1723	255	2022	871	1320	671	368	284	219	537	246	489	267	351	820	603	1341	821	506	1488	1195	860	430	872	573	283	841	922	351	506	555	752	0	1983	944	523
Las Vegas, NV	2609	576	876	1947	1297	2408	1060	1822	662	2765	1573	2254	2247	2119	2173	1749	1921	2059	2162	1995	1249	2316	743	1399	2011	722	1535	2530	1878	1203	1889	2237	2675	1468	1816	1650	2238	1345	1983	0	1224	1483
Lincoln, NE	1386	837	596	1013	851	1192	836	953	1205	1500	1216	1057	1287	960	1151	527	802	867	1199	776	648	1401	507	203	819	946	451	1670	686	648	699	1202	1378	892	673	874	1321	211	944	1224	0	616
Little Rock, AK	1370	883	607	540	520	1207	1439	394	1781	1472	819	1046	814	707	743	675	608	851	759	713	317	904	992	562	850	960	1091	1184	711	349	799	778	1344	446	608	251	843	409	523	1483	616	0
Los Angeles, CA	2911	823	1095	2197	1410	2676	1254	2067	837	2993	1678	2587	2521	2394	2617	1989	2164	2392	2426	2254	1401	2407	1009	1654	2270	818	1844	2704	2137	1361	2148	2478	2829	1581	2075	1880	2402	1589	2201	275	1476	1678
Louisville, KY	868	1332	1041	421	1022	608	1550	373	1908	976	1321	543	608	258	438	300	105	349	494	211	819	801	1127	591	365	1467	949	1078	222	851	373	462	867	948	129	575	729	519	246	1861	730	502
Memphis, TN	1232	1021	721	397	658	900	1557	239	1833	1379	957	908	689	653	604	551	469	713	612	575	455	749	1151	599	712	1103	1224	989	592	487	690	640	1209	584	470	211	697	470	385	1581	647	138
Miami, FL	1439	1994	1694	665	1338	1095	2710	788	2860	1516	1580	1524	630	1046	745	1338	1086	1264	658	1210	1321	259	2131	1582	1386	1958	1986	24	1326	1353	1356	810	1427	1207	1208	907	356	1475	859	2570	1673	1208
Milwaukee, WI	933	1443	1143	784	1203	794	1143	766	1777	1078	1530	640	1032	566	835	92	388	445	891	448	1013	1180	1070	365	389	1528	576	1443	256	1059	275	826	948	1155	283	884	1067	568	643	1752	560	772
Minneapolis, MN	1215	1256	1062	1105	1120	1105	812	1088	1488	1362	1456	948	1316	874	1143	405	696	753	1276	753	1013	1458	956	251	698	1520	244	1723	564	1001	583	1135	1257	1266	591	1123	1376	459	932	1630	409	881
Mobile, AL	1322	1265	965	340	656	990	1854	269	2343	1379	851	1184	607	825	575	908	745	989	555	834	592	502	1372	954	988	1236	1413	705	839	624	1006	681	1290	478	749	178	413	819	449	1841	1039	430
Montgomery, AL	1178	1345	1042	164	804	833	1836	93	2346	1232	1041	1076	464	632	405	762	561	815	379	707	677	458	1412	1311	814	1325	1521	671	686	701	819	512	1133	709	590	255	379	867	348	2015	975	470
Nashville, TN	993	1232	932	243	869	688	1640	195	2059	1062	1168	722	576	458	399	474	283	527	458	389	666	639	1167	712	536	1314	1136	900	385	698	534	429	973	795	302	422	592	590	174	1792	770	349
New Orleans, LA	1453	1187	875	493	535	1136	1820	352	2191	1526	730	1273	727	891	721	925	820	1078	701	940	530	632	1323	978	1077	1127	1494	843	916	519	1071	810	1436	367	857	193	551	857	607	1800	1114	430
New York City, NY	146	1995	1695	855	1728	201	1926	1019	2571	203	2002	390	786	524	625	794	628	446	715	551	1525	1054	1775	1070	620	2173	1450	1289	691	1557	706	561	101	1679	730	1192	957	1192	771	2520	1274	1235
Norfolk, VA	505	1905	1632	551	1403	237	2098	711	2551	660	1735	569	454	369	341	851	681	493	412	559	1359	702	1800	1202	711	1998	1581	964	709	1382	802	227	471	1362	669	948	632	1179	412	2534	1354	1025
Oakland, CA	2982	1134	1430	2488	1786	2864	1218	2321	671	3124	2034	2745	2788	2600	2755	2098	2317	2498	2703	2391	1803	2831	1223	1742	2350	1194	1870	3041	2257	1723	2308	2809	2909	1957	2212	2270	2771	1799	2509	582	1604	1984
Oklahoma City, OK	1523	559	267	863	414	1322	1168	701	1451	1659	680	1242	1176	1031	1069	804	835	1047	1091	909	211	1257	660	576	1030	708	989	1481	852	210	932	1118	1546	454	730	575	1181	373	847	1119	433	324
Omaha, NE	1308	905	754	989	847	1143	904	904	1274	1443	1249	1005	1303	899	1135	464	721	824	1283	795	693	1402	559	146	726	1256	464	1604	634	634	640	1208	1321	949	616	914	1305	195	930	1249	57	690
Orlando, FL	1249	1751	1451	446	1142	917	2277	545	2695	1297	2034	1306	401	814	559	1127	892	1046	440	997	1078	81	1896	1363	1143	1735	1826	208	1059	1110	1188	648	1208	964	989	697	138	1266	665	2311	1452	965
Philadelphia, PA	251	1922	1622	766	1630	97	2051	880	2488	327	1954	397	688	517	522	757	559	430	627	460	1427	914	1762	998	585	2075	1370	1127	604	1459	672	438	220	1581	624	1094	859	1134	646	2449	1260	1110
Phoenix, AZ	2512	446	746	1810	1030	2311	1220	1700	1022	2644	1289	2269	2222	2045	2061	1776	1808	2045	2025	1907	1013	2101	802	1497	2019	438	1791	2244	1831	983	1906	2099	2523	1110	1719	1500	2100	1277	1845	284	1236	1379
Pittsburgh, PA	471	1654	1354	712	1412	245	1681	778	2203	584	1713	219	778	211	504	470	291	128	572	186	1209	859	1475	770	304	1833	1112	1216	336	1241	397	438	486	1345	349	965	882	851	515	2181	965	899
Portland, Or	2869	1378	1636	2763	2059	2765	867	2571	439	3149	2468	2677	2952	2615	2757	2140	2474	2416	2972	2478	2051	3018	1283	1816	2368	1661	1484	3204	2299	2003	2251	2823	2877	2369	2335	2518	3042	1809	2550	991	1641	2270
Providence, RI	178	2156	1856	1027	1898	356	2238	1189	2701	41	2222	454	956	699	785	924	790	600	888	713	1695	1201	1961	1256	746	2335	1566	1459	799	1727	859	706	73	1849	892	1362	1127	1378	935	2683	1451	1395
Raleigh, NC	656	1759	1459	397	1355	324	2273	557	2560	713	1506	721	300	297	162	802	540	559	215	453	1152	559	1694	1123	643	1800	1485	794	603	1184	754	73	624	1233	635	815	486	1086	356	2319	1263	851
Reno, NV	2763	1056	1345	2411	1775	2562	1021	2363	404	2871	2068	2433	2765	2407	2570	1897	2221	2238	2626	2295	1731	2758	1030	1606	2190	1183	1660	3008	2056	1608	2067	2591	2749	1932	2116	2143	2716	1606	2363	478	1411	1986
Richmond, VA	482	1833	1533	527	1463	155	1655	699	2594	544	1646	552	462	251	280	341	356	583	390	498	1313	713	1904	1293	609	2023	1481	946	635	1333	722	191	455	2291	907	946	693	1205	440	2406	1249	963
Rochester,NY	219	1857	1557	1015	1623	300	1922	965	2352	381	1891	81	871	495	689	608	502	268	789	397	1420	1176	1637	932	424	2036	1249	1410	464	1452	499	600	324	1555	551	1183	1102	1062	710	2371	1135	1111
Saint Louis, MO	1028	1054	754	588	806	827	1381	539	1727	1184	1216	747	884	544	689	292	340	552	737	414	641	956	859	377	585	1238	872	1208	369	698	437	762	1030	835	251	495	859	251	497	1581	462	422
Saint Paul, MN	1215	1362	1062	1105	1120	1095	812	1118	1398	892	1565	948	1316	870	1143	405	696	753	1320	745	1013	1458	956	251	698	1541	244	1753	564	987	583	1138	1257	1266	591	1160	1376	459	951	1630	408	881
Salt Lake City, UT	2290	621	1324	1900	1341	2051	579	1825	349	2417	1775	1922	2254	1896	2059	1386	1710	1727	2115	1711	1287	2283	519	1085	1679	892	1172	2578	1527	1184	1556	2059	2238	1460	1605	1742	2286	1095	1766	413	900	1054
San Antonio, TX	1986	684	530	965	81	1646	1600	895	1709	2052	300	1638	1371	1419	1272	1208	1208	1443	1180	1305	284	1175	975	1022	1500	576	1402	1378	1269	283	1353	1321	1965	203	1200	649	1086	795	1150	1273	916	592
San Diego, CA	2855	787	1078	2174	1313	2714	1309	2034	1010	2992	1574	2613	2505	2402	2423	2335	2193	2334	2389	2277	1369	2418	1054	1760	2419	721	1934	2621	2189	1332	2269	2457	2944	1484	2067	1783	2329	1627	2269	349	1573	1743
San Francisco, CA	2966	1135	1396	2511	1776	2765	1239	2371	595	3133	2044	2403	2923	2616	2756	2108	2329	2408	2738	2461	1865	2827	1233	1832	2360	1184	1886	3073	2304	1735	2318	2740	3019	1947	2224	2183	2781	1869	2549	592	1614	1994
Seattle, WA	2855	1500	1805	2656	2157	2685	815	2475	524	2961	2521	2531	2960	2748	2765	2043	2334	2336	2971	2408	2203	3070	1371	1889	2299	1775	1440	3882	2202	2071	2221	2773	2918	2498	2229	2585	3090	1884	2553	1209	1636	2320
Shreveport, LA	1599	868	568	624	340	1229	1691	474	1912	1618	644	1265	945	899	885	916	826	1070	833	592	196	903	1112	827	1069	844	1229	1144	909	228	1018	937	1519	271	827	223	814	624	729	1468	727	219
Spokane, WA	2652	1346	1563	2367	1981	2417	541	2469	369	2693	2359	2263	2700	2503	2505	1775	2066	2068	2572	2115	1978	2811	1095	1556	2020	1686	1166	3014	1921	1978	1941	2503	2650	2222	1961	2205	2822	1727	2298	1119	1460	2092
Tallahassee, FL	1249	1508	1208	268	899	932	2306	302	2512	1312	1094	1155	364	868	559	957	706	949	408	828	835	259	1727	1216	957	1492	1598	462	871	867	1022	608	1223	721	818	421	170	1045	584	2068	1227	679
Tampa, FL	1281	1759	1459	476	1150	949	2143	553	2763	1329	1345	1346	479	903	584	1143	908	1091	497	1013	1086	141	1858	1460	1200	1743	1849	268	1092	1118	1219	673	1240	972	1069	672	195	1296	730	2319	1477	958
Toledo, OH	633	1526	1220	641	1315	454	1557	673	2020	742	1622	309	973	284	533	243	203	114	683	138	1112	1063	1272	567	65	1699	885	1289	105	1144	170	516	624	1249	243	876	989	717	449	1954	762	803
Tuscon, AZ	2442	486	656	1785	908	2246	1342	1621	1144	2571	1176	2166	2100	2039	1913	1711	1750	1971	2080	1833	964	1999	835	1484	1938	316	1897	2271	1783	932	1856	2059	2433	1079	1668	1378	2010	1281	1755	389	1246	1257
Tulsa, OK	1409	674	336	803	462	1208	1293	636	2020	1532	835	1128	1103	941	989	673	721	933	1018	795	259	1156	714	471	916	788	972	1409	738	305	818	1037	1411	504	616	510	1167	283	782	1224	416	259
Washington, DC	378	1864	1564	630	1509	41	2006	781	2441	430	1787	429	559	299	334	697	478	341	498	418	1306	802	1654	1054	506	1954	1322	1062	531	1338	608	309	341	1220	551	965	730	1046	554	2376	1184	832
West Palm Beach, FL	1396	1938	1638	632	1329	1046	2736	702	2942	1426	1524	1443	568	982	673	1289	1063	1192	586	1146	1265	195	2157	1646	1305	1922	2028	41	1157	1297	1476	737	1339	1151	1176	851	284	1052	806	2498	1598	1101
Youngstown, OH	462	1632	1346	719	1368	298	1632	738	2090	568	1695	190	709	251	502	413	275	74	561	170	1193	986	1421	737	239	1804	1038	1219	275	1225	340	482	470	1322	341	949	958	843	521	2124	923	876

	Los Angeles, CA	Louisville, KY	Memphis, TN	Miami, FL	Milwaukee, WI	Minneapolis, MN	Mobile, AL	Montgomery, AL	Nashville, TN	New Orleans, LA	New York City NY	Norfolk, VA	Oakland, CA	Oklahoma City, OK	Omaha, NE	Orlando, FL	Philadelphia, PA	Phoenix, AZ	Pittsburgh, PA	Portland, OR	Providence, RI	Raleigh, NC	Reno, NV	Richmond, VA	Rochester, NY	Saint Louis, MO	Saint Paul, MN	Salt Lake City, UT	San Antonio, TX	San Diego, CA	San Francisco, CA	Seattle, WA	Shreveport, LA	Spokane, WA	Tallahassee, FL	Tampa, FL	Toledo, OH	Tucson, AZ	Tulsa, OK	Washington, DC	West Palm Beach, FL	Youngstown, OH
Albany, NY	2911	868	1232	1439	933	1215	1322	1178	993	1453	146	505	2982	1523	1308	1249	251	2512	471	2869	178	656	2763	482	219	1028	1215	2290	1986	2855	2966	2855	1599	2652	1249	1281	633	2442	1409	378	1396	462
Albuquerque, NM	823	1332	1021	1994	1443	1256	1265	1345	1232	1187	1995	1905	1134	559	905	1751	1922	446	1654	1378	2156	1759	1056	1833	1857	1054	1362	621	684	787	1135	1500	868	1346	1508	1759	1526	486	674	1864	1938	1646
Amarillo, TX	1095	1041	721	1694	1143	1062	965	1045	932	875	1695	1632	1430	267	754	1451	1622	746	1354	1636	1856	1458	1345	1533	1557	754	1062	917	530	1078	1396	1805	568	1563	1208	1459	1220	656	336	1564	1638	1346
Atlanta, GA	2197	421	397	665	784	1105	340	164	243	493	855	551	2488	863	989	446	766	1810	712	2763	1027	397	2411	527	1015	588	1105	1900	965	2174	2511	2656	624	2367	268	476	641	1785	803	630	632	719
Austin, TX	1410	1022	658	1338	1203	1120	656	804	869	535	1728	1403	1786	414	847	1142	1630	1030	1412	2059	1898	1355	1775	1463	1623	806	1120	1341	81	1313	1776	2157	340	1981	899	1150	1315	908	462	1509	1329	1368
Baltimore, MD	2676	608	900	1095	794	1105	990	833	688	1136	201	237	2864	1322	1143	917	97	2311	245	2765	356	324	2562	155	300	827	1095	2051	1646	2714	2765	2686	1229	2417	932	949	454	2246	1208	41	1046	298
Billings, MT	1254	1550	1557	2710	1143	812	1854	1836	1640	1820	1926	2098	1218	1168	904	2277	2051	1220	1681	867	2238	2273	1021	1655	1922	1381	812	579	1600	1309	1239	815	1691	541	2306	2143	1557	1342	1293	2006	2736	1632
Birmingham, AL	2067	373	239	788	766	1088	269	93	195	352	1019	711	2321	701	904	545	880	1700	778	2571	1189	557	2363	699	965	539	1118	1825	895	2034	2371	2475	474	2469	302	553	673	1621	636	781	702	738
Boise, ID	837	1908	1833	2860	1777	1488	2143	2346	2059	2191	2571	2551	671	1451	1274	2695	2498	1022	2203	439	2701	2560	404	2594	2352	1727	1398	349	1709	1010	595	524	1912	369	2512	2763	2020	1144	1582	2441	2492	2090
Boston, MA	2993	976	1379	1516	1078	1362	1379	1232	1062	1525	203	560	3124	1659	1443	1297	327	2644	584	3149	41	713	2871	544	381	1184	892	2417	2052	2992	3133	2961	1618	2693	1312	1329	742	2571	1532	430	1426	568
Brownsville, TX	1678	1321	957	1580	1530	1456	851	1041	1168	730	2002	1735	2034	680	1249	2034	1954	1289	1713	2468	2222	1506	2068	1646	1891	1216	1565	1609	300	1574	2044	2521	644	2359	1094	1345	1622	1176	835	1787	1524	1695
Buffalo, NY	2587	543	908	1424	640	948	1184	1076	722	1273	390	569	2745	1242	1005	1306	397	2269	219	2677	454	721	2433	552	81	747	948	1922	1638	2613	2667	2531	1265	2263	1155	1346	309	2166	1128	429	1443	190
Charleston, SC	2521	608	689	630	1032	1316	607	464	576	727	787	454	2788	1176	1303	401	688	2222	778	2952	956	300	2765	462	871	884	1316	2254	1371	2505	2923	2960	945	2700	364	479	973	2100	1103	559	568	709
Charleston, WV	2394	258	653	1046	566	874	825	632	458	891	524	369	2600	1031	899	814	517	2045	211	2615	699	297	2407	251	495	544	870	1896	1419	2402	2616	2748	899	2503	868	903	284	2039	941	299	982	251
Charlotte, NC	2417	438	592	604	835	1143	575	415	399	721	625	341	2755	1069	1135	559	522	2061	504	2757	785	162	2570	280	689	689	1143	2059	1272	2423	2756	2765	885	2505	559	584	583	1913	989	334	673	502
Chicago, IL	1989	300	551	1338	92	405	908	762	474	925	794	851	2098	804	454	1127	757	1776	470	2140	924	802	1897	341	608	292	405	1386	1208	2306	2108	2043	916	1775	957	1143	243	1711	673	697	1289	413
Cincinnati, OH	2164	105	469	1086	388	696	712	561	283	810	628	601	2317	835	721	892	559	1808	291	2369	790	540	2201	503	502	340	696	1671	1208	2193	2329	2334	813	2066	706	908	203	1756	721	478	1051	275
Cleveland, OH	2392	349	713	1264	445	753	989	815	527	1078	446	493	2498	1047	824	1046	430	2045	128	2416	600	559	2238	583	268	552	753	1727	1443	2384	2408	2336	1070	2068	949	1091	114	1971	933	341	1192	74
Columbia, SC	2426	494	612	658	891	1276	555	379	458	701	715	412	2703	1091	1283	440	627	2025	572	2972	888	215	2626	390	789	737	1320	2115	1180	2389	2738	2971	833	2572	408	497	683	2080	1018	498	586	561
Columbus, OH	2254	211	575	1210	448	753	834	707	389	940	551	559	2391	909	795	997	460	1907	186	2478	713	453	2295	498	397	414	745	1711	1305	2277	2461	2408	592	2115	828	1513	138	1833	795	418	1146	170
Dallas, TX	1401	819	455	1321	1013	1013	592	677	666	530	1525	1359	1803	211	693	1078	1427	1013	1209	2059	1695	1152	1731	1313	1420	641	1013	1287	284	1369	1865	2203	196	1978	835	1086	1112	964	259	1306	1265	1193
Daytona Beach, FL	2407	801	749	259	1180	1458	502	458	639	632	1054	702	2831	1257	1402	81	914	2102	859	3018	1201	559	2758	713	1176	956	1458	2283	1175	2418	2827	3070	903	2811	259	141	1063	1999	1156	802	195	986
Denver, CO	1009	1127	1151	2131	1070	956	1372	1412	1167	1323	1775	1800	1223	660	559	1896	1762	802	1475	1283	1961	1694	1030	1904	1637	859	956	519	975	1054	1233	1371	1112	1095	1727	1858	1272	835	714	1654	2157	1421
Des Moines, IA	1654	591	599	1582	365	251	954	1131	712	978	1070	1202	1742	576	146	1363	1037	1479	770	1816	1256	1123	1606	1293	932	377	251	1085	1022	1760	1832	1889	827	1556	1216	1460	567	1484	471	1054	1646	737
Detroit, MI	2270	365	712	1386	389	698	988	814	536	1077	620	711	2350	1030	726	1143	585	2019	304	2368	746	643	2190	609	424	535	698	1679	1500	2419	2360	2299	1069	2020	957	1200	65	1938	916	506	1305	239
El Paso, TX	818	1467	1103	1958	1528	1520	1236	1325	1314	1127	2173	1998	1194	708	1256	1735	2073	438	1833	1661	2335	1800	1185	2023	2036	1238	1541	894	576	721	1184	1775	844	1686	1492	1743	1699	316	788	1954	1922	1804
Fargo, ND	1844	949	1224	1987	576	244	1413	1525	1138	1521	1450	1581	1870	989	464	1826	1370	1791	1112	1484	1566	1485	1660	1481	1249	872	244	1172	1402	1934	1886	1440	1229	1166	1598	1849	885	1897	972	1322	2028	1038
Fort Lauderdale	2704	1078	989	24	1443	1723	705	671	900	843	1289	964	3041	1481	1604	208	1127	2244	1216	3204	1459	794	3008	946	1410	1208	1753	2578	1378	2621	3073	3382	1144	3014	462	268	1289	2271	1409	1062	41	1219
Fort Wayne, IN	2137	222	592	1326	256	564	839	686	385	916	691	709	2257	852	634	1059	604	1831	336	2299	799	603	2056	635	464	369	564	1527	1269	2189	2304	2202	909	1921	871	1092	105	1783	738	531	1157	275
Fort Worth, TX	1361	851	487	1353	1059	1001	624	701	698	519	1557	1382	1723	210	634	1110	1459	983	1241	2003	1727	1184	1608	1333	1452	698	987	1184	283	1332	1735	2071	228	1978	867	1118	1144	932	305	1338	1297	1225
Grand Rapids, MI	2148	373	690	1356	275	583	1006	819	534	1071	706	802	2308	932	640	1188	672	1906	397	2251	859	754	2067	722	499	437	583	1556	1353	2269	2318	2221	1018	1941	1022	1219	170	1856	818	608	1476	340
Greensboro, NC	2478	462	640	810	826	1135	681	512	429	810	561	227	2809	1118	1208	648	438	2099	438	2823	706	73	2591	191	600	762	1138	2059	1321	2457	2740	2773	937	2503	608	673	516	2059	1037	309	737	482
Hartford, CT	2829	867	1209	1427	948	1257	1290	1133	973	1436	101	471	2909	1546	1321	1208	220	2523	486	2877	73	624	2749	455	324	1030	1257	2238	1965	2944	3019	2918	1529	2656	1223	1240	624	2433	1411	341	1339	470
Houston, TX	1581	948	584	1207	1155	1266	478	709	795	367	1679	1362	1957	454	949	964	1581	1110	1345	2369	1849	1233	1932	2291	1555	835	1266	1460	203	1484	1947	2498	271	2222	721	972	1249	1079	504	1420	1151	1322
Indianapolis, IN	2075	129	470	1208	283	591	749	590	302	857	730	669	2212	730	616	989	624	1719	349	2335	892	635	2116	907	551	251	591	1605	1200	2067	2224	2229	827	1961	818	1069	223	668	616	551	1176	341
Jackson, MS	1880	575	211	907	884	1123	178	255	422	193	1192	948	2270	575	914	697	1094	1500	965	2518	1362	815	2143	946	1183	495	1160	1742	649	1783	2183	2585	223	2205	421	672	876	1378	510	965	851	949
Jacksonville, FL	2402	729	697	356	1067	1374	413	379	592	551	957	632	2771	1181	1305	138	859	2100	882	3030	1127	584	2716	693	1102	867	1374	2286	1086	2329	2781	3042	814	2822	170	195	989	2010	1167	730	284	958
Kansas City, MO	1589	519	470	1475	568	459	819	867	590	857	1192	1179	1799	373	195	1266	1134	1277	851	1809	1378	1086	1606	1205	1062	251	459	1095	795	1627	1809	1834	624	1727	1045	1296	717	1281	283	1052	1440	794
Knoxville, TN	2201	246	385	859	643	932	449	348	174	607	753	412	2509	847	930	665	646	1845	515	2550	951	356	2363	440	710	497	935	1766	1150	2269	2549	2553	729	2298	584	730	449	1755	782	554	806	521
Las Vegas, NV	275	1861	1581	2570	1752	1630	1841	2015	1792	1800	2520	2534	582	1119	1249	2311	2449	284	2181	991	2683	2319	478	2406	2371	1581	1630	413	1273	349	592	1209	1468	1119	2068	2319	1954	389	1224	2376	2498	2124
Lincoln, NE	1476	730	647	1673	560	409	1039	975	770	1014	1274	1354	1604	433	57	1452	1260	1236	965	1641	1451	1263	1411	1249	1135	462	408	900	916	1573	1614	1636	727	1460	1227	1477	762	1246	416	1184	1598	923
Little Rock	1678	502	138	1208	772	881	430	470	349	430	1235	1025	1984	324	690	965	1110	1379	899	2270	1395	851	1986	963	1111	422	881	1054	592	1743	1994	2368	219	2092	679	958	803	1257	259	832	1101	876
Los Angeles, CA	0	2136	1816	2828	2238	1905	2013	2035	2027	1883	2790	2809	372	1354	1508	2585	2717	389	2449	989	2902	2554	511	2641	2400	1849	1905	672	1378	121	382	1159	1687	1406	2342	2578	2213	502	1459	2659	2772	2424
Louisville, KY	2136	0	364	1102	397	705	626	466	178	729	707	607	2333	738	671	907	664	1782	381	2298	421	525	2132	686	608	290	705	1638	1103	2119	2388	2320	721	2075	664	915	300	1697	633	533	1094	373
Memphis, TN	1816	364	0	1013	673	949	389	332	211	397	1095	876	2122	462	705	770	989	2948	795	2408	1257	712	2124	825	973	300	949	1613	730	1881	2129	2506	357	2230	527	778	665	1370	397	363	957	738
Miami, FL	2828	1102	1013	0	1435	1743	729	695	908	867	1313	988	3087	1524	1670	227	1215	2448	1248	3366	1483	818	3032	988	1435	1231	1743	2602	1402	2645	3097	3406	1130	3138	486	292	1293	2326	1483	1086	65	1264
Milwaukee, WI	2238	397	673	1435	0	332	981	859	571	1045	851	948	2171	884	503	1224	834	1873	567	2002	1021	899	1930	832	697	389	332	1419	1305	2109	2175	1970	1013	1702	1053	1240	332	1808	770	770	1386	510
Minneapolis, MN	1905	705	949	1743	332	0	1227	1281	892	1346	1160	1337	2065	803	381	1673	1126	1848	868	1670	1322	1241	1776	1237	1005	628	1	1475	1265	1975	2075	1638	985	1370	1354	1589	641	1702	705	1078	1737	794
Mobile, AL	2013	626	389	729	981	1227	0	176	462	146	1176	884	2351	786	1011	486	1078	1593	1050	2611	1346	738	2278	867	1273	673	1158	1903	697	1971	2361	2710	401	2342	243	494	940	1542	713	949	673	1005
Montgomery, AL	2035	466	332	695	859	1281	176	0	288	322	1010	715	2295	794	1037	452	930	1655	843	2632	1191	561	2456	792	1179	632	1281	1918	904	2127	2464	2838	478	2562	209	460	766	1633	765	794	639	831
Nashville, TN	2027	178	211	908	571	892	462	288	0	551	859	665	2374	673	735	689	761	1671	575	2376	1029	502	2189	614	770	323	892	1678	941	2092	2375	2384	669	2124	486	737	478	1581	608	632	875	543
New Orleans, LA	1883	729	397	867	1045	1346	146	322	551	0	1322	1054	2317	681	1362	624	1224	1540	1078	2505	1492	876	2278	1114	1362	681	1346	1842	551	1824	2327	2574	309	2409	381	632	1005	1419	657	1095	811	1095
New York, NY	2790	707	1095	1313	851	1160	1176	1010	859	1322	0	389	2876	1436	1208	1094	101	2425	381	2330	162	510	2635	366	320	941	1160	2124	1832	2773	2858	2837	1415	2569	1109	1126	556	2360	1331	252	1223	456
Norfolk, VA	2809	607	876	988	948	1337	884	715	665	1054	389	0	2957	1349	1362	770	268	2393	365	2968	527	197	2789	98	535	927	1337	2262	1606	2669	2967	2975	1203	2700	802	827	592	2271	1234	190	916	438
Oakland, CA	372	2333	2122	3087	2171	2065	2351	2295	2374	2317	2876	2957	0	1660	1596	2844	2913	744	2528	614	2974	2865	201	2988	2681	2003	2065	545	1734	493	9	777	2052	979	2601	2836	2293	878	1766	2772	3055	2463
Oklahoma City, OK	1354	738	462	1524	884	803	786	794	673	681	1436	1349	1660	0	495	1281	1363	998	1095	1946	1597	1200	1662	1287	1298	495	803	1151	478	1345	1670	2044	389	1768	1038	1289	961	908	105	1305	1468	1087
Omaha, NE	1508	671	705	1670	503	381	1110	1037	735	1362	1208	1362	1596	495	0	1421	1200	1427	908	1605	1394	1281	1395	1400	1078	446	381	947	949	1641	1606	1679	729	1403	1241	1492	705	1400	401	1151	1671	857
Orlando, FL	2585	907	770	227	1224	1673	486	452	689	624	1094	770	2844	1281	1421	0	1005	2205	1025	3123	1273	608	2789	776	1200	1030	1551	2359	1159	2402	2854	3163	920	2895	243	89	1086	2083	1240	876	194	1052
Philadelphia, PA	2717	664	989	1215	834	1126	1078	930	761	1224	101	268	2913	1363	1200	1005	0	1025	292	2830	259	412	2627	252	324	868	1126	2209	1734	2911	2923	2780	1270	2512	1020	1037	502	2287	1249	133	1134	357
Phoenix, AZ	389	1782	1377	2448	1873	1848	1593	1655	1671	1540	2425	2393	744	998	1427	2205	1025	0	2084	1322	2586	2172	754	2285	2281	1484	1808	673	989	357	754	1492	1282	1386	1962	2213	1950	122	1103	2367	2392	2061
Pittsburgh, PA	2449	381	795	1248	567	868	1050	843	575	1078	381	365	2528	1095	908	1025	292	2084	0	2538	559	519	2335	333	284	600	868	1824	1468	2441	2538	2513	1087	2190	932	998	227	2021	981	219	1111	65
Portland, OR	985	2298	2408	3366	2002	1670	2611	2632	2376	2505	2330	2968	614	1946	1605	3123	2830	1322	2538	0	3000	2903	616	3012	2676	2068	1670	764	2168	1078	624	170	2255	365	2880	3131	2311	1483	1987	2846	3310	2481
Providence, RI	2902	421	1257	1483	1021	1322	1346	1191	1029	1492	162	527	2974	1597	1394	1273	259	2586	559	3000	0	673	2814	511	381	1102	1322	2303	2002	2978	2984	2967	1585	2644	1288	1322	689	252	1483	397	1402	538
Raleigh, NC	2554	525	713	818	899	1241	738	561	502	876	510	197	2865	1200	1281	608	412	2172	519	2903	673	0	2716	175	600	835	1241	2205	1427	2529	2797	2911	938	2651	624	657	584	2124	1103	283	754	535
Reno, NV	511	2132	2124	3032	1930	1776	2278	2456	2189	2278	2635	2789	201	1662	1395	2789	2627	754	2335	616	2814	2716	0	2803	2489	1881	1776	511	1768	535	211	810	1927	770	2546	2797	2133	867	1702	2579	2976	2303
Richmond, VA	2641	686	825	988	832	1237	867	792	614	1114	366	98	2988	1287	1400	776	252	2285	333	3012	511	175	2803	0	455	976	1237	2324	1555	2643	2989	3029	1173	2761	794	827	630	2425	1222	114	924	662
Rochester, NY	2400	608	973	1435	697	1005	1273	1179	770	1362	320	535	2681	1298	1078	1200	324	2281	284	2676	381	600	2489	455	0	803	1005	1978	1686	2674	2691	2660	1361	2384	1208	1257	381	2222	1398	341	1346	265
Saint Louis, MO	1849	290	300	1231	389	628	673	632	323	681	941	927	2003	495	446	1030	868	1484	600	2068	1102	835	1881	976	803	0	628	1370	916	1840	2075	2076	624	1881	795	1030	466	1419	381	795	1241	592
Saint Paul, MN	1905	705	949	1743	332	1	1158	1281	892	1346	1160	1337	2065	803	381	1551	1126	1808	868	1670	1322	1241	1776	1237	1005	628	0	1475	1265	1975	2075	1638	985	1370	1354	1589	641	1702	705	1078	1737	794
Salt Lake City, UT	672	1638	1613	2602	1419	1475	1903	1918	1678	1842	2124	2262	545	1151	947	2359	2209	673	1824	764	2303	2205	511	2324	1978	1370	1475	0	1447	762	714	851	1563	706	2116	2318	1715	795	1223	2141	2490	1805
San Antonio, TX	1378	1103	794	1402	1305	1265	697	904	941	551	1832	1606	1734	478	949	1159	1734	989	1468	2168	2002	1427	1768	1555	1686	916	1265	1447	0	1274	1774	2255	474	2110	916	1151	1387	876	535	1605	1370	1477
San Diego, CA	121	2119	1881	2645	2109	1975	1971	2127	2092	1824	2773	2669	493	1345	1641	2402	2911	357	2441	1078	2978	2529	535	2643	2674	1840	1975	762	1274	0	527	1276	1565	1403	2213	2464	2604	405	1403	2733	2072	2456
San Francisco, CA	382	2388	2132	3097	2175	2075	2361	2464	2375	2327	2886	2967	9	1670	1606	2854	2923	754	2538	624	2984	2797	211	2989	2691	2075	2075	714	1774	527	0	787	2061	852	2611	2846	2415	868	1776	2949	3065	2569
Seattle, WA	1159	2343	2506	3406	1970	1638	2710	2838	2384	2574	2837	2975	777	2044	1679	3163	2780	1492	2513	170	2967	2911	810	3029	2660	2076	1638	851	2255	1276	787	0	2335	274	2920	3155	2231	1573	2034	2684	3388	2456
Shreveport, LA	1687	721	357	1130	1013	985	401	478	669	309	1415	1203	2052	389	729	920	1270	1282	1087	2255	1585	538	1927	1173	1361	624	985	1563	474	1565	2061	2335	0	2038	644	895	1099	1160	356	953	507	1081
Spokane, WA	1406	2075	2230	3138	1702	1370	2342	2562	2124	2409	2569	2700	979	1768	1403	2895	2512	1386	2190	365	2644	2651	770	2761	2384	1816	1370	706	2110	1403	852	274	2038	0	2652	2887	2100	1496	1727	2417	3196	2125
Tallahassee, FL	2342	664	527	486	1053	1354	243	209	486	381	1109	802	2601	1038	1241	243	1020	1962	932	2880	1288	624	2546	794	1208	795	1354	2116	916	2213	2611	2920	644	2652	0	251	900	1840	955	891	430	1005
Tampa, FL	2578	915	778	292	1240	1589	494	460	737	632	1126	827	2836	1289	1492	89	1037	2213	998	3131	1322	657	2797	827	1251	1030	1589	2318	1151	2464	2846	3155	895	2887	251	0	1143	2076	1182	908	219	1088
Toledo, OH	2213	300	665	1293	332	641	940	766	478	1005	556	592	2293	961	705	1086	502	1950	227	2311	689	584	2133	630	381	466	641	1715	1387	2604	2415	2231	1099	2100	900	1143	0	2051	867	438	1248	170
Tuscon, AZ	502	1697	1370	2326	1808	1702	1542	1633	1581	1419	2360	2271	878	908	1400	2083	2287	122	2021	1483	252	2124	867	2425	2222	1419	1702	795	876	405	868	1573	1160	1496	1840	2076	2051	0	1038	2254	2270	2003
Tulsa, OK	1459	633	397	1483	770	705	713	765	608	657	1331	1234	1766	105	401	1240	1249	1103	981	1987	1483	1103	1702	1222	1398	381	705	1223	535	1403	1776	2034	356	1727	955	1182	867	1038	0	1284	1167	964
Washington, DC	2659	533	363	1086	770	1078	949	796	632	1095	252	190	2772	1305	1151	876	133	2367	219	2846	397	283	2579	114	341	795	1078	2141	1605	2733	2949	2684	953	2417	891	908	438	2254	1284	0	1005	283
West Palm Beach, FL	2772	1094	957	65	1386	1737	673	639	875	811	1223	916	3055	1468	1671	194	1134	2392	1111	3310	1402	754	2976	924	1346	1241	1737	2490	1370	2072	3065	3388	507	3196	430	219	1248	2270	1167	1005	0	1167
Youngstown, OH	2424	373	738	1238	510	794	1005	831	543	1095	403	438	2463	1087	875	1052	357	2076	65	2481	527	535	2303	662	265	592	794	1877	1477	2432	2569	2456	1181	2125	1005	1088	170	2003	964	283	1167	0

TIME & DISTANCE MAP

The Time & Distance Map has been specially prepared to help the interstate traveler estimate time between major cities throughout the 48 states. The mileages and times shown have been calculated giving ample consideration to normal driving conditions. Topography, congested areas, peak traffic periods, speed limits, roadwork and highway construction may have an unfavorable effect on these estimates. Additional time should also be allowed for rest periods, sightseeing and eating.

Limited access highways are not always the shortest distance, however, they have been used in these calculations, since they normally represent the shortest driving time and best over-all driving conditions.

Driving times have been calculated using an average speed of 50 miles per hour. Your actual driving time will depend on traffic, road conditions and your personal driving habits.

BLACK NUMERALS INDICATE MILEAGE

RED NUMERALS INDICATE DRIVING TIME ONLY

Drive safely and cautiously at all times. Obey all traffic signs.

Creative Sales Corporation
Publisher of Quality Road Maps

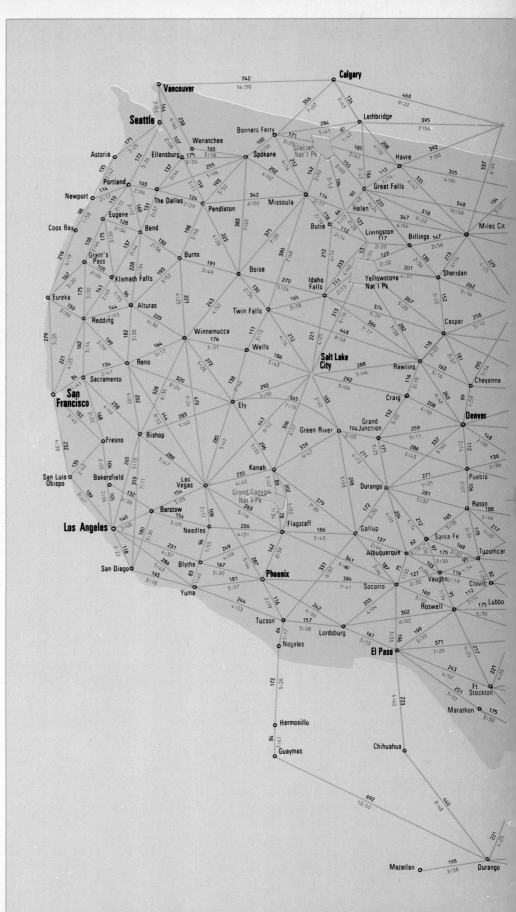

1   2   3   4   5   6   7

A B C D E F G H J K

BRITISH COLUMBIA   ALBERTA   Calgary   Saskatoon   CANADA   SASKATCHEWAN   MANITOBA   Winnipeg   Regina   Moose Jaw   Riding Mountain Nat'l Park

Vancouver   Seattle   Tacoma   Olympia   Spokane   WASHINGTON   Walla Walla   Portland   Salem   Eugene   OREGON

UNITED STATES   MONTANA   Great Falls   Helena   Butte   Billings   NORTH DAKOTA   Williston   Bismarck   Fargo   Theodore Roosevelt Nat'l Park

IDAHO   Boise   Twin Falls   Pocatello   Yellowstone Nat'l Park   Grand Teton Nat'l Park   Jackson   WYOMING   Casper   Custer Battlefield Nat'l Mon.   Devil's Tower Nat'l Mon.   Black Hills   Rapid City   Mt. Rushmore Nat'l Mem.   Wind Cave Nat'l Park   Hot Springs   Badlands Nat'l Park   SOUTH DAKOTA   Pierre   Sioux Falls

NEVADA   Reno   Carson City   Winnemucca   Ely   GREAT SALT LAKE DESERT   Salt Lake City   Provo   UTAH   Golden Spike Nat'l Hist. Site   Rock Springs   Dinosaur Nat'l Mon.   Boulder   Denver   Cheyenne   COLORADO   Colorado Springs   Pueblo   NEBRASKA   North Platte   Lincoln   Scottsbluff

San Francisco   Oakland   San Jose   Sacramento   Monterey   Fresno   Bakersfield   CALIFORNIA   Las Vegas   Death Valley Nat'l Mon.   Yosemite Nat'l Park   Sequoia Nat'l Park   Kings Canyon Nat'l Park   Zion Nat'l Park   Bryce Canyon   Grand Canyon Nat'l Park   Mesa Verde Nat'l Park   Durango   KANSAS   Dodge City   Wichita

Los Angeles   San Bernardino   Anaheim   San Diego   Tijuana   Mexicali   Yuma   ARIZONA   Phoenix   Globe   Tucson   Flagstaff   Prescott   Petrified Forest Nat'l Park   Albuquerque   Santa Fe   NEW MEXICO   Amarillo   Oklahoma City   OKLAHOMA   Lubbock   Wichita Falls

BAJA CALIFORNIA   UNITED STATES   MEXICO   SONORA   Nogales   Douglas   Ciudad Juarez   El Paso   CHIHUAHUA   Carlsbad   Guadalupe Mtns Nat'l Park   Odessa   Midland   San Angelo   TEXAS   Waco   Austin   Abilene   Ft. Worth   Dallas

PACIFIC OCEAN

U.S.S.R.   Wainwright   Barrow   Arctic Ocean   Point Hope   Prudhoe Bay   Gates of the Arctic Nat'l Park & Preserve   Nome   Fort Yukon   ALASKA   Fairbanks   College   Delta Junction   Tok   Anchorage   Valdez   Denali Nat'l Park and Preserve   Glennallen   Palmer   Wrangell-St. Elias Nat'l Park   Kenai Fjords Nat'l Park   Katmai Nat'l Park & Preserve   Kodiak Island   Bering Sea   Bristol Bay   Gulf of Alaska   Juneau   Sitka   Ketchikan   B.C.   Aleutian Islands

YUKON   Kluane Nat'l Park

HAWAII   Lihue   Wahiawa   Kaneohe   Pearl City   Honolulu   Lahaina   Wailuku   Haleakala Nat'l Park   Hilo   Hawaii Volcanoes Nat'l Park   City of Refuge Nat'l Hist. Park   Pacific Ocean

CHIHUAHUA   Big Bend Nat'l Park   Nuevo Casas Grandes   Old Ft. Davis Nat'l Hist. Site   COAHUILA   Piedras Negras   Nueva Rosita   San Antonio   Laredo   Corpus Christi   Padre Island Nat'l Seashore   NUEVO LEON   Monterrey   Brownsville   TAMAULIPAS

PACIFIC TIME ZONE   MOUNTAIN TIME ZONE   CENTRAL TIME ZONE   CONTINENTAL DIVIDE

8 • 9 • 10 • 11 • 12 • 13 • 14

USE ONLY FOR ORIENTATION TO NATIONAL PARKS AND LANDMARKS. FOR MORE DETAILED HIGHWAY INFORMATION SEE INTERSTATE HIGHWAY MAP, PAGES 4-5, AND STATE MAP SECTION , PAGES 17-98.

A • B • C • D • E • F • G • H • J • K

QUEBEC
NEW BRUNSWICK
ONTARIO
Laurentides Prov. Park
La Verendrye Prov. Park
Mastigouche Prov. Park
Maurice Nat'l Park
Algonquin Prov. Park
Georgian Bay
Georgian Bay Is. Park
Lake St. Jean
St. Lawrence River
Presque Isle
Roosevelt Campobello Int'l Park
MAINE
Bangor
Acadia Nat'l Park
Quebec
Montreal
Ottawa
Sudbury
North Bay
Peterborough
Toronto
Rochester
Syracuse
Albany
Concord
Portland
Augusta
White Mts. Nat'l Forest
Green Mtn. Nat'l Forest
VT.
N.H.
MASS.
Boston
Cape Cod Nat'l Seashore
Providence
New Bedford
CONN.
R.I.
Hartford
New Haven
New York
ADIRONDACK MTNS.
Adirondack Nat'l Park
Catskill Park
Montpelier

Lake Winnipeg
Lake Nipigon
Kenora
Lake of the Woods
Red River of the North
Thunder Bay
Pukaskwa Nat'l Park
Isle Royale Nat'l Park
Superior
Lake Superior
Voyageurs Nat'l Park
Chippewa Nat'l Forest
Apostle Islands Nat'l Lakeshore
Ottawa Nat'l Forest
Nicolet Nat'l Forest
Chequamegon Nat'l Forest
Pictured Rocks Nat'l Lakeshore
Sault Ste. Marie
Hiawatha Nat'l Forest
Lake Michigan
Sleeping Bear Dunes Nat'l Lakeshore
Huron Nat'l Forest
Manistee Nat'l Forest
Lake Huron
Pt. Pelee Nat'l Park

MINNESOTA
St. Paul
Minneapolis
Rochester
WISCONSIN
Madison
Milwaukee
Green Bay
La Crosse
MICHIGAN
Grand Rapids
Lansing
Detroit
Windsor
Toledo
London
Cleveland
Akron
Youngstown
Pittsburgh
Harrisburg
Scranton
Allentown
Trenton
Philadelphia
NEW JERSEY
NEW YORK
Buffalo
Erie
Lake Erie
Allegheny Nat'l Forest
Hopewell Village Nat'l Hist. Site
Eisenhower Nat'l Hist. Site
Wilmington
Baltimore
Dover
DELAWARE
Annapolis
MARYLAND
Washington D.C.
Richmond
Assateague Island Nat'l Seashore
PENNSYLVANIA
Roosevelt Inaug. Nat'l Hist. Site
Delaware R.
Susquehanna R.

IOWA
Sioux City
Des Moines
Cedar Rapids
Davenport
Rockford
Omaha
Council Bluffs
Dodge House Nat'l Mon.
Chicago
Gary
South Bend
Ft. Wayne
ILLINOIS
Peoria
Springfield
INDIANA
Indianapolis
Hoosier Nat'l Forest
OHIO
Columbus
Cincinnati
Dayton
Mound City Group Nat'l Mon.
Wayne Nat'l Forest
Victory & Int'l Peace Mem.
Charleston
Huntington
WEST VIRGINIA
George Washington Nat'l Forest
Monongahela Nat'l Forest
Shenandoah Nat'l Park
George Washington Birthplace Nat'l Mon.
VIRGINIA
Lynchburg
Roanoke
Norfolk
Newport News
APPALACHIAN MTNS.
Jefferson Nat'l Forest

Topeka
Kansas City
Columbia
Jefferson City
MISSOURI
St. Louis
Springfield
Mark Twain Nat'l Forest
Shawnee Nat'l Forest
Louisville
Frankfort
Lexington
KENTUCKY
Mammoth Cave Nat'l Park
Cumberland Gap Nat'l Hist. Park
Daniel Boone Nat'l Forest
Kentucky Lake
Ohio River
Andrew Johnson Nat'l Mon.
Winston-Salem
Greensboro
Raleigh
NORTH CAROLINA
Uwharrie Nat'l Forest
Croatan Nat'l Forest
Wright Brothers Nat'l Memorial
Cape Hatteras Nat'l Seashore
Cape Lookout Nat'l Seashore

Tulsa
Ft. Smith
Ozark Nat'l Forest
ARKANSAS
Little Rock
Pine Bluff
Ouachita Nat'l Forest
Hot Springs Nat'l Park
Texarkana
Memphis
Holly Springs Nat'l Forest
Arkansas Post Nat'l Mon.
TENNESSEE
Nashville
Knoxville
Chattanooga
Great Smoky Mtns. Nat'l Park
Cherokee Nat'l Forest
Nantahala Nat'l Forest
Pisgah Nat'l Forest
Chattahoochee Nat'l Forest
Cowpens Nat'l Battlefield
Kings Mtn. Nat'l Mil. Park
Charlotte
SOUTH CAROLINA
Columbia
Sumter Nat'l Forest
Moore's Creek Nat'l Battlefield
Francis Marion Nat'l Forest

Tyler
Shreveport
Monroe
Jackson
MISSISSIPPI
Bienville Nat'l Forest
Homochitto Nat'l Forest
Rocky Springs Nat'l Forest
De Soto Nat'l Forest
ALABAMA
Birmingham
Montgomery
Talladega Nat'l Forest
William B. Bankhead Nat'l Forest
Little Mtn. Nat'l Forest
Tombigbee Nat'l Forest
Delta Nat'l Forest
Conecuh Nat'l Forest
Columbus
Macon
GEORGIA
Atlanta
Kennesaw Mtn. Nat'l Battlefield Park
Chattahoochee Nat'l Forest
Oconee Nat'l Forest
Ocmulgee Nat'l Mon.
Augusta
Savannah
Ft. Frederica Nat'l Mon.
Cumberland Island Nat'l Seashore
Ft. Sumter Nat'l Mon.
ATLANTIC OCEAN
Congaree Swamp Nat'l Mon.

Texarkana
Davy Crockett Nat'l Forest
Angelina Nat'l Forest
Sabine Nat'l Forest
Sam Houston Nat'l Forest
LOUISIANA
Baton Rouge
Houston
Galveston
New Orleans
Lake Charles
Mobile
Biloxi
Pensacola
Panama City
Gulf Islands Nat'l Seashore
Apalachicola Nat'l Forest
Tallahassee
Osceola Nat'l Forest
Jacksonville
Ft. Matanzas Nat'l Mon.
Sabine River

FLORIDA
Ocala Nat'l Forest
Daytona Beach
Canaveral Nat'l Seashore
John F. Kennedy Space Center
Orlando
Tampa
St. Petersburg
Lake Okeechobee
Desoto Nat'l Mon.
West Palm Beach
Ft. Myers
Naples
Ft. Lauderdale
Miami
Everglades Nat'l Park
Biscayne Nat'l Park

GULF OF MEXICO

CENTRAL TIME ZONE
EASTERN TIME ZONE
ATLANTIC TIME ZONE

ALBERTA

Banff	J-4
Calgary	J-4
Camrose	H-5
Cardston	J-4
Drumheller	H-5
Edmonton	H-5
Edson	H-4
Fitzgerald	F-5
Fort Chipewyn	F-4
Ft. McMurray	G-5
Ft. Vermillion	F-4

Grande Centre	G-5
Grande Prairie	G-4
Habay	F-4
High Level	F-4
High River	J-4
Hinton	H-4
Jasper	H-4
Lethbridge	J-5
Medicine Hat	J-5
Peace Point	G-4
Rainbow Lake	F-4

Red Deer	H-5
Rocky Mtn. House	H-4
Waterways	G-5
Wetaskiwin	H-4
Whitecourt	H-4

BRITISH COLUMBIA

Alert Bay	J-2
Atlin	F-2
Bella Coola	H-2
Campbell River	J-2

Cassiar	F-2
Courtnay	J-2
Cranbrook	J-4
Dawson Creek	G-3
Ft. Nelson	F-3
Ft. St. John	F-3
Hazelton	G-2
Kamloops	J-3
Kelowna	J-4
Kimberley	J-4
Kitimat	H-2
Masset	G-1
Nanaimo	J-2

Nelson	J-4
New Westminster	J-3
Ocean Falls	H-2
Penticton	J-4
Port Alberni	J-2
Port Alice	J-2
Powell River	J-3
Prince George	H-3
Prince Rupert	G-2
Quesnel	H-3
Revelstoke	H-3
Sandpit	H-1

Smithers	G-2
Stewart	G-2
Telegraph Creek	F-2
Trail	J-4
Ucluelet	J-2
Vancouver	J-3
Vernon	J-4
Victoria	J-3
Ware	G-3
Williams Lake	H-3

MANITOBA

Berens River	G-7
Brandon	H-7
Brochet	F-6
Churchill	F-7
Dauphin	H-7
Flin Flon	G-6
Gillam	F-7
Gods Lake	G-8
Grand Rapids	G-7
Island Lake	G-7

Lynn Lake	F-6
Norway House	G-7
Portage la Prairie	H-7
Selkirk	H-8
Snow Lake	G-7
S. Indian Lake	F-7
Swan River	H-7
The Pas	G-6
Thompson	G-7
Virden	J-7
Winnipeg	H-8

NEW BRUNSWICK

Bathurst	E-13
Campbellton	E-12
Chatam	E-13
Edmundston	E-12
Fredricton	F-13
Moncton	E-13
Newcastle	E-13
St. John	F-13
St. Stephen	F-13
Tracadie	E-13

Woodstock	F-13

NEWFOUNDLAND

Battle Harbour	C-13
Bonavista	C-14
Cartwright	C-12
Channel-Port aux Basques	D-14
Churchill Falls	D-12
Corner Brook	D-13
Gander	C-14

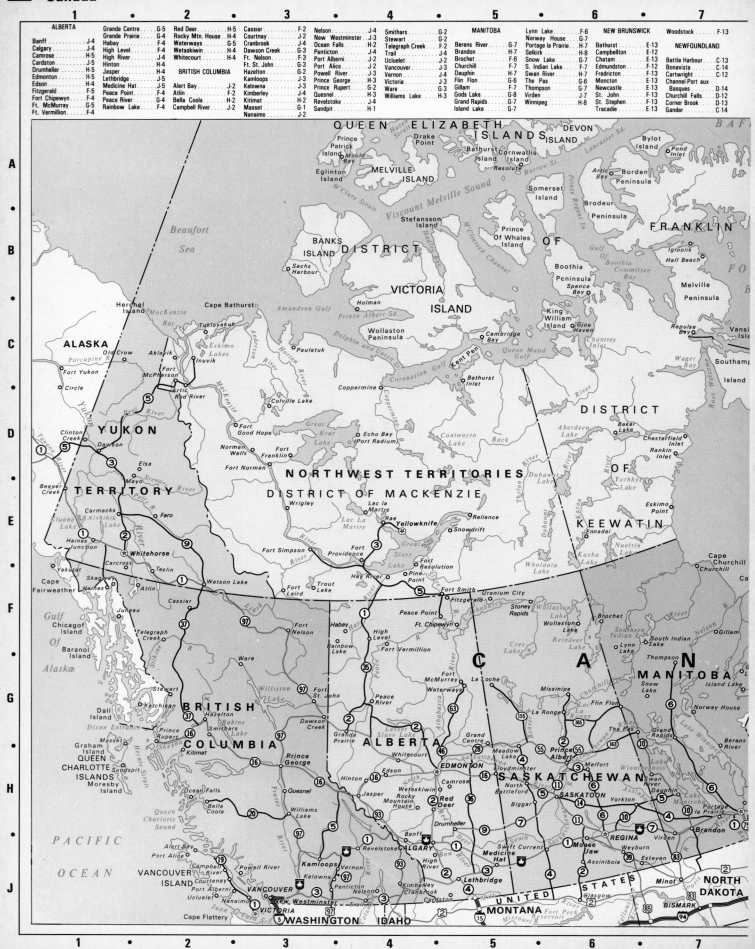

Goose Bay C-12	St. Pierre (France) .D-14	Cape Dorset C-8	Ft. Laird F-3	Inuvik C-2	Resolute A-5	Ft. Albany F-9	Toronto H-11	La Tugue F-12	SASKATCHEWAN
Grand Falls ..C-14	Stephenville D-13	Cape Dyer A-9	Ft. McPherson .D-2	Lac la Martre ..E-4	Resolution Island .A-9	Ft. Frances ..H-8	Trenton H-12	Lac-Allard E-12	Assiniboia J-6
Hebron C-11	Wabana C-14	Chesterfield Inlet .D-7	Ft. Norman ..D-3	Lake Harbour ..B-9	Sachs Harbour ..B-3	Ft. Severn H-9	Wawa H-10	Levis F-12	Biggar H-5
Hopedale C-11		Clyde A-8	Ft. Providence ..E-4	Mould Bay A-4	Snowdrift E-5	Geraldton H-9	Windsor J-11	Maniwaki G-11	Estevan J-7
Labrador City .D-11	N.W. TERRITORY	Colville Lake ..D-3	Ft. Resolution ..F-4	Norman Wells ..D-3	Spence Bay B-6	Goderich J-11	Winisk F-9	Maricourt (Wakeham)C-9	La Loche G-5
Makkovik C-12		Coppermine ..D-4	Ft. Simpson ..E-4	Panguirtung ..A-9	Trout Lake F-3	Guelph H-11		Matagami F-10	La Rouge H-5
Marystown ..D-14	Aklavik C-2	Echo Bay (Port	Ft. Smith F-4	Paulatuk C-3	Tukloy.kuk C-2	Hamilton H-11	PRINCE EDWARD	Matane F-12	Lloydminister ..H-5
Northwest River .C-12	Artic Bay A-6	Radium) D-4	Frobisher Bay ..B-9	Pine Point F-4	Yellowknife ..E-4	Hearst G-10	ISLAND	Mont-Laurier ..G-12	Meadow lake ..H-5
Nutak C-11	Artic Red River .D-2	Ennadai E-6	Gjoa Haven ..C-6	Pond Inlet A-7		Kapuskasing ..G-10		Montreal G-12	Melfort H-6
Placentia C-14	Baker Lake ..D-6	Eskimo Point ..E-7	Hall Beach B-7	Rae E-4		Kenora H-8	Charlottetown ..E-13	Nitchequon ..E-11	Missinipe G-5
St. Anthony ..C-13	Bathurst Inlet ..C-5	Ft. Franklin ..D-3	Hay River E-4	Rankin Inlet ..D-7		Kingston H-12	Summerside ..E-13	Noranda G-10	Moose Jaw J-6
St. John's C-14	Cambridge Bay .C-5	Ft. Good Hope .D-3	Holman C-4	Reliance E-5		Kirkland Lake .G-10		Nouveau-Quebec	North Battleford .H-5
			Igloolik B-7	Repulse Bay ..C-7	NOVA SCOTIA	Kitchener H-11	QUEBEC	(George River) .C-10	Prince Albert ..H-6
						Lec Seul H-8		Port Alfred ..F-12	Regina J-6
					Amherst E-13	London J-11	Alma F-12	Port Cartier ..E-12	Saskatoon H-6
					Bridgewater ..F-14	Marathon H-9	Amos G-11	Poste-de-la-	Stoney Rapids ..F-5
					Canso E-14	Moosonee F-10	Arvida F-12	Baleine E-10	Swift Current ..J-5
					Glace Bay E-14	Nakina G-9	Baie Comeau ..E-12	Povungnitak ..D-9	Uranium City ..F-5
					Halifax F-14	Niagra Falls ..H-12	Belin (Payne) ..C-10	Quebec F-12	Weyburn J-6
					Kentville F-13	Nipigon H-9	Cape Smith ..D-9	Rimouski F-12	Wollaston Lake ..G-5
					New Glasgow ..E-14	North Bay H-11	Chandler F-12	Riviere-du-Loup .F-12	Yorkton H-6
					Shelburne F-14	Oshawa H-11	Chicoutimi ..F-12	Rouyn G-10	
					Sydney E-14	Ottawa G-12	Deception C-9	St. Hyacinthe ..G-12	YUKON
					Truro E-13	Owen Sound ..H-11	Desmaraisville ..F-11	St. Jean G-12	
					Yarmouth F-13	Parry Sound ..H-11	Drummondville ..G-12	St. Jerome ..G-12	Beaver Creek ..E-1
						Pembroke G-11	Eastmain F-10	Ste. Anne-des-	Carcross E-1
					ONTARIO	Peterborough .H-12	Ft. Chimo C-10	Monts E-12	Carmacks E-1
						Pickle Lake ..G-9	Ft. George ..F-10	Schefferville ..D-11	Clinton Creek ..D-1
					Armstrong G-9	Red Lake H-8	Ft. Rupert ..F-10	Senneterre ..G-11	Dawson D-1
					Atikokan H-8	Renfrew G-11	Gagnon E-11	Sept. Iles E-12	Elsa D-2
					Barrie H-11	St. Catharines .H-12	Gaspe F-12	Shawinigan ..G-12	Faro E-2
					Belleville H-12	St. Thomas ..J-11	Granby G-12	Sherbrooke ..G-12	Haines Jct. ..E-1
					Blind River ..H-10	Sault Ste. Marie .H-10	Harve St. Pierre .E-12	Shibougamau ..F-11	Mayo E-1
					Brantford J-11	Sioux Lookout ..H-8	Hull G-12	Sorel G-12	Old Crow C-1
					Brockville G-12	Smith's Falls ..G-12	Inoucdjouac (Port	Thetford Mines .F-12	Teslin F-2
					Chatham J-11	Sudbury H-10	Harrison) D-9	Trois-Rivieres ..G-12	Watson Lake ..F-2
					Cochrane G-10	Thunder Bay ..H-9	Ivujivik C-9	Val-d'Or G-12	Whitehcrse ..F-2
					Cornwall G-12	Timmins G-10	Koartac C-9		
					Deep River ..G-11				
					Favourable Lake .G-8				

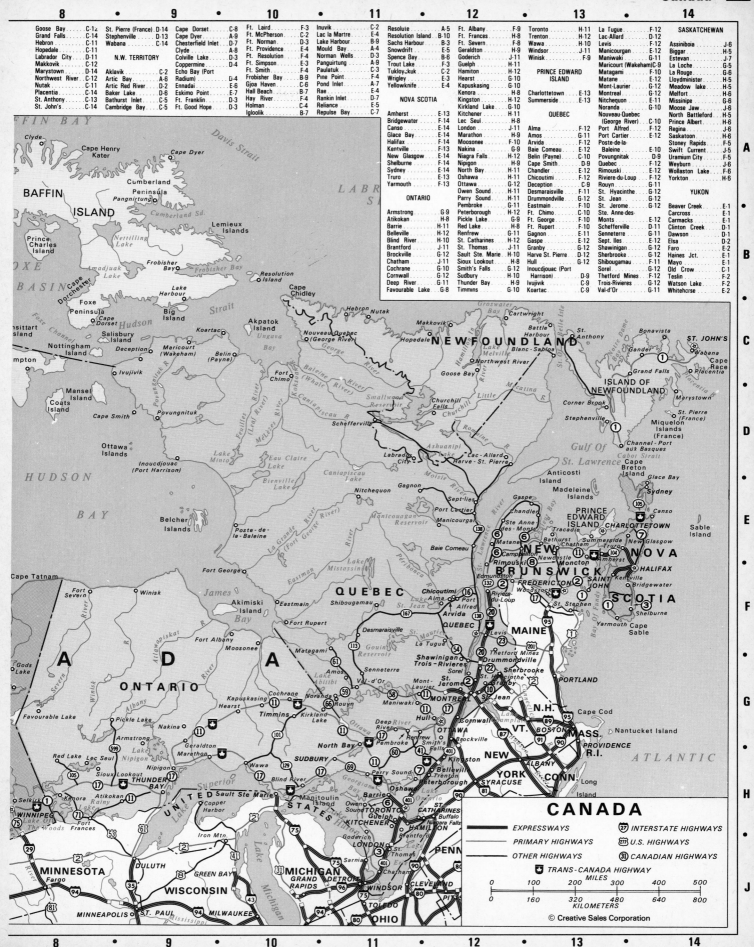

CANADA

▬▬▬ EXPRESSWAYS	(27) INTERSTATE HIGHWAYS
▬▬▬ PRIMARY HIGHWAYS	(277) U.S. HIGHWAYS
▬▬▬ OTHER HIGHWAYS	(31) CANADIAN HIGHWAYS

✚ TRANS-CANADA HIGHWAY

MILES
0   100   200   300   400   500

KILOMETERS
160   320   480   640   800

© Creative Sales Corporation

MEXICO

Legend	
▬▬ EXPRESSWAYS	(38) MEXICAN HIGHWAYS
▬ PRIMARY THROUGH ROUTES	(31) INTERSTATE HIGHWAYS
▬ OTHER THROUGH ROADS	(83) U.S. HIGHWAYS
···· OTHER ROADS	(31) STATE HIGHWAYS

Approximate distances are shown between red markers on map.
Red numbers are kilometers, black numbers are miles.

MILES: 0 — 100 — 200 — 300
KILOMETERS: 0 — 160 — 320 — 480

© Creative Sales Corporation

UNITED STATES
ARIZONA
NEW MEXICO
MEXICO
BAJA CALIFORNIA
BAJA CALIFORNIA SUR
SONORA
CHIHUAHUA
COAHUILA
DURANGO
SINALOA
ZACATECAS
NAYARIT
AGUASCALIENTES
JALISCO
COLIMA

Pacific Ocean
Gulf of California
Rio Grande

Tijuana, Tecate, Mexicali, Ensenada, San Felipe, El Rosario, Punta Prieta, Rasarito, San Ignacio, Santa Rosalia, Rosarito, Ejido Insurgentes, El Medano, La Paz, Todos Santos, San Jose del Cabo
Yuma, San Luis, Sonorita, Puerto Penasco, Caborca, Altar, Magdalena, Santa Ana, Puerto de la Libertad, Hermosillo, Bahia Kino, Guaymas, Empalme, Rosario, Ciudad Obregón, Navojoa, El Fuerte, Los Mochis, Topolobampo, Sinaloa, Guasave, Tameapa, Culiacán, Altata, Cosalá, Eldorado, La Cruz, Mazatlán, Villa Union, Rosario
Ajo, Tucson, Nogales, Agua Prieta, Douglas, Cananea, Bavispe, Sahuaripa, Tonichi, Yecora
Safford, Silver City, Las Cruces, El Paso, Ciudad Juarez, Alamogordo, Artesia, Hobbs, Carlsbad, Midland, Odessa, Pecos, Rankin, Alpine, Sanderson, Presidio, Ojinaga
Janos, Nueva Casas Grandes, Buenaventura, Moctezuma, Villa Ahumada, Gallego, Madera, Ciudad Guerrero, El Sauz, Chihuahua, Cuauhtémoc, Delicias, La Perla, Ciudad Camargo, Jiménez, Hidalgo del Parral, Santa Barbara, Escalón
Boquillas del Carmen, La Cuesta, Nacimiento, Sabinas, Ocampo, La Cadena, San Pedro de las Colonias, Gómez Palacio, TORREÓN, Parras, Concepción del Oro, Camacho, Cuencamé, Abasolo, Tepehuanes, Canatlán, Durango, El Salto, Sombrerete, Rio Grande, Fresnillo, Zacatecas, Monte Escobedo
Tuxpan, Los Corchos, Tepic, Las Varas, Moyahua, Jalpa, Lagos de Moreno, Aguascalientes, Tepatitlan, Puerto Vallarta, El Tuito, GUADALAJARA, Tlaquepaque, Ocotlán, Salamanca, Irapuato, Sahuayu, Autlán, Sayula, Ciudad Guzmán, Tomatlán, Uruapan, Melaque, Manzanillo, Colima, Apatzingán, Arteaga, Playa Azul, Ixtapa

MEXICO

Cities and Towns

Abasolo	D-5	Ciudad del Maiz	E-7	La Pesca	D-7	Paraiso
Acambaro	F-6	Coatzacoalcos	F-9	La Piedad	E-6	Parras
Acapulco	G-6	Colima	F-5	Las Varas	E-5	Peto
Acatlan	F-7	Comitan	G-9	Leon	E-6	Piedras Negras
Acayucan	F-8	Conception de Oro	D-6	Linares	D-7	Pijijiapan
Agua Prieta	A-3	Cordoba	F-8	Los Corchos	E-5	Pinotepa Nacional
Aguascalientes	E-6	Cosala	D-4	Los Mochis	C-3	Piste
Altar	A-3	Cuauhtemoc	B-4	Madera	B-4	Playa Azul
Altata	D-4	Cuencame	D-5	Magdalena	A-3	Pochutla
Alvarado	F-8	Cuernavaca	F-7	Malpaso	G-9	Poza Pica
Apatzingan	F-6	Culiacan	D-4	Manuel	E-7	Progreso
Arcelia	F-6	Delicias	B-5	Manzanillo	F-5	Puebla
Arriga	G-9	Durango	D-5	Matamoros	C-7	Puerto de la
Arteaga	F-6	Dzilam de Bravo	E-10	Matehuala	D-6	Libertad
Arlixco	F-7	Ejido Insurgentes	C-3	Matias Romero	G-8	Puerto Escondido
Autlan	F-5	Eldorado	D-4	Mazatlan	D-4	Puerto Juarez
Bahia Kino	B-2	El Fuerte	C-4	Melaque	F-5	Puerto Madero
Bavispe	B-4	El Medana	D-3	Merida	E-10	Puerto Penasco
Becal	E-10	El Rosario	A-1	Mexicali	A-1	Punta Prieta
Boquillas de		El Sauz	B-4	Mexico City	F-7	Queretaro
Carmen	B-6	El Tuito	E-5	Miahuatlan	G-8	Rasarito
Buenaventura	B-4	Empalme	B-3	Mier	C-7	Reynosa
Caborca	A-2	Ensanada	A-1	Minatitlan	F-8	Rio Grande
Camacho	D-6	Escalon	C-5	Moctezuma	B-4	Rio Lagartos
Campeche	E-10	Escarcega	F-10	Molango	E-7	Rosario
Cananea	A-3	Fresnillo	D-5	Monclova	C-6	Rosario
Canatlan	D-5	Gallego	B-4	Monte Escobedo	E-5	Sabinas
Cardenas	F-9	Gomez Palacio	C-5	Montemorelos	D-7	Sabinas Hidagalo
Celaya	E-6	Guadalajara	E-5	Monterrey	C-6	Sahuaripa
Celestun	E-10	Guasave	C-4	Morelia	F-6	Salamanca
Champoton	F-10	Guaymas	B-3	Morelos	B-6	Salinas
Chetumal	F-11	Hermosillo	B-3	Moyahua	E-5	Salina Cruz
Chilpancingo	F-7	Hidalgo del Parral	C-5	Nacimiento	C-6	Saltillo
China	C-7	Hopelchen	E-10	Nautla	E-8	San Andres Tuxtla
Chihuahua	B-5	Huajuapan de Leon	F-7	Navojoa	C-3	San Cristobal
Ciudad Acuna	B-6	Iguala	F-7	Nogales	A-3	San Felipe
Ciudad Camargo	C-5	Irapuato	E-6	Nueva Casas		San Fernando
Ciudad Guerrero	B-4	Iturbide	F-10	Grandes	B-4	San Ignacio
Ciudad Guzman	F-5	Jalapa	F-8	Nueva Rosita	C-6	San Jose del Cabo
Ciudad Juarez	A-4	Jalpa	E-6	Nuevo Laredo	C-7	San Luis
Ciudad Mante	E-7	Janos	A-4	Oaxaca	F-7	San Luis Potosi
Ciudad Madero	E-7	Jimenez	C-5	Ocampo	C-6	San Pedro de las
Ciudad Victoria	D-7	Juchitan	G-8	Ocotlan	E-6	Colonias
Ciudad de Carmen	F-9	La Cruz	D-4	Ojinaga	B-5	Santa Ana
Ciudad de Valles	E-7	La Cadena	C-5	Ometepec	G-7	Santa Barbara
		La Cuesta	B-6	Orizaba	F-8	Santa Rosalia
		Lagos de Morena	E-6	Pachuca	E-7	Sayula
		La Paz	D-3	Palenque	F-9	Sinaloa
		La Perla	B-5	Papantla	E-7	Sombrerete

Paraiso	F-9	Sonorita	A-2
Parras	C-6	Soto La Marina	D-7
Peto	E-10	Tameapa	C-4
Piedras Negras	B-6	Tampico	E-7
Pijijiapan	G-9	Tapachula	G-9
Pinotepa Nacional	G-7	Tapanatepec	G-9
Piste	E-11	Taxco	F-7
Playa Azul	F-6	Teapa	F-9
Pochutla	G-8	Tecate	A-1
Poza Pica	E-7	Tehuacan	F-7
Progreso	E-10	Tehuantepec	G-8
Puebla	F-7	Temporal	E-7
Puerto de la		Tepatitlan	E-6
Libertad	B-2	Tepehuanes	D-5
Puerto Escondido	G-8	Tepic	E-5
Puerto Juarez	E-11	Ticul	E-10
Puerto Madero	G-9	Tijuana	A-1
Puerto Penasco	A-2	Tiquicheo	G-7
Punta Prieta	B-2	Tlaciaco	G-7
Queretaro	E-6	Tlaxcala	F-7
Rasarito	A-1	Tlaxiaco	G-7
Reynosa	C-7	Todos Santos	D-3
Rio Grande	D-6	Toluca	F-7
Rio Lagartos	E-11	Tomatlan	F-5
Rosario	C-3	Tonala	B-3
Rosario	D-4	Topolobampo	C-5
Sabinas	C-6	Torreon	C-5
Sabinas Hidagalo	C-6	Tototalpan	G-8
Sahuaripa	B-3	Tulancingo	F-7
Salamanca	E-6	Tulum	E-11
Salinas	D-6	Tuxpan	E-5
Salina Cruz	G-8	Tuxpan	E-7
Saltillo	C-6	Tuxtepec	F-8
San Andres Tuxtla	F-8	Tuxtla Gutierrez	G-9
San Cristobal	G-9	Uruapan	F-6
San Felipe	A-2	Valladolid	E-11
San Fernando	D-7	Villa Ahumada	A-4
San Ignacio	C-2	Villagran	D-7
San Jose del Cabo	D-3	Villahermosa	F-9
San Luis	A-2	Villa Union	D-4
San Luis Potosi	E-7	Xcan	E-11
San Pedro de las		Yecora	B-4
Colonias	C-6	Zacatal	F-9
Santa Ana	A-3	Zacatecas	E-6
Santa Barbara	C-5	Zamora	F-6
Santa Rosalia	C-2	Zihuatanejo	F-6
Sayula	C-4	Zimapan	E-7
Sinaloa	C-4	Zitacuaro	F-6
Sombrerete	D-5		

STATE MAP LEGEND

ROAD CLASSIFICATIONS & RELATED SYMBOLS

Free Interstate Hwy.	90
Toll Interstate Hwy.	76
Divided Federal Hwy.	14
Federal Hwy.	20
Divided State Hwy.	31
State Hwy.	147
Other Connecting Road	258
Trans - Canada Hwy.	
Point to Point Milage	17
State Boundaries	- - - - - - -

LAND MARKS & POINTS OF INTEREST

Indian Reservation		Desert	
National & State Forest or Wildlife Preserve		River, Lake, Ocean or other Drainage	
Military Installation		Urban Area	**Denver**
National & State Park or Recreation Area		Airport	✈
		State Capital	⊛
		Park, Monument, University or other Point of Interest	▪
Grassland		Roadside Table or Rest Areas	▲

ABBREVIATIONS

A.F.B. - Air Force Base	Mgmt. - Management	Prov. - Province	S. F. - State Forest
Hist. - Historical	Mon. - Monument	Rec. - Recreation	St. Pk. - State Park
Mem. - Memorial	Nat. - Natural	Ref. - Refuge	W.M.A. - Wildlife Management Area

CITIES & TOWNS - Type size indicates the relative population of cities and towns

Mapleton	Kenhorst	Somerset	Butler	Auburn	Harrisburg	Madison	Chicago
under 1000	1000-5,000	5,000-10,000	10,000-25,000	25,000-50,000	50,000-100,000	100,000-500,000	500,000 and over

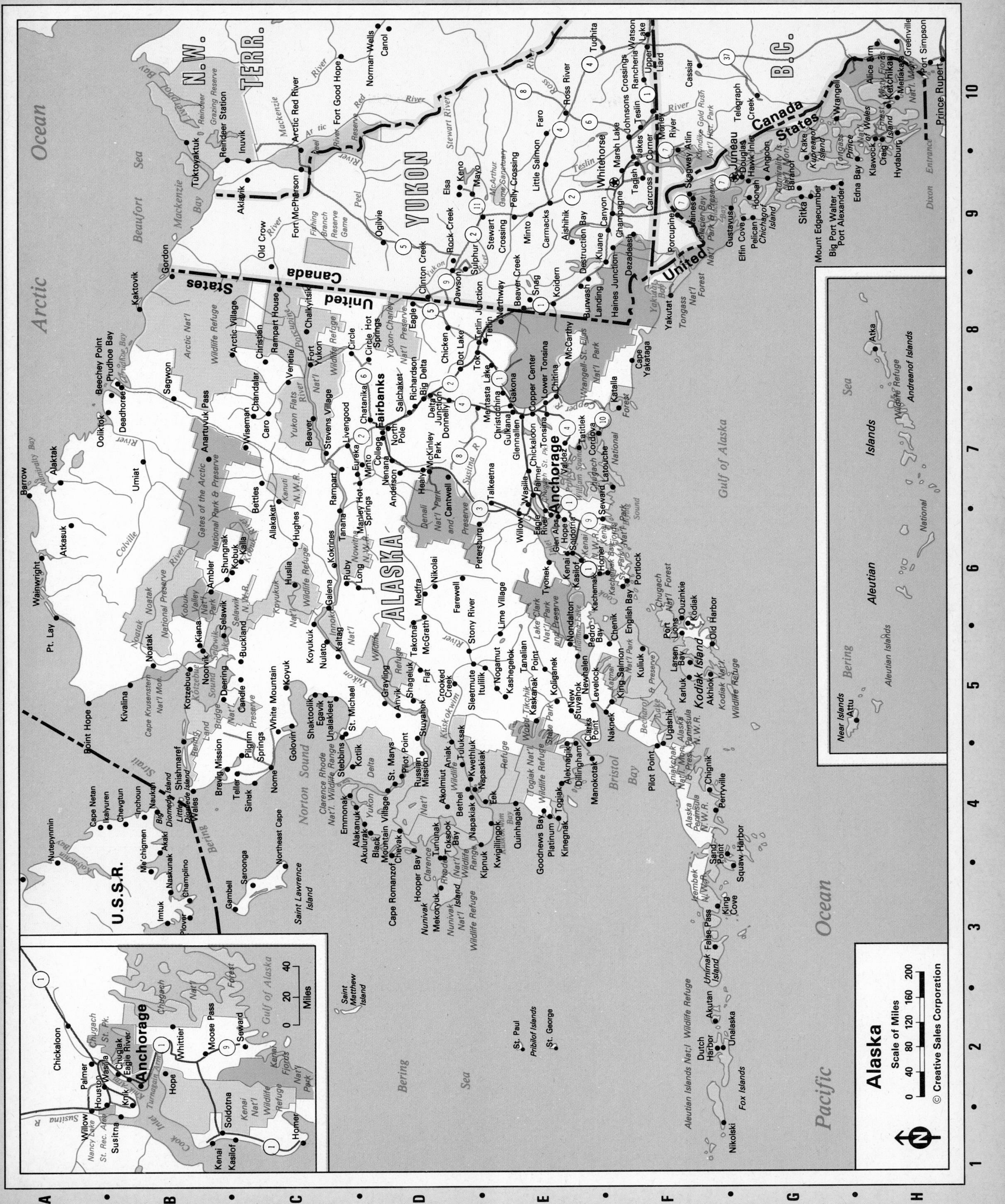
Alaska
Scale of Miles
0 40 80 120 160 200
© Creative Sales Corporation
ALASKA
YUKON
N.W. TERR.
B.C.
U.S.S.R.
Canada
United States
Arctic Ocean
Beaufort Sea
Bering Sea
Pacific Ocean
Gulf of Alaska
Norton Sound
Bristol Bay
Aleutian Islands
Pribilof Islands
Near Islands
Fox Islands
Saint Lawrence Island
Nunivak Island
Kodiak Island
Anchorage
Fairbanks
Juneau
Whitehorse
Miles
0 20 40
A B C D E F G H
1 2 3 4 5 6 7 8 9 10

Hawaii

Scale of Miles

0 4 8 12 16 20

© Creative Sales Corporation

N

Maui

Kalahu Pt.
Hana
Muolea Pt.
Kipahulu
Pukailua Pt.
360
Waialua
Kaupo
Apole Pt.
Haleakala Crater
Haleakala Nat'l Park
Waianapanapa St. Pk.
Keoneoio
Ulupalakua
378
Makawao
377
Haiku
Pauwela
37
Keokea
Paia
Pauwela
36
Spreckelsville
Puunene
Kihei
31
Kahului
Wailuku
Waiehu Bay
Waihee Pt.
Kahakuloa
Nakalele Pt.
340
Iao Valley
Wailuku
Mopua
Maalaea
30
Maalaea Bay
Kamaole Beach Park
Wailea
Makena
Nukuele Pt.
Honokahua
Hekili Pt.
Olowalu
30
Lahaina
Hanamanioa
Maui
Pacific Ocean

Molokai

Halawa
Lamaloa Head
Wailau
Pauwalu
Cape Halawa
Kikipua Pt.
Pukoo
Ujapue
Kalae
Kamalo
450
Kamiloloa
Kaunakakai
Kualapuu
Kualae
Mauna Loa
460
Kolo
Makanalua Pen.
Kahiu Pt.
Lilo Pt.
Laau Pt.
Kalohi Channel
Pailolo Channel
Molokai
Pacific Ocean

Niihau

Anahola
56
Lihue
Lawai
Haena
50
Waianae
Mana
Kauai
Niihau (Private)
Puuwai
Kaulakahi Channel
Lehua
Pacific Ocean

Lanai

Maui
Hana
360
Honokahua Nat'l Park
Haiku
36
Kahului
37
Ulupalakua
31
Honokohau
Lahaina
30
Kaunolu
Kaomoku
Koele
Lanai City
Kahoolawe
Kamalo
Maunalei
460
Mauna Loa
450
Kualapuu
Molokai
Kalohi Channel
Kalaikahiki Channel
Auau Channel
Pailolo Channel
Alalakeiki Channel
Kaka Pt.
Halawa
Kawi Channel
HAWAII

Maui Co.
Hawaii Co.
Maui Co.
Honolulu Co.
Kauai Co.
Honolulu Co.

Oahu

Kahuku
Kahana
83
Kaneohe
Kailua
Haleiwa
Pearl City
2
Waikiki
1
Makaha
Nanakuli
Honolulu
Oahu
Pacific Ocean

Hawaii (Big Island)

Waiakea
Wailea
Pepeekeo Pt.
Pohoiki
Black Sands
Kalaipana
Honomu
Honohina
Hakalau
Papaikou
130
Pahoa
Kaimu
Apua Pt.
Kaena Pt.
Papaaloa
Hilo
Keaau
Punaluu Black Sand Beach
Kukuihaele
Honokaa
Ookala
19
Paukaa
Rainbow Falls
Kurtistown
Mountain View
Glenwood
Hawaii Volcanoes National Park
Waipio
Kukaiau
Waimea
Mauna Kea 13,796 ft.
200
Mauna Loa 13,680 ft.
Honuapo
Hawi
Niulii
270
250
Waiaka
190
Kalaoa
Honokohau
Captain Cook
Keokea
Pahala
Naalehu
Kaalualu
Kawaihae
Puako
19
Kailua
Keauhou
Napoopoo
Honaunau
Hookena
Papa
Milolii
11
Waiohinu
Waiahukini
Ka Lee
Upola Pt.
Mahukona
Keahole Pt.
Kauna Pt.
Hanamalo Pt.
Kaena Pt.
Hawaii
Alenuihaha Channel
Pacific Ocean

Oahu (detail)

Waimanalo
Life Park
Makapuu
Makapuu Head
Koko Head
Waimanalo Bay
Kailua
Kaneohe Bay
Mokapu Pt.
Kaneohe
Marine Air Station
3
61
Hawaii Kai
72
Maunalua Bay
Diamond Head
Waikiki
92
1
Honolulu
63
Pali Lookout
Kualoa Pt.
78
Aiea
99
Pearl City
Waipahu
2
Ewa
95
1
Makakilo City
750
Barbers Pt.
Barbers Air Sta.
Mililani Town
Wahiawa
Schofield Barracks
Range
780
Waialua
99
83
Haleiwa
Sunset Beach
Sacred Falls
Kahana
Hauula
Laie
Polynesian Cultural Center
Kahuku Pt.
Kahuku
Koolau Range
Waianae
Maili
Nanakuli
Waianae
930
Dillingham Air Force Base
Makaha
Kepuhi Pt.
Keaau Pt.
Kaena Pt.
Oahu
Kaui Channel
Pacific Ocean

Kauai

Anahola
Kealia
Moloaa
Kapaa
Wailua
56
Kilauea
Hanamaulu
Lihue Airport
Nawiliwili
Ninini Pt.
Hanalei
580
583
Puhi
50
Lihue
Koloa
Mt. Waialeale 5243 ft.
Haena Pt.
Haena
Kalalau
Kokee State Park
Makaha Pt.
Waimea Canyon
550
Eleele
Port Allen
Lawai
Kalaheo
Koheo Pt.
Makahuena Pt.
Kaumakani
Hanapepe
50
Waimea
Kekaha
Kaumakani
Mana
Kauai
Kaui Channel
Pacific Ocean

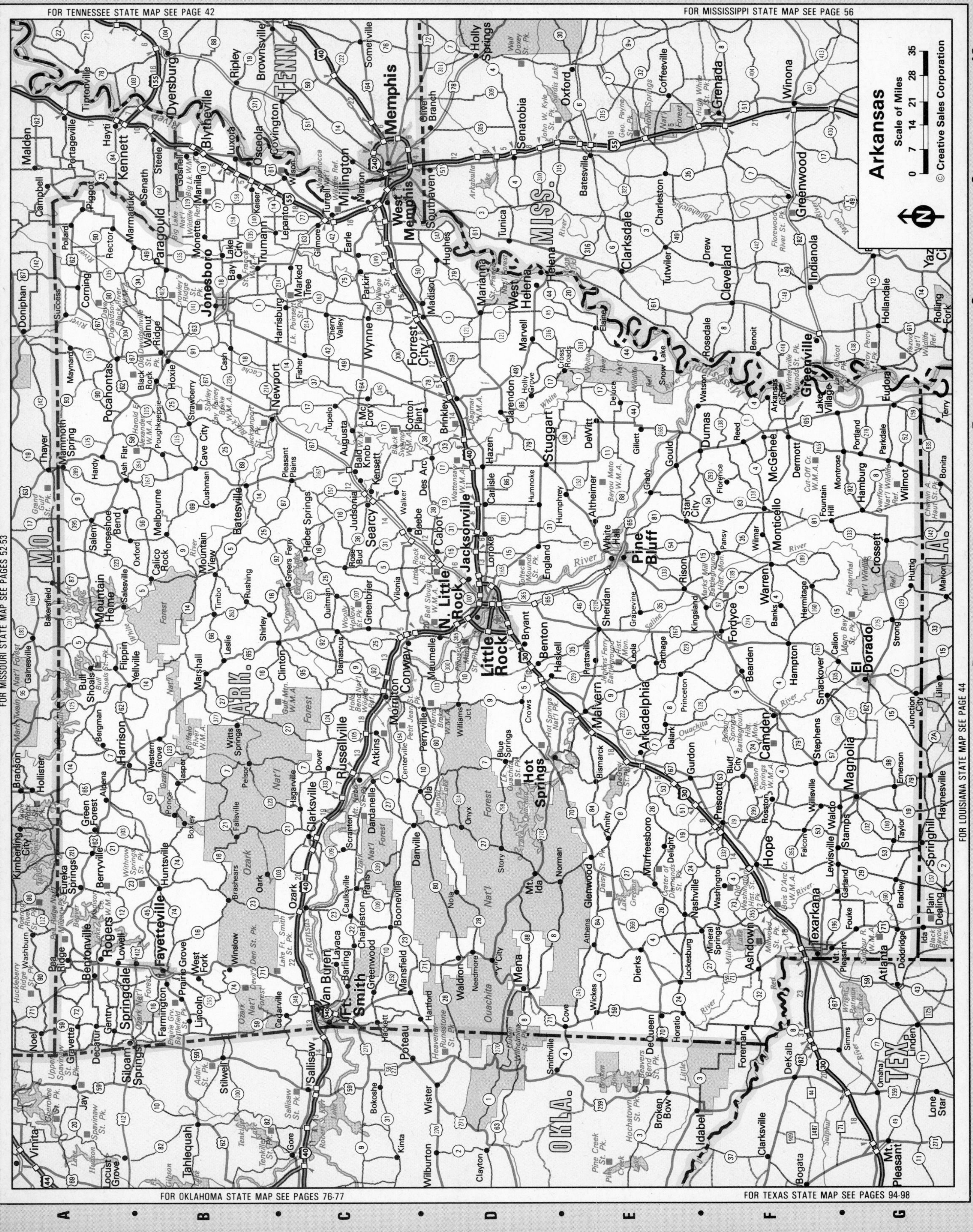

FOR TENNESSEE STATE MAP SEE PAGE 42
FOR MISSISSIPPI STATE MAP SEE PAGE 56
FOR MISSOURI STATE MAP SEE PAGES 52-53
FOR LOUISIANA STATE MAP SEE PAGE 44
FOR OKLAHOMA STATE MAP SEE PAGES 76-77
FOR TEXAS STATE MAP SEE PAGES 94-98
Arkansas
Scale of Miles
0 7 14 21 28 35
© Creative Sales Corporation
ARK.
MO.
TENN.
MISS.
LA.
TEX.
OKLA.
Little Rock
N. Little Rock
Memphis
West Memphis
Fort Smith
Pine Bluff
Hot Springs
Texarkana
Jonesboro
Fayetteville

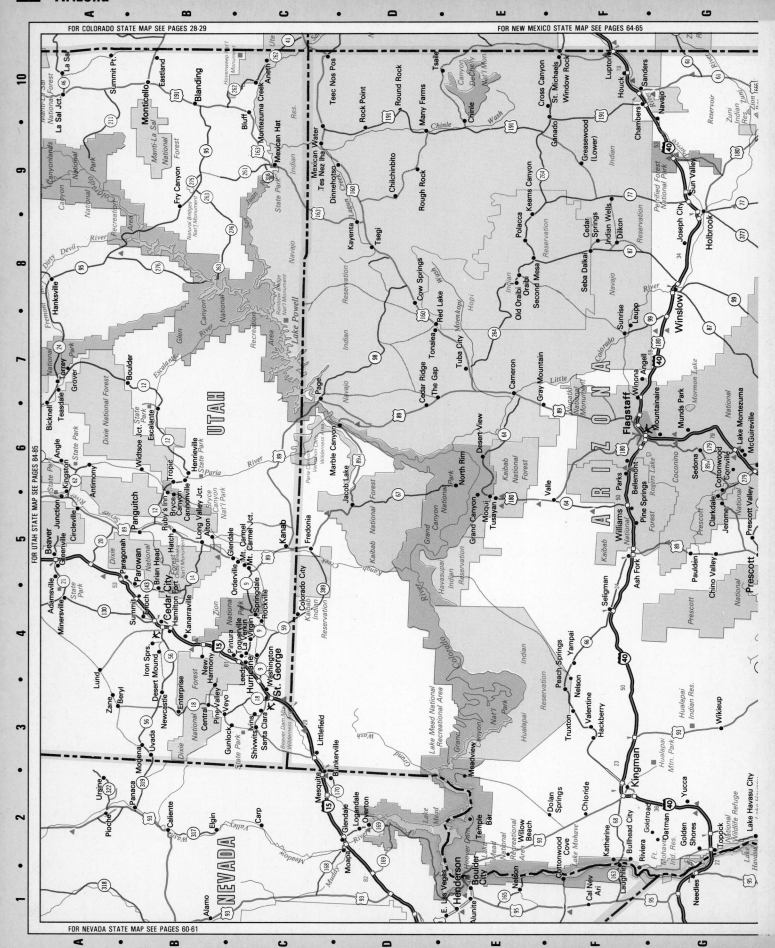

FOR COLORADO STATE MAP SEE PAGES 28-29

FOR NEW MEXICO STATE MAP SEE PAGES 64-65

FOR UTAH STATE MAP SEE PAGES 84-85

FOR NEVADA STATE MAP SEE PAGES 60-61

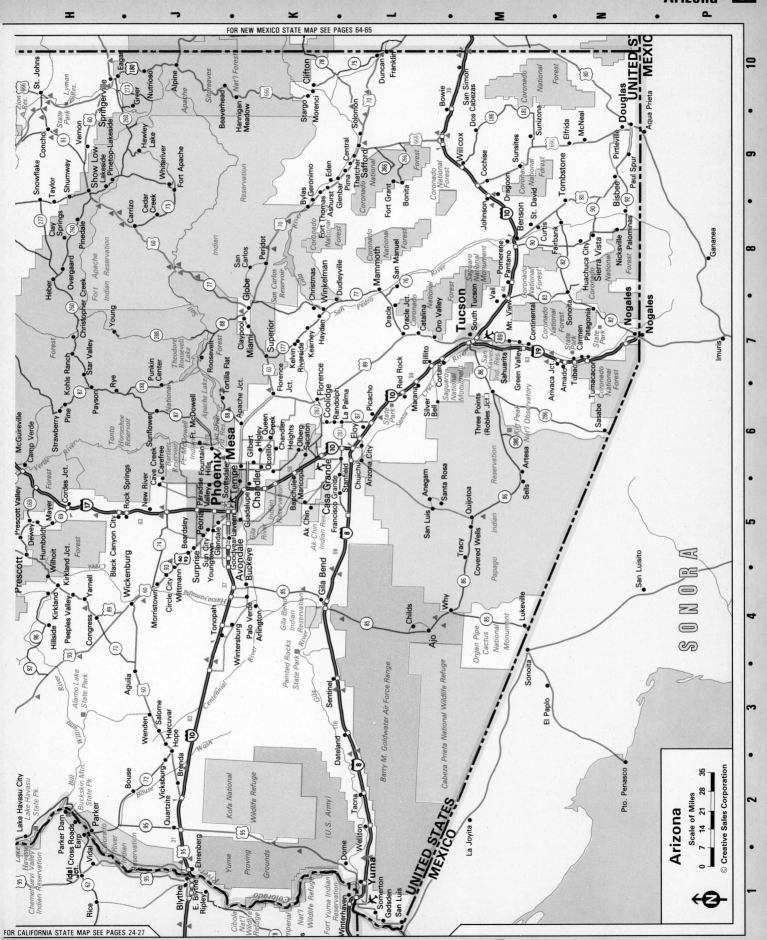

FOR NEW MEXICO STATE MAP SEE PAGES 64-65

FOR CALIFORNIA STATE MAP SEE PAGES 24-27

Arizona

Scale of Miles

0 7 14 21 28 35

© Creative Sales Corporation

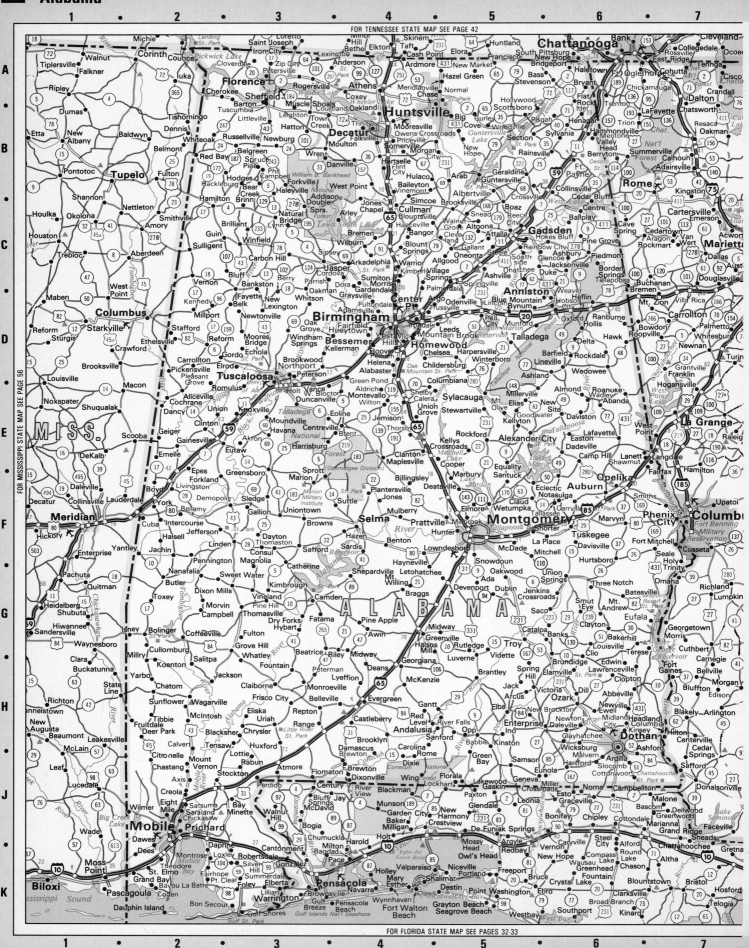

FOR TENNESSEE STATE MAP SEE PAGE 42

FOR FLORIDA STATE MAP SEE PAGES 32-33

FOR MISSISSIPPI STATE MAP SEE PAGE 56

FOR NORTH CAROLINA STATE MAP SEE PAGES 70-71

Alabama/Georgia

Scale of Miles
0 7 14 21 28 35

© Creative Sales Corporation

N

FOR SOUTH CAROLINA STATE MAP SEE PAGE 71

GEORGIA

SOUTH CAROLINA

Atlanta
Columbia
Augusta
Macon
Savannah
Warner Robins
Albany
Valdosta
Brunswick
Tallahassee
Jacksonville

Atlantic Ocean

FOR FLORIDA STATE MAP SEE PAGES 32-33

California

Scale of Miles

0 7 14 21 28 35

© Creative Sales Corporation

FOR NEVADA STATE MAP SEE PAGES 60-61

FOR OREGON STATE MAP SEE PAGES 78-79

OREGON

NEVADA

CALIFORNIA

Medford · Ashland · Talent · Klamath Falls · Lakeview · Ft. Bidwell · Davis Cr. · Lake City · Cedarville · Eagleville · Gerlach · Sparks · Reno · Carson City · Virginia City · Fernley · Wadsworth · Nixon · Silver Springs · Fallon · Wabuska

Brookings · Smith River · Crescent City · Cave Junction · Happy Camp · Klamath · Merrill · Tulelake · Newell · Dorris · Macdoel · Montague · Yreka · Hornbrook · Hilt · Alturas · Canby · Likely · Madeline · Termo · Ravendale · Herlong · Litchfield · Standish · Milford · Doyle · Loyalton · Portola · Beckwourth · Vinton · Hallelujah Jct. · Sierraville · Calpine · Sattley · Sierra City · Truckee · Tahoe City · Kings Beach · Soda Sprs.

Eureka · Arcata · McKinleyville · Trinidad · Blue Lake · Kneeland · Fortuna · Scotia · Rio Dell · Ferndale · Petrolia · Honeydew · Weott · Redway · Redway · Garberville · Leggett · Laytonville · Covelo · Willits · Ukiah · Redwood Valley · Potter Valley · Upper Lake · Lucerne · Clearlake · Kelseyville · Lakeport · Hopland · Boonville · Philo · Navarro · Mendocino · Ft. Bragg · Westport

Weed · Mt. Shasta · Dunsmuir · McCloud · Big Bend · Burney · Fall River Mills · McArthur · Old Sta. · Chester · Westwood · Greenville · Quincy · Oroville · Paradise · Chico · Orland · Willows · Colusa · Williams · Arbuckle · Maxwell · Red Bluff · Corning · Los Molinos · Gerber · Vina · Redding · Anderson · Cottonwood · Shasta · Weaverville · Hayfork · Junction City · Platina · Covelo

McCloud · Shasta Lake · Whiskeytown · Igo · Ono · Douglas City · Lewiston · Trinity Ctr. · Coffee Creek · Callahan · Etna · Ft. Jones · Greenview · Scott Bar · Happy Camp · Somes Bar · Orleans · Weitchpec · Hoopa · Willow Cr. · Salyer · Burnt Ranch · Big Bar · Big Bend · Forest Glen

Susanville · Janesville · Johnstonville · Herlong · Doyle · Loyalton · Taylorsville · Crescent Mills · Canyon Dam · Almanor · Twain · Belden · Storrie · Pulga · Berry Creek · Stirling City · Butte Mdws. · Mineral · Manton · Shingletown · Whitmore · Montgomery Creek · Round Mtn.

Marysville · Yuba City · Linda · Sutter · Live Oak · Gridley · Biggs · Durham · Nord · Hamilton City · Artois · Princeton · Glenn · Elk Creek · Stonyford · Sites · Maxwell · Grimes · Meridian · Knights Landing · Wheatland · Oroville · Palermo · Bangor · Grass Valley · Nevada City · Rough And Ready · Penn Valley · Browns Valley · Smartville · Camptonville · Downieville · Sierra City · Graniteville · Washington · Colfax · Meadow Vista

Pyramid Lk. · Indian Reservation · Honey Lk. · Eagle Lake · Clear Lake Res. · Goose Lk. · Tule Lk. · Lewiston Lk. · Shasta Lk. · Whiskeytown Lk. · Lake Almanor · Lake Pillsbury · Ruth Res.

Klamath Nat'l Forest · Modoc Nat'l Forest · Shasta Nat'l Forest · Trinity Nat'l Forest · Six Rivers Nat'l Forest · Lassen Nat'l Forest · Plumas Nat'l Forest · Tahoe Nat'l Forest · Mendocino Nat'l Forest · Eldorado Nat'l Forest · Redwood Nat'l Park · Lassen Volcanic Nat'l Park · Lava Beds Nat'l Mon. · Humboldt Redwoods St. Park · Eureka · Reno

FOR CONTINUATION SEE GRID P-1

FOR CONTINUATION SEE PAGES 26-27

FOR CONTINUATION SEE PAGE 27

FOR NEVADA STATE MAP SEE PAGES 60-61

4 • 5 • 6 • 7 • 8 • 9 • 10

FOR CONTINUATION SEE PAGES 24-25

Carmel
Pt. Lobos St. Reserve
Carmel Valley
Gonzales
Pinnacles Nat'l Mon.
Tranquillity
San Joaquin
Malaga
Fowler
Sanger
Orange Cove
Badger
Park

Andrew Molera St. Park
Big Sur
Soledad
Greenfield
New Idria
Five Points
Caruthers
Selma
Orosi
Cutler
Giant Forest Village
Sequoia Nat'l Park

Pfeiffer - Big Sur St. Park
Los Padres Nat'l Forest
Santa Lucia Range
King City
Riverdale
Kingsbury
Cross
Woodlake
Three Rivers

Julia Pfeiffer Burns St. Park
Ft. Hunter Liggett
San Lucas
Coalinga
Huron
Lemoore
Hanford
Goshen
Visalia
Exeter
Farmersville
Lindsay
Camp Nelson

Jolon
Lockwood
San Ardo
Stratford
Corcoran
Woodville
Strathmore
Sequoia Nat'l Forest

San Antonio Res.
Bradley
Avenal
Kettleman City
Tipton
Poplar
Pixley
Earlimart
Springville
Tule River Ind. Res.

Nacimiento Res.
Parkfield
Devils Den
Col. Allensworth St. Hist. Pk.
Delano
Alpaugh
Ducor
California Hot Sprs.
Forest

San Miguel
Cholame
Lost Hills
Wasco
McFarland
Glennville
Kernville
Isabella Res.

San Simeon
Wm. R. Hearst Mem. St. Beach
San Simeon St. Beach
Hearst San Simeon St. Hist. Mon.
Shandon
Blackwells Corner
Wasco
Woody
Wofford Heights
Onyx
Bodfish

Cambria
Paso Robles
Templeton
Shafter
Green Acres
Bakersfield
Edison
Sequoia

Cayucos St. Beach
Cayucos
Atascadero
Santa Margarita
Simmler
Buttonwillow
McKittrick
Tule Elk St. Reserve
Nat'l Forest

Atascadero St. Beach
Morro Bay
Morro Bay St. Park
Pozo
Taft
Fellows
Pumpkin Center
Lamont
Caliente
Keene

Baywood Pk.
San Luis Obispo
Santa Margarita Res.
Ford City
Maricopa
Arvin
Tehachapi

Montana De Oro St. Park
Pismo Beach
Sierra Madre
Cuyama
Frazier Pk.
Ft. Tejon St. Hist. Pk.
Willow Sprs.
Mojave

Grover City
Arroyo Grande
Nipomo
Oceano
Twitchell Res.
New Cuyama
Gorman
Rosamond

Pismo St. Beach
San Luis Obispo Bay
Guadalupe
Santa Maria
Los Padres Nat'l Forest
Castaic Lake St. Rec. Area
Palmdale

Pt. Sal St. Beach
Orcutt
Sisquoc
La Purisima Mission St. Hist. Park
Los Olivos
Castaic
Acton

Casmalia
Los Alamos
Lake Cachuma
Fillmore
Valencia
San Fernando

Surf
Lompoc
Buellton
Solvang
Gaviota
Montecito
Summerland
Carpinteria
Ojai
Santa Paula
Moorpark
Simi Valley
Glendale

Gaviota St. Park
El Capitan St. Beach
Refugio St. Beach
Goleta
Santa Barbara
Carpenteria St. Beach
Emma Wood St. Beach
Ventura
Oxnard
Saticoy
Agoura Hills
Thousand Oaks
Pasadena

Port Hueneme
Pt. Mugu St. Park
Leo Carrillo St. Beach
Malibu
Beverly Hills
Santa Monica
Los Angeles

San Miguel Is.
Santa Cruz Is.
San Miguel Passage
Santa Cruz Channel
Channel Islands Nat'l Mon.
Santa Monica Bay
Redondo Beach
Long Beach
Huntington Beach
Newport Beach
Laguna

Santa Rosa Is.
Santa Barbara Is.
Rancho Palos Verdes

Pacific

San Nicolas Is.
Channel Islands Nat'l Mon.
Santa Catalina Is.
Avalon
San Pedro Channel
Outer Santa Barbara Channel
Doheny

Ocean

San Clemente Is.

California

Scale of Miles

0 7 14 21 28 35

N

© Creative Sales Corporation

4 • 5 • 6 • 7 • 8 • 9 • 10

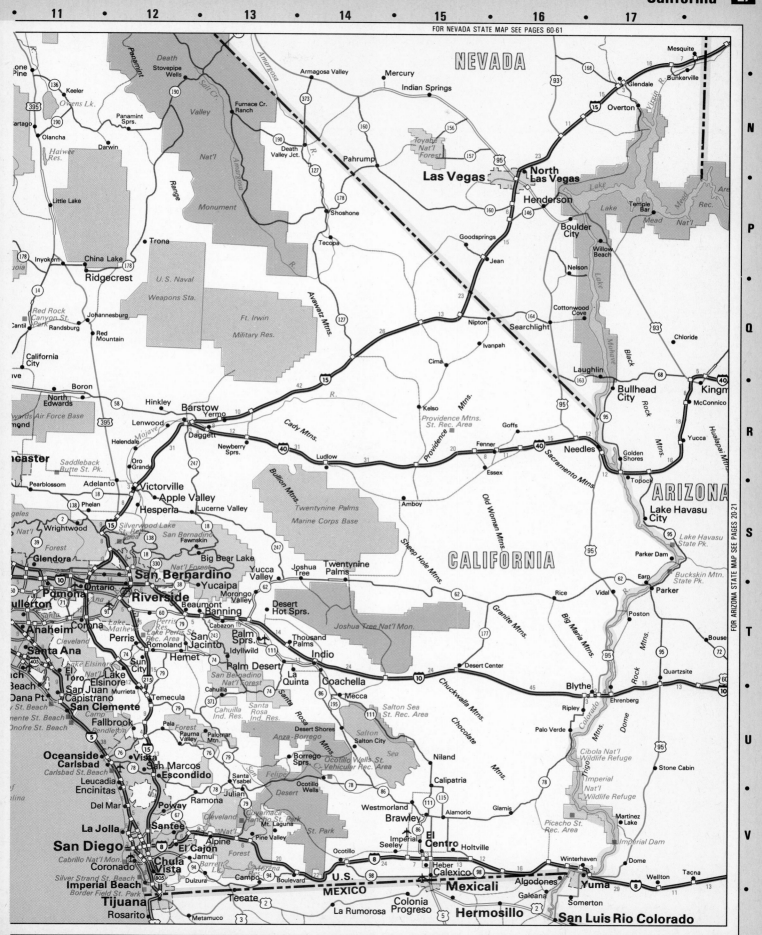

FOR NEVADA STATE MAP SEE PAGES 60-61

FOR ARIZONA STATE MAP SEE PAGES 20-21

NEVADA

ARIZONA

CALIFORNIA

U.S.

MEXICO

FOR WYOMING STATE MAP SEE PAGES 92-93

WYOMING

UTAH

Carter · Lyman · Urie · Mountain View · Robertson · Lonetree · Burntfork · McKinnon · Manila · Green Lake · Ashley · Oak Park Res. National · Forest · State Park · Steinaker Res. · Whiterocks · Monarch · Neola · Maeser · Vernal · Naples · Jensen · Boneta · Altamont · Bluebell · Cedarview · Leeton · Gusher · Lapoint · Mt. Emmons · Upalco · Arcadia · Ioka · Roosevelt · Fort Duchesne · Bridgeland · Myton · Ouray · Leota · Duchesne · Sunnyside · East Carbon City · Hill Creek Extension · Uintah and Ouray Indian Reservation · Woodside · Green River · Thompson · Crescent Jct · Cisco · Mack · Loma · Fruita · Grand Junction · Clifton · Moab · Gateway · Uravan · Paradox · Bedrock · La Sal Jct · La Sal · Nucla · Vancorum · Naturita · Slick Rock · Summit Pt. · Egnar · Monticello · Dove Creek · Eastland · Cahone · Fry Canyon · Blanding · Pleasant View · Yellow Jacket · Lewis · Arriola · Dolores · Lebanon · Cortez · Bluff · Montezuma Creek · Aneth · Towaoc · Mexican Hat · Beklabito · Shiprock · Flora Vista · Kirtland · Turley · Aztec · Archuleta · Farmington · Bloomfield · Blanco

Green River · Flaming Gorge Res. · Flaming Gorge National Recreation Area · Dinosaur National Monument · Hiawatha · Sunbeam · Maybell · Craig · Lay · Milner · Steamboat Sprs. · Coalmont · Hamilton · Hayden · Rand · Elk Springs · Blue Mountain · Dinosaur · Rangely · Meeker · Buford · Oak Creek · Phippsburg · Yampa · Hot Sulphur Springs · Toponas · McCoy · Parshall · Kremmling · Tabernash · Fraser · Rio Blanco · Bond · State Bridge · Winter Park · New Castle · Dotsero · Gypsum · Wolcott · Silverthorne · Vail · Frisco · Georgetown · Echo Lake · Rifle · Silt · Eagle · Edwards · Avon · Dowd · Gilman · Dillon · Breckenridge · Parachute · Glenwood Sprs. · Red Cliff · Climax · Blue River · Jefferson · DeBeque · Carbondale · Basalt · Snowmass · Woody Creek · Alma · Como · Collbran · Molina · Redstone · Aspen · Leadville · Fairplay · Cameo · Mesa · Marble · Snowmass Village · Twin Lakes · Granite · Garo Park · Palisade · Skyway · Grand Mesa National Forest · Whitewater · Cedaredge · Bowie · Somerset · Crested Butte · Buena Vista · Orchard City · Austin · Paonia · Mount Princeton Hot Springs · Nathrop · Delta · Lazear · Hotchkiss · Crawford · Almont · Johnson Village · Maher · Gunnison · Garfield · Salida · Olathe · Montrose · Parlin · Doyleville · Poncha Springs · Howard · Cimarron · Sapinero · Sargents · Coaldale · Powderhorn · Lake City · Saguache · Villa Grove · Ridgway · Ouray · Mineral Hot Springs · Moffat · Redvale · Norwood · Placerville · Saw Pit · Telluride · Red Mountain · Creede · Center · Hooper · Ophir · Gladstone · Silverton · Wagon Wheel Gap · Dunton · Rico · South Fork · Spar City · Del Norte · Mosca · Stoner · Homelake · Rockwood · Monte Vista · Alamosa · Hermosa · Summitville · Platoro · Capulin · Mancos · Hesperus · Durango · Chimney Rock · Pagosa Sprs. · La Jara · Romeo · Sanford · Fort Lewis · Breen · Kline · Oxford · Bayfield · Ignacio · Allison · Arboles · Chromo · Conejos · Antonito · Marvel · Redmesa · Dulce · Lumberton · Monero · Chama · Tres Piedras · La Plata · Cedar Hill · Navajo Lake State Park · Los Ojos · Rutheron · Ensenada · Tierra Amarilla · Brazos

Saratoga · Centennial · Albany · Riverside · Encampment · Savery · Baggs · Dixon · Woods Landing · Mountain Home · Cowdrey · Walden · Rustic · Lake John · Routt National Forest · Estes Park · Deer Ridge · Grand Lake · Raymond · Granby · Nederland · Rollinsville · Empire · Black Hawk · Winter Park · Arapaho National Forest · Medicine Bow Nat'l Forest · Platte River

White River National Forest · Gunnison National Forest · San Isabel National Forest · Pike National Forest · Uncompahgre National Forest · San Juan National Forest · Rio Grande National Forest · Curecanti National Recreation Area · Blue Mesa Res. · Black Canyon of the Gunnison National Monument · Great Sand Dunes National Monument · Southern Ute Indian Reservation · Mesa Verde National Park · Ute Mountain Indian Reservation · Hovenweep Nat'l Monument · Natural Bridges Nat'l Monument · Canyonlands National Park · Arches National Park · Colorado National Monument · Manti-La Sal National Forest · Glen Canyon National Recreation Area

FOR UTAH STATE MAP SEE PAGES 84-85

Colorado
Scale of Miles
0 7 14 21 28 35

N

© Creative Sales Corporation

FOR NEW MEXICO STATE MAP SEE PAGES 64-65

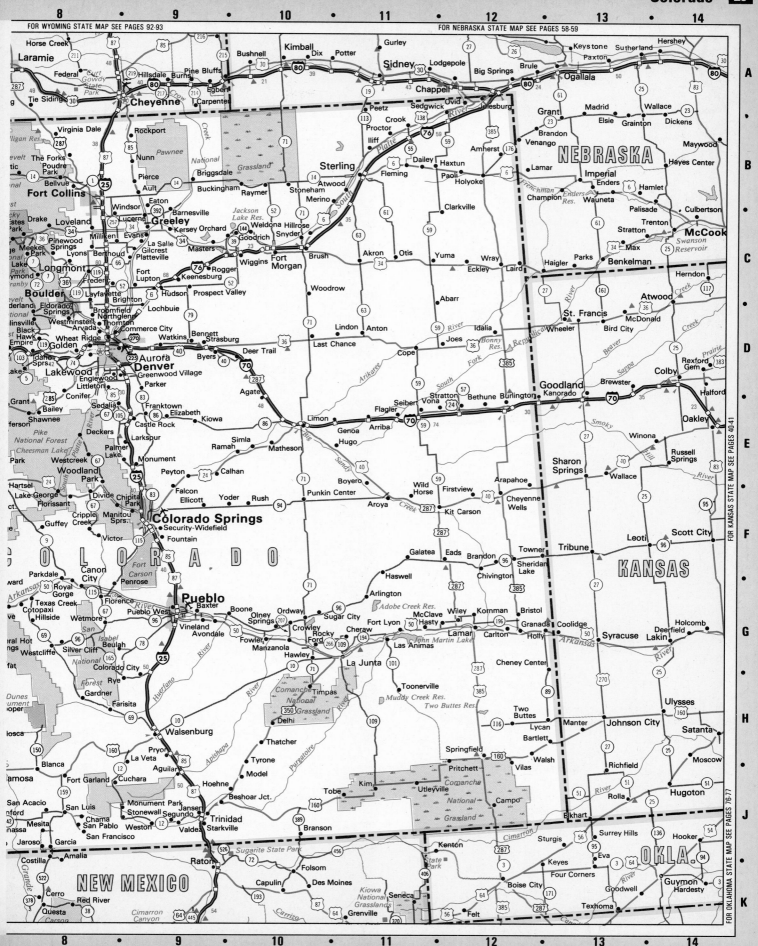

FOR VERMONT STATE MAP SEE PAGE 57

FOR NEW YORK STATE MAP SEE PAGES 66-69

Long Island Sound

N.Y.

VT.

N.H.

MASS.

CONN

Selected place names:

Troy, Albany, Rensselaer, Williamstown, North Adams, Adams, Pittsfield, Dalton, Hinsdale, Lenox, Richmond, West Stockbridge, Stockbridge, Lee, Great Barrington, Sheffield, New Marlborough, Sandisfield, Monterey, Otis, West Becket, Becket, Chester, Washington, Middlefield, Chesterfield, Worthington Ctr., Cummington, Williamsburg, Northampton, Westhampton, Easthampton, Huntington, Russell, Montgomery, Westfield, Holyoke, Chicopee, Springfield, West Springfield, Agawam, Suffield, Granby, Windsor Locks, East Granby, Enfield, Somers, Stafford, Woodstock, Eastford, Pomfret, Putnam, Thompson, Killingly, Brooklyn, Plainfield, Sterling, Webster, Southbridge, Dudley, Sturbridge, Brimfield, Palmer, Monson, Wales, Holland, Wilbraham, Longmeadow, East Longmeadow, Hampden, Ware, West Brookfield, Brookfield, Spencer, Leicester, Worcester, Holden, Paxton, Rutland, Barre, Princeton, Westminster, Gardner, Leominster, Fitchburg, Ashburnham, Winchendon, Royalston, Athol, Orange, Templeton, Petersham, Hardwick, Belchertown, South Hadley, Hadley, Amherst, Sunderland, Leverett, Montague, Millers Falls, Greenfield, Deerfield, Whately, Conway, Shelburne, Shelburne Falls, Buckland, Charlemont, Colrain, Leyden, Bernardston, Gill, Northfield, Warwick, Winchester, Swanzey, Peterborough, Jaffrey, Rindge, Ashby, Baldwinville

Pownal, Clarksburg, Stamford, Readsboro, Whitingham, Wilmington, Guilford, Florida, Savoy, Cheshire, Windsor, Hawley, Plainfield, Peru, Worthington, Goshen, Cornwall, Torrington, Litchfield, Warren, Kent, Cornwall Bridge, Sharon, Falls Village, Canaan, Norfolk, Colebrook, Hartland, East Hartland, Barkhamsted, New Hartford, Canton, Simsbury, Avon, Bloomfield, Windsor, South Windsor, East Hartford, Manchester, Vernon, Coventry, Andover, Columbia, Hebron, Bolton, Storrs, Mansfield Center, Chaplin, Hampton, Willington, Ashford, Westford, Ellington, Tolland, Melrose

Salisbury, Lakeville, Amenia, Dover Plains, Pawling, Sherman, New Fairfield, New Milford, Brookfield, Southbury, Woodbury, Bethlehem, Morris, Washington, Roxbury, Bridgewater, Newtown, Monroe, Shelton, Derby, Ansonia, Seymour, Oxford, Naugatuck, Beacon Falls, Bethel, Danbury, Redding, Ridgefield, Georgetown, Wilton, New Canaan, Norwalk, Westport, Weston, Fairfield, Bridgeport, Trumbull, Stratford, Milford, West Haven, New Haven, Woodbridge, Hamden, North Haven, Wallingford, Cheshire, Southington, Plainville, Bristol, Plymouth, Thomaston, Watertown, Waterbury, Wolcott, Meriden, New Britain, Newington, Wethersfield, Rocky Hill, Cromwell, Berlin, Farmington, West Hartford, Hartford, Glastonbury, Middletown, Durham, Middlefield, Haddam, East Hampton, Marlborough, Colchester, Lebanon, Windham, Scotland, Canterbury, Franklin, Bozrah, Norwich, Preston City, Jewett City, Hopeville, Voluntown, Sterling

North Branford, Branford, East Haven, Guilford, Madison, Clinton, Westbrook, Old Saybrook, Essex, Deep River, Chester, Haddam, Killingworth, Durham, Old Lyme, East Lyme, Waterford, New London, Groton, Mystic, Pawcatuck, North Stonington, Ledyard Ctr., Oakdale Hts., Salem, Montville, Gales Ferry

Greenwich, Stamford, Darien, Bedford, Cross River, Brewster, Salem Ctr., Poughquag, Stanfordville

Greenport, Southold, Shelter Island, Peconic, Gardiners Island, Fishers Island, Montauk

Long Island Sound

8 9 10 11 12 13 14 15

FOR NEW HAMPSHIRE STATE MAP SEE PAGE 57

Atlantic

Ocean

Wilton, Merrimack, Derry, Hampstead, Amesbury, Salisbury, Salisbury Beach St. Res.
Milford, Litchfield, Londonderry, Atkinson, Merrimac, West Newbury, Newburyport, Newbury, Parker River Nat'l Wildlife Ref.
Nashua, Windham, Hudson, Salem, Groveland, Haverhill, Georgetown, Rowley, Plum Is. St. Pk.
Hollis, Methuen, Lawrence, Boxford, Ipswich, Topsfield, Essex, Rockport
Townsend, Tyngsborough, Dracut, Andover, North Reading, Wenham, Hamilton, Gloucester
Pepperell, Lowell, Tewksbury, Reading, Danvers, Manchester
Groton, Westford, Chelmsford, Billerica, Wilmington, Lynnfield, Beverly, Salem, Marblehead
Shirley, Littleton, Carlisle, Concord, Wakefield, Peabody, Saugus, Swampscott
Harvard, Acton, Bedford, Woburn, Lexington, Lynn, Nahant
Sterling, Clinton, Stow, Maynard, Lincoln, Cambridge, Revere, Chelsea, Winthrop
Boylston, Hudson, Wayland, Newton, Boston
Northborough, Marlborough, Cochituate, Wellesley, Hull, Massachusetts Bay
Shrewsbury, Natick, Milton, Quincy, Scituate
Westborough, Framingham, Westwood, Dedham, Hingham, Weymouth, Norwell
Grafton, Upton, Hopkinton, Medfield, Norwood, Braintree, Randolph, Hanover, Marshfield
Millbury, Milford, Millis, Walpole, Canton, Holbrook, Avon, Rockland
Northbridge, Hopedale, Norfolk, Sharon, Stoughton, Brockton, Abington, Hanson, Pembroke
Whitinsville, Mendon, Wrentham, Foxborough, Easton, Whitman, East Bridgewater, Duxbury
Uxbridge, Bellingham, Mansfield, Bridgewater, Halifax, Kingston, Plymouth
Blackstone, N. Attleborough, Norton, Raynham, Plympton, Carver
Slatersville, Woonsocket, Attleboro, Taunton, Middleborough
Harrisville, Nasonville, Berkley, Rehoboth, Dighton, Provincetown, Truro
Pascoag, Ashton, Pawtucket, Seekonk, Somerset, Freetown, Wareham, Wellfleet, Eastham
Chepachet, Esmond, Providence, Dighton, Buzzards Bay, Sagamore, Sandwich, Brewster, Orleans
Glocester, Harmony, Cranston, East Providence, Auburn, Swansea, Bourne, Barnstable, Dennis, Yarmouth, Harwich, Chatham
Foster Center, Clayville, Barrington, Warren, Bristol, Rochester, Acushnet, Marion, Centerville, Hyannis, South Yarmouth, Dennis Port, West Dennis
Vernon, Hope, Fiskeville, Warwick, Mattapoisett, Osterville
West Greenwich, East Greenwich, Tiverton, Westport, Fairhaven, New Bedford, Falmouth, East Falmouth
Nooseneck, Arcadia, Exeter, Portsmouth, Dartmouth, Buzzards Bay
Millville, Wickford, Middletown, Tisbury, Vineyard Haven, Oak Bluffs, Nantucket Sound
Hope Valley, Saunderstown, Jamestown, Newport, Little Compton, North Tisbury
Wood River Jct., Woodville, Kingston, Wakefield, Narragansett Pier, Gay Head, Chilmark, Edgartown, West Tisbury, Nantucket
Charlestown, Rhode Island Sound, Elizabeth Islands, Martha's Vineyard, Chappaquidick Island, Nantucket Island

Cape Cod Bay
Nantucket Sound
Monomoy Island
Cape Cod Nat'l Seashore
Block Island

Connecticut
Massachusetts
Rhode Island

Scale of Miles
0 3 6 9 12 15

N

© Creative Sales Corporation

A B C D E F G H J K

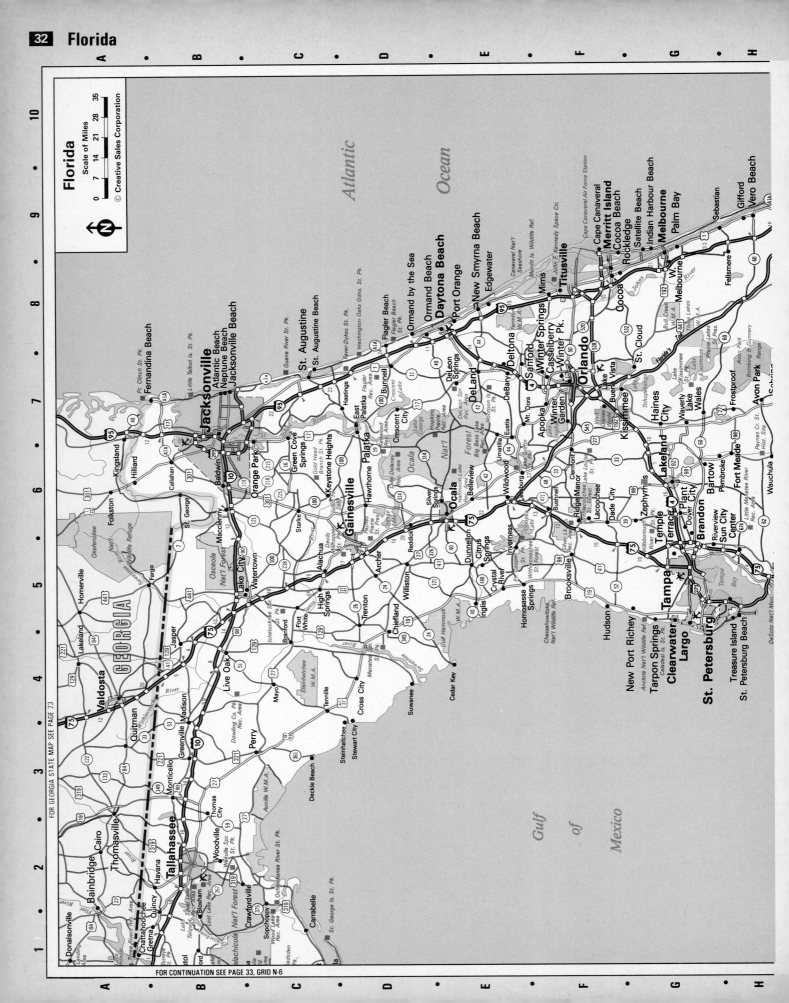

Florida

Gulf of Mexico

FOR CONTINUATION SEE PAGE 32, GRID B-1

FOR MISSISSIPPI STATE MAP SEE PAGE 56

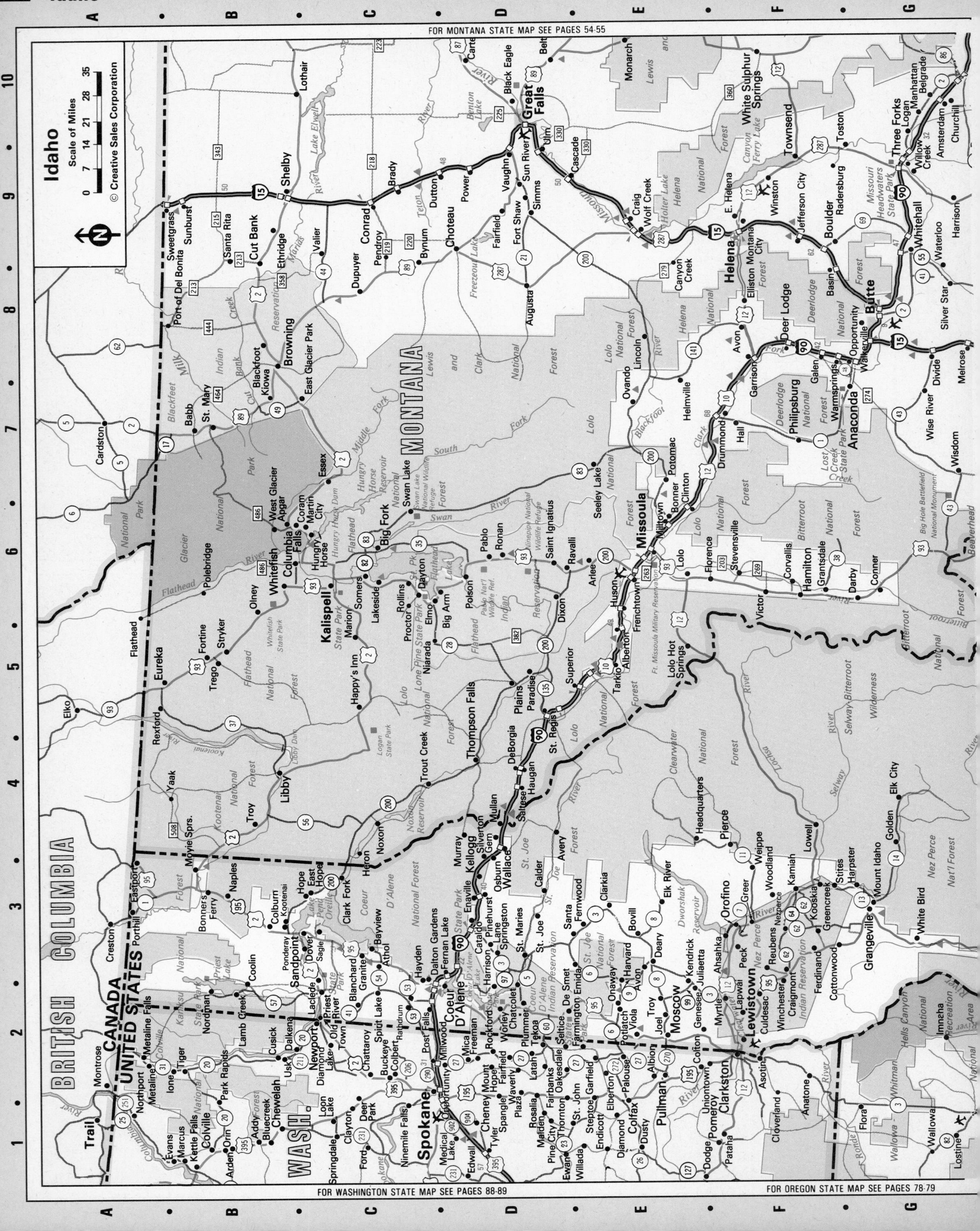

Idaho

Scale of Miles

© Creative Sales Corporation

0 7 14 21 28 35

N

FOR WASHINGTON STATE MAP SEE PAGES 88-89

FOR OREGON STATE MAP SEE PAGES 78-79

FOR WYOMING STATE MAP SEE PAGES 92-93

FOR OREGON STATE MAP SEE PAGES 78-79

FOR UTAH STATE MAP SEE PAGES 84-85

FOR NEVADA STATE MAP SEE PAGES 60-61

IDAHO

MONTANA

WYOMING / WY

OREGON

NEVADA

UTAH

Bozeman, Gallatin Gateway, Emigrant, Chico Hot Springs, Bozeman Hot Sprs., Big Sky, Cameron, Norris, Sheridan, Twin Bridges, Alder, Laurin, Ennis, Virginia City, Glen, Dillon, Grant, Jackson, Gibbonsville, North Fork, Salmon, Tendoy, Lemhi, May, Leadore, Patterson, Baker, Challis, Clayton, Sunbeam, Stanley, Cape Horn, Warm Lake, Cascade, Donnelly, McCall, Meadows, New Meadows, Tamarack, Council, Fruitvale, Midvale, Cambridge, Weiser, New Bridge, Halfway, Richland, Joseph, Huntington, Ontario, Nyssa, Adrian, Parma, Notus, Caldwell, Nampa, Kuna, Meridian, Boise, Eagle, Emmett, Payette, Fruitland, New Plymouth, Gardena, Sweet, Letha, Middleton, Marsing, Homedale, Wilder, Murphy, Silver City, Melba, Givens Hot Sprs., Grand View, Mountain Home, Bruneau, Hammett, Glenns Ferry, King Hill, Hagerman, Bliss, Gooding, Wendell, Jerome, Twin Falls, Buhl, Filer, Kimberly, Hansen, Murtaugh, Castleford, Hollister, Rogerson, Jackpot, Contact, Jarbidge, Mountain City, Owyhee

Salmon, Challis, Sawtooth, Boise, Payette National Forest, Sawtooth National Recreation Area, Craters of the Moon Nat'l Mon.

Idaho Falls, Rexburg, St. Anthony, Ashton, Chester, Newdale, Teton, Sugar City, Parker, Menan, Lewisville, Roberts, Rigby, Ririe, Ucon, Ammon, Iona, Shelley, Basalt, Firth, Blackfoot, Moreland, Rockford, Pingree, Springfield, Sterling, Aberdeen, American Falls, Pocatello, Chubbuck, Inkom, McCammon, Arimo, Lava Hot Springs, Downey, Bancroft, Grace, Thatcher, Soda Springs, Conda, Bern, Montpelier, Paris, St. Charles, Fish Haven, Bloomington, Dingle, Georgetown, Bennington, Swan Lake, Virginia, Robin, Malad City, Holbrook, Samaria, Snowville, Portage, Plymouth, Clarkston, Preston, Franklin, Dayton, Clifton, Oxford, Banida, Mink Creek, Richmond, Smithfield, Lewiston, Cove, Newton, Amalga, Fielding, Cornish

Pocatello, Raft River, Malta, Elba, Albion, Oakley, Burley, Rupert, Paul, Acequia, Minidoka, Eden, Hazelton, Heyburn, Declo, Marion, Rock Creek

Dubois, Spencer, Hamer, Mud Lake, Howe, Arco, Darlington, Moore, Mackay, Butte City, Atomic City, Carey, Picabo, Richfield, Dietrich, Shoshone, Gannett, Bellevue, Hailey, Ketchum, Sun Valley, Fairfield, Corral, Hill City

Island Park, Macks Inn, Warm River, Drummond, Tetonia, Driggs, Victor, Swan Valley, Irwin, Heise, Palisades Reservoir, Alpine Jct., Etna, Freedom, Thayne, Turnerville, Bedford, Grover, Afton, Smoot, Fairview, Auburn, Border, Cokeville, Sage, Sage Jct.

Jackson, Moose, Jenny Lake, Teton Village, Wilson, Moran, Kelly, Old Faithful, W. Thumb Jct., Mammoth, Norris Jct., Madison Jct., Yellowstone National Park, Grand Teton National Park, Targhee National Forest, Caribou National Forest

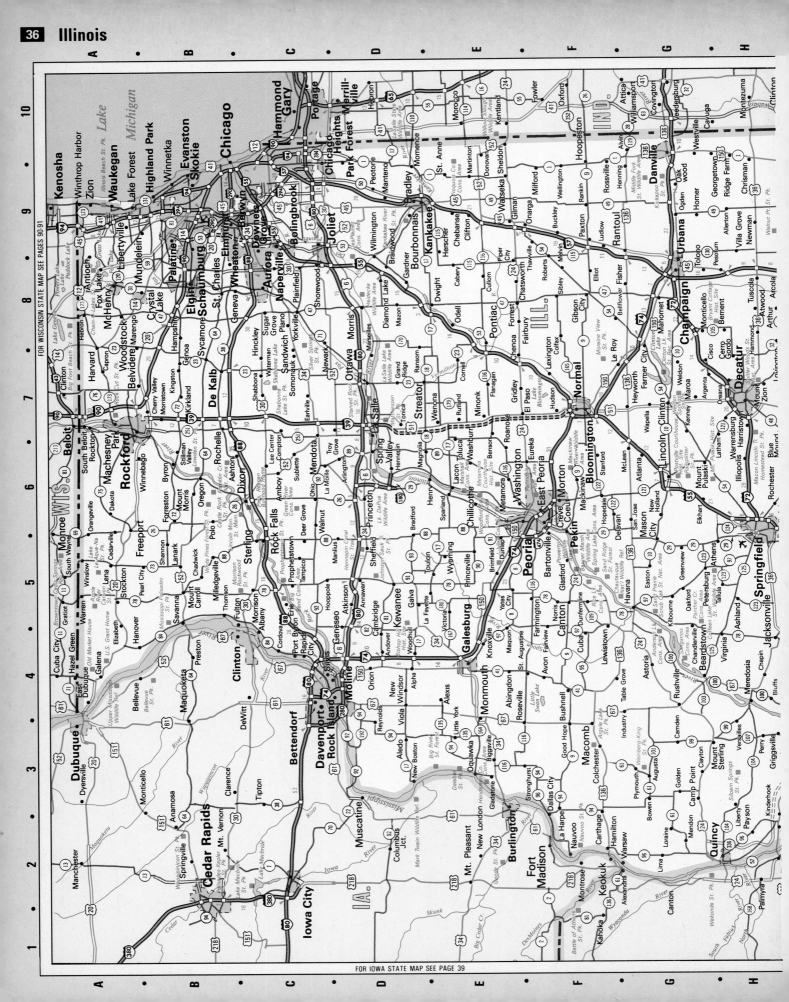

FOR WISCONSIN STATE MAP SEE PAGES 90-91

FOR IOWA STATE MAP SEE PAGE 39

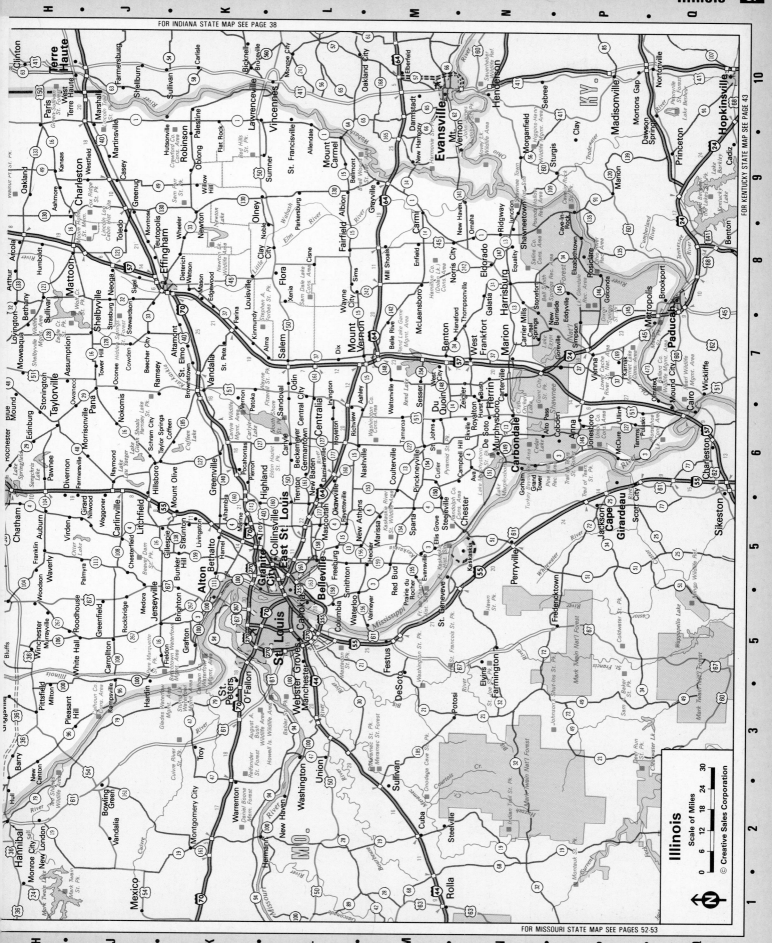

FOR INDIANA STATE MAP SEE PAGE 38

FOR KENTUCKY STATE MAP SEE PAGE 43

FOR MISSOURI STATE MAP SEE PAGES 52-53

Illinois

Scale of Miles

0 6 12 18 24 30

© Creative Sales Corporation

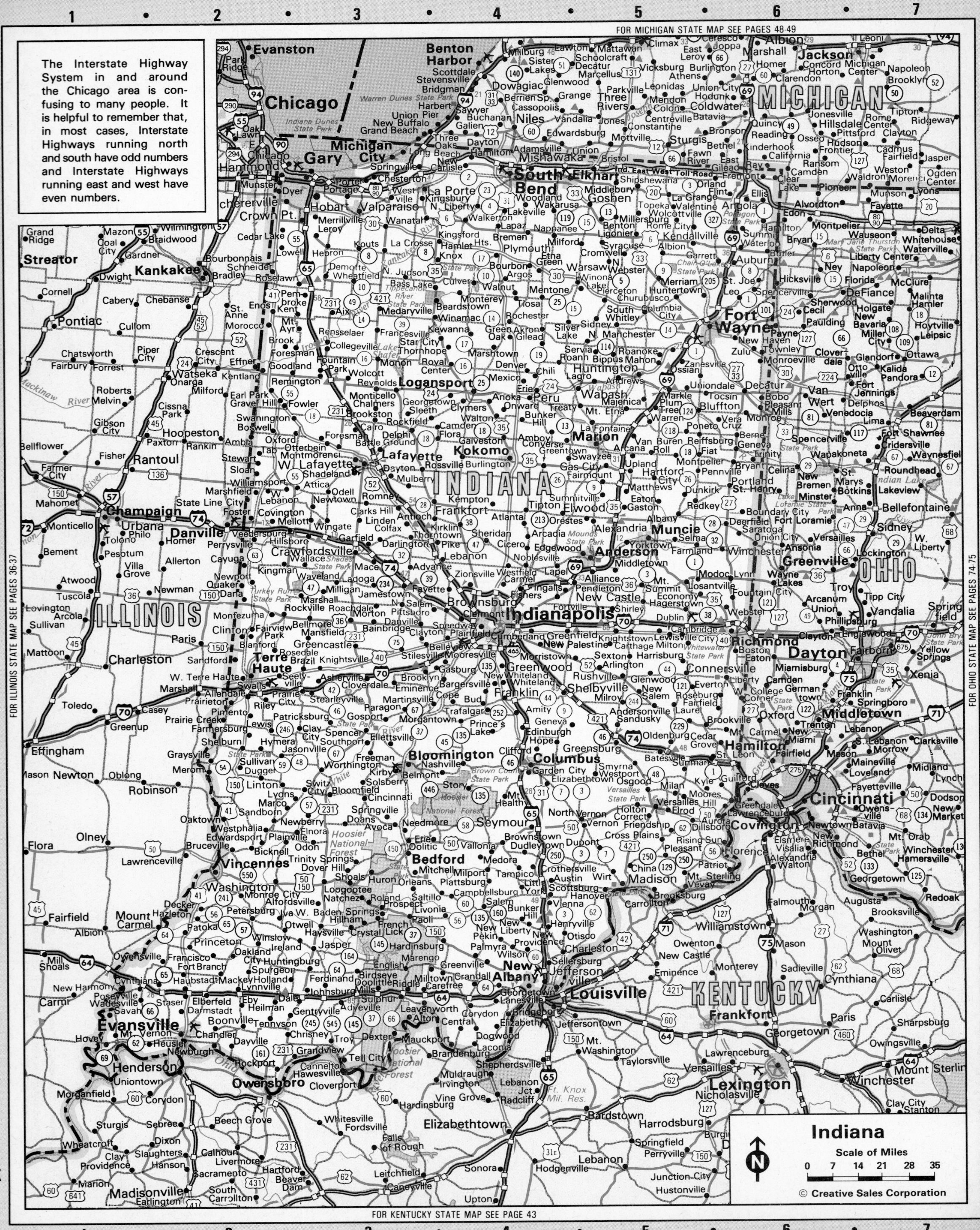

FOR MICHIGAN STATE MAP SEE PAGES 48-49

The Interstate Highway System in and around the Chicago area is confusing to many people. It is helpful to remember that, in most cases, Interstate Highways running north and south have odd numbers and Interstate Highways running east and west have even numbers.

MICHIGAN

ILLINOIS

INDIANA

OHIO

KENTUCKY

Chicago

Gary

South Bend

Fort Wayne

Lafayette

Kokomo

Indianapolis

Muncie

Anderson

Terre Haute

Bloomington

Columbus

Cincinnati

Louisville

Evansville

Henderson

Owensboro

Indiana

Scale of Miles

0   7   14   21   28   35

© Creative Sales Corporation

FOR ILLINOIS STATE MAP SEE PAGES 36-37

FOR OHIO STATE MAP SEE PAGES 74-75

FOR KENTUCKY STATE MAP SEE PAGE 43

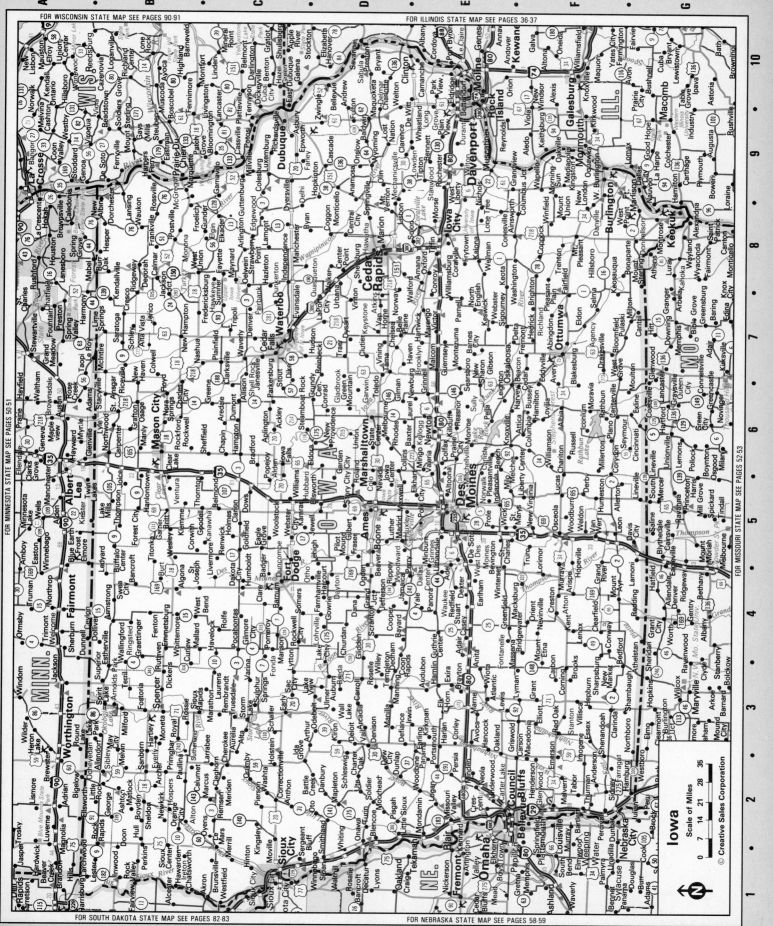

Iowa

Scale of Miles

0 7 14 21 28 35

© Creative Sales Corporation

FOR NEBRASKA STATE MAP SEE PAGES 58-59

NEBRASKA

KANSAS

COL.

FOR COLORADO STATE MAP SEE PAGES 28-29

Kansas

Scale of Miles

0   7   14   21   28   35

N

© Creative Sales Corporation

FOR OKLAHOMA STATE MAP SEE PAGES 76-77

Clarkville, Imperial, Champion, Enders, Wauneta, Hamlet, Palisade, Hayes Center, Stockville, Elwood, Smithfield, Bertrand, Loomis, Holdrege, Axtell, Minden, Holstein, Hastings, Otis, Yuma, Eckley, Wray, Laird, Haigler, Parks, Benkelman, Max, Stratton, Trenton, Culbertson, McCook, Cambridge, Bartley, Indianola, Arapahoe, Edison, Oxford, Atlanta, Funk, Wilcox, Ragan, Huntley, Republican City, Franklin, Naponee, Riverton, Inavale

Cope, Joes, Idalia, St. Francis, Wheeler, Bird City, McDonald, Atwood, Oberlin, Norcatur, Almena, Long Island, Herndon, Danbury, Lebanon, Alma, Wilsonville, Beaver City, Stamford, Orleans

St. Francis, Bird City, McDonald, Atwood, Oberlin, Norcatur, Norton, Prairie View, Phillipsburg, Kensington, Athol, Lebanon, Jennings, Clayton, Edmond, Logan, Glade, Agra, Smith Center, Dresden, Selden, Lenora, Kirwin, Cedar, Gaylord, Portis

Vona, Stratton, Burlington, Goodland, Brewster, Colby, Gem, Rexford, Menlo, Morland, Hill City, Stockton, Woodston, Alton, Osborne, Halford, Hoxie, Bogue, Damar, Palco, Zurich, Plainville, Natoma, Paradise, Luray, Lucas

Oakley, Winona, Grinnell, Park, Grainfield, Quinter, Collyer, WaKeeney, Waldo, Firstview, Arapahoe, Cheyenne Wells, Sharon Springs, Wallace, Russell Springs, Gove, Saline River, Ellis, Hays, Victoria, Gorham, Russell, Bunker Hill, Wilson, Ellsworth

Sheridan Lake, Towner, Brandon, Tribune, Leoti, Healy, Utica, Ransom, Brownell, McCracken, LaCrosse, Galatia, Schoenchen, Holyrood, Bushton, Dighton, Ness City, Bazine, Otis, Bison, Olmitz, Claflin, May, Valley, Bristol, Carlton, Granada, Holly, Coolidge, Syracuse, Deerfield, Garden City, Holcomb, Lakin, Scott City, Alexander, Rush Center, Timken, Hoisington, Great Bend, Burdett, Rozel, Pawnee Rock, Larned, Seward, Hudson, St. John, Abbeyville, Plevna, Sylvia, Stafford, Byers

Lamar, Cheney Center, Two Buttes, Lycan, Johnson City, Ulysses, Montezuma, Ensign, Ford, Dodge City, Wright, Spearville, Offerle, Kinsley, Lewis, Macksville, Belpre, Iuka, Turon, Preston, Pratt, Coats, Sawyer, Isabel, Zenda, Nashville

Vilas, Bartlett, Manter, Saunders, Walsh, Richfield, Moscow, Satanta, Sublette, Copeland, Minneola, Kingsdown, Bucklin, Mullinville, Greensburg, Cullison, Haviland, Johnson City, Meade, Fowler, Plains, Kismet, Ashland, Coldwater, Medicine Lodge, Sharon, Attica

Sturgis, Surrey Hills, Eva, Four Corners, Elkhart, Rolla, Liberal, Tyrone, Baker, Forgan, Mocane, Knowles, Englewood, Hardtner, Kiowa, Hazelton

Guymon, Goodwell, Optima, Hooker, Turpin, Beaver, Gate, Rosston, Buffalo, Laverne, Plainview, Camp Houston, Cora, Capron, Burlington, Driftwood, Ingersoll, Cherokee, Alva, Amorita

Hardesty, Bryan's Corner, Boyd, Balko, Gray, Elmwood, Slapout, Ft. Supply, Tegarden, Waynoka, Hopeton, Carmen, McWillie, Aline, Cleo Springs, Orienta

Perry, Booker, Follett, Tangier, Woodward, Mooreland, Gage

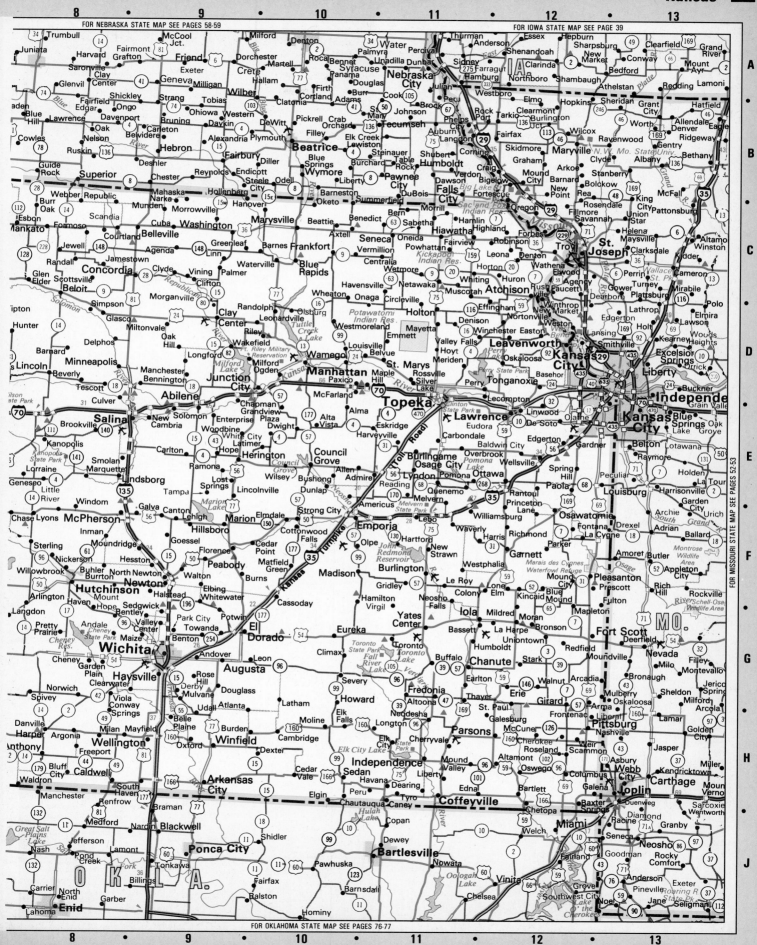

FOR NEBRASKA STATE MAP SEE PAGES 58-59
FOR IOWA STATE MAP SEE PAGE 39
FOR MISSOURI STATE MAP SEE PAGES 52-53
FOR OKLAHOMA STATE MAP SEE PAGES 76-77

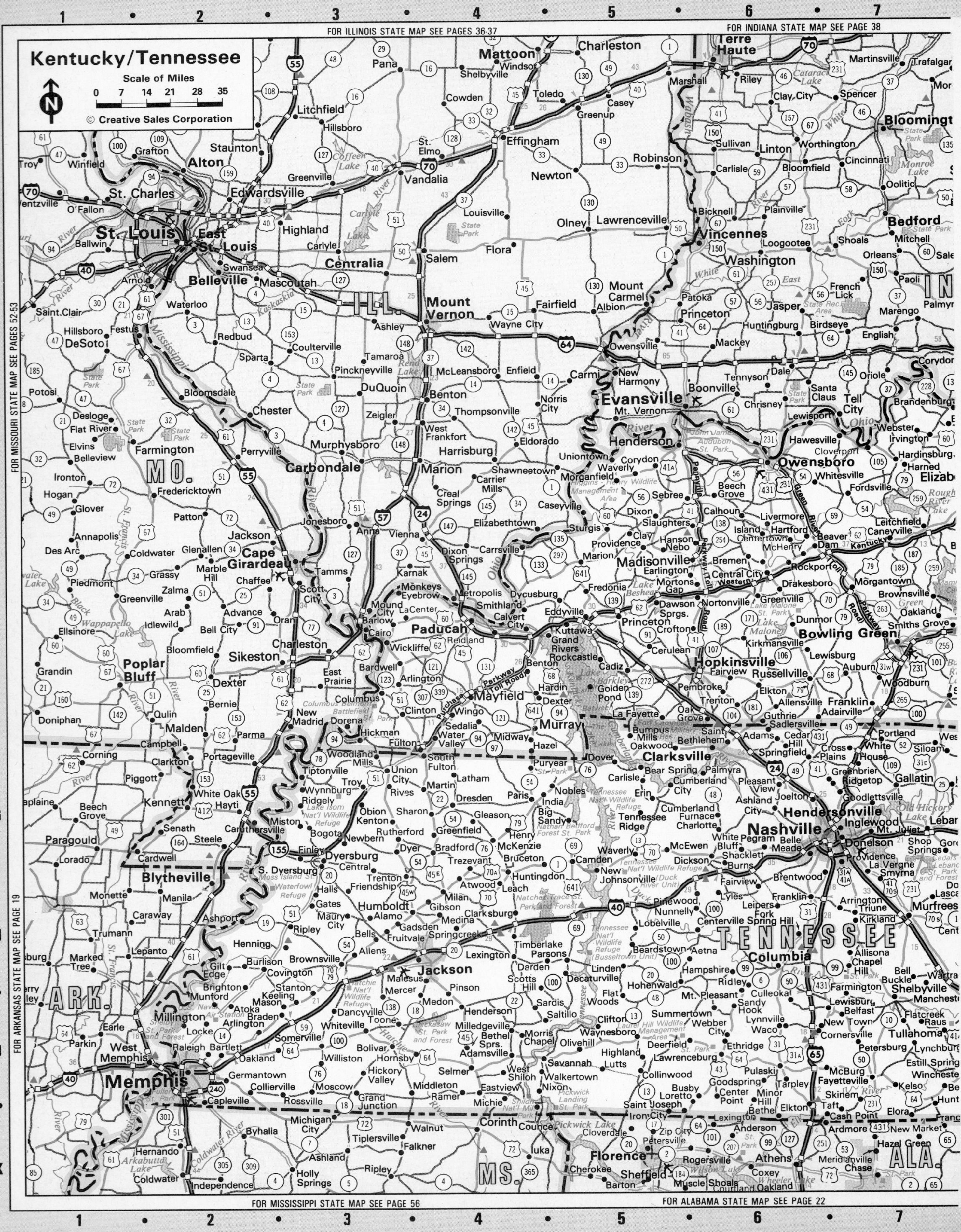

Kentucky/Tennessee

Scale of Miles
0 7 14 21 28 35

© Creative Sales Corporation

N

FOR ILLINOIS STATE MAP SEE PAGES 36-37
FOR INDIANA STATE MAP SEE PAGE 38
FOR MISSOURI STATE MAP SEE PAGES 52-53
FOR ARKANSAS STATE MAP SEE PAGE 19
FOR MISSISSIPPI STATE MAP SEE PAGE 56
FOR ALABAMA STATE MAP SEE PAGE 22

Major place names visible on map:

Illinois: Pana, Mattoon, Charleston, Shelbyville, Windsor, Toledo, Cowden, Casey, Greenup, Effingham, St. Elmo, Newton, Vandalia, Greenville, Litchfield, Hillsboro, Staunton, Alton, Edwardsville, Highland, Centralia, Mount Vernon, Salem, Flora, Fairfield, Albion, Carmi, Mt. Carmel, Benton, DuQuoin, Murphysboro, Carbondale, Marion, Harrisburg, Eldorado, Anna, Vienna, Cairo, Chester

Missouri: St. Louis, East St. Louis, Belleville, Ballwin, Arnold, Festus, DeSoto, Potosi, Farmington, Fredericktown, Ironton, Cape Girardeau, Jackson, Chaffee, Sikeston, Dexter, Poplar Bluff, Kennett, Caruthersville, Malden, Doniphan, Piedmont, Annapolis

Indiana: Terre Haute, Martinsville, Bloomington, Vincennes, Washington, Princeton, Evansville, Boonville, Tell City, Owensboro, Huntingburg, Jasper, Paoli, Bedford

Kentucky: Henderson, Owensboro, Madisonville, Central City, Bowling Green, Hopkinsville, Russellville, Franklin, Cadiz, Murray, Mayfield, Paducah, Benton, Princeton, Eddyville, Morganfield, Providence, Marion

Tennessee: Memphis, Millington, Bartlett, Collierville, Brownsville, Jackson, Humboldt, Dyersburg, Union City, Martin, Dresden, Paris, Camden, Waverly, Dickson, Clarksville, Nashville, Hendersonville, Donelson, Brentwood, Franklin, Columbia, Lawrenceburg, Pulaski, Fayetteville, Tullahoma, Shelbyville, Lynchburg, Winchester, Murfreesboro, Gallatin, Lebanon, Smyrna

Arkansas: Paragould, Jonesboro, Blytheville, Marked Tree, West Memphis, Trumann, Manila

Mississippi: Corinth, Iuka, Holly Springs, Byhalia, Walnut, Hernando

Alabama: Florence, Athens, Sheffield, Muscle Shoals, Courtland, Rogersville

FOR OHIO STATE MAP SEE PAGES 74-75

FOR WEST VIRGINIA STATE MAP SEE PAGES 86-87

FOR VIRGINIA STATE MAP SEE PAGES 86-87

FOR NORTH CAROLINA STATE MAP SEE PAGES 70-71

FOR SOUTH CAROLINA STATE MAP SEE PAGE 71

FOR MISSISSIPPI STATE MAP SEE PAGE 56

Louisiana

Scale of Miles

0   7   14   21   28   35

© Creative Sales Corporation

N

FOR ARKANSAS STATE MAP SEE PAGE 19

Gulf of Mexico

LOUISIANA

MS

TEX

Major cities and places shown on the map include:

New Orleans, Baton Rouge, Shreveport, Monroe, Alexandria, Lafayette, Lake Charles, Houma, Opelousas, New Iberia, Natchitoches, Ruston, Bastrop, Minden, Bossier City, Slidell, Covington, Hammond, Morgan City, Thibodaux, Gretna, Metairie, Kenner, Westwego, Abbeville, Crowley, Jennings, Sulphur, De Ridder, Leesville, Many, Winnfield, Jonesboro, Columbia, Ferriday, Vidalia, Bunkie, Marksville, Ville Platte, Eunice, Port Allen, Plaquemine, Donaldsonville, Gonzales, Denham Springs, Franklinton, Bogalusa, Amite, Kentwood

Jackson, Vicksburg, Natchez, McComb, Brookhaven, Hattiesburg, Laurel, Meridian, Canton, Yazoo City, Picayune, Gulfport

Beaumont, Port Arthur, Orange, Nederland, Groves, Carthage, Center

Canadian Citizens Visiting the United States

Passports or visas are not required of Canadian citizens or British subjects residing in Canada entering the United States for a period of six months or less; however, evidence of citizenship is rigidly controlled. Check with customs officials for complete regulations and requirements.

United States Citizens Visiting Canada

All persons entering Canada must report to the Canadian Immigration and Customs Office at the Port of Entry and secure the necessary permits for admission of their person and possessions. The transportation of plants and produce is rigidly controlled. Check with customs officials for complete regulations and requirements.

QUEBEC

MAINE

NEW BRUNSWICK

NH

Atlantic

Ocean

FOR NEW HAMPSHIRE STATE MAP SEE PAGE 57

Maine

Scale of Miles

0 7 14 21 28 35

© Creative Sales Corporation

1 • 2 • 3 • 4 • 5 • 6 • 7 • 8

FOR PENNSYLVANIA STATE MAP SEE PAGES 80-81

A

Confluence
Meyersdale
Hyndman
Fayetteville
Mont Alto
Gettysb
Mercersburg
Greencastle
Waynesboro
Warfordsburg
Riney Grove
Grantsville
Corriganville
Pratt
Hancock
Millstone
Clear Spring
Fountain Head
Cascade
Emmit
Friendsville
Frostburg
La Vale
Rush
Cumberland
Halfway
Hagerstown
Thurmont
Accident
Midland
Cresaptown
Ridgeley Potomac Park
Berkeley Springs
Hedgesville
Boonsboro
Myersville
Walkersville
Hoyes
McHenry
Lonaconing
Oldtown
Martinsburg
Middletown
Frederick
Paw Paw
Sharpsburg
Shepherdstown
Braddock Heights
Luke
Westernport
Fort Ashby
Piedmont
Keyser
Romney
Gerrardstown
Inwood
Harpers Ferry
Brunswick
Rosemont
Buckeystown
Terra Alta
Oakland
Mtn. Lake Park
Elk Garden
Kitzmiller
Swanton
Altamont
Junction
Augusta
Ranson
Charles Town
Purcellville
Barnesville
Germantown
Redhouse
Scherr
Winchester
Berryville
Poolesville
Gaithersb
Thomas
Davis
Moorefield
Baker
Wardensville
Stephens City
Leesburg
Herndon
Potomac
Harman
Petersburg
Strasburg
Front Royal
Upperville
Middleburg
Vienna
Seneca Rocks
Lost City
Woodstock
Manassas
Fairfax
Franklin
Oak Flat
Timberville
Warrenton
Opal
Dale City
Luray
Stanley
Triangle
Harrisonburg
Elkton
Culpeper
Falmouth
Bridgewater
Madison
Fredericksburg
Churchville
Orange
Gordonsville
Staunton
Waynesboro
Charlottesville
Louisa
Stuarts Draft
Scottsville
Ashland
Lovington
Rockville

WEST VIRGINIA

VIRGINIA

Maryland/Delaware

Scale of Miles

0 3 6 9 12 15

N

© Creative Sales Corporation

FOR PENNSYLVANIA STATE MAP SEE PAGES 80-81
FOR NEW JERSEY STATE MAP SEE PAGES 62-63

FOR VIRGINIA STATE MAP SEE PAGES 86-87

FOR CONTINUATION SEE GRID B-1

CANADA
UNITED STATES

When travelling in wilderness areas or on unfamiliar roads, it is always best to be cautious and particularly attentive to local driving conditions. Be alert at all times and use the designated rest areas as often as necessary.

CANADA
UNITED STATES

Lake Superior

Lake Huron

Lake Michigan

North Channel

Georgian Bay

Green Bay

Keweenaw Bay

Saginaw Bay

MICH

Ironwood

Silver City · White Pine · North Merriweather · Ironwood · Bessemer · Ramsay · Wakefield · Bergland · Rockland · Ewen · Matchwood · Marenisco · Manitowish · Lac Du · Hurley · Butternut

Popuple Mtns. State Park

Eagle Harbor · Copper Harbor · Fort Wilkins State Park · Eagle River · Cliff · Phoenix · Mohawk · Ahmeek · Allouez · Kearsarge · Calumet · Laurium · Lake Linden · Hubbell · Oskar · **Houghton** · Hancock · Atlantic Mine · South Range · Painesdale · Donken · Toivola · Greenland · Mass City · Rockland · Ontonagon · Nisula · Twin Lakes · Winona · Beechwood · Kenton · Sidnaw · Watton · Covington · Three Lakes · L'Anse · Alberta · Baraga · Arnheim · Assinins · Keweenaw Bay · Big Bay · Skanee

Pictured Rocks National Lakeshore

Marquette · **Negaunee** · **Ishpeming** · Harvey · Au Train · Christmas · Munising · Chatham · Wetmore · Deerton · Palmer · Sands · Gwinn · Little Lake · Trenary · Forest Lake · Rumely · Kiva · Traunik · Princeton · National Mine · Michigamme · Three Lakes · Republic · Witch Lake · Amasa · Crystal Falls · Alpha · Mastodon · Iron River · Stambaugh · Caspian · Gaastra · Beechwood

Tahquamenon Falls State Park · Paradise · Deer Park · Grand Marais · Seney National Wildlife Refuge · Germfask · McMillan · Newberry · Soo Junction · Hulbert · Eckerman · Strongs · Hiawatha · Trout Lake · Rexton · Engadine · Garnet · Naubinway · Gould City · Gulliver · Blaney Park · Curtis · Helmer · Shingleton · Seney · Steuben · Manistique

Indian Lake State Park · Thompson · Garden Corners · Fayette · Garden · Cooks · Isabella · Ensign · Rapid River · Gladstone · **Escanaba** · Wells · Ford River · Bark River · Hyde · Perronville · Cornell · Brampton · Masonville

Chippewa Falls · Batchawana Bay · Hayden

Sault Ste. Marie · Brimley · Dafter · Kinross · Rudyard · Pickford · Donaldson · Stalwart · Cedarville · Hessel · Goetzville · De Tour Village · Drummond Is. · Thessalon · Iron Bridge · Blind River · Algoma · Sprague · Serpent · Elliot Lake

Iron Mountain · Kingsford · Quinnesec · Norway · Vulcan · Loretto · Hardwood · Felch · Foster City · Theodore · Granite Bluff · Sagola · Ralph · Floodwood · Channing · Sawyer · Metropolitan · Hermansville · Spalding · Powers · Daggett · Carney · Nadeau · Wilson · Bark River · Gourley · Harris · Ingalls · Cedar River · Stephenson · Wallace · Carbondale · Menominee · Marinette · Peshtigo · Coleman

Beaver Is. · St. James

Father Marquette National Memorial · Mackinac Island · St. Ignace · Mackinaw City · Carp Lake · Levering · Pellston · Alanson · Brutus · Pleasantview · Good Hart · Harbor Springs · Cross Village · Bliss

Petoskey · Conway · Bay View · Walloon Lake · Boyne City · Boyne Falls · Clarion · Horton Bay · Charlevoix · Ironton · East Jordan · Ellsworth · Central Lake · Bellaire · Alba · Elmira · Vanderbilt · Wolverine · Afton · Indian River · Tower · Onaway · Ocqueoc · Millersburg · Metz · Posen · Rogers City · Presque Isle · Hawks · Cathro · **Alpena** · Ossineke · Lachine · Hubbard Lake · Spratt · Herron · Long Rapids · Lincoln · Spruce · Harrisville · Greenbush · Black River · Alcona

Cheboygan · Aloha · Mullett Lake · Topinabee · Wolverine

Gaylord · Johannesburg · Vienna · Atlanta · Hillman · Comins · Fairview · Curran · Mio · Luzerne · Lewiston · McKinley · Glennie · Barton City · South Branch · Hale · National City · Whittemore · Turner · Twining · Prescott · Sterling · Alabaster · Au Sable · Oscoda · Greenbush · Tawas City · East Tawas

Grayling · Frederic · Lovells · Waters · Otsego Lake · Higgins Lake · Roscommon · St. Helen · Houghton Lake · Prudenville · Meredith · Gladwin · Harrison · Skidway Lake · Rose City · West Branch · Lupton

Traverse City · Acme · Kewadin · Williamsburg · Elk Rapids · Kalkaska · South Boardman · Fife Lake · Manton · Sherman · Buckley · Interlochen · Grawn · Karlin · Kingsley · Walton · Sharon · Darragh · Mayfield · Lake City · McBain · Marion · Le Roy · Ashton · Tustin · Dighton · Lucas · **Cadillac** · Boon · Mesick · Brethren · Wellston · Irons · Dublin · Harrietta · Copemish · Thompsonville · Benzonia · Beulah · Honor · Empire · Glen Arbor · Glen Haven · Leland · Northport · Omena · Suttons Bay · Cedar · Lake Leelanau · Maple City · Cedar

Sleeping Bear Dunes National Lakeshore · Frankfort · Elberta · Arcadia · Pierport · Onekama · Bear Lake · Eastlake · **Manistee** · Parkdale · Filer City · Wellston · Stronach · Free Soil · Fountain · Kaleva · Wolf Lake · Walhalla · Custer · Scottville · Ludington · Hamlin Lake

North Manitou Is. · S. Manitou Is. · N. Manitou Is.

Appleton · **Green Bay** · Kaukauna · Menasha · Neenah · Kimberly · Little Chute · De Pere · Ashwaubenon · Allouez · Howard · Seymour · Shawano · Keshena · Bonduel · Pulaski · Oconto · Oconto Falls · Abrams · Suring · Gillett · Cecil · Crivitz · Wausaukee · Amberg · Pembine · Niagara · Coleman · Pound · Lena

Oshkosh · Neenah · Weyauwega · Waupaca · New London · Clintonville · Embarrass · North Fond du Lac · Fond du Lac · St. Cloud · Mount Calvary · Kiel · New Holstein · Chilton · Brillion · Reedsville · Valders · Kellnersville · Brandon · Ripon · Rosendale

Manitowoc · **Two Rivers** · Mishicot · Denmark · Casco · Kewaunee · Algoma · Luxemburg · Cleveland

Door County · Sturgeon Bay · Egg Harbor · Ephraim · Sister Bay · Fish Creek · Forestville · Baileys Harbor

FOR CONTINUATION SEE GRID A-10

FOR WISCONSIN STATE MAP SEE PAGES 90-91

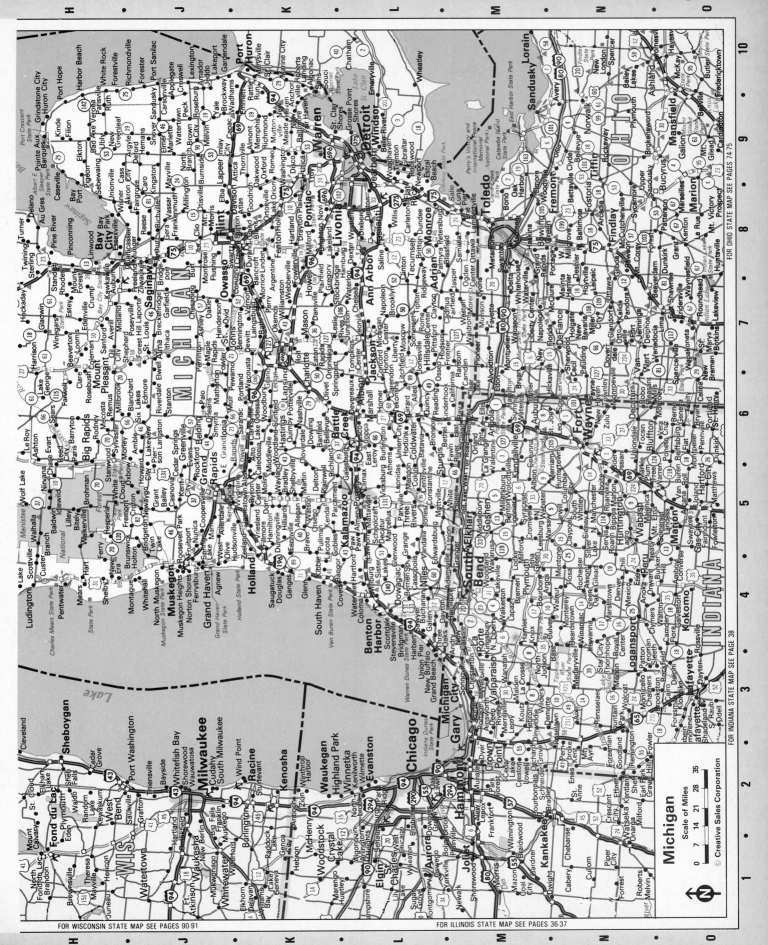

FOR OHIO STATE MAP SEE PAGES 74-75

FOR INDIANA STATE MAP SEE PAGE 38

FOR WISCONSIN STATE MAP SEE PAGES 90-91

FOR ILLINOIS STATE MAP SEE PAGES 36-37

Michigan

Scale of Miles

0 7 14 21 28 35

© Creative Sales Corporation

FOR CONTINUATION SEE GRID A-9
FOR WISCONSIN STATE MAP SEE PAGES 90-91

FOR CONTINUATION SEE GRID C-10

Grand Portage Indian Res.

Grand Portage State Forest
Judge C. R. Magney State Park
Cascade River State Park

Grand Portage
Howland
Croftville
Grand Marais
Lutsen

ONTARIO

Shebandowan

Grand Marais
Lutsen
Schroeder
Taconite Harbor
Little Marais State Park
Finland
Silver Bay
Beaver Bay
Tettegouche State Park
Temperance River State Park
Geo. H. Crosby Manitou State Park
Split Rock Lighthouse

Isabella

Superior
National Forest

CANADA
UNITED STATES

Superior

Two Harbors
Larsmont
Knife River
Duluth
Superior
Proctor

Ashland
Washburn
Bayfield
Iron River
Poplar
Solon Springs

Hurley
Montreal
Mellen
Mason
Nebagamon

Park Falls
Butternut
Fifield
Phillips

Ely
Winton
Babbitt
Hoyt Lakes
Aurora
Biwabik
Virginia
Gilbert
Eveleth

Tower
Soudan
Vermilion Lake

Hibbing
Chisholm
Buhl
Keewatin
Nashwauk

Grand Rapids
Coleraine
Bovey

Bemidji

Brainerd
Baxter

MINNESOTA

Fergus Falls

Detroit Lakes

Moorhead
Dilworth

Fargo
West Fargo

Wahpeton
Breckenridge

Crookston
East Grand Forks

Thief River Falls

Warren

Roseau
Warroad

International Falls

Baudette

Red Lake Indian Reservation

Leech Lake Indian Reservation

FOR NORTH DAKOTA STATE MAP SEE PAGES 72-73

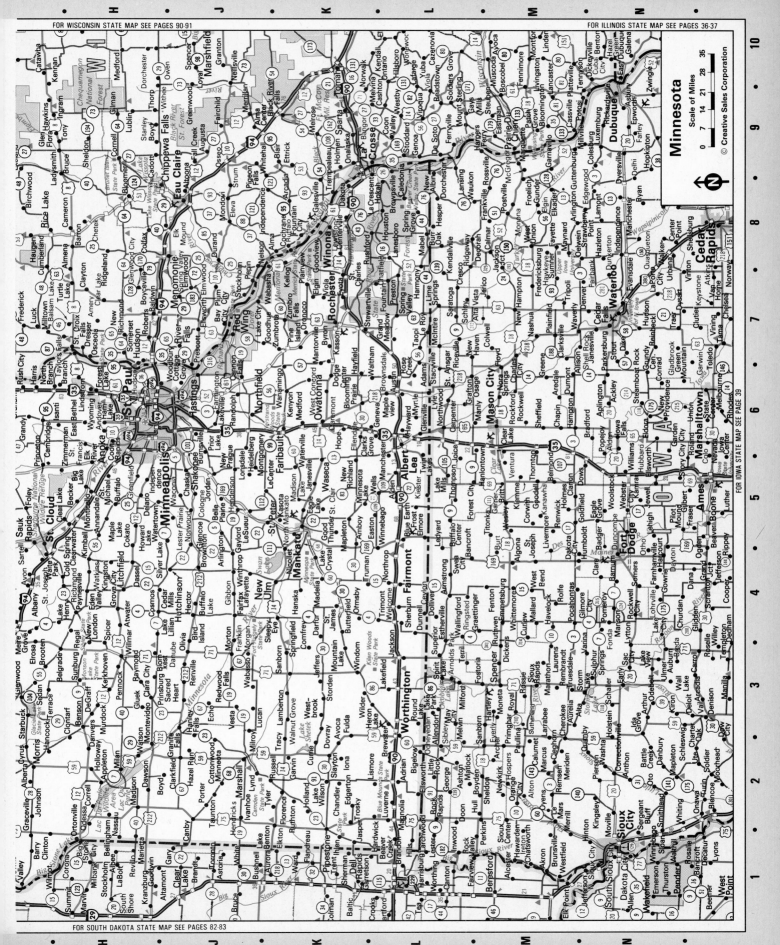

FOR WISCONSIN STATE MAP SEE PAGES 90-91

FOR ILLINOIS STATE MAP SEE PAGES 36-37

Minnesota

Scale of Miles

0 7 14 21 28 35

© Creative Sales Corporation

FOR IOWA STATE MAP SEE PAGE 39

FOR SOUTH DAKOTA STATE MAP SEE PAGES 82-83

FOR ILLINOIS STATE MAP SEE PAGES 36-37

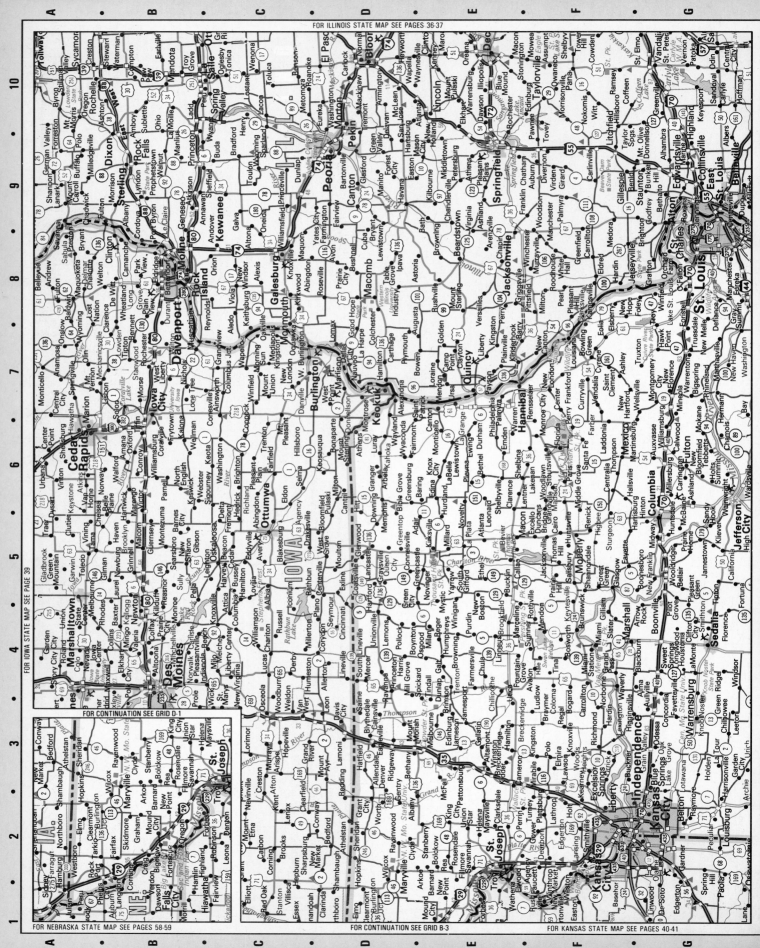

FOR IOWA STATE MAP SEE PAGE 39

FOR CONTINUATION SEE GRID D-1

FOR NEBRASKA STATE MAP SEE PAGES 58-59

FOR CONTINUATION SEE GRID B-3

FOR KANSAS STATE MAP SEE PAGES 40-41

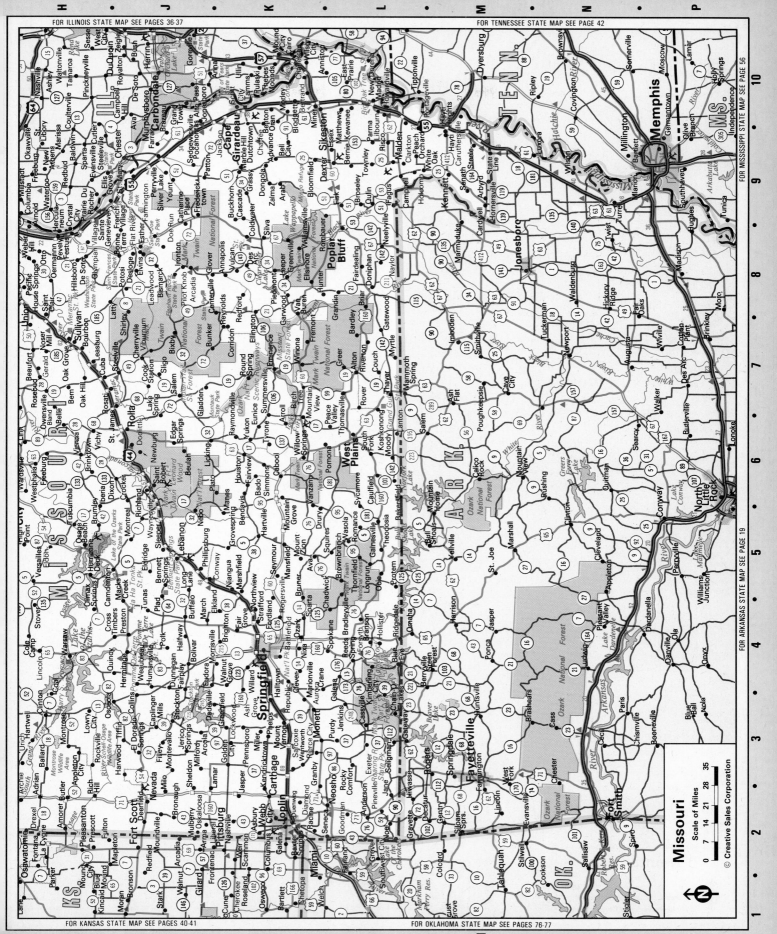

FOR ILLINOIS STATE MAP SEE PAGES 36-37
FOR TENNESSEE STATE MAP SEE PAGE 42
FOR MISSISSIPPI STATE MAP SEE PAGE 56
FOR ARKANSAS STATE MAP SEE PAGE 19
FOR KANSAS STATE MAP SEE PAGES 40-41
FOR OKLAHOMA STATE MAP SEE PAGES 76-77

Missouri

Scale of Miles

0 7 14 21 28 35

© Creative Sales Corporation

BRITISH COLUMBIA

ALBERTA

CANADA
UNITED STATES

IDAHO

Glacier National Park

Flathead National Forest

Lolo National Forest

Kootenai National Forest

Lewis and Clark National Forest

Helena National Forest

Deerlodge National Forest

Bitterroot National Forest

Selway-Bitterroot Wilderness

Gallatin National Forest

Beaverhead National Forest

Blackfeet Indian Reservation

Flathead Indian Reservation

Rocky Boy's Indian Reservation

Yellowstone National Park

Grand Teton National Park

FOR IDAHO STATE MAP SEE PAGES 34-35

Elko, Flathead, Cardston

Eastport, Naples, Movie Sprs., Yaak, Rexford, Eureka, Fortine, Trego, Stryker, Polebridge, Olney, Whitefish, Columbia Falls, West Glacier, Apgar, Coram, Martin City, Essex, Babb, St. Mary, Blackfoot, Kiowa, Browning, East Glacier Park, Port of Del Bonita, Sweetgrass, Sunburst, Santa Rita, Cut Bank, Shelby, Ethridge, Valier, Inverness, Rudyard, Joplin, Hingham, Gildford, Kremlin, Lothair, Chester, Box Elder, Big Sandy

Hope, East Hope, Heron, Noxon, Troy, Libby, Happy's Inn, Marion, Somers, Kalispell, Lakeside, Big Fork, Rollins, Proctor, Dayton, Elmo, Niarada, Big Arm, Polson, Pablo, Ronan, Hot Springs, Dupuyer, Conrad, Pendroy, Brady, Bynum, Dutton, Power, Choteau, Loma, Fort Benton, Carter, Montague, Geraldine

Murray, Kellogg, Silverton, Gem, Mullan, Wallace, Osburn, Saltese, DeBorgia, Haugan, St. Regis, Plains, Paradise, Superior, Tarkio, Alberton, Frenchtown, Huson, Thompson Falls, Trout Creek, Dixon, Ravalli, Saint Ignatius, Arlee, Fairfield, Augusta, Fort Shaw, Simms, Sun River, Vaughn, Ulm, Great Falls, Black Eagle, Belt, Raynesford, Geyser, Coffee, Denton, Stanford, Moccasin, Hobson, Monarch, Neihart

Headquarters, Pierce, Weippe, Woodland, Kamiah, Lowell, Kooskia, Stites, Harpster, Mount Idaho, Missoula, Milltown, Bonner, Clinton, Potomac, Lolo, Lolo Hot Springs, Florence, Stevensville, Victor, Corvallis, Hamilton, Grantsdale, Darby, Conner, Seeley Lake, Ovando, Lincoln, Helmville, Avon, Drummond, Hall, Garrison, Helena, E. Helena, Elliston, Montana City, Winston, Canyon Creek, Craig, Wolf Creek, Cascade, White Sulphur Springs, Checkerboard, Martinsdale, Twodot, Ringling, Judith Gap, Melville

Golden, Elk City, Philipsburg, Galen, Warmsprings, Deer Lodge, Opportunity, Anaconda, Walkerville, Butte, Basin, Boulder, Radersburg, Toston, Townsend, Jefferson City, Three Forks, Logan, Manhattan, Belgrade, Clyde Park, Wilsall, Wise River, Divide, Silver Star, Whitehall, Waterloo, Willow Creek, Amsterdam, Churchill, Bozeman, Livingston, McLeod, Springdale, Big Timber, Wisdom, Melrose, Twin Bridges, Harrison, Norris, Bozeman Hot Sprs., Gallatin Gateway, Emigrant, Pray, Big Sky

Gibbonsville, North Fork, Jackson, Glen, Sheridan, Laurin, Ennis, Alder, Virginia City, Cameron, Chico Hot Springs, Gardiner

Salmon, Baker, Grant, Dillon, Dell, Lima, West Yellowstone, Macks Inn, Island Park, Mammoth Springs Jct., Norris Jct., Tower Jct., Canyon Jct., Madison Jct., Lake Jct., Old Faithful, W. Thumb Jct.

Warm Lake, May, Leadore, Tendoy, Lemhi, Challis, Cape Horn, Patterson, Sunbeam, Spencer, Blue Dome, Dubois, St. Anthony, Parker, Chester, Hamer, MacKay, Mud Lake, Warm River

Montana

Scale of Miles

0 9 18 27 36 45

N

© Creative Sales Corporation

8 9 10 11 12 13 14

SASKATCHEWAN

A
Claydon Frontier
Val Marie
Rock Glen
Minton Lake Alma Oungre
Climax Bracken Orkney
Coronach Big Beaver
Port of Coronoch
Regway
Port of Oungre
Fortuna

Port of Climax Monchy
W. Poplar
Port of Whitetail Port of Raymond Westby
Alkabo

NADA STATES

Turner
Port of Morgan
Port of Opheim Opheim
Whitetail Redstone Raymond
Loring
Richland Four Buttes Flaxville Plentywood
Peerless Scobey
Antelope
Reserve
Grenora 50

B
232 233
241
242
24
Medicine Lake
Zahl
85
Lohman
Chinook Zurich
Harlem
248
13
Plentywood
Medicine Lakes Nat'l Wildlife Refuge
2
Havre
Bearpaw State Recreational Area
Fort Belknap Agency
Dodson
Saco
Hinsdale
Homestead
Froid
Williston

234 240 66
Chief Joseph Battleground State Mon.
Wagner Malta
251
344
Bainville
Fort Union Nat'l Hist. Site
87
Lloyd
Fort Belknap Indian Reservation
Glasgow
Nashua
Wolf Point
Poplar Brockton Culbertson
Cleveland

C
Cleveland
66
Oswego
Frazer
13
201
Fort Buford State Hist. Site
Fairview
Cartwright
200
Charbonneau

N TA N A
Missouri River
Fort Peck
Bear Creek Recreational Area
Rock Creek Recreational Area
Vida
58
Sidney
23
68

U.S. Bend Nat'l Wildlife Refuge
Fort Peck Lake
Richey
Lambert
Crane

Charles M. Russel Nat'l Wildlife Refuge
Nelson Creek Recreational Area
200
Savage

D
Winifred
236
Suffolk Christina
James Kipp Recreational Area
Devils Creek Recreational Area
Charles M. Russel Nat'l Wildlife Refuge
Circle
Bloomfield
Intake
16

Coffee Creek
81
Roy
191
Hilger
Crooked Creek Recreational Area
Jordan
200
Brockway
Lindsay
254
Glendive
ND

19
Box Elder Creek
59
200
Makoshika State Park
Wibaux
10 34

E
Lewistown
Grassrange
200
Teigen
Winnett
Cohagen
253
37
Fallon
Terry
94
7
Beach
41

Moore
87
244
Flatwillow
Rock Springs
253
16
Golva

Forestgrove
Garneill
Lewis and Clark National Forest
Melstone Sumatra
Angela
38 Yellowstone
Plevna
Baker

F
Gap
297
Musselshell
Ingomar
12
59
Medicine Rocks State Park

Harlowtown
Roundup
Klein
Hysham
Cartersville
Miles City
12
7

Shawmut
87
Lavina
Bighorn
10
Forsyth
Rosebud
447
Ladner

Ryegate
Musselshell River
Broadview
Custer
Worden
Pompeys Pillar
39
Colstrip
59
Volborg
Powderville
Ekalaka
20

G
Rapelje
306
58
Ballantine
47
Medicine Rocks
Capitol
Custer National Forest

Reedpoint
10
Columbus
Huntley
212
Acton
302
Billings
Hardin
384
Lame Deer Ashland
Broadus
323

Yellowstone
Laurel
90
Crow Agency
Busby
212
Northern Cheyenne Indian Reservation
Custer National Forest
20

H
Absarokee
78
Park City Silesia
Garryowen
31
Birney
Hammond 212

Nye
419
Joliet Boyd
Crow Indian Reservation
90
Tongue River
Biddle
Alzada 323
SD

Dean
Edgar Fromberg
Bighorn Canyon Nat'l Recreational Area
Lodge Grass
Ford
Lightning Flat

Fishtail
Roberts
212
Bridger
Wyola
314 Decker
Tongue River Res.
Rockypoint
Colony

J
Red Lodge
Bearcreek Belfry
310
Parkman Parkman
338
Acme
59
Recluse
New Haven
Hulett
112
Belle Fourche

Cooke City
212 297
Clark Elk Basin
Frannie Deaver Cowley
Ranchester Dayton
45 366
Sheridan
Leiter
Spotted Horse
Weston Oshoto
24 Alva Aladdin
111 Beulah

296 292
294 295 114
Lovell
Burgess Jct.
Beckton 331
Big Horn
16
Devils Tower Jct.
14
Spearfish

K
Powell
120
Ralston
310 32
14
Banner Story
Clearmont Arvada
16
Rozet
81
Sundance
585

Cody
291
16 20
Emblem
Shell
Ucross
Lake DeSmet
59 Gillette
Moorcroft
116
Four Corners

Buffalo Bill State Park
20
Otto
Greybull
Basin
National Forest
Buffalo
WYOMING
87
Keyhole Res.
Upton
116 Osage

16
Burlington
30
Hyattville
Ten Sleep
90
Newcastle

Valley Pitchfork
290
Meeteetse
Manderson
433 436 435
25
196
50 59

FOR WYOMING STATE MAP SEE PAGES 92-93
FOR NORTH DAKOTA STATE MAP SEE PAGES 72-73
FOR SOUTH DAKOTA STATE MAP SEE PAGES 82-83

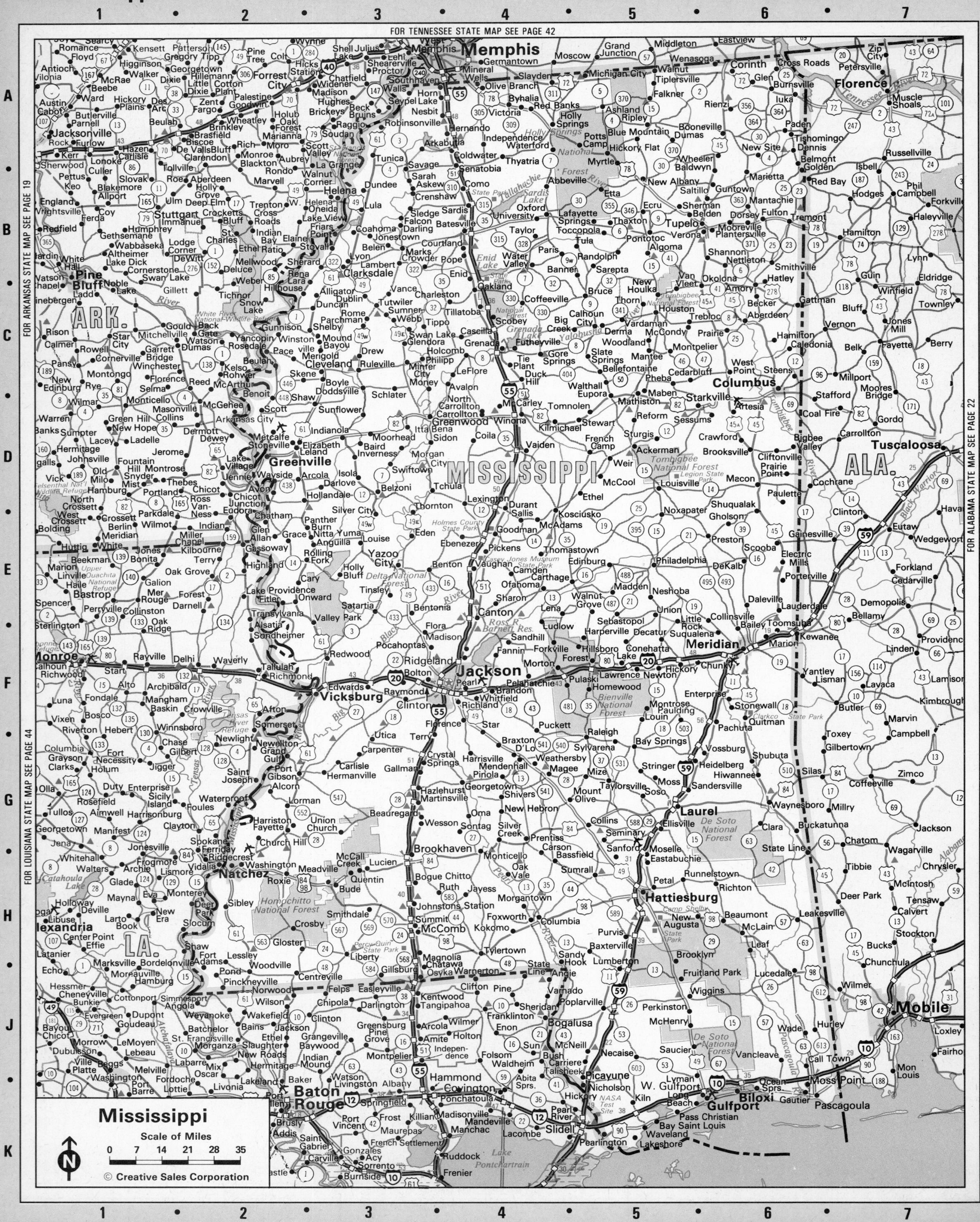

1 2 3 4 5 6 7

FOR TENNESSEE STATE MAP SEE PAGE 42

A
B
C
D
E
F
G
H
J
K

FOR ARKANSAS STATE MAP SEE PAGE 19

FOR LOUISIANA STATE MAP SEE PAGE 44

FOR ALABAMA STATE MAP SEE PAGE 22

MISSISSIPPI

ARK.

LA.

ALA.

Memphis
Tupelo
Columbus
Greenville
Greenwood
Jackson
Vicksburg
Natchez
Hattiesburg
Laurel
Meridian
Tuscaloosa
Mobile
Biloxi
Gulfport
Baton Rouge
Pine Bluff
Monroe
Alexandria
Florence

Mississippi

Scale of Miles

0   7   14   21   28   35

N

© Creative Sales Corporation

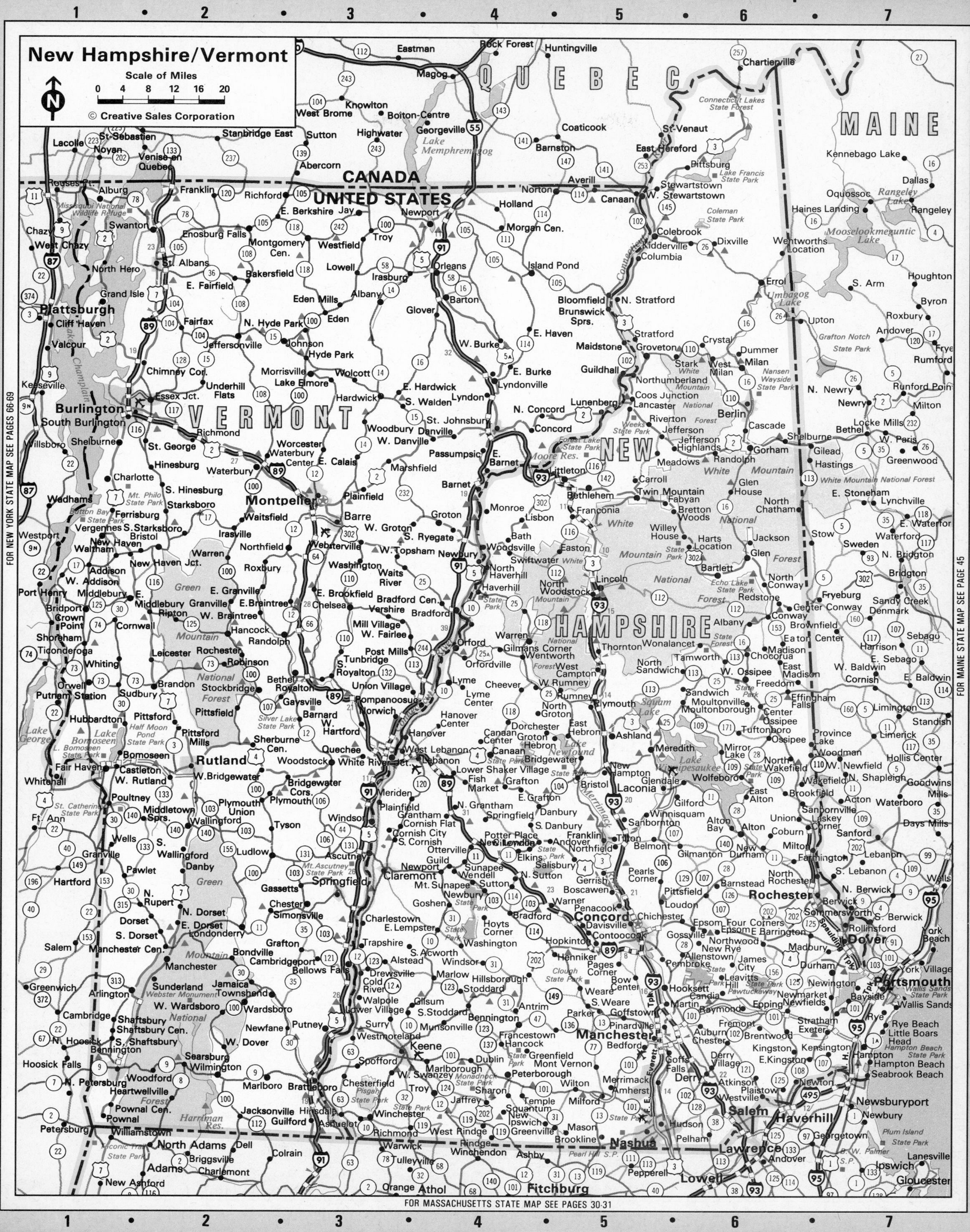
New Hampshire/Vermont
Scale of Miles
0 4 8 12 16 20
N
© Creative Sales Corporation
QUEBEC
CANADA
UNITED STATES
MAINE
VERMONT
NEW HAMPSHIRE
FOR NEW YORK STATE MAP SEE PAGES 66-69
FOR MAINE STATE MAP SEE PAGE 45
FOR MASSACHUSETTS STATE MAP SEE PAGES 30-31
Lake Memphremagog
Lake Champlain
Lake George
Connecticut Lakes State Forest
Lake Francis State Park
Coleman State Park
Umbagog Lake
Mooselookmeguntic Lake
Rangeley Lake
Grafton Notch State Park
Nansen Wayside State Park
White Mountain National Forest
Green Mountain National Forest
Lake Winnipesaukee
Squam Lake
Newfound Lake
Moore Res.
Harriman Res.
Plum Island
Burlington
Montpelier
Barre
Rutland
Bennington
Brattleboro
St. Johnsbury
Newport
St. Albans
Middlebury
Springfield
Plattsburgh
Concord
Manchester
Nashua
Portsmouth
Dover
Rochester
Keene
Laconia
Claremont
Lebanon
Hanover
Littleton
Berlin
Lancaster
Colebrook
Pittsburg
Conway
Salem
Haverhill
Lawrence
Lowell
Fitchburg
Newburyport
Gloucester
Magog
Coaticook
Rangeley
1 2 3 4 5 6 7
A B C D E F G H J K

FOR SOUTH DAKOTA STATE MAP SEE PAGES 82-83

FOR WYOMING STATE MAP SEE PAGES 92-93

FOR COLORADO STATE MAP SEE PAGES 28-29

WY · WYO · COL. · NEBR

Mule Co. Jct. · Hot Springs · Gap · Edgemont · Redbird · Provo · Lance Creek · Manville · Lusk · Node · Van Tassell · Harrison · Crawford · Whitney · Chadron · Kyle · Long Valley · White River · Wood · Oglala · Wounded Knee · Pine Ridge · Allen · Martin · Batesland · Parmelee · Okreek · Mission · Rosebud · Saint Francis · Merriman · Eli · Cody · Nenzel · Kilgore · Crookston · Sparks · Norden · Valentine · Jay Em · Oelrichs · Hay Springs · Clinton · Rushville · Gordon · Wood Lake · Johnstown · Ainsworth · Fort Laramie · Lingle · Torrington · Hemingford · Niobrara · Brownlee · Elsmere · Purdum · Alliance · Antioch · Lakeside · Ellsworth · Bingham · Hyannis · Whitman · Mullen · Seneca · Thedford · Halsey · Dunning · Morrill · Mitchell · Scottsbluff · Gering · Terrytown · Minatare · Angora · Ashby · Arthur · Tryon · Stapleton · Gandy · Arnold · Callaway · Melbeta · McGrew · Bayard · Bridgeport · Broadwater · Lisco · Dalton · Gurley · Oshkosh · Lewellen · Lemoyne · Keystone · Harrisburg · Bushnell · Kimball · Dix · Potter · Sidney · Lodgepole · Chappell · Big Springs · Brule · Ogallala · Paxton · Sutherland · Hershey · North Platte · Maxwell · Brady · Gothenburg · Willow Island · Cozad · Pine Bluffs · Egbert · Sedgwick · Ovid · Julesburg · Crook · Proctor · Grant · Madrid · Elsie · Wallace · Maywood · Moorefield · Farnam · Eustis · Elwood · Briggsdale · Buckingham · Raymer · Sterling · Fleming · Haxtun · Paoli · Amherst · Brandon · Venango · Grainton · Dickens · Wellfleet · Curtis · Stockville · Stoneham · Willard · Atwood · Marino · Holyoke · Imperial · Champion · Enders · Wauneta · Hayes Center · Cambridge · Arapahoe · Edison · Jackson Lake Res. · Weldona · Log Lane Village · Snyder · Clarkville · Hamlet · Palisade · Bartley · Indianola · McCook · Orchard · Wiggins · Fort Morgan · Brush · Akron · Otis · Yuma · Eckley · Wray · Laird · Haigler · Parks · Benkelman · Stratton · Max · Trenton · Culbertson · Wilsonville · Beaver City · Danbury · Lebanon · Last Chance · Lindon · Anton · Cope · Joes · Idalia · St. Francis · Wheeler · Bird City · McDonald · Atwood · Herndon · Oberlin · Norcatur · Almena · River Bend · Limon · Arriba · Seibert · Vona · Stratton · Burlington · Goodland · Brewster · Colby · Gem · Rexford · Selden · Dresden · Lenora · Edmond · Logan · Genoa · Hugo · Menlo · Halford · Hoxie · Morland · Norton · Jennings · Clayton · Colorado

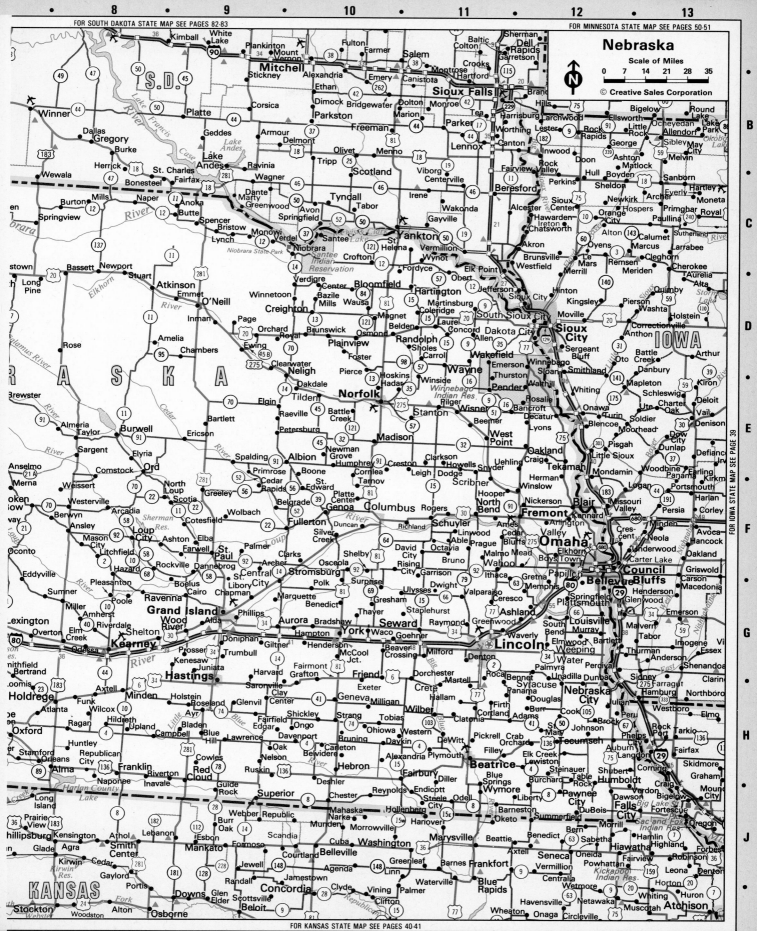

Nebraska

Scale of Miles

0 7 14 21 28 35

© Creative Sales Corporation

FOR UTAH STATE MAP SEE PAGES 84-85

FOR IDAHO STATE MAP SEE PAGES 34-35

FOR OREGON STATE MAP SEE PAGES 78-79

FOR CALIFORNIA STATE MAP SEE PAGES 24-27

IDAHO

OREGON

CAL.

NEVADA

UTAH

Marion
Oakley
Hollister
Rogerson
Three Creek
Riddle
Jackpot
Etna
Montello
Thousand Springs
Contact
Jarbidge
Mountain City
Owyhee
Oasis
Wells
Deeth
Halleck
Toana Range
Wendover
White Horse Pass
Currie
Lage's
Cherry Creek
McGill
East Ely
Ely
Ruth
Kimberly
Preston
Lund
Currant
Duckwater
Eureka
Baker
Major's Place
Wheeler Peak Scenic Area
Lehman Caves Nat'l Monument
Sacramento Pass
Connors Pass
Lamoille
Lee
Jiggs
Ruby Valley
Harrison Pass
Shantytown
Elko
Carlin
Crescent Valley
Beowawe
Beowawe Geysers
Tuscarora
Jack Creek
Midas
Valmy
Battle Mountain
Golconda
Paradise Valley
McDermitt
Orovada
Winnemucca
Mill City
Unionville
Oreana
Imlay
Lovelock
Sulphur
Gerlach
Empire
Denio Junction
Denio
Fields
Pueblo
Lakeview
Adel
Cedarville
Eagleville
Lake City
Ravendale
Gabbs
Ione
Austin
Round Mt.
Carver's
Berlin - Ichthyosaur State Park
Middle Gate
Cold Spring
Frenchman
Stillwater
Fallon
Hazen
Silver Springs
Fernley
Wadsworth
Nixon
Reno
Sparks
Verdi
Truckee
Virginia City
Gold Hill
Silver City
Dayton
Carson City
Stewart
Genoa
Minden
Gardnerville
Wellington
Smith
Yerington
Mason
Wabuska
Schurz
Babbitt
Wassuk
S. Lake Tahoe
Stateline
Zephyr Cove
Glenbrook
Markleeville
Coleville
Topaz
Woodfords
Meyers
Loyalton
Doyle
Herlong
Vinton
Chilcoot
Beckwourth Pass
Floriston
Sutcliffe
Empire
Pyramid Lake
Walker Lake
Carson Lake
Carson Sink
U.S. Naval Air Station
Rye Patch Reservoir
Rye Patch Dam
Eagle Picher Mine
Dixie Valley
Black Rock Desert
Smoke Creek Desert
Granite Range
High Rock Canyon
Jackson Mts.
Quinn River
Santa Rosa Range
Pine Forest Range
Trout Creek Mts.
Sawtooth National Forest
Humboldt National Forest
Humboldt River
Ruby Mountains
East Humboldt Range
Independence Mts.
Tuscarora Mts.
Emigrant Pass
Sonoma Range
Humboldt Range
Stillwater Range
Clan Alpine Mts.
Desatoya Mts.
Simpson Park Mts.
Shoshone Range
Toiyabe Range
Toquima Range
Monitor Range
Egan Range
Schell Creek Range
Snake Range
Antelope Range
Goshute Range
Pequop Mts.
Goose Creek Mts.
Goshute Indian Reservation
Te-Moak Indian Res.
Fort McDermitt Indian Reservation
Pyramid Lake Indian Reservation
Walker River Indian Reservation
Fallon Indian Res.
Duck Valley Indian Reservation
Charles Sheldon National Antelope Range
Toiyabe National Forest
New Pass
Railroad Pass
Garden Pass
Garden Pass
Railroad Pass
Connors Pass
Blue Mtn. Pass
Beckwourth Pass
Chilcoot Pass
Lamoille
Rock Creek
Pine Creek
Willow Creek

Route markers: 80, 95, 93, 50, 6, 305, 306, 376, 361, 338, 208, 395, 89, 140, 225, 226, 228, 229, 232, 233, 30, 51, 93A, 489, 893, 318, 379, 278, 892, 399, 400, 446, 447, 445, 34, 50A, 290, 293, 53, 72, 21, 299, 31

FOR CALIFORNIA STATE MAP SEE PAGES 24-27

Nevada

Scale of Miles

0 7 14 21 28 35

© Creative Sales Corporation

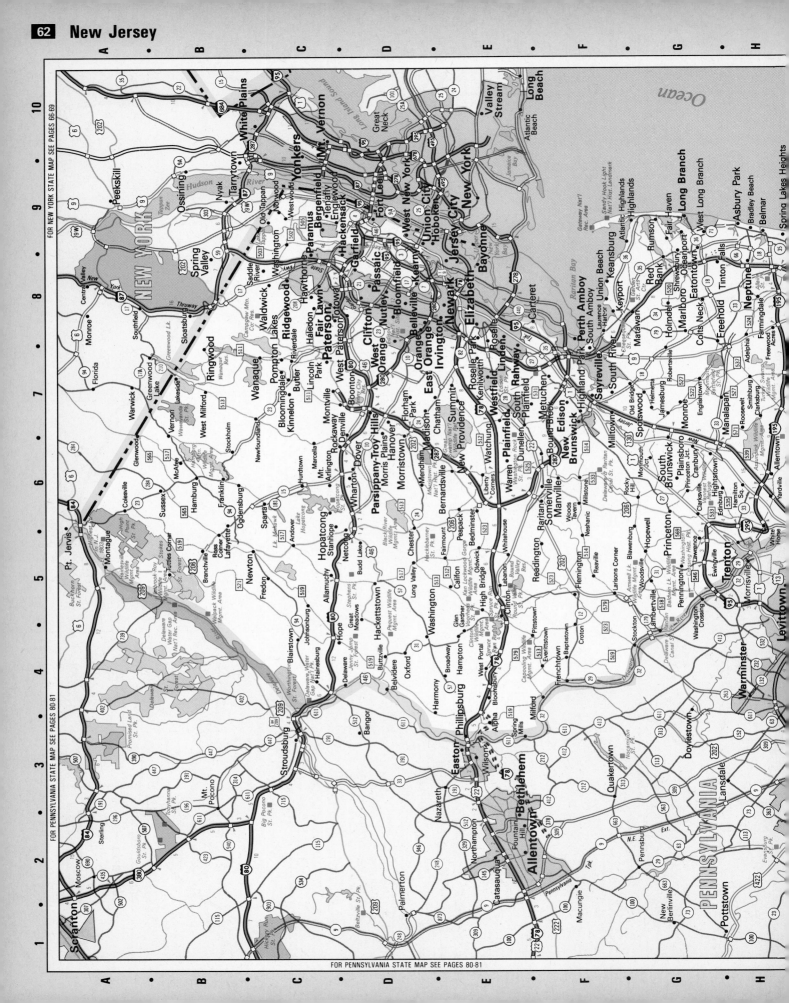

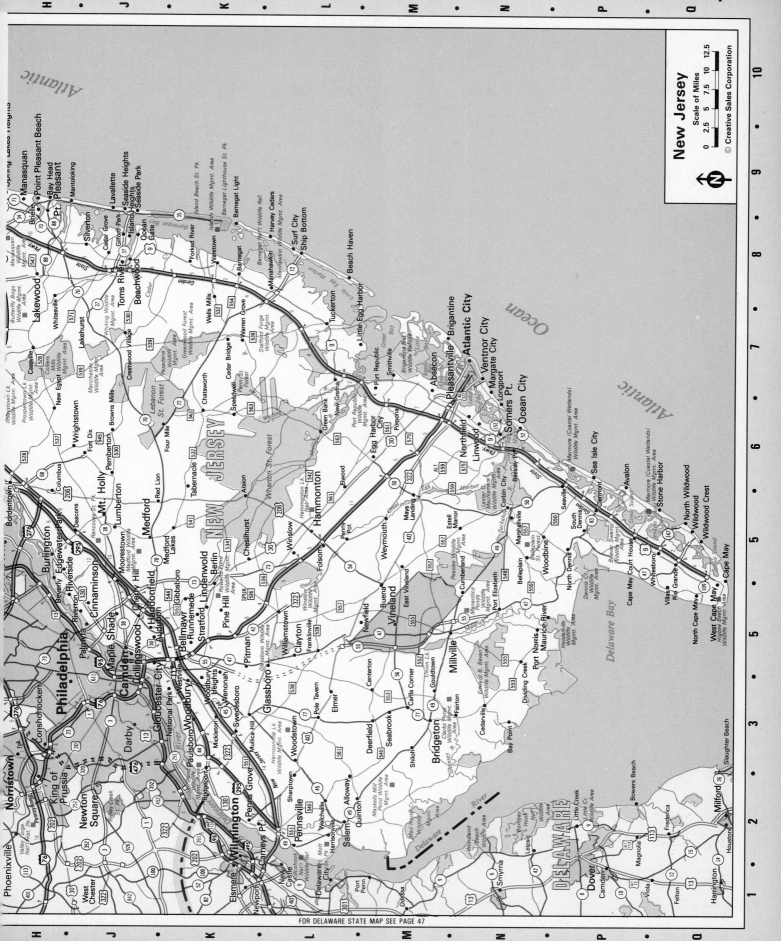

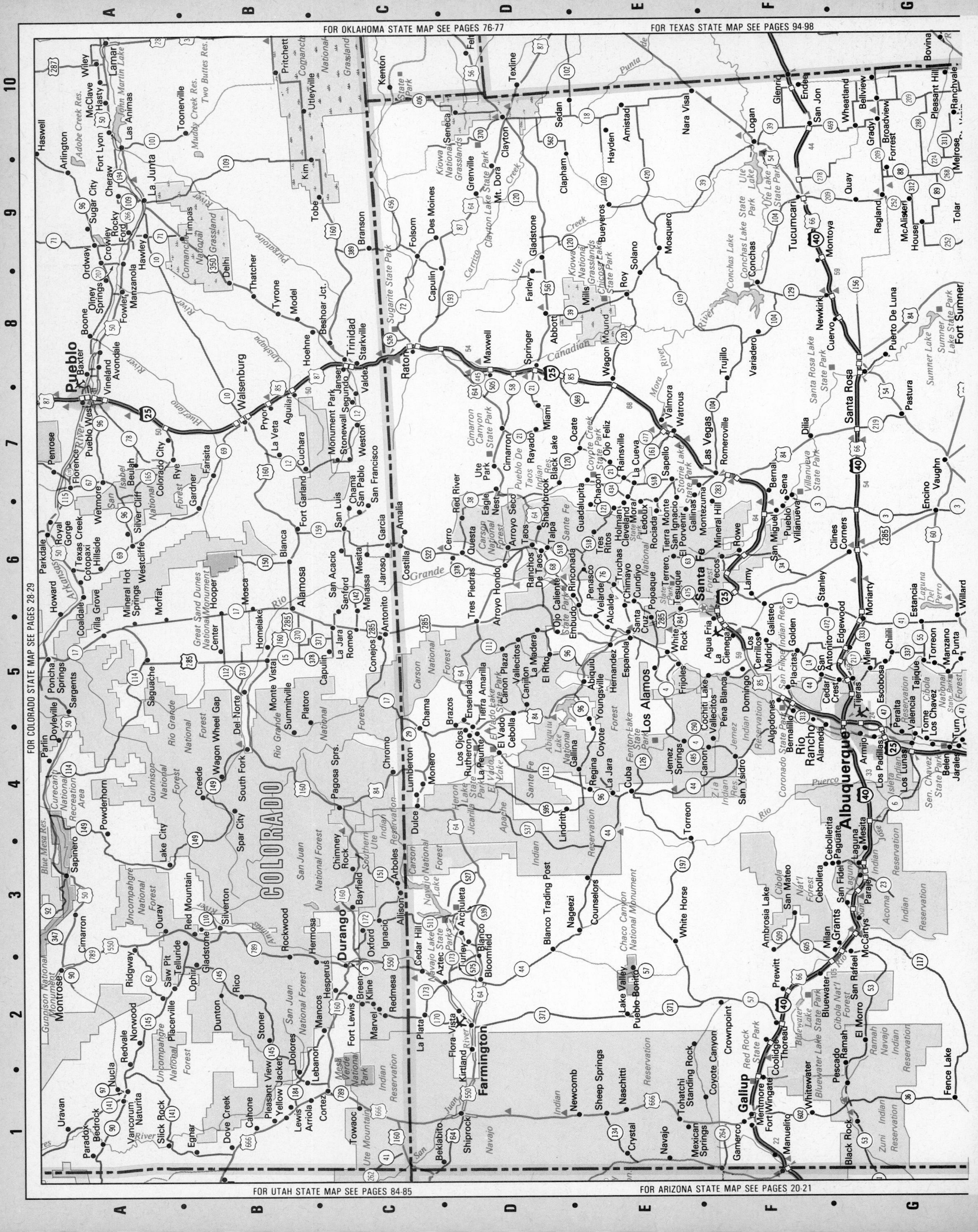

FOR OKLAHOMA STATE MAP SEE PAGES 76-77
FOR TEXAS STATE MAP SEE PAGES 94-98
FOR COLORADO STATE MAP SEE PAGES 28-29
FOR UTAH STATE MAP SEE PAGES 84-85
FOR ARIZONA STATE MAP SEE PAGES 20-21
COLORADO
Pueblo
Santa Fe
Albuquerque
Los Alamos
Farmington
Gallup
Durango
Raton
Trinidad
Las Vegas
Santa Rosa
Tucumcari
Alamosa
Walsenburg
La Junta
Clayton
Grants
Rio Rancho
Taos
Espanola
Springer
Fort Sumner

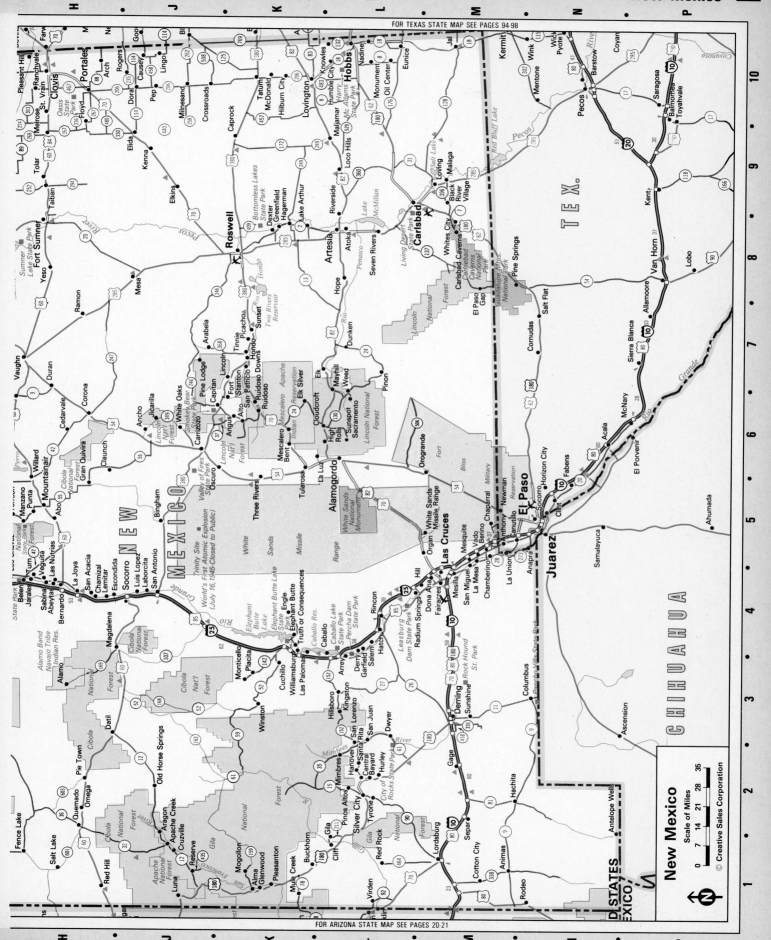

New Mexico

Scale of Miles

0   7   14   21   28   35

© Creative Sales Corporation

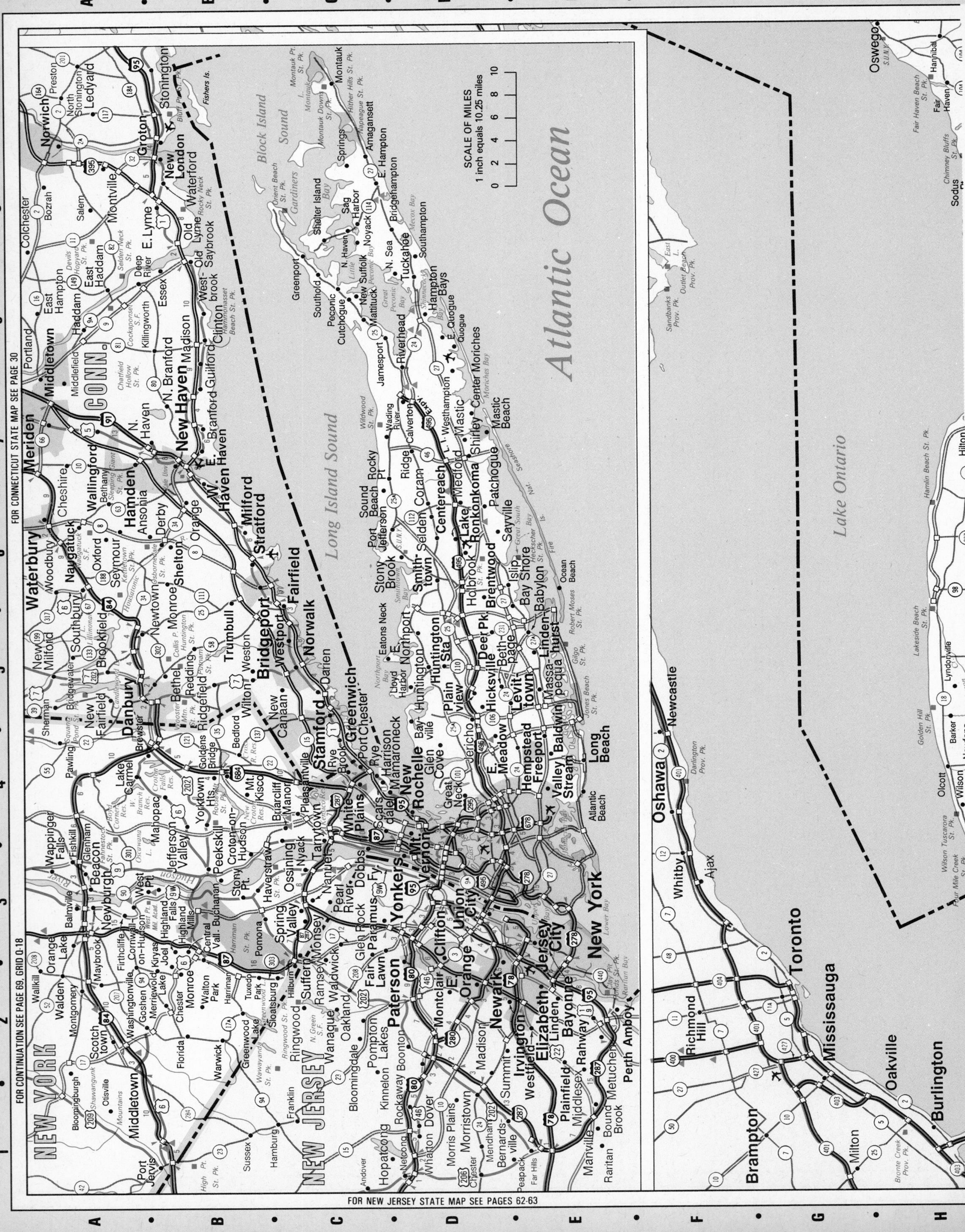

NEW YORK

NEW JERSEY

CONN

New York

Atlantic Ocean

Long Island Sound

Block Island Sound

Lake Ontario

SCALE OF MILES
1 inch equals 10.25 miles
0 2 4 6 8 10

FOR CONTINUATION SEE PAGE 69, GRID O-18
FOR CONNECTICUT STATE MAP SEE PAGE 30
FOR NEW JERSEY STATE MAP SEE PAGES 62-63

FOR CONTINUATION SEE PAGE 69

New York

Scale of Miles

0 4 8 12 16 20

© Creative Sales Corporation

PENNSYLVANIA

ONTARIO

CANADA
UNITED STATES

Lake Erie

Major cities and towns:
Buffalo, Rochester, Niagara Falls, Tonawanda, N. Tonawanda, Kenmore, Lackawanna, Hamburg, Lockport, Olean, Jamestown, Warren, Bradford, Elmira, Corning, Horseheads, Auburn, Geneva, Canandaigua, Batavia, Geneseo, Hornell, Dunkirk, Fredonia, Salamanca, Dansville, Penn Yan, Bath, Wellsville, Cuba, Naples, Silver Springs, Perry, Warsaw, Attica, Arcade, Springville, Gowanda, Cattaraugus, Little Valley, Randolph, Falconer, Lakewood, Celoron, Westfield, Mayville, Panama, Sherman, Angola, Silver Creek, Brocton, Angola-on-the-Lake, Lake Erie Beach, Farnham, N. Collins, Eden, Blasdell, Orchard Pk., E. Aurora, Elma, Lancaster, Depew, Williamsville, Clarence Center, Akron, Corfu, Alexander, Darien, Wyoming, Castile, LeRoy, Bergen, Churchville, Spencerport, Brockport, Holley, Albion, Medina, Middleport, Barker, Newfane, Olcott, Wilson, Youngstown, Lewiston, Ransomville, Wilson

Canada side: Burlington, Hamilton, Dundas, Stoney Creek, Grimsby, St. Catharines, Niagara-on-the-Lake, Niagara Falls, Thorold, Welland, Port Colborne, Dunnville

NEW YORK

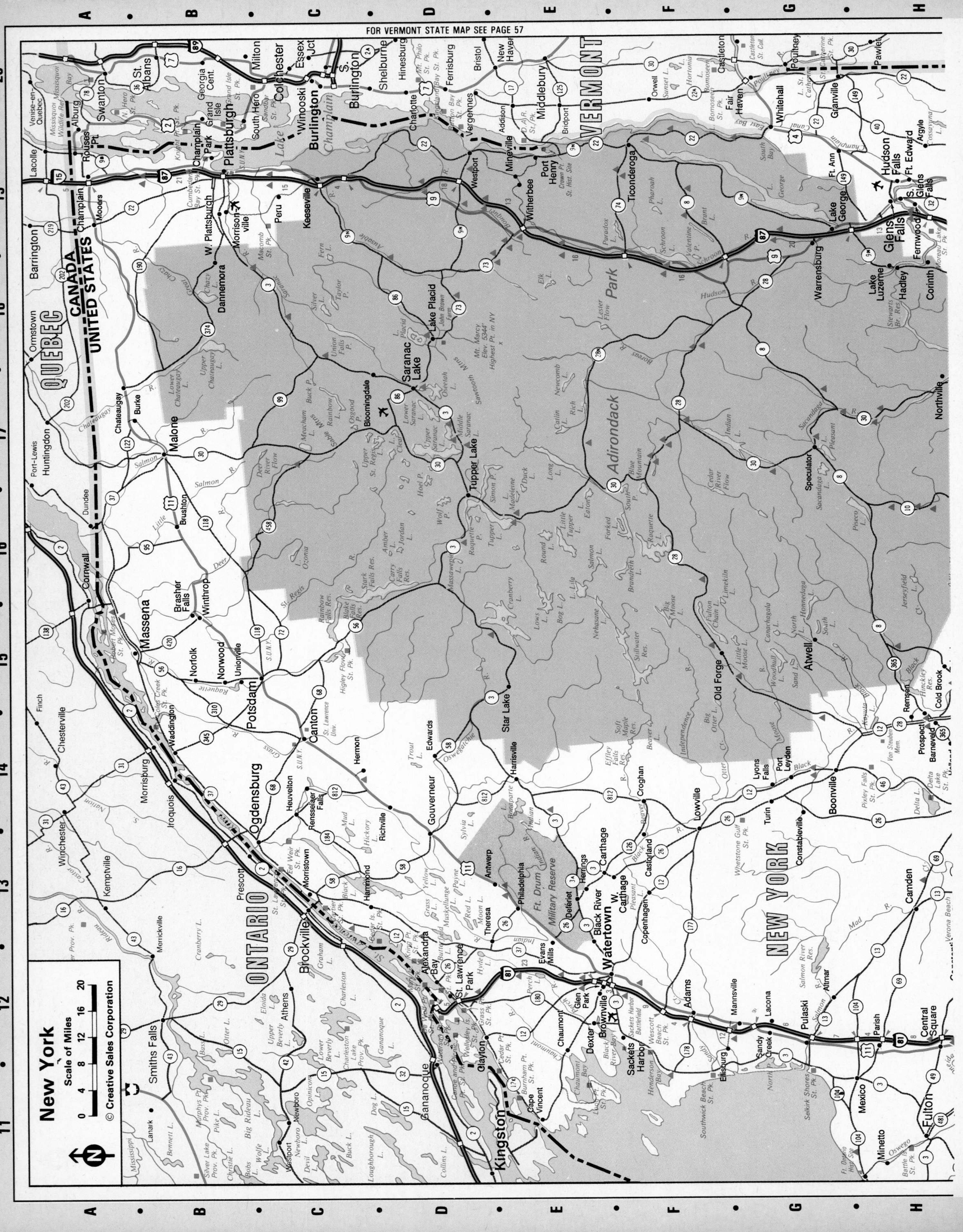

FOR VERMONT STATE MAP SEE PAGE 57

New York

Scale of Miles

0 4 8 12 16 20

© Creative Sales Corporation

N

CANADA
UNITED STATES

QUEBEC

ONTARIO

VERMONT

NEW YORK

Adirondack Park

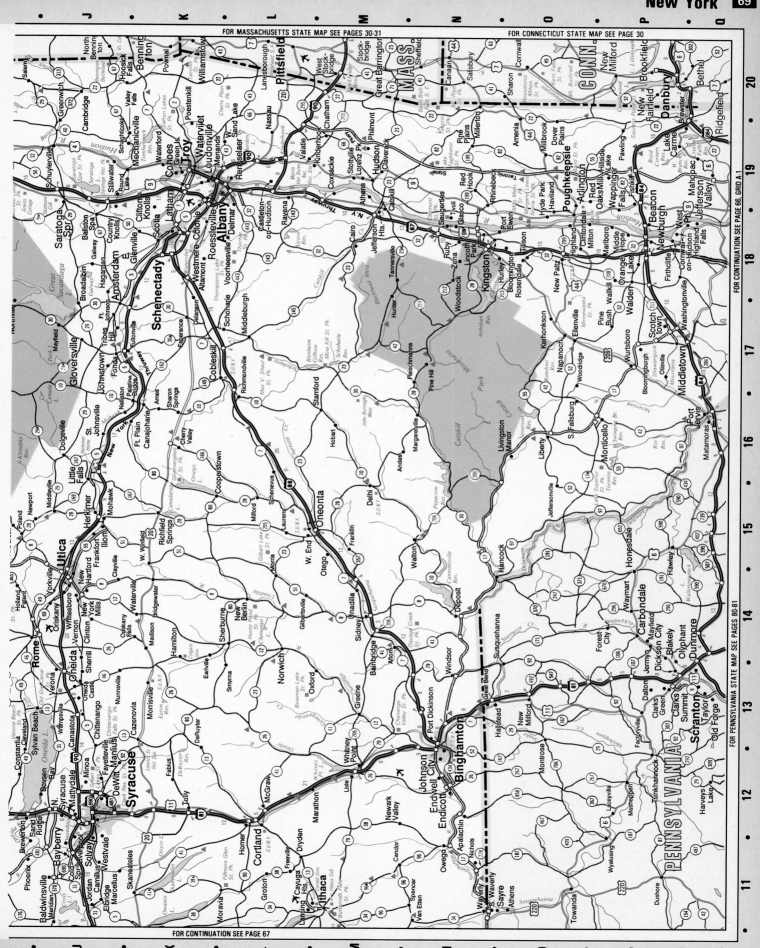

FOR MASSACHUSETTS STATE MAP SEE PAGES 30-31

FOR CONNECTICUT STATE MAP SEE PAGE 30

FOR CONTINUATION SEE PAGE 66, GRID A-1

FOR PENNSYLVANIA STATE MAP SEE PAGES 80-81

FOR CONTINUATION SEE PAGE 67

FOR KENTUCKY STATE MAP SEE PAGE 43
FOR VIRGINIA STATE MAP SEE PAGES 86-87
FOR TENNESSEE STATE MAP SEE PAGE 42
FOR GEORGIA STATE MAP SEE PAGE 23

FOR VIRGINIA STATE MAP SEE PAGES 86-87

A • B • C • D • E • F • G • H • J • K

8 • 9 • 10 • 11 • 12 • 13 • 14

Chatham, Halifax, Chase City, South Hill, Lawrenceville, Emporia, Franklin, Corapeake, Gates, St. Park, Morgans Corner, Barco

Martinsville, Danville, Clarksville, John H. Kerr Reservoir, Roanoke Rapids Lake, Roanoke Rapids, Pleasant Hill, Garysburg, Roduco, Sunbury, Elizabeth City, Camden, Coinjock, Bertha, Grandy

Yanceyville, Leasburg, Brooksdale, Roxboro, Stovall, Middleburg, Norlina, Weldon, Jackson, Winton, U.S. Coast Guard Air Station, Point Harbor, Jarvisburg, Powells Point, Harbinger

Williamsburg, Hightowers, Picks, Gordonton, Oxford, Kittrell, Henderson, Liberia, Rheasville, Halifax, Woodland, Ahoskie, Colerain, Hertford, Edenton, Albemarle Sound, Columbia, East Lake, Manns Harbor, Nags Head, Whalebone, Wanchese, Manteo

Burlington, Hillsborough, Creedmoor, Ingleside, Louisburg, Justice, Gold Rock, Rich Square, Scotland Neck, Ashland, Midway, Edenhouse, Woodley, Creswell, Rodanthe, Waves, Salvo

Greensboro, Durham, Raleigh, Chapel Hill, Cary, Wake Forest, Nashville, Rocky Mount, Tarboro, Robersonville, Williamston, Plymouth, Roper, Phelps Lake, New Lake, Kilkenny, Englehard, Lake Landing

Asheboro, Siler City, Bear Creek, Moncure, Fuquay-Varina, Smithfield, Bagley, Micro, Wilson, Fountain, Greenville, Bethel, Stokes, Mineola, Pantego, Belhaven, Leechville, Scranton, New Holland

Sanford, Swann, Lillington, Benson, Goldsboro, Walnut Creek, Snow Hill, Winterville, Ayden, Chocowinity, Wilmar, Edward, Aurora, Mesic, Pamlico Sound, Buxton, Frisco, Hatteras

Fayetteville, Fort Bragg, Spring Lake, Pope A.F.B., Salemburg, Newton Grove, Mount Olive, Kinston, Grifton, Graingers, Vanceboro, Hollyville, Bridgeton, New Bern, Arapahoe, Ocracoke, Portsmouth

Aberdeen, Raeford, Hope Mills, Clinton, Warsaw, Kenansville, Beulaville, Trenton, Pollocksville, Comfort, Maysville, Belgrade, Kuhns, Newport, Morehead City, Beaufort, Raleigh Bay

Rockingham, Hamlet, Lumberton, Cedar Creek, Saint Pauls, Magnolia, Rose Hill, Teachey, Chinquapin, Wallace, Maple Hill, Midway Park, Hubert, Swansboro, Fort Macon St. Park

Lumber Bridge, Pembroke, Maxton, Bladenboro, Elizabethtown, Harrells, Delway, Willard, Burgaw, Folkstone, Onslow Bay, West Onslow Beach, Del Mar Beach, Surf City

McColl, Fair Bluff, Chadbourn, Whiteville, Bolton, Council, Currie, Hampstead, Scotts Hill, Topsail Beach

Bennettsville, Dillon, Fairmont, Evergreen, Maco, Freeman, Holly Ridge, Wrightsville Beach, U.S.S. North Carolina Battleship Memorial St. Park

Florence, Marion, Mullins, Nichols, Tabor City, Brunswick, Old Dock, Wilmington, Seabreeze, Carolina Beach, Wilmington Beach, Kure Beach

Green Sea, Loris, Supply, Shallotte, Southport, Long Beach, Smith Island

Conway, Aynor, Cool Spring, Hickory Grove, Little River, Cresent Beach, Long Bay

Kingstree, Stuckey, Yauhannah, Myrtle Beach, Surfside Beach, Garden City, Litchfield Beach, Pawleys Island

Andrews, Georgetown, Debidue Beach, North Island

Jamestown, Hampton Plantation St. Park, Cape Romain National Wildlife Refuge, Bulls Bay

Moncks Corner, Goose Creek, Hanahan, Awendaw, Cainhoy, Whitehall, Mt. Pleasant, Isle of Palms, Sullivans Island, Charleston, James Island, Folly Beach

Atlantic Ocean

**North Carolina
South Carolina**

Scale of Miles

0 7 14 21 28 35

N

© Creative Sales Corporation

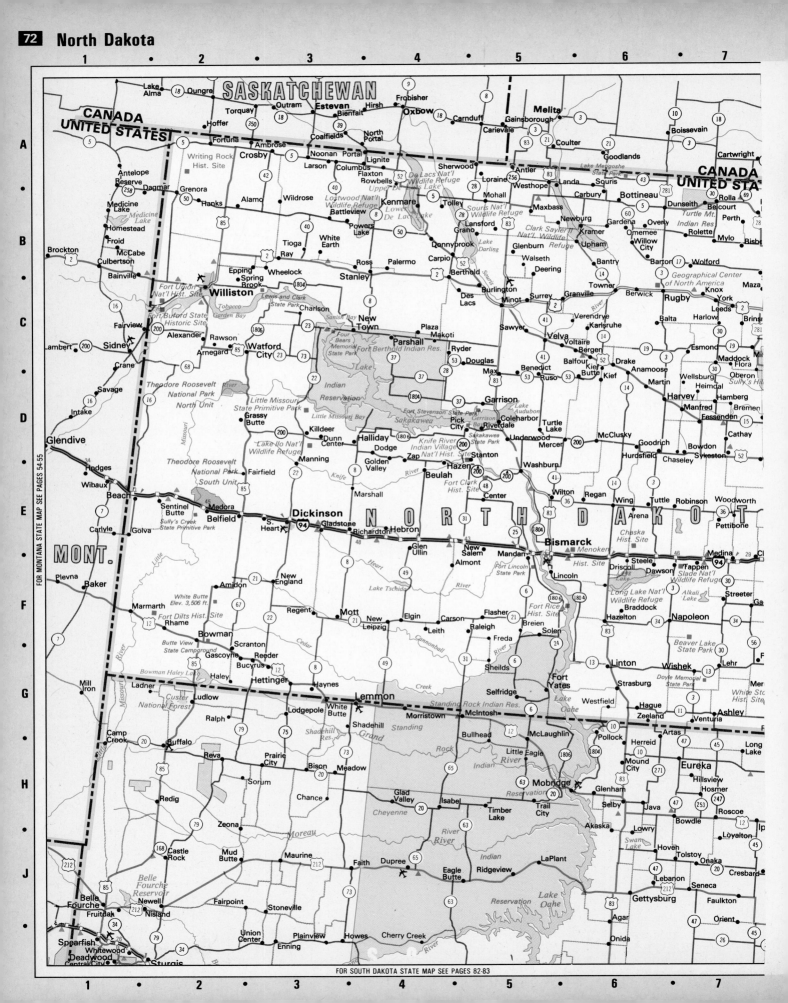

Canadian Citizens Visiting the United States

Passports or visas are not required of Canadian citizens or British subjects residing in Canada entering the United States for a period of six months or less; however, evidence of citizenship is required. Check with customs officials for complete regulations and requirements.

United States Citizens Visiting Canada

All persons entering Canada must report to the Canadian Immigration and Customs Office at the Port of Entry and secure the necessary permits for admission of their person and possessions. The transportation of plants and produce is rigidly controlled. Check with customs officials for complete regulations and requirements.

MANITOBA

CANADA
UNITED STATES

MINNESOTA

SOUTH DAKOTA

North Dakota

Scale of Miles

0 7 14 21 28 35

N

© Creative Sales Corporation

FOR MINNESOTA STATE MAP SEE PAGES 50-51

FOR SOUTH DAKOTA STATE MAP SEE PAGES 82-83

FOR PENNSYLVANIA STATE MAP SEE PAGES 80-81

CANADA
UNITED STATES

ONTARIO

MICHIGAN

OHIO

Lake Erie

Lake St. Clair

Lake Huron

Pelee Is.

Major cities and places:

London, St. Thomas, Sarnia, Port Huron, Chatham, Wallaceburg, Leamington, Windsor, Detroit, Warren, Sterling Hts., Troy, Royal Oak, Pontiac, Southfield, Farmington Hills, Livonia, Westland, Dearborn, Taylor, Lincoln Park, Ann Arbor, Flint, Burton, Lansing, E. Lansing, Jackson

Toledo, Oregon, Bowling Green, Sylvania, Maumee, Perrysburg, Findlay, Lima, Defiance, Van Wert, St. Marys, Wapakoneta, Marion, Bucyrus, Galion, Mansfield, Ashland, Wooster, Massillon, Canton, Dover, Akron, Barberton, Cuyahoga Falls, Kent, Stow, Ravenna, Youngstown, Warren, Niles, Girard, Struthers, Campbell, Hubbard

Cleveland, Lakewood, Parma, Euclid, Cleveland Hts., Garfield Hts., Willoughby, Willowick, Eastlake, Mentor, Painesville, Geneva, Ashtabula, Conneaut, N. Kingsville, Jefferson, Chardon, Elyria, Lorain, Sheffield Lake, Avon Lake, N. Ridgeville, Westlake, Medina, Brunswick, Strongsville, Berea, Olmsted, Amherst, Oberlin, Wellington, Vermilion, Sandusky, Huron, Norwalk, Bellevue, Fremont, Clyde, Tiffin, Fostoria

Marblehead, Put-in-Bay, Kelleys Island, South Bass Island, Catawba

FOR MICHIGAN STATE MAP SEE PAGES 48-49

FOR MICHIGAN STATE MAP SEE PAGES 48-49

FOR INDIANA STATE MAP SEE PAGE 38

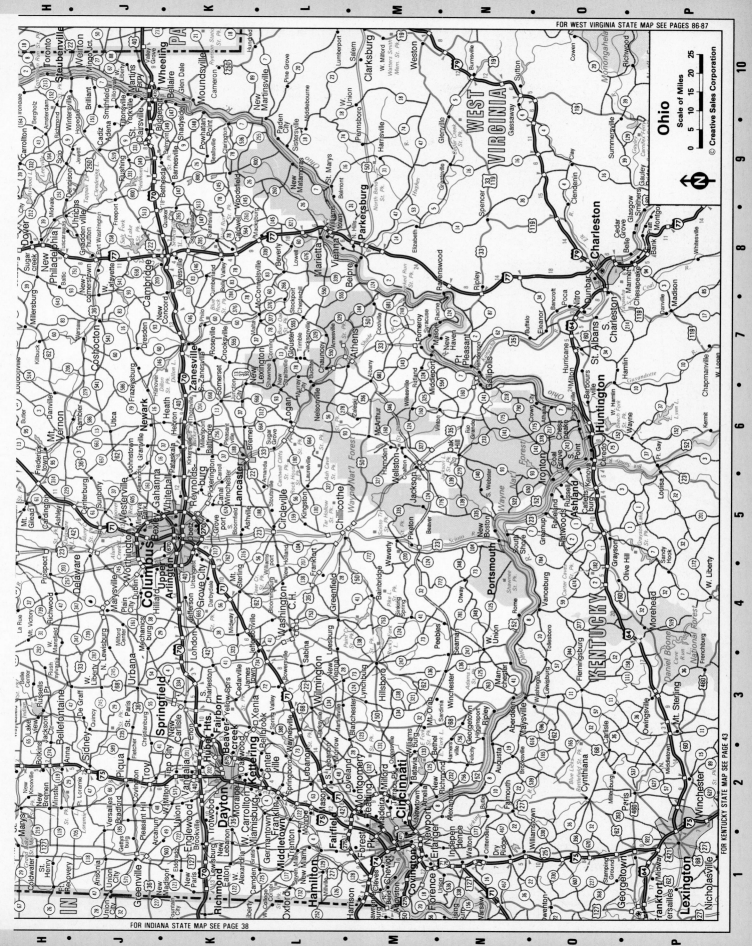

FOR WEST VIRGINIA STATE MAP SEE PAGES 86-87

Ohio

Scale of Miles

0   5   10   15   20   25

© Creative Sales Corporation

FOR KENTUCKY STATE MAP SEE PAGE 43

FOR INDIANA STATE MAP SEE PAGE 38

1 · 2 · 3 · 4 · 5 · 6 · 7

FOR COLORADO STATE MAP SEE PAGES 28-29 FOR KANSAS STATE MAP SEE PAGES 40-41

COLORADO

KANSAS

N.M.

TEXAS

Dodge City
Johnson Montezuma Greensburg Cullison
Pritchett Springfield Bartlett Sublette Bucklin Minneola
Kim Vilas Richfield Meade Coldwater
Utleyville Campo Hugoton Kismet Ashland Protection
Kenton Elkhart Liberal Englewood Hardtner
Sturgis Surrey Hills Tyrone Lookout
Wheeless Keyes Hough Hooker Floris Forgan Mocane Knowles Buffalo Plainview
Mt. Dora Boise City Eva Turpin Gate Selman Edith Tegarden Cora Alva
Clayton Felt Four Corners Optima Rosston Lovedale Freedom Brace Avard Waynoka
Griggs Guymon Boyd Laverne May Ft. Supply Hopeton
Goodwell Hardesty Balko Slapout Catesby Tangier Mooreland Curtis Quinlan
Texline Texhoma Gray Elmwood Booker Darrouzett Fargo Gage Woodward
Stratford Perryton Farnsworth Follett Shattuck Goodwin Sharon Seiling
Sedan Gruver Waka Lipscomb Arnett Vici Cestos
Cactus Etter Spearman Higgins Harmon Camargo Taloga
Dalhart Sunray Morse Glazier Durham Crawford Trail Leedey Rhea Oakwood
Hartley Stinnett Canadian Roll Angora Aledo Burmah
Channing Masterson Miami Reydon Strong City Butler Custer City
Boys Ranch Sanford Borger Allison Rankin Cheyenne Hammon Arapaho Weatherford
Tascosa Fritch Phillips Bunavista New Mobeetie Briscoe Dempsey Foss Clinton
Adrian Vega Skellytown Pampa Mobeetie Wheeler Sweetwater Elk City Corn
Amarillo White Deer Kings Mill Lefors Kellerville Mayfield Burns Flat Bessie
Glenrio Endee Wildorado Bushland Panhandle McLean Lela Twitty Sayre Doxey Forty One Dill Cordell
San Jon Conway Groom Lark Alanreed Shamrock Erick Texola Retrop Rocky Sentinel Lake Valley
Canyon Claude Goodnight Ashtola Dozier Samnorwood Willow Goteho Mountain View
Umbarger Dawn Clarendon Lutie Brinkman Granite Lone Wolf Hobart Babbs
Hereford Happy Lelia Lake Hedley Quail Madge Vinson Reed Mangum Cooperton Lugert
Summerfield Wayside Brice Memphis Wellington Blair Roosevelt
Black Friona Tulia Lakeview Newlin Hollis Gould Martha Warren Snyder
Dimmitt Nazareth Hart Silverton Parnell Estelline Duke Altus Ozark
Clovis Farwell Bovina Kress Quitaque Turkey Tell McQueen Creta Eldorado Elmer
Texico Lariat Edmonson Childress Lincoln Olustee Humphreys Indiahoma Faxon
Muleshoe Earth Springlake Olton Aiken Lockney Whiteflat Kirkland Goodlett Tipton Manitou Chattanooga Frederick
Rogers Needmore Fieldton Sudan Plainview South Plains Flomot Northfield Quanah Acme Medicine Mound Hollister Loveland
Goodland Enochs Bula Hale Center Cotton Center Floydada Matador Paducah Rayland Lockett Oklaunion Electra Grayback
Lingo Maple Morton Spade Petersburg Dougherty Crowell Thalia Harrold Burkburnett Iowa
Whitharral Anton Abernathy Glenn Dumont Vernon Davidson
Bledsoe Lehman Shallowater New Deal Ralls McAdoo Finney Gilliland Kamay
Whiteface Reese Vill. Idalou Crosbyton Dickens Guthrie Vera Red Springs Mankins
Leveland Hurlwood Lorenzo Benjamin Dundee
Smyer Lubbock Spur Knox City Munday Goree Seymour Bomarton Westover Archer City
Sundown Wolfforth Posey Kalgary Girard O'Brien Weinert Megargel Olney
Bronco Slaton Rochester Elbert Lovi
New Home Southland Jayton Swenson Old Glory Haskell Newcastle
Meadow Wilson Clairemont Rule Sagerton Graham Woodson
Tahoka Post Aspermont South Bend
Grassland Draw Justiceburg Lake Stamford
O'Donnell

Oklahoma
Scale of Miles
0 7 14 21 28 35
© Creative Sales Corporation

N

FOR TEXAS STATE MAP SEE PAGES 94-98

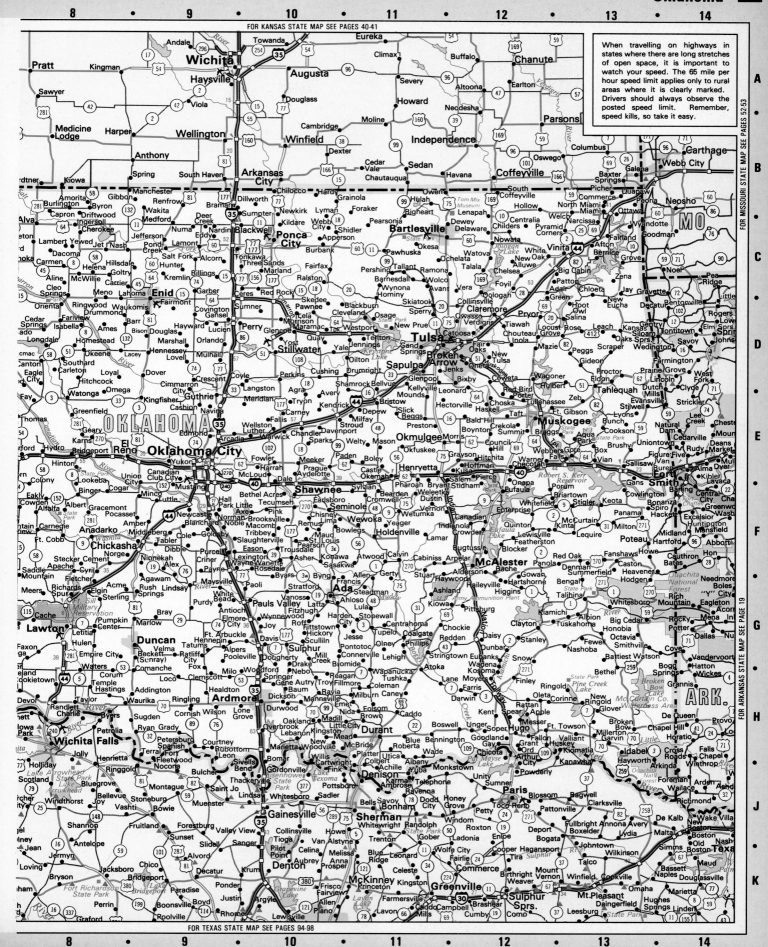

FOR KANSAS STATE MAP SEE PAGES 40-41

When travelling on highways in states where there are long stretches of open space, it is important to watch your speed. The 65 mile per hour speed limit applies only to rural areas where it is clearly marked. Drivers should always observe the posted speed limit. Remember, speed kills, so take it easy.

FOR MISSOURI STATE MAP SEE PAGES 52-53

FOR ARKANSAS STATE MAP SEE PAGE 19

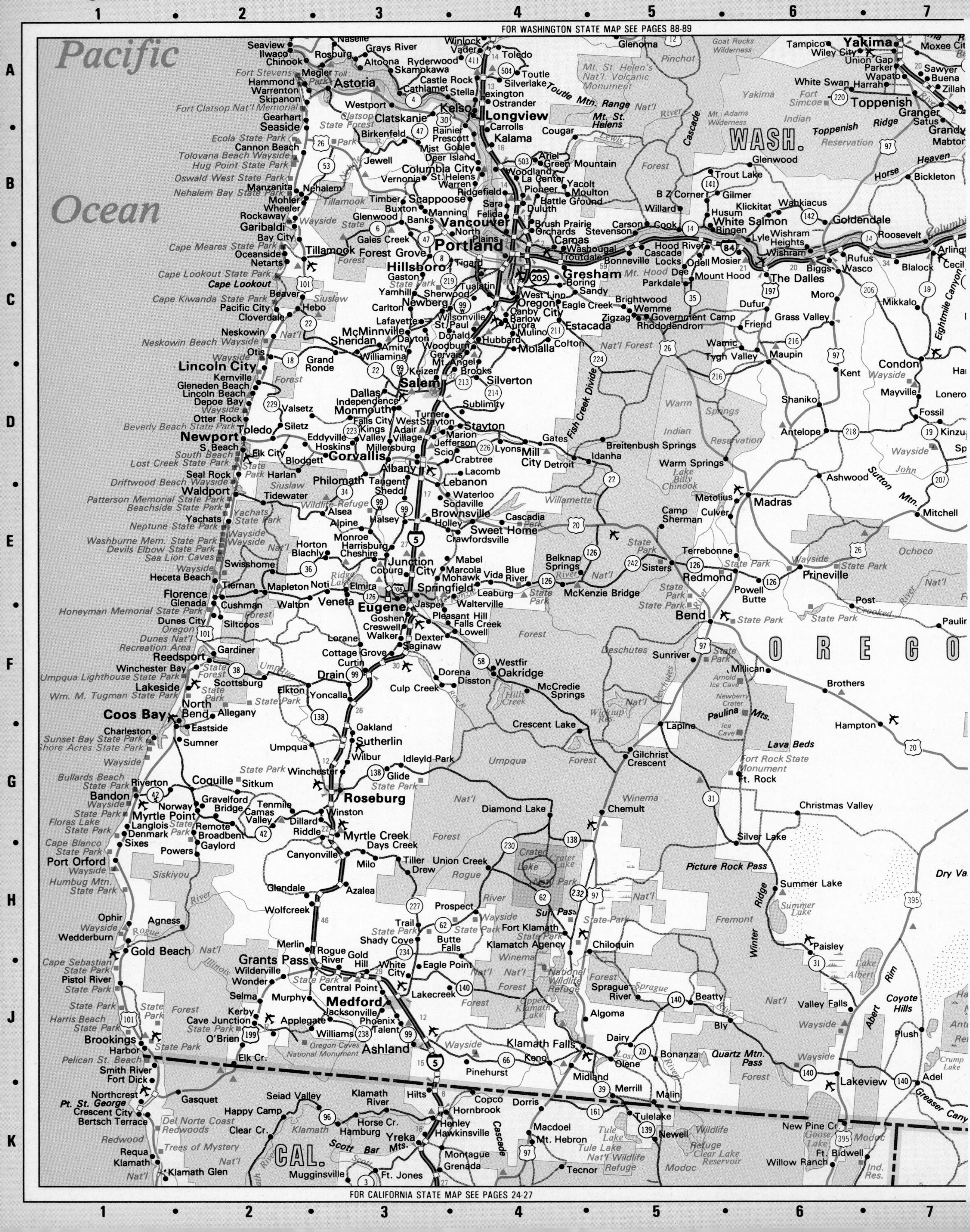

1
2
3
4
5
6
7
A
B
C
D
E
F
G
H
J
K
FOR WASHINGTON STATE MAP SEE PAGES 88-89
FOR CALIFORNIA STATE MAP SEE PAGES 24-27
Pacific
Ocean
WASH.
OREGO
CAL.
Naselle
Seaview
Ilwaco
Chinook
Rosburg
Grays River
Altoona
Skamokawa
Ryderwood
Winlock
Vader
Toledo
Toutle
Silverlake
Toutle Mtn. Range
Glenoma
Pinchot
Goat Rocks Wilderness
Mt. St. Helen's Nat'l. Volcanic Monument
Tampico
Wiley City
Yakima
Moxee City
Union Gap
Parker
Wapato
Sawyer
Buena
Zillah
Fort Stevens
Megler
Toll
Hammond
Astoria
Warrenton
Skipanon
Cathlamet
Castle Rock
Stella
Lexington
Ostrander
Kelso
Longview
White Swan
Harrah
Fort Simcoe
Toppenish
Granger
Satus
Grandview
Mabton
Yakima
Indian
Toppenish
Reservation
Ridge
Fort Clatsop Nat'l Memorial
Gearhart
Seaside
Westport
Clatskanie
Clatsop State Forest
Rainier
Prescott
Goble
Carrolls
Kalama
Mt. St. Helens
Cougar
Cascade
Mt. Adams Wilderness
Ecola State Park
Cannon Beach
Tolovana Beach Wayside
Hug Point State Park
Oswald West State Park
Nehalem Bay State Park
Birkenfeld
Jewell
Mist
Deer Island
Columbia City
St. Helens
Vernonia
Warren
Ariel
Green Mountain
Woodland
La Center
Yacolt
Moulton
Pioneer
Ridgefield
Battle Ground
Forest
Glenwood
Trout Lake
Horse
Heaven
Bickleton
Manzanita
Nehalem
Mohler
Wheeler
Rockaway
Garibaldi
Bay City
Tillamook
Wayside
Timber
Scappoose
Buxton
Manning
Banks
Glenwood
Sara
Felida
Duluth
Vancouver
B Z Corner
Willard
Gilmer
Husum
Klickitat
Wahkiacus
White Salmon
Bingen
Goldendale
Cape Meares State Park
Oceanside
Netarts
Gales Creek
Forest Grove
North Plains
Portland
Brush Prairie
Orchards
Camas
Washougal
Carson
Stevenson
Cook
Lyle
Wishram Heights
Wishram
Roosevelt
Columbia
Arlington
Cape Lookout State Park
Cape Lookout
Hillsboro
Tigard
Gaston
State Park
Tualatin
Troutdale
Bonneville
Cascade Locks
Hood River
Odell
Mosier
Dee
Rufus
Wasco
Biggs
Blalock
Cecil
Gresham
Boring
Sandy
West Linn
Mt. Hood
Parkdale
Mount Hood
The Dalles
Cape Kiwanda State Park
Beaver
Siuslaw
Pacific City
Hebo
Cloverdale
Yamhill
Carlton
Sherwood
Newberg
Wilsonville
Oregon City
Canby
Barlow
Aurora
Eagle Creek
Brightwood
Wemme
Zigzag
Government Camp
Rhododendron
Dufur
Moro
Mikkalo
Grass Valley
Eightmile Canyon
Neskowin
Neskowin Beach Wayside
Nat'l
Lafayette
McMinnville
Sheridan
Dayton
St. Paul
Donald
Mulino
Estacada
Friend
Otis
Grand Ronde
Amity
Williamina
Woodburn
Hubbard
Molalla
Colton
Nat'l Forest
Wamic
Tygh Valley
Maupin
Condon
Wayside
Lincoln City
Kernville
Gleneden Beach
Lincoln Beach
Depoe Bay
Forest
Keizer
Gervais
Mt. Angel
Brooks
Salem
Silverton
Kent
Mayville
Lonerock
Valsetz
Dallas
Independence
Monmouth
Sublimity
Fish Creek Divide
Warm
Springs
Shaniko
Fossil
Beverly Beach State Park
Otter Rock
Wayside
Newport
Toledo
Siletz
Falls City
Kings Valley
Eddyville
Turner
West Stayton
Stayton
Adair Village
Marion
Jefferson
Lyons
Mill City
Gates
Detroit
Indian
Reservation
Breitenbush Springs
Antelope
Kinzua
South Beach
S. Beach
Elk City
Hoskins
Millersburg
Corvallis
Scio
Crabtree
Idanha
Warm Springs
Lake Billy Chinook
Spray
Lost Creek State Park
Seal Rock
Driftwood Beach Wayside
Waldport
Blodgett
Harlan
Siuslaw
Philomath
Albany
Tangent
Shedd
Lacomb
Lebanon
Waterloo
Sodaville
Ashwood
John
Sutton Mtn.
Patterson Memorial State Park
Beachside State Park
Yachats
Neptune State Park
Tidewater
Alsea
Wildlife Refuge
Alpine
Halsey
Brownsville
Holley
Cascadia
Sweet Home
Willamette
Metolius
Culver
Madras
Camp Sherman
Mitchell
Yachats State Park
Washburne Mem. State Park
Devils Elbow State Park
Sea Lion Caves
Wayside
Horton
Blachly
Monroe
Harrisburg
Cheshire
Crawfordsville
Belknap Springs
Terrebonne
Ochoco
Swisshome
Heceta Beach
Tiernan
Mapleton
Noti
Ridge Lake
Junction City
Coburg
Mabel
Marcola
Mohawk
Vida
Blue River
McKenzie Bridge
Sisters
Redmond
Prineville
Florence
Glenada
Cushman
Walton
Veneta
Elmira
Springfield
Leaburg
Walterville
Jasper
State Park
Powell Butte
Post
Crooked
Honeyman Memorial State Park
Dunes City
Siltcoos
Eugene
Goshen
Creswell
Pleasant Hill
Falls Creek
Lowell
Bend
Paulina
Oregon Dunes Nat'l Recreation Area
Gardiner
Reedsport
Lorane
Cottage Grove
Walker
Dexter
Saginaw
Curtin
Westfir
Oakridge
Deschutes
Sunriver
Millican
Brothers
Winchester Bay
Umpqua Lighthouse State Park
Lakeside
Wm. M. Tugman State Park
Scottsburg
Elkton
Drain
Yoncalla
Dorena
Disston
Culp Creek
Row R.
McCredie Springs
Hills Creek
Arnold Ice Cave
Newberry Crater
Paulina Mts.
Coos Bay
North Bend
Allegany
Charleston
Eastside
Sunset Bay State Park
Shore Acres State Park
Sumner
Oakland
Sutherlin
Umpqua
Wilbur
Crescent Lake
Wickiup Res.
Lapine
Hampton
Lava Beds
Bullards Beach State Park
Riverton
Coquille
Sitkum
Winchester
Idleyld Park
Glide
Umpqua
Gilchrist
Crescent
Fort Rock State Monument
Ft. Rock
Bandon
Wayside
Norway
Gravelford
Bridge
Tenmile
Camas Valley
Roseburg
Winston
Dillard
Diamond Lake
Winema
Chemult
Christmas Valley
Myrtle Point
Langlois
Denmark
Remote
Broadbent
Floras Lake State Park
Riddle
Myrtle Creek
Days Creek
Silver Lake
Cape Blanco State Park
Sixes
Powers
Gaylord
Port Orford
Wayside
Canyonville
Milo
Tiller
Drew
Union Creek
Crater Lake
Crater Lake Nat'l Park
Picture Rock Pass
Humbug Mtn. State Park
Siskiyou
Glendale
Azalea
Rogue
Summer Lake
Dry Valley
Ophir
Agness
Wayside
Wedderburn
Gold Beach
Wolfcreek
Prospect
River
Trail
Shady Cove
Butte Falls
Fort Klamath
Klamath Agency
Sun Pass
State Park
Chiloquin
Fremont
Winter Ridge
Summer Lake
Cape Sebastian State Park
Pistol River
Illinois
Merlin
Grants Pass
Wilderville
Wonder
Rogue River
Gold Hill
White City
Eagle Point
Central Point
Lakecreek
Winema Nat'l Forest
Upper Klamath Nat'l Wildlife Refuge
Sprague River
Paisley
Lake Albert
Abert Rim
Harris Beach State Park
Brookings
Harbor
Pelican St. Beach
Selma
Murphy
Kerby
Cave Junction
O'Brien
Applegate
Medford
Jacksonville
Phoenix
Talent
Williams
Ashland
Oregon Caves National Monument
Beatty
Bly
Algoma
Valley Falls
Coyote Hills
Plush
Smith River
Fort Dick
Elk Cr.
Wayside
Klamath Falls
Keno
Pinehurst
Dairy
Olene
Bonanza
Quartz Mtn. Pass
Midland
Merrill
Malin
Lakeview
Adel
Crump Lake
Northcrest
Pt. St. George
Crescent City
Bertsch Terrace
Gasquet
Seiad Valley
Happy Camp
Klamath River
Hilts
Copco
Hornbrook
Dorris
Tulelake
Greaser Canyon
Del Norte Coast Redwoods
Redwood
Requa
Klamath
Klamath Glen
Trees of Mystery
Clear Cr.
Horse Cr.
Hamburg
Henley
Hawkinsville
Yreka
Scott Bar Mts.
Macdoel
Mt. Hebron
Tule Lake Nat'l Wildlife Refuge
Newell
Clear Lake Reservoir
Modoc
New Pine Cr.
Goose Lake
Ft. Bidwell
Willow Ranch
Montague
Grenada
Mugginsville
Ft. Jones
Tecnor
Ind. Res.

FOR WASHINGTON STATE MAP SEE PAGES 88-89

8 9 10 11 12 13 14

A B C D E F G H J K

FOR IDAHO STATE MAP SEE PAGES 34-35

Vernita U.S. Dept. of Energy Basin City Connell Hay Penawawa Pullman Almota Joel Troy Dworshak Reservoir National Forest
Outlook Mesa Ringold Ayer Riparia Gould City Illia Wawawai 195 Colton Juliaetta Kendrick Cavendish Ahsahka Headquarters Selway-Bitterro
Sunnyside West Richland 240 Pleasant View Kahlotus Starbuck River 261 Pomeroy Pataha Uniontown Genesee Lenore Peck Orofino Greer Grangemont Pierce
Benton City Glade Page Clyde Eureka Dodge 126 Clarkston Spalding Myrtle Gifford Mohler Weippe Wilderness
Richland Kennewick Burbank Prescott Dayton Lewistown Nez Perce Nezperce Kamiah Clearwater Mountains Nezperce
Prosser Klona Finley Hover 124 125 Waitsburg 128 Asotin Reubens Craigmont Ferdinand Kooskia Lowell Selway River
Paterson Plymouth Umatilla Touchet College Place Walla Walla Cloverland Anatone 129 Greencreek 62 Kooskia Clearwater National
Irrigon McNary Lowden Sudbury Dixie Kooskooskie Umatilla Nat'l Forest Rogersburg Keuterville Cottonwood 13 Clearwater
Boardman Hermiston Stanfield Milton-Freewater Wenaha Tucannon Wilderness Fenn Harpster
National Wildlife Refuge Echo Adams Weston Troy Flora White Bird Grangville Mount Idaho Golden Elk City Forest
Ione Helix Athena Umatilla Flora Lucile Orogrande
Lexington Pendleton Mission Gibbon National Wallowa Imnaha Hell's Canyon Riggins Dixie Salmon River Breaks Primitive Area
Heppner Pilot Rock Meacham Elgin Minam 82 Wallowa Nat'l Recreation Pollock Burgdorf Warren Gospel Hump Wilderness Idaho
Kamela Summerville Lostine Enterprise Area Payette Primitive
Boardman Ukiah Alicel Island City Whitman Joseph Tamarack Meadows National Area
Meadow Br. Pass Ritter LaGrande Cove Union Homestead Cuprum New Meadows State Park Yellow Pine IDAHO
Monument Wayside Wallowa Telocaset Medical Springs Fruitvale McCall Lake Fork Stibnite
Kimberly Long Creek Granite North Powder Whitman Halfway Starkey Council Donnelly Cape Horn
Hamilton Sumpter Haines Nat'l New Bridge Richland 86 Warm Lake Sunbeam
Fox Greenhorn Austin Baker Forest Pleasant Valley Durkee 71 Mesa Cascade Reservoir Casacade Stanley
Dayville Prairie City Whitney State Park 30 245 Bridgeport Cambridge Smiths Ferry Sawtooth
Mount Vernon John Day Canyon City Hereford Unity Midvale Ola Crouch Garden Valley Lowman Sawtooth Wilderness National Recreation
Seneca Ironside Huntington State Park Weiser Banks Centerville Placerville Pioneerville Area
Jamieson Brogan Payette Gardena Idaho City Atlanta
Willow Creek Westfall Vale Ontario Fruitland New Plymouth Sweet Horse Shoe Bend Sawtooth
Burns Hines Drewsey Drinkwater Pass Harper Nyssa Letha Montour Pearl National
Riley Lawen Juntura Owyhee Emmett Eagle Garden Valley Forest
Warm Springs Valley Crane Roswell Parma Notus Middleton Boise Mayfield Pine
Crow Camp Hills Adrian Wilder Caldwell Star Meridian Anderson Ranch Reservoir Fairfield
New Princeton Homedale Nampa Kuna Orchard Corral Hill City
Harney Lake Malheur Caves Marsing Bowmont Melba 46
Diamond Duck Pond Ridge Reynolds Murphy Mountain Home King Hill
Frenchglen Mahogany Mts. Sheaville Silver City Grand View Hammett Glenns Ferry Bliss
Wayside The Craters Jordon Valley Oreana 78 Bruneau Bruneau Hot Sprs. Hagerman Tuttle
Andrews Arock Lava Beds Triangle Grasmere Castleford Buhl Filer
Alvord Rome Antelope Res. Hollister
Fields Burns Jct. Bowden Hills Riddle
Bowden Hills Blue Mtn. Pass
Trout Creek Mts. Charles Sheldon Denio 51
Denio Junction McDermitt Fort McDermitt Indian Reservation Humboldt Duck Valley Owyhee

Oregon
Scale of Miles
0 7 14 21 28 35
N
© Creative Sales Corporation

FOR NEVADA STATE MAP SEE PAGES 60-61

NV.

1 • 2 • 3 • 4 • 5 • 6 • 7

FOR NEW YORK STATE MAP SEE PAGES 66-69

A

Lake Erie

Presque Isle St. Pk.

Gowanda
Fredonia
Brocton
Westfield
Mayville
N. East
Sherman
Cassadaga
Cherry Creek
Sinclairville
Randolph
E. Randolph
Little Valley
Cattaraugus
Ellicottville
Franklinville
Lime Lake
Machias
Houghton
Fillmore
Canaseraga
Arkport
Angelica
Almond

B

Erie
Fairview
Lake City
Wesleyville
Panama
Lakewood
Celoron
Jamestown
Frewsburg
Allegany St. Pk.
Salamanca
Allegany
Olean
Cuba
Friendship
Andover
Belmont
Richburg
Wellsville
Stannards
Bolivar
Portville
Cuba Reservation St. Pk.

C

Conneaut
Girard
Platea
Cranesville
McKean
Waterford
Union City
Edinboro
Albion
Springboro
Conneautville
Cambridge Springs
Venango
Saegertown
Blooming Valley
Mill Village
Townville
Centerville
Spartansburg
Corry
Sugar Grove
Youngsville
Warren
Clarendon
Allegheny Res.
Bradford
Eldred
Shinglehouse
Oswayo
Port Allegany
Coudersport
Denton Hill St. Pk.

OH

D

Andover
Linesville
Pymatuning Res.
Meadville
Cochranton
Pleasantville
Hydetown
Titusville
Oil Creek St. Pk.
Cooperstown
Rouseville
Tidioute
Allegheny National Forest
Kane
Mt. Jewett
Sizerville St. Pk.
Elk St. Pk.
Austin
Lyman Run St. Pk.
Sinnemahoning St. Pk.
Emporium
Johnsonburg
Bendigo St. Pk.
Ridgway
St. Marys
Renovo
S. Renovo
Kettle Creek St. Pk.
Driftwood
Goddard St. Pk.
Jamestown
Greenville
New Lebanon
Sugarcreek
Franklin
Polk
Stoneboro
Sandy Lake
Oil City
Tionesta
Cook Forest St. Pk.
Clarion

E

Pymatuning St. Pk.
Cortland
Sharon
Farrell
Wheatland
Mercer
W. Middlesex
Jackson Center
Clintonville
Knox
Shippenville
Strattanville
Clarion
Corsica
Falls Creek
Brockway
PENNSYLVANIA
Parker Dam St. Pk.
Emlenton
St. Petersburg
Callensburg
Sligo
Eau Claire
Harrisville
Parker
Grove City
Brookville
Summerville
Reynoldsville
Du Bois
Snow Shoe
Milesburg
Bald Eagle St. Pk.

F

Youngstown
New Castle
Bessemer
Portersville
Wampum
Ellwood City
Ellport
New Beaver
Big Beaver
Slippery Rock
Petrolia
Karns City
W. Liberty
Moraine St. Pk.
Chicora
E. Butler
Butler
Bruin
Rimersburg
New Bethlehem
S. Bethlehem
Hawthorn
Dayton
Punxsutawney
Big Run
Troutville
Sykesville
Grampian
Curwensville
Clearfield
Philipsburg
Lumber City
Osceola Mills
Chester Hill
Houtzdale
Port Matilda
Bellefonte
Centre Hall
State College
Penn. St. Univ.

G

Beaver Falls
New Brighton
Monaca
Industry
Beaver
Baden
Economy
Conway
Mars
Saxonburg
Callery
Evans City
Connoquenessing
Worthington
W. Kittanning
Kittanning
Ford Cliff
Ford City
Rural Valley
Plumville
Creekside
Glen Campbell
Marion Center
Cherry Tree
Barnesboro
Spangler
Hastings
Carrolltown
Patton
Ashville
Loretto
Gallitzin
Bellwood
Tyrone
Altoona
Sankertown
Cresson
Williamsburg
Canoe Creek St. Pk.
Petersburg
McVeytown
Huntingdon
Greenwood Furnace St. Pk.
Indiana
Indiana Univ.
Homer City
Clymer
Westover
Coalport
Irvona
Ramey
Glen Hope
Newburg
Philipsburg

H

Pittsburgh
Carnegie
Dormont
W. Mifflin
Wilkinsburg
Murrysville
Monroeville
Bethel Park
McKeesport
Clairton
White Oak
Jeanette
Latrobe
Greensburg
Blairsville
Seward
S. Fork
Johnstown
Windber
Hollidaysburg
Duncansville
Roaring Spring
Martinsburg
Woodbury
Mill Creek
Mt. Union
Shirleysburg
New Alexandria
Bolivar
New Florence
Derry
Ligonier
Westmont
Geistown
Scalp Level
Cassandra
Lily
Portage
Summerhill
Newry
Marklesburg
Blue Knob St. Pk.
Saxton
Dudley
Saltillo
Orbisonia
Blain
Three Springs
Shade Gap

J

Washington
Canonsburg
Houston
Jefferson
New Eagle
Donora
Monessen
Charleroi
Belle Vernon
N. Belle Vernon
California
W. Brownsville
Brownsville
S. Connellsville
Connellsville
Dunbar
Scottdale
Mt. Pleasant
Youngwood
W. Newton
New Stanton
Donegal
Boswell
Jennerstown
Stoystown
Central City
New Paris
Pleasantville
Hooversville
Somerset
Rockwood
Berlin
Garrett
Meyersdale
Rainsburg
Bedford
Everett
Chambersburg
Cowans Gap St. Pk.
Mercersburg
Greencastle

K

WV
Waynesburg
Carmichaels
Rices Landing
New Salem
Masontown
Greensboro
Point Marion
Fairchance
Smithfield
Uniontown
Ohiopyle
Friendship Hill Nat. Hist. Site
Ft. Necessity Nat. Battlefield
Ursina
Mt. Davis Elev. 3213' Highest Pt. in PA
Salisbury
Addison
Wellersburg
Grantsville
Coopers Rock S.F.
Cameron
Westover
Morgantown
Star City
Friendsville
New Germany St. Pk.
Accident
Frostburg
Midland
Cumberland
Hancock
Hagerstown
MD
Williamsport
Mannington
Barrackville
Rivesville
Masontown
Lonaconing
Barton

FOR OHIO STATE MAP SEE PAGES 74-75

FOR WEST VIRGINIA STATE MAP SEE PAGES 86-87

FOR MARYLAND STATE MAP SEE PAGES 46-47

Pennsylvania

Scale of Miles

N

0 5 10 15 20 25

© Creative Sales Corporation

NEW YORK

Catskill Park

Avoca • Hammondsport • Montour Falls • Watkins Glen • Ithaca • Dryden • Oxford
Bath • Savona • Millport • Odessa • Lisle • Whitney Point • Greene • Sidney
Painted Post • Corning • Horseheads • Van Etten • Spencer • Candor • Newark Valley • Afton • Bainbridge • Andes • Margaretville
Gang Mills • Elmira Hts. • Owego • Endwell • Binghamton • Windsor • Walton
Addison • Woodhull • S. Corning • Elmira • Southport • Waverly • Apalachin • Johnson City • Endicott • Deposit • Livingston Manor
Knoxville • Elkland • Tioga • Sayre • Athens • Nichols • Little Meadows • Great Bend • Oakland • Lanesboro • Hancock • Liberty
Westfield • Mansfield • Sylvania • Troy • Rome • Le Raysville • Montrose • New Milford • Susquehanna • Jeffersonville • Monticello
Galeton • Wellsboro • Blossburg • Canton • West Franklin • Wyalusing • Meshoppen • Nicholson • Waymart • Honesdale
Liberty • Forksville • Dushore • New Albany • Tunkhannock • Factoryville • Jermyn • Carbondale • Archbald • Hawley
Williamsport • Montoursville • Hughesville • Laporte • Harveys Lake • Clarks Summit • Dickson City • Blakely • Olyphant • Matamoras
Lock Haven • Jersey Shore • Watsontown • Benton • Stillwater • Scranton • Taylor • Old Forge • Dunmore • Moosic • Moscow • Milford
Mill Hall • Milton • Lewisburg • Danville • Bloomsburg • Berwick • Nescopeck • Kingston • Wilkes-Barre • Pittston • Newton
Mifflinburg • Northumberland • Catawissa • Nanticoke • Ashley • White Haven • Mt. Pocono • E. Stroudsburg
Shamokin Dam • Sunbury • Mt. Carmel • Shenandoah • Hazleton • Freeland • Weatherly • Jim Thorpe • Stroudsburg • Delaware Water Gap
Selinsgrove • Shamokin • Frackville • Mahanoy City • Tamaqua • Lansford • Lehighton • Palmerton • Bangor • Easton
Middleburg • Freeburg • Kulpmont • St. Clair • New Philadelphia • Port Carbon • Summit Hill • Bowmanstown • Slatington • Nazareth • Phillipsburg • Washington
Beavertown • Herndon • Pillow • Gratz • Tremont • Minersville • Pottsville • Orwigsburg • Walnutport • Northampton • Catasauqua • Wilson
Lewistown • Millerstown • Liverpool • Paxtang • Williamstown • Cressona • Schuylkill Haven • Hamburg • Whitehall • Bethlehem
Mifflintown • Millersburg • Elizabethville • Pine Grove • Shoemakersville • Emmaus • Allentown • Freemansburg
Port Royal • Newport • New Buffalo • Halifax • Jonestown • Strausstown • Leesport • Kutztown • Fountain Hill
Duncannon • Dauphin • Myerstown • Richland • Womelsdorf • Robesonia • Temple • Topton • Macungie • Richlandtown • Quakertown
Marysville • Lebanon • Cleona • W. Reading • Laureldale • E. Greenville • Pennsburg • Perkasie • Sellersville • Doylestown
Harrisburg • Hershey • Palmyra • Cornwall • Wyomissing • Reading • Boyertown • Telford • Souderton • Lansdale • Hatboro • Ambler
Carlisle • Lemoyne • Hummelstown • Denver • Adamstown • Shillington • Pottstown • Trappe • Collegeville • Chalfont
Mechanicsburg • New Cumberland • Middletown • Lincoln • Birdsboro • Royersford • Spring City • N. Wales • Norristown • Conshocken
Newville • Dillsburg • Elizabethtown • Ephrata • Akron • Terre Hill • Honey Brook • Phoenixville • Collegeville • Levittown • Trenton
Shippensburg • Mt. Holly Springs • Mt. Wolf • Mt. Joy • Manheim • Lititz • New Holland • Downingtown • Philadelphia • Bristol
Orrstown • Newburg • Wellsville • Manchester • Marietta • Mountville • Lancaster • Coatesville • W. Chester • Narberth • Camden
Mont Alto • Shippensburg • Dover • Wrightsville • Columbia • Strasburg • Parkesburg • Goatesville • Media • Yeadon • Darby • Collingswood
Gettysburg • York • Dallastown • Millersville • Quarryville • Kennett Square • Chester • Brookhaven • Bellmawr • Strafford
Waynesboro • Hanover • Spring Grove • Jacobus • Red Lion • Oxford • W. Grove • Wilmington • Elsmere • Chester Hts. • Runnemede • Linwood • Berlin
Emmitsburg • Littlestown • Glen Rock • Winterstown • Fawn Grove • Delta • Newport • Penns Grove • Pitman • Clayton
Taneytown • Manchester • New Freedom • Shrewsbury • Rising Sun • Port Deposit • New Castle • Glassboro • Folsom
Westminster • Hampstead • Bel Air • Perryville • Elkton • Delaware City • Salem • Woodstown • Newfield • Buena
Thurmont • Woodsboro • North East • Charlestown • Delaware City • Buena

NJ • **DE** • **MD**

FOR NEW JERSEY STATE MAP SEE PAGES 62-63

2 · 3 · 4 · 5 · 6 · 7 ·

FOR NORTH DAKOTA STATE MAP SEE PAGES 72-73

NORTH DAKOTA

SOUTH DAK

NEBRASKA

MT.

WY.

FOR MONTANA STATE MAP SEE PAGES 54-55

FOR WYOMING STATE MAP SEE PAGES 92-93

Bismarck, Medina, 94, Glen Ullin, New Salem, Mandan, Menoken, Steele, Driscoll, Dawson, Tappen, Almont, Lincoln, Fort Lincoln State Park, Hist. Site, Slade Nat'l Wildlife Refuge, Long Lake Nat'l Wildlife Refuge, Alkali Lake, Braddock, Napoleon, Hazelton, Freda, Raleigh, Carson, Elgin, Leith, Mott, New Leipzig, Regent, New England, Amidon, White Butte Elev. 3,506 ft., Fort Dilts Hist. Site, Marmarth, Rhame, Bowman, Gascoyne, Scranton, Reeder, Bucyrus, Haley, Hettinger, Haynes, Lemmon, Plevna, Baker, Ekalaka, Mill Iron, Ladner, Ludlow, Ralph, Lodgepole, White Butte, Shadehill, Morristown, McIntosh, Standing Rock Indian Res., Selfridge, Shields, Solen, Breien, Fort Yates, Linton, Strasburg, Westfield, Hague, Zeeland, Venturia, Ashley, Wishek, Doyle Memorial State Park, Beaver Lake State Park, Napoleon

Camp Crook, Buffalo, Reva, Prairie City, Bison, Meadow, Shadehill Res., Grand, Bullhead, McLaughlin, Little Eagle, Pollock, Herreid, Mound City, Eureka, Hillsview, Hosmer, Artas, Mobridge, Glenham, Selby, Java, Bowdle, Roscoe, Onaka, Tolstoy, Hoven, Lowry, Swan Lake, Akaska, LaPlant, Ridgeview, Eagle Butte, Dupree, Faith, Isabel, Timber Lake, Trail City, Glad Valley, Chance, Sorum, Redig, Zeona, Mud Butte, Maurine, Castle Rock, Alzada, Colony, Moreau, Cheyenne, Indian, Reservation, Lake Oahe, Gettysburg, Seneca, Faulkton, Agar, Onida, Orient, Blunt, Harrold, Highmore, Ree Heights, Pierre, Fort Pierre, Stephan, Fort Thompson, Reliance, Oacoma, Chamberlain, Pukwana, Kennebec, Presho, Vivian, Draper, Murdo, Belvidere, Kadoka, Interior, Scenic, Cottonwood, Quinn, Wall, Wasta, Box Elder, Rapid City, Farmingdale, Hermosa, Keystone, Rockerville, Hill City, Mt. Rushmore, Crazy Horse Mon., Custer, Pringle, Fairburn, Buffalo Gap, Hot Springs, Edgemont, Provo, Newcastle, Horton, Spearfish, Whitewood, Deadwood, Central City, Lead, Sturgis, Black Hawk, Elm Springs, Creighton, Plainview, Howes, Cherry Creek, Enning, Union Center, Stoneville, Fairpoint, Newell, Nisland, Fruitdale, Belle Fourche, Beulah, Aladdin, Alva, Mule Cr. Jct., Philip, Midland, Bad River, Missouri River, Crow Creek, Lower Brule Indian Reservation, White River, Long Valley, Wood, Kyle, Allen, Martin, Bateland, Pine Ridge, Wounded Knee, Wounded Knee Battle Site, Oglala, Oelrichs, Parmelee, Okreek, Mission, Rosebud, Saint Francis, Winner, Dallas, Gregory, Burke, Herrick, Bonesteel, Wewela, Eli, Merriman, Cody, Nenzel, Kilgore, Crookston, Valentine, Sparks, Norden, Burton, Mills, Naper, Springview, Chadron, Whitney, Crawford, Harrison, Fort Robinson State Park, Chadron State Park, Hay Springs, Clinton, Rushville, Gordon, Nebraska National Forest, Samuel R. McKelvie Nat'l Forest, Niobrara Nat'l Wildlife Refuge, Merritt Res., Valentine Migratory Waterfowl Refuge, Wood Lake, Johnstown, Ainsworth, Long Pine, Bassett, Newport, Stuart, Elsmere, Rose, Morrill, Mitchell, Scottsbluff, Terrytown, Alliance, Antioch, Lakeside, Angora, Ellsworth, Bingham, Hyannis, Whitman, Mullen, Brownlee, Hemingford, Agate Fossil Beds Nat'l Monument, Angostura Res., Cheyenne, Badlands National Park, Pine Ridge Indian Reservation, Oglala National Grasslands, Buffalo Gap National Grassland

FOR NEBRASKA STATE MAP SEE PAGES 58-59

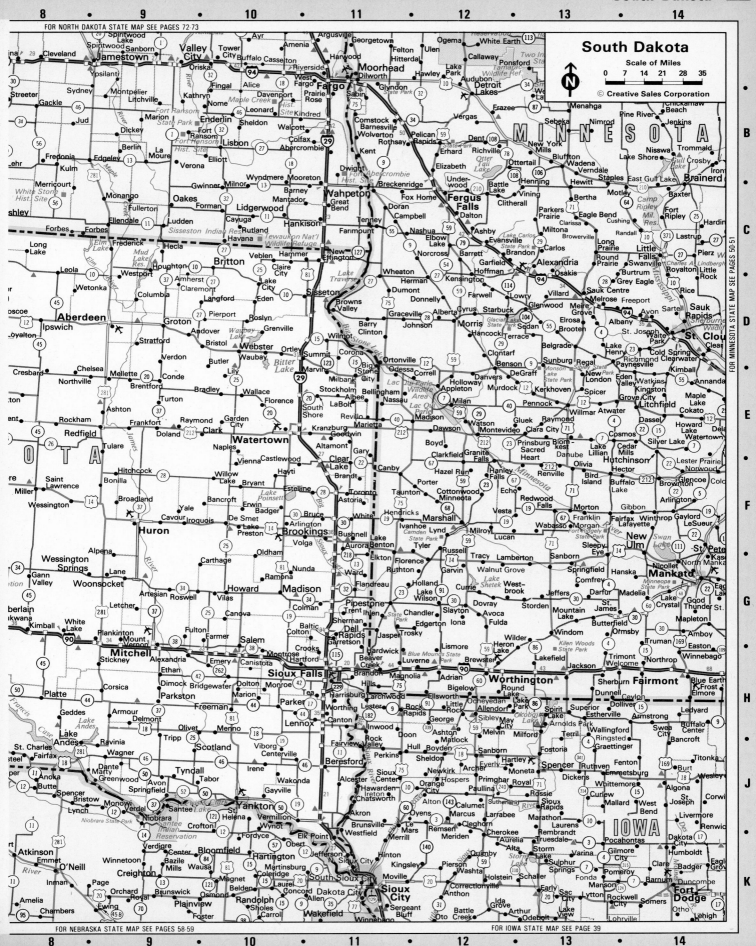

South Dakota
Scale of Miles
0 7 14 21 28 35
© Creative Sales Corporation

FOR MINNESOTA STATE MAP SEE PAGES 50-51

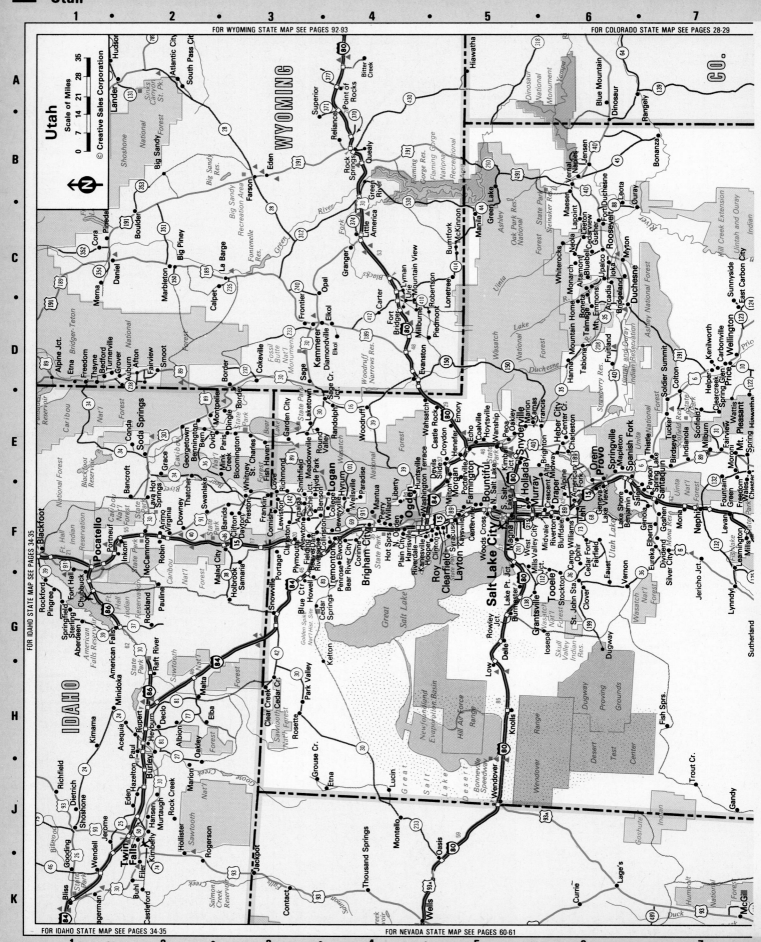

Utah
Scale of Miles
© Creative Sales Corporation

FOR COLORADO STATE MAP SEE PAGES 28-29

FOR NEW MEXICO STATE MAP SEE PAGES 64-65

FOR ARIZONA STATE MAP SEE PAGES 20-21

UTAH

NEVADA

ARIZONA

N.M.

Grand Junction, Fruita, Loma, Mack, Cisco, Thompson, Green River, Crescent Jct., Moab, Arches National Park, Canyonlands National Park, Monticello, Blanding, Bluff, Mexican Hat, Montezuma Creek, Aneth

Nucla, Naturita, Slick Rock, Egnar, Dove Creek, Cahone, Pleasant View, Yellow Jacket, Lewis, Arriola, Cortez, Towaoc, Mesa Verde National Park

Beklabito, Shiprock, Newcomb, Sheep Spr., Naschitti, Tohatchi, Crystal, Navajo, Teec Nos Pos, Rock Point, Round Rock, Many Farms, Chinle, Tsaile, Kayenta, Tsegi

East Carbon City, Woodside, Price, Cleveland, Huntington, Castle Dale, Ferron, Emery, Hanksville, Fry Canyon, Natural Bridges Nat'l Monument

Mt. Pleasant, Spring City, Ephraim, Manti, Sterling, Gunnison, Centerfield, Salina, Richfield, Aurora, Sigurd, Elsinore, Joseph, Monroe, Koosharem, Greenwich, Antimony, Kingston, Junction, Circleville, Marysville, Beaver, Manderfield, Greenville, Cove Fort, Minersville, Milford

Fremont, Loa, Bicknell, Lyman, Teasdale, Torrey, Grover, Boulder, Escalante, Henrieville, Tropic, Cannonville, Bryce Canyon, Panguitch, Hatch, Paragonah, Parowan, Brian Head, Cedar City, Enoch, Summit

Fillmore, Holden, Meadow, Kanosh, Scipio, Oak City, Delta, Hinckley, Oasis, Deseret, Sutherland, Abraham, Leamington

Kanarraville, New Harmony, Pintura, Toquerville, La Verkin, Virgin, Rockville, Springdale, Zion National Park, Hurricane, Washington, St. George, Santa Clara, Ivins, Shivwits, Gunlock, Leeds, Central, Pine Valley, Veyo, Newcastle, Enterprise, Beryl, Zane, Lund

Page, Marble Canyon, Jacob Lake, Fredonia, Kanab, Mt. Carmel, Glendale, Orderville, Colorado City, Alton, Long Valley Jct.

Littlefield, Mesquite, Bunkerville, Glendale, Logandale, Overton, Meadview, Temple Bar, Lake Mead National Recreation Area

Garrison, Baker, McGill, Ursine, Panaca, Pioche, Caliente, Elgin, Carp, Modena, Uvada, Desert Mound

Grand Canyon, North Rim, Tusayan, Kaibab National Forest, Cameron, Desert View, Tuba City, The Gap, Cedar Ridge, Red Lake, Cow Springs, Kaibito, Tonalea, Chilchinbito, Dinnehotso, Mexican Water, Rough Rock, Keams Canyon, Polacca, Second Mesa, Old Oraibi, Moqui, Hopi Indian Reservation, Navajo Indian Reservation

Lake Powell, Glen Canyon National Recreation Area

FOR NEVADA STATE MAP SEE PAGES 276-277

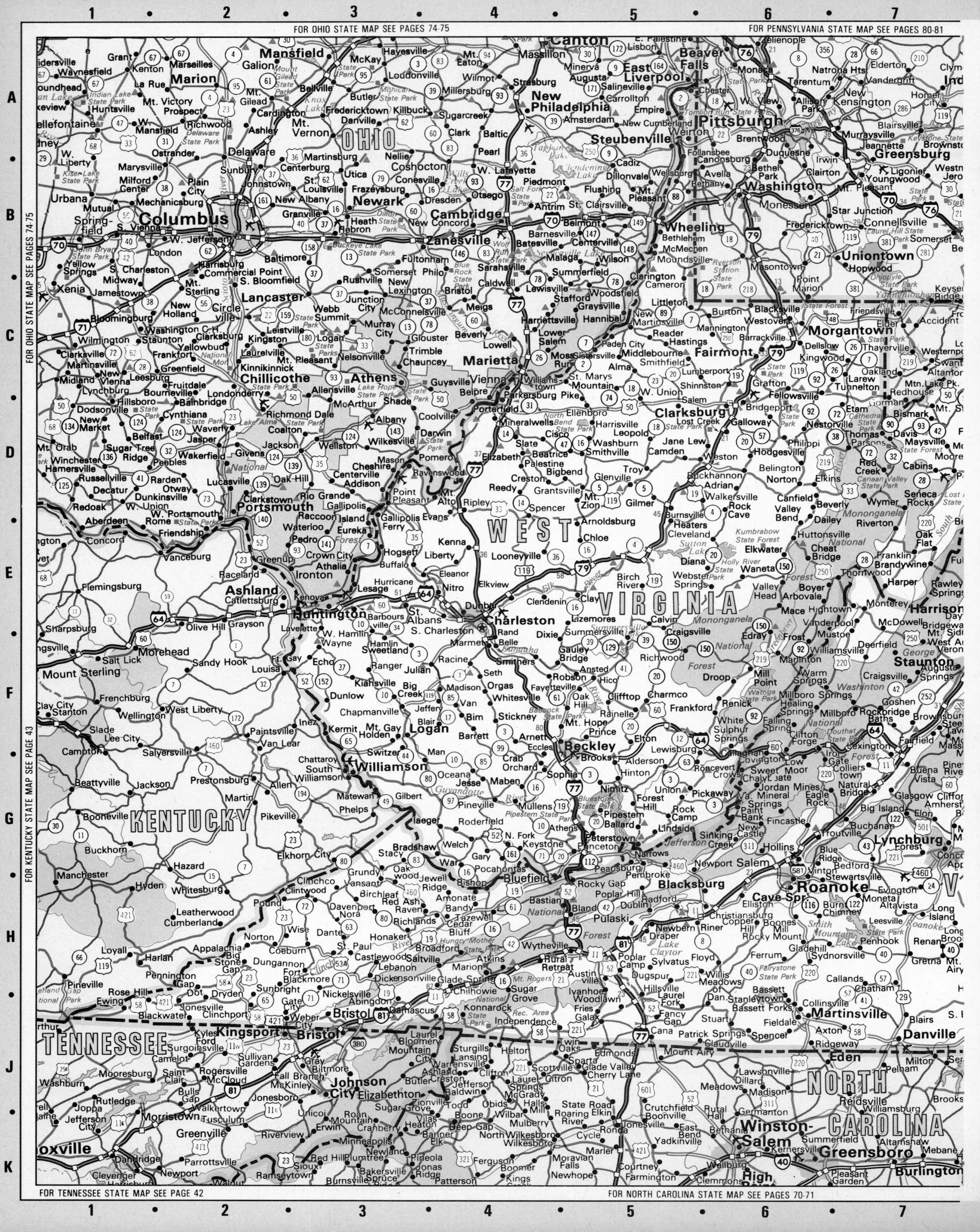
FOR OHIO STATE MAP SEE PAGES 74-75
FOR PENNSYLVANIA STATE MAP SEE PAGES 80-81
FOR KENTUCKY STATE MAP SEE PAGE 43
FOR TENNESSEE STATE MAP SEE PAGE 42
FOR NORTH CAROLINA STATE MAP SEE PAGES 70-71
OHIO
WEST VIRGINIA
KENTUCKY
TENNESSEE
NORTH CAROLINA
Columbus
Mansfield
Marion
Canton
Pittsburgh
Steubenville
Wheeling
Zanesville
Cambridge
Newark
Lancaster
Chillicothe
Athens
Marietta
Parkersburg
Morgantown
Fairmont
Clarksburg
Uniontown
Washington
Greensburg
Portsmouth
Ashland
Huntington
Charleston
Logan
Williamson
Beckley
Bluefield
Blacksburg
Roanoke
Lynchburg
Staunton
Danville
Martinsville
Bristol
Kingsport
Johnson City
Winston-Salem
Greensboro

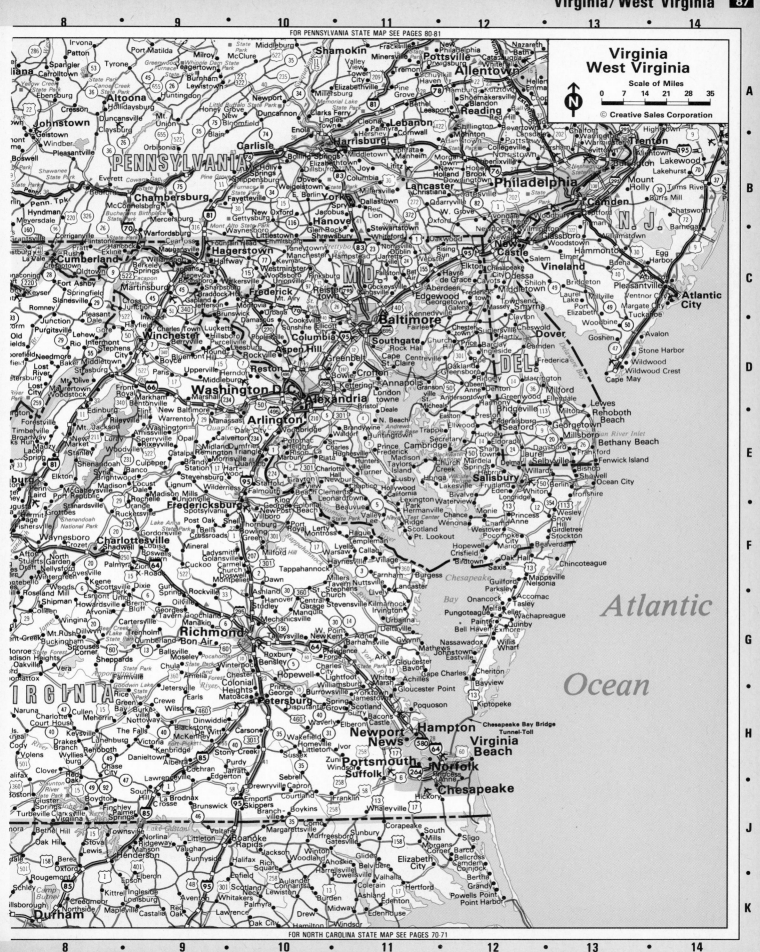

Virginia
West Virginia

Scale of Miles

0 7 14 21 28 35

© Creative Sales Corporation

BRITISH COLUMBIA

Vancouver Island

CANADA
U.S.

Strait of Juan De Fuca

Strait of Georgia

Barkley Sound · Nitinat Lake · Cowichan Lake · Ladysmith · Duncan · Saltspring Is. · Sidney · Sooke Lake · Port Renfrew · Galiano Is. · Mayne Is. · Pender Is. · Saturna Is. · Waldron Is. · Orcas Is. · Shaw Is. · Blakely Is. · Friday Harbor · San Juan Is. Nat'l Hist. Park · Victoria · Sooke · Lopez Is. · Guemes Is. · Cypress Is. · Fidalgo Is.

White Rock · Langley · Mission · Chilliwack · Chilliwack Lake · Skagit Valley Prov. Rec. Area

Blaine · Lynden · Sumas · Everson · Deming · Mount Baker · Mt. Baker · North Cascades Nat'l · Ross Lake · Ross Lake Nat'l Rec. Area

Ferndale · Lummi Indian Res. · Bellingham · Lake Whatcom · Acme · Wickersham · Upper Baker Dam · Baker Lake · Noisy Diobsud Wilderness

Anacortes · Sedro-Woolley · Lyman · Hamilton · Concrete · Lower Baker Dam · Rockport · Glacier Peak Wilderness

Mount Vernon · Burlington · Lake Shannon · Darrington · Boulder River Wilderness

Oak Harbor · Whidbey Is. · Coupeville · Stanwood · Arlington · Henry M. Jackson Wilderness

Neah Bay · Makah Indian Res. · Ozette · Lake Ozette · Sappho · Joyce · Fairholm · Crescent Lake · Port Angeles · Sequim · Port Townsend · Discovery Bay · Marysville · Everett · Granite Falls · Lake Stevens

Forks · La Push · Olympic Nat'l Forest · Olympic Nat'l Park · Mukilteo · Snohomish · Sultan · Gold Bar · Index · Wallace Falls St. Pk. · Snoqualmie Nat'l

Queets · Quinault Indian Res. · Lake Quinault · Poulsbo · Edmonds · Lynnwood · Brier · Bothell · Monroe · Duvall · Skykomish · Alpine Lakes Wilderness

Taholah · Neilton · Seattle · Kirkland · Redmond · Carnation · Snoqualmie · North Bend · Hyak · Salmon La Sac

Pacific Beach · Pacific Beach St. Pk. · Copalis Beach · Humptulips · Eldon · Bremerton · Mercer Island · Bellevue · Issaquah · Kachess Lake · Kachess Dam

Ocean Shores · Aberdeen · Hoquiam · Montesano · Elma · McCleary · Shelton · Port Orchard · Tukwila · Renton · Kent · Black Diamond · Keechelus Lake · South Cle Elum

Westport · Cosmopolis · Olympia · Lacey · Tumwater · Des Moines · Normandy Park · Auburn · Pacific · Sumner · Enumclaw · Buckley

North Cove · Oakville · Rochester · Yelm · Rainier · Eatonville · Gig Harbor · Tacoma · Fircrest · Steilacoom · Puyallup · Bonney Lake · Orting · Carbonado · Mt. Rainier Nat'l Park

Raymond · Menlo · Lebam · Pe Ell · Napavine · Tenino · Bucoda · Centralia · Chehalis · Morton · Glenoma · Randle · Packwood · Gifford Pinchot

South Bend · Ocean Park · Long Beach · Ilwaco · Naselle · Rosburg · Ryderwood · Winlock · Toledo · Vader · Mossyrock · Mayfield Lake · Riffe Lake · Goat Rocks Wilderness

Astoria · Warrenton · Cathlamet · Stella · Castle Rock · Silver Lake · Mt. St. Helens Nat'l Volcanic Mon. · Spirit Lake

Clatskanie · Kelso · Longview · Kalama · Woodland · Yacolt · Trout Lake · Mt. Adams Wilderness

Seaside · Cannon Beach · Vernonia · Ridgefield · La Center · Battle Ground · Orchards · Stevenson · North Bonneville · Husum · White Salmon · Klickitat

Manzanita · Tillamook · Forest Grove · Hillsboro · Vancouver · Camas · Washougal · Bonneville Dam · Hood River · Bingen · The Dalles

Garibaldi · Gresham · Portland · Oregon City · Newberg · Sandy · Dufur · Wishram

Pacific Ocean · Willapa Bay · Grays Harbor · Columbia R. · Lake Cushman

Washington

Scale of Miles

0 · 6 · 12 · 18 · 24 · 30

N

© Creative Sales Corporation

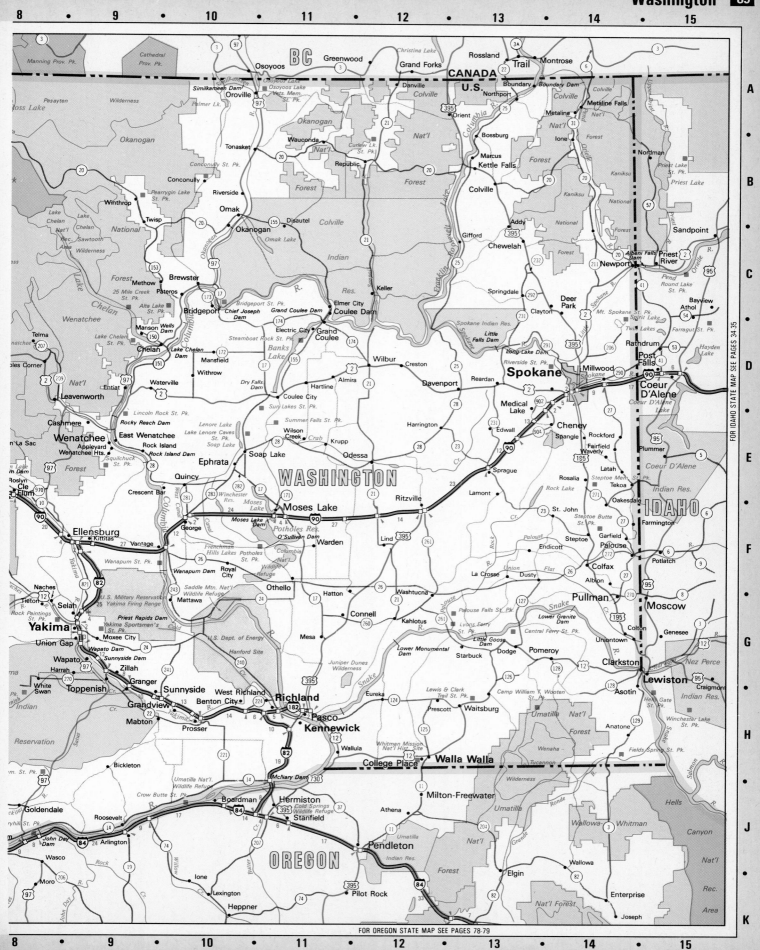

FOR IDAHO STATE MAP SEE PAGES 34-35

FOR OREGON STATE MAP SEE PAGES 78-79

FOR MICHIGAN STATE MAP SEE PAGES 48-49

United States Citizens Visiting Canada

All persons entering Canada must report to the Canadian Immigration and Customs Office at the Port of Entry and secure required permits for admission for their person and possessions. The transportation of plants and produce is rigidly controlled. Check with customs officials for complete regulations and requirements.

Canadian Citizens Visiting the United States

Passports or visas are not required of Canadian citizens or British subjects residing in Canada entering the United States for a period of six months or less, however, evidence of citizenship is required. Check with customs officials for complete regulations and requirements.

The Interstate Highway System in and around the Chicago area is confusing to many people. It is helpful to remember that, in most cases, Interstate Highways running north and south have odd numbers, and Interstate Highways running east and west have even numbers

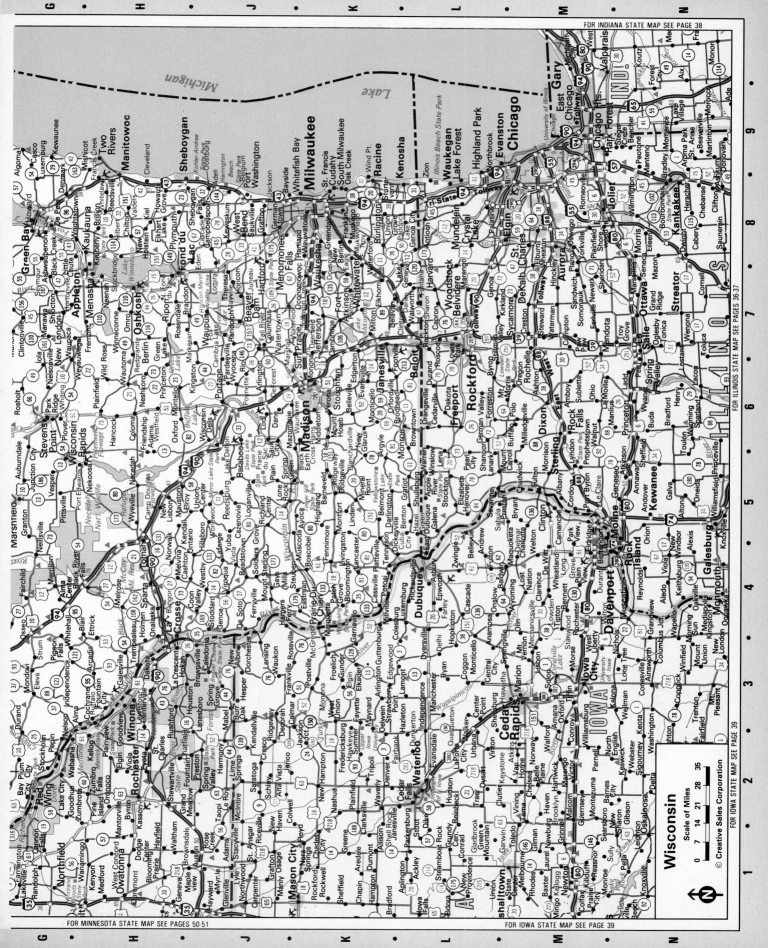

FOR INDIANA STATE MAP SEE PAGE 38

FOR ILLINOIS STATE MAP SEE PAGES 36-37

FOR IOWA STATE MAP SEE PAGE 39

Wisconsin

Scale of Miles

0 7 14 21 28 35

© Creative Sales Corporation

Wyoming

Scale of Miles
0 7 14 21 28 35

© Creative Sales Corporation

N

FOR IDAHO STATE MAP SEE PAGES 34-35
FOR MONTANA STATE MAP SEE PAGES 54-55
FOR UTAH STATE MAP SEE PAGES 84-85
FOR COLORADO STATE MAP SEE PAGES 28-29

MT.

IDAHO

WYOMING

UTAH

COLORADO

Grant, Dell, Lima, Lima Reservoir, Spencer, Blue Dome, Dubois, Cameron, Big Sky, Chico Hot Springs, Emigrant, Pray, Gardiner, Nye, Dean, Fishtail, Joliet, Boyd, Edgar, Roberts, Fromberg, Bridger, Red Lodge, Bearcreek, Belfry, Cooke City, Clark, Elk Basin, Frannie, Deaver, Cowley, Lovell, Burges

Mammouth Springs Jct., Tower Jct., Norris Jct., Canyon Jct., Madison Jct., Lake Jct., Old Faithful, W. Thumb Jct., Yellowstone, Shoshone Lake, Lewis Lake, Heart Lake, Yellowstone Lake

Powell, Ralston, Cody, Garland, Byron, Emblem, Shell, Greybull, Burlington, Otto, Basin, Meeteetse, Manderson, Worland, Pitchfork, Valley, Grass Creek, Kirby, Lucerne, Hamilton Dome, Thermopolis, E. Thermopolis

Macks Inn, Island Park, Warm River, Ashton, St. Anthony, Parker, Chester, Newdale, Sugar City, Teton, Rexburg, Tetonia, Driggs, Heise, Victor, Teton Village, Moose, Kelly, Wilson, Jackson, Hoback Jct.

Grand Teton National Park, Jenny Lake, Jackson Lake, Moran Jct., Bridger-Teton National Forest

Dubois, Burris, Crowheart, Morton, Pavillion, Kinnear, Ethete, Fort Washakie, Arapahoe, Lander, Hudson, St. Stephens, Riverton, Shoshoni, Lysite, Moneta, Boysen Res., Ocean Lake, Bull Lake, Wind River

St. Anthony, Newdale, Sugar City, Teton, Menan, Lorenzo, Roberts, Lewisville, Rigby, Ririe, Idaho Falls, Iona, Ammon, Shelley, Basalt, Firth, Blackfoot, Moreland, Rockford, Pingree, Fort Hall, Chubbuck, Pocatello, Portneuf, Inkom

Bancroft, Conda, Soda Springs, Grace, Georgetown, Bennington, Bern, Ovid, Paris, Montpelier, Dingle, Border, Bloomington, St. Charles, Fish Haven, Cokeville

Alpine Jct., Etna, Freedom, Thayne, Bedford, Turnerville, Grover, Auburn, Afton, Fairview, Smoot, Merna, Cora, Pinedale, Daniel, Boulder, Big Sandy, Marbleton, Big Piney, Calpet, La Barge, Farson, Eden

Bondurant, Fremont Lake, Fontenelle Res., Big Sandy Res., Big Sandy Recreation Area

Atlantic City, South Pass City, Jeffre, Sweetwa

Kemmerer, Diamondville, Elkol, Opal, Frontier, Sage, Granger, Little America, Green River, Rock Springs, Qualey, Reliance, Superior, Point of Rocks, Bitter Creek, Table Rock, Red Desert, Wamsutt

Fossil Butte Nat'l Monument, Woodruff, Randolph, Sage Jct., Round Valley, Laketown, Garden City

Evanston, Fort Bridger, Lyman, Urie, Millburne, Mountain View, Robertson, Piedmont, Lonetree, McKinnon, Burntfork, Manila, Green Lake, Hiawatha

Flaming Gorge Res., Flaming Gorge National Recreation Area

Salt Lake City, Ogden, Brigham City, Logan, Tremonton, Bear River City, Corinne, Hyrum, Wellsville, Paradise, Mantua, Willard, Layton, Clearfield, Roy, Bountiful, Snyderville, Holladay

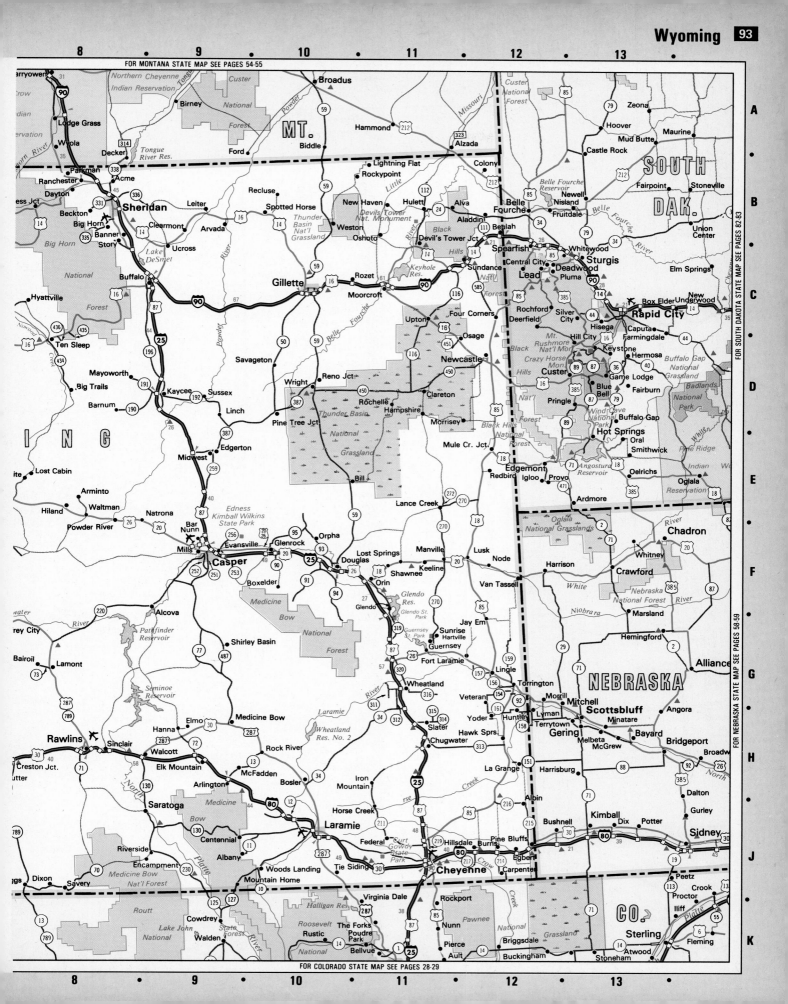

6   7   8   9   10   11

FOR NEW MEXICO STATE MAP SEE PAGES 64-65

FOR CONTINUATION SEE PAGE 98

FOR CONTINUATION SEE PAGE 96

NEW MEXICO

TEXAS

T E X A S

Grenville · Mt. Dora · Clayton · Griggs · Bryan's Corner · Balko · Hardesty · Elmwood · Slapout · May · Ft. Supply · Brace · Avard · Waynoka · Lambert · Yewed

Felt · Goodwell · Bado · Gray · Catesby · Tangier · Mooreland · Curtis · Belva · Carmen · Dacoma

Texline · Stratford · Texhoma · Perryton · Booker · Darrouzett · Follett · Fargo · Woodward · Quinlan · Cleo · Aline · McW

Sedan · Dalhart · Gruver · Waka · Lipscomb · Shattuck · Goodwin · Vici · Cestos · Seiling · Orienta · Ring

Hayden · Amistad · Cactus · Etter · Sunray · Spearman · Morse · Higgins · Arnett · Camargo · Taloga · Canton · Eagle City

Nara Visa · Dumas · Channing · Hartley · Stinnett · Sanford · Canadian · Durham · Crawford · Angora · Roll · Oakwood · Putnam · Fay

Logan · Masterson · Borger · Phillips · Miami · New Mobeetie · Briscoe · Dempsey · Cheyenne · Rankin · Strong City · Butler · Custer City

Adrian · Vega · Panhandle · Pampa · Skellytown · White Deer · Lefors · Mobeetie · Wheeler · Sweetwater · Elk City · Foss · Clinton · Weatherford · Hydro

Amarillo · Wildorado · Bushland · Conway · Groom · McLean · Lela · Shamrock · Erick · Texola · Sayre · Doxey · Forty One · Burns Flat · Bessie · Corn · Colony

Glenrio · Endee · **Canyon** · Claude · Alanreed · Twitty · Mayfield · Retrop · Dill City · Cloud Chief · Eakly · Cordell

San Jon · Goodnight · Ashtola · Dozier · Samnorwood · Vinson · Carter · Sentinel · Rocky · Lake Valley · Cowden · Alfalfa

Wheatland · Umbarger · Dawn · Happy · Clarendon · Lelia Lake · Hedley · Quail · Lutie · Madge · Wellington · Granite · Lone Wolf · Hobart · Mountain View · Carnegie · Ft. Cobb

Grady · Hereford · Summerfield · Brice · Memphis · Newlin · Mangum · Kugert · Babbs · Gotebo

Bellview · Broadview · Black · Friona · Nazareth · Tulia · Silverton · Lakeview · Estelline · Hollis · Gould · Duke · Altus · Ozark · Headrick · Humphreys · Indiahoma · Lawton

Pleasant Hill · Bovina · Dimmitt · Hart · Kress · Parnell · Lincoln · Olustee · Creta · Elmer · Cache

Clovis · Farwell · Texico · Lariat · Edmonson · Quitaque · Turkey · Tell · Kirkland · Goodlett · Quanah · Manitou · Faxon · Chattanooga · Hollister

Portales · Muleshoe · Springlake · Olton · Plainview · Aiken · Lockney · Whiteflat · Northfield · Acme · Medicine Mound · Chillicothe · Davidson · Loveland · Cookietown · Grandfield

Rogers · Needmore · Fieldton · Sudan · Hale Center · Cotton Center · Floydada · Matador · Paducah · Rayland · Vernon · Lockett · Oklaunion · Burkburnett · Devol · Randlett · Charlie

Dora · Pep · Goodland · Lingo · Maple · Morton · Enochs · Bula · Littlefield · Spade · Anton · Petersburg · Abernathy · Glenn · Dumont · Finney · Crowell · Harrold · Electra · Grayback · Iowa Park · Wichita

Milnesand · Bledsoe · Whitharral · Shallowater · New Deal · Idalou · Ralls · McAdoo · Guthrie · Gilliland · Red Springs · Kamay · Holliday · Scotland

Tatum · Lehman · Whiteface · Levelland · Hurlwood · Smyer · Lorenzo · Crosbyton · Dickens · Vera · Benjamin · Seymour · Dundee · Archer City · Windthorst

Bronco · Sundown · Wolfforth · **Lubbock** · Posey · Slaton · Kalgary · Spur · Knox City · Munday · Goree · Bomarton · Westover

McDonald · Hilburn City · Plains · Brownfield · New Home · Southland · Wilson · Girard · Jayton · O'Brien · Rochester · Weinert · Olney · Jean · Jermyn

Allred · Denver City · Wellman · Meadow · Tahoka · Post · Clairemont · Swenson · Old Glory · Haskell · Sagerton · Throckmorton · Elbert · Loving · Bryson

Humble City · Knowles · Loop · Welch · Grassland · Draw · Justiceburg · Aspermont · Old Rule · Newcastle · Graham

Hobbs · Seagraves · O'Donnell · Fluvanna · Rotan · Hamlin · Avoca · Fort Griffin · Woodson · South Bend · Mineral

Monument · Nadine · Seminole · Lamesa · Gail · Snyder · McCaulley · Anson · Funston · Lueders · Albany · Caddo · Palo Pinto

Oil Center · Eunice · Patricia · Ackerly · Vealmoor · Vincent · Ira · Dunn · Inadale · Longworth · Noodle · Moran · Morton Valley · Mingus · Strawn · Ranger

Frankel City · Andrews · Knott · Fairview · Westbrook · Loraine · Roscoe · Sweetwater · Merkel · Tye · **Abilene** · Baird · Putnam · Cisco · Eastland · Olden

Jal · Tarzan · Lenorah · Coahoma · Colorado City · Nolan · Trent · Caps · Clyde · Scranton · Carbon · Gorman · Desdemona · Lingleville

Kermit · Notrees · **Midland** · Stanton · **Big Spring** · Maryneal · Blackwell · Tuscola · Ovalo · Lawn · Oplin · Cross Plains · Pioneer · Rising Star · May · De Leon · Dublin

Wink · Penwell · **Odessa** · Gardendale · Lomax · Silver · Wingate · Bradshaw · Goldsboro · Cross Cut · Burkett · Proctor

Monahans · Pyote · Wickett · Royalty · Crane · Garden City · Sterling City · Robert Lee · Norton · Hatchel · Novice · Glen Cove · Coleman · Santa Anna · Bangs · Early · **Brownwood** · Blanket · Lamk · Energy

Coyanosa · Grandfalls · Imperial · Rankin · Water Valley · Tennyson · Rowena · Ballinger · Valera · Voss · Talpa · Sidney · Comanche · Gustin

Carlsbad · Miles · Paint Rock · Rockwood · Mullin · Goldthwaite · Priddy · Indian Gap

O. C. Fisher Lake · Twin Butte Lake · Tankersley · **San Angelo** · Wall · Vancourt · Millersview · Doole · Richland Springs

Mertzon · Sherwood · Knickerbocker · Rochelle · Adams

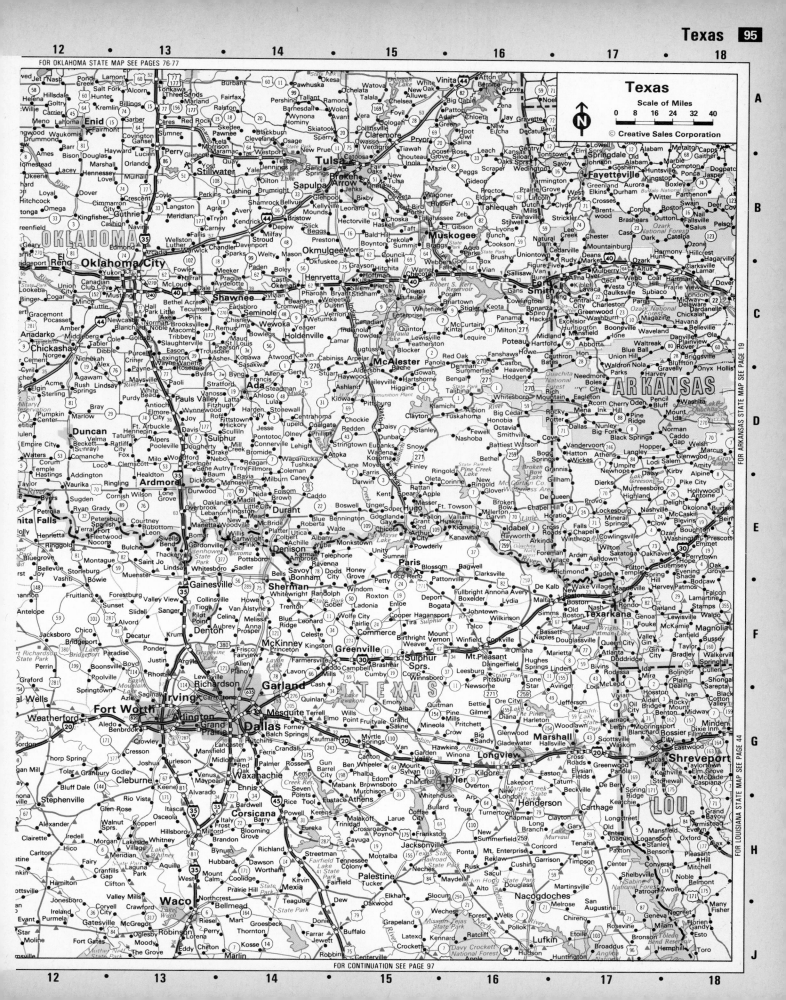

FOR CONTINUATION SEE PAGE 94

FOR CONTINUATION SEE PAGE 98

6 7 8 9 10 11

J

McCamey Big Lake Barnhart Christoval Eden Melvin Rochelle Springs Lometa Adamsv
Girvin 18 Brady San Saba Cop Lampas
Fort Stockton 385 349 Calf Creek 71 Voca Fredonia Cherokee
Bakersfield 35 Iraan 190 Menard Katemcy Hext 29 Pontotoc Valley Spring Bluffton Tow Buchanan Lake Burnet
23 137 Eldorado Fort McKavett London Grit Mason Llano Kingsland Marble Falls Buchanan Dam
Sheffield 42 I-10 290 Ozona 277 190 29 Loyal Valley 16 87 Lake Lyndon B. Johnson

K

Port Lancaster State Park 37 Sonora Roosevelt Junction Doss Cherry Spring Willow City Round Mountain Spicev
Big Canyon 163 Segovia Enchanted Rock State Park Johnson City State Park
Sanderson 349 290 Harper Fredericksburg Stonewall Hye Lyndon B. Johnson State Park
Dryden Telegraph Mountain Home Hunt Ingram Luckenbach Blanco Twin Si
Juno 55 Kerrville Center Pt Comfort Sisterdale Spring Branch S

L

Langtry 90 Loma Alta Rocksprings 41 39 16 Camp Verde I-10 Boerne 46 N Bra
Rio Grande Carta Valley 377 Barksdale Camp Wood Leakey Vanderpool Medina Pipecreek 87 Leon Springs 281
Seminole Canyon State Park Comstock Devils Lake Amistad National Recreation Area 55 Utopia Bandera Tarpley Lake Hills Mico Castle Hills Universal City
Basin Lake Walk Concan 127 D'Hanis Riomedina Castroville Leon Valley San
Boquillas del Carmen Del Rio Ciudad Acuna Knippa Sabinal Hondo 90 Dunlay 410 Martinez Elme

M

Fort Clark Springs Brackettville 90 Uvalde 173 Natalia Lytle Somerset
Spofford Dabney Blewett Frio Town Moore 81 Devine Leming
131 Quemado Normandy La Pryor Batesville 35 Bigfoot Poteet 281 Pleasan
Piedras Negras Eagle Pass 57 Crystal City Divot Derby 85 97 Christine
277 Brundage Big Wells Woodward Millett Hindes Campbellton Whitsett

N

Carrizo Springs Asherton Los Angeles Cotulla 97 72 Tilden Three Rivers
Catarina 16 TEXAS George We
Nueva Rosita 57 UNITED STATES MEXICO 83 Artesia Wells 20 Calliham
44 Encinal Nueces

P

COAHUILA 57 44 Freer 44 Ora
Rio Grande 81 59 44 San Diego 339 Ben
Benavides 339 Ri
Nuevo Laredo Laredo 359 Oilton 16 Realitos Concepcion
Nueva Rosita Mirando City Bruni Ramirez
Hebbronville 285

Q

30 Monclova San Ygnacio Escobas Randado
83 Bustamante 16
Falcon Res

R

57 Sabinas Hidalgo Lopeno La Gloria Santa Ele San Isidr
Falcon Falcon State Park La Reforma
53 Nuevo Guerrero El Sauz
NUEVO LEON Cd. Mier Roma Rio Grande City Edinbur
54 Cd. Camargo La Grulla La Joya Mission 102
Presa De El Azucar Sullivan City Bentsen Rio Grande Valley State Park
San Pedro de las Colonias 40 Hidalgo Reynosa

S

6 7 8 9 10 11

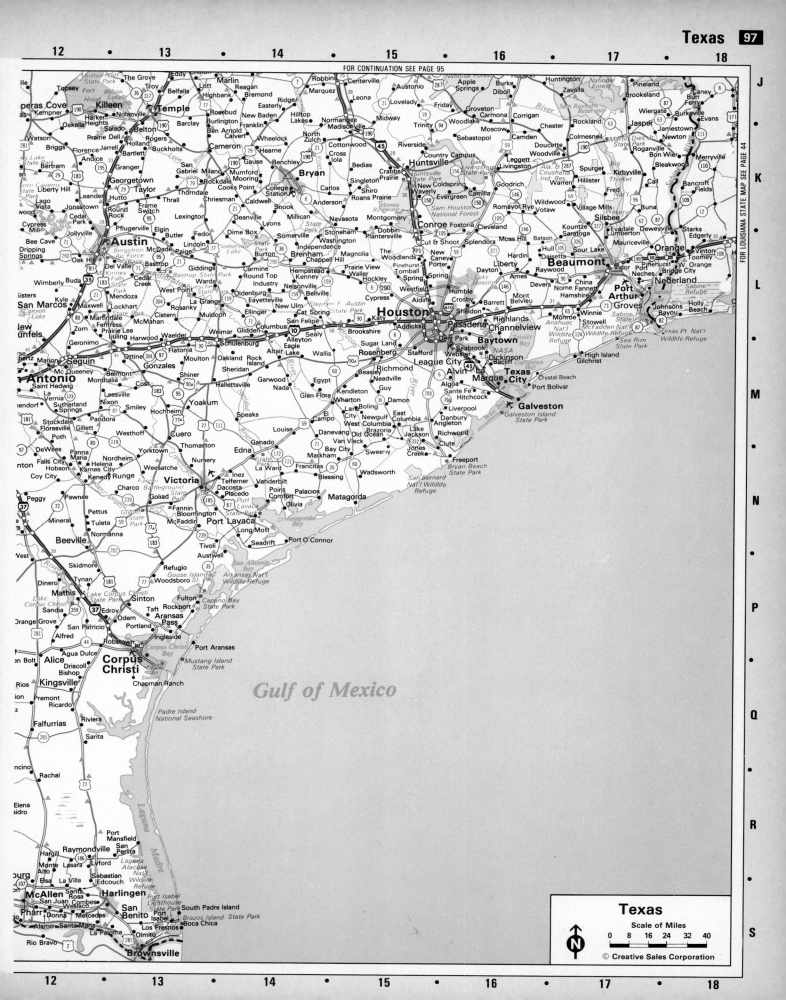

FOR LOUISIANA STATE MAP SEE PAGE 44

Gulf of Mexico

Texas

Scale of Miles

0 8 16 24 32 40

© Creative Sales Corporation

Texas

Scale of Miles

0 8 16 24 32 40

© Creative Sales Corporation

N

NEW MEXICO

TEXAS

CHIHUAHUA

UNITED STATES
MEXICO

FOR NEW MEXICO STATE MAP SEE PAGES 64-65
FOR CONTINUATION SEE PAGE 94
FOR CONTINUATION SEE PAGE 96

Ancho
Jicarilla
Mesa
White Oaks
Carrizozo
Pine Lodge
Arabela
Elida
Rogers
Needmore
Circle Back
Amherst
Littlefield
Sudan
Earth
Fieldton
Dora
Pep
Goodland
Enochs
Bula
Capitan
Lincoln
Angus
Alto
San Patricio
Ruidoso Downs
Hondo
Tinnie
Picacho
Sunset
Two Rivers Res.
Roswell
Dexter
Greenfield
Hagerman
Milnesand
Morton
Lingo
Maple
Bledsoe
Whitharral
Levelland
Three Rivers
Ruidoso
Crossroads
Caprock
Tatum
McDonald
Bronco
Plains
Brownfield
Smyer
Whiteface
Reese V.
Bent
Mescalero
Elk Silver
Apache Mescalero Indian Reservation
Lake Arthur
Hilburn City
Lovington
Allred
Denver City
Seagraves
Loop
Wellman
Tularosa
La Luz
High Rolls
Cloudcroft
Alamogordo
Dunken
Hope
Artesia
Riverside
Loco Hills
Maljamar
Humble City
Knowles
Sacramento
Mayhill
Weed
Elk
Pinon
Atoka
Seven Rivers
Lake McMillan
Monument
Nadine
Oil Center
Eunice
Hobbs
Seminole
White Sands Nat'l Mon.
Lincoln National Forest
Carlsbad
Black River Village
Loving
Malaga
Whites City
Jal
Frankel City
Andrews
Patricia
Rincon
Las Cruces
Mesilla
San Miguel
La Mesa
Chamberino
Dona Ana
Organ
White Sands Missile Range
Orogrande
Fort Bliss
Carlsbad Caverns
Carlsbad Caverns National Park
Gardendale
Midland
Anthony
Newman
El Paso
Ciudad Juarez
San Elizario
Clint
Fabens
Tornillo
Socorro
Horizon City
Huencol Tanks State Park
Dell City
Guadalupe Mtns. National Park
Cornudas
Salt Flat
Kermit
Notrees
Odessa
Magoffin House State Park
Acala
Fort Hancock
McNary
Sierra Blanca
Allamoore
Van Horn
Kent
Toyah
Pecos
Barstow
Wickett
Monahans
Pyote
Penwell
Royalty
Crane
Grandfalls
Imperial
Coyanosa
McCamey
Girvin
Bakersfield
Fort Stockton
Balmorhea
Saragosa
Balmorhea State Park
Lobo
Valentine
Davis Mountains State Park
Fort Davis
Alpine
Marfa
Marathon
Sanderson
Dryden
Plata
Shafter
Presidio
Ojinaga
Fort Leaton State Park
Redford
Terlingua
Study Butte
Chisos Basin
Big Bend National Park
Boquillas del Carmen
Chihuahua
Monahans Sandhills State Park

Rio Grande
Rio Hondo
Penasco
Sulphur
Pecos

Alabama
Population: 3,893,888
Capital: Montgomery (F-5)
Largest City: Birmingham 284,413 (D-4)
Highest Elevation: Cheaha Mtn. 2,407 ft.
Land Area (sq. miles): 50,767

Alaska
Population: 401,851
Capital: Juneau (G-9)
Largest City: Anchorage 174,431 (E-6)
Highest Elevation: Mt. McKinley 20,320 ft.
Land Area (sq. miles): 570,833

Arizona
Population: 2,718,215
Capital: Phoenix (J-6)
Largest City: Phoenix 789,704 (J-6)
Highest Elevation: Humphreys Peak 12,633 ft.
Land Area (sq. miles): 113,508

Arkansas
Population: 2,286,435
Capital: Little Rock 158,461 (D-5)
Largest City: Little Rock 158,461 (D-5)
Highest Elevation: Magazine Mtn. 2,753 ft.
Land Area (sq. miles): 52,078

California
Population: 23,667,902
Capital: Sacramento (J-5)
Largest City: Los Angeles 2,966,850 (T-8)
Highest Elevation: Mount Whitney 14,494 ft.
Land Area (sq. miles): 156,299

Colorado
Population: 2,889,964
Capital: Denver (D-9)
Largest City: Denver 492,365 (D-9)
Highest Elevation: Mount Elbert 14,433 ft.
Land Area (sq. miles): 103,595

Connecticut
Population: 3,107,576
Capital: Hartford (D-3)
Largest City: Bridgeport 142,546 (F-2)
Highest Elevation: Mount Frissell 2,380 ft.
Land Area (sq. miles): 4,872

Delaware
Population: 594,338
Capital: Dover (H-2)
Largest City: Wilmington 70,195 (F-2)
Highest Elevation: Near Brandywine 442 ft.
Land Area (sq. miles): 1,932

District of Columbia
Population: 638,333
Capital: Washington (F-5)
Largest City: Washington 638,333 (F-5)
Highest Elevation: Tenleytown 410 ft.
Land Area (sq. miles): 63

Florida
Population: 9,746,324
Capital: Tallahassee (D-2)
Largest City: Jacksonville 540,920 (D-6)
Highest Elevation: Near Gaskin 345 ft.
Land Area (sq. miles): 58,560

Georgia
Population: 5,463,105
Capital: Atlanta (C-8)
Largest City: Atlanta 425,022 (C-8)
Highest Elevation: Brasstown Bald 4,784 ft.
Land Area (sq. miles): 54,153

Hawaii
Population: 964,691
Capital: Honolulu (C-5)
Largest City: Honolulu 365,048 (C-5)
Highest Elevation: Mauna Kea 13,796 ft.
Land Area (sq. miles): 6,425

Idaho
Population: 943,935
Capital: Boise (M-3)
Largest City: Boise 102,451 (M-3)
Highest Elevation: Borah Peak 12,662 ft.
Land Area (sq. miles): 82,413

Illinois
Population: 11,426,518
Capital: Springfield (J-5)
Largest City: Chicago 3,005,072 (E-8)
Highest Elevation: Charles Mound 1,235 ft.
Land Area (sq. miles): 55,645

Indiana
Population: 5,490,224
Capital: Indianapolis (F-4)
Largest City: Indianapolis 700,807 (F-4)
Highest Elevation: Near Fountain City 1,257 ft.
Land Area (sq. miles): 35,932

Iowa
Population: 2,913,808
Capital: Des Moines (E-5)
Largest City: Des Moines 191,003 (E-5)
Highest Elevation: Near Allendorf 1,670 ft.
Land Area (sq. miles): 55,965

Kansas
Population: 2,363,679
Capital: Topeka (D-11)
Largest City: Wichita 279,272 (G-9)
Highest Elevation: Mount Sunflower 4,039 ft.
Land Area (sq. miles): 81,781

Kentucky
Population: 3,660,777
Capital: Frankfort (C-9)
Largest City: Louisville 298,451 (C-8)
Highest Elevation: Black Mtn. 4,145 ft.
Land Area (sq. miles): 39,669

Louisiana
Population: 4,205,900
Capital: Baton Rouge (E-7)
Largest City: New Orleans 557,515 (F-9)
Highest Elevation: Driskill Mtn. 535 ft.
Land Area (sq. miles): 44,521

Maine
Population: 1,124,660
Capital: Augusta (G-3)
Largest City: Portland 61,572 (J-3)
Highest Elevation: Mt. Katahdin 5,268 ft.
Land Area (sq. miles): 30,995

Maryland
Population: 4,216,975
Capital: Annapolis (D-11)
Largest City: Baltimore 786,775 (D-11)
Highest Elevation: Backbone Mtn. 3,360 ft.
Land Area (sq. miles): 9,837

Massachusetts
Population: 5,737,037
Capital: Boston (B-8)
Largest City: Boston 562,994 (B-8)
Highest Elevation: Mt. Greylock 3,491 ft.
Land Area (sq. miles): 7,824

Michigan
Population: 9,262,078
Capital: Lansing (K-6)
Largest City: Detroit 1,203,339 (L-9)
Highest Elevation: Mt. Curwood 1,980 ft.
Land Area (sq. miles): 56,954

Minnesota
Population: 4,075,970
Capital: St. Paul (H-6)
Largest City: Minneapolis 370,951 (J-5)
Highest Elevation: Eagle Mtn. 2,301 ft.
Land Area (sq. miles): 79,548

Mississippi
Population: 2,520,638
Capital: Jackson (F-4)
Largest City: Jackson 202,895 (F-4)
Highest Elevation: Woodall Mtn. 806 ft.
Land Area (sq. miles): 47,233

Missouri
Population: 4,916,686
Capital: Jefferson City (G-5)
Largest City: St. Louis 453,085 (G-9)
Highest Elevation: Taum Sauk Mtn. 1,772 ft.
Land Area (sq. miles): 68,945

Montana
Population: 786,690
Capital: Helena (F-5)
Largest City: Billings 66,798 (G-9)
Highest Elevation: Granite Peak 12,799 ft.
Land Area (sq. miles): 145,398

Nebraska
Population: 1,569,825
Capital: Lincoln (G-12)
Largest City: Omaha 314,255 (F-12)
Highest Elevation: near Bushnell 5,426 ft.
Land Area (sq. miles): 76,644

Nevada
Population: 800,493
Capital: Carson City (F-2)
Largest City: Las Vegas 164,674 (M-8)
Highest Elevation: Boundary Peak 13,143 ft.
Land Area (sq. miles): 109,893

New Hampshire
Population: 920,610
Capital: Concord (H-5)
Largest City: Manchester 90,936 (J-5)
Highest Elevation: Mt. Washington 6,288 ft.
Land Area (sq. miles): 8,993

New Jersey
Population: 7,364,823
Capital: Trenton (D-4)
Largest City: Newark 329,248 (C-6)
Highest Elevation: High Point 1,803 ft.
Land Area (sq. miles): 7,468

New Mexico
Population: 1,302,894
Capital: Santa Fe (F-6)
Largest City: Albuquerque 331,767 (G-4)
Highest Elevation: Wheeler Peak 13,161 ft.
Land Area (sq. miles): 121,335

New York
Population: 17,558,072
Capital: Albany (L-19)
Largest City: New York 7,071,639 (E-3)
Highest Elevation: Mount Marcy 5,344 ft.
Land Area (sq. miles): 47,377

North Carolina
Population: 5,881,766
Capital: Raleigh (B-10)
Largest City: Charlotte 314,447 (D-7)
Highest Elevation: Mt. Mitchell 6,684 ft.
Land Area (sq. miles): 48,843

North Dakota
Population: 652,717
Capital: Bismark (F-6)
Largest City: Fargo 61,383 (F-10)
Highest Elevation: White Butte 3,506 ft.
Land Area (sq. miles): 69,300

Ohio
Population: 10,797,630
Capital: Columbus (J-4)
Largest City: Cleveland 573,822 (E-7)
Highest Elevation: Campbell Hill 1,550 ft.
Land Area (sq. miles): 41,004

Oklahoma
Population: 3,025,487
Capital: Oklahoma City (E-9)
Largest City: Oklahoma City 403,213 (E-9)
Highest Elevation: Black Mesa 4,973 ft.
Land Area (sq. miles): 68,655

Oregon
Population: 2,633,105
Capital: Salem (D-3)
Largest City: Portland 366,383 (C-4)
Highest Elevation: Mt. Hood 11,239 ft.
Land Area (sq. miles): 96,184

Pennsylvania
Population: 11,863,895
Capital: Harrisburg (H-9)
Largest City: Philadelphia 1,688,210 (J-13)
Highest Elevation: Mt. Davis 3,213 ft.
Land Area (sq. miles): 44,888

Rhode Island
Population: 947,154
Capital: Providence (D-6)
Largest City: Providence 156,804 (D-6)
Highest Elevation: Jerimoth Hill 812 ft.
Land Area (sq. miles): 1,055

South Carolina
Population: 3,121,820
Capital: Columbia (F-6)
Largest City: Columbia 101,208 (F-6)
Highest Elevation: Sassafrass Mtn. 3,560 ft.
Land Area (sq. miles): 30,203

South Dakota
Population: 690,768
Capital: Pierre (F-6)
Largest City: Sioux Falls 81,343 (H-10)
Highest Elevation: Harney Peak 7,242 ft.
Land Area (sq. miles): 75,952

Tennessee
Population: 4,591,120
Capital: Nashville (G-6)
Largest City: Memphis 646,356 (J-1)
Highest Elevation: Clingmans Dome 6,643 ft.
Land Area (sq. miles): 41,155

Texas
Population: 14,229,191
Capital: Austin (L-13)
Largest City: Houston 1,595,138 (L-15)
Highest Elevation: Guapalupe Peak 8,749
Land Area (sq. miles): 262,017

Utah
Population: 1,461,037
Capital: Salt Lake City (E-5)
Largest City: Salt Lake City 163,033 (E-5)
Highest Elevation: Kings Peak 13,528 ft.
Land Area (sq. miles): 82,073

Vermont
Population: 511,456
Capital: Montpelier (D-3)
Largest City: Burlington 37,712 (D-1)
Highest Elevation: Mt. Mansfield 4,393 ft.
Land Area (sq. miles): 9,273

Virginia
Population: 5,346,818
Capital: Richmond (G-10)
Largest City: Norfolk 266,979 (H-12)
Highest Elevation: Mt. Rogers 5,729 ft.
Land Area (sq. miles): 39,703

Washington
Population: 4,132,156
Capital: Olympia (E-4)
Largest City: Seattle 493,846 (C-5)
Highest Elevation: Mt. Rainier 14,410 ft.
Land Area (sq. miles): 66,511

West Virginia
Population: 1,949,644
Capital: Charleston (E-4)
Largest City: Charleston 63,968 (E-4)
Highest Elevation: Spruce Knob 4,863 ft.
Land Area (sq. miles): 24,119

Wisconsin
Population: 4,705,767
Capital: Madison (K-6)
Largest City: Milwaukee 636,212 (K-8)
Highest Elevation: Timms Hill 1,951 ft.
Land Area (sq. miles): 54,426

Wyoming
Population: 469,559
Capital: Cheyenne (J-11)
Largest City: Casper 51,016 (F-9)
Highest Elevation: Gannet Peak 13,804 ft.
Land Area (sq. miles): 96,989

Atlanta, GA
Land Area (sq. miles): 131.0
City Population: 425,022
Metropolitan Population: 1,613,357

Baltimore, MD
Land Area (sq. miles): 80.3
City Population: 786,775
Metropolitan Population: 1,755,477

Boston, MA
Land Area (sq. miles): 47.2
City Population: 562,994
Metropolitan Population: 2,678,762

Chicago, IL
Land Area (sq. miles): 228.1
City Population: 3,005,072
Metropolitan Population: 6,779,799

Cincinnati, OH
Land Area (sq. miles): 78.1
City Population: 385,457
Metropolitan Population: 1,123,412

Cleveland, OH
Land Area (sq. miles): 79.0
City Population: 573,822
Metropolitan Population: 1,752,424

Dallas, TX
Land Area (sq. miles): 333.0
City Population: 904,078
Metropolitan Population: including Ft. Worth 2,451,390

Denver, CO
Land Area (sq. miles): 110.6
City Population: 492,365
Metropolitan Population: 1,352,070

Detroit, MI
Land Area (sq. miles): 135.6
City Population: 1,203,339
Metropolitan Population: 3,809,327

Fort Worth, TX
Land Area (sq. miles): 240.2
City Population: 385,164
Metropolitan Population: including Dallas 2,451,390

Houston, TX
Land Area (sq. miles): 556.4
City Population: 1,595,138
Metropolitan Population: 2,412,644

Indianapolis, IN
Land Area (sq. miles): 352.0
City Population: 700,807
Metropolitan Population: 836,472

Kansas City, MO
Land Area (sq. miles): 316.3
City Population: 448,159
Metropolitan Population: 1,097,793

Los Angeles, CA
Land Area (sq. miles): 464.7
City Population: 2,966,850
Metropolitan Population: 9,479,436

Louisville, KY
Land Area (sq. miles): 60.0
City Population: 298,451
Metropolitan Population: 761,002

Memphis, TN
Land Area (sq. miles): 264.1
City Population: 646,305
Metropolitan Population: 774,551

Miami, FL
Land Area (sq. miles): 34.3
City Population: 346,865
Metropolitan Population: 1,608,159

Milwaukee, WI
Land Area (sq. miles): 95.8
City Population: 636,212
Metropolitan Population: 1,207,008

Minneapolis, MN
Land Area (sq. miles): 55.1
City Population: 370,951
Metropolitan Population: including St. Paul 1,787,564

New Orleans, LA
Land Area (sq. miles): 199.4
City Population: 557,515
Metropolitan Population: 1,078,299

New York City, NY
Land Area (sq. miles): 301.5
City Population: 7,071,639
Metropolitan Population: 15,590,274

Oakland, CA
Land Area (sq. miles): 59.3
City Population: 339,337
Metropolitan Population: including San Francisco 3,190,698

Oklahoma City, OK
Land Area (sq. miles): 603.6
City Population: 388,599
Metropolitan Population: 674,322

Omaha, NE
Land Area (sq. miles): 90.9
City Population: 314,255
Metropolitan Population: 512,438

Philadelphia, PA
Land Area (sq. miles): 136.0
City Population: 1,688,210
Metropolitan Population: 4,112,933

Phoenix, AZ
Land Area (sq. miles): 324.0
City Population: 789,704
Metropolitan Population: 1,437,392

Pittsburgh, PA
Land Area (sq. miles): 55.4
City Population: 423,938
Metropolitan Population: 1,810,038

Portland, OR
Land Area (sq. miles): 103.3
City Population: 366,383
Metropolitan Population: 1,026,144

Saint Louis, MO
Land Area (sq. miles): 61.4
City Population: 453,085
Metropolitan Population: 1,848,590

Saint Paul, MN
Land Area (sq. miles): 52.4
City Population: 270,230
Metropolitan Population: including Minneapolis 1,787,564

Saint Petersburg, FL
Land Area (sq. miles): 55.5
City Population: 238,647
Metropolitan Population: 833,337

Salt Lake City, UT
Land Area (sq. miles): 75.2
City Population: 163,033
Metropolitan Population: 674,201

San Diego, CA
Land Area (sq. miles): 320.0
City Population: 875,538
Metropolitan Population: 1,704,352

San Francisco, CA
Land Area (sq. miles): 46.4
City Population: 678,974
Metropolitan Population: including Oakland 3,190,698

Seattle, WA
Land Area (sq. miles): 144.6
City Population: 493,846
Metropolitan Population: 1,391,535

Tampa, FL
Land Area (sq. miles): 84.4
City Population: 271,523
Metropolitan Population: 520,912

Washington, DC
Land Area (sq. miles): 62.7
City Population: 638,333
Metropolitan Population: 2,763,105

Grid columns: 1 2 3 4 5 6 7
Grid rows: A B C D E F G H J K

DELIGHT, CRONHARDT, POT SPRING, TIMONIUM, HAMPTON, GERMANTOWN, PROVIDENCE, CUB HILL, BELLTOWN, OWINGS MILLS, BROOKLANDVILLE, STEVENSON, LUTHERVILLE, PERRY HALL, DEER PARK, HOLBROOK, GARRISON, CHATTOLANEE, FISHTOWN, RIDERWOOD, TOWSON, ROCKLAND, RUXTON, CARNEY, NECKER, WHITE MARSH, HARRISONVILLE, MT. WILSON, PIKESVILLE, RODGERS FORGE, PARKVILLE, PUTTY HILL, HERNWOOD HEIGHTS, HERNWOOD, RANDALLSTOWN, ROCKDALE, MILFORD, LOCHEARN, FULLERTON, OVERLEA, GRANITE, HEBBVILLE, WOODLAWN, BALTIMORE, ROSEDALE, MIDDLE RIVER, DANIELS, JOSENHANS CORNER, ESSEX, NORTH POINT, DUNDALK, GRAY MANOR, INVERNESS, ELLICOTT CITY, CATONSVILLE, EDMONDSON, TURNER, BLOOMSBURY, ARBUTUS, LANSDOWNE, BROOKLYN, EDGEMERE, COLUMBIA HILLS, ILCHESTER, HALETHORPE, RELAY, PUMPHREY, SPARROWS POINT, OAKLAND MILLS, JONESTOWN, ELKRIDGE, FORT HOWARD, ALLVIEW ESTATES, HANOVER, HARWOOD, LINTHICUM, FOREMANS CORNER, GUILFORD, DORSEY, WATERLOO, FERNDALE, SOLLEY, ORCHARD BEACH, RIVIERA BEACH, JESSUP, MC PHERSON, HARMANS, GLEN BURNE, FAIRVIEW, BAYSIDE BEACH, BURLEYTOWN, SEVERN, GREEN HAVEN, ANNAPOLIS JUNCTION, GEORGETOWN, RIDGEWAY, HARUNDALE, LIPINS CORNER, ARMIGER, JACOBSVILLE, PINEHURST, MARYLAND CITY, MAYFIELD, PASADENA, LAKE SHORE, LAUREL, ODENTON, BENFIELD, ROBINSON, MACEY'S COR., MAGO VISTA BEACH, DORRS CORNER, SEVERNA PARK, SHORE ACRES, GAMBRILLS, MILLERSVILLE, JOYCE, ARN, CROWNSVILLE, CAPE ST. CLAIRE

Scale of Miles: 0 1 2 3

© C.S.C.

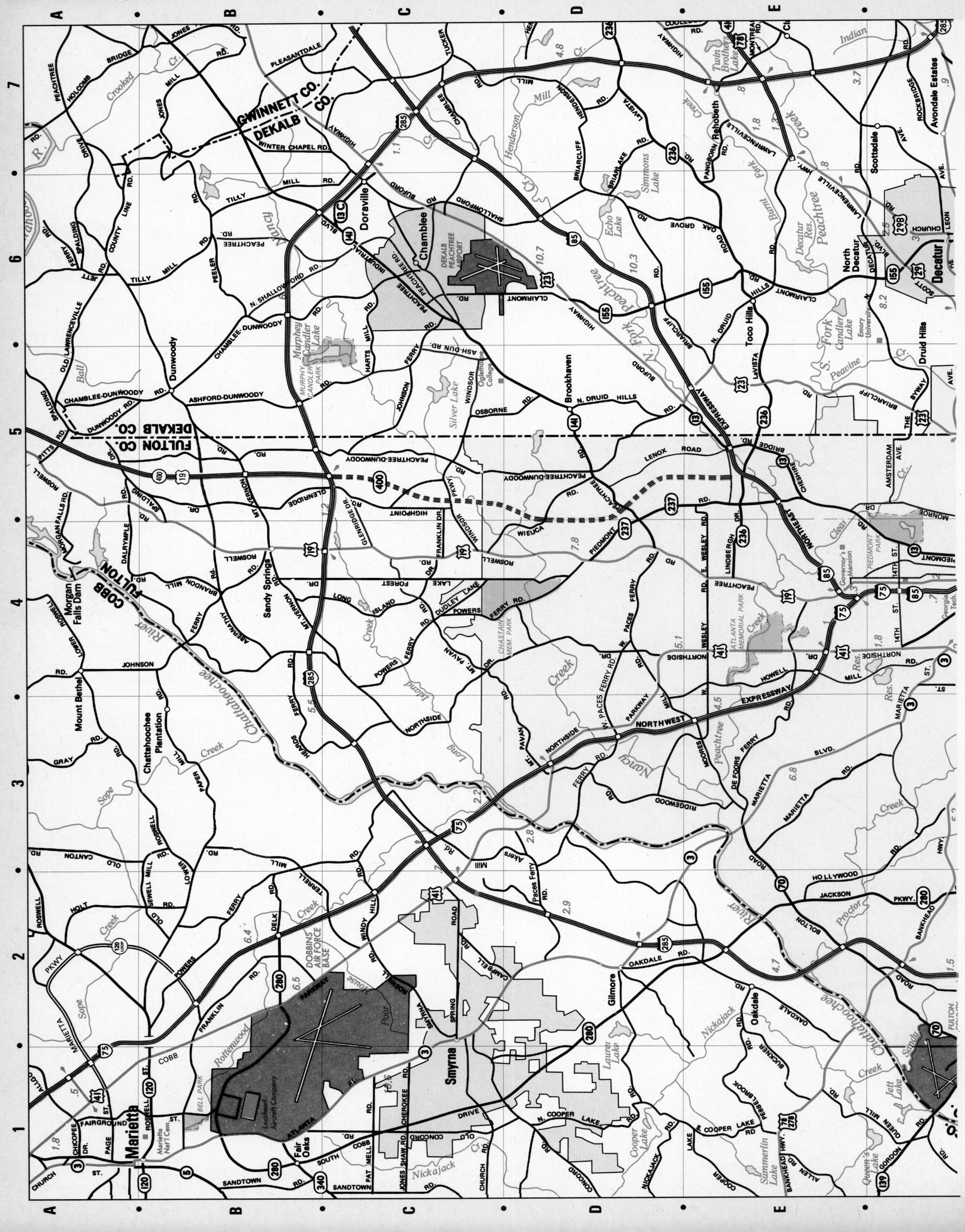

GWINNETT CO.
DEKALB CO.
FULTON CO.
COBB
FULTON
Doraville
Chamblee
DEKALB PEACHTREE AIRPORT
Dunwoody
Brookhaven
Oglethorpe College
Silver Lake
Murphey Candler Lake
MURPHY CANDLER PARK
Sandy Springs
Morgan Falls Dam
Mount Bethel
Chattahoochee Plantation
Chattahoochee River
CHASTAIN MEM. PARK
ATLANTA MEMORIAL PARK
Governor's Mansion
PIEDMONT PARK
Georgia Tech.
Toco Hills
North Decatur
Decatur
Druid Hills
Emory University
Candler Lake
Scottdale
Avondale Estates
Echo Lake
Simmons Lake
Twin Brothers Lake
Decatur Res.
Peachtree Creek
Nancy Creek
Proctor Creek
Nickajack Creek
Sope Creek
Rottenwood Creek
DOBBINS AIR FORCE BASE
Lockheed Aircraft Company
Marietta
Marietta Nat'l Cem.
Fair Oaks
Smyrna
Gilmore
Oakdale
Laurel Lake
Cooper Lake
Summerlin Lake
Jett Lake
Queen's Lake
NORTHWEST EXPRESSWAY
NORTHEAST EXPRESSWAY

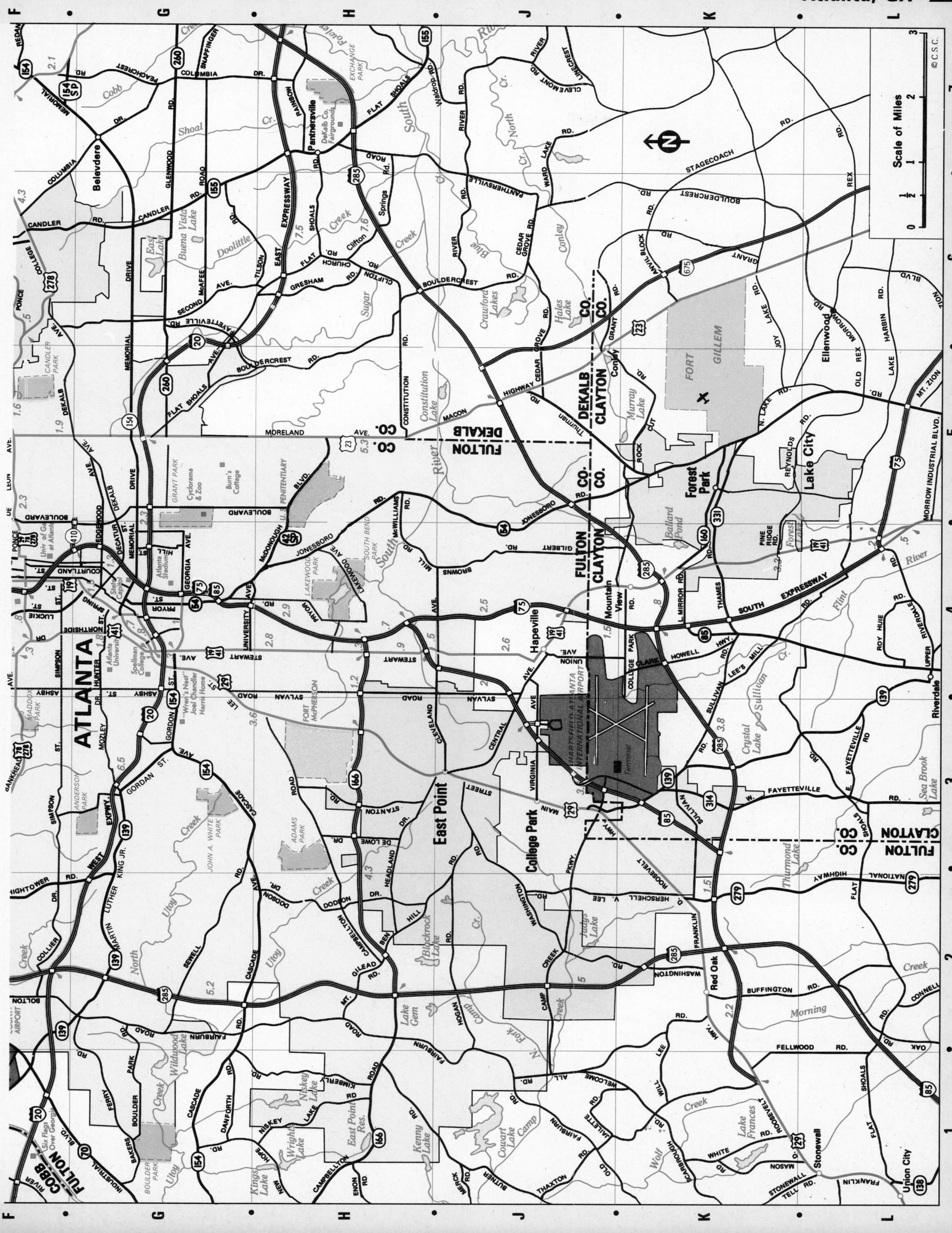
ATLANTA
East Point
College Park
Hapeville
Forest Park
Lake City
Riverdale
Red Oak
Stonewall
Union City
Conley
Ellenwood
Belvedere
Panthersville
Mountain View
FORT GILLEM
FORT McPHERSON
HARTSFIELD ATLANTA INTERNATIONAL AIRPORT
Terminal
DEKALB CO.
FULTON CO.
CLAYTON CO.
COBB
FULTON
Scale of Miles
0 ½ 1 2 3
© C.S.C.

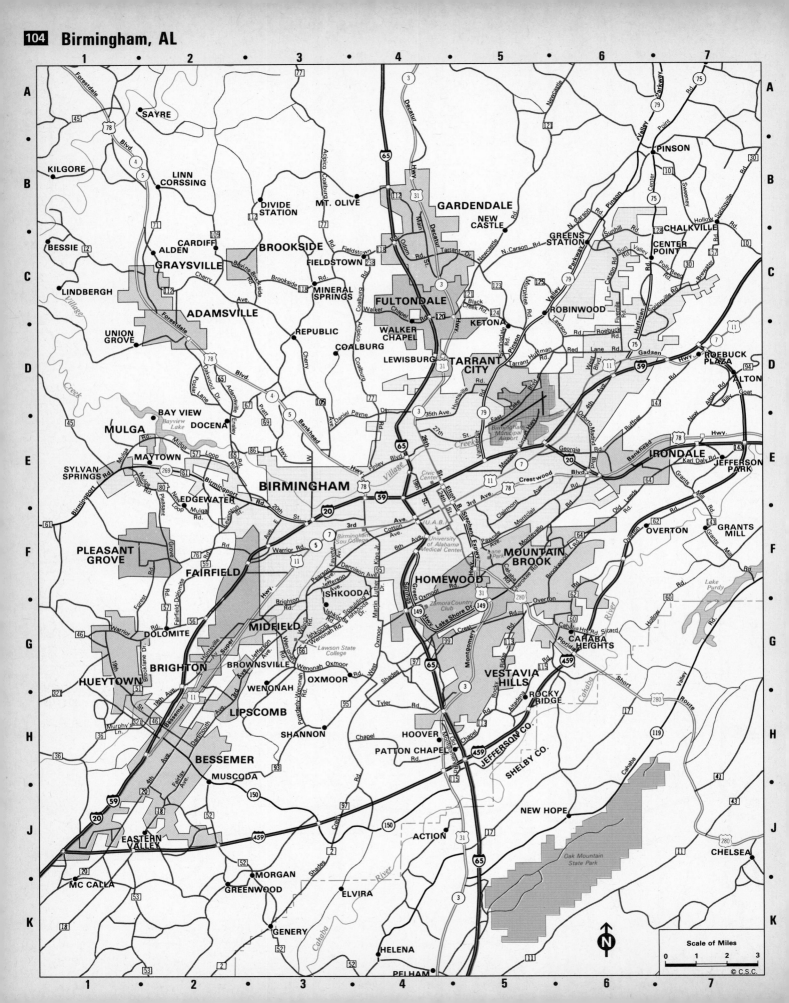

NIAGARA FALLS
ECHOTA
BERKHOLTZ
BEACH RIDGE
PENDLETON
RAPIDS
MILLERSPORT
ST. JOHNSBURG
NIAGARA FALLS
LA SALLE
NASHVILLE
HOFFMAN
WENDELVILLE
SAWYER
WURLITZER PARK
MARTINSVILLE
ELSERS CORNERS
PEACH HAVEN
NIAGARA CO.
ERIE CO.
CHIPPAWA
SANDY BEACH
EDGEWATER
SWORMVILLE
NORTH TONAWANDA
GETZVILLE
EAST AMHERST
CLARENCE CENTER
GRANDYLE VILLAGE
TONAWANDA
KENMORE
NORTH BAILEY
AMHERST
EGGERTSVILLE
SNYDER
WILLIAMSVILLE
HARRIS HILL
FERRY VILLAGE
SNYDER
STEVENSVILLE
BOWMANSVILLE
FORT ERIE NORTH
DEPEW
LANCASTER
POINT ABINO
RIDGEWAY
CRESCENT PARK
FORT ERIE
ERIE BEACH
SLOAN
CHEEKTOWAGA
BELLEVUE
THUNDER BAY
CRYSTAL BEACH
BUFFALO
BLOSSOM
ELMA
GARDENVILLE
ELMA CENTER
WEST SENECA
EAST SENECA
EBENEZER
SPRINGBROOK
LACKAWANNA
BLASDELL
WOODLAND
WINDOM
WEBSTER CORNERS
BAY VIEW
EAST HAMBURG
ATHOL SPRINGS
BIG TREE
ORCHARD PARK
LOCKSLEY PARK
MT. VERNON
WANAKAH
CARNEGIE
DUELLS CORNERS
ELLICOTT
ELLICOTT HEIGHTS
CLIFTON HEIGHTS
PINEHURST
SCRANTON
ARMOR
JEWETTVILLE
GRIFFINS MILLS
HIGHLAND-ON-THE-LAKE
LAKE VIEW
HAMBURG
WATER VALLEY
WEST FALLS
NORTH EVANS
JERUSALEM CORNERS
DERBY
EDEN VALLEY
NORTH BOSTON
ANGOLA-ON-THE-LAKE
EVANS
EAST EDEN
PATCHIN

CANADA
UNITED STATES
ONTARIO
NEW YORK
WELLAND CO.
ERIE CO.
Lake Erie
Buffalo Harbor
Niagara River

N

Scale of Miles
0 1 2 3

© C.S.C.

Beverly
Salem
Peabody
Danvers
DANVERS
Swampscott
Nahant Bay
Lynn
LYNN WOODS
Winthrop
SUFFOLK
ESSEX COUNTY
Saugus
Lynnfield
LYNNFIELD
Wakefield
Melrose
Revere
Chelsea
Everett
NORTH READING
North Reading
MIDDLESEX
ESSEX
Stoneham
Malden
Medford
Somerville
Reading
Wilmington
Woburn
Winchester
Arlington
Belmont
Cambridge
Watertown
Lexington
Burlington
Pinehurst
BILLERICA
Billerica
Waltham

Scale of Miles

© C.S.C.

A map of the Chicago, IL northwest suburban area, with a grid labeled columns 1–4 and rows A–E.

Places and features labeled include:

Wonder Lake, Ringwood, Johnsburg, McCullom Lake, Sunnyside, Fox Lake, Lake Villa, Lake Villa Sand, Venetian Village, Stearns School, Grand, Duck Lake, Rollins, Round Lake Heights, West Miltmore, Monaville, Third Lake, Round Lake Beach, Round Lake Park, Washington, Druce L., Wildwood, Long Lake, Round Lake, Highland, Gages Lake, Grayslake, Grays L., Hainesville, McHenry, Lilymoor, Lakemoor, Volo, Sullivan Lake, Fish Lake, Wooster Lake, Belvidere, McHenry Shores, Defiance Lake, Moraine Hills State Park, Holiday Hills, Fremont Center, Ivanhoe, Loch Lomond, St. Marys Lake, Minear Lake, Butler L., Libertyville, Green Oaks, Mason Hill, Crystal Springs, Oak Ridge, Terra Cotta, Ridgefield, Prairie Grove, Burtons Bridge, Island Lake, Wauconda, Bangs Lake, Davis Lake, Countryside L., Diamond Lake, Mundelein, Lake Charles, Mettawa, Crystal Lake, Lakewood, Fox River Valley Gardens, Fox River Grove, Lake Barrington, North Barrington, Grassy Lake, Honey Lake, Lake Zurich, Hawthorn Woods, Indian Creek, Vernon Hills, Everett, Lake in the Hills, Fox Trails, Cuba, Oak Knoll, Barrington, Deer Park, Kildeer, Long Grove, Aptakisic, Highwood, Prairie View, Half Day, Lincolnshire, Huntley-Algonquin, Algonquin, McHenry Co., Kane Co., Cook County, Lake County, Buffalo Park, Carpentersville, Hawley L., Goose L., Keene, Crabtree Lake, Inverness, Palatine, Buffalo Grove, Wheeling, Arlington Heights, Prospect Heights, Mount Prospect, Des Plaines, Binnie, Gilberts, Sleepy Hollow, East Dundee, West Dundee, South Barrington, Mundhank, Hoffman Estates, Rolling Meadows, Arlington Park Race Track, Elk Grove Village, Elgin, Elgin Com. College, Elgin Mental Health Center, South Elgin, Streamwood, Bartlett, Schaumburg, Roselle, Medinah, Itasca, Bensenville, Wood Dale, Hanover Park, Keeneyville, Mallard Lake, Bloomingdale, Valley View, Chicago O'Hare International Airport.

Highways labeled include: 41, 94, 45, 21, 132, 59, 83, 12, 120, 134, 137, 60, 176, 14, 31, 25, 22, 53, 62, 68, 72, 58, 90, 290, 20, 19.

CHICAGO AND VICINITY

LAKE MICHIGAN

Waukegan — Gurnee — North Chicago — Park City — Green Oaks — Knollwood — Rondout — Lake Bluff — Lake Forest — Mettawa — Everett — Half Day — Lincolnshire — Bannockburn — Riverwoods — Deerfield — Highland Park — Northbrook — Wheeling — Glencoe — Northfield — Winnetka — Kenilworth — Glenview — Wilmette — Morton Grove — Niles — Skokie — Evanston — Des Plaines — Park Ridge — Lincolnwood — Rosemont — Schiller Park — Harwood Heights — Norridge

Great Lakes Naval Training Station — Victory Mem. Hospital — Lake Co. General Hosp. — St. Therese Hospital — V.A. Hospital — Lake Forest College — Fort Sheridan — Trinity College — Barat College — Mallinckrodt College — National College of Education — Kendall College — Northwestern University — Loyola University — Glenview Naval Air Station

Beach State Park — Lake Forest Oasis — Des Plaines Oasis — O'Hare Oasis — Lincoln Park

O'Hare International Airport

Indiana: Whiting — East Chicago — Hammond — Gary — Munster — Highland — Griffith — Schererville — Dyer — St. John — Merrillville — Ainsworth — Deep River — New Chicago — East Gary — Hobart

Wolf Lake — Lake George — Gary Municipal Airport — Purdue Univ. Regional Campus — Indiana Univ. Regional Campus — Wicker Memorial Park — Marquette Park — Grand Calumet River Lagoon — Little Calumet — Calumet River — Burns Ditch — Deep River — Turkey Creek

East-West Toll Road — Tri-State Tollway — Edens Expressway — Dickey Guthries St. Industrial Hwy. — Dunes Hwy.

Lake County

Scale of Miles
0   1   2   3

N

© C.S.C.

1　2　3　4

ST. Dominic College
Cloverdale
ADDISON
294
BU
DEAN ST.
COUNTRY CLUB RD.
DUNHAM
SMITH
INGALTON
TRAIL ROAD
GARY
GRAND AVE.
1.7
DU PAGE CO.
STATE LINE
64
PRAIRIE ST.
ST. CHARLES
NORTH
AVENUE
5.7
FAIR OAKS
Branch
KUHN
CAROL STREAM
GLENDALE HEIGHTS
53
3.2
NORTH
ADDISON
AVENUE
2.1
NORTH
38
25
GENEVA
2.0
HAWTHORNE LA.
Prince Crossing
6.7
64
GLEN ELLYN
GENEVA
2.5
2.7
ELMHURST
Elmhurst College
2.6
WOLF

F
KESLINGER RD.
WEST CHICAGO
ROOSEVELT
GENEVA RD.
6.1
HIGH LAKE RD.
4.0
JEWELL RD.
59
WINFIELD
Wheaton College
Flowerfield
York Center
LOMBARD
VILLA PARK
83
ST. CHARLES ROAD
1.9
56
2.5
88
CAMPANA
Illinois Youth Center Geneva
Kress Creek
WHEATON
38
Roosevelt
Maryknoll Seminary
2.0
Highland Hills
1.3
22ND
OAKBROOK TERRACE
1.1 2.0
1.5
1.0

MAIN
BATAVIA
4.7
WILSON RD.
NATIONAL ACCELERATOR LABORATORY
4.3
Du Page
WINFIELD RD.
BATAVIA RD.
NAPERVILLE
56
College of DuPage
4.0
Morton Arboretum
4.3
G. Williams College
31ST
OAKBROOK
2.5
HWY
290

Mooseheart
31
NORTH AURORA
KIRK
BUTTERFIELD
Herrick Lake
WARRENVILLE
88
EAST-WEST TOLLWAY
Du Page
OGDEN AVE.
6.8
CHICAGO AVE.
HINSDALE
294
WOLF

G
88
OAK RD.
2.0
Marywood
CHURCH AVE.
56
6.2
WEST AVE.
OGDEN
LISLE
34
Illinois Benedictine College
DOWNERS GROVE
MAPLE ST.
55TH
WEST-MONT
CLARENDON HILLS
83
Hinsdale Oasis
3.4

INDIAN TRAIL RD.
FARNSWORTH
KANE CO.
DU PAGE CO.
EOLA RD.
N. AURORA
3.5
North Central College
MAPLE AVE.
63RD
MAIN ST.
DARIEN
KINGERY
BURR RIDGE
AURORA
W. GALENA BLVD.
25
Eola
AURORA AVE.
HOBSON
COLLEGE RD.
8.2
75TH
PLAINFIELD
WILLOW BROOK

H
Aurora College
JERICHO RD.
MONTGOMERY
34
Frontenac
5TH AVE.
KAUTZ
1.6
75TH
WASHINGTON ST.
LISSON RD.
77TH
79TH ST.
83RD
WOODWARD AVE.
75TH
79TH
GERMAN CHURCH RD.

31
25
MONTGOMERY RD.
3.4
83RD
DU PAGE WILL
91ST ST.
ROYCE
COUNTY COUNTY
East Branch
JOLIET
7.5
91ST
ROBERT

2.6
30
2.0
95TH ST.
59
55
ARGONNE NATIONAL LABORATORY
Illinois River

34
4.4
WOLFS CROSSING
Wolfs
9.7
BOUGHTON
53
BOLINGBROOK
Sag Bridge
171

OSWEGO
30
111TH
LINCOLN HIGHWAY
244TH
NAPERVILLE ST.
JOLIET ROAD
DAVEY RD.
DES PLAINES
127TH ST.
Hastings
CALUMET
McCARTHY

3.4
Normantown
NORMANTOWN RD.
9.6
Lily Cache Creek
ROMEOVILLE
ROMEOVILLE RD.
LEMONT
131ST
BELL
4.0
126
55
WEBER RD.
53
143RD
ARCHER AVE.
Long Run
Goodings Grove
GOODINGS GROVE
COOK

J
Plainfield
PLAINFIELD
11.3
151ST
COUNTY COUNTY
RENWICK
DRAUDEN RD.
2.5
Lake Renwick
Mink Creek
Lewis University
7
Stateville Correctional Center
53
Lockport
167TH
CEDAR
WILL COOK

CATON FARM RD.
Caton Farm
5.8
59
4.6
Du Page River
30
CREST HILL
THEODORE ST.
South Lockport
Fairmont
Rosalind
SOUTHWEST
15.6
Marley
80

K
KENDALL WILL COUNTY
SHOREWOOD
BLACK RD.
52
BLACK
LARKIN AVE.
2.3
JOLIET
College of St. Francis
171
Illinois Chem. Lab.
Ridgewood
WASHINGTON ST.
NEW LENOX
LINCOLN HWY
30
Caton Farm
Aux Sable Creek
E. Aux Sable
MINOOKA
52
80
2.1
ROCKDALE
6
Illinois & Michigan Canal
Preston Heights
Ingalls Park
5.1
MILLS RD.
SPENCER
LARAWAY
CEDAR ROAD
SPENCER
7.5

Scale of Miles
0　1　2　3
© C.S.C.

1　2　3　4

4 5 6 7

N

ELMWOOD PARK

FRANKLIN PARK
NORTHLAKE
STONE PARK
MELROSE PARK
RIVER GROVE
OAK PARK
RIVER FOREST
HUMBOLDT PARK
GARFIELD PARK
MAYWOOD
BERKELEY
BELLWOOD
WASHINGTON
HILLSIDE
WESTCHESTER
BROAD VIEW
BERWYN
CICERO
FIELD MUS. OF NATURAL HISTORY
MEIGS FIELD
GRANT PARK

F

NORTH RIVERSIDE
LA GRANGE PARK
BROOKFIELD
26TH RIVERSIDE
LA GRANGE
WESTERN SPRINGS
STICKNEY
FOREST VIEW
LYONS
STEVENSON
ADLAI
ARCHER
BURNHAM PARK

G

MC COOK
INDIAN HEAD PARK
COUNTRYSIDE
LA GRANGE EAST
SUMMIT
Chicago Midway Airport
GARFIELD BLVD.
WASHINGTON PARK
JACKSON PARK
Hinsdale Oasis
BURR RIDGE
JUSTICE
BRIDGEVIEW
BEDFORD PARK
MARQUETTE PARK
HODGKINS

H

WILLOW SPRINGS
HICKORY HILLS
PALOS HILLS
BURBANK
HOMETOWN
EVERGREEN PARK
OAK LAWN
CHICAGO RIDGE
WORTH
PALOS HEIGHTS
PALOS PARK
MERRIONETTE PARK
BLUE ISLAND
CALUMET PARK
FENGER-SOUTHEAST COLLEGE
Lake Calumet
WILLIAM W. POWERS CONSERVATION AREA
WHITING

Sag Bridge
Trinity Christian College
McCarthy
ALSIP
CRESTWOOD
ROBBINS
DIXMOOR
RIVERDALE
DOLTON
BURNHAM
EAST CHICAGO
COLUMBUS

I

Goodings Grove
Orland Park
MIDLOTHIAN
POSEN
HARVEY
PHOENIX
SOUTH HOLLAND
CALUMET CITY
HAMMOND
Purdue Univ. Reg. Campus

J

Marley
ORLAND HILLS
TINLEY PARK
Tinley Park Mental Health Center
COUNTRY CLUB HILLS
MARKHAM
OAK FOREST
HAZEL CREST
EAST HAZEL CREST
HOMEWOOD
THORNTON
Abraham Lincoln Oasis
LANSING
Ridge
MUNSTER
WICKER MEMORIAL PARK
HIGHLAND

Mokena
Aubury Hills
ST. FRANCIS
Lincoln Estates
FLOSSMOOR
GLENWOOD
LYNWOOD
EAST CHICAGO HEIGHTS
Olympia Field
Prairie State College
Joe Orr

K

FRANKFORT
Matteson
RICHTON PARK
CHICAGO HEIGHTS
PARK FOREST
STEGER
SOUTH CHICAGO HEIGHTS
Sauk Village
SCHERERVILLE
DYER

WILL CO. / COOK CO.
COOK CO. / LAKE CO.
ILLINOIS / INDIANA

4 5 6 7

Scale of Miles

0   1   2   3

©C.S.C.

1　2　3　4　5　6　7

Lake Erie

EUCLID
WICKLIFFE

N

RICHMOND HEIGHTS

BRATENAHL

SOUTH EUCLID

CLEVELAND

EAST CLEVELAND

LYNDHURST

MAYFIELD HEIGHTS

CLEVELAND HEIGHTS

LAKEWOOD

UNIVERSITY HEIGHTS

Institute of Art

Case Western Reserve University

Rockefeller Park

John Carroll University

PEPPER PIKE

SHAKER HEIGHTS

BEECHWOOD

Ursuline College

ROCKY RIVER

WARRENSVILLE HEIGHTS

MORELAND HILLS

FAIRVIEW PARK

BROOKLYN

GARFIELD HEIGHTS

EMERY

ORANGE

BEDFORD HTS.

Cleveland Zoological Park

South Chagrin Reservation

Cleveland Hopkins Airport

BROOK PARK

MAPLE HEIGHTS

BEDFORD

SOLON

SEVEN HILLS

VALLEY VIEW

PARMA HEIGHTS

PARMA

Bedford Reservation

WALTON HILLS

MIDDLEBURG HEIGHTS

INDEPENDENCE

BEREA

CUYAHOGA CO.
SUMMIT CO.

Rocky River Reservation

NORTH ROYALTON

BRECKSVILLE

SAGAMORE HILLS

STRONGSVILLE

MACEDONIA

TWINSBURG

BROADVIEW HEIGHTS

Rocky River Reservation

N. ROYALTON

CUYAHOGA CO.
MEDINA CO.

BENNETTS CORNERS

HUDSON

HINCKLEY

W. RICHFIELD

RICHFIELD

PENINSULA

BRUNSWICK

EVERETT

ABBEYVILLE

BATH

STOW

WEYMOUTH

REMSEN CORNERS

BATH CENTER

GRANGER

GHENT

BOTZUM

Scale of Miles
0　1　2　3

© C.S.C.

A B C D E F G H J K

1　2　3　4　5　6　7

1   2   3   4   5   6

A

Newark

287
81

EAGLE MOUNTAIN NATIONAL GUARD BASE

156

35 W

377

Roanoke

114

Westlake

Grapevine Lake

AVONDALE-HASLET RD.

KELLER RD.

HASLET RD.

Haslet

HASLET-ROANOKE RD.

B

BLUE MOUND RD.

KELLER-HICKS RD.

Southlake

Grapevine

1709

1220

SKEET RICHARDSON RD.

81
287

HICKS RD.

B.R. 287

WAGLEY-ROBERTSON RD.

1709

Big

Keller

1938

Colleyville

26

157

114

North Car Rental & Return Area for:
Metro Flight
Braniff
Ozark
Frontier
& Texas Internat'l.

Braniff, Mexicana & Metro-Flight

Hotel

Eagle Mountain Lake

PARK DR.

HALSTON-BAILEY-BOSWELL RD.

ALTA VISTA RD.

DENTON HWY.

Watauga

377

North Richland Hills

Return Area for:
American, Continental, Delta & Eastern

BOWMAN-ROBERTS RD.

OLD DECATUR RD.

Saginaw Airfield

SAGINAW RD.

Saginaw

156

Blue Mound

81

WATAUGA

SMITHFIELD RD.

1938

Harwood

Bedford

Euless

South Contl Plaz

C

1220

Lake Worth

199

AZLE AVE.

Meacham Field

Lakeside

Lake Worth

Sansom Park

JACKSBORO HWY.

820

NORTH FRWY.

35 W

AIRPORT FREEWAY

BEACH ST.

Haltom City

DAVIS

26

Glenview

Richland Hills

Hurst

121

Pipeline

183

10

157

360

FT. WORTH

MILL LN.

RANDOL

River

MIDWAY FRWY.

28TH

183

BELKNAP ST.

RIVERSIDE

26

377

Trinity

DALLAS FT. WORTH TURNPIKE

COLLINS

D

CARSWELL A.F.B.

River Oaks

820

183

Westworth

West Fork of the Trinity River

NORTHSIDE DR.

N. MAIN

HOUSTON DR.

COMMERCE

199

E. 1ST ST.

OAKLAND

30

820

COOKS

SANDY LN.

RANDOL MILL

Arlington Stadium

Village

DIVISION

E. ABRAM ST.

80

White Settlement

820

30

Westover Hills

West

BOWIE BLVD.

80
18 0

B.R.

LANCASTER

FOREST PARK

8TH AVE.

S. MAIN

81

ROSEDALE

180

80

AVE.

Arlington

Pantego

303

COOPER

COLLINS AVE.

157

PIONEER

WATSON

360

Univ. of Texas at Arlington

E

80
180

CAMP BOWIE BLVD.

FRWY.

80
377

University

BERRY ST.

RIVERSIDE DR.

MITCHELL

VAUGHN

BERRY

287

POLY FRWY.

Lake Arlington

ARKANSAS

Dalingworth Gardens

LITTLE

MATLOCK

MC KNIGHT RD.

Fish

2871

VICKERY BLVD.

20

SPUR 20

377

Texas Christian Univ.

SEMINARY DR.

JAMES ST.

35 W

SOUTH FRWY.

WICHITA

287

20

Arlington Municipal Airfield

RD.

Benbrook

183

20

MC CART

Edgecliff

731

SCHOOL RD.

OAK GROVE

FOREST HILL

Forest Hill

20

ANGLIN

287

Kennedale

EDEN RD.

RD.

HARRIS RD.

WEBB

RD.

F

Benbrook Lake

Clear

DIRKS RD.

CLEBURNE RD.

SYCAMORE

OLD GRANBURY RD.

Everman

81

RENDON RD.

B.R. 287

Watsonville

157

Mansfield

MANSFIELD RD.

LILLIAN

MARSFIELD RD.

N

Crowley

1187

731

174

35 W

Burleson

Rendon

1187

Retta

RETTA

MANSFIELD RD.

2738

917

287

G

Scale of Miles
0 1 2 3 4 5

© C.S.C.

1   2   3   4   5   6

DALLAS

Lewisville
Hebron
Plano
Murphy
Richardson
Sachse
Coppell
Carrollton
Addison
Renner
Garland
Farmers Branch
Buckingham
North Lake
Ozark Frontier & Texas Internat'l.
Eastern & American
Continental & Delta
DALLAS FT. WORTH REGIONAL AIRPORT
South-Car Rental & Return Area
Univ. of Dallas
Texas Stadium
Love Field
Southern Methodist Univ.
University Park
Highland Park
White Rock Lake
Garland
Mesquite
Sunnyvale
Irving
Shady Grove
Hunter
Ferrell
DALLAS
Cotton Bowl
Grand Prairie
Naval Air Station
Mountain Creek Lake
Cockrell Hill
Illinois
Bruton
Lake June
Elam
Balch Springs
Kleburg
Duncanville
Hutchins
Dowdy
Woodland Hills
Lancaster
Wilmer
Cedar Hill
Pleasant Run
De Soto
Parkerville
Bear Creek
Glenn Heights
Ovilla
Red Oak
Ferris

North Control Plaza
White Rock Creek
Trinity River
Elm Fork of the Trinity River

Grid columns: 1 2 3 4 5 6 7
Grid rows: A B C D E F G H J K

HYATTS, LEWIS CENTER, GALENA, Vans Valley
RATHBONE, Hyatts, Hollenback, Rome Corners, Trenton
JEROME, Duffy, Home, AFRICA, Jaycox, CENTER VILLAGE, Woodtown
SHAWNEE HILLS, Merchant, POWELL, Freeman, HARLEM, Gorsuch
DELAWARE, FRANKLIN, MOUNT AIR, FLINT, WESTERVILLE, Maxtown, Robins
Summit View, Smothers, Fancher, Bevelheimer
KILEVILLE, DUBLIN, LINWORTH, WORTHINGTON, HUBER RIDGE, NEW ALBANY
Plain City, RIVERLEA, MINERVA PARK, GOULD PARK
AMLIN, CLINTON, Columbus Park of Roses, Thompson
HAYDEN, COLUMBUS, Morse
HILLARD, UPPER ARLINGTON, GAHANNA
MUDSOCK, Columbus Dominican College, BLACKLICK
SAN MARGHERITA, Ohio State Univ, Port Columbus International Airport
MARBLE CLIFF, GRANDVIEW HEIGHTS, WHITEHALL, REYNOLDSBURG
VALLEYVIEW, State Capitol, BEXLEY
NEW ROME, ALTON, Capital University
BRIGGSDALE, BRICE
GALLOWAY, EDGEWATER PARK
GEORGEVILLE, URBANCREST, GROVE CITY, OBETZ
REESE, GROVEPORT
DARBYDALE, PLEASANT CORNERS, CANAL WINCHESTER, WATERLOO
SHADEVILLE, LOCKBOURNE
HARRISBURG, ORIENT, FRANKLIN PICKAWAY, U.S. Military Res. Rickenbacker Air Force Base, LITHOPOLIS

Ohio History Museum
Beulah Park
Scale of Miles 0 1 2 3
© C.S.C.

MARSHALL

McCastlin Blvd.

BOULDER COUNTY
JEFFERSON COUNTY

U.S. Atomic
Energy Commission

(Rocky Flats Plant)

BROOMFIELD

BOULDER COUNTY
ADAMS COUNTY

Jefferson Co.
Airport

W. 128th Ave.
EASTLAKE

E. 128th Ave.

HENDERSON

120th Ave.

NORTHGLENN

W. 112th Ave.
E. 112th Ave.

108th Ave.

104th

THORNTON

100th Ave.

96th Ave.

WESTMINSTER

Stanley Lake

92nd Ave.

FEDERAL
HEIGHTS

88th Ave.

84th Ave.

96th Ave.

90th Ave.

80th Ave.

Coal Creek Canyon Rd.

EL DORADO
ESTATES

W. 82nd Ave.

80th

WELBY

DUPONT

Rocky Mountain Arsenal

72nd

ARVADA

Mayhorn Lake

70th Ave.

64th

64th

58th

COMMERCE
CITY

56th Ave.

52nd Ave.

Ridge Rd.

ADAMS COUNTY
DENVER COUNTY

44th Ave.

MOUNTAIN
VIEW

GOLDEN

Camp George
West
(National Guard)

WHEAT RIDGE

38th

32nd

26th Ave.

29th Ave.

31st Ave.

23rd

DENVER

Stapleton
International
Airport

AURORA

20th Ave.

Colfax

EDGEWATER

18th
17th

Montview

PLEASANT VIEW

6th Ave.

6th

8th Ave.
6th Ave.
1st Ave.

Lowry
Air Force
Base

6th Ave.

Alameda

LAKEWOOD

Alameda

JEFFERSON COUNTY
DENVER COUNTY

Morrison Rd.

Washington
Park

GLENDALE

Mississippi Ave.

Mississippi

IDLEDALE

Red Rocks
Park

Jefferson
Co. Park

Mississippi

Jewell Ave.

Florida

MORRISON

Federal
Correctional
Institute

Denver University

Yale

ENGLEWOOD

SHERIDAN

Quincy

CHERRY HILL
VILLAGE

Cherry
Creek
Park

INDIAN HILLS

Mount Falcon
County Park

Marston
Lake

Belleview

DENVER COUNTY
ARAPAHOE COUNTY

Cherry Creek
Reservoir

TINY TOWN

TWIN FORKS

LITTLETON

GREENWOOD VILLAGE

Littleton Blvd.

Orchard

Bowles Ave.

FENDERS

Coal Mine Rd.

Arapahoe

Dry Creek Rd.

Arapahoe
County
Airport

Ken Caryl Rd.

COLUMBINE

Rangeview Dr.

McClellan Res.

ARAPAHOE COUNTY
DOUGLAS COUNTY

County Line

GRANDVIEW
ESTATES

HOMEWOOD
PARK

PHILLIPSBURG

RIVERSIDE

CHATFIELD ACRES

DEERMONT

N

Scale of Miles
0   1   2   3

© C.S.C.

Highland Rd.
Lone Tree Rd.
Pettibone Lake Rd.
Beaumont Rd.
Highland State Recreational Area
Elizabeth Lake Rd.
WATERFORD
Voorheis Rd.
Dixie Hwy. Dr.
PONTIAC

Honeywell Lake Rd.
Cooley Lake Rd.
Duck Lake Rd.
Oxbow Lake
Union Lake
Williams Lake Rd.
Hospital Rd.
Cass-Elizabeth Rd.
Cooley Lake Rd.
Sylvan Lake
Hickory Grove Rd.
1

Auto Proving Grounds
General Motors Rd.
MILFORD
Commerce Rd.
Carey
Commerce Rd.
Bogie Lake Rd.
Carroll Lake Rd.
Richardson Rd.
Union Lake
Lochaven Rd.
Greer Rd.
Great Lake
Union Lake
Cass Lake
Orchard Lake Rd.
ORCHARD LAKE
Orchard Lake
Long Lake Rd.
Franklin Rd.
BLOOMFIELD HILLS

Stobart Rd.
Pearson Rd.
Dawson Rd.
Sleeth Rd.
State Recreational Area
Lake Rd.
WOLVERINE LAKE
Green Lake
Middle Straits Lake
Pontiac Tr.
Walnut Lake Rd.
Quarton Rd.
Quarton Rd.

Jacoby
Munn
Buno Rd.
Loon Lake
Welch Rd.
Long Pine Rd.
Scott Lake
BEVERLY

Valley
Pleasant
Island Lake State Recreational Area
West Maple Rd.
Plank Rd.
West Maple Rd.
WALLED LAKE
14 Mile Rd.
FRANKLIN
Lincoln Dr.

Kensington Rd.
Kent Lake
WIXOM
Wixom Rd.
Beck Rd.
13 Mile Rd.
Halstead Rd.
Drake Rd.
Farmington Rd.
Orchard Lake Rd.
Middle Belt Rd.

Huron R.
96
South Hill Rd.
Grand River Ave.
12 Mile Rd.
696
Bell Rd.
SOUTHFIELD

New Hudson Airport
Davis Creek
11 Mile Rd.
NOVI
FARMINGTON HILLS
Powers Rd.
Rouge River

LIVINGSTON CO.
OAKLAND CO.
10 Mile Rd.
102
FARMINGTON
8 Mile Rd.
24

SOUTH LYON
9 Mile Rd.
Taft Rd.
102

OAKLAND CO.
WASHTENAW CO.
Hass Rd.
8 Mile Rd.
NORTHVILLE
Meadowbrook Rd.
8 Mile Rd.
7 Mile Rd.
5 Points Rd.
Telegraph Rd.
Lahser Rd.
5

Rushton Rd.
Napier Rd.
Garfield Rd.
7 Mile Rd.
Haggerty Hwy.
275
Newburgh Rd.
Merriman Rd.
Farmington Rd.
6 Mile Rd.
Inkster Rd.
Beech-Daly Rd.

Dixboro Rd.
Pontiac Trail
Angle
6 Mile Rd.
96
5 Mile Rd.

Earhart Rd.
Tower Rd.
Curtis Rd.
5 Mile Rd.
LIVONIA
Middle Belt Rd.
96
River Rouge Park

Brookville Rd.
PLYMOUTH
North Territorial Rd.
REDFORD
River Rouge Park

14
Powell Rd.
Ann Arbor Trail
Ann Arbor Rd.
Plymouth Rd.
Levan Rd.
Plymouth Rd.
W. Chicago Rd.

14
Joy Rd.
Main St.
Joy Rd.
Riverside Park
Joy Rd.

Warren Rd.
Warren Rd.
GARDEN CITY
DEARBORN HEIGHTS

14
153
WASHTENAW CO.
WAYNE CO.
Saltz Rd.
WESTLAND
Ford Rd.
DEARBORN

Stommel Rd.
Fraine Lake Rd.
Cherry Hill Rd.
Proctor Rd.
Marquette
Cherry Hill Rd.
Avondale
INKSTER

ANN ARBOR
Dixboro Rd.
Vreeland Rd.
Burk Rd.
Beck Rd.
Canton Center Rd.
Sheldon Rd.
Lilley Rd.
John Hix Rd.
Wayne Rd.
Venoy
Palmer Rd.
Glenwood
Harrison Rd.
Inkster Rd.
John Daly
Carlisle

23
Gale Rd.
Geddes Rd.
Ridge Rd.
Ward Rd.
Michigan Ave.
12
Annapolis
Van Born Rd.

Washtenaw Ave.
Clark Rd.
Clark Rd.
WAYNE
Beverly Rd.

17
Packard Rd.
YPSILANTI
Holmes Rd.
Forest Ave.
Cross St.
12a
12
Ecorse Rd.
Hannan Rd.
ROMULUS
Ecorse Rd.

94
Ellsworth Rd.
Tyler Rd.
Willow Run Airport
Belleville Rd.
Taylor Rd.
Wick Rd.
Wick Rd.
TAYLOR
Goddard Rd.

12
Ford Lake
Huron River
Tyler Rd.
94
Detroit Industrial Pkwy.

Textile Rd.
Goddard Rd.
Detroit Metropolitan Wayne County Airport
North Line Rd.

94
12
Whitaker Rd.
Huron River Dr.
BELLEVILLE
Savage Rd.
275
Eureka Rd.
24

Platt Rd.
Carpenter Rd.
Merritt Rd.
Stony Creek Rd.
Hitchingham Rd.
Tuttle Hill Rd.
Hoggt Rd.
Hull Rd.
Rawsonville Rd.
Sumpter Rd.
Martinsville Rd.
Martz Rd.
Viking Hwy.
Beach-Daly Rd.
Pardee Rd.

8 • 9 • 10 • 11 • 12 • 13 • 14

A
B
C
D
E
F
G
H
J
K

STERLING HEIGHTS
TROY
BIRMINGHAM
CLAWSON
ROYAL OAK
HILLS
LATHRUP VILLAGE
BERKLEY
HUNTINGTON WOODS
PLEASANT RIDGE
OAK PARK
FERNDALE
HAZEL PARK
MADISON HEIGHTS
WARREN
CENTER LINE
MACOMB CO.
WAYNE CO.
HIGHLAND PARK
DETROIT
HAMTRAMCK
MELVINDALE
RIVER ROUGE
ALLEN PARK
ECORSE
LINCOLN PARK
WYANDOTTE
SOUTHGATE
WINDSOR
UTICA
MOUNT CLEMENS
FRASER
ROSEVILLE
EAST DETROIT
SAINT CLAIR SHORES
HARPER WOODS
GROSSE POINTE WOODS
GROSSE POINTE SHORES
GROSSE POINTE FARMS
GROSSE POINTE
GROSSE POINTE PARK

Lake St. Claire

U.S.A.
CANADA

Detroit River

Ambassador Bridge (Toll)
Detroit-Windsor Tunnel (Toll)
Douglas McArthur Br.

N

Scale of Miles
0 1 2 3

© C.S.C.

8 • 9 • 10 • 11 • 12 • 13 • 14

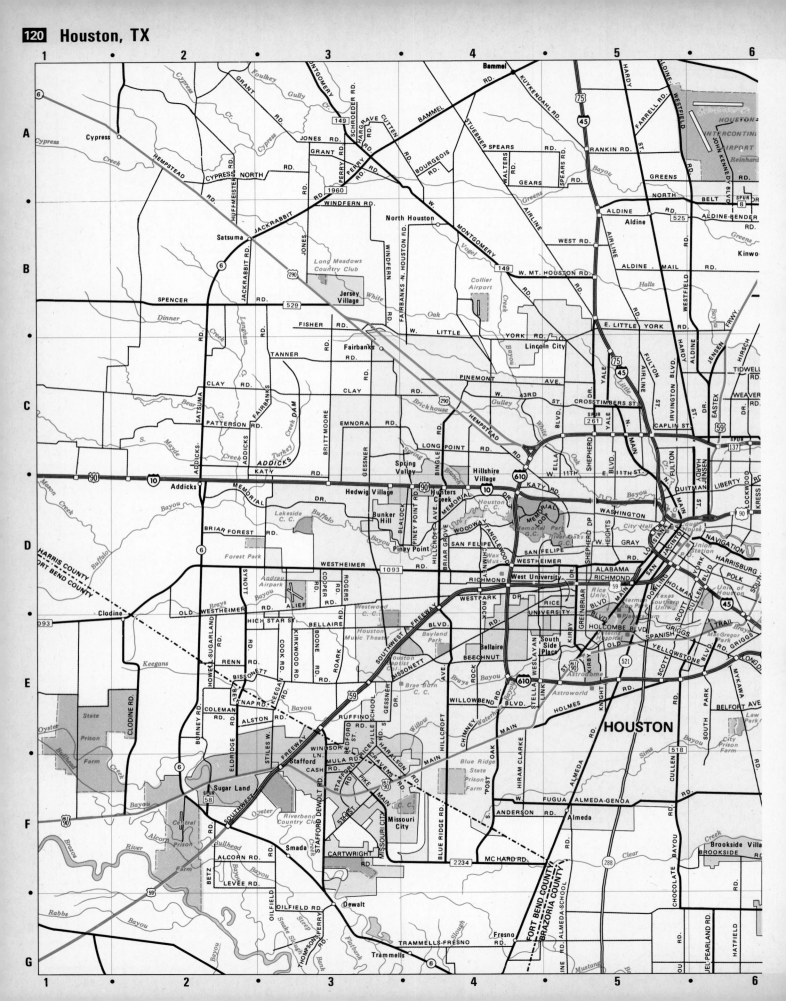

7   8   9   10   11

A

HUMBLE   WESTFIELD   RD.
Garners Tejas G.C.   ATASCOCITA   RD.
PETERO   OPOSSUM PARK RD.   RD.
HUMBLE   G.C.
Humble   HUMBLE   RD.   2100   PETERSON RD.   STROKER   RD.   RAMSEY   LOUIS RD.   OIL FIELD   146   Day
Harris County Prison Farm   Bayou   FOLEY   RD.   HARE & COOK RD.   RD.   LORD   RD.   90   GUM ISLAND CUT-OFF   RD.

LOCKWOOD RD.   LAKE   WILSON   HATCHERVILLE

ATASCOCITA   Williams   Bayou   HOUSTON   RD.   146

B
59   WOODLAWN   El Dorado Golf Course Greens   N. LAKE HOUSTON PKWY.   ALEXANDER DEUSSEN COUNTY PARK   San   Crosby   90   Barrett   KENNING   BOHEMIAN HALL   BRODT RD.   LIBERTY CO.
E. MT. HOUSTON   RD.   KRENEK   CHAMBERS CO.
Dyersdale   GARRETT   RD.   Jacinto   CROSBY   CEDAR   WOLCEK RD.
527   Sheldon Reservoir   Sheldon   RALSTON ST.   Sheldon Wildlife Refuge   River   LYNCHBURG   SARALLA   HOLY RD.   146   Mont

C
Brock Park G.C.   CROSS TIMBERS RD.   1942   BARBERS HILL RD.   BARBERS HILL RD.
LEY   GREEN RIVER DR.   ST. HWY.   MILLER   BARBERS   HILL   HARRIS CO.   CHAMBERS CO.
HOMESTEAD   N. WAYSIDE   MESA   BEAUMONT   526   CARPENTERS   Bear Lake   Highlands   CANAL RD.   ORCHARD RD.   JOHN MARTIN   GARTH   Smith Gully
MC CARTY   Hunting   Bayou   WALLISVILLE   RD.   Highlands Reservoir   WALLISVILLE   10
N. HOUSTON   SHELDON-DEER PARK   BATTLE   BELL   RD.   McNair

D
610   Busch Gardens   Texaco C.C.   Cloverleaf   Channelview   10   Old River   BURNETT   WADE   Coady   LYNCHBURG-CEDAR BAYOU   ARCHER   N. MAIN   BARKULOO   146
WALLISVILLE   OATES   UVALDE   MARKET ST.   Lost Lake   134   WOOSTER RD.   Baytown Airport
90   MARKET ST.   Jacinto City   MAXEY   FEDERAL   Lynchburg   Battleship Texas Museum   BURNETT DR.   Crystal Lake   CEDAR BAYOU   SPUR 330   Baytown   CEDAR BAYOU BAY RD.
10   MC CARTY   MARKET ST.   RD.   HOLLAND   Houston   San Jacinto Monument   Scott Bay   BAYWAY   1405
WAYSIDE   CLINTON DR.   Galena Park   MAIN   CLINTON   DR.   Ship   San Jacinto Battlefield State Park   Peggy Lake   Goat Island   BAYWAY DR.

E
75   Executive G.C.   Mason Park   BROADWAY   225   Milby Park   Little   RED   SOUTH ST.   San Jacinto Battlefield   Alexander Island   Upper San Jacinto Bay   Black Duck Bay   Tabbs Bay   Hogg Is.   IJAMS LAKE   TRI-CITY BEACH
LAWNDALE   610   Glenbrook Park Municipal G.C.   RICHEY   S. SHAVER   SOUTHMORE   BLUFF   6   Deer Park   Lomax   225   Lower San Jacinto Bay
35   TELEPHONE RD.   VINCE   ALLENDALE   PASADENA   PASADENA   BLVD.   146   Morgans Point
WINKER   SOUTH   ALLEN-GENOA   SPENCER   SPENCER   HWY.   GRANVIEW AVE.   Atkinson Island   TRI-CITY BEACH
BROADWAY   DR.   VINCE   BAYOU   La Porte Municipal Airport   MAIN ST.   Sylvan Beach Park

F
William P. Hobby Airport   GALVESTON RD.   EDGEBROOK   Pasadena   FAIRMONT   La Porte PKWY.   La Porte   16TH ST.
MONROE RD.   South Houston   SHAVER   CRENSHAW   GENOA-RED BLUFF   RD.   MC CADE RD.   Shoreacres
ALMEDA   GENOA RD.   3   SPRING GULLY   BROADWAY   GALVESTO
TELEPHONE RD.   HALL   45   FUQUA   CHOATE RD.   Ellington Air Force Base   RED BLUFF RD.   TODVILLE   EL JARDIN DR.   BAY
HARRIS CO.   BRAZORIA CO.   HORSEPEN   SPACE CENTER AREA BLVD.   Taylor Lake Village   Taylor Lake   Seabrook

G
35   HALL RD.   GULF FREEWAY   GALVESTON AVE.   2351   75   EL DORADO BLVD.   NASA   EL CAMINO REAL   Mud Lake   El Lago   146   Seabrook
Pearland   518   C.C.   Clear   NASA RD. NO. 1   Clear Lake   Clear Lake Shores   Kemah
GARLAND-SITES RD.   DIXIE FARM RD.   BRAZORIA CO.   GALVESTON CO.   EDGEWOOD AVE.   FRIENDSWOOD   3   45

N

GALVESTON BAY

Scale of Miles
0   1   2   3   4   5

© C.S.C.

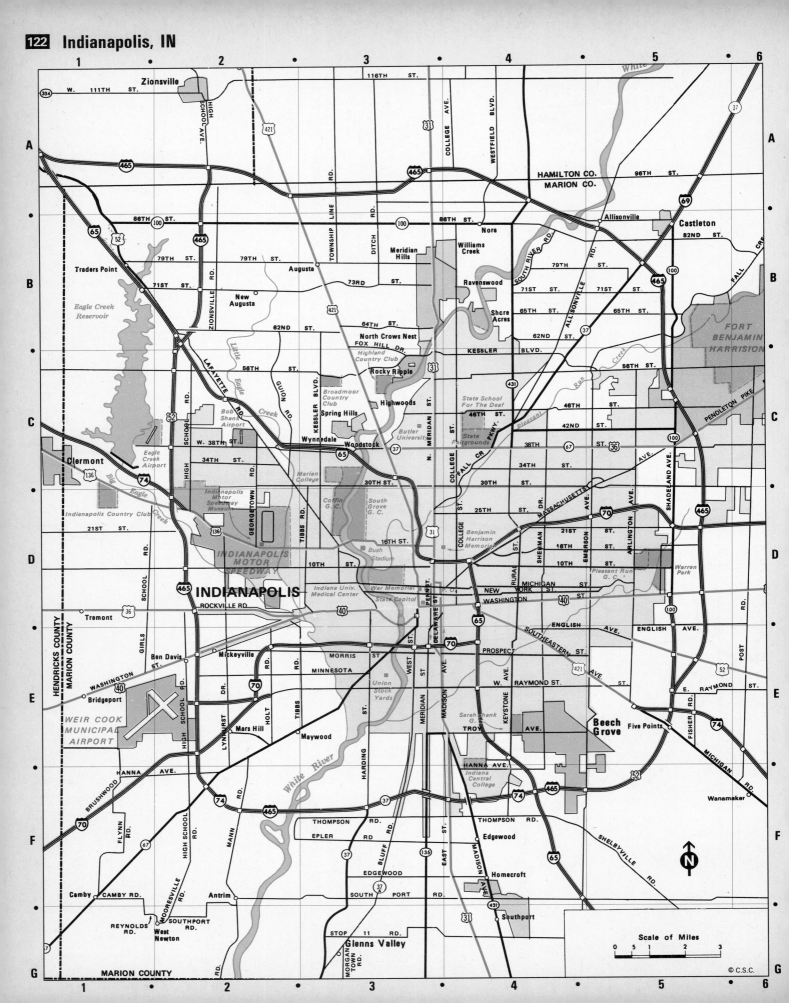

NASSAU CO.
DUVAL CO.

TISONIA

BARFORD

PECAN PARK

DUVAL

Jacksonville International Airport

BEEGHLY HEIGHTS

DUNN CREEK

CARY

OCEANWAY

PLUMMER

DINSMORE

GARDEN CITY

POLLY TOWN

SPAULDING

HOLLY FORD

EASTPORT

Jacksonville Zoo

NEW BERLIN

DAME POINT

CHASEVILLE

Ft. Carolina National Mem.

PICKETTVILLE

GILMORE

COSMO
FORT CAROLINE
SHORES

JACKSONVILLE

Jacksonville University

EGGLESTON HEIGHTS

Craig Airport

CAMBON

ARLINGTON

MARIETTA

OAKWOOD VILLA

WHITEHOUSE

Gator Bowl
Coliseum

HOGAN

SOUTHSIDE
ESTATES

CENTER PARK

Herlong Airport

CEDAR HILLS

University of
North Florida

JACKSONVILLE HEIGHTS

BOWDEN

SKINNERS

Cecil Field Naval Air Station

WESCONNETT

VENETIA

SAN JOSE

YUKON

Timuquana Country Club Golf Course

Willow Lakes Golf and Country Club

Jacksonville Naval Air Station

SUNBEAM

DUVAL CO.
CLAY CO.

GOODBYS

Orange Park

PLUMMERS

GREENLAND

MANDARIN

LORETTO

BAYARD

EAST MANDARIN

Julington Creek

Julington

Durbin

FRUIT COVE

Scale of Miles
0 1 2 3

© C.S.C.

N

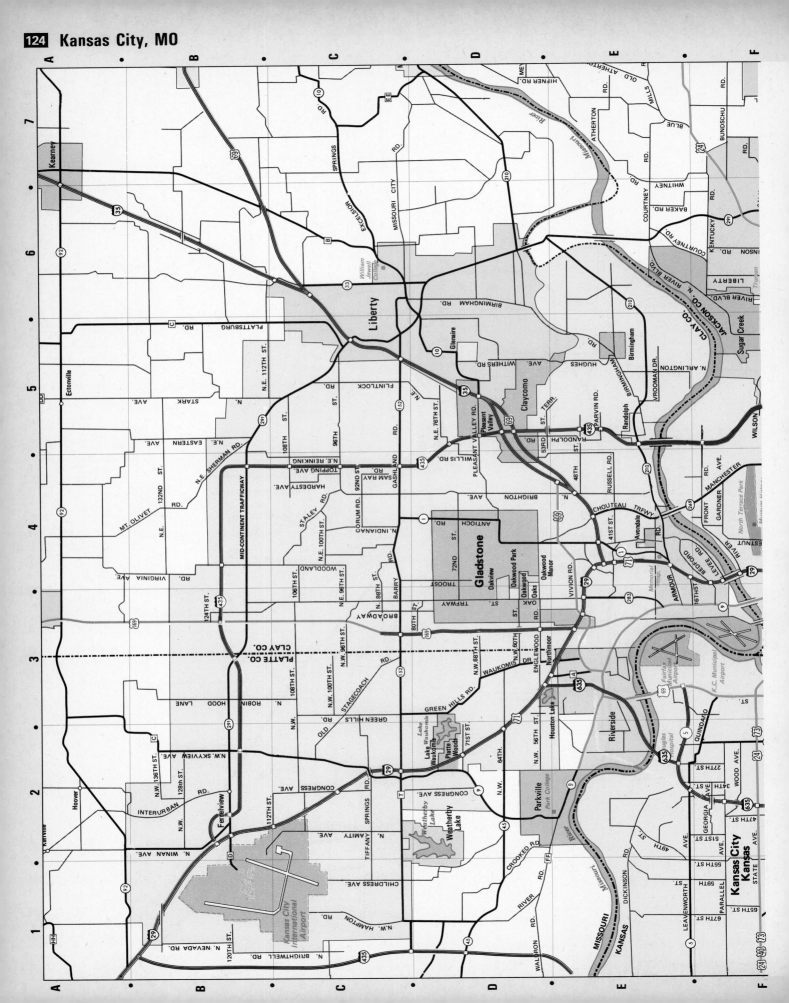

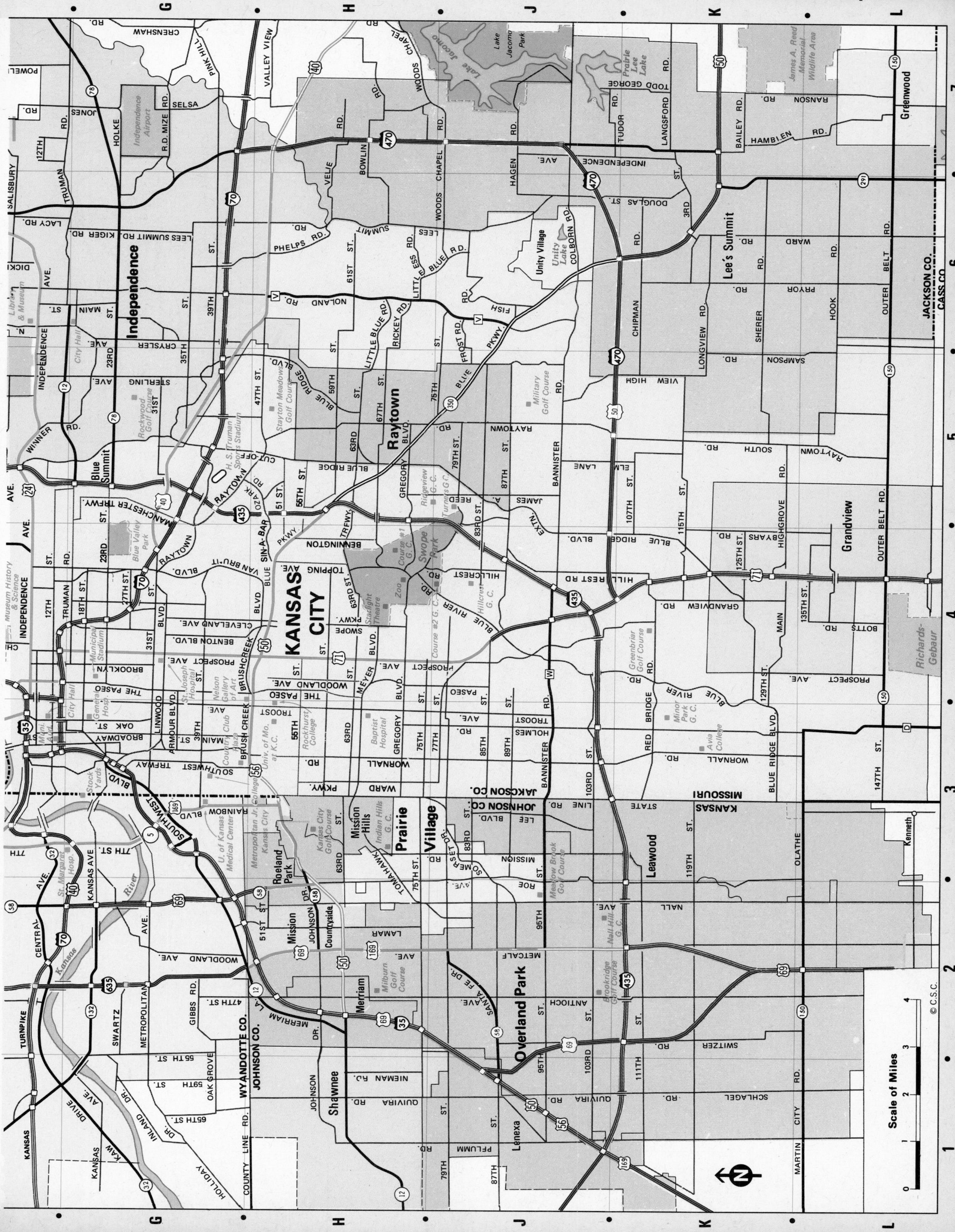

Independence

Blue Summit

KANSAS CITY

Raytown

Lee's Summit

Grandview

Prairie Village

Mission Hills

Roeland Park

Mission

Merriam

Shawnee

Overland Park

Leawood

Lenexa

Greenwood

WYANDOTTE CO.
JOHNSON CO.

JACKSON CO.
JOHNSON CO.

JACKSON CO.
CASS CO.

MISSOURI
KANSAS

STATE LINE RD.

Swope Park

Zoo

Starlight Theatre

Military Golf Course

Unity Village

Lake Jacomo

Prairie Lee Lake

James A. Reed Memorial Wildlife Area

H.S. Truman Sports Stadium

Municipal Stadium

Nelson Gallery of Art

Rockhurst College

Univ. of Mo. at K.C.

Baptist Hospital

St. Joseph Hospital

Avila College

Richards-Gebaur

Scale of Miles

© C.S.C.

ANGELES NATIONAL FOREST

SIERRA MADRE

TEMPLE CITY

EL MONTE

SOUTH EL MONTE

PICO RIVERA

ALTADENA

PASADENA

SAN GABRIEL

ROSEMEAD

MONTEBELLO

COMMERCE

BELL GARDENS

SOUTH PASADENA

SAN MARINO

ALHAMBRA

MONTEREY PARK

EAST LOS ANGELES

HUNTINGTON PARK

BELL

MAYWOOD

GLENDALE

VERDUGO MOUNTAINS

BURBANK

GRIFFITH PARK

LOS ANGELES

HOLLYWOOD

NORTH HOLLYWOOD

UNIVERSAL CITY

WEST HOLLYWOOD

BEVERLY HILLS

CENTURY CITY

CULVER CITY

BALDWIN HILLS

SANTA MONICA MOUNTAINS

SAN VINCENTE MTN.

BEL AIR

WESTWOOD

UNIV. OF SOUTHERN CALIF.

EXPOSITION PARK

HYDE PARK

SAN FERNANDO

PANORAMA CITY

SHERMAN OAKS

VAN NUYS

MISSION HILLS

SEPULVEDA

ENCINO

TARZANA

NORTHRIDGE

RESEDA

CANOGA PARK

WOODLAND HILLS

SANTA MONICA

PACIFIC PALISADES

MARINA DEL REY

VENICE

Freeways: 210, 110, 10, 710, 605, 5, 101, 170, 405, 2, 134

Vetter Pk. + 5908
Josephine Pk. + 5558
Strawberry Pk. + 6164
San Gabriel Pk. + 6161
Brown Mtn. + 4454
Mt. Harvard + 5440
Condor Pk. + 5439
Mt. Lukens + 5074
Verdugo Pk. + 3126

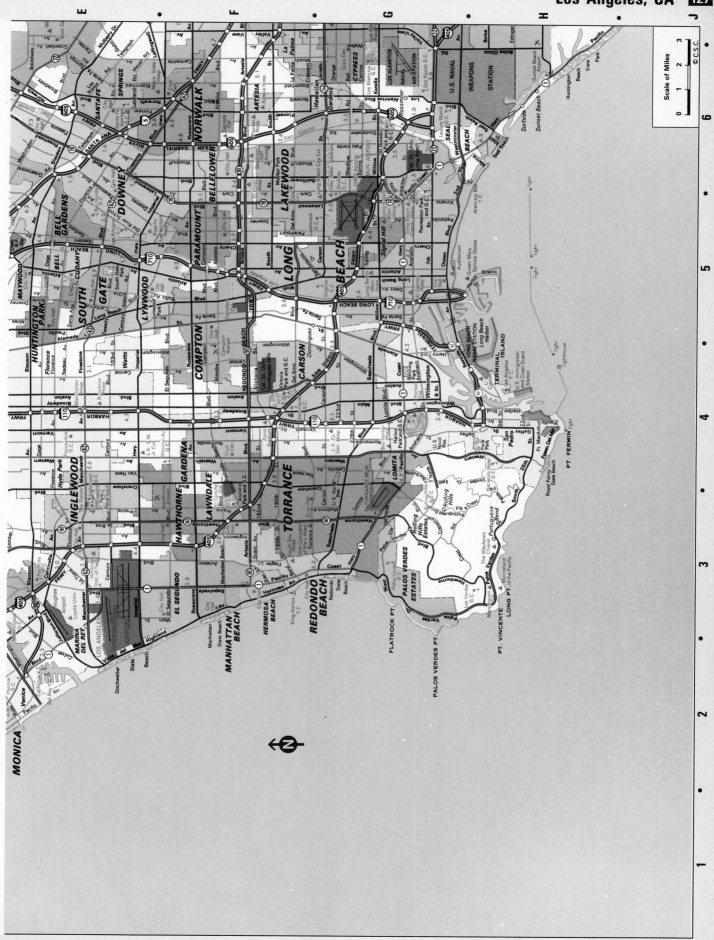

A · B · C · D

12 · 11 · 10 · 9 · 8 · 7

SAN BERNARDINO NATIONAL FOREST

+ HARRISON MTN. 4743

+ MCKINLEY MTN. 3795

SAN BERNARDINO

REDLANDS

NORTON AIR FORCE BASE

COLTON

RIALTO

FONTANA

Tri-City Airport

Loma Linda

RIALTO

RIALTO Airport

For continuation of inset, see main map

RIALTO

FONTANA

Ontario Motor Speedway

ONTARIO INTERNATIONAL AIRPORT

UPLAND

MONTCLAIR

CLAREMONT

POMONA

CHINO

CHINO AIRPORT

CALIFORNIA INSTITUTE FOR MEN

JURUPA HILLS

PEDLEY

Mira Loma

LOS ANGELES COUNTY
SAN BERNARDINO COUNTY

ANGELES NATIONAL FOREST

+ MT. SALLY 5408

+ MT. BLISS 3725

Falling Springs

GLENDORA

AZUSA

DUARTE

MONROVIA

ARCADIA

BALDWIN PARK

COVINA

WEST COVINA

SAN DIMAS

LA VERNE

PUDDINGTON RESERVOIR STATE REC. AREA

LOS ANGELES COUNTY FAIRGROUNDS

CALIF. STATE POLYTECHNIC UNIV.

SAN JOSE HILLS

LA PUENTE

PUENTE HILLS

WORKMAN HILL 1387

WHITTIER

Scale of Miles
0 1 2 3

© C.S.C.

N

CLEVELAND NATIONAL FOREST

RIVERSIDE
RIVERSIDE MUNICIPAL AIRPORT
NORCO
CORONA
HOME GARDENS
U.S. NAVAL RESERVATION
CHINO AIRPORT
CALIF. INST. FOR WOMEN
COUNTY
FLOOD CONTROL BASIN
CALIFORNIA INSTITUTE FOR MEN
SAN BERNARDINO
RIVERSIDE
CHINO HILLS
EL CERRITO
Silverado
Santiago
Modjeska
Trabuco Canyon
Lake Forest
El Toro

SAN BERNARDINO COUNTY
ORANGE COUNTY

LOS ANGELES COUNTY
ORANGE COUNTY

WORKMAN HILL 1367
HILLS
ROWLAND HTS.
LA HABRA
BREA
FULLERTON
PLACENTIA
YORBA LINDA
Villa Park Res.
Santiago Res.
Orange Park
IRVINE
EL TORO U.S.M.C. AIR STATION
UNIV. OF CALIFORNIA IRVINE CAMPUS

LA MIRADA
BUENA PARK
ANAHEIM
STANTON
GARDEN GROVE
WESTMINSTER
ORANGE
SANTA ANA
TUSTIN
COSTA MESA
SANTA ANA U.S.M.C. AIR FACILITY
NEWPORT BEACH
HUNTINGTON BEACH
FOUNTAIN VALLEY

LOUISVILLE

New Albany
Clarksville
Jeffersonville
Shively

Robinswood
Riverwood
Indian Hills
Cherokee Section
Indian Hills
Mockingbird Valley
Rolling Fields
Maryhill Estates
Druid Hills
Cherrywood Estates
Bellewood
Norburne Estates
Broadfields
Plymouth Village

Shawnee Park
North
Miles Park Race Track
Gibson
Seneca Gardens
Bowman Field
Strathmoor Village
Wellington
Kingsley
Parkway Village
Audubon Park
Zoological Gardens
Churchill Downs
Kentucky State Fair & Exposition Center
West Buechel
General Electric Appliance Park
Buechel
Lynnview
Iroquis Park
U.S. Navy Ordinance Plant
Standford Field
Ford Car Plant
Minor Lane Hts

Shermon Minton Bridge
Kentucky-Indiana Bridge (Toll)
George Rodgers Clark Bridge
J.F. Kennedy Mem. Bridge
Cox Park
Bandman Park
Cherokee Park

OHIO RIVER

Riverside Pkwy.
Western Pkwy.
Portland
Bank St.
Main St.
Market St.
Broadway
Chestnut St.
Liberty St.
Lexington
Frankfort
Brownsboro
Grinstead
Bardstown
Baxter Ave.
Barret Ave.
Winter Ave.
Goss Ave.
Kentucky St.
Virginia Ave.
Oak St.
Hill St.
Burnett
Shelby
Eastern Pkwy.
Preston St.
Poplar Level
Newburgh Rd.
Trevilian
Richmond Dr.
Alta Vista Rd.
Rock Creek
Cannons La.
Breckenridge
Westport Rd.
Willis
Dutchmans La.
Goldsmith
Bashford Manor La.
6 Mile La.
Bishop La.
Jennings La.
Indian Trail
Poplar Level Rd.
Shepherdsville Rd.
Buechel Bank Rd.
Fegenbush La.
Watterson Expwy.
Henry Watterson Expwy.
Woodlawn Av.
Longfield Av.
Berry Blvd.
Taylor Blvd.
Manslick Rd.
Bluegrass Av.
Hazelwood Av.
Gagel Av.
Southern Av.
New Cut Rd.
Southside Dr.
Strawberry La.
Kenwood Dr.
Crittenden Dr.
Norton Av.
Kentucky Turnpike
Preston Hwy.
Fern Valley Rd.
National Turnpike
Grade La.
Outer Loop
Palatka Rd.
St. Andrews Church Rd.
St. Anthony Church Rd.
3rd St.
Blanton Rd.
Church Rd.
Arnoldtown Rd.
Rockford La.
Dixie Hwy.
Crums La.
Algonquin Pkwy.
Wilson Av.
Greenwood Av.
South Western Pkwy.
River Park Dr.
Bells La.
Camp Ground Rd.
Cane Run Rd.
Millers La.
Ralph Av.
Winkler Av.
Central Blvd.
Park Dr.
Gardiner La.
Mansick Rd.
Grant Line Rd.
Graybrook Rd.
Beechwood Av.
Charlestown Rd.
Silver St.
Slate Run Rd.
State St.
Spring St.
Main St.
8th St.
Vincennes
Ekin Av.
Harrison Av.
Emery Crossing Rd.
McCulloch
Eastern Blvd.
Charlestown Pike
Hamburg Pike
Dutch La.
Spring St.
10th St.
8th St.
Penn St.
Springdale Dr.
Chippewa
Mullins La.
Middle Rd.
Allison La.
Utica Pike
River Rd.
Mellwood Av.
Story Ave.
Zorn Ave.
Mockingbird Valley Rd.
Indian Hill Trail
Chenoweth La.
Hubbard La.
Blankenbaker
Payne St.
Logan St.
Campbell St.
Jackson St.
Shippingport I.
Towhead I.
Six Mile I.

Scale of Miles
0 1 2 3

N

© C.S.C.

Scale of Miles

0 1 2 3

© C.S.C.

TENNESSEE / MISSISSIPPI

TENNESSEE / ARKANSAS

SHELBY CO. / CRITTENDEN CO.

SHELBY CO. / DE SOTO CO.

Mississippi River

Wolf River

Loosahatchie River

Cities and places:
ARLINGTON, BOLTON, GILDFIELD, BRUNSWICK, LUCY, WOODSTOCK, EGYPT, RAMSEY, BENJESTOWN, SPRING LAKE, ELLENDALE, BARTLETT, RALEIGH, ELMORE PARK, LENOW, PISGAH, FISHERVILLE, CORDOVA, SHELBY FARMS, GERMANTOWN, FOREST HILL, COLLIERVILLE, BAILEY, MINERAL WELLS, CAPLEVILLE, PLUM POINT, MEMPHIS, OAKVILLE, HARVARD, GAMMON, REDMAN POINT, ST. CLAIR, MOUND CITY, BLANTON, WEST MEMPHIS, GALET, WYANOKE, HULBERT, LAKE VIEW

Meeman Shelby Forest State Park

Shelby County Penal Farm

Shelby County Airport

Gen. DeWitt Spain Downtown Airport

Memphis International Airport

McKellar Park

Overton Park

Firestone Park

Fuller State Park

Mississippi Park

Presidents Island

Robinson Crusoe Island

Chicken Island

North Horn Lake

Rob-co Lake

Coro Lake

Beef Island

Bear Creek

Fletcher Lake

McKellar Lake

Southwestern University

Memphis State University

Fox Meadows Country Club

Elvis Presley Blvd.

1 2 3 4 5 6

N.W. 69TH AVE.
Canal
N.W. 57TH AVE.
N.W. 47TH AVE.
N.W. 42ND AVE.
N.W. 37TH AVE.
N.W. 32ND AVE.
N.W. 27TH AVE.
N.W. 17TH AVE.
MIAMI
GARDENS DR.
FLORIDA'S TURNPIKE
TOLL GATE
N.W. 2ND AVE. EXT.
MIAMI AVE.
95
441
North Miami Beach
Greynold Pk.
N.E. 179TH DR.
Greynolds Pk. G.C.
N.E. 20TH AVE.
Snake Creek
N.E. 18TH AVE.
N.E. 167TH ST.
826
Maule Lake
A1A

PALMETTO
826
EXPRESSWAY
Bunche Park
Biscayne College
Biscayne Canal
INTERAMA
N.E. 160TH ST.
N.E. 159TH ST.
N.E. 149TH ST.
North Miami
Florida Int'l Univ.
East Greynolds Pk.
Haulover Beach

A

LUDLAM RD.
N.W. 68TH
DAIRY RD.
OPA-LOCKA AIRPORT
ORIENTAL BLVD.
N.W. 151ST ST.
N.W. 143RD ST.
9
S. RIVER
Memorial Hwy.
6TH AVE.
Biscayne Canal
DIXIE HWY.
N.E. 135TH ST.
N.E. 123RD ST.
Bay Harbor Is.
Bal Harbour
96TH ST.
Surfside

Lake Sable
Lake Cecile
Gratigny Regional Park
Opa-Locka
N.W. 135TH ST.
OPA-LOCKA BLVD.
441
N.W. 126TH ST.
N.W. 119TH ST.
GRATIGNY DR.
Biscayne Park
Barry Coll.
N.E. 115TH ST.
N.E. 108TH ST.
Indian Creek Village
Indian Creek C.C.
Surfside
88TH ST.

B

ke Lawrence
819
GRATIGNY RD.
Westview C.C.
N.W. 111TH ST.
Biscayne Dog Kennel
103RD ST.
Miami Shores
N.E. 96TH ST.
Miami Shores C.C.
Waterway
Belle Meade Is.
Normandy Shores G.C.
N. Shore Dr.
85TH ST.
A1A

Lake Tahoe
Little River
Miami Dade Jr. Coll.
N.W. 27TH AVE.
N.W. 22ND AVE.
N.W. 17TH
95TH ST.
LITTLE RIVER DR.
El Portal
81ST ST.
79TH ST.
N.E. 79TH ST.
North Bay Village
Normandy
71ST ST.
77TH ST.

850
Hialeah
W. 41ST ST.
E. 41ST ST.
E. 49TH ST.
Normandy
John F. Kennedy Causeway
Treasure Is.
La Gorce Is.
Collins Ave.
Alton Dr.
51ST ST.
47TH ST.
Miami Beach

C

W. 40TH PL.
E. 33RD ST.
E. 32ND ST.
N.W.
Hialeah Park Race Track
71ST ST.
62ND ST.
61ST ST.
North Bay Is.
Bird Key
Morningside Park
La Groce C.C.
BISCAYNE BAY

W. 29TH
W. 23RD
W. 17TH
E. 17TH ST.
E. 9TH ST.
W. 9TH
54TH ST.
54TH ST.
25A
815
A. Godfrey Rd.
D

Miami Springs
WESTWARD DR.
ALBATROSS
25A
46TH ST.
Airport Expwy
Toll Gate
195
JULIA TUTTLE CAUSEWAY
Bayshore Mun. G.C.
Sunset Islands
Par 3
Pine Tree Dr.

Miami Springs G.C.
Virginia Gardens
36TH ST.
CURTISS PKWY
S. ROYAL POINCIANA BLVD.
27
Airport Expwy
N.W. 36TH ST.
N.E. 36TH ST.
9
N.E. 29TH ST.
Venetian Islands
Venetian Causeway (Toll)
Belle Isle
Flamingo

MIAMI INTERNATIONAL AIRPORT
N.W. 67TH AVE.
Terminal
N.W. N. RIVER DR.
N.W. S. RIVER DR.
N.W. 28TH ST.
N.E. 20TH ST.
1
MIAMI
Civic Center
Hibiscus Is.
Palm Is.
Star Is.
Lincoln Rd.
Alton Rd.
Meridian
Washington Ave.
Collins Ave.
A1A

E

WETHERFORD BLVD.
PERIMETER RD.
EAST DR.
N.W. 21ST ST.
Le Jeune G.C.
N.W. 14TH ST.
WEST
395
MAC ARTHUR CAUSEWAY
Watson Park
5TH ST.

TAMIAMI CANAL
Blue Lagoon
51ST AVE.
49TH AVE.
42ND AVE.
37TH
11TH
N.W. 32ND CT.
836
TOLL GATE
7TH ST.
N.W. 11TH ST.
N.W. 5TH ST.
Port of Miami
Bay Front Park
Dodge Is.

FLAGLER ST.
Orange Bowl
W. FLAGER
E. FLAGER
S.W. 1ST ST.
Burlingame Is.
Lummus Is.
Fisher Is.

F

West Miami
Granada G.C.
TAMIAMI TRAIL 41
S.W. 12TH
S.W. 13TH ST.
S.W. 11TH
95
Brickell
Rickenbacker Causeway Toll
Norris Cut
Virginia Key
ATLANTIC

S.W. 16TH ST.
42ND AVE.
27TH AVE.
22ND
17TH
9
S.W. 22ND ST.
Coral Gables
Vizcaya
Fisher Is.
Duck Lake

GRANADA BLVD.
PONCE DE LEON BLVD.
DIXIE HIGHWAY
1
BIRD AVE.
SOUTH BAY SHORE DR.
Fair Isle
Marine Stadium
Virginia Beach Park
Bear Cut

Coral Gable Biltmore G.C.
Riviera C.C.
Douglas Park
Dinner Key
Seaquarium
Bear Cut Causeway Toll

G

Park Track
S.W. 33RD ST.
S.W. 48TH ST.
MILLER
Univ. of Miami
PONCE DE LEON
HARDEE
POINCIANA
MAIN HWY.
Coconut Grove Bayfront Park
Intracoastal
N
South Miami

Scale of Miles
0 5 1 2

©C.S.C.

MEEKER
GERMANTOWN
COLGATE
MEQUIN
MENOMONEE FALLS
BROWN DEER
RIVER HILLS
BAYSIDE
LANNON
FOX POINT
SUSSEX
GLENDALE
WHITEFISH BAY
BUTLER
SHOREWOOD
PEWAUKEE
BROOKFIELD
DUPLAINVILLE
ELM GROVE
WAUWATOSA
MILWAUKEE
GOERKES CORNER
WAUKESHA
WEST MILWAUKEE
SAINT FRANCIS
NEW BERLIN
WEST ALLIS
GREENFIELD
CUDAHY
HALES CORNERS
GREENDALE
VERNON
MUSKEGO
OAK CREEK
SOUTH MILWAUKEE
BIG BEND
FRANKLIN
Lake Michigan
UNION CHURCH
CADDY VISTA
TICHIGAN
KNEELAND
HUSHER
RAYMOND
CALEDONIA
TABOR
BUENA PARK
NORTH CAPE
THOMPSONVILLE

Scale of Miles
0   1   2   3

© C.S.C.

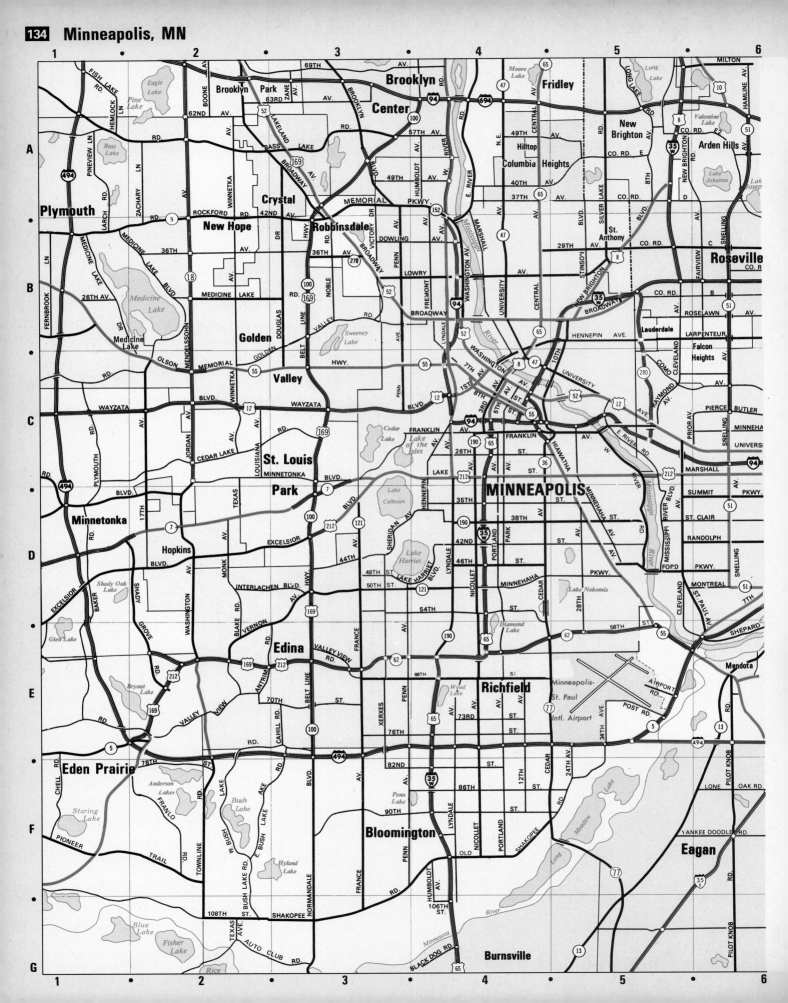

6 7 8 9 10 11

Snail Lake
Shoreview
CO. RD. 96
CO. RD. G
Vadnais Heights
McMENEMY
Gem Lake
White Bear Lake
Mahtomedi
Birchwood
CEDAR
CEDAR AV.
Willernie
75TH ST.
White Bear Lake
Lake Vadnais
CO. RD. E
BELLAIRE
EAST CO. LINE
Pine Springs
36
KEATS AVE.
MANNING AVE.
694
DALLWOOD RD.

A

Lake Owasso
OWASSO BLVD.
LITTLE CANADA RD.
EDGERTON
Kohlman Lake
CO. RD. D
HAZELWOOD
WHITE BEAR
120
North St. Paul
Silver Lake
CO. RD. C
Lake De Montreville
JANE
Lake Jane
40TH ST. N.

B

Little Canade
Gervais Lake
MAPLEWOOD
Maplewood
ROSELAWN
CO. RD. B
FROST AV.
PROSPERITY
7TH AV.
Larpenteur
5
Lake Elmo
Sunfish Lake
30TH ST. N.
15

Lake Elmo
ARLINGTON AV.
MARYLAND AVE.
MCKNIGHT RD.
EAST CO. LINE
STILLWATER
Oakdale
HARVESTER AV.
Eagle Point Lake
EAGLE POINT
Lake Elmo
10TH ST.

C

L. Como
COMO AV.
ST. PAUL
EDGERTON
ARCADE ST.
EARL ST.
Minnehaha
212
120
Landfall
694
HUDSON RD.
17
94

PIERCE BUTLER RTE.
MINNEHAHA
UNIVERSITY AV.
DAYTON AVE.
SUMMIT AVE.
WARNER
BURNS AV.
UPPER AFTON
Battle Creek Lake
BROOKVIEW DR.
19
Markgrafs Lake
Powers Lake
ST. JOHNS DR.

D

Lilydale
13
BUTLER
ANNAPOLIS ST.
GEORGE ST.
St. Paul Downtown Airport (Holman Field)
Pigs Eye Lake
LOWER AFTON
LINWOOD AV.
HIGHWOOD AV.
494
STEEPLE VIEW RD.
Woodbury
Colby Lake
WOODBURY
Afton
40TH ST. S.

Mendota Heights
WACHTLER
CHARLTON
West St. Paul
WENTWORTH
THOMPSON AV.
South St. Paul
SOUTHVIEW BLVD.
CARVER AV.
61
BAILEY RD.
RADIO DR.

E

Sunfish Lake
MENDOTA
110
DELAWARE
DODD RD.
Rogers Lake
ROBERT ST.
OAKDALE
15TH AV.
9TH AV.
5TH AV.
Newport
POINT DOUGLAS
MILITARY RD.
TOWER
DALE
GLEN RD.
WOODLANE
KEATS
COTTAGE GROVE
MANNING

494
49
52
70TH
LONE OAK
55
Inver Grove
BABCOCK
CAHILL
CUNEEN TR.
CONCORD BLVD.
St. Paul Park
65TH
70TH ST.
95
MILITARY
Cottage Grove

F

YANKEE DOODLE RD.
ALVERNO AV.
Heights
COLLEGE TR.
BARNES AV.
INVER GROVE TR.
Mississippi River
HASTINGS AV.
HADLEY AV.
61
95

DIFFLEY RD.
DODD RD.
ROBERT ST.
RICH VALLEY TR.
105TH ST.
52
56
3RD ST.

N

0 1 2
Scale of Miles
© C.S.C.

G

6 7 8 9 10 11

Scale of Miles
0 1 2 3

©C.S.C.

NEW ORLEANS

KENNER
METAIRIE
EAST END
HARAHAN
AIRLINE PARK
JEFFERSON HTS.
AVONDALE
WAGGAMAN
WILLSWOOD
LIVE OAK MANOR
AMA
ST. ROSE
LONE STAR
DESTREHAN
MARRERO
WESTWEGO
GRETNA
HARVEY
ARABI
CHALMETTE
MERAUX
POYDRAS
ST. BERNARD
CAERNARVON
BRAITHWAITE
ENGLISH TURN
SAINT CLAIR
BELLE CHASSE
SCARSDALE
CONCESSION
STELLA
DALCOUR
BERTRANDVILLE
WILLS POINT
AUGUSTA
CEDAR GROVE
OAKVILLE
LIVE OAK
JESUIT BEND
CROWN POINT
JEAN LAFITTE
ESTELLE

ORLEANS PARISH
JEFFERSON PARISH
ST. BERNARD PARISH
PLAQUEMINES PARISH
JEFFERSON PARISH
ST. BERNARD
PLAQUEMINES
JEFFERSON PARISH
ST. CHARLES PARISH

Lake Pontchartrain
Lake
Lake Pontchartrain Causeway (Toll)
Lake Salvador
Lake Cataouatche
Couba Island

Mississippi River

New Orleans Lakefront Airport
New Orleans International Airport

Scale of Miles
0 1 2 3
© C.S.C.

NEW YORK
NEW JERSEY

ORANGE CO.
ROCKLAND CO.

PASSAIC CO.
BERGEN CO.

ROCKLAND CO.
BERGEN CO.

WESTCHESTER CO.
BRONX CO.

BERGEN CO.
HUDSON CO.

PASSAIC CO.
ESSEX CO.

Hudson River
Tappan Zee
Tappan Zee Bridge

THORNWOOD
HAWTHORNE
CHAPPAQUA
PLEASANTVILLE
VALHALLA
WHITE PLAINS
HARTSDALE
SCARSDALE
EASTCHESTER
GREENVILLE
ARDSLEY
DOBBS FERRY
HASTINGS-ON-HUDSON
IRVINGTON
EAST IRVINGTON
DOBBS FERRY
BRONXVILLE
MT. VERNON
PELHAM
PELHAM MANOR
NEW ROCHELLE
YONKERS
BRONX
RIVERDALE

POCANTICO HILL
EAST VIEW
GLENVILLE
TARRYTOWN
NORTH TARRYTOWN
SOUTH TARRYTOWN
ARCHVILLE
NYACK
UPPER NYACK
CENTRAL NYACK
WEST NYACK
VALLEY COTTAGE
BARDONIA
GRAND VIEW
PIERMONT
SPARKILL
PALISADES
NORTHVALE
NORWOOD
ROCKLEIGH
HARRINGTON PARK
ALPINE
CLOSTER
CRESSKILL
DUMONT
BERGENFIELD
TENAFLY
ENGLEWOOD
FORT LEE
PALISADES PARK
RIDGEFIELD PARK
HACKENSACK

ORANGEBURG
TAPPAN
OLD TAPPAN
MONTVALE
PARK RIDGE
WOODCLIFF LAKE
RIVER VALE
HILLSDALE
WESTWOOD
EMERSON
ORADELL
PARAMUS
MAYWOOD
LITTLE FERRY
BLAUVELT
PEARL RIVER
SPRING VALLEY
HILL CREST
MT. IVY
LADENTOWN
VIOLA
MONSEY
TALLMAN
AIRMONT
UPPER SADDLE RIVER
SADDLE RIVER
ALLENDALE
WALDWICK
HOHOKUS
RIDGEWOOD
GLEN ROCK
FAIR LAWN
ELMWOOD PARK
SADDLE BROOK
GARFIELD
LODI
PASSAIC
HASBROUCK HTS.
WOOD RIDGE
NEW ROCHELLE

RAMSEY
MAHWAH
SUFFERN
HILLBURN
SLOATSBURG
TUXEDO PARK
HEWITT
RINGWOOD
ERSKINE
WANAQUE
OAKLAND
FRANKLIN LAKES
WYCKOFF
MIDLAND PARK
WALDWICK
HAWTHORNE
N. HALEDON
HALEDON
WAYNE
TOTOWA
PATERSON
WEST PATERSON
LITTLE FALLS
CLIFTON
CEDAR GROVE
N. CALDWELL
WEST CALDWELL
FAIRFIELD
PINE BROOK
POMPTON PLAINS
BLOOMINGDALE
POMPTON LAKES
PEQUANNOCK
LINCOLN PARK

Kensico Res.
Lake de Forest
Oradell Res.
Tallman Mtn. State Park
Wanaque Res.
Point View Res.
Black Oak Ridge Rd.

Scale of Miles

© C.S.C.

Atlantic Ocean

Manhattan

QUEENS
FLUSHING
JAMAICA
SPRINGFIELD GDNS.
QUEENS VILL.
FOREST HILLS
RICHMOND HILL
OZONE PARK
JACKSON HTS.
ASTORIA
LONG ISLAND CITY
GREEN POINT
COLLEGE POINT
BAYSIDE
SADDLE ROCK
KINGS POINTS

John F. Kennedy International Airport
La Guardia Airport
Rikers Is.

FAR ROCKAWAY
EDGEMERE
Jamaica Bay
CANARSIE
E. NEW YORK
BROOKLYN
FLATBUSH
BENSON HURST
CONEY ISLAND
BAY RIDGE

KINGS CO.
QUEENS CO.
KINGS CO.
RICHMOND CO.

NEW YORK
Lower Bay
Verrazano Narrows Bridge

STATEN ISLAND
NEW BRIGHTON
CASTLETON CORNERS
DONGAN HILLS
NEW DORP
NEW DORP BEACH
GREAT KILLS
PORT RICHMOND
WILLOW BROOK
CHELSEA
ROSSVILLE
HUGUENOT
HUGUENOT PARK
PERTH AMBOY

BAYONNE
JERSEY CITY
HUDSON CO.
SECAUCUS
NORTH BERGEN
WEST NEW YORK
UNION CITY
WEEHAWKEN
HOBOKEN
GUTTENBERG
CLIFFSIDE PARK
RIDGEFIELD

NEWARK
Newark International Airport
KEARNY
HARRISON
IRVINGTON
EAST ORANGE
ORANGE
SOUTH ORANGE
MAPLEWOOD
MILLBURN
SPRINGFIELD
UNION
ELIZABETH
LINDEN
ROSELLE
ROSELLE PARK
CRANFORD
GARWOOD
CLARK
RAHWAY
AVENEL
WOODBRIDGE
PORT READING
SEWAREN
CARTERET
COLONIA
ISELIN
FORDS

EAST RUTHERFORD
RUTHERFORD
LYNDHURST
NORTH ARLINGTON
BELLEVILLE
NUTLEY
BLOOMFIELD
CALDWELL
ROSELAND
LIVINGSTON
WEST ORANGE

ESSEX CO.
UNION CO.
MIDDLESEX CO.

Hudson River
East River
Harlem River
Passaic River
Hackensack River
Newark Bay
Upper Bay
Gravesend Bay
Jamaica Bay
Arthur Kill
Kill van Kull

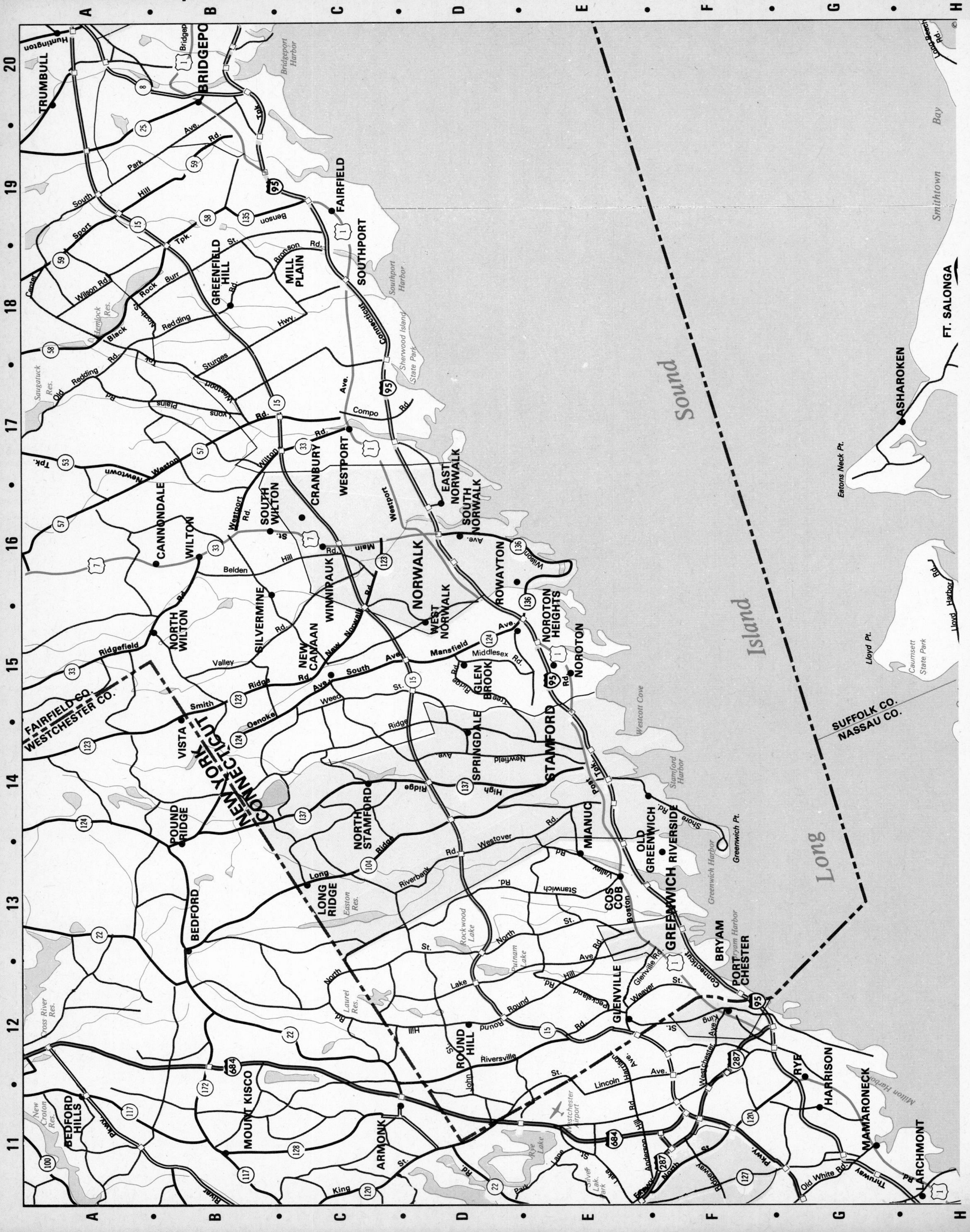

TRUMBULL
BRIDGEPORT
FAIRFIELD
SOUTHPORT
GREENFIELD HILL
MILL PLAIN
WESTPORT
CRANBURY
EAST NORWALK
SOUTH NORWALK
ROWAYTON
NOROTON HEIGHTS
NOROTON
CANNONDALE
WILTON
SOUTH WILTON
NORWALK
WEST NORWALK
NORTH WILTON
SILVERMINE
WINNIPAUK
NEW CANAAN
MANSFIELD
GLEN BROOK
STAMFORD
SPRINGDALE
VISTA
POUND RIDGE
BEDFORD
NORTH STAMFORD
LONG RIDGE
MIANUC
OLD GREENWICH
RIVERSIDE
COS COB
BYRAM
PORT CHESTER
GREENWICH
GLENVILLE
ROUND HILL
RIVERSVILLE
BEDFORD HILLS
MOUNT KISCO
ARMONK
RYE
HARRISON
MAMARONECK
LARCHMONT
ASHAROKEN
FT. SALONGA

Long Island Sound
Sound
Island
Long

NEW YORK
CONNECTICUT

FAIRFIELD CO.
WESTCHESTER CO.

SUFFOLK CO.
NASSAU CO.

Scale of Miles

© C.S.C.

SMITH TOWN
NORTH SMITH TOWN
VILLAGE OF THE BRANCH
HAUPPAUGE
CENTRAL ISLIP
EAST ISLIP
ISLIP
BAY SHORE
BRIGHTWATERS
FAIR HARBOR
SAN REMO
KINGS PARK
BRENTWOOD
MIDDLEVILLE
NORTHPORT
EAST NORTHPORT
ELWOOD
GREEN LAWN
CENTER PORT
HALESITE
HUNTINGTON STATION
MELVILLE
DEER PARK
WYANDANCH
WEST BABYLON
BABYLON
LINDENHURST
OAK BEACH
LLOYD HARBOR
HUNTINGTON
COLD SPRING HARBOR
WOODBURY
PLAINVIEW
BETHPAGE
FARMINGDALE
COPIAGUE
AMITYVILLE
NASSAU SHORES
MASSAPEQUA
OYSTER BAY
EAST NORWICH
SYOSSET
HICKSVILLE
LEVITTOWN
WANTAGH
SEAFORD
BELLMORE
BAYVILLE
LOCUST VALLEY
JERICHO
NEW CASSEL
EAST MEADOW
MERRICK
FREEPORT
ROOSEVELT
BALDWIN
ISLAND PARK
LIDO BEACH
LATTINGTOWN
GLEN COVE
SEA CLIFF
GLENWOOD LANDING
GREENVALE
EAST HILLS
WESTBURY
CARLE PLACE
UNIONDALE
ROCKVILLE CENTRE
OCEANSIDE
LONG BEACH
SANDS POINT
MANORHAVEN
PORT WASHINGTON
FLOWER HILL
MANHASSET
ROSLYN HTS.
MUNSEY PARK
WILLISTON PARK
ALBERTSON
GARDEN CITY PARK
NEW HYDE PARK
FRANKLIN SQUARE
ELMONT
LYNBROOK
HEWLETT
EAST ROCKAWAY
BAYPARK
CEDARHURST
LAWRENCE
ATLANTIC BEACH
THOMASTON
GREAT NECK
SADDLE ROCK
BELLE ROSE
QUEENS VILLAGE
VALLEY STREAM
INWOOD
NASSAU CO.
QUEENS CO.

Great South Bay
Fire Island
Atlantic Ocean
Long Island Sound
Oyster Bay
Hempstead Harbor
Manhasset Bay
Jones Beach State Park
Robert Moses State Park
Belmont Lake State Park
Bethpage State Park
Captree State Park
Republic Airport
Kennedy International

Robert Moses Causeway

N

Cities and Towns

NEWPORT NEWS
TABB
POQUOSON
HAMPTON
FOX HILL
BUCKROE BEACH
NORFOLK
VIRGINIA BEACH
PORTSMOUTH
CHURCHLAND
WEST NORFOLK
BARTLETT
ECLIPSE
CRITTENDEN
HOBSON
SANDY BOTTOM
TWIN PINES
HUNTERSVILLE
BELLEVILLE
NANSEMOND SHORES
SLEEPY HOLE
PUGHSVILLE
BENNETT CORNER
DRIVER
CHADSWYCK
BEAMON
GENEVA PARK
GILMERTON
CRESTWOOD
SOUTH NORFOLK
SUFFOLK
MILLVILLEO
DEEP CREEK
GRASSFIELD
CAMDEN MILLS
GREAT BRIDGE
FENTRESS
MOUNT PLEASANT
OAK GROVE
BUTTS
ESSEX MEADOWS
KEMPSVILLE
EUCLID
ACREDALE
SALEM
MEARS CORNER
ARAGONA VILLAGE

Labels and Features

Patrick Henry Airport
Yorktown
Plum Tree Island National Wildlife Refuge
Plum Tree Island Bombing Range
Plum Tree Pt.
YORK CO.
Back River
N.A.S.A.
Langley AFB
Chesapeake Bay
Virginia Assoc. Research Center
Christopher Newport College
Thomas Nelson Comm. College
Mariners Museum Park
NEWPORT NEWS CITY ISLE OF WIGHT CO.
Apprentice School of Newport News
Newport News Shipbuilding and Dry Dock
James River
Batten Bay
NANSEMOND CO.
Hampton Roads
HAMPTON CITY
U.S. Military Reservation Fort Monroe
Old Point Comfort
Willoughby Bay
U.S. Naval Shipyard
Athletic Center
Little Creek Amphibious Naval Base
Lynnhaven Roads
Chesapeake Bay Bridge-Tunnel Toll
Lake Whitehurst
Norfolk Airport
Virginia Wesleyan College
Old Dominion Univ.
Tidewater Comm. College
U.S. Army Corps of Engr. Disposal Area
Elizabeth River
PORTSMOUTH CITY
VIRGINIA BEACH CITY
Lake Smith
U.S. Naval Shipyard
Hampton Roads Airport
U.S. Naval Ammunition Depot
Dismal Swamp National Wildlife Refuge
Tidewater Comm. College
Stumpy Lake
NANSEMOND CO. CHESAPEAKE CITY
VIRGINIA BEACH CITY CHESAPEAKE CITY

ARCADIA

Arcadia Lake

Central State Univ.

Edmond Mem. Hosp.

EDMOND

Okla. Christian College

Turner Turnpike

JONES

THE VILLAGE

NICHOLS HILLS

Lake Hefner

Oklahoma City G.C.

Belle Isle Lake

Midwest Christian College

National Cowboy Hall of Fame

Expressway Junction Airport

LAKE ALUMA

FOREST PARK

SPENCER

NICOMA PARK

YUKON

CANADIAN CO.
OKLAHOMA CO.

Wiley Post Airport

WARR ACRES

BETHANY

Deaconess Hosp.

Will Rogers Park

WOODLAWN PARK

Bethany Gen. Hosp.

OKLAHOMA CITY

Okla. City Univ.

State Capitol

Lincoln Park

Univ. of Okla. Med. Center

O.S.U. Tech.

Civic Center

Downtown Airport

CHOCTAW

MIDWEST CITY

Midwest City Mem. Hosp.

SMITH VILLAGE

DEL CITY

Rose State College

Tinker

South Comm. Hosp.

Will Rogers World Airport

F.A.A. Ctr.

Tinker Air Force Base

Oklahoma City Air Force Station

Diagonal

MUSTANG

Okla. City Comm. College

OKLAHOMA CO.
CLEVELAND CO.

VALLEY BROOK

Stanly Draper Lake

GRADY CO.
CLEVELAND CO.
MC CLAIN CO.

Canadian River

MOORE

NEWCASTLE

NORMAN

Scale of Miles
0   1   2   3

© C.S.C.

Northwest Expy.

Proposed Outer Loop

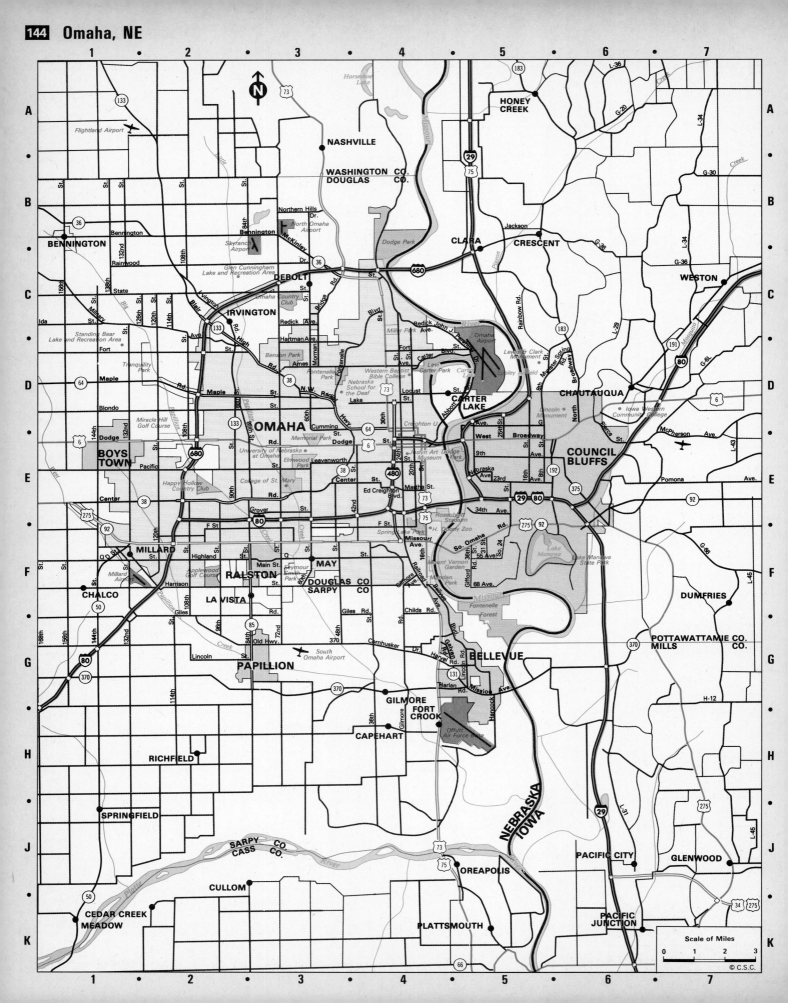

Scale of Miles

0   1   2   3

1 2 3 4 5 6 7

A B C D E F G H J K

Plymouth
Peterson Rd.
Main St.
Lake Ave.
Votaw Rd.
Thompson Rd.
Pleasant Hill Rd.
Wekiwa Springs Rd.
Line Dr.
Acre Rd.
Wekiwa Springs
Sanlando Springs
Lake Brantley
Wekiwa River
4
17
92

Apopka
441
1st St.
Cleveland Ave.
Sheeler Ave.
Lake Ave.
Green Rd.
Bear Lake
Forest City
Semoran
Altamonte Springs
Blvd.

Lust Rd.
Boy Scout Rd.
Hooper Farms Rd.
Binion Rd.
Keene Rd.
Marden Rd.
Lake Rd.
Lake Lotus
Spring Lake
Oranole Rd.
Maitland
Haratio Ave.
Lake Howell Rd.
Branch Rd.

LAKE APOPKA
437
McCormick Rd.
Ingram Rd.
Beggs Rd.
Rose Rd.
Rundle Rd.
Riverside Park Rd.
Lockhart
Lake
Eatonville
Lake Maitland
Winter Park
Goldenrod
Webster Ave.
Aloma Ave.

Clarcona
Clarcona-Ocoee
Sully Rd.
Long Rd.
Lee Rd.
Fairbanks Ave.
Loch Ferry Rd.
Lake Virginia
Lakemont

Ocoee
Clarona Ocoee
Apopka Vineland
Northlin Rd.
Lake Wekiwa
Big Lake Fairview
Edgewater Dr.
John Young Park Way
New Hampshire St.
Princeton Ave.
Lake Baldwin

Fuller Cross Rd.
E. Crown Point Rd.
Silver Star Rd.
Fairvilla
Pine Hills
Powers Dr.
Pine St.

Winter Garden
Starke Lake
Tildenville
Park Ave.
50
Winter Garden Rd.
Old Winter Garden Rd.
Colonial Dr.
Herndon Airport
East-West Expwy.

545
Black Lake
Lake Rd.
Lake Hiawassee
Orlovista
Lake Mann
Washington
Church St.
Central Ave.
ORLANDO
435
Gotha
Steer
Hiawassee Rd.
Cleveland Ave.
Miles Ave.
Curry Ford Rd.
Grant Ave.
15

Tilden Rd.
Lake Down
Conroy Rd.
Turkey Lake
Kirkman Rd.
L.B. McLeod Rd.
Clear Lake
Trail
Kaley St.
Michigan Ave.
527
Lake Holden
Pershing Ave.

Lake Speer
Lake Hancock
Lake Butler
Orlando Vineland Rd.
Americana Blvd.
Texas Ave.
Rio Grande Ave.
Orange Ave.
Holden Ave.
Lake Jessamine
Edgewood
Gatlin Ave.
Conway Hoffner Rd.
436

Lake Tibet Butler
Winter Garden Rd.
Vineland Rd.
Lake
Oak Ridge Rd.
Sand Lake Rd.
Lancaster Rd.
Lake Conway
Belle Isle
Conway Rd.
McCoy Rd.

Lake Mabel
Lake Sheen
Little Sand Lake
Big Sand Lake
Sunshine State Pkwy.
Pine Castle
J Rd.

WALT DISNEY WORLD
Bay Lake
Reams Rd.
Lake Hancock Rd.
Apopka Vineland Rd.
Turkey Lake Rd.
528
Bee Line Expwy.
Thorpe St.
Fourth St.
Taft
NAVAL TRAINING CENTER
ORLANDO INTERNATIONAL AIRPORT

VACATION KINGDOM
Disney Entrance Rd.
Sea World
Vineland
Gatorland
McCoy Rd.

Lake Buena Vista
441
17
92
N
Canal
Boggy Creek Rd.

4
Lake Bryan
Reedy Creek
192

Scale of Miles
0 1 2 3
© C.S.C.

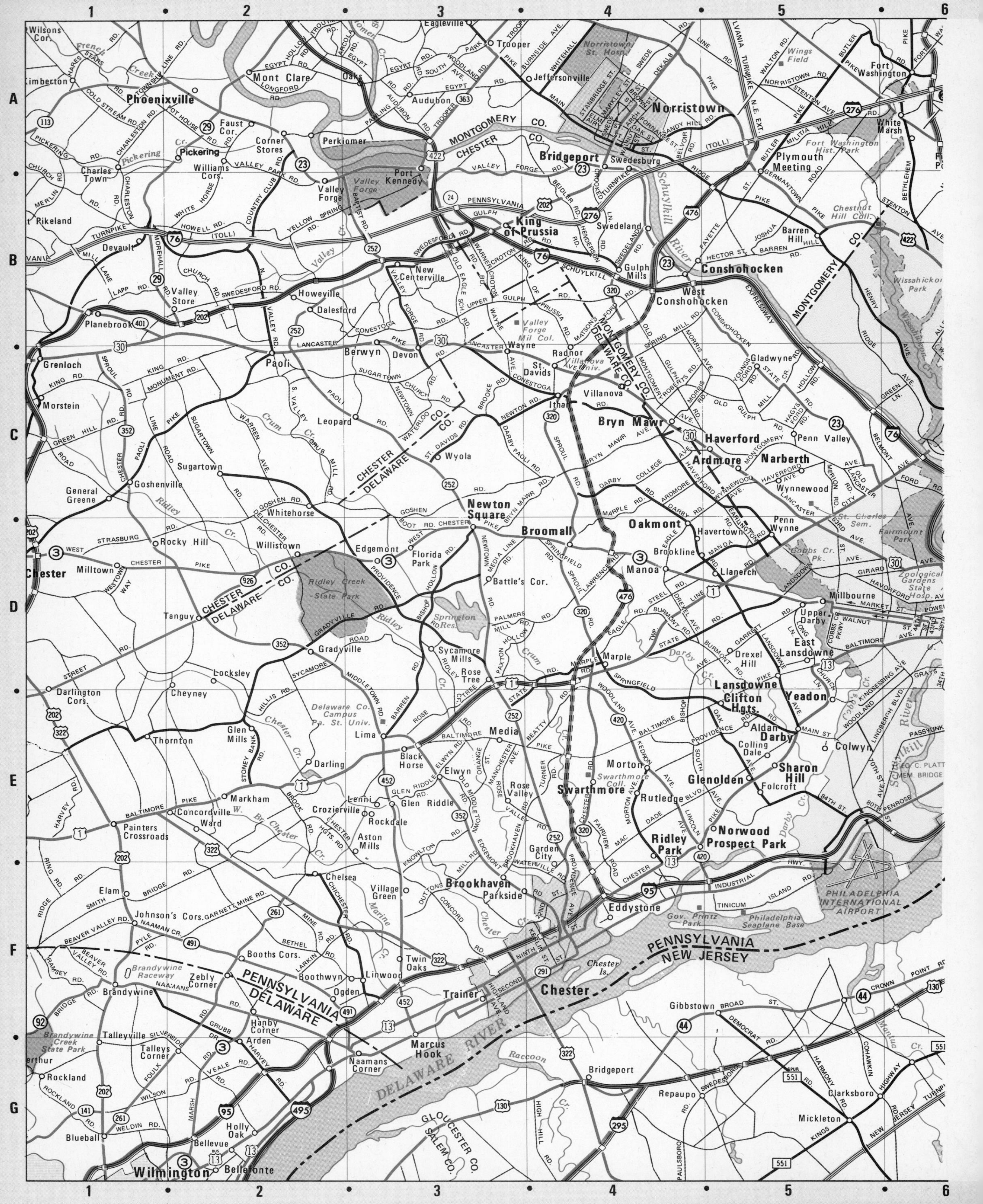

Grid columns: 1 2 3 4 5 6
Grid rows: A B C D E F G

Places and labels:

Wilsons Cor., Limberton, French Creek, Hares Stars Rd., Mont Clare, Oaks, Eagleville, Trooper, Norristown St. Hosp., Wings Field, Fort Washington, Phoenixville, Egypt Rd., Audubon, Jeffersonville, Norristown, White Marsh, Faust Cor., Corner Stores, Williams Cors., Pickering, Perkiomer, Port Kennedy, Bridgeport, Swedesburg, Plymouth Meeting, Fort Washington Hist. Park, Chestnut Hill Coll., Charles Town, Merlin Rd., Rikeland, Valley Forge, King of Prussia, Swedeland, Barren Hill, Devault, Valley Store, Planebrook, Howeville, Dalesford, New Centerville, Gulph Mills, West Conshohocken, Conshohocken, Wissahickon Park, Grenloch, Morstein, Paoli, Berwyn, Devon, Wayne, Radnor, St. Davids, Villanova, Bryn Mawr, Haverford, Penn Valley, Gladwyne, Narberth, Ardmore, Wynnewood, Sugartown, General Greene, Goshenville, Whitehorse, Leopard, Wyola, Newton Square, Broomall, Oakmont, Havertown, Penn Wynne, St. Charles Sem., Fairmount Park, Chester, Milltown, Rocky Hill, Willistown, Edgemont, Florida Park, Battle's Cor., Brookline, Manoa, Llanerch, Millbourne, Zoological Gardens, Tanguy, Ridley Creek State Park, Gradyville, Sycamore Mills, Rose Tree, Palmers, Marple, Drexel Hill, Upper Darby, East Lansdowne, Darlington Cors., Cheyney, Locksley, Glen Mills, Thornton, Darling, Lima, Black Horse, Media, Morton, Lansdowne, Clifton Hgts., Yeadon, Aldan, Darby, Colwyn, Markham, Concordville, Crozierville, Glen Riddle, Rose Valley, Swarthmore, Rutledge, Glenolden, Sharon Hill, Folcroft, Painters Crossroads, Ward, Lenni, Rockdale, Aston Mills, Garden City, Ridley Park, Norwood, Prospect Park, Elam, Chelsea, Village Green, Brookhaven, Parkside, Eddystone, Philadelphia International Airport, Johnson's Cors., Zebly Corner, Booths Cors., Boothwyn, Linwood, Twin Oaks, Trainer, Chester, Gov. Printz Park, Philadelphia Seaplane Base, Tinicum, Brandywine, Ogden, Naamans Corner, Marcus Hook, Bridgeport, Gibbstown, Talleyville, Talleys Corner, Arden, Hanby Corner, Raccoon, Repaupo, Clarksboro, Rockland, Blueball, Bellevue, Bellefonte, Wilmington, Mickleton

Counties: MONTGOMERY CO., CHESTER CO., DELAWARE CO., GLOUCESTER CO., SALEM CO.

State lines: PENNSYLVANIA / NEW JERSEY, PENNSYLVANIA / DELAWARE

Rivers: Schuylkill River, DELAWARE RIVER, French Creek, Ridley Creek, Crum Creek, Chester Creek, Brandywine Creek

Route markers: 113, 29, 23, 422, 202, 276, 76, 252, 401, 30, 3, 352, 926, 322, 491, 452, 1, 13, 476, 320, 420, 291, 95, 495, 551, 44, 130, 295, 92, 141, 261

Parks: Brandywine Creek State Park, Brandywine Raceway, Delaware Co. Campus Pa. St. Univ.

PHILADELPHIA

Places (Pennsylvania side)

Willow Grove, Trevose, Oakford, Middletown, Feasterville, Lincoln, Edgely, Bryn Athyn, Bucks Co., Montgomery Co., Fitzwatertown, Roslyn, Abington, Bethayres, Philmont, Philmont, Newportville, Croydon, Bristol, Oreland, Edge Hill, Glenside, Jenkintown, Ogontz Campus Pa. St. Univ., North Philadelphia Airport, Cornwells Hgts., Andalusia, Burlington Island, Memorial Bridge, Ogontz, Rockledge, Elkins Park, Melrose Park, Cheltenham, Holy Family Coll., Liberty Bell Race Track, Philadelphia State Hospital Co. Prison, State Hospital, La Salle Coll., Juniata Park, Hunting Park, Frankford Arsenal, Tacony-Palmyra Bridge (Toll), PHILADELPHIA, Temple Univ., Girard Coll., Pettys Is., Benjamin Franklin Bridge (Toll), Independence Hall, Walt Whitman House, Camden, Woodlynne, Collingswood, Gloucester City, U.S. Naval Base, John F. Kennedy Sta., I.C.I. F.D. Roosevelt Park, Westmont, Oaklyn, Audubon, Haddon Hgts., Mt. Ephraim, Barrington, National Park, Westville, Brooklawn, Bellmawr, Woodbury, Woodbury Hgts., Deptford, Almonesson, Blackwood, Mantua, Wenonah, Fairview, Runnemede, Glendora, Somerdale, Stratford, Laurel Springs, Lindenwold, Clementon, Berlin, Pine Hill, Albion, Tansboro

Places (New Jersey side)

PENNSYLVANIA / NEW JERSEY, Burlington, Cooper & Lawrence House, Beverly, Delanco, Riverside, Willingboro, Deacons, Bridgeboro, Fairview, Riverton, Palmyra, Delair, Morrisville, Cinnaminson, Moorestown, Centerton, Rancocas, Rancocas State Park, Old Sch House, Mesonville, Hainesport, Delanco, County Home, House of Corr., Jordentown, Pennsauken, Maple Shade, Stanwick, Lenola, Merchantville, Mt. Laurel, Medford Fish & Wildlife Man. Area, Garden State Race Track, Cherry Hill, Ellisburg, Fellowship, Evesboro, Marlton, Haddonfield, Springdale, Springdale, Cox Corners, Indian King Tavern, Kirkwood, Gibbsboro, Coffins Corner, Ashland, Lawnside, Magnolia, Glendale, Kresson, Lake Pine, Taunton Lake, Taunton Lake, W. Berlin, Whitman Stafford House, Hopewell, Clementon

Counties / regions

Bucks Co., Montgomery Co., Burlington / Camden Co., Camden / Gloucester Co.

Route numbers (selected)

263, 532, 276, 413, 73, 63, 611, 152, 309, 232, 1, 13, 95, 132, 513, 543, 541, 528, 130, 537, 38, 90, 676, 30, 76, 561, 70, 41, 295, 42, 45, 47, 551, 168, 154, 573, 534, 553, 4, 3

Scale of Miles
0 1 2 3

N

© C.S.C.

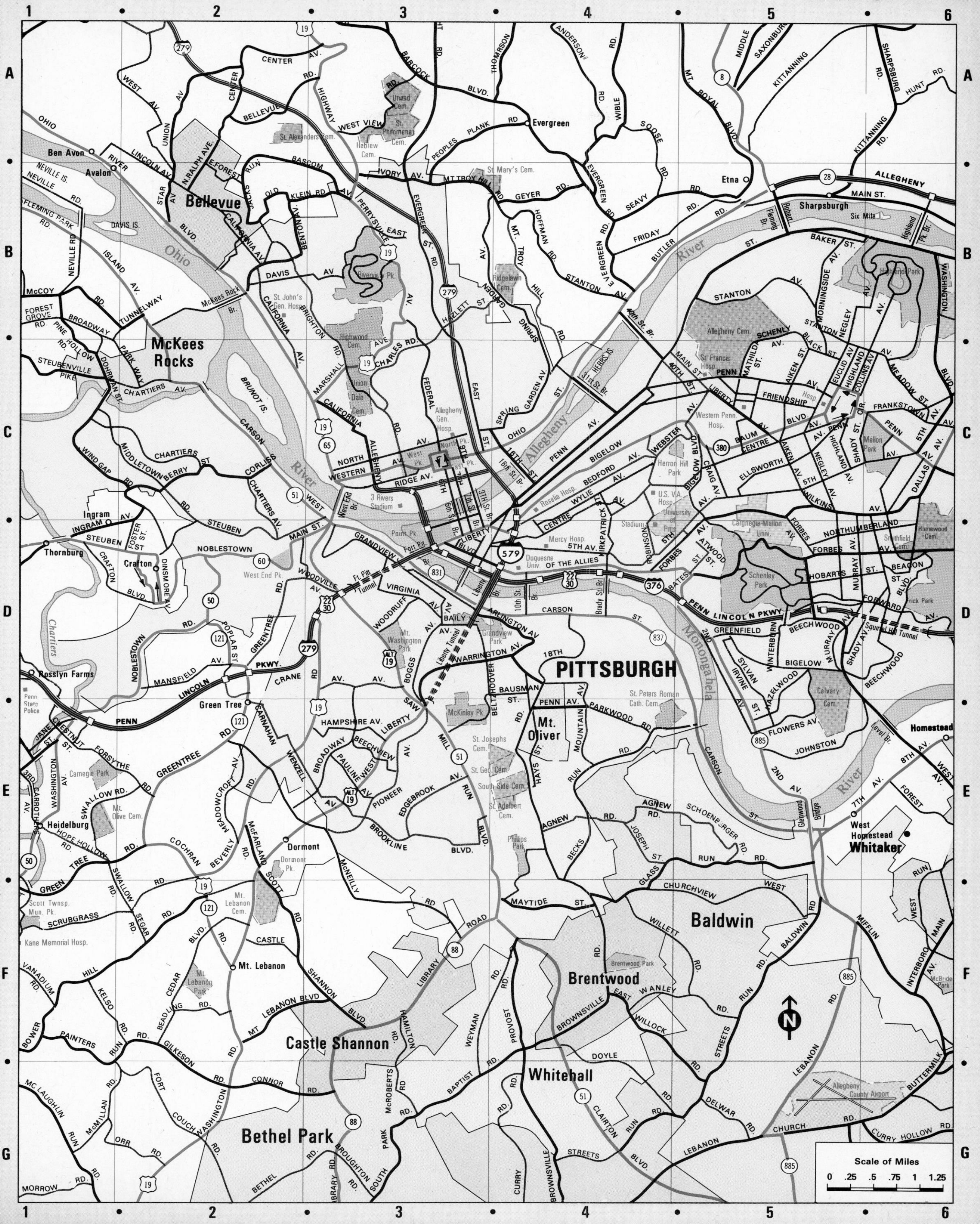
PITTSBURGH
Bellevue
McKees Rocks
Mt. Oliver
Baldwin
Brentwood
Castle Shannon
Whitehall
Bethel Park
Whitaker
Homestead
West Homestead
Sharpsburgh
Etna
Evergreen
Ben Avon
Avalon
Ingram
Thornburg
Crafton
Rosslyn Farms
Green Tree
Heidelburg
Dormont
Mt. Lebanon
Ohio River
Allegheny River
Monongahela River
Chartiers
Allegheny County Airport
Allegheny Cem.
Highland Park
Schenley Park
Riverview Pk.
3 Rivers Stadium
Duquesne Univ.
Carnegie-Mellon Univ.
University of Pitts.
Liberty Tunnel
Squirrel Hill Tunnel
Ft. Pitt Tunnel
PENN LINCOLN PKWY
BLVD. OF THE ALLIES
Scale of Miles
0 .25 .5 .75 1 1.25

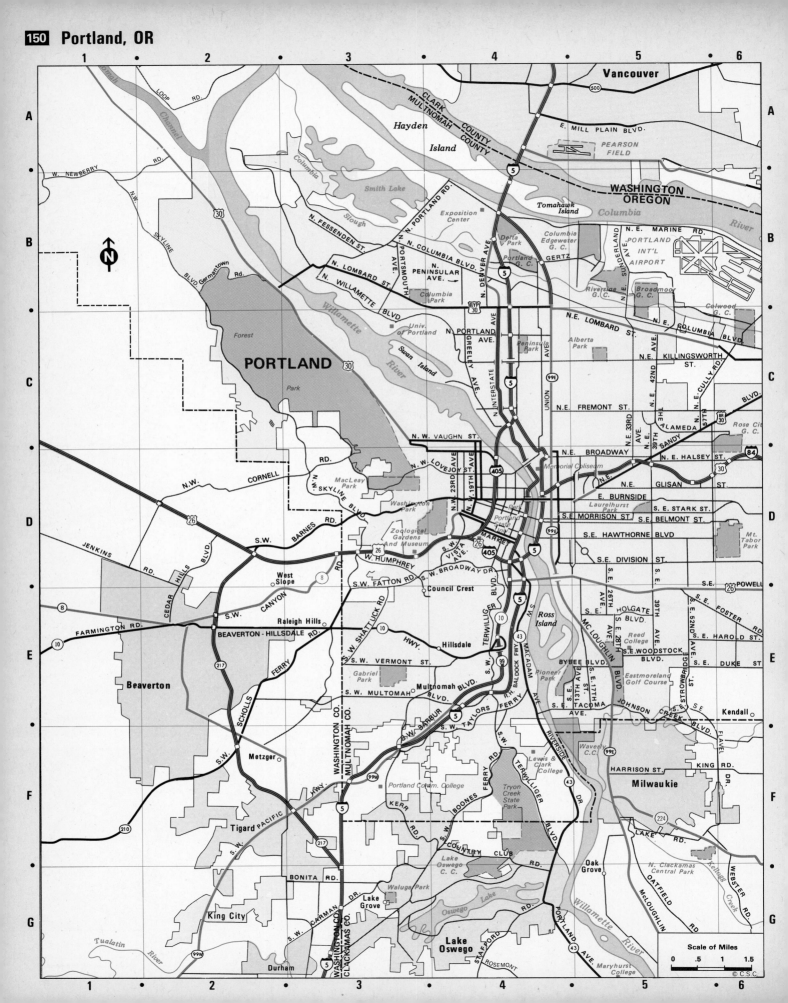

Scale of Miles
0   .5   1   1.5

©C.S.C.

Map Grid Reference (columns 1–7, rows A–K)

DAVIS COUNTY
SALT LAKE COUNTY

Great Salt Lake

Googin Drain

Consolidated Canal

N. Point

WOODS CROSS

BOUNTIFUL

68

15

NORTH SALT LAKE

215

2400 N. St.

Salt Lake City International Airport

Jordan River

Beck St.

Victory Rd.

City Creek Canyon Rd.

4000 W. St.

6th N. St.

11th Ave.

State Fair Ground

Fort Douglas Military Res.

I-80

North Temple St.

186

40

80

4th St.

3rd St.

S. Temple St.

Wasatch Dr.

Pioneer Trail State Park

65

Hogle Zoo

Utah State Capital

University of Utah

186

Mount Olivet Cemetery

Bonneville Golf Course

Tailings Pond

13th South St.

Liberty Park

9th E. St.

11th E. St.

1300 E. St.

California

Ave.

80

I-80

21st South

50A

201

3600 W. St.

215

SALT LAKE CITY

9th W. St.

71

40

186

WEST VALLEY CITY

3100 S. St.

3500 South

171

56th St.

4100 South

2700 W. St.

3900 South

MAGNA

West

West

West

Utah & Salt Lake Canal

21st South

Fairmont Dale

Sugarhouse Park

Forest Dale Golf Course

Briar's Way

Salt Lake Country Club Golf Course

3300 South

EAST MILLCREEK

4500 South

2300 E.

700 East

SOUTH SALT LAKE

171

State St.

7th E. St.

HOLLADAY

215

BACCHUS

111

8000

7200

4700 South

5400 South

266

215

TAYLORS-VILLE

MURRAY

KNUDSEN CORNER

KEARNS

6200 South

BENNION

Redwood Rd.

Jordan River

UNION

East

215

152

WEST JORDAN

Salt Lake City Municipal Airport

7800 South

48

MIDVALE

15

50A

2000 E.

210

210

National

Wasatch

COPPERTON

48

9000 South

89

91

700 East

SANDY

9400 South

1300 E.

GRANITE

10200 South

10400 South

10600 South

SOUTH JORDAN

CRESCENT

71

TOOELE CO.

N

11800 South

12600 South

71

RIVERTON

68

111

DRAPER

LARK

111

HERRIMAN

Proto

91

SALT LAKE COUNTY

UTAH CO.

BLUFFDALE

Reservoir

15

50A

UTAH CO.

Camp Williams Military Res.

Scale of Miles

0   1   2   3

© C.S.C.

Alton

Wood River

North Wood River

MADISON COUNTY
ST. CHARLES COUNTY

ILLINOIS
MISSOURI

West Alton

Missouri River

Spanish Lake

Black Jack

Florissant

Ferguson

Hazelwood

Berkeley

Bridgeton

Bridgeton Terr.

St. Ann

St. John

Breckenridge Hills

Overland

Olivette

Creve Coeur

Granite City

Venice

Madison

MADISON COUNTY
ST. CLAIR COUNTY

MADISON COUNTY
ST. LOUIS COUNTY

MISSOURI
ILLINOIS

Mississippi River

Bellefontaine Neighbors

Jennings

Delwood

Normandy

Northwoods

Pine Lawn

Cool Valley

Bellerive

Bel-Ridge

Kinloch

Pagedale

University City

DELBALIVIERE

Woodson Terr.

Mary Ridge

ST. CHARLES COUNTY
ST. LOUIS COUNTY

LAMBERT ST. LOUIS INTERNATIONAL

Creve Coeur Memorial Park

St. Charles Airport

Bischertown

St. Charles

Elm Point

Creve Coeur Airport

© C.S.C.

ST. LOUIS

East St. Louis

Brooklyn · National City · Centreville · Cahokia · Sauget · Dupo · Columbia

Clayton · Richmond Heights · Maplewood · Brentwood · Webster Groves · Shrewsbury

Ladue · Frontenac · Des Peres · Kirkwood · Rock Hill · Glendale · Watson Woods · Crestwood · Sunset Hills

Town and Country · Fenton · Arnold · Oakville · Maxville

MISSOURI / ILLINOIS

ST. LOUIS COUNTY / ST. CLAIR COUNTY

ST. CLAIR / MONROE COUNTY

ST. LOUIS COUNTY / JEFFERSON CO.

MERAMEC CO. / JEFFERSON CO.

Forest Park · Tower Grove Park · Carondelet Park

Meramec River · Mississippi River

National Museum Of Transportation

Scale of Miles
0 1 2 3 4

N

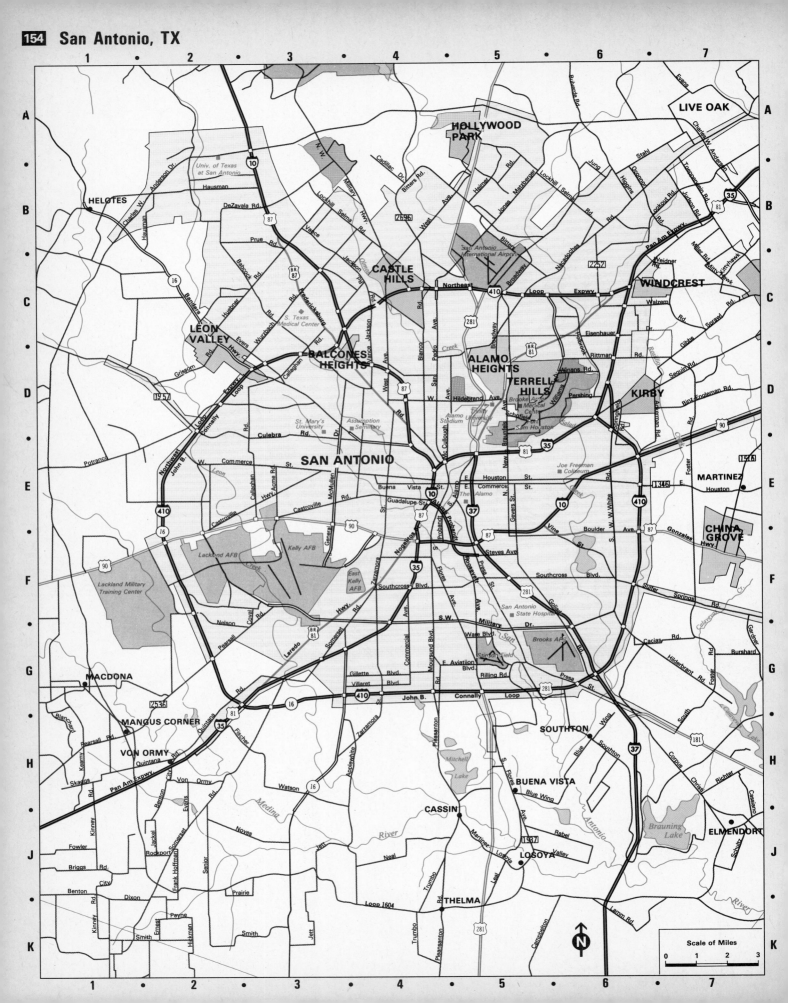

SOLANA BEACH
DEL MAR
SORRENTO
SAN DIEGO
MIRAMAR
POWAY
FERNBROOK
EUCALYPTUS HILLS
MORENO
LAKESIDE FARMS
CARLTON HILLS
LAKESIDE
LA JOLLA
SANTEE
LAKEVIEW
WINTER GARDENS
JOHNSTOWN
GLENVIEW
EL CAJON
MISSION BEACH
BALBOA PARK
GROSSMONT
MT. HELIX
CALAVO GARDENS
LA MESA
JAMACHA JUNCTION
JAMACHA
SPRING VALLEY
LEMON GROVE
DICTIONARY HILL
CORONADO
LA PRESA
NATIONAL CITY
LINCOLN ACRES
SUNNYSIDE
BONITA
LYNWOOD HILLS
HARBOR SIDE
CHULA VISTA
CASTLE PARK
OTAY
IMPERIAL BEACH
SAN YSIDRO
OTAY MESA

Pacific Ocean

Scale of Miles
0 1 2 3
© C.S.C.

Chipps Islan.
Pittsburg
Sacramento River
Seal Islands
U.S. NAVAL MAGAZINE PORT CHICAGO
Shore Acres
Clyde
Avon
Concord
Walnut Creek
Pleasant Hill
STATE GAME REFUGE
MT. DIABLO STATE PARK
Clayton
DOUGHERTY RD.
JOB CORPS TRAINING CENTER
San Ramon
Dublin
Danville
BLACKHAWK
TASSAJARA
SAN RAMON VALLEY
BOLLINGER CANYON
Las Trampas Regional Park
CULL CANYON
Lake Chabot
Crockett
Benicia
Martinez
Rodeo
Hercules
Pinole
Lafayette
Moraga
BRIONES REGIONAL PARK
St. Mary's College
San Pablo Res.
Upper San Leandro Res.
ANTHONY CHABOT REGIONAL PARK
Mills College
OAKLAND
Piedmont
Emeryville
Berkeley
U.C. BERKELEY
Albany
El Cerrito
Richmond
TILDEN REGIONAL PARK
WILDCAT CANYON REGIONAL PARK
Robert Sibley Regional Park
REDWOOD REGIONAL PARK
Alameda
OAKLAND METROPOLITAN INTERNATIONAL AIRPORT
ALAMEDA NAVAL AIR STATION
Treasure Island
Yerba Buena Island
OAKLAND BAY BRIDGE (TOLL)
SAN FRANCISCO
Angel Island State Park
Alcatraz Island
Tiburon
Belvedere
Sausalito
GOLDEN GATE
GOLDEN GATE BRIDGE (TOLL)
Ft. Baker
Cavallo Pt.
Hunters Point Naval Shipyard
Candlestick Park
SAN PABLO BAY
San Pablo Strait
San Rafael Bay
RICHMOND SAN RAFAEL BRIDGE (TOLL)
U.S. Naval Fuel Depot
San Rafael
San Pedro
Marin Is.
Carquinez Strait

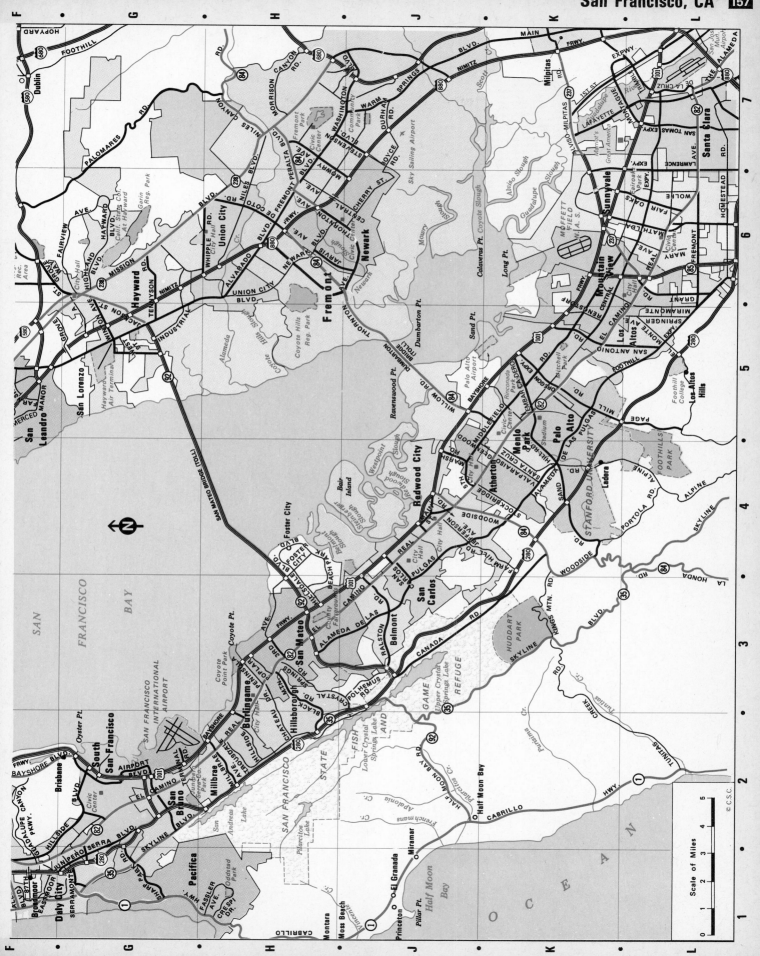

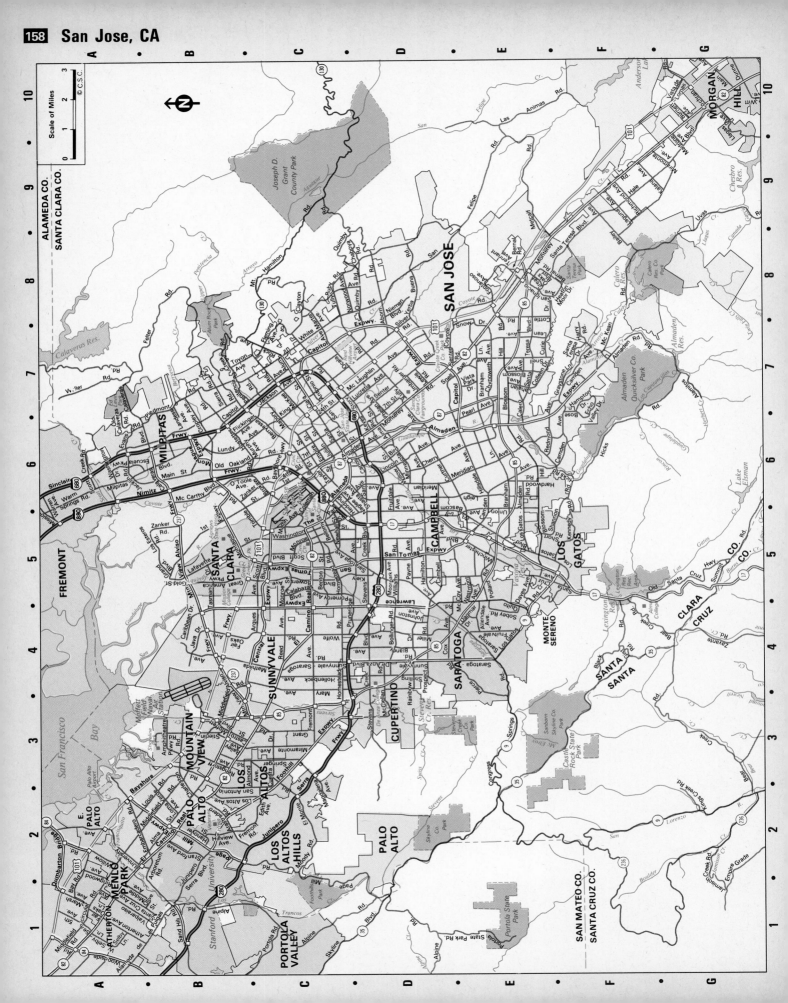

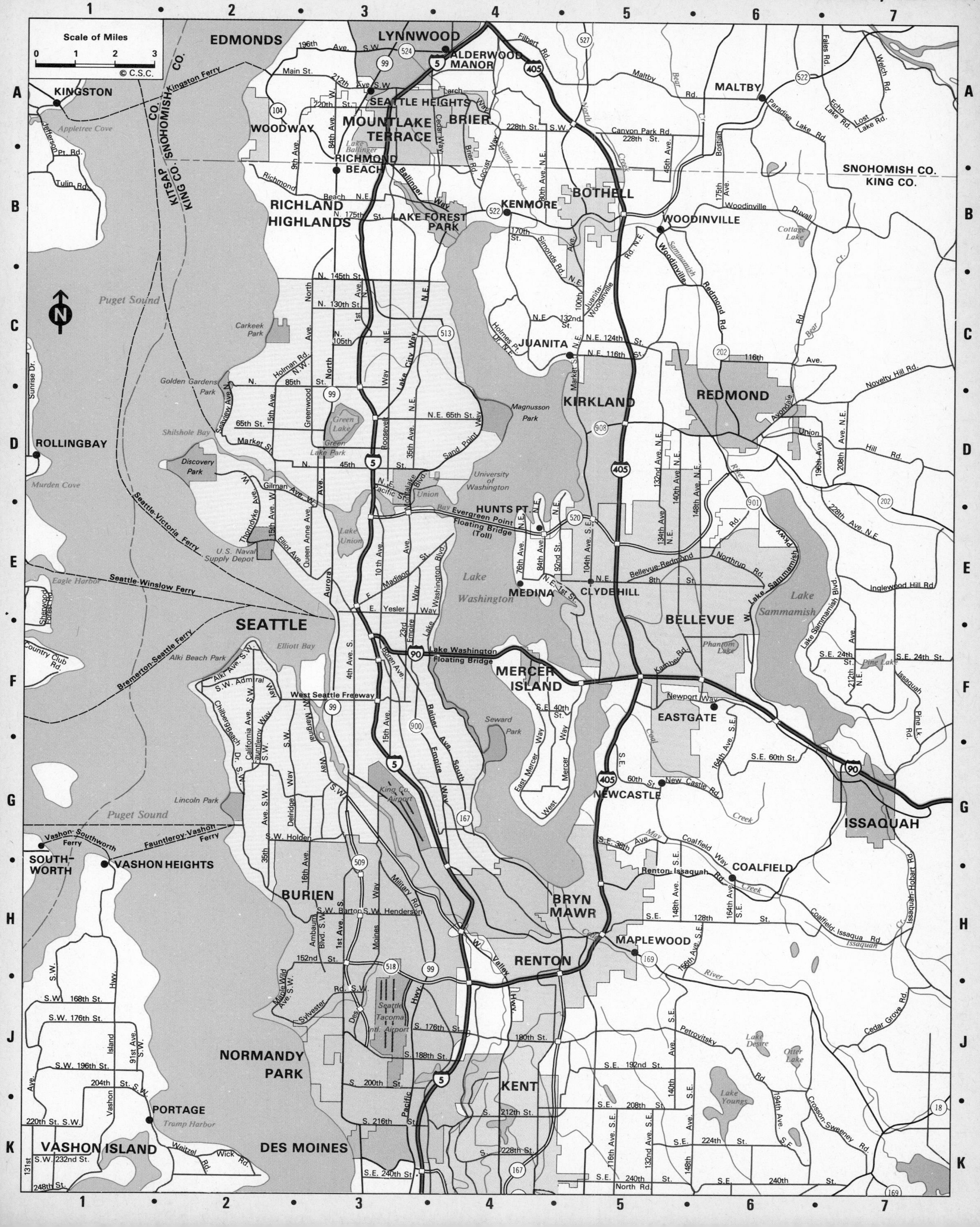
Scale of Miles
0 1 2 3
© C.S.C.
EDMONDS
LYNNWOOD
ALDERWOOD MANOR
KINGSTON
MALTBY
SEATTLE HEIGHTS
MOUNTLAKE TERRACE
BRIER
WOODWAY
RICHMOND BEACH
SNOHOMISH CO.
KING CO.
KITSAP CO.
BOTHELL
KENMORE
RICHLAND HIGHLANDS
LAKE FOREST PARK
WOODINVILLE
Puget Sound
Carkeek Park
Golden Gardens Park
JUANITA
KIRKLAND
REDMOND
Magnusson Park
Green Lake
Shilshole Bay
ROLLINGBAY
Discovery Park
Murden Cove
University of Washington
Lake Union
HUNTS PT.
Evergreen Point Floating Bridge (Toll)
U.S. Naval Supply Depot
Eagle Harbor
Seattle-Winslow Ferry
Seattle-Victoria Ferry
Lake Washington
MEDINA
CLYDE HILL
Lake Sammamish
BELLEVUE
SEATTLE
Elliott Bay
Bremerton-Seattle Ferry
Alki Beach Park
Lake Washington Floating Bridge
MERCER ISLAND
West Seattle Freeway
EASTGATE
Phantom Lake
Seward Park
King Co. Airport
Lincoln Park
NEWCASTLE
ISSAQUAH
Vashon-Southworth Ferry
Fauntleroy-Vashon Ferry
SOUTHWORTH
VASHON HEIGHTS
COALFIELD
BURIEN
BRYN MAWR
MAPLEWOOD
RENTON
Seattle Tacoma Intl. Airport
Lake Desire
Otter Lake
NORMANDY PARK
KENT
Lake Youngs
PORTAGE
Tramp Harbor
VASHON ISLAND
DES MOINES

Scale of Miles

0 1 2 3

© C.S.C.

Scale of Miles

0 1 2 3

© C.S.C.

Gulf of Mexico

SUNSET BEACH
ST. PETERSBURG BEACH
PASS-A-GRILLE BEACH
TIERRA VERDE

RUSKIN
GULF CITY
Park

Big Bayou
Lake Maggiore
St. Petersburg
Aquarium
Gordon Wax Museum
Florida Presbyterian College
Pinellas Bayway
Boca Ciega Bay

34th St. S.
22nd Ave. S.
62nd Ave. S.
66th Ave. S.
6th St.
4th St.
Country Club Way
Pinellas Pt. Dr.
693
699
19

Airport

N

Big

U.S. 89
Hwy.

Tucson-Florence

De Oesta
Camino
Thornydale
Magee
La
Cholla
Naranja
Dr.
Ln.
Lambert
Overton
Linda Vista Blvd.
La Canada
Hardy Rd.
Sage St.
Romero Rd.
Magee
Northway
89
Cortaro Farms
Casa Grande Hwy.
Ina
Shannon Rd.
Cholla
Orange Grove Dr.
La Canada
Ave.
Campbell Ave.
Skyline Dr.
Alvernon Way
Rd.
JAYNES
Sunrise Dr.
Snyder
Sunset Rd.
Camino De Oesta
Del Cerro
El Camino
Silverbell
Rillito
Ruthrauff Rd.
Creek
River
Canyon Rd.
Bear Canyon Rd.
Sweetwater
Dr.
Wetmore
Roger
Rd.
Rd.
Sabino
River Rd.
Freeway Airport
Goret Rd.
Flowing Wells
Fairview
Oracle
N. 1st
Ave.
Prince Ave.
Rd.
Swan Rd.
Craycroft
River Rd.
Camino Del Oesta
Ironwood Hill Dr.
Miracle Mile
Ft. Lowell
Ft. Lowell Rd.
Rd.
Teague Rd.
Wrightstown
Tanque
Ina
Grant
Miracle Mile
Stone
Grant
Way
Rd.
TUCSON
Sweetwater
Camino
Anklam Rd.
Marve Rd.
Speedway
Campbell Blvd.
Club Rd.
Speedway
Wilmot Rd.
Blvd.
Pantano
Freeway
Broadway
Randolph Park Municipal Golf Course
Alvernon
Swan
Rd.
Golf Links Rd.
22nd
Camino Seco
10
22nd
Fairland
St.
Davis-Monthan Air Force Base
36th
St.
Country
Stru.
Craycroft
Kolb Rd.
Escalante Rd.
Downtown Airport
86
Ajo Way
Irvington
Rd.
Golf Links Rd.
Irvington
SOUTH TUCSON
Tucson Ajo
Hwy.
Santa Cruz
Valley Rd.
Drexel
Rd.
Rd.
Tucson-Benson Hwy.
Davis-Monthan Air Force B.
LITTLETOWN
Valencia
Valencia
Missiondale
Valencia
Rd.
EMERY PARK
19
12th Ave.
Tucson-Nogales Hwy.
Tucson International Airport
Los Reales Rd.
Mission Rd.
6th Ave.
Access
Hughes
10
San Xavier Indian Reservation
San Xavier Indian Reservation
89
19
John F. Kennedy Park
Tucson

1 • 2 • 3 • 4 • 5 • 6 • 7

A
CLOPPER
BROWNSTOWN
GAITHERSBURG
118
117
124
Seneca Creek
State Park
Germantown
Blackrock Rd.
Goshen
Laytonville
Muncaster
Bowie Mill Rd.
108
OLNEY
SANDY SPRING
108
97
Ashton
ASHTON
650
Clarksville
108
Lime Kiln
Browns Rd.
HAMMOND PARK
FULTON
SCAGGSVILLE
216
HOWARD
29
Gorman Rd.

EMORY GROVE
REDLAND
WASHINGTON GROVE
NORBECK ESTATES
Needwood
270
Frederick
Redland Mill
115
Emory
182
Norwood
SYCAMORE ACRES
NORBECK
SPENCERVILLE
198
Spencerville
W. LAUREL
BURTONSVILLE
198
216
Riding Stable Rd.
Brooklyn Bridge Rd.

B
112
DARNESTOWN
MITCHELLS RANGE
QUINCE ORCHARD
HUNTING HILL
Darnestown
28
124
Quince Orchard
Lake Bernard Frank
Gude
Dr.
Avery
28
Norbeck
Bel Pre Rd.
LAYHILL
COLESVILLE
MEADOWOOD
FAIRLAND
EAST SPRINGBROOK
COLVERTON
MULRKIRK
LAUREL
Cherry
Contee

GLEN HILLS
ROCKVILLE
Montgomery Av.
189
586
Viers Mill Rd.
185
GLENMONT
97
182
HOLLYWOOD PARK
650
29
WHITE OAK
HILLONDALE
BELTSVILLE
AMMENDALE
212

C
WATTS
THE GLEN
REGENCY ESTATES
MONROSE
VEIRS MILL
355
187
WHEATON
Wheaton Regional Arcola Av.
University
Beltway
495
Powder Mill Rd.
COLLEGE PARK
Odell
SHADY OAK
VIRGINIA
MARYLAND
Potomac

D
POTOMAC
189
OAKMONT
191
495
Georgetown
97
193
Beltway
MONTGOMERY
PRINCE GEORGES
212
Metzerott Rd.
1
Glenn Dale
193
95
295

GREAT FALLS
TRUXTON
CROPLEY
188
BETHESDA
185
CHEVY CHASE
SILVER SPRING
193
College Park
TAKOMA PARK
UNIVERSITY PARK
RIVERDALE
410
500
NEW CARROLLTON
201
50

E
GREENWAY
PROSPECT HILL
BELLEVIEW
KENMORE
738
ASH GROVE
MC LEAN HAMLET
193
LANGLEY
Dulles Airport
7
Leesburg
123
Old McLean
CABIN JOHN
GLEN ECHO
190
FRIENDSHIP HEIGHTS
396
Military Rd.
Western
HYATTSVILLE
MT. RAINIER
COLMAR MANOR
BLADENSBURG
LANDOVER HILLS
450
Ardmore

F
VIENNA
PIMMIT HILLS
123
309
120
MC LEAN
Dolly Madison
123
Great Falls
Old Dominion
Kirby
WASHINGTON
National Zoological Park
M
Florida
New York
1A
50
CHEVERLY
National Arboretum
FAIRMOUNT HEIGHTS
202
Sheriff
704
650

G
FAIRFAX
29
211
ARLINGTON
211
Hwy.
29
FALLS CHURCH
66
237
Wilson
Glebe
395
Arlington National Cemetery
Lincoln Memorial
Constitution
The Mall
Independence
U.S. Capitol
Pentagon
295
SEAT PLEASANT
CAPITOL HEIGHTS
DISTRICT HEIGHTS
214
Ritchie

BAILEY'S CROSSROADS
649
617
Columbia
244
120
P. Walter Reed
Washington National Airport
210
Suitland Rd.
4
SUITLAND
FORESTVILLE
4
Westphalia

H
620
KINGS PARK
ANNANDALE
236
244
ALEXANDRIA
395
Quaker
7
Duke
ALEXANDRIA
Beltway
95
DISTRICT OF COLUMBIA
MARYLAND
FOREST HEIGHTS
414
MARLOW HEIGHTS
TEMPLE HILLS
MORNINGSIDE
5
Andrews Air Force Base

BURKE
620
Braddock
Lake Accotink Park
Edsail
236
648
Huntington
Capitol
95
CAMP SPRINGS
337

J
645
638
SPRINGFIELD
FRANCONIA
644
611
PENDAW
SOUTH LAWN
BELLE HAVEN
OXON HILL
OAKLAWN
CLINTON
BALLARD
COLES CORNER

KEENE MILL HEIGHTS
BEVERLY FOREST
GROVETON
633
1
FT. FOOT VILLAGE
BUCKNELL MANOR
WINDSOR ESTATES
WELLINGTON
FRIENDLY
TIPPETT

K
123
CHAPEL ACRES
636
POHICK ESTATES
611
Military Reservation
Fort Belvoir
235
WAYNEWOOD
626
OAKWOOD
SILESIA
210
223
Piscataway
TANTALLON
235

Scale of Miles
0 1 2 3

N

©C.S.C.

INDEX
To The United States

Index to Canadian Cities and Towns on Pages 12-13.
Index to Mexican Cities and Towns on Page 15.

ALABAMA
Page 22

Abanda E-6
Abbeville H-6
Ada G-5
Adamsville D-4
Vicinity Pg. 104, C-2
Addison B-4
Akron E-3
Alabaster D-4
Albertville B-5
Aldrich D-4
Alexander City E-5
Aliceville E-2
Allgood C-5
Almond E-6
Altoona C-5
Andalusia H-4
Anderson A-4
Anniston C-5
Arab B-5
Arcus H-5
Ardilla H-6
Ardmore A-4
Argo D-5
Arkadelphia C-4
Arley C-4
Ashbury C-6
Ashford H-7
Ashland D-6
Ashville C-5
Athens A-4
Atmore J-3
Attalla C-5
Auburn F-6
Awin G-4
Axis J-2
Babbie H-5
Bailyton B-4
Bakerhill G-6
Ballplay C-6
Bangor C-4
Banks G-6
Bankston C-3
Barfield D-6
Barton A-3
Bass A-6
Batesville G-7
Bay Minette J-3
Bayou LaBatre K-2
Bear Creek B-3
Beatrice G-3
Belgreen B-3
Belk D-3
Bellamy F-2
Belleville H-4
Benton F-4
Berry C-3
Bessemer D-4
Vicinity Pg. 104, H-2
Big Cove B-5
Billingsley E-4
Birmingham D-4
Vicinity Pg. 104
Blacksher H-3
Blount Springs C-4
Blountsville C-4
Blue Mountain D-5
Bluff C-3
Boaz C-5
Bolinger G-2
Bon Secour K-3
Borden Springs C-6
Boyd F-2
Braggs G-4
Brantley H-5
Bremen C-4
Brent E-4
Brewton J-4
Bridgeport A-6
Brilliant C-3
Brinn B-3
Brooklyn H-4
Brooksville C-5
Brookwood D-3
Browns F-4
Brundidge G-6
Bryant A-6
Butler G-2
Bynum D-5
Calera E-4
Calvert H-2
Camden G-4
Campbell G-3
Camphill E-6
Carbon Hill C-3
Carrollton D-2
Carrville F-6
Castleberry H-4
Catalpa G-6
Catherine F-3
Cedar Bluff B-6
Center Point C-4
Vicinity Pg. 104, C-6
Centre C-6
Centreville E-4
Chase A-4
Chastang J-2
Chatom H-2
Chelsea D-5
Vicinity Pg. 104, J-7
Cherokee A-3
Chickasaw J-2
Childersburg D-5
Chrysler H-3
Citronelle H-2
Claiborne H-3
Clanton E-4
Claud F-5
Clayhatchee H-6
Clayton G-6
Cleveland C-5
Clinton E-2
Clio G-6
Clopton H-6
Cloverdale A-3
Cochrane E-2
Coden K-2
Coffeeville G-2
Collinsville B-6
Columbia H-7
Columbiana D-5
Consul F-3
Cooper E-5
Cordova C-4
Cottonwood J-6
Courtland B-4
Coxey A-4
Creola J-2
Crossville B-6
Cuba F-2
Cullman C-4
Cullomburg G-2
Dadeville E-6
Daleville H-6
Damascus H-4
Dancy E-2
Danville B-4
Daphne J-3
Dauphin Island K-2
Daviston E-6
Davisville F-6
Dawes J-2
Dayton F-3
Deans H-4
Deatsville F-5
Decatur B-4
Deer Park H-2
Dees K-2
Delta D-6
Demopolis F-3
Devenport G-5
Dill H-6
Dixie J-4
Dixon Mills G-2
Dixonville J-4
Dora C-4
Dothan H-7
Double Sprs. C-3
Dry Forks G-3
Dublin G-5
Duke C-6
Duncanville E-3
E. Brewton J-4
Easton E-6
Echola D-3
Eclectic F-6
Edwin G-6
Eight Mile J-2
Elamville H-6
Elba H-5
Elberta K-3
Elias E-5
Eliska H-3
Elmore F-5
Elrod D-3
Emelle E-2
Enterprise H-5
Eoline E-4
Epes E-2
Equality E-5
Ethelsville D-2
Eufaula G-7
Eunola J-6
Eutaw E-3
Evergreen H-4
Ewell H-6
Fairfax E-7
Fairfield D-4
Vicinity Pg. 104, F-2
Fairhope K-2
Falkville B-4
Fatama G-4
Fayette D-3
Flat Rock A-6
Flint City B-4
Flomaton J-4
Florala J-5
Florence A-3
Foley K-3
Forkland F-2
Forkville B-3
Fort Mitchell F-7
Fort Payne B-6
Fountain H-3
Francisco A-5
Frisco City H-3
Fruitdale H-2
Fulton G-3
Fultondale D-4
Vicinity Pg. 104, C-4
Gadsden C-6
Gainesville E-2
Gallant C-5
Gallion F-3
Gantt H-5
Gardendale C-4
Vicinity Pg. 104, B-5
Geiger E-2
Geneva J-5
Georgiana G-4
Geraldine B-5
Glencoe C-6
Goodwater E-5
Gordo D-3
Grand Bay K-2
Graysville C-4
Vicinity Pg. 104, C-2
Green Bay H-5
Green Pond D-4
Greensboro E-3
Greenville G-5
Grove Hill G-3
Guin C-2
Gulf Shores K-3
Guntersville B-5
Gurly B-5
Hackleburg B-3
Haleyville B-3
Halsell F-2
Halsos Mill G-5
Hamilton B-2
Hammondville B-6
Hanceville C-4
Harpersville D-5
Harrisburg E-3
Hartford J-6
Hartselle B-4
Hatton B-3
Havana E-3
Hawk D-6
Hayneville F-4
Hazel Green A-5
Hazen F-4
Headland H-7
Helena D-4
Vicinity Pg. 104, K-4
Henagar B-6
Hobson City D-6
Hodges B-3
Hokes Bluff C-6
Hollis D-6
Hollywood A-6
Holt D-3
Holy Trinity F-7
Homewood D-4
Vicinity Pg. 104, F-4
Hoover D-4
Vicinity Pg. 104, H-4
Hueytown D-4
Vicinity Pg. 104, G-1
Hulaco B-4
Hunter F-5
Huntsville A-5
Hurtsboro F-6
Huxford H-3
Hybart G-3
Ider B-6
Ino H-5
Intercourse F-2
Irondale D-4
Vicinity Pg. 104, E-7
Isney G-2
Jachin F-2
Jack H-5
Jackson H-3
Jacksonville C-6
Jasper C-4
Jefferson F-2
Jemison E-4
Jenkins Crossroads G-6
Jones F-4
Jones Chapel C-4
Kellerman D-4
Kelly's Crossroads E-5
Kellyton E-5
Kennedy D-2
Kimberly C-4
Kimbrough G-3
Kinsey H-6
Kinston H-5
Knoxville E-3
Koenton H-2
La Place F-6
Lafayette E-6
Lanett E-6
Langdale E-7
Lawrenceville H-6
Leeds D-5
Leighton A-3
Letohatchee G-4
Lexington A-3
Lillian K-3
Lincoln D-5
Linden F-3
Lineville D-6
Littleville B-3
Livingston F-3
Lockhart J-5
Lottie H-3
Louisville G-6
Lowndesboro F-5
Loxley K-3
Luverne G-5
Lyeffion H-4
Lynn C-3
Magnolia F-3
Malvern J-6
Maplesville E-4
Marbury E-5
Marion E-3
Marvyn F-6
McDade F-5
McIntosh H-2
McKenzie H-5
Mentone B-6
Meridianville A-5
Midland City H-6
Midway G-4
Millbrook F-5
Millerville E-5
Millport D-2
Millry G-2
Mitchell F-6
Mobile J-2
Monroeville H-4
Montevallo E-4
Montgomery F-5
Montrose K-2
Moores Bridge D-3
Mooresville B-4
Morgan City B-5
Morris C-4
Morvin G-3
Moulton B-4
Moundville E-3
Mount Andrew G-6
Mount Olive E-5
Vicinity Pg. 104, B-4
Mount Vernon J-2
Mount Willing G-4
Mountain Brook D-4
Vicinity Pg. 104, F-5
Mulberry F-4
Munford D-6
Muscle Shoals A-3
Nanafalia G-2
Natural Bridge C-3
New Brockton H-5
New Hope B-5
Vicinity Pg. 104, J-6
New Lexington D-3
New Market A-5
Newburg B-3
Newsite E-6
Newton H-6
Newtonville D-3
Newville H-6
Normal A-5
Northport D-3
Notasulga F-6
Oak Grove D-4
Oakland B-4
Oakman C-3
Oakwood F-5
Odenville C-5
Ohatchee C-5
Omaha G-7
Oneonta C-5
Opelika E-6
Opp H-5
Owens Crossroads B-5
Oxford D-6
Ozark H-6
Palmerdale C-4
Vicinity Pg. 104, A-7
Parrish C-4
Pelham D-4
Vicinity Pg. 104, K-4
Pell City D-5
Pennington F-2
Perdido J-3
Peterman H-3
Peterson D-3
Petersville A-3
Phenix City F-7
Phil Campbell B-3
Pickensville D-2
Piedmont C-6
Pine Apple G-4
Pine Grove C-6
Pine Hill G-3
Pisgah B-6
Plantersville F-4
Pleasant Grove D-2
Vicinity Pg. 104, F-1
Prattville F-5
Priceville B-4
Prichard J-2
Pt. Clear K-2
Rabun J-3
Rainbow City C-5
Rainsville B-6
Ranburne D-6
Range H-3
Red Bay B-2
Red Level H-4
Reece City C-5
Reform D-3
Repton H-3
Riley G-4
River Falls H-5
River View J-4
Roanoke E-6
Robertsdale K-3
Rockdale D-6
Rockford E-5
Rogersville A-3
Rome H-5
Romulus E-3
Russellville B-3
Rutledge G-5
Saco G-6
Safford F-3
Saint Elmo K-2
Salitpa G-2
Samson H-5
Sanford H-5
Santuck E-5
Saraland J-2
Sardis F-4
Satsuma J-2
Scottsboro B-5
Seale F-7
Section B-5
Selma F-4
Shawmut E-7
Sheffield A-3
Shelby E-5
Shepardville G-4
Shorter F-6
Silver Hill K-3
Simcoe B-4
Sipsey C-4
Sledge F-3
Slocomb J-6
Smiths F-7
Smut Eye G-6
Snead C-5
Snowdoun F-5
Somerville B-4
Southside C-5
Spring Hill H-6
Springville C-5
Sprott E-3
Spruce Pine B-3
Stafford D-2
Steele C-5
Stevenson A-6
Stewartville E-5
Stockton J-3
Sulligent C-2
Sumiton C-4
Summerdale K-3
Sunflower H-2
Suttle F-4
Sweet Water G-3
Sylacauga E-5
Sylvania B-6
Talladega D-5
Tallassee F-6
Tensaw H-3
Terese G-7
Theodore K-2
Thomaston F-3
Thomasville G-3
Thorsby E-4
Three Notch G-6
Tibbie H-2
Town Creek B-4
Toxey G-2
Trinity B-4
Troy G-5
Trussville D-5
Tuscaloosa D-3
Tuscumbia A-3
Tuskegee F-6
Union E-3
Union Grove E-5
Vicinity Pg. 104, D-1
Union Springs G-6
Uniontown F-3
Uriah H-3
Valley Head B-6
Vance E-3
Vernon C-2
Vestavia Hills D-4
Vicinity Pg. 104, G-5
Victoria H-6
Vidette G-5
Village Springs C-5
Vineland G-3
Vinemont B-4
Wadley E-6
Wagarville H-2
Walnut Grove C-5
Walnut Hill E-6
Warrior C-4
Weaver C-6
Wedowee D-6
West Blockton D-4
West Point B-4
Wetumpka F-5
Whatley G-3
Whiteoak B-2
Whitson D-3
Wicksburg H-6
Wilburn C-4
Wilmer J-2
Wilton E-4
Windham Springs D-3
Winfield C-3
Wing J-4
Winterboro D-5
Woodville B-5
Wren B-3
Yantley F-2
Yarbo H-2
York F-2
Zip City A-3

ALASKA
Page 17

Akhiok F-5
Akolmiut D-4
Akulurak D-4
Akutan F-2
Alakanuk C-4
Alaktak A-7
Aleknagik E-4
Alice Arm H-10
Allakaket C-6
Ambler B-6
Anartuvuk Pass B-7
Anchorage E-6
Inset Map B-2
Anderson D-7
Angoon G-9
Aniak D-4
Anvik D-5
Arctic Village C-8
Atka H-8
Atkasuk A-6
Attu H-5
Baranof G-9
Barrow A-7
Beaver C-7
Beechey Pt A-7
Bethel D-4
Bettles C-7
Big Delta D-7
Big Port Walter G-9
Black D-4
Brevig Mission B-4
Buckland C-5
Candle C-5
Cantwell D-7
Cape Romanzof D-3
Cape Yakataga F-8
Caro C-7
Chalkyitsik C-8
Chatanika D-7
Chenik F-5

★ Denotes City only on Vicinity map. City not located on State map.

ALASKA

CALIFORNIA

Chevak D-4
Chickaloon E-7
  Inset Map A-2
Chicken D-8
Chignik F-4
Chitina E-7
Christian C-8
Christochina E-7
Chugiak B-2
Circle C-8
Circle Hot Springs D-8
Clarks Pt. E-5
College D-7
Copper Center E-7
Cordova E-7
Craig H-9
Crooked Creek D-5
Deadhorse B-7
Deering B-5
Delta Junction D-7
Dillingham E-4
Donnelly D-7
Dot Lake D-8
Douglas G-9
Dutch Harbor F-2
Eagle D-8
Eagle River E-6
  Inset Map B-2
Edna Bay H-9
Eek E-4
Egavic C-5
Elfin Cove G-9
Emmonak C-4
English Bay F-6
Eureka D-7
Fairbanks D-7
False Pass F-3
Farewell D-6
Flat D-5
Fort Yukon C-8
Gakona E-7
Galena C-6
Gambell C-3
Glen Alps E-6
Glennallen E-7
Golovin C-5
Goodnews Bay E-4
Gordon B-8
Grayling D-5
Gulkana E-7
Gustavus G-9
Haines F-9
Hawk Inlet G-9
Healy D-7
Homer E-6
  Inset Map C-1
Hoonah G-9
Hooper Bay D-3
Hope E-6
  Inset Map B-2
Houston A-2
Hughes C-6
Huslia C-6
Hydaburg H-9
Itullick E-5
Juneau G-9
Kachemak E-6
Kake G-9
Kaktovik B-8
Kalla C-6
Kaltag C-5
Karluk F-5
Kashegelok E-6
  Inset Map B-1
Kaskanak E-5
Katalla F-7
Kenai B-1
Ketchikan H-10
Kiana B-5
Kinegnak E-4
King Cove F-3
King Salmon F-5
Kipnuk E-4
Kivalina B-5
Klawock H-9
Knik B-2
Kobuk C-6
Kodiak F-6
Kokrines C-6
Koliganek E-5
Kotlick C-4
Kotzebue B-5
Koyuk C-5
Koyukuk C-6
Kuliuk F-5
Kwethluk D-4
Kwigillingok E-4
Larsen Bay F-5
Latouche F-7
Levelock E-5
Lime Village E-5
Livengood D-6
Long D-6
Lower Tonsina E-7
Manley Hot Springs . . . D-6
Manokotak E-4
McCarthy E-8
McGrath D-5
McKinley Park D-6
Medfra D-6
Mekoryuk D-3
Mentasta Lake E-7
Metlakatla H-10
Minto D-7

Moose Pass B-2
Mount Edgecumber . . . G-9
Mountain Village D-4
Naknek F-5
Napakiak E-4
Napaskiak E-4
Nenana D-7
New Stuyahok E-5
Newhalen E-5
Nikolai D-6
Nikolski F-1
Noatak B-5
Nogamut K-9
Nome C-4
Nondalton E-5
Noorvik B-5
North Pole D-7
Northeast Cape C-2
Northway E-8
Nulato C-5
Old Harbor F-5
Ooliktok A-7
Ouzinkie F-5
Palmer E-7
  Inset Map A-2
Pedro Bay E-5
Pelican G-9
Perryville F-4
Petersburg E-6
Pilgrim Springs B-4
Pilot Point F-4
  Inset Map D-4
Platinum E-4
Point Hope A-5
Point Lay A-5
Porcupine F-9
Port Alexander G-9
Port Lions F-5
Portlock F-6
Prudhoe Bay B-8
Quinhagak E-4
Rampart C-7
Rampart House C-8
Richardson D-7
Ruby C-6
Russian Mission D-4
Sagwon B-7
Salchaket D-7
Sand Pt. F-4
Saroonga C-3
Selawik B-5
Seward E-6
  Inset Map C-2
Shageluk D-5
Shaktoolik C-5
Shishmaref B-4
Shungnak B-6
Sinuk C-4
Sitka G-9
Skagway F-9
Sleetmute D-5
Soldotna E-6
  Inset Map B-1
Squaw Harbor G-3
St. George E-2
St. Marys D-4
St. Michael C-5
St. Paul E-2
Stebbins C-4
Stevens Village C-7
Stony River D-5
Stuyahok D-5
Susitna B-2
Takotna D-5
Talkeetna C-6
  Inset Map A-1
Tanalian Pt E-5
Tanana C-6
Tatitlek E-7
Teller C-4
Tetlin E-8
Tetlin Junction E-8
Togiak E-4
Tok D-8
Toksook Bay D-4
Tonsina E-7
Tuluksak D-4
Tununak D-4
Tyonek E-6
  Inset Map B-1
Ugashik F-5
Umiat B-7
Unalakleet C-5
Unalaska F-2
Valdez E-7
Venetie C-8
Wainwright A-6
Wales B-4
Wasilla A-2
Wasilla A-7
White Mountain C-5
Whittier B-2
Willow E-6
  Inset Map A-1
Wiseman C-7
Wrangell G-10
Yakutat F-8

ARIZONA
Pages 20-21

Adobe . . . . ★
  Vicinity . . . . Pg. 148, B-4
Aguila J-3

Ajo L-4
Ak Chin K-5
Alpine J-10
Amado N-7
Anegam L-5
Angell F-7
Apache Jct. K-6
Arivaca Jct. N-7
Arizona City L-6
Arlington K-4
Artesia A-6
Ash Fork F-5
Ashurst K-9
Avondale K-5
  Vicinity . . . . Pg. 148, K-4
Bagdad G-4
Bapchule K-6
Beaverhead J-10
Bellemont F-6
Benson M-8
Bisbee N-9
Black Canyon City H-5
Bonita L-9
Bouse J-2
Bowie M-10
Brenda J-2
Buckeye K-5
Bullhead City F-2
Bylas K-9
Cameron E-7
Camp Verde H-6
Carefree J-6
Carmen N-7
Carrizo J-8
Casa Grande K-6
  Vicinity . . . . Pg. 148, E-2
Catalina L-7
Cave Creek J-6
Cedar Creek J-8
Cedar Ridge D-7
Cedar Springs F-8
Central L-9
Chambers F-9
Chandler K-6
  Vicinity . . . . . . Pg. 148, F-7
Chandler Heights K-6
Chilchinbito D-9
Childs L-4
Chinle E-10
Chino Valley G-5
Chloride F-2
Christmas K-8
Christopher Creek H-7
Chuichu L-6
Circle City J-4
Clarkdale G-5
Clay Spring H-8
Claypool K-7
Clifton K-10
Cochise M-9
Colorado City C-4
Concho H-9
Congress H-4
Continental M-7
Coolidge K-6
Cordes Jct. H-5
Cornville G-6
Cortaro L-7
Cottonwood G-6
Covered Wells M-5
Cow Springs D-8
Cross Canyon E-10
Currys Corner . . . . ★
  Vicinity . . . . . . Pg. 148, B-6
Curtis M-8
Dateland K-3
Desert View E-6
Dewey H-5
Dilkon F-8
Dinnehotso D-9
Dolan Springs F-2
Dome L-2
Dos Cabezas M-10
Douglas N-10
Dragoon M-9
Dudleyville L-8
Duncan L-10
Eager H-10
Eden K-9
Ehrenberg J-2
Elfrida N-9
Eloy L-6
Emery Park . . . . ★
  Vicinity . . . . . . Pg. 161, H-3
Fairbank M-8
Flagstaff F-6
Florence K-7
Florence Jct. K-7
Fort Apache J-9
Fort Defiance E-10
Fort Grant L-9
Fort McDowell J-6
Fort Thomas K-9
Fountain Hills J-6
Francisco Grande L-6
Franklin L-10
Fredonia C-5
Gadsden L-1
Ganado F-9
Gila Bend K-5
Gilbert K-6
  Vicinity . . . . . . Pg. 148, C-3
Glendale J-5
  Vicinity . . . . . . Pg. 148, C-3
Globe K-7
Golden Shores G-2

Goldroad F-2
Goodyear K-5
  Vicinity . . . . . . Pg. 148, E-1
Grand Canyon E-5
Gray Mountain E-7
Greasewood (Lower) . . F-9
Green Valley M-7
Greer J-10
Guadalupe K-5
  Vicinity . . . . . . Pg. 148, F-5
Hackberry F-3
Hannigan Meadow K-10
Harcuvar J-3
Hawley Lake J-9
Hayden K-8
Heber H-8
Higley K-6
Hillside H-4
Holbrook G-8
Hope J-3
Hotevilla E-8
Houck F-9
Huachuca City N-8
Humbolt H-7
Indian Wells F-8
Jacob Lake D-5
Jaynes . . . . ★
  Vicinity . . . . . . Pg. 161, D-2
Jerome G-5
Johnson M-8
Joseph City G-8
Katherine F-2
Kayenta D-8
Keams Canyon E-9
Kearney K-7
Kelvin K-7
Kingman F-2
Kirkland H-4
Kirkland Jct. H-5
Kohls Ranch H-7
Kyrene . . . . ★
  Vicinity . . . . . . Pg. 148, F-6
La Palma L-6
Lake Havasu City G-2
Lake Montezuma G-6
Lakeside H-9
Laveen . . . . ★
  Vicinity . . . . . . Pg. 148, E-3
Leupp F-7
Litchfield J-5
Littlefield C-3
Littletown . . . . ★
  Vicinity . . . . . . Pg. 161, H-5
Lukeville M-4
Lupton F-10
Mammoth L-8
Many Farms D-10
Marana L-6
Marble Canyon D-6
Maricopa K-5
Mayer H-5
McGuireville G-6
McNeal N-9
Meadview E-2
Mesa J-6
Mexican Water C-9
Miami K-7
Moenkopi E-7
Moqui E-5
Morenci K-10
Morristown J-4
Mountainaire G-6
Mt. View M-7
Munds Park G-6
Naco N-9
Navajo G-10
Nelson F-3
New River J-5
Nicksville N-8
Nogales N-7
North Rim E-6
Nutrioso J-10
Oatman G-2
Ocotillo K-6
Olberg K-6
Old Oraibi E-8
Oracle L-7
Oracle Jct. L-7
Oraibi E-8
Oro Valley L-7
Overgaard H-8
Page C-7
Palm Springs K-6
Palo Verde K-4
Palominas N-8
Pantano M-8
Paradise City . . . . ★
  Vicinity . . . . . . Pg. 148, B-5
Paradise Valley J-5
Parker H-2
Parks F-6
Patagonia N-7
Paul Spur N-9
Paulden G-5
Payson H-6
Peach Springs F-4
Peeples Valley H-4
Peoria J-5
  Vicinity . . . . . . Pg. 148, C-3
Peridot K-8
Phoenix J-6
  Vicinity . . . . . . Pg. 148
Picacho L-6
Pima K-9
Pine H-6

Pine Springs F-5
Pinedale H-8
Pinetop H-9
Pirtleville N-9
Polacca E-8
Pomerene M-8
Prescott G-5
Prescott Valley G-5
Punkin Center J-7
Quartzite J-2
Queen Creek K-6
Quijotoa M-5
Randolph K-6
Red Lake D-7
Red Rock L-7
Rillito L-7
Riverside K-7
Riviera F-2
Rock Point D-10
Rock Springs J-5
Roosevelt J-7
Rough Rock D-9
Round Rock D-10
Rye H-7
Sacaton K-6
Safford L-9
Sahuarita M-7
Saint David M-9
Saint Johns H-10
Saint Michaels F-10
Salome J-3
San Carlos K-8
San Luis L-1
San Luis L-5
San Manuel L-8
San Simon M-10
Sanders F-10
Sasabe N-6
Scottsdale . . . . ★
  Vicinity . . . . . . Pg. 148, D-6
Seba Dalkai F-8
Second Mesa E-8
Sedona G-6
Seligman F-4
Sells M-5
Sentinel K-3
Shonto D-8
Show Low H-9
Shumway H-9
Sierra Vista N-8
Silver Bell N-6
Snowflake H-9
Solomon L-9
Somerton L-1
Sonoita N-7
South Tuscon M-7
South Tucson M-7
  Vicinity . . . . . . Pg. 161, G-2
Springerville H-10
Stanfield L-6
Star Valley H-7
Stargo K-10
Sun City J-5
  Vicinity . . . . . . Pg. 148, C-2
Sun City West J-5
Sun Lake K-6
Sun Valley J-6
Sunflower J-6
Sunizona M-9
Sunrise F-7
Sunsites M-9
Superior K-7
Suprise J-5
Tacna L-2
Taylor H-9
Teec Nos Pas D-10
Tempe K-6
  Vicinity . . . . . . Pg. 148, E-6
Tes Nez Iha C-9
Thatcher L-9
The Gap D-7
Three Points (Robles Jct.) M-6
Tolleson K-5
  Vicinity . . . . . . Pg. 148, E-2
Tombstone N-9
Tonalea D-8
Tonopah J-4
Topock G-2
Tortilla Flat J-7
Tracy M-5
Truxton F-3
Tsaile D-10
Tsegi D-8
Tuba City E-7
Tubac N-7
Tucson M-7
Tucson M-7
  Vicinity . . . . . . Pg. 161
Tumacacori N-7
Tusayan E-5
Vail M-8
Valentine F-3
Valle F-5
Vernon H-9
Vicksburg J-2
Wellton L-2
Wenden J-3
Whiteriver J-9
Why M-4
Wickenburg J-4
Wikieup G-3
Wilhoit H-5
Willcox M-9
Williams F-5

Window Rock F-10
Winkelman K-8
Winona F-7
Winslow G-7
Wintersburg K-4
Wittmann J-4
Yampai F-4
Yarnell H-4
Young H-7
Youngtown J-5
  Vicinity . . . . . Pg. 148, C-2
Yucca G-2
Yuma L-1

ARKANSAS
Page 19

Alpena A-4
Altheimer E-6
Amity E-4
Arkadelphia E-4
Arkansas City F-7
Ash Flat A-7
Ashdown F-3
Athens E-3
Atkins C-4
Augusta C-7
Bald Knob C-7
Banks F-5
Barling C-2
Batesville B-6
Bay B-8
Bearden F-5
Beebe D-6
Benton D-5
Bentonville A-3
Bergman A-4
Berryville A-3
Bismark E-4
Black Rock B-7
Blue Springs D-4
Bluff City F-4
Blytheville B-9
Booneville C-3
Boxley B-4
Bradley G-3
Brashears B-3
Brinkley D-7
Bryant D-5
Bull Shoals A-5
Cabot D-6
Calico Rock B-6
Calion F-5
Camden F-4
Carlisle D-6
Carthage E-5
Cash B-8
Caulksville C-3
Cave City B-7
Cedarville C-2
Centerville C-4
Charleston C-3
Cherry Valley C-8
Clarksville C-3
Clinton C-5
Conway C-5
Corning A-8
Cotton Plant D-7
Cove E-2
Crossett G-6
Crossroads E-7
Crows D-5
Cushman B-6
Dalark E-4
Damascus C-5
Danville D-4
Dardanelle A-5
DeQueen E-2
DeWitt E-7
Decatur A-2
Delight E-3
Deluce E-3
Des Arc D-7
Dermott F-7
Dierks E-3
Dodridge G-3
Dover C-4
Dumas F-7
Earle C-8
El Dorado G-5
Elaine E-8
Emerson G-4
England D-6
Eudora G-8
Eureka Springs A-3
Falcon F-4
Fallsville B-4
Farmington B-2
Fayetteville B-3
Fisher C-7
Flippin A-5
Florence F-6
Fordyce F-5
Foreman F-2
Forrest City D-8
Fouke G-3
Fountain Hill F-6
Ft. Smith C-2
Garland G-3
Gentry A-2
Gillett E-7
Gillham E-2
Gilmore C-8
Glenwood E-3
Gosnell B-9

Gould E-7
Grady E-6
Grapevine E-5
Gravette A-2
Green Forest A-4
Greenbrier C-5
Greenwood C-2
Greers Ferry C-6
Gurdon E-4
Hackett C-2
Hagarville C-4
Hamburg G-6
Hampton F-5
Hardy A-7
Harrisburg C-8
Harrison A-4
Hartford D-2
Haskell E-5
Hazen D-7
Heber Springs C-6
Helena D-8
Hermitage F-6
Holly Grove D-7
Horatio E-2
Horseshoe Bend A-6
Hot Springs D-4
Hoxie B-7
Hughes D-8
Humnoke D-6
Humphrey E-6
Huntsville B-3
Huttig G-6
Jacksonville D-6
Jasper B-4
Jonesboro B-8
Judsonia C-6
Junction City G-5
Keiser B-9
Kensett C-6
Kingsland F-5
Lake City B-8
Lake Village F-7
Lavaca C-3
LePanto C-9
Lead Hill A-5
Leslie B-5
Lewisville F-3
Lincoln B-2
Little Rock D-5
Lockesburg E-3
Lonoke D-6
Lowell A-3
Luxora B-9
Madison D-8
Magnolia G-4
Malvern E-5
Mammoth Spring A-7
Manila B-9
Mansfield C-2
Marianna C-9
Marion C-9
Marked Tree C-8
Marmaduke B-8
Marshall B-5
Marvell D-8
Maumelle D-5
Maynard A-7
McCroy C-7
McGehee F-7
Melbourne B-6
Mena E-2
Mineral Springs F-3
Monette B-9
Monticello F-6
Montrose G-7
Morrilton C-5
Mountain Home A-5
Mountain View B-6
Mt. Ida D-3
Mt. Pleasant B-6
Murfreesboro E-3
N. Little Rock D-5
Nashville E-3
Needmore C-7
Newport C-7
Nola D-3
Norman D-3
Oark B-3
Ola D-4
Onyx D-4
Osceola B-9
Oxford B-6
Ozark C-3
Pansy F-6
Paragould B-8
Paris C-3
Parkdale G-7
Parkin C-8
Pea Ridge A-3
Pelsor B-4
Perryville D-5
Piggot A-9
Pine Bluff E-6
Pleasant Plains C-7
Pocahontas A-7
Pollard A-9
Ponca B-4
Portland G-7
Poughkee A-6
Prairie Grove B-3
Prattsville E-5
Prescott F-4
Princeton E-5
Quitman C-6

Rector A-8
Reed F-7
Rison E-6
Rogers A-3
Rose Bud C-6
Rosston F-4
Rushing B-6
Russellville C-4
Salem A-6
Salesville A-6
Scranton C-4
Searcy C-6
Sherdian E-5
Shirley B-5
Siloam Springs A-2
Smackover F-5
Snow Lake E-7
Springdale A-2
St. Francis G-4
Star City E-6
Stephens F-4
Story D-3
Strawberry B-7
Strong G-5
Stuggart D-7
Success A-8
Taylor G-4
Texarkana F-3
Timbo B-5
Truman B-8
Tupelo C-7
Turrell C-9
VanBuren C-2
Vilonia C-6
Waldo F-4
Waldron D-2
Walker C-6
Walnut Ridge B-8
Warren County F-6
Washington F-3
Watson F-7
West Fork B-2
West Helena D-8
West Memphis C-9
Western Grove B-4
White Hall E-6
Wickes E-2
Williams Jct. D-5
Willisville F-4
Wilmar F-6
Wilmot G-8
Wilson C-9
Winslow B-3
Witt Springs B-4
Wynne C-8
Y City D-3
Yellville B-5

CALIFORNIA
Pages 24-27

Acton S-10
Adelanto S-11
Adin C-7
Agoura Hills S-9
Ahwahnee L-8
Alameda . . . . ★
  Vicinity . . . . . . Pg. 156, E-3
Alamorio V-15
Albany . . . . ★
  Vicinity . . . . . . Pg. 156, C-3
Albion G-2
Alder Springs F-3
Alderpoint E-2
Alhambra . . . . ★
  Vicinity . . . . . . Pg. 126, C-5
Alleghany F-6
Almanor E-6
Alpaugh P-8
Alpine V-12
Alta Loma . . . . ★
  Vicinity . . . . . Pg. 128, C-11
Altadena . . . . ★
  Vicinity . . . . . . Pg. 126, B-6
Altaville J-6
Alton D-1
Alturas C-7
Amboy S-15
Anaheim T-11
  Vicinity . . . . . . Pg. 129, G-7
Anderson D-4
Angels Camp J-7
Angwin H-3
Annapolis H-2
Antioch J-5
Apple Valley S-12
Aptos L-4
Arbuckle G-4
Arcadia . . . . ★
  Vicinity . . . . . . Pg. 128, C-7
Arcata C-1
Arnold J-7
Arroyo Grande Q-6
Artesia . . . . ★
  Vicinity . . . . . Pg. 127, F-6
Artois F-4
Arvin Q-9
Atascadero P-6
Atherton . . . . ★
  Vicinity . . . . . . Pg. 158, A-1
Atwater L-6
Auberry L-8
Auburn H-6
Avalon U-10

★ Denotes City only on Vicinity map. City not located on State map.

CALIFORNIA

Avenal ... N-7
Avon ... ★
  Vicinity ... Pg. 156, A-6
Azusa ... ★
  Vicinity ... Pg. 128, C-8
Badger ... M-9
Bakersfield ... Q-9
Balboa Park ... ★
  Vicinity ... Pg. 155, F-3
Baldwin Park ... ★
  Vicinity ... Pg. 128, C-7
Banning ... T-13
Barstow ... R-12
Bartlett Sprs. ... G-3
Bass Lake ... L-8
Baxter ... G-6
Baywood Park ... Q-5
Bear Valley ... J-8
Bear Valley ... K-7
Beaumont ... T-12
Beckwourth ... F-7
Bel Air ... ★
  Vicinity ... Pg. 126, C-2
Belden ... E-6
Bell ... ★
  Vicinity ... Pg. 127, E-5
Bella Vista ... D-4
Bellflower ... ★
  Vicinity ... Pg. 127, F-6
Bells Station ... L-5
Belmont ... ★
  Vicinity ... Pg. 157, J-3
Belvedere ... ★
  Vicinity ... Pg. 156, D-1
Ben Lomond ... L-4
Bend ... E-4
Benicia ... ★
  Vicinity ... Pg. 156, A-5
Benton ... K-10
Berenda ... L-7
Berkeley ... J-4
  Vicinity ... Pg. 156, D-3
Berry Creek ... F-6
Bertsch Terr. ... A-1
Beverly Hills ... S-10
  Vicinity ... Pg. 126, D-3
Bieber ... C-6
Big Bar ... D-3
Big Bear Lake ... S-13
Big Bend ... C-5
Big Creek ... L-9
Big Oak Flat ... K-7
Big Pine ... L-10
Big Sur ... N-4
Biggs ... G-5
Bishop ... L-10
Blackwells Corner ... P-7
Blairsden ... F-7
Bloomington ... ★
  Vicinity ... Pg. 128, B-10
Blue Lake ... C-2
Blythe ... U-16
Bodega Bay ... H-2
Bodfish ... P-10
Bolinas ... J-3
Bonita ... ★
  Vicinity ... Pg. 155, H-5
Boonville ... G-2
Boron ... R-11
Borrego Springs ... U-13
Boulder Creek ... L-4
Boulevard ... V-13
Bowman ... G-6
Bradley ... P-6
Brawley ... V-15
Brea ... ★
  Vicinity ... Pg. 129, E-8
Brentwood ... J-5
Bridgeport ... J-9
Bridgeville ... D-2
Broderick ... H-5
Browns Valley ... G-5
Brownsville ... G-6
Bryn Mawr ... ★
  Vicinity ... Pg. 128, B-12
Buellton ... R-6
Buena Park ... ★
  Vicinity ... Pg. 129, F-7
Burbank ... ★
  Vicinity ... Pg. 126, B-4
Burlingame ... ★
  Vicinity ... Pg. 157, H-2
Burney ... D-5
Burnt Ranch ... C-3
Butte City ... F-4
Butte Meadows ... E-5
Buttonwillow ... Q-8
Cabazon ... T-13
Cahuilla ... U-13
Calexico ... V-15
Caliente ... Q-10
California City ... Q-11
California Hot Sprs. ... P-9
Calipatria ... V-15
Calistoga ... H-3
Callahan ... C-4
Calpella ... G-2
Calpine ... F-7
Cambria ... P-5
Cameron Park ... H-7
Camino ... H-7
Camp Nelson ... N-10
Camp Richardson ... H-8
Campbell ... ★
  Vicinity ... Pg. 158, E-6

Campo ... V-13
Camptonville ... G-6
Canby ... C-7
Canoga Park ... ★
  Vicinity ... Pg. 126, B-1
Cantil ... Q-10
Canyon Dam ... E-6
Capay ... H-4
Capetown ... D-1
Capitola ... L-4
Carlotta ... D-1
Carlsbad ... U-11
Carmel Valley ... M-4
Carnelian Bay ... G-8
Carpinteria ... S-8
Carson ... ★
  Vicinity ... Pg. 127, F-4
Carson Hill - Cartago ... N-11
Caruthers ... M-7
Casmalia ... R-6
Caspar ... F-1
Castaic ... S-9
Castella ... C-4
Castroville ... M-4
Cayucos ... P-5
Cedar Grove ... M-10
Cedarville ... C-8
Century City ... ★
  Vicinity ... Pg. 126, D-3
Ceres ... K-6
Chalfant ... L-10
Challenge ... F-6
Chatsworth ... ★
  Vicinity ... Pg. 126, B-1
Chester ... E-6
Chico ... F-5
China Lake ... P-11
Chino ... ★
  Vicinity ... Pg. 128, D-10
Cholame ... P-7
Chowchilla ... L-7
Chula Vista ... V-12
Cima ... Q-15
Claremont ... ★
  Vicinity ... Pg. 128, C-10
Clarksburg ... H-5
Clay ... J-6
Clayton ... ★
  Vicinity ... Pg. 156, C-7
Clearlake ... G-3
Clovis ... M-8
Clyde ... ★
  Vicinity ... Pg. 156, A-6
Coachella ... U-14
Coalinga ... N-6
Coarsegold ... L-8
Cobb ... G-3
Colfax ... G-6
Coloma ... H-6
Colton ... ★
  Vicinity ... Pg. 128, B-11
Colusa ... G-4
Commerce ... ★
  Vicinity ... Pg. 126, D-5
Compton ... ★
  Vicinity ... Pg. 127, F-4
Concord ... J-4
  Vicinity ... Pg. 156, B-6
Copperopolis ... J-6
Corcoran ... N-8
Corning ... E-4
Corona ... ★
  Vicinity ... Pg. 129, F-11
Coronado ... V-12
Costa Mesa ... ★
  Vicinity ... Pg. 129, H-8
Cottonwood ... D-4
Coulterville ... K-7
Courtland ... J-5
Covelo ... E-3
Covina ... ★
  Vicinity ... Pg. 128, C-8
Crannell ... C-1
Crescent City ... B-1
Crescent Mills ... E-6
Crestmore ... ★
  Vicinity ... Pg. 128, B-10
Crockett ... ★
  Vicinity ... Pg. 156, A-4
Cucamonga ... ★
  Vicinity ... Pg. 128, C-11
Cudahy ... ★
  Vicinity ... Pg. 127, E-5
Culver City ... ★
  Vicinity ... Pg. 126, D-3
Culver City ... ★
  Vicinity ... Pg. 126, D-3
Cummings ... E-2
Cupertino ... ★
  Vicinity ... Pg. 158, D-4
Cutler ... N-9
Cutten ... C-1
Cuyama ... R-8
Cypress ... ★
  Vicinity ... Pg. 129, G-6
Daggett ... R-12
Dairyville ... E-4
Dales ... E-4
Daly City ... ★
  Vicinity ... Pg. 157, G-1
Dana Point ... U-10
Danville ... ★
  Vicinity ... Pg. 156, D-6
Darwin ... N-11
Davis ... H-5

Davis Creek ... B-8
Death Valley Jct. ... N-13
Del Mar ... V-11
Delano ... P-9
Desert Center ... T-15
Desert Hot Springs ... T13
Desert Shores ... U-14
Devils Den ... P-7
Diamond Sprs. ... H-6
Dictionary Hill ... ★
  Vicinity ... Pg. 155, G-6
Dillon Beach ... J-2
Dinkey Creek ... L-9
Dixon ... H-5
Dobbins ... G-6
Dominguez ... ★
  Vicinity ... Pg. 127, F-5
Dorris ... B-5
Dos Palos ... L-6
Dos Rios ... F-2
Douglas City ... D-3
Downey ... ★
  Vicinity ... Pg. 127, E-5
Doyle ... F-8
Duarte ... ★
  Vicinity ... Pg. 128, C-7
Ducor ... N-9
Dulzura ... V-12
Dunsmuir ... C-4
Durham ... F-5
Eagle Rock ... ★
  Vicinity ... Pg. 126, C-5
Eagleville ... C-8
Earlimart ... P-9
Earp ... T-17
East Highlands ... ★
  Vicinity ... Pg. 128, A-12
East Los Angeles ... ★
  Vicinity ... Pg. 126, D-5
East Palo Alto ... ★
  Vicinity ... Pg. 158, A-2
Edison ... Q-9
El Cajon ... V-12
El Centro ... V-15
El Cerrito ... ★
  Vicinity ... Pg. 156, C-3
El Granada ... ★
  Vicinity ... Pg. 157, J-1
El Monte ... ★
  Vicinity ... Pg. 126, C-6
El Nido ... L-7
El Portal ... K-8
El Segundo ... ★
  Vicinity ... Pg. 127, F-3
El Toro ... T-11
Elk Creek ... F-4
Elk Grove ... J-5
Elmira ... J-4
Emeryville ... ★
  Vicinity ... Pg. 156, D-3
Encinitas ... V-11
Encino ... ★
  Vicinity ... Pg. 126, C-2
Enterprise ... D-4
Escalon ... K-6
Escondido ... U-11
Esparto ... H-4
Essex ... R-15
Etiwanda ... ★
  Vicinity ... Pg. 128, C-12
Etna ... B-4
Eucalyptus Hills ... ★
  Vicinity ... Pg. 155, C-6
Eureka ... C-1
Exeter ... N-9
Fairfield ... J-4
Fall River Mills ... C-6
Fallbrook ... U-12
Farmersville ... N-9
Farmington ... J-6
Fawnskin ... S-12
Feather Falls ... F-6
Fellows ... P-7
Fenner ... R-15
Ferndale ... D-1
Fields Landing ... D-1
Fillmore ... S-9
Firebaugh ... M-6
Fish Camp ... L-8
Fish Rock ... G-2
Five Points ... N-7
Flint Ridge ... ★
  Vicinity ... Pg. 126, B-5
Florence ... ★
  Vicinity ... Pg. 127, G-6
Florin ... H-5
Floriston ... G-8
Flournoy ... E-4
Folsom ... H-6
Fontana ... ★
  Vicinity ... Pg. 128, C-12
Forbestown ... F-5
Ford City ... Q-8
Forest Glen ... D-3
Forest Ranch ... F-5
Foresthill ... G-6
Forks Of Salmon ... B-3
Fortuna ... D-1
Foster City ... ★
  Vicinity ... Pg. 157, H-4
Fountain Valley ... ★
  Vicinity ... Pg. 129, H-7
Fowler ... M-8

Frazier Park ... R-9
Fredericksburg ... H-8
Fremont ... K-4
  Vicinity ... Pg. 157, A-5
Frenbrook ... ★
  Vicinity ... Pg. 155, B-7
French Gulch ... D-4
Fresno ... M-8
  Vicinity ... Pg. 126, E-5
Ft. Bidwell ... B-8
Ft. Bragg ... F-1
Ft. Dick ... A-1
Ft. Jones ... B-4
Fullerton ... ★
  Vicinity ... Pg. 129, F-7
Furnace Creek Ranch ... N-13
Galt ... J-5
Garberville ... E-2
Garden Grove ... ★
  Vicinity ... Pg. 129, G-7
Gardena ... ★
  Vicinity ... Pg. 127, F-4
Gasquet ... A-2
Gaviota ... R-7
Gazelle ... B-4
Georgetown ... H-6
Gerber ... E-4
Geyserville ... H-3
Giant Forest Village ... N-10
Gilroy ... L-5
Glamis ... V-16
Glen Avon ... ★
  Vicinity ... Pg. 128, D-12
Glen Ellen ... H-3
Glendale ... S-10
Glendora ... S-11
  Vicinity ... Pg. 128, C-8
Glenn ... F-4
Glennville ... P-10
Glenview ... ★
  Vicinity ... Pg. 155, E-7
Goffs ... R-16
Goleta ... S-7
Gonzales ... M-5
Gorman ... R-9
Goshen ... N-8
Graeagle ... F-7
Granada Hills ... ★
  Vicinity ... Pg. 126, A-1
Grand Terrace ... ★
  Vicinity ... Pg. 128, B-11
Graniteville ... G-6
Grass Valley ... G-6
Green Acres ... Q-9
Greenfield ... N-5
Greenview ... B-4
Greenville ... E-6
Grenada ... B-4
Gridley ... G-5
Grimes ... G-5
Grossmont ... ★
  Vicinity ... Pg. 155, F-6
Groveland ... K-7
Grover City ... Q-6
Guadalupe ... Q-6
Gualala ... G-2
Guerneville ... H-2
Guinda ... H-4
Gustine ... L-6
Hacienda Heights ... ★
  Vicinity ... Pg. 128, D-7
Half Moon Bay ... K-3
Hallelujah Jct. ... F-8
Hamburg ... B-3
Hamilton City ... F-4
Hanford ... N-8
Happy Camp ... B-3
Harbor Side ... ★
  Vicinity ... Pg. 155, J-4
Harden Flat ... K-7
Hawaiian Gardens ... ★
  Vicinity ... Pg. 127, G-6
Hawthorne ... ★
  Vicinity ... Pg. 127, F-3
Hayfork ... D-3
Hayward ... K-4
  Vicinity ... Pg. 157, G-6
Healdsburg ... H-3
Heber ... V-15
Helena ... D-3
Helendale ... R-12
Hemet ... T-12
Hercules ... ★
  Vicinity ... Pg. 156, B-3
Herlong ... E-8
Hermosa Beach ... ★
  Vicinity ... Pg. 127, F-3
Herndon ... M-7
Hesperia ... S-12
Highland ... ★
  Vicinity ... Pg. 128, A-12
Highland Park ... ★
  Vicinity ... Pg. 126, C-5
Hillsborough ... ★
  Vicinity ... Pg. 157, H-2
Hilmar ... L-6
Hilt ... A-4
Hinkley ... R-12
Hobart Mills ... G-7
Hollister ... M-5
Hollywood ... ★
  Vicinity ... Pg. 126, C-3
Holtville ... V-15
Homewood ... G-7
Honcut ... G-5
Honeydew ... D-1

Hoopa ... C-2
Hopland ... G-2
Hornbrook ... B-4
Hornitos ... K-7
Hume ... M-9
Huntington Beach ... T-10
  Vicinity ... Pg. 129, H-7
Huntington Park ... ★
  Vicinity ... Pg. 126, E-5
Huron ... N-7
Idyllwild ... T-13
Igo ... D-4
Imperial ... V-15
Imperial Beach ... V-12
  Vicinity ... Pg. 155, K-3
Independence ... M-10
Indio ... T-14
Industry ... ★
  Vicinity ... Pg. 128, D-7
Inglewood ... ★
  Vicinity ... Pg. 127, E-3
Ingot ... D-5
Inverness ... J-3
Inyokern ... P-11
Ione ... J-6
Irvine ... ★
  Vicinity ... Pg. 129, H-9
Isleton ... J-5
Ivanpah ... Q-15
Jackson ... J-6
Jamacha ... ★
  Vicinity ... Pg. 155, F-7
Jamacha Junction ... ★
  Vicinity ... Pg. 155, F-6
Jamestown ... K-7
Jamul ... V-12
Janesville ... E-7
Johannesburg ... Q-11
Johnsondale ... O-10
Johnstown ... E-7
Jolon ... N-5
Joshua Tree ... S-13
Julian ... V-13
Junction City ... D-3
June Lake ... K-9
Keddie ... E-6
Keeler ... N-11
Keene ... Q-10
Kelseyville ... G-3
Kelso ... R-15
Kenwood ... H-3
Kerman ... M-7
Kernville ... P-10
Kettleman City ... N-7
King City ... N-5
Kings Beach ... G-8
Kingsburg ... N-8
Kirkwood ... H-8
Kit Carson ... H-7
Klamath Glen ... B-2
Klamath River ... B-4
Kneeland ... D-2
Knights Ferry ... K-6
Knights Landing ... H-5
Kyburz ... H-7
La Canada ... ★
  Vicinity ... Pg. 126, B-5
La Crescenta ... ★
  Vicinity ... Pg. 126, B-4
La Grange ... K-7
La Habra ... ★
  Vicinity ... Pg. 129, E-7
La Honda ... K-3
La Jolla ... V-11
La Jolla Mesa ... ★
  Vicinity ... Pg. 155, D-1
La Mesa ... ★
  Vicinity ... Pg. 155, F-5
La Mirada ... ★
  Vicinity ... Pg. 129, F-7
La Palma ... ★
  Vicinity ... Pg. 127, F-6
La Presa ... ★
  Vicinity ... Pg. 155, G-6
La Puente ... ★
  Vicinity ... Pg. 128, D-7
La Quinta ... T-13
Lafayette ... ★
  Vicinity ... Pg. 156, C-5
Laguna Beach ... U-10
Lake City ... B-8
Lake Elsinore ... T-12
Lakehead ... D-4
Lakeport ... G-3
Lakeside ... ★
  Vicinity ... Pg. 155, D-7
Lakewood ... ★
  Vicinity ... Pg. 127, F-5
Lamont ... Q-9
Lancaster ... R-10
Lawndale ... ★
  Vicinity ... Pg. 127, F-3
Laytonville ... F-2
Lee Vining ... K-9
Leggett ... E-2
Lemon Grove ... ★
  Vicinity ... Pg. 155, F-5
Lemoore ... N-7
Lenwood ... R-12
Leucadia ... V-11
Likely ... C-7
Lincoln ... H-5
Lincoln Acres ... ★
  Vicinity ... Pg. 155, H-4

Linda ... G-5
Linden ... J-6
Lindsay ... N-9
Litchfield ... E-7
Little Lake ... P-11
Live Oak ... G-5
Livermore ... K-4
Livingston ... L-6
Lockeford ... J-6
Lockwood ... N-5
Lodi ... J-5
Loleta ... D-1
Loma Linda ... ★
  Vicinity ... Pg. 128, B-11
Lomita ... ★
  Vicinity ... Pg. 127, G-4
Lompoc ... R-6
Lone Pine ... N-10
Long Beach ... T-10
  Vicinity ... Pg. 127, G-5
Longvale ... F-2
Lookout ... C-6
Loomis ... H-6
Los Alamos ... R-7
Los Altos ... ★
  Vicinity ... Pg. 157, C-3
Los Altos Hills ... ★
  Vicinity ... Pg. 158, C-2
Los Angeles ... T-9
  Vicinity ... Pg. 126-129
Los Banos ... L-6
Los Gatos ... L-4
  Vicinity ... Pg. 158, F-5
Los Molinos ... E-4
Los Olivos ... R-7
Lost Hills ... P-8
Lower Lake ... G-3
Loyalton ... F-7
Lucerne ... G-3
Lucerne Valley ... S-12
Ludlow ... R-14
Lynwood ... ★
  Vicinity ... Pg. 127, E-5
Lynwood Hills ... ★
  Vicinity ... Pg. 155, J-5
Macdoel ... B-5
Mad River ... D-2
Madeline ... D-7
Madera ... M-7
Malaga ... M-8
Malibu ... S-9
Mammoth Lakes ... K-9
Manchester ... G-2
Manhattan Beach ... ★
  Vicinity ... Pg. 127, F-3
Manteca ... K-5
Manton ... D-5
Maricopa ... Q-8
Marina ... M-4
Markleeville ... H-8
Martinez ... ★
  Vicinity ... Pg. 155, D-1
Marysville ... G-5
Maxwell ... G-4
Maywood ... ★
  Vicinity ... Pg. 126, E-5
McArthur ... C-6
McCloud ... C-5
McFarland ... P-9
McKinleyville ... C-1
McKittrick ... Q-8
Meadow Valley ... F-6
Meadow Vista ... G-6
Mecca ... U-14
Meeks Bay ... H-6
Mendocino ... F-2
Mendota ... M-7
Menlo Park ... ★
  Vicinity ... Pg. 158, A-2
Merced ... L-7
Mercy Hot Springs ... M-6
Meridian ... G-5
Meyers ... H-8
Mi-wuk Village ... K-7
Middletown ... H-3
Midpines ... K-8
Milford ... E-7
Millbrae ... ★
  Vicinity ... Pg. 157, H-2
Millville ... D-4
Milpitas ... K-4
Mineral ... D-5
Mira Loma ... ★
  Vicinity ... Pg. 128, E-12
Miramar ... ★
  Vicinity ... Pg. 157, J-1
Miranda ... E-2
Mission Beach ... ★
  Vicinity ... Pg. 155, F-1
Mission Hills ... ★
  Vicinity ... Pg. 126, B-2
Modesto ... K-6
Mojave ... R-10
Mokelumne Hill ... J-6
Mono Hot Springs ... L-9
Mono Lake ... K-9
Monrovia ... ★
  Vicinity ... Pg. 128, C-7
Montague ... B-4
Montara ... ★
  Vicinity ... Pg. 157, J-1
Montclair ... ★
  Vicinity ... Pg. 128, D-10
Monte Rio ... H-2

Monte Serona ... ★
Montebello ... ★
  Vicinity ... Pg. 126, D-6
Montecito ... R-7
Monterey ... M-4
Monterey Park ... ★
  Vicinity ... Pg. 126, D-5
Montgomery Creek ... C-5
Montrose ... ★
  Vicinity ... Pg. 126, B-5
Moorpark ... S-9
Moraga ... ★
  Vicinity ... Pg. 156, D-5
Moraga ... ★
  Vicinity ... Pg. 156, D-5
Moreno ... ★
  Vicinity ... Pg. 155, C-7
Morgan ... ★
  Vicinity ... Pg. 158, G-10
Morgan Hill ... L-5
Mormon Bar ... K-7
Morongo Valley ... T-13
Morro Bay ... Q-5
Moss Beach ... ★
  Vicinity ... Pg. 157, J-1
Moss Landing ... M-4
Mountain View ... ★
  Vicinity ... Pg. 158, B-3
Mt. Bullion ... K-7
Mt. Helix ... ★
  Vicinity ... Pg. 155, F-6
Mt. Laguna ... V-13
Mt. Shasta ... C-4
Mugginsville ... B-4
Murphys ... J-7
Murrieta ... U-12
Napa ... J-4
National City ... ★
  Vicinity ... Pg. 155, H-4
Navarro ... G-2
Needles ... R-16
Nevada City ... G-6
New Cuyama ... R-7
New Idria ... N-6
Newark ... ★
  Vicinity ... Pg. 157, J-6
Newberry Springs ... R-13
Newell ... B-6
Newport Beach ... T-10
  Vicinity ... Pg. 129, J-8
Nice ... G-3
Niland ... U-15
Nipomo ... Q-6
Nipton ... Q-15
Norco ... ★
  Vicinity ... Pg. 129, E-11
Nord ... F-5
North Edwards ... R-11
North Fork ... L-8
North Hollywood ... ★
  Vicinity ... Pg. 126, C-3
Northridge ... ★
  Vicinity ... Pg. 126, B-1
Norwalk ... ★
  Vicinity ... Pg. 127, F-6
Novato ... J-3
Noyo ... F-2
Nubieber ... C-6
O'Neals ... L-8
Oakdale ... K-6
Oakhurst ... L-8
Oakland ... K-4
  Vicinity ... Pg. 156, E-4
Oasis ... L-11
Oceano ... Q-6
Oceanside ... U-11
Ocotillo ... V-14
Ocotillo Wells ... V-14
Ojai ... S-8
Olancha ... N-11
Old Station ... D-6
Olema ... J-3
Olinda ... D-4
Ono ... D-4
Ontario ... T-11
  Vicinity ... Pg. 128, D-10
Onyx ... P-10
Orange ... ★
  Vicinity ... Pg. 129, G-8
Orange Cove ... M-9
Orcutt ... R-6
Ordbend ... F-5
Orick ... B-1
Orland ... F-4
Orleans ... C-2
Oro Grande ... R-12
Orosi ... N-9
Oroville ... F-5
Otay ... ★
  Vicinity ... Pg. 155, K-5
Otay Mesa ... ★
  Vicinity ... Pg. 155, K-7
Oxnard ... S-8
Pacific Grove ... M-4
Pacific Palisades ... ★
  Vicinity ... Pg. 126, D-1
Pacifica ... ★
  Vicinity ... Pg. 157, G-1
Paicines ... M-5
Pala ... U-12
Palermo ... F-5
Palm Desert ... T-13
Palm Springs ... T-13
Palmdale ... S-10

Palms ... ★
  Vicinity ... Pg. 126, D-3
Palo Alto ... K-4
  Vicinity ... Pg. 158, B-2
Palo Verde ... U-16
Palomar Mountain ... U-13
Palos Verdes Estates ... ★
  Vicinity ... Pg. 127, G-3
Panamint Sprs. ... N-12
Panoche ... M-6
Panorama City ... ★
  Vicinity ... Pg. 126, B-2
Paradise ... F-5
Paramount ... ★
  Vicinity ... Pg. 127, F-5
Parker Dam ... S-17
Parkfield ... P-6
Pasadena ... ★
  Vicinity ... Pg. 126, C-5
Paskenta ... E-4
Paso Robles ... P-6
Patterson ... K-6
Patton ... ★
  Vicinity ... Pg. 128, A-12
Pauma Valley ... U-12
Pearblossom ... S-11
Pebble Beach ... M-4
Pedley ... ★
  Vicinity ... Pg. 129, E-12
Penn Valley ... G-6
Perris ... T-12
Petrolia ... D-1
Phelan ... S-11
Philo ... G-2
Pico Rivera ... ★
  Vicinity ... Pg. 126, E-6
Piedmont ... ★
  Vicinity ... Pg. 156, D-4
Piercy ... E-2
Pine Grove ... J-6
Pine Valley ... V-13
Pinecrest ... J-8
Pinedale ... M-8
Pinole ... ★
  Vicinity ... Pg. 156, B-3
Pioneer Station ... J-7
Pismo Beach ... Q-6
Pittsburg ... ★
  Vicinity ... Pg. 156, A-7
Pixley ... P-9
Placentia ... ★
  Vicinity ... Pg. 129, F-8
Placerville ... H-6
Planada ... L-7
Pleasant Hill ... ★
  Vicinity ... Pg. 156, B-6
Plymouth ... H-6
Point Arena ... G-2
Pollock Pines ... H-7
Pomona ... T-11
  Vicinity ... Pg. 128, D-9
Pondosa ... C-5
Poplar ... P-9
Port Hueneme ... S-8
Portola ... F-7
Portola Valley ... ★
  Vicinity ... Pg. 158, C-1
Portuguese Bend ... ★
  Vicinity ... Pg. 127, H-3
Potter Valley ... G-2
Poway ... V-12
  Vicinity ... Pg. 155, B-5
Pozo ... Q-6
Princeton ... G-4
  Vicinity ... Pg. 157, J-1
Project City ... D-4
Pulga ... F-6
Pumpkin Center ... Q-9
Quincy ... F-6
Raisin ... M-7
Ramona ... V-12
Rancho Palos Verdes ... T-9
Randsburg ... Q-11
Ravendale ... D-7
Red Bluff ... E-4
Red Mountain ... Q-11
Redcrest ... D-1
Redding ... D-4
Redlands ... ★
  Vicinity ... Pg. 128, B-12
Redondo Beach ... T-9
  Vicinity ... Pg. 127, G-3
Redway ... E-2
Redwood City ... ★
  Vicinity ... Pg. 157, J-4
Redwood Valley ... G-2
Requa ... B-1
Reseda ... ★
  Vicinity ... Pg. 126, B-1
Rialto ... ★
  Vicinity ... Pg. 128, A-10
Richmond ... ★
  Vicinity ... Pg. 156, C-2
Richvale ... F-5
Ridgecrest ... Q-11
Rio Dell ... D-1
Rio Linda ... H-5
Rio Oso ... H-5
Rio Vista ... J-5
Ripley ... U-16
Ripon ... K-5
River Pines ... H-6
Riverdale ... N-7
Riverside ... T-12
  Vicinity ... Pg. 129, E-12

★ Denotes City only on Vicinity map. City not located on State map.

CALIFORNIA

Rocklin ... H-5
Rockport ... F-2
Rodeo ... ★
  Vicinity ... Pg. 156, A-3
Rohnert Park ... J-3
Rolling Hills ... ★
  Vicinity ... Pg. 127, G-3
Rolling Hills Estates ... ★
  Vicinity ... Pg. 127, G-3
Romoland ... T-12
Rosamond ... R-10
Rosemead ... ★
  Vicinity ... Pg. 126, D-6
Roseville ... H-5
Rough And Ready ... G-6
Round Mountain ... D-5
Rovana ... L-10
Rowland Heights ... ★
  Vicinity ... Pg. 128, E-8
Rutherford ... H-4
Sacramento ... H-5
Salinas ... M-5
Salton City ... U-14
Salyer ... C-2
San Andreas ... J-7
San Ardo ... N-6
San Bernardino ... T-12
  Vicinity ... Pg. 128, A-11
San Carlos ... ★
  Vicinity ... Pg. 157, J-3
San Clemente ... U-11
  Vicinity ... Pg. 129, G-7
San Diego ... V-12
  Vicinity ... Pg. 155
San Dimas ... ★
  Vicinity ... Pg. 128, C-9
San Fernando ... S-10
  Vicinity ... Pg. 126, A-2
San Francisco ... K-3
  Vicinity ... Pg. 157
San Gabriel ... ★
  Vicinity ... Pg. 126, C-6
San Jacinto ... T-12
San Joaquin ... M-7
San Jose ... L-5
  Vicinity ... Pg. 158, D-8
San Juan Bautista ... M-5
San Juan Capistrano ... U-11
San Leandro ... ★
  Vicinity ... Pg. 157, F-5
San Lorenzo ... ★
  Vicinity ... Pg. 157, G-5
San Lucas ... N-5
San Luis Obispo ... Q-6
San Marcos ... U-12
San Marino ... ★
  Vicinity ... Pg. 126, C-6
San Martin ... L-5
San Mateo ... K-3
  Vicinity ... Pg. 157, H-3
San Miguel ... P-6
San Pablo ... ★
  Vicinity ... Pg. 156, B-3
San Pedro ... ★
  Vicinity ... Pg. 127, H-4
San Rafael ... J-3
  Vicinity ... Pg. 156, B-1
San Simeon ... P-5
Sanger ... M-8
Santa Ana ... T-11
  Vicinity ... Pg. 129, H-8
Santa Barbara ... S-7
Santa Clara ... ★
  Vicinity ... Pg. 158, C-5
Santa Cruz ... L-4
Santa Fe Springs ... ★
  Vicinity ... Pg. 127, E-6
Santa Margarita ... Q-6
Santa Maria ... R-7
Santa Monica ... ★
  Vicinity ... Pg. 126, E-2
Santa Nella ... L-6
Santa Paula ... S-8
Santa Rosa ... H-3
Santa Ysabel ... V-13
Santee ... V12
  Vicinity ... Pg. 155, D-6
Saratoga ... ★
  Vicinity ... Pg. 158, E-4
Saticoy ... S-9
Sattley ... F-7
Sausalito ... J-3
  Vicinity ... Pg. 156, D-1
Sawyers Bar ... C-3
Scotia ... D-1
Scotts Valley ... L-4
Scottys Castle ... M-12
Seeley ... V-14
Selma ... M-8
Shafter ... Q-8
Shandon ... P-6
Shasta ... D-4
Shaver Lake ... L-8
Shelter Cove ... E-1
Shingletown ... D-5
Short Acres ... ★
  Vicinity ... Pg. 156, A-6
Shoshone ... P-14
Sierra City ... F-7
Sierraville ... F-7
Signal Hill ... ★
  Vicinity ... Pg. 127, G-5
Simi Valley ... S-9
Simmler ... Q-7
Sisquoc ... R-7
Sites ... G-4

Sloat ... F-7
Smith River ... A-2
Snelling ... K-7
Soda Springs ... G-7
Solana Beach ... ★
  Vicinity ... Pg. 155, A-1
Soledad ... N-5
Solvang ... R-7
Somerset ... H-7
Somes Bar ... B-3
Sonoma ... J-3
Sonora ... K-7
Soquel ... L-4
Sorrento ... ★
South El Monte ... ★
  Vicinity ... Pg. 126, D-6
South Gate ... ★
  Vicinity ... Pg. 127, E-5
South Lake Tahoe ... H-8
South Pasadena ... ★
  Vicinity ... Pg. 126, C-5
South San Francisco ... ★
  Vicinity ... Pg. 157, G-2
Spring Valley ... ★
  Vicinity ... Pg. 155, G-6
Springville ... N-9
Squaw Valley ... K-8
St. Helena ... H-3
Standish ... E-7
Stanton ... ★
  Vicinity ... Pg. 129, G-7
Stewarts Point ... H-2
Stirling City ... F-5
Stockton ... K-5
Stonyford ... F-4
Stovepipe Wells ... N-12
Stratford ... N-8
Strathmore ... N-9
Studio City ... ★
  Vicinity ... Pg. 126, C-3
Suisun City ... J-4
Summerland ... S-8
Summit City ... D-4
Sun City ... T-12
Sun Valley ... ★
  Vicinity ... Pg. 126, B-3
Sunland ... ★
  Vicinity ... Pg. 126, A-3
Sunnyside ... ★
  Vicinity ... Pg. 155, H-6
Sunnyvale ... K-5
  Vicinity ... Pg. 158, C-4
Surf ... R-6
Susanville ... E-7
Sutter ... G-5
Sutter Creek ... J-7
Taft ... Q-8
Tahoe City ... G-7
Talmage ... G-3
Tarzana ... ★
  Vicinity ... Pg. 126, C-1
Taylorsville ... E-7
Tecopa ... P-14
Tehachapi ... Q-10
Temecula ... U-12
Temple City ... ★
  Vicinity ... Pg. 126, C-6
Templeton ... P-6
Terminous ... J-5
Termo ... D-7
Terra Bella ... N-9
Thornton ... J-5
Thousand Oaks ... S-9
Thousand Palms ... T-13
Three Rivers ... N-9
Tiburon ... ★
  Vicinity ... Pg. 156, D-1
Tipton ... N-8
Tomales ... J-3
Topanga ... ★
  Vicinity ... Pg. 126, D-1
Topanga Beach ... ★
  Vicinity ... Pg. 126, D-1
Topaz ... H-8
Torrance ... ★
  Vicinity ... Pg. 127, F-3
Tracy ... K-5
Tranquility ... M-7
Tres Pinos ... M-5
Trinidad ... C-1
Trinity Center ... C-3
Trona ... P-12
Truckee ... G-7
Tujunga ... ★
  Vicinity ... Pg. 126, A-4
Tulelake ... B-6
Tuolumne ... K-7
Turlock ... K-6
Tustin ... ★
  Vicinity ... Pg. 129, G-9
Tuttletown ... K-7
Twain ... F-6
Twain Harte ... K-7
Twentynine Palms ... S-14
Ukiah ... G-2
Union City ... ★
  Vicinity ... Pg. 157, H-6
Universal City ... ★
  Vicinity ... Pg. 126, C-3
Upland ... ★
  Vicinity ... Pg. 128, C-10
Upper Lake ... G-3
Vacaville ... H-4

Valencia ... S-9
Vallejo ... J-4
Valley Springs ... J-6
Van Nuys ... ★
  Vicinity ... Pg. 126, B-2
Venice ... ★
  Vicinity ... Pg. 126, E-2
Ventura ... S-8
Victorville ... S-12
Vidal ... T-17
Vina ... E-4
Vinton ... F-8
Visalia ... N-8
Vista ... U-12
Walker ... J-8
Walnut ... ★
  Vicinity ... Pg. 128, D-8
Walnut Creek ... K-4
  Vicinity ... Pg. 156, C-6
Walnut Grove ... J-5
Wasco ... P-8
Washington ... G-7
Waterford ... K-6
Waterloo ... J-6
Watsonville ... L-4
Watts ... ★
  Vicinity ... Pg. 127, E-4
Wawona ... K-8
Weaverville ... D-3
Weed ... C-4
Weitchpec ... C-2
Wendel ... E-8
Weott ... D-1
West Covina ... ★
  Vicinity ... Pg. 128, D-8
West Hollywood ... ★
  Vicinity ... Pg. 126, D-3
West Los Angeles ... ★
  Vicinity ... Pg. 126, D-2
West Point ... J-7
West Riverside ... ★
  Vicinity ... Pg. 128, D-12
Westley ... K-6
Westminister ... ★
  Vicinity ... Pg. 129, G-7
Westmorland ... V-14
Westport ... F-2
Westwood ... E-6
Wheatland ... G-5
Whitmore ... D-5
Whittier ... ★
  Vicinity ... Pg. 129, E-7
Williams ... F-2
Willits ... F-2
Willow Creek ... C-2
Willow Ranch ... B-8
Willow Springs ... R-10
Willows ... F-4
Wilmington ... ★
  Vicinity ... Pg. 127, G-4
Winter Gardens ... ★
  Vicinity ... Pg. 155, D-6
Winterhaven ... V-16
Winters ... H-4
Winton ... L-6
Wofford Heights ... P-10
Woodfords ... H-8
Woodlake ... N-9
Woodland ... H-4
Woodville ... N-9
Woody ... P-9
Wrightwood ... S-11
Yermo ... R-12
Yolo ... H-5
Yorba Linda ... ★
  Vicinity ... Pg. 129, F-9
Yorkville ... G-2
Yosemite Village ... K-8
Yreka ... B-4
Yuba City ... G-5
Yucaipa ... T-12
Yucca Valley ... S-13

COLORADO
Pages 28-29

Abarr ... C-12
Agate ... D-10
Aguilar ... J-9
Akron ... C-11
Alamosa ... J-7
Allison ... J-5
Alma ... E-7
Almont ... F-6
Amherst ... B-12
Antero Jct. ... F-7
Anton ... D-11
Antonito ... J-7
Arapahoe ... E-12
Arboles ... J-5
Arlington ... G-11
Aroya ... F-11
Arriba ... E-11
Arriola ... J-3
Arvada ... D-8
  Vicinity ... Pg. 117, C-3
Aspen ... E-6
Atwood ... B-11
Ault ... B-9
Aurora ... D-9
  Vicinity ... Pg. 117, D-7
Austin ... F-4
Avon ... D-7
Avondale ... G-9

Bailey ... E-8
Barnesville ... B-9
Bartlett ... H-12
Basalt ... E-6
Baxter ... G-9
Bayfield ... J-5
Bedrock ... G-3
Bellvue ... B-9
Bennett ... D-9
Berthoud ... C-8
Beshoar Jct. ... J-10
Bethune ... D-12
Beulah ... H-8
Black Hawk ... D-8
Blanca ... J-7
Blue Mountain ... C-3
Blue River ... E-7
Bond ... D-6
Boone ... G-9
Boulder ... C-8
  Vicinity ... Pg. 117, A-3
Bowie ... F-5
Boyero ... E-11
Brandon ... F-12
Branson ... J-10
Breckenridge ... D-7
Breen ... J-4
Briggsdale ... B-9
Brighton ... C-8
Bristol ... G-12
Broomfield ... C-8
  Vicinity ... Pg. 117, A-3
Brush ... C-10
Buckingham ... B-9
Buena Vista ... F-7
Buford ... D-5
Burlington ... D-12
Byers ... D-9
Cahone ... H-3
Calhan ... E-10
Cameo ... E-4
Campo ... J-11
Canon City ... F-8
Capulin ... J-7
Carbondale ... E-5
Carlton ... G-12
Castle Rock ... D-8
Cedaredge ... F-4
Center ... H-7
Chama ... J-8
Chatfield Acres ... ★
  Vicinity ... Pg. 117, K-4
Cheney Center ... G-12
Cheraw ... G-11
Cherry Hill Village ... ★
  Vicinity ... Pg. 117, G-5
Cheyenne Wells ... F-12
Chimney Rock ... J-5
Chipita Park ... F-9
Chivington ... F-12
Chromo ... J-6
Cimarron ... F-5
Clarkville ... B-12
Clifton ... E-4
Climax ... E-7
Coaldale ... G-7
Coalmont ... C-6
Collbran ... E-4
Colorado City ... G-8
Colorado Springs ... F-9
Columbine ... ★
  Vicinity ... Pg. 117, J-3
Commerce City ... ★
  Vicinity ... Pg. 117, D-6
Como ... E-7
Conejos ... J-7
Conifer ... D-8
Cope ... D-11
Cortez ... J-3
Cotopaxi ... G-8
Cowdrey ... B-6
Craig ... B-5
Crawford ... F-5
Creede ... H-6
Crested Butte ... F-6
Cripple Creek ... F-8
Critchell ... ★
  Vicinity ... Pg. 117, K-1
Crook ... B-11
Crowley ... G-10
Cuchara ... J-9
Dailey ... B-11
DeBeque ... E-4
Deckers ... E-8
Deer Ridge ... C-7
Deer Trail ... D-10
Deertmont ... ★
  Vicinity ... Pg. 117, K-2
Del Norte ... H-7
Delhi ... H-10
Delta ... F-4
Denver ... D-9
  Vicinity ... Pg. 117
Dillon ... D-7
Dinosaur ... C-3
Divide ... F-8
Dolores ... H-4
Dotsero ... D-6
Dove Creek ... H-3
Dowd ... D-6
Doyleville ... F-6
Drake ... C-8
Dunton ... H-4
Dupont ... ★
  Vicinity ... Pg. 117, D-6
Durango ... J-4

Eads ... F-12
Eagle ... D-6
Eastlake ... ★
  Vicinity ... Pg. 117, A-5
Eaton ... B-9
Echo Lake ... D-7
Eckley ... C-12
Edgewater ... ★
  Vicinity ... Pg. 117, E-3
Edwards ... D-6
Egnar ... H-3
El Dorado Estates ... ★
  Vicinity ... Pg. 117, C-1
Eldorado Springs ... D-8
Elizabeth ... E-9
Elk Springs ... C-4
Ellicott ... F-9
Empire ... D-7
Englewood ... D-8
  Vicinity ... Pg. 117, G-5
Estes Park ... C-7
Evans ... C-9
Fairplay ... E-7
Falcon ... F-9
Farisita ... H-8
Federal Heights ... ★
  Vicinity ... Pg. 117, B-4
Fenders ... ★
  Vicinity ... Pg. 117, J-1
Firstview ... F-12
Flagler ... E-11
Fleming ... B-11
Florence ... G-8
Florissant ... F-8
Ford ... G-10
Fort Collins ... B-8
Fort Garland ... J-8
Fort Lewis ... J-4
Fort Lupton ... C-9
Fort Lyon ... G-11
Fort Morgan ... C-10
Fountain ... F-9
Fowler ... G-10
Franktown ... E-9
Fraser ... D-7
Frederick ... C-8
Frisco ... D-7
Fruita ... E-3
Galatea ... F-11
Garcia ... J-8
Gardner ... H-8
Garo Park ... E-7
Gateway ... F-3
Genoa ... E-11
Georgetown ... D-7
Gilcrest ... C-9
Gilman ... D-7
Gladstone ... H-5
Glendale ... ★
  Vicinity ... Pg. 117, F-5
Glenwood Springs ... D-5
Golden ... D-8
  Vicinity ... Pg. 117, E-1
Goodrich ... C-10
Gould ... B-7
Granada ... G-12
Granby ... C-7
Grand Junction ... E-3
Grand Lake ... C-7
Grandview Estates ... ★
  Vicinity ... Pg. 117, J-7
Granite ... E-7
Grant ... E-7
Greeley ... C-9
Greenwood Village ... ★
  Vicinity ... Pg. 117, H-5
Guffey ... F-8
Gunnison ... F-6
Gypsum ... D-6
Hamilton ... C-5
Hartsel ... E-7
Hasty ... G-11
Haswell ... F-11
Hawley ... G-10
Haxtun ... B-12
Hayden ... C-5
Henderson ... ★
  Vicinity ... Pg. 117, A-6
Hermosa ... J-5
Hesperus ... J-4
Hiawatha ... B-3
Hillrose ... C-10
Hillside ... G-8
Hoehne ... J-9
Holly ... G-12
Holyoke ... B-12
Homelake ... H-7
Homewood Park ... ★
  Vicinity ... Pg. 117, K-1
Hooper ... H-7
Hot Sulphur Springs ... C-7
Hotchkiss ... F-5
Howard ... G-8
Hudson ... C-9
Hugo ... E-11
Idaho Sprs. ... D-8
Idalia ... D-12
Idledale ... ★
  Vicinity ... Pg. 117, F-1
Ignacio ... J-5
Iliff ... B-11
Indian Hills ... ★
  Vicinity ... Pg. 117, H-1
Jansen ... J-9

Jaroso ... J-8
Jefferson ... E-7
Joes ... D-12
Johnson Village ... F-7
Julesburg ... A-12
Keenesburg ... C-9
Kersey ... C-9
Kim ... J-11
Kiowa ... E-9
Kit Carson ... F-11
Kline ... J-4
Komman ... G-12
Kremmling ... C-7
La Jara ... J-7
La Junta ... G-11
La Salle ... C-9
La Veta ... H-9
Lafayette ... C-8
Laird ... B-12
Lake City ... G-5
Lake George ... F-8
Lakewood ... D-8
  Vicinity ... Pg. 117, F-2
Lamar ... G-12
Larkspur ... E-9
Las Animas ... G-11
Last Chance ... D-10
Lay ... C-4
Lazear ... F-5
Leadville ... E-7
Lebanon ... J-4
Lewis ... J-3
Limon ... E-10
Lindon ... D-11
Littleton ... D-8
  Vicinity ... Pg. 117, H-4
Lochbule ... C-9
Log Lane Village ... C-10
Loma ... E-3
Longmont ... C-8
Loveland ... C-8
Lucerne ... C-9
Lycan ... H-12
Lyons ... C-8
Mack ... E-3
Maher ... F-5
Malta ... E-6
Manassa ... J-7
Mancos ... J-4
Manitou Springs ... F-8
Manzanola ... G-10
Marble ... E-5
Marshall ... ★
  Vicinity ... Pg. 117, A-1
Marvel ... J-4
Masters ... C-9
Matheson ... E-10
Maybell ... B-4
McClave ... G-11
McCoy ... D-6
Meeker ... C-4
Meeker Park ... C-8
Merino ... B-10
Mesa ... E-4
Mesita ... J-8
Milliken ... C-8
Milner ... B-5
Mineral Hot Springs ... G-7
Minturn ... D-7
Model ... J-10
Moffat ... G-7
Molina ... E-4
Monte Vista ... H-7
Montrose ... F-4
Monument ... E-9
Monument Park ... J-9
Morrison ... ★
  Vicinity ... Pg. 117, G-2
Mosca ... H-7
Mount Princeton Hot Springs ... F-7
Mountain View ... ★
  Vicinity ... Pg. 117, D-3
Nathrop ... F-7
Naturita ... G-3
Nederland ... D-7
New Castle ... D-5
Northglenn ... C-8
  Vicinity ... Pg. 117, B-5
Norwood ... G-4
Nucla ... G-4
Nunn ... B-9
Oak Creek ... C-6
Olathe ... F-4
Olney Springs ... G-10
Ophir ... H-4
Orchard ... C-9
Orchard City ... F-4
Ordway ... G-10
Otis ... C-11
Ouray ... H-4
Ovid ... A-12
Oxford ... J-5
Pagosa Sprs. ... J-6
Palisade ... E-4
Palmer Lake ... E-9
Paoli ... B-12
Paonia ... F-5
Parachute ... E-4
Paradox ... G-3
Park ... F-9
Parkdale ... F-8
Parker ... D-9
Parlin ... F-6
Parshall ... C-7
Peetz ... A-11

Penrose ... F-9
Peyton ... E-9
Phillipsburg ... ★
  Vicinity ... Pg. 117, K-2
Phippsburg ... C-6
Pierce ... B-9
Pinewood Springs ... C-8
Placerville ... G-4
Platoro ... J-6
Platteville ... C-9
Pleasant View ... H-3
  Vicinity ... Pg. 117, C-1
Poncha Springs ... F-7
Poudre Park ... B-8
Powderhorn ... G-6
Pritchett ... H-12
Proctor ... B-11
Prospect Valley ... C-9
Pryor ... H-9
Pueblo ... G-9
Pueblo West ... G-8
Punkin Center ... F-10
Ramah ... E-9
Rand ... C-7
Rangely ... C-3
Raymer ... B-10
Raymond ... C-8
Red Mountain ... H-5
Redcliff ... E-6
Redmesa ... J-4
Redstone ... E-5
Redvale ... G-4
Rico ... H-4
Ridgway ... G-4
Rifle ... D-4
Rio Blanco ... D-4
Rockport ... B-9
Rockwood ... H-5
Rocky ... G-10
Roggen ... C-9
Rollinsville ... D-7
Romeo ... J-7
Royal Gorge ... G-8
Rush ... F-10
Rustic ... B-8
Rye ... H-8
Saguache ... G-7
Salida ... F-7
San Acacio ... J-8
San Francisco ... J-8
San Luis ... J-8
San Pablo ... J-8
Sanford ... J-7
Sapinero ... G-5
Sargents ... G-7
Saw Pit ... G-4
Sedalia ... E-8
Sedgewick ... A-11
Segundo ... J-9
Seibert ... E-11
Shawnee ... E-8
Sheridan ... ★
  Vicinity ... Pg. 117, G-4
Sheridan Lake ... F-12
Silt ... D-5
Silver Cliff ... G-8
Silverthorne ... D-7
Silverton ... H-5
Simla ... E-10
Skyway ... E-4
Slick Rock ... G-3
Snow Mass ... E-6
Snow Mass Village ... E-6
Snyder ... C-10
Somerset ... F-5
South Fork ... H-6
Spar City ... H-6
Springfield ... H-12
Starkville ... J-9
State Bridge ... D-6
Steamboat Springs ... B-6
Sterling ... B-11
Stoneham ... B-10
Stoner ... H-4
Stonewall ... J-9
Strasburg ... D-9
Stratton ... D-12
Sugar City ... G-11
Summitville ... H-7
Sunbeam ... B-4
Superior ... ★
  Vicinity ... Pg. 117, A-2
Swink ... G-10
Tabernash ... D-7
Telluride ... H-4
Texas Creek ... G-8
Thatcher ... H-10
The Forks ... B-8
Thronton ... D-9
  Vicinity ... Pg. 117, B-5
Timpas ... H-10
Tiny Town ... ★
  Vicinity ... Pg. 117, H-1
Tobe ... H-11
Toonerville ... H-11
Toponas ... C-6
Towaoc ... J-3
Towner ... F-12
Trinidad ... J-9
Twin Forks ... ★
  Vicinity ... Pg. 117, H-1
Twinlakes ... E-6

Two Buttes ... H-12
Tyrone ... H-10
Uravan ... G-3
Utleyville ... J-11
Vail ... D-7
Valdez ... J-9
Vancorum ... G-3
Victor ... F-8
Vilas ... H-12
Villa Grove ... G-7
Vineland ... G-9
Virginia Dale ... A-8
Vona ... E-11
Wagon Wheel Gap ... H-6
Walden ... B-6
Walsenburg ... H-9
Walsh ... H-12
Watkins ... D-9
Welby ... ★
  Vicinity ... Pg. 117, C-5
Weldona ... C-10
Westcliffe ... G-8
Westcreek ... E-8
Westminster ... D-8
  Vicinity ... Pg. 117, B-3
Weston ... J-9
Wetmore ... G-8
Wheat Ridge ... E-7
  Vicinity ... Pg. 117, E-3
Whitewater ... F-4
Wiggins ... C-10
Wild Horse ... F-11
Wiley ... G-12
Windsor ... B-8
Winter Park ... D-7
Wolcott ... D-6
Woodland Park ... F-8
Woodrow ... C-10
Woody Creek ... E-6
Wray ... C-12
Yampa ... C-6
Yellow Jacket ... H-3
Yoder ... F-9
Yuma ... C-12

CONNECTICUT
Page 30

Andover ... F-6
Ansonia ... H-3
Ashford ... F-7
Avon ... F-4
Barkhamsted ... E-4
Berlin ... G-4
Bethany ... H-2
Bethel ... H-2
Bethlehem ... G-3
Bloomfield ... F-4
Branford ... J-4
Bridgeport ... J-2
Bristol ... F-4
Brookfield ... G-2
Brooklyn ... F-7
Burlington ... F-4
Canaan ... E-2
Canterbury ... F-7
Canton ... F-4
Chaplin ... F-7
Cheshire ... G-4
Chester ... H-6
Clinton ... J-5
Colchester ... G-6
Colebrook ... E-3
Columbia ... F-6
Cornwall ... F-2
Cornwall Bridge ... F-2
Coventry ... F-6
Cromwell ... G-5
Darien ... J-2
Dayville ... F-8
Deep River ... H-6
Derby ... H-3
Durham ... G-5
E. Hartland ... E-4
East Granby ... F-4
East Hampton ... G-5
East Hartford ... F-5
East Haven ... J-4
East Lyme ... H-3
Eastford ... E-7
Ellington ... E-5
Enfield ... E-5
Essex ... H-6
Fairfield ... J-2
Falls Vill. ... E-2
Farmington ... F-4
Franklin ... F-6
Georgetown ... J-2
Glastonbury ... F-5
Goshen ... F-3
Granby ... E-4
Greenwich ... K-1
Groton ... H-7
Guilford ... J-5
Haddam ... H-5
Hamden ... H-4
Hampton ... F-7
Hartford ... F-5
Harwinton ... F-3
Hebron ... G-6
Kent ... F-2
Killingworth ... H-5
Lebanon ... G-7
Ledyard Ctr. ... H-7
Litchfield ... F-3

★ Denotes City only on Vicinity map. City not located on State map.

CONNECTICUT

City	Grid
Madison	H-5
Manchester	F-5
Marlborough	G-6
Melrose	E-4
Meriden	G-4
Middlefield	G-5
Middletown	G-5
Milford	J-3
Monroe	H-2
Morris	G-3
N. Canton	E-4
Naugatuck	G-3
New Britain	G-4
New Canaan	J-1
New Fairfield	H-1
New Hartford	F-3
New Haven	H-4
New London	H-7
New Milford	G-2
Newington	F-4
Newtown	H-2
No. Stonington	H-8
Norfolk	E-3
North Branford	H-4
North Haven	H-4
Norwalk	J-2
Norwich	G-7
Old Saybrook	J-6
Plainfield	G-7
Plymouth	F-3
Pomfret	E-7
Prospect	H-3
Putnam	E-8
Redding	H-2
Ridgefield	H-1
Rocky Hill	G-5
Salem	G-6
Salisbury	E-2
Scotland	F-7
Seymour	H-3
Sharon	E-2
Shelton	H-3
Simsbury	F-4
Somers	E-6
South Windsor	F-5
Southbury	G-2
Southington	G-4
Stafford	E-6
Stamford	K-1
Sterling	F-8
Stratford	J-3
Suffield	E-5
Thomaston	G-3
Thompson	E-8
Tolland	E-6
Torrington	F-3
Trumbull	J-2
Union	E-7
Vernon	F-5
Voluntown	G-8
Wallingford	H-4
Warren	F-2
Washington	G-2
Waterbury	G-3
Waterford	H-7
Watertown	G-3
West Hartford	F-4
West Haven	J-4
Westbrook	H-5
Westchester	G-6
Weston	J-2
Westport	J-2
Wethersfield	F-5
Willington	F-6
Wilton	J-2
Windsor	F-5
Windsor Locks	E-5
Wolcott	G-4
Woodbridge	H-3
Woodbury	G-2
Woodstock	E-7

DELAWARE
Page 47

City	Grid
Angola	F-15
Bethany Beach	F-15
Blades	F-13
Bowers Beach	D-14
Bridgeville	E-14
Camden	D-13
Cheswold	C-13
Clayton	C-13
Delaware City	B-13
Dewey Beach	E-15
Dover	C-13
Ellendale	E-14
Elsmere	A-13
Felton	D-13
Fenwick Is.	F-15
Frankford	F-15
Frederica	D-14
Georgetown	F-14
Greenwood	E-13
Gumboro	F-14
Harbeson	E-15
Hardscrabble	F-14
Harrington	E-13
Hartly	D-13
Houston	E-14
Laurel	F-14
Leipsic	C-14
Lewes	E-15
Middletown	B-13
Milford	D-14
Millsboro	F-15
Millville	F-15
Milton	E-14
Mission	F-14
New Castle	A-13
Newark	A-13
Newport	A-13
Odessa	B-13
Porter	B-13
Seaford	F-13
Selbyville	F-15
Slaughter Beach	E-15
Smyrna	C-14
Staytonville	E-14
Townsend	C-13
Wilmington	A-14
Wyoming	D-13

DIST. OF COLUMBIA
Page 47

District of Columbia	D-10
Vicinity	Pg. 162, F-5

FLORIDA
Pages 32-33

City	Grid
Adamsville	★
Vicinity	Pg. 160, F-9
Alachua	C-5
Apalachicola	Q-6
Apopka	F-7
Appollo Beach	★
Arcadia	J-6
Archer	D-5
Atlantic Beach	B-7
Avon Pk.	H-7
Baldwin	B-6
Bartow	G-6
Bay Harbor Is.	★
Vicinity	Pg. 132, B-5
Bay Pines	★
Vicinity	Pg. 160, F-2
Bayview	★
Vicinity	Pg. 160, C-4
Belle Glade	K-9
Belleair	★
Vicinity	Pg. 160, D-2
Belleair Beach	★
Vicinity	Pg. 160, D-1
Belleair Bluffs	★
Vicinity	Pg. 160, D-1
Belleair Shores	★
Vicinity	Pg. 160, D-1
Belleview	E-6
Big Island	★
Vicinity	Pg. 160, E-5
Biscayne Park	★
Vicinity	Pg. 132, B-4
Blountstown	P-6
Bloxham	B-1
Boca Ciega	★
Vicinity	Pg. 160, G-2
Boca Raton	L-10
Bonifay	N-5
Bonita Spr.	L-6
Bradenton	H-5
Brandon	G-5
Branford	C-4
Bridgeport	★
Vicinity	Pg. 160, B-3
Bristol	P-6
Brooksville	F-5
Bunnell	D-7
Bushnell	F-6
Callahan	B-6
Callaway	P-5
Cantonment	N-2
Cape Coral	K-6
Carrabelle	C-6
Casselberry	F-7
Cedar Key	E-4
Chattahoochee	A-1
Chiefland	D-4
Chipley	N-5
Citrus Park	★
Vicinity	Pg. 160, A-6
Citrus Spr.	E-5
Clarcona	★
Vicinity	Pg. 145, C-3
Clearwater	★
Vicinity	Pg. 160, C-2
Clearwater Beach Island	★
Vicinity	Pg. 160, B-2
Clermont	F-6
Clewiston	K-8
Coachman	★
Vicinity	Pg. 160, C-2
Cocoa Beach	F-8
Conway	★
Vicinity	Pg. 145, F-7
Cooper City	L-9
Coral Gables	M-9
Vicinity	Pg. 132, F-2
Coral Gables	M-9
Vicinity	Pg. 132, F-2
Crawfordville	C-2
Crescent City	D-7
Crestview	N-3
Cross City	D-4
Crystal Beach	★
Vicinity	Pg. 160, A-2
Crystal River	E-5
Cutler Ridge	M-9
Dade City	E-6
Daytona Beach	E-8
DeBary	E-7
DeFuniak Spr.	N-4
DeLeon Springs	E-7
Delray Beach	K-10
Deltona	E-7
Dover	G-5
Dunedin	H-4
Vicinity	Pg. 160, B-2
East Palatka	D-7
East Tampa	★
Vicinity	Pg. 160, E-9
Eastpoint	Q-6
Eatonville	★
Vicinity	Pg. 145, C-6
Edgewater	E-8
El Portal	★
Vicinity	Pg. 132, C-4
Ellenton	H-5
Englewood	J-5
Ensley	N-2
Eustis	E-6
Everglades City	M-7
Fairvilla	★
Vicinity	Pg. 145, D-5
Fellsmere	H-9
Fernandina Beach	B-7
Flagler Beach	D-7
Florida City	M-9
Forest City	★
Vicinity	Pg. 145, B-5
Four Corners	★
Vicinity	Pg. 160, D-3
Freeport	N-4
Frost Proof	H-7
Ft. Basinger	H-8
Ft. Lauderdale	L-10
Ft. Meyers Beach	K-6
Ft. Walton Beach	N-3
Ft. White	C-5
Gainesville	D-5
Gardenville	★
Vicinity	Pg. 160, F-9
Gibsonton	★
Vicinity	Pg. 160, F-10
Gifford	H-9
Gotha	★
Vicinity	Pg. 145, E-3
Graceville	M-5
Green Cove Spr.	C-6
Greenville	B-3
Gretna	B-1
Grove City	J-5
Gulfport	★
Vicinity	Pg. 160, G-4
Haines City	G-7
Harney	★
Vicinity	Pg. 160, B-10
Hastings	D-7
Havana	B-2
Hawthorne	D-6
Hialeah	M-9
Vicinity	Pg. l32, C-2
High Springs	C-5
Hilliard	A-6
Hobe Sound	J-10
Hollywood	L-10
Holmes Beach	H-5
Homestead	M-9
Homosassa	E-5
Hosford	P-6
Hudson	F-5
Indian Creek Village	★
Vicinity	Pg. 132, B-5
Indian Harbour Beach	G-8
Indian Rocks Beach	★
Vicinity	Pg. 160, E-1
Indian Shores	★
Vicinity	Pg. 160, E-1
Indiantown	J-9
Inglis	E-5
Islamorada	P-9
Jacksonville	B-7
Jacksonville Beach	B-7
Jasper	B-4
Jay	M-1
Kenneth City	★
Vicinity	Pg. 160, F-4
Key Biscayne	★
Vicinity	Pg. 132, G-5
Key Largo	N-9
Key West	P-6
Keystone Hts.	C-6
Kissimmee	F-7
LaBelle	K-7
Lacoochee	E-6
Lake Buena Vista	F-7
Lake Buena Vista	★
Vicinity	Pg. 145, J-3
Lake City	C-5
Lake Park	K-9
Lake Wales	G-7
Lakeland	G-6
Lantana	K-10
Largo	★
Vicinity	Pg. 160, D-2
Lealman	★
Vicinity	Pg. 160, F-5
Leesburg	E-6
Lehigh Acres	K-7
Lighthouse Pt.	L-10
Live Oak	B-4
Lockhart	★
Vicinity	Pg. 145, C-5
Longboat Key	H-5
Lynn Haven	P-5
Macclenny	B-6
Madeira Beach	★
Vicinity	Pg. 160, G-1
Madison	B-3
Marathon	P-8
Marco Is.	L-6
Marianna	N-5
Mayo	C-4
Medley	★
Vicinity	Pg. 132, C-1
Melbourne	G-9
Merritt Is.	F-8
Miami	M-9
Vicinity	Pg. 132
Miami Beach	M-10
Vicinity	Pg. 132, D-6
Miami Shores	★
Vicinity	Pg. 132, D-1
Miami Spr.	M-9
Vicinity	Pg. 132, D-1
Miami Springs	★
Vicinity	Pg. 132, D-1
Milton	N-2
Mims	F-8
Monticello	B-3
Moore Haven	K-8
Mount Dora	E-7
Mullis City	★
Vicinity	Pg. 160, B-7
N. Lauderdale	L-9
Naples	L-6
Naples Pk.	L-6
Neptune Beach	B-7
New Port Richey	G-5
New Smyrna Beach	E-8
Niceville	N-3
North Bay Village	★
Vicinity	Pg. 132, C-5
North Miami	M-9
Vicinity	Pg. 132, B-4
North Miami Beach	★
Vicinity	Pg. 132, A-4
North Palm Beach	K-10
North Port	J-6
North Redington Beach	★
Vicinity	Pg. 160, F-2
North Ruskin	★
Vicinity	Pg. 160, G-10
Nowatney	★
Vicinity	Pg. 160, A-8
Oakhurst	★
Vicinity	Pg. 160, F-1
Oakland Pk.	L-10
Ocala	E-6
Ocoee	★
Vicinity	Pg. 145, D-3
Okeechobee	J-8
Oldsmar	★
Vicinity	Pg. 160, B-4
Opa-Locka	L-9
Vicinity	Pg. 132, B-2
Orange Pk.	C-6
Orient Park	★
Vicinity	Pg. 160, C-9
Orlando	F-7
Orlando	F-7
Vicinity	Pg. 145, E-6
Orlouista	★
Vicinity	Pg. 145, E-4
Ormond Beach	D-8
Ormand by the Sea	D-8
Osprey	J-5
Ozona	★
Vicinity	Pg. 160, A-2
Pace	N-2
Palatka	D-6
Palm	★
Vicinity	Pg. 160, D-9
Palm Bay	G-9
Palm Beach	K-10
Palm Harbor	★
Vicinity	Pg. 160, A-2
Panama City	P-5
Pembroke	G-6
Pembroke Pines	G-6
Pensacola	N-2
Perrine	M-9
Perry	C-3
Pine Castle	★
Vicinity	Pg. 145, G-6
Pinellas Park	★
Vicinity	Pg. 160, F-4
Plant City	G-6
Plymouth	★
Vicinity	Pg. 145, A-2
Pompano Beach	L-10
Port Charlotte	J-6
Port St. Joe	Q-5
Port St. Lucie	H-9
Port Tampa	★
Vicinity	Pg. 160, E-7
Punta Gorda	J-6
Quincy	B-1
Rattlesnake	★
Vicinity	Pg. 160, E-7
Reddick	D-5
Redington Beach	★
Vicinity	Pg. 160, F-1
Redington Shores	★
Vicinity	Pg. 160, F-1
Richmond Hts.	M-9
Ridge Manor	F-6
Riviera Beach	K-10
Rockledge	F-8
Rotonda	K-6
Safety Harbor	★
Vicinity	Pg. 160, C-4
Sanford	E-7
Sanibel	K-6
Sanlando Springs	★
Vicinity	Pg. 145, A-5
Sarasota	J-5
Satellite Beach	G-8
Sebastian	H-9
Sebring	H-7
Seminole	★
Vicinity	Pg. 160, F-2
Sneads	N-6
Sopchoppy	C-1
South Bay	K-8
South Miami	★
Vicinity	Pg. 132, G-1
South Pasadena	★
Vicinity	Pg. 160, G-3
South Venice	J-5
Spivey	★
Vicinity	Pg. 160, B-6
Spring Lake	H-7
Springfield	P-5
St. Augustine	C-7
St. Augustine Beach	C-7
St. Cloud	F-7
St. Petersburg	G-4
Vicinity	Pg. 160, G-4
St. Petersburg Beach	H-4
Stuart	J-10
Sun City Ctr.	H-5
Sunshine Beach	★
Vicinity	Pg. 160, G-2
Tallahassee	B-2
Tampa	G-5
Vicinity	Pg. 160, B-8
Tarpon Spr.	G-4
Temple Terrace	★
Vicinity	Pg. 160, B-10
Tennille	B-2
Thomas City	B-2
Tice	K-6
Titusville	F-8
Treasure Island	H-4
Vicinity	Pg. 160, G-2
Trenton	D-4
Umitilla	E-6
Valparaiso	N-3
Venice	J-5
Vero Beach	H-9
Virginia Gardens	★
Vicinity	Pg. 132, D-1
W. Melbourne	G-9
Wall Springs	★
Vicinity	Pg. 160, A-2
Walsingham	★
Vicinity	Pg. 160, E-2
Warrington	N-2
Watertown	C-5
Wauchula	H-6
Wausau	N-5
Waverly	G-7
West Miami	★
Vicinity	Pg. 132, F-1
West Palm Beach	K-10
Westwood Lake	M-9
Wewahitchka	N-6
White City	Q-5
Wildwood	E-6
Williston	D-5
Wilma	P-6
Winter Garden	F-7
Winter Park	★
Vicinity	Pg. 145, C-6
Winter Pk.	F-7
Winter Spr.	F-7
Woodville	B-2
Zephyrhills	F-6
Zolfo Spr.	H-6

GEORGIA
Page 23

City	Grid
Abbeville	G-10
Adairsville	B-7
Adel	H-9
Adrian	F-11
Alamo	G-10
Alapaha	H-9
Albany	G-8
Aldora	E-8
Allentown	F-10
Alma	H-11
Alpharetta	C-8
Alston	G-11
Alto	B-9
Alvaton	E-8
Ambrose	H-10
Americus	F-8
Amsterdam	J-8
Andersonville	F-8
Apalachee	D-9
Appling	D-11
Arabi	G-9
Aragon	B-7
Arlington	H-7
Arnoldsville	C-10
Ashburn	G-9
Athens	C-9
Atlanta	C-8
Vicinity	Pg. 102-103
Attapulgus	J-8
Augusta	D-11
Austell	C-7
Avalon	B-10
Avondale Estates	★
Vicinity	Pg. 102, F-7
Axson	H-11
Baconton	H-8
Baldwin	B-9
Ball Ground	B-7
Barnesville	E-8
Barney	J-9
Barwick	J-9
Baxley	G-11
Bellville	H-7
Belvidere	★
Vicinity	Pg. 103, G-7
Benevolence	G-8
Berlin	J-9
Berryton	B-6
Between	C-9
Bishop	C-9
Blackshear	H-11
Blairsville	A-8
Blakely	H-7
Blue Ridge	A-8
Bluffton	H-7
Bonaire	F-9
Boston	J-9
Bowdon	D-7
Bowersville	B-10
Bowman	B-10
Bremen	C-8
Bridgeboro	H-8
Bristol	H-11
Bronwood	G-8
Brookhaven	★
Vicinity	Pg. 102, D-5
Broxton	H-10
Brunswick	H-13
Buchanan	C-8
Buena Vista	F-8
Buford	C-9
Byron	E-8
Cadwell	F-10
Cairo	J-8
Calhoun	B-7
Calvary	J-8
Camilla	H-8
Candler	B-9
Canon	B-9
Canoochee	F-11
Canton	B-8
Carnegie	G-7
Carrollton	D-7
Cartersville	C-7
Cave Spring	C-7
Cecil	J-10
Cedar Springs	H-7
Cedartown	C-7
Center	C-9
Centerville	H-7
Vicinity	Pg. 102, C-6
Chatsworth	B-7
Chatthoochee Plantation	★
Vicinity	Pg. 102, B-3
Chauncey	G-10
Chester	F-10
Chickamauga	A-6
Cisco	A-7
Clarkesville	B-9
Clarkston	★
Vicinity	Pg. 102, E-7
Claxton	F-11
Cleveland	B-9
Climax	J-8
Clyattville	J-9
Clyo	F-12
Cobbtown	F-11
Cochran	F-10
Cogdell	H-10
Cohutta	A-7
Colemans Lake	E-11
College Park	★
Vicinity	Pg. 103, J-3
Colquitt	H-7
Columbus	F-7
Comer	C-10
Commerce	C-9
Conley	★
Vicinity	Pg. 103, J-5
Conyers	C-9
Coolidge	J-9
Copperhill	A-8
Cordele	G-9
Cornelia	B-9
Cotton	H-8
Covena	F-11
Covington	D-9
Crandall	A-7
Crawford	C-10
Crawfordville	D-10
Culloden	E-8
Cumming	C-8
Cusseta	F-7
Cuthbert	G-7
Dacula	C-9
Dahlonega	B-8
Dallas	C-7
Dalton	A-7
Damascus	H-7
Danielsville	C-10
Darien	H-12
Dasher	J-10
Davisboro	E-11
Dawson	G-8
Dawsonville	C-8
Decatur	C-8
Vicinity	Pg. 102, F-6
Demorest	B-9
Dexter	F-10
Doerun	H-9
Donalsonville	J-7
Doraville	★
Vicinity	Pg. 102, C-6
Douglas	H-10
Douglasville	C-7
Druid Hills	★
Vicinity	Pg. 102, F-5
Dublin	F-10
Duluth	C-8
Dunwoody	★
Vicinity	Pg. 102, B-5
East Dublin	F-10
East Point	★
Vicinity	Pg. 103, J-3
Eastman	F-10
Eatonton	D-10
Edgehill	E-10
Edison	G-7
Elberton	C-10
Elko	F-9
Ellaville	F-8
Ellenton	H-9
Ellijay	A-8
Emerson	C-7
Empire	F-10
Enigma	H-10
Evans	C-11
Faceville	J-7
Fair Oaks	★
Vicinity	Pg. 102, B-1
Fairmount	B-8
Fargo	J-11
Fayetteville	D-8
Finleyson	G-9
Fitzgerald	G-10
Flemington	G-12
Folkston	J-11
Forest Beach	F-13
Forest Park	C-8
Forsyth	E-9
Fort Gaines	H-7
Fort Oglethorpe	A-6
Fort Valley	E-8
Franklin	D-7
Franklin Springs	B-9
Gainesville	C-8
Garden City	G-13
Georgetown	G-7
Gibson	E-11
Gillsville	B-9
Gilmore	★
Vicinity	Pg. 102, D-2
Girard	E-12
Glennville	G-12
Glenwood	G-11
Gordon	E-10
Gracewood	D-11
Grantville	D-7
Gray	E-9
Greensboro	D-10
Greenville	E-8
Griffin	D-8
Grovania	F-9
Grovetown	D-11
Haddock	E-10
Hagan	F-11
Hahira	J-9
Hamilton	E-7
Hampton	D-8
Hapeville	★
Vicinity	Pg. 103, J-4
Hapeville	★
Vicinity	Pg. 103, J-4
Haralson	E-8
Harlem	D-11
Harrison	E-11
Hartwell	B-10
Hawkinsville	F-9
Hazlehurst	G-10
Helen	B-9
Helena	G-10
Hephzibah	D-11
Herod	H-8
Hiawassee	A-9
Hickox	H-12
Hilton	H-7
Hiltonia	E-12
Hinesville	G-12
Hoboken	H-11
Hogansville	D-7
Holly Springs	B-8
Homeland	J-11
Homer	B-9
Homerville	H-11
Ideal	F-8
Irwinton	E-10
Irwinville	G-9
Ivey	E-10
Jackson	D-9
Jacksonville	G-10
Jasper	B-8
Jefferson	C-9
Jeffersonville	F-9
Jesup	G-12
Jonesboro	D-8
Juno	E-12
Kingsland	J-12
Kingston	B-7
Kite	E-11
Knoxville	E-9
La Grange	E-7
LaFayette	B-7
Lake Park	J-10
Lakeland	J-10
Lakemont	A-9
Lavonia	B-10
Lawrenceville	C-8
Leary	H-8
Leesburg	G-8
Lenox	H-9
Leslie	G-8
Lexington	C-10
Lilburn	F-9
Lilly	F-9
Lincolnton	C-10
Lithia	C-8
Locust Grove	D-8
Loganville	C-9
Louisville	E-11
Lovett	F-10
Ludowici	G-12
Lula	B-9
Lumber City	G-10
Lumpkin	G-7
Lyons	F-11
Macon	E-9
Madison	D-9
Manchester	E-7
Manor	H-11
Margret	A-8
Marietta	C-7
Vicinity	Pg. 102, A-1
Marshallville	F-9
Maxeys	C-9
Maysville	B-9
McCaysville	A-8
McIntyre	E-10
McRae	G-10
Meigs	J-8
Merrillville	J-8
Metcalf	J-9
Metter	F-11
Middleton	C-10
Midville	E-11
Milan	G-10
Milledgeville	E-10
Millen	E-12
Mineral Bluff	A-8
Modoc	E-11
Molena	E-8
Moncrief	J-8
Monroe	C-9
Montezuma	F-9
Monticello	D-9
Morgan	H-7
Morganton	A-8
Morris	G-7
Morven	J-9
Moultrie	H-9
Mount Airy	A-9
Mount Bethel	★
Vicinity	Pg. 102, A-4
Mount Vernon	F-11
Mountain City	A-9
Mt. Zion	D-7
Nahunta	H-12
Nashville	H-10
Naylor	J-10
Nelson	B-8
Newington	F-12
Newnan	D-7
Newton	H-8
Nicholls	H-11
Norman Park	H-9
Norristown	F-11
North Decatur	★
Vicinity	Pg. 102, E-6
Oak Park	F-11
Oakdale	★
Vicinity	Pg. 102, E-2
Oakfield	G-9
Oakland	G-8
Oakman	B-7
Oakwood	B-9
Ochlocknee	J-8
Ocilla	H-10
Odum	G-12
Offerman	H-11
Oglethorpe	F-8
Ohoopee	F-11
Oliver	F-12
Omega	H-9
Oxford	D-9
Palmetto	D-7
Pantherville	★
Vicinity	Pg. 103, H-7
Parrott	G-8
Patterson	H-11
Pavo	H-8
Peachtree City	D-7
Pearson	H-10
Pelham	J-8
Pembroke	F-12
Percale	E-9
Perry	F-9
Philomath	C-10
Pine Park	J-8
Pinehurst	F-9
Pineview	F-9

★ Denotes City only on Vicinity map. City not located on State map.

GEORGIA

Pitts G-9
Plains G-8
Pooler F-12
Port Wentworth F-13
Portal F-12
Poulan H-9
Preston G-8
Pulaski F-12
Quitman J-9
Radium Springs H-8
Raleigh E-7
Ray City J-10
Rayle C-10
Rebecca G-9
Red Oak .... ★
  Vicinity .... Pg. 103, K-2
Rehobeth .... ★
  Vicinity .... Pg. 102, E-7
Reidsville G-11
Resaca A-7
Reynolds E-8
Rhine G-10
Richland G-7
Richmond Hill F-12
Rincon F-12
Riverdale .... ★
  Vicinity .... Pg. 103, L-4
Roberta E-8
Rochelle G-9
Rockmart C-7
Rocky Ford E-12
Rome B-6
Roopville D-7
Rossville A-6
Roswell C-8
Royston B-10
Saffold J-7
Sale City H-9
Sandersville E-10
Sandy Springs .... ★
  Vicinity .... Pg. 102, B-4
Sardis E-12
Sasser G-8
Savannah F-13
Scottsdale .... ★
  Vicinity .... Pg. 102, F-7
Screven H-11
Senoia D-7
Seville G-9
Shady Dale D-9
Shellman G-8
Shiloh E-7
Smithville G-8
Smyrna .... ★
  Vicinity .... Pg. 102, C-2
Social Circle D-9
Soperton F-11
Sparks H-9
Sparta D-10
Springfield F-12
St. Marys J-12
St. Simons Island H-13
Statenville J-10
Statesboro F-12
Stillmore F-11
Stockbridge D-8
Stockton J-10
Stone Mtn. C-8
Stonewall .... ★
  Vicinity .... Pg. 103, L-1
Suches B-8
Sugar Hill B-8
Summertown E-11
Summerville B-7
Sumner H-9
Surrency G-11
Suwanee B-8
Swainsboro F-11
Sycamore H-9
Sylvania E-12
Sylvester H-9
Tallapoosa C-6
Tallulah Falls B-9
Talmo H-11
Tarrytown F-10
Tarver J-10
Tarversville F-9
Tazewell F-8
Tennga A-7
Tennille E-10
Thomaston E-8
Thomasville J-8
Thomson D-11
Thunderbolt G-13
Tifton H-9
Tignall C-10
Toccoa B-9
Toco Hills .... ★
  Vicinity .... Pg. 102, E-6
Toombsboro E-9
Towns G-10
Trenton A-6
Trion A-6
Twin City F-11
Ty Ty H-9
Unadilla F-9
Union City .... ★
  Vicinity .... Pg. 103, L-1
Union Point C-9
Upatoi F-7
Uvalda G-11
Valdosta J-10
Van Wert C-7
Vanna B-10
Vidalia F-11

Vienna G-9
Villa Rica C-7
Wadley E-11
Waleska B-8
Waresboro H-11
Warner Robins F-9
Warrenton D-10
Warthen E-10
Warwick G-8
Washington C-10
Watkinsville C-9
Waycross H-11
Waynesboro E-11
West Point E-7
Whigham J-8
White B-8
Whitesburg D-7
Willacoochee H-10
Winder C-9
Woodbine J-12
Woodbury E-8
Woodland F-7
Wrens D-11
Wrightsville E-10
Zebulon E-8

HAWAII
Page 18

Aiea G-6
Anahola D-3
Apole Pt C-9
Apua Pt G-10
Barbers Pt G-4
Cape Halawa A-6
Cape Hanamanioa C-8
Captain Cook F-9
Eleele F-2
Ewa G-5
Glenwood F-9
Haena D-2
Haena Pt D-2
Haiku A-9
Hakalau F-10
Halawa A-6
Haleiwa F-4
Hana B-10
Hanalei D-2
Hanamalo Pt G-8
Hanamaulu E-3
Hanapepe F-1
Hauula F-6
Hawaii Kai G-6
Hawi E-9
Hekili Pt B-7
Hilo F-10
Honaunau F-8
Honohina E-10
Honokaa E-9
Honokahau F-8
Honokahua A-7
Honolulu G-5
Honuapo G-9
Hookena F-8
Ka Lae G-9
Kaalualu G-9
Kaena Pt G-10
Kahakuloa Pt A-8
Kahaluu F-6
Kahana F-6
Kahlu Pt A-4
Kahuku E-5
Kahuku Pt E-5
Kahului A-8
Kailua (Hawaii) F-8
Kailua (Oahu) G-7
Kaimu F-10
Kainaliu F-8
Kaka Pt E-7
Kalae A-5
Kalaheo F-2
Kalahu Pt B-10
Kalalau D-2
Kalaoa F-8
Kalapana G-10
Kamalo A-5
Kamiloloa A-5
Kaneohe G-6
Kapaa E-3
Kaumakani F-1
Kauna Pt G-8
Kaunakakai A-5
Kaupo B-9
Kawahae E-8
Keaau F-10
Keahole Pt F-8
Kealia E-3
Keauhou F-8
Kekaha E-1
Kekoea B-8
Keomuku B-7
Kepuhi Pt F-4
Kihei B-8
Kikipua Pt A-5
Kilauea D-2
Kipahulu B-10
Koele D-6
Koheo Pt F-2
Koko Head G-7
Kolo A-4
Kualapua A-4
Kualoa Pt F-6

Kukaiau E-9
Kukuihaele E-9
Kurtistown F-10
Laau Pt A-3
Lahaina A-7
Laie E-6
Lamaloa Head A-6
Lanai City D-6
Lawai F-2
Lihue E-3
Lilo Pt A-3
Maalaea B-8
Mahukona E-8
Maili G-4
Makaha F-4
Makaha Pt D-1
Makahuena Pt F-3
Makakilo City G-4
Makanalua Pen A-5
Makapuu Pt G-7
Makawao A-9
Makena B-8
Mana E-1
Mauna Loa A-4
Mililani Town F-5
Milolii G-8
Mokapu Pt. F-7
Moloaa D-3
Mopua B-7
Mountain View F-9
Muolea Pt. B-10
Naalehu G-9
Nakalele Pt. A-7
Nanakuli G-4
Napoopoo F-8
Nawiliwili E-3
Ninini Pt. E-3
Niulii E-9
Nukuele Pt. A-8
Olowalu B-7
Ookala E-9
Opihikao F-10
Pahala G-9
Pahoa F-10
Paia A-8
Papa G-9
Papaaloa E-10
Papaikou F-10
Paukaa F-10
Pauwalu A-8
Pauwela A-8
Pauwela Pt. A-8
Pearl City F-5
Pearl Harbor G-5
Pepeekeo F-9
Pepeekeo Pt. F-10
Pohoiki F-10
Port Allen F-2
Puako E-8
Puhi E-2
Pukaulua Pt. A-10
Pukoo A-5
Puunene A-8
Puuwai B-1
Spreckelsville A-8
Sunset Beach E-5
Ulapue A-5
Ulupalakua B-9
Upola Pt. E-8
Wahiawa F-5
Waiahukini G-9
Waiaka A-7
Waiakea F-10
Waialua (Molokai) A-5
Waialua (Ohau) F-5
Waianae F-4
Waihee Pt. A-8
Waikiki G-6
Wailea B-8
Wailua (Kauai) E-3
Wailua (Maui) A-9
Wailuku A-8
Waimanalo G-7
Waimea (Hawaii) E-8
Waimea (Kauai) E-1
Waiohinu G-9
Walpahu G-5

IDAHO
Pages 34-35

Aberdeen M-7
Acequia N-6
Ahsahka F-3
Albion N-6
American Falls M-7
Ammon L-9
Arco L-7
Arimo N-8
Ashton K-9
Athol C-3
Atlanta L-4
Atomic City L-7
Avery E-3
Avon E-3
Baker H-6
Bancroft N-9
Banida N-9
Banks K-3
Basalt M-8
Bayview C-3
Bellevue L-6
Bennington N-9
Bern N-9

Blackfoot M-8
Blanchard C-2
Bliss M-4
Bloomington P-9
Blue Dome K-8
Boise L-3
Bonners Ferry B-3
Bovill E-3
Bowmont L-2
Bruneau M-3
Buhl N-5
Burley N-6
Butte City L-7
Calder D-3
Caldwell L-2
Cambridge J-2
Cape Horn J-4
Carey M-6
Cascade J-3
Castleford N-4
Cataldo D-3
Centerville K-3
Challis J-5
Chatcolet D-2
Chestet K-9
Chubbuck M-8
Clark Fork C-3
Clarkia E-3
Clayton K-5
Clifton P-8
Coeur D'Alene D-2
Colburn B-3
Conda N-9
Coolin B-3
Corral L-4
Cottonwood F-3
Council J-3
Craigmont F-2
Crouch K-3
Culdesac F-2
Dalton Gardens C-3
Darlington L-7
Dayton P-8
De Smet D-2
Deary E-3
Declo N-6
Dietrich M-5
Dingle P-10
Donnelly J-3
Dover C-3
Downey N-9
Driggs L-10
Dubois K-8
Eagle L-3
East Hope C-3
Eastport A-3
Eden N-5
Elba N-6
Elk City G-4
Elk River E-3
Emida E-3
Emmett K-2
Enaville D-3
Ferdinand F-3
Fernan Lake D-3
Fernwood E-3
Filer N-5
Firth M-8
Fish Haven P-9
Fort Hall M-8
Franklin P-9
Fruitland K-2
Fruitvale J-2
Gannett L-6
Garden City L-3
Garden Valley K-3
Gardena K-3
Garfield Bay C-3
Garwood C-3
Gem D-4
Genesee E-2
Georgetown N-9
Gibbonsville H-6
Givens Hot Springs L-2
Glens Ferry M-4
Golden G-4
Gooding M-5
Grace N-9
Grand View M-2
Grangeville G-3
Granite C-3
Greencreek F-3
Greer F-3
Hagerman M-4
Hailey L-5
Hammett M-3
Hansen N-5
Harpster G-3
Harrison D-3
Harvard E-3
Hauser C-2
Hayden C-3
Hazelton N-6
Headquarters E-4
Heise L-9
Heyburn N-6
Hill City L-4
Holbrook P-8
Hollister N-5
Homedale L-2
Hope C-3
Horseshoe Bend K-3
Howe L-7
Idaho City K-3

Idaho Falls L-9
Inkom N-8
Iona L-9
Irwin L-10
Island Park K-10
Jerome M-5
Joel E-2
Juliaetta F-3
Kamiah F-3
Kellogg D-4
Kendrick E-3
Ketchum L-5
Kimama M-6
Kimberly N-5
King Hill M-4
Kooskia F-3
Kootenai B-3
Kuna L-2
Laclede C-3
Lamb Creek B-2
Lane D-3
Lapwai F-2
Lava Hot Springs N-9
Leadore J-7
Lemhi J-6
Letha K-2
Lewiston F-2
Lewisville L-9
Lorenzo L-9
Lowell F-3
Lowman K-4
Mackay K-7
Malad City N-8
Malta N-7
Marion L-2
Marsing L-2
May J-6
McCall H-3
McCammon N-8
Meadows H-3
Melba L-2
Menan L-9
Meridian K-2
Middleton K-2
Midvale J-2
Minidoka M-7
Mink Creek N-9
Montour K-3
Montpelier N-10
Moreland M-8
Morre L-7
Moscow E-2
Mount Idaho G-3
Mountain Home M-3
Moyie Springs B-3
Mud Lake L-8
Mullan D-4
Murphy L-2
Murray D-4
Murtaugh N-5
Myrtle F-2
Nampa L-2
Naples B-3
New Meadows H-2
New Plymouth K-2
Newdale L-9
Nezperce F-3
Nordman B-2
North Fork H-6
Notus K-2
Oakley N-6
Onaway E-2
Orofino F-3
Osburn D-3
Ovid N-9
Paris N-9
Parker K-9
Parma K-2
Patterson J-6
Paul N-6
Pauline M-8
Payette K-2
Peck F-3
Picabo M-6
Pierce F-4
Pinehurst D-3
Pingree M-8
Pioneerville K-3
Plummer D-2
Pocatello M-8
Pollock H-3
Ponderay B-3
Porthill A-3
Portneuf M-8
Post Falls C-2
Potlatch E-3
Preston P-9
Priest River B-3
Raft River N-7
Rathdrum C-2
Reubens F-3
Rexburg L-9
Richfield M-6
Rigby L-9
Riggins H-3
Ririe L-9
Roberts L-9
Robin N-8
Rock Creek N-5
Rockford M-8
Rockland N-7
Rogerson N-4
Rupert N-6
Sagle C-3
Salmon H-6

Samaria P-8
Sandpoint B-3
Santa D-3
Shelley M-9
Shoshone M-5
Silver City M-2
Silverton D-4
Smelterville D-3
Soda Springs N-9
Spirit Lake C-2
Springfield M-7
Springston D-3
St. Anthony K-9
St. Charles P-9
St. Joe D-3
St. Maries D-3
Stanley K-5
Starkey H-2
Sterling M-7
Stites F-3
Sugar City L-9
Sun Valley L-5
Sunbeam K-5
Swan Valley L-10
Swanlake N-9
Sweet K-2
Tamarack H-2
Tendoy J-6
Tensed D-2
Teton L-9
Tetonia L-10
Thatcher N-9
Thornton L-9
Troy E-2
Twin Falls N-5
Ucon L-9
Victor L-10
Viola E-2
Virginia N-8
Wallace D-3
Warm Lake J-4
Warm River K-10
Weippe F-4
Weiser J-2
Wendell M-5
White Bird G-3
Whitney P-9
Wilder L-2
Winchester F-2
Woodland F-3
Worley D-2

ILLINOIS
Page 36-37

Abingdon C-5
Addison .... ★
  Vicinity .... Pg. 110, F-3
Albany D-3
Albion H-11
Aledo B-4
Alexis C-4
Algonquin .... ★
  Vicinity .... Pg. 108, C-1
Alhambra D-10
Allendale H-11
Allerton H-7
Alma F-11
Alorton .... ★
  Vicinity .... Pg. 153, G-7
Alpha C-4
Alpine .... ★
  Vicinity .... Pg. 111, J-4
Alsip .... ★
  Vicinity .... Pg. 111, H-5
Altamont F-10
Alto Pass E-14
Alton D-10
  Vicinity .... Pg. 111, H-6
Alvin J-6
Amboy E-3
Andover C-4
Anna E-14
Annawan D-4
Antioch G-1
Aptakisik .... ★
  Vicinity .... Pg. 108, C-4
Arcola G-8
Argenta F-7
Arlington E-3
Arlington Heights .... ★
  Vicinity .... Pg. 108, D-3
Arthur G-8
Ashland D-8
Ashley F-12
Ashmore H-8
Ashton E-2
Assumption F-9
Astoria C-7
Athens D-7
Atkinson D-3
Atlanta E-7
Atwood G-8
Auburn D-8
Aubury Hills .... ★
  Vicinity .... Pg. 152, D-7
Augusta B-7
Aurora G-3
  Vicinity .... Pg. 110, G-4
Ava E-13
Avon C-6
Bannockburn .... ★
  Vicinity .... Pg. 109, C-4
Barrington .... ★
  Vicinity .... Pg. 108, C-2

Barrington Hills .... ★
  Vicinity .... Pg. 108, D-2
Barry B-8
Bartlett .... ★
  Vicinity .... Pg. 108, E-2
Bartonville D-6
Batavia .... ★
  Vicinity .... Pg. 110, F-1
Beardstown C-7
Beckemeyer E-11
Bedford Park .... ★
  Vicinity .... Pg. 111, G-5
Beecher City F-9
Belle Rive F-12
Belleville D-11
Bellflower G-6
Bellmont H-11
Bellwood .... ★
  Vicinity .... Pg. 111, F-4
Belvidere F-1
Bement G-7
Bensenville .... ★
  Vicinity .... Pg. 110, G-4
Benson E-6
Benton F-12
Berkeley .... ★
  Vicinity .... Pg. 111, F-4
Berwyn .... ★
  Vicinity .... Pg. 111, F-5
Bethalto D-10
Bethany G-8
Biggsville B-5
Bloomingdale .... ★
  Vicinity .... Pg. 108, E-3
Bloomington E-6
Blue Island .... ★
  Vicinity .... Pg. 111, H-6
Blue Mound F-8
Bluffs C-8
Bolingbrook .... ★
  Vicinity .... Pg. 110, H-3
Bourbonnais H-4
Bowen B-7
Bradford E-5
Bradley H-4
Braidwood H-4
Bridgeview .... ★
  Vicinity .... Pg. 111, G-5
Brighton C-10
Brimfield D-5
Broadview .... ★
  Vicinity .... Pg. 111, F-4
Brookfield .... ★
  Vicinity .... Pg. 111, G-5
Brookport G-15
Brownstown F-10
Buckley H-6
Buffalo Grove .... ★
  Vicinity .... Pg. 108, C-4
Bunker Hill D-10
Burbank .... ★
  Vicinity .... Pg. 111, H-5
Burnham .... ★
  Vicinity .... Pg. 111, J-7
Burr Ridge .... ★
  Vicinity .... Pg. 110, G-4
Burtons Bridge .... ★
  Vicinity .... Pg. 108, B-2
Bush F-13
Bushnell C-6
Byron E-2
Cabery G-5
Cahokia C-11
  Vicinity .... Pg. 153, H-7
Cairo F-15
Calumet City .... ★
  Vicinity .... Pg. 111, J-7
Calumet Park .... ★
  Vicinity .... Pg. 111, H-6
Cambridge C-4
Camden B-7
Camp Point B-7
Campbell Hill E-13
Canton D-6
Capron F-1
Carbondale E-13
Carlinville D-9
Carlyle E-11
Carmi G-12
Carol Stream .... ★
  Vicinity .... Pg. 110, F-2
Carpentersville .... ★
  Vicinity .... Pg. 108, D-1
Carriers Mills G-13
Carrollton C-9
Carterville F-13
Carthage A-6
Cary .... ★
  Vicinity .... Pg. 108, C-1
Casey H-9
Caton Farm .... ★
  Vicinity .... Pg. 110, J-2
Cave-In-Rock H-14
Cedar Pk .... ★
  Vicinity .... Pg. 152, D-7
Cedarville E-1
Central City E-11
Centralia E-11
Centreville .... ★
  Vicinity .... Pg. 153, H-7
Cerro Gordo F-7
Chadwick D-2
Champaign G-7
Chandlerville C-8
Chapin C-8

Charleston H-9
Chatham D-8
Chatsworth G-5
Chebanse H-5
Chenoa F-5
Cherry Valley F-1
Chester D-13
Chesterfield D-9
Chicago J-2
  Vicinity .... Pg. 108
Chicago Heights J-3
  Vicinity .... Pg. 111, K-6
Chicago Ridge .... ★
  Vicinity .... Pg. 111, H-5
Chillicothe E-5
Chrisman H-8
Cicero .... ★
  Vicinity .... Pg. 111, F-5
Cisco F-7
Cisne G-11
Clarendon Hills .... ★
  Vicinity .... Pg. 110, G-4
Clay City G-11
Clayton B-7
Clifton H-5
Clinton F-7
Cloverdale .... ★
  Vicinity .... Pg. 111, F-2
Cobden E-14
Coffeen E-10
Colchester B-6
Colfax F-6
Collinsville D-11
Columbia C-11
  Vicinity .... Pg. 153, K-6
Compton E-3
Cordova C-3
Cornell F-5
Coulterville E-12
Country Club Hills .... ★
  Vicinity .... Pg. 111, J-5
Countryside .... ★
  Vicinity .... Pg. 111, G-4
Cowden F-9
Creal Springs F-13
Crest Hill .... ★
  Vicinity .... Pg. 110, J-2
Crestwood .... ★
  Vicinity .... Pg. 111, J-5
Crete .... ★
  Vicinity .... Pg. 111, K-6
Creve Coeur E-6
Crystal Lake G-1
Cuba C-6
Cullom G-5
Cutler E-12
Dakota E-1
Dallas City B-6
Damiansville E-11
Danville J-7
Darien .... ★
  Vicinity .... Pg. 110, G-4
De Kalb F-2
De Soto E-13
Decatur F-8
Deer Grove .... ★
  Vicinity .... Pg. 108, C-3
Deer Park .... ★
  Vicinity .... Pg. 108, C-3
Deerfield .... ★
  Vicinity .... Pg. 109, C-4
Delavan E-6
Des Plaines .... ★
  Vicinity .... Pg. 109, D-4
Diamond Lake .... ★
  Vicinity .... Pg. 109, D-4
Dieterich G-10
Divernon E-9
Dix F-11
Dixmoor .... ★
  Vicinity .... Pg. 111, J-6
Dixon E-2
Dolton .... ★
  Vicinity .... Pg. 111, J-6
Donovan H-5
Downers Grove H-3
  Vicinity .... Pg. 110, G-4
Du Quoin E-12
Dunfermline D-6
Dunlap D-5
Dupo .... ★
  Vicinity .... Pg. 153, J-6
Dwight G-4
Earlville F-3
East Carondelet .... ★
  Vicinity .... Pg. 153, J-5
East Chicago Heights .... ★
  Vicinity .... Pg. 111, K-7
East Dubuque C-1
East Dundee .... ★
  Vicinity .... Pg. 108, D-1
East Hazelcrest .... ★
  Vicinity .... Pg. 111, J-6
East Peoria E-5
East St. Louis .... ★
  Vicinity .... Pg. 153, G-7
Easton D-7
Eddyville G-14
Edgewood G-10
Edinburg E-8
Effingham G-10
El Paso F-5
Eldorado G-13
Elgin G-2
  Vicinity .... Pg. 108, D-1

★ Denotes City only on Vicinity map. City not located on State map.

ILLINOIS

INDIANA

Elizabeth C-1
Elizabethtown G-14
Elk Grove Village .... ★
  Vicinity .... Pg. 108, E-3
Elkhart E-7
Elkville E-13
Elliot .... ★
Ellis Grove D-12
Elmhurst H-2
  Vicinity .... Pg. 110, F-4
Elmwood Park .... ★
  Vicinity .... Pg. 111, F-5
Enfield G-12
Eola .... ★
  Vicinity .... Pg. 110, G-2
Equality G-13
Erie D-3
Eureka E-5
Evanston J-2
  Vicinity .... Pg. 109, E-6
Evansville D-12
Evergreen Park .... ★
  Vicinity .... Pg. 111, H-6
Fairbury G-5
Fairfield G-11
Fairmont H-2
  Vicinity .... Pg. 110, J-3
Fairmont City .... ★
  Vicinity .... Pg. 153, F-7
Fairview C-6
Farina F-10
Farmer City F-7
Farmersville E-9
Farmington D-5
Fayetteville D-11
Fieldon C-10
Fisher G-6
Flanagan F-5
Flat Rock H-10
Flora G-11
Flossmoor .... ★
  Vicinity .... Pg. 111, K-6
Flower Field .... ★
  Vicinity .... Pg. 110, F-3
Forest Park .... ★
  Vicinity .... Pg. 111, F-5
Forest View .... ★
  Vicinity .... Pg. 111, G-6
Forrest G-5
Forreston E-2
Fox Lake G-1
  Vicinity .... Pg. 108, A-2
Fox Lake Hills .... ★
  Vicinity .... Pg. 108, A-2
Fox River Grove .... ★
  Vicinity .... Pg. 108, C-2
Fox River Valley Gardens .... ★
  Vicinity .... Pg. 108, B-2
Frankfort .... ★
  Vicinity .... Pg. 111, K-4
Franklin D-8
Franklin Park .... ★
  Vicinity .... Pg. 111, F-4
Freeburg D-11
Freeport D-1
Fremont Center .... ★
  Vicinity .... Pg. 108, B-3
Frontenac .... ★
  Vicinity .... Pg. 110, H-2
Fulton D-2
Galatia G-13
Galena C-1
Galesburg C-5
Galva D-4
Gardner G-4
Geneseo C-3
Geneva G-2
  Vicinity .... Pg. 110, F-1
Genoa F-2
Georgetown H-7
Germantown E-11
Gibson City G-6
Gilberts .... ★
  Vicinity .... Pg. 108, D-1
Gillespie D-10
Gilman H-5
Gilmer .... ★
  Vicinity .... Pg. 108, B-3
Girard D-9
Gladstone B-5
Glasford D-6
Glen Ellyn .... ★
  Vicinity .... Pg. 110, F-3
Glencoe .... ★
  Vicinity .... Pg. 109, C-5
Glendale Heights .... ★
  Vicinity .... Pg. 110, F-3
Glenview .... ★
  Vicinity .... Pg. 109, D-5
Glenwood .... ★
  Vicinity .... Pg. 111, K-6
Golconda G-14
Golden B-7
Good Hope B-6
Goodings Grove .... ★
  Vicinity .... Pg. 110, J-4
Goreville F-14
Gorham E-13
Grafton C-10
Grand Ridge F-4
Grand Tower E-13
Granite City .... ★
  Vicinity .... Pg. 152, E-7
Grayslake .... ★
  Vicinity .... Pg. 108, A-3

Grayville H-12
Green Oaks .... ★
  Vicinity .... Pg. 108, B-4
Greenfield C-9
Greenup H-9
Greenview D-7
Greenville E-10
Gridley F-5
Griggsville B-8
Gurnee .... ★
  Vicinity .... Pg. 109, A-4
Hainesville .... ★
  Vicinity .... Pg. 108, A-3
Half Day .... ★
  Vicinity .... Pg. 109, C-4
Hamel D-10
Hamilton A-6
Hammond G-8
Hampshire G-2
Hanaford F-13
Hanover C-1
Hanover Park .... ★
  Vicinity .... Pg. 108, E-2
Hardin B-9
Harrisburg G-13
Harristown F-8
Harvard F-1
Harvey .... ★
  Vicinity .... Pg. 111, J-6
Harwood Heights .... ★
  Vicinity .... Pg. 109, E-5
Hastings .... ★
  Vicinity .... Pg. 110, H-4
Havana D-6
Hawthorn Woods .... ★
  Vicinity .... Pg. 108, C-3
Hazel Crest .... ★
  Vicinity .... Pg. 111, J-6
Hebron G-1
Hecker D-12
Hennepin E-4
Henning H-6
Henry E-4
Herrin F-13
Herscher H-5
Heyworth F-6
Hickory Hills .... ★
  Vicinity .... Pg. 111, H-5
Highland E-11
Highland Hills .... ★
  Vicinity .... Pg. 110, F-3
Highland Park H-1
  Vicinity .... Pg. 109, C-5
Highwood .... ★
  Vicinity .... Pg. 109, C-5
Hillsboro E-9
Hillside .... ★
  Vicinity .... Pg. 111, F-4
Hinckley G-3
Hinsdale .... ★
  Vicinity .... Pg. 110, G-4
Hodgkins .... ★
  Vicinity .... Pg. 111, G-4
Hoffman Estates .... ★
  Vicinity .... Pg. 108, D-2
Holiday Hills .... ★
  Vicinity .... Pg. 108, B-2
Homer H-7
Hometown .... ★
  Vicinity .... Pg. 111, H-5
Homewood .... ★
  Vicinity .... Pg. 111, J-6
Hoopeston J-6
Hoopole D-3
Hopedale E-5
Hoyleton E-11
Hudson F-6
Hull A-8
Humboldt G-8
Hurst E-13
Hutsonville H-10
Illiopolis E-8
Imbs Station .... ★
  Vicinity .... Pg. 153, J-7
Indian Creek .... ★
  Vicinity .... Pg. 108, C-4
Indian Head Park .... ★
  Vicinity .... Pg. 111, G-4
Industry B-6
Ingalls Park .... ★
  Vicinity .... Pg. 110, K-3
Inverness .... ★
  Vicinity .... Pg. 108, D-3
Irvington F-11
Island Lake .... ★
  Vicinity .... Pg. 108, B-2
Itasca .... ★
  Vicinity .... Pg. 108, E-3
Ivanhoe .... ★
  Vicinity .... Pg. 108, B-3
Jacksonville C-8
Jerseyville C-9
Johnsburg .... ★
  Vicinity .... Pg. 108, A-1
Joliet .... ★
  Vicinity .... Pg. 110, K-2
Jonesboro E-14
Junction City H-13
Justice .... ★
  Vicinity .... Pg. 111, G-5
Kampsville B-9
Kankakee H-4
Kansas H-8
Karnak F-14
Kaskaskia D-13

Keeneyville .... ★
  Vicinity .... Pg. 108, E-2
Kenilworth .... ★
  Vicinity .... Pg. 109, D-6
Kenney F-7
Kewanee D-4
Kilbourne D-7
Kildeer .... ★
  Vicinity .... Pg. 108, C-3
Kinderhook B-8
Kingston F-2
Kinmundy F-10
Kirkland F-2
Knollwood .... ★
  Vicinity .... Pg. 109, B-4
Knoxville C-5
La Fayette D-4
La Grange .... ★
  Vicinity .... Pg. 111, G-4
La Grange Park .... ★
  Vicinity .... Pg. 111, G-4
La Harpe A-6
La Moille E-3
La Salle F-4
Lacon E-5
Lake Barrington .... ★
  Vicinity .... Pg. 108, C-2
Lake Bluff .... ★
  Vicinity .... Pg. 109, B-5
Lake Forest H-1
  Vicinity .... Pg. 109, B-5
Lake Villa .... ★
  Vicinity .... Pg. 108, A-3
Lake Zurich .... ★
  Vicinity .... Pg. 108, C-3
Lake in the Hills .... ★
  Vicinity .... Pg. 108, C-1
Lakemoor .... ★
  Vicinity .... Pg. 108, B-2
Lakewood .... ★
  Vicinity .... Pg. 108, C-1
Lanark D-2
Lansing .... ★
  Vicinity .... Pg. 111, J-7
Latham E-7
Lawrenceville J-10
Le Roy F-6
Lee Center E-3
Lemont .... ★
  Vicinity .... Pg. 110, H-3
Lena D-1
Lewistown C-6
Lexington F-6
Liberty A-8
Libertyville H-1
  Vicinity .... Pg. 108, B-4
Lilymoor .... ★
  Vicinity .... Pg. 108, A-2
Lima A-7
Lincoln E-7
Lincoln Estates .... ★
  Vicinity .... Pg. 111, K-5
Lincolnshire .... ★
  Vicinity .... Pg. 109, C-4
Lincolnwood .... ★
  Vicinity .... Pg. 109, E-5
Lindenhurst .... ★
  Vicinity .... Pg. 108, A-3
Lisle .... ★
  Vicinity .... Pg. 110, G-3
Litchfield D-9
Little York B-5
Livingston D-10
Lockport .... ★
  Vicinity .... Pg. 110, J-3
Lombard .... ★
  Vicinity .... Pg. 110, F-3
Long Grove .... ★
  Vicinity .... Pg. 108, C-3
Long Lake .... ★
  Vicinity .... Pg. 108, A-2
Loraine A-7
Louisville G-10
Lovington F-8
Ludlow H-6
Lynwood .... ★
  Vicinity .... Pg. 111, K-7
Lyons .... ★
  Vicinity .... Pg. 111, G-5
Machesney Park E-1
Mackinaw E-6
Macomb B-6
Madison .... ★
  Vicinity .... Pg. 152, E-7
Magnolia E-4
Mahomet G-7
Manlius D-3
Manteno H-4
Maquon C-5
Marengo G-1
Marine D-10
Marion F-13
Marissa D-12
Markham .... ★
  Vicinity .... Pg. 111, J-6
Marley .... ★
  Vicinity .... Pg. 110, K-4
Maroa F-7
Marseilles G-4
Marshall J-9
Martinsville H-9
Martinton H-5
Marywood .... ★
  Vicinity .... Pg. 110, G-1
Mascoutah D-11

Mason G-10
Mason City D-7
Matteson .... ★
  Vicinity .... Pg. 111, K-5
Mattoon G-9
Maywood .... ★
  Vicinity .... Pg. 111, F-5
Mazon G-4
McClure E-14
McCook .... ★
  Vicinity .... Pg. 111, G-4
McCullom Lake .... ★
  Vicinity .... Pg. 108, A-1
McHenry G-1
  Vicinity .... Pg. 108, A-1
McHenry Shores .... ★
  Vicinity .... Pg. 108, B-1
McLean E-6
McLeansboro G-12
Medinah .... ★
  Vicinity .... Pg. 108, E-3
Medora C-9
Melrose Park .... ★
  Vicinity .... Pg. 111, F-4
Melvin G-6
Mendon A-7
Mendota E-3
Meredosia C-8
Merrionette Park .... ★
  Vicinity .... Pg. 111, H-6
Metamora E-5
Metropolis G-15
Mettawa .... ★
  Vicinity .... Pg. 109, B-4
Midlothianb .... ★
  Vicinity .... Pg. 111, J-5
Milford H-5
Mill Shoals G-12
Milledgeville D-2
Milton B-8
Minonk F-5
Minooka .... ★
  Vicinity .... Pg. 110, K-1
Mokena .... ★
  Vicinity .... Pg. 111, K-4
Moline C-3
Momence J-4
Monmouth C-5
Montgomery .... ★
  Vicinity .... Pg. 110, H-1
Monticello G-7
Montrose G-9
Mooseheart .... ★
  Vicinity .... Pg. 110, G-1
Morris G-4
Morrison D-2
Morrisonville E-9
Morristown F-2
Morton E-6
Morton Grove .... ★
  Vicinity .... Pg. 109, D-5
Mound City F-15
Mount Carmel H-11
Mount Carroll D-2
Mount Morris E-2
Mount Olive D-10
Mount Prospect .... ★
  Vicinity .... Pg. 108, D-4
Mount Pulaski E-7
Mount Sterling B-7
Mount Vernon F-12
Mount Zion F-8
Moweaqua F-8
Mundelein G-1
  Vicinity .... Pg. 108, B-3
Murphysboro E-13
Murrayville C-8
Nameoki Acres .... ★
  Vicinity .... Pg. 152, D-7
Naperville .... ★
  Vicinity .... Pg. 110, G-2
Nashville E-12
National City .... ★
  Vicinity .... Pg. 153, F-7
Neoga G-9
New Athens D-12
New Baden E-11
New Boston B-4
New Burnside F-14
New Canton B-8
New Haven H-13
New Holland E-7
New Lenox .... ★
  Vicinity .... Pg. 110, K-4
New Windsor C-4
Newark F-3
Newman H-8
Newton G-10
Niles .... ★
  Vicinity .... Pg. 109, E-5
Nilwood D-9
Noble G-11
Nokomis E-9
Normal F-6
Normantown .... ★
  Vicinity .... Pg. 110, H-1
Norridge .... ★
  Vicinity .... Pg. 109, E-5
Norris D-5
Norris City G-13
North Aurora .... ★
  Vicinity .... Pg. 110, G-1
North Barrington .... ★
  Vicinity .... Pg. 108, C-2

North Chicago .... ★
  Vicinity .... Pg. 109, A-4
North Dupo .... ★
  Vicinity .... Pg. 153, H-6
North Riverside .... ★
  Vicinity .... Pg. 111, F-5
North Wood River .... ★
  Vicinity .... Pg. 152, A-7
Northbrook .... ★
  Vicinity .... Pg. 109, D-4
Northfield .... ★
  Vicinity .... Pg. 109, D-5
Northfield .... ★
  Vicinity .... Pg. 109, D-5
Northlake .... ★
  Vicinity .... Pg. 111, F-4
Oak Brook .... ★
  Vicinity .... Pg. 110, G-4
Oak Forest .... ★
  Vicinity .... Pg. 111, J-5
Oak Lawn .... ★
  Vicinity .... Pg. 111, H-5
Oak Park .... ★
  Vicinity .... Pg. 111, F-5
Oakbrook Terrace .... ★
  Vicinity .... Pg. 110, F-4
Oakford D-7
Oakland H-8
Oakwood H-7
Oakwood Hills .... ★
  Vicinity .... Pg. 108, B-2
Oblong H-10
Oconee F-9
Odell G-5
Odin F-11
Ogden H-7
Ohio E-3
Okawville D-11
Old Mill Creek .... ★
  Vicinity .... Pg. 108, A-4
Olmsted F-15
Olney H-10
Olympia Fields .... ★
  Vicinity .... Pg. 111, K-6
Omaha G-13
Onarga H-5
Oquawka B-5
Orangeville F-1
Oreana F-7
Oregon E-2
Orion C-4
Orland Hills .... ★
  Vicinity .... Pg. 111, K-5
Orland Park .... ★
  Vicinity .... Pg. 111, J-4
Oswego F-8
Ottawa F-3
Owaneco F-9
Palatine G-2
  Vicinity .... Pg. 108, D-3
Palestine J-10
Palmyra D-9
Palos Heights .... ★
  Vicinity .... Pg. 111, H-5
Palos Hills .... ★
  Vicinity .... Pg. 108, A-2
Palos Park .... ★
  Vicinity .... Pg. 111, H-5
Pana F-9
Paris J-8
Park City .... ★
  Vicinity .... Pg. 109, A-4
Park Forest J-3
Park Ridge .... ★
  Vicinity .... Pg. 109, E-5
Parkersburg H-11
Patoka F-10
Pawnee E-8
Paxton H-6
Payson A-8
Pearl City D-1
Pekin D-6
Peoria D-5
Peotone H-4
Perry B-8
Pesotum G-7
Petersburg D-7
Phoenix .... ★
  Vicinity .... Pg. 111, J-6
Pierron E-10
Pinckneyville E-12
Piper City G-5
Pittsfield B-8
Plainfield G-3
  Vicinity .... Pg. 110, J-2
Plano G-3
Pleasant Hill B-9
Plymouth B-6
Pocahontas E-10
Polo E-2
Pontiac G-5
Port Byron C-3
Posen .... ★
  Vicinity .... Pg. 111, J-6
Prairie Grove .... ★
  Vicinity .... Pg. 108, B-1
Prairie View .... ★
  Vicinity .... Pg. 108, C-4
Prairie du Rocher F-12
Preston Heights .... ★
  Vicinity .... Pg. 110, K-3
Prince Crossing .... ★
  Vicinity .... Pg. 110, F-2

Princeton E-4
Princeville D-5
Prophetstown D-3
Prospect Heights .... ★
  Vicinity .... Pg. 108, D-4
Pulaski E-15
Quincy A-7
Ramsey F-9
Rankin H-6
Ransom F-4
Rantoul H-6
Rapids City C-3
Raymond E-9
Red Bud D-12
Reynolds C-4
Richton Park .... ★
  Vicinity .... Pg. 111, K-5
Richview E-11
Ridge Farm H-7
Ridgefield .... ★
  Vicinity .... Pg. 108, B-1
Ridgeway G-13
Ridgewood .... ★
  Vicinity .... Pg. 110, K-3
Ringwood .... ★
  Vicinity .... Pg. 108, A-1
River Forest .... ★
  Vicinity .... Pg. 111, F-5
River Grove .... ★
  Vicinity .... Pg. 111, F-5
Riverdale .... ★
  Vicinity .... Pg. 111, J-6
Riverside .... ★
  Vicinity .... Pg. 111, G-5
Riverwoods .... ★
  Vicinity .... Pg. 109, C-4
Roanoke F-5
Robbins .... ★
  Vicinity .... Pg. 111, J-6
Roberts G-6
Robinson H-10
Rochelle E-2
Rochester E-8
Rock Falls D-3
Rock Island B-3
Rockbridge C-9
Rockdale .... ★
  Vicinity .... Pg. 110, K-2
Rockford D-1
Rockton E-1
Rolling Meadows .... ★
  Vicinity .... Pg. 108, D-3
Romeoville .... ★
  Vicinity .... Pg. 110, J-3
Rondout .... ★
  Vicinity .... Pg. 109, B-4
Roodhouse C-9
Roselle .... ★
  Vicinity .... Pg. 108, E-3
Rosemont .... ★
  Vicinity .... Pg. 109, E-4
Roseville C-5
Rosiclare G-14
Rossville H-6
Round Lake .... ★
  Vicinity .... Pg. 108, A-3
Round Lake Beach .... ★
  Vicinity .... Pg. 108, A-3
Round Lake Heights .... ★
  Vicinity .... Pg. 108, A-3
Round Lake Park .... ★
  Vicinity .... Pg. 108, A-3
Royalton E-13
Rushville C-7
Rutland F-5
Sag Bridge .... ★
  Vicinity .... Pg. 109, G-5
Salem F-11
San Jose E-6
Sandoval E-11
Sandwich F-3
Sauget .... ★
  Vicinity .... Pg. 153, G-6
Sauk Village .... ★
  Vicinity .... Pg. 111, K-7
Savanna D-2
Schaumburg G-2
  Vicinity .... Pg. 108, E-3
Schiller Park .... ★
  Vicinity .... Pg. 109, E-4
Schram City E-9
Sesser F-12
Shabbona F-2
Shannon D-2
Shawneetown G-13
Sheffield D-4
Shelbyville F-9
Sheldon J-5
Sherwood .... ★
  Vicinity .... Pg. 110, K-2
Sibley G-6
Sigel G-9
Silvis B-3
Simpson F-14
Sims G-11
Skokie H-2
Skokie .... ★
  Vicinity .... Pg. 109, E-5
Sleepy Hollow .... ★
  Vicinity .... Pg. 108, D-1
Smithton D-11
Somonauk F-3
South Barrington .... ★
  Vicinity .... Pg. 108, D-2
South Beloit E-1

South Chicago Heights .... ★
  Vicinity .... Pg. 111, K-6
South Elgin .... ★
  Vicinity .... Pg. 108, E-1
South Holland .... ★
  Vicinity .... Pg. 111, J-6
South Lockport .... ★
  Vicinity .... Pg. 110, J-3
Sparland E-4
Sparta D-12
Spencer .... ★
  Vicinity .... Pg. 110, K-4
Spring Valley E-4
Springfield D-8
St. Anne H-4
St. Augustine C-5
St. Charles G-2
St. Charles .... ★
  Vicinity .... Pg. 110, F-1
St. Elmo F-10
St. Francisville H-11
St. Johns E-12
St. Peter F-10
Stanford E-6
Staunton D-10
Steeleville D-12
Steger .... ★
  Vicinity .... Pg. 111, K-6
Sterling D-2
Stewardson F-9
Stickney .... ★
  Vicinity .... Pg. 111, G-5
Stillman Valley E-2
Stockton D-1
Stolle .... ★
  Vicinity .... Pg. 153, H-7
Stone Park .... ★
  Vicinity .... Pg. 111, F-4
Stonefort G-13
Stonington F-8
Strasburg F-9
Streamwood .... ★
  Vicinity .... Pg. 108, E-2
Streator F-4
Stronghurst B-5
Sublette E-3
Sugar Grove G-3
Sugarloaf Hts. .... ★
  Vicinity .... Pg. 153, K-6
Sullivan G-8
Summit .... ★
  Vicinity .... Pg. 111, G-5
Sumner H-11
Sunnyside .... ★
  Vicinity .... Pg. 108, A-2
Sunrise Ridge .... ★
  Vicinity .... Pg. 108, A-1
Sycamore G-2
Table Grove C-6
Tallula D-7
Tamaroa E-12
Tamms E-14
Tampico D-3
Taylor Springs E-9
Taylorville F-8
Teutopolis G-9
Thawville G-5
Third Lake .... ★
  Vicinity .... Pg. 108, A-3
Thompsonville G-13
Thomson D-2
Thornton .... ★
  Vicinity .... Pg. 111, J-6
Tinley Park .... ★
  Vicinity .... Pg. 111, J-5
Toledo G-9
Toluca E-5
Tonica F-4
Toulon D-4
Tower Hill F-9
Tower Lakes .... ★
  Vicinity .... Pg. 108, C-2
Trenton E-11
Troy D-11
Troy Grove E-3
Tuscola G-8
Urbana H-7
Valley View .... ★
  Vicinity .... Pg. 108, E-1
Valmeyer C-12
Vandalia F-10
Venetian Village .... ★
  Vicinity .... Pg. 152, F-7
Venice .... ★
Vernon F-10
Vernon Hills .... ★
  Vicinity .... Pg. 108, B-4
Versailles B-8
Victoria D-4
Vienna F-14
Villa Grove H-8
Villa Park .... ★
  Vicinity .... Pg. 110, F-3
Viola C-4
Virden D-9
Virginia C-7
Volo .... ★
  Vicinity .... Pg. 108, B-2
Wadsworth .... ★
  Vicinity .... Pg. 108, A-4

Waggoner D-9
Walnut E-3
Waltonville F-12
Wapella F-7
Warren D-1
Warrensburg F-7
Warrenville .... ★
  Vicinity .... Pg. 110, G-2
Warsaw A-6
Washburn E-5
Washington E-5
Waterloo C-12
Waterman F-3
Watseka H-5
Watson G-10
Wauconda .... ★
  Vicinity .... Pg. 108, B-2
Waukegan H-1
  Vicinity .... Pg. 108, A-4
Waverly D-8
Wayne .... ★
  Vicinity .... Pg. 108, E-1
Wayne City G-11
Weldon F-7
Wellington H-6
Wenona F-4
West Chicago .... ★
  Vicinity .... Pg. 110, F-2
West City F-12
West Dundee .... ★
  Vicinity .... Pg. 108, D-1
West Frankfort F-13
West Miltmore .... ★
  Vicinity .... Pg. 108, A-3
Westchester .... ★
  Vicinity .... Pg. 110, F-4
Western Springs .... ★
  Vicinity .... Pg. 110, G-4
Westfield H-9
Westmont .... ★
  Vicinity .... Pg. 110, G-3
Westville J-7
Wheaton G-2
  Vicinity .... Pg. 110, F-3
Wheeler G-10
Wheeling .... ★
  Vicinity .... Pg. 108, D-4
White Hall C-9
Wildwood .... ★
  Vicinity .... Pg. 108, A-4
Willow Hill H-10
Willow Springs .... ★
  Vicinity .... Pg. 110, H-4
Willowbrook .... ★
  Vicinity .... Pg. 110, G-4
Wilmette .... ★
  Vicinity .... Pg. 109, D-6
Wilmington H-4
Winchester C-8
Winfield .... ★
  Vicinity .... Pg. 110, F-2
Winnebago E-1
Winnetka H-2
  Vicinity .... Pg. 109, D-5
Winslow D-1
Winthrop Harbor H-1
Wolfs .... ★
  Vicinity .... Pg. 110, H-1
Wonder Lake .... ★
  Vicinity .... Pg. 108, A-1
Wood Dale .... ★
  Vicinity .... Pg. 108, E-3
Wood River .... ★
  Vicinity .... Pg. 152, B-7
Woodhull C-4
Woodridge .... ★
  Vicinity .... Pg. 110, H-3
Woodson C-8
Woodstock G-1
Worth .... ★
  Vicinity .... Pg. 111, H-5
Wyoming D-5
Xenia G-11
Yates City D-5
York Center .... ★
Yorkville G-3
Zeigler F-13
Zion H-1
Zion H-1

INDIANA
Page 38

Advance E-4
Adyeville J-3
  Vicinity .... Pg. 109, C-7
Aix C-3
Akron C-4
Albany E-5
Albion C-5
Alexandria E-5
Alfordsville H-3
Allendale F-2
Alliance E-5
Allisonville .... ★
  Vicinity .... Pg. 122, B-5
Alton J-3
Amboy D-4
Amity F-4
Anderson E-5
Andersonville F-5
Andrews D-5
Angola B-6

★ Denotes City only on Vicinity map. City not located on State map.

INDIANA

Anoka D-4
Antioch E-4
Antrim . . . . ★
  Vicinity . . . . . Pg. 122, F-2
Arcadia E-4
Arcana D-5
Argos C-4
Arlington F-5
Asherville F-3
Atlanta E-4
Attica D-3
Auburn C-6
Augusta . . . . ★
  Vicinity . . . . . Pg. 122, B-3
Aurora G-6
Austin H-5
Avoca G-3
Bainbridge F-3
Bargersville F-4
Bass Lake C-4
Batesville G-5
Battle Ground D-3
Beardstown C-4
Bedford H-4
Beech Grove . . . . . ★
  Vicinity . . . . . Pg. 122, E-5
Belleview F-4
Bellmore F-3
Belmont G-4
Ben Davis . . . . ★
  Vicinity . . . . . Pg. 122, E-5
Benton B-5
Berne D-6
Bicknell G-2
Bippus C-5
Birdseye H-3
Bloomfield G-3
Bloomington G-4
Bluffton D-6
Bobo D-6
Boonville J-2
Boston F-6
Boswell D-2
Boundary City E-6
Bourbon C-4
Brazil F-3
Bremen B-4
Bridgeport . . . . ★
  Vicinity . . . . . Pg. 122, E-1
Brook C-3
Brooklyn F-4
Brooksburg H-5
Brookston D-3
Brookville F-6
Brownsburg E-4
Brownstown G-4
Bruceville G-2
Bryan D-6
Bud F-4
Bunker Hill H-4
Burlington D-4
Butler C-6
Cairo D-3
Cambridge City F-5
Camby . . . . ★
  Vicinity . . . . . Pg. 122, F-1
Camden D-4
Campbellsburg H-4
Cannelton J-3
Carefree J-4
Carmel E-4
Carthage F-5
Castleton . . . . ★
  Vicinity . . . . . Pg. 122, B-5
Cayuga E-2
Cedar Grove G-6
Cedar Lake B-3
Central J-4
Chalmers D-3
Chandler J-2
Charleston H-5
Chesterton B-3
Chile D-4
China H-5
Chrisney J-3
Churubusco C-5
Cicero E-4
Cincinnati G-3
Clarks Hill E-3
Clarksville . . . . ★
  Vicinity . . . . . Pg. 130, A-2
Clarmont E-4
Clay City F-3
Clayton F-4
Clear Lake B-6
Clermont . . . . ★
  Vicinity . . . . . Pg. 122, C-1
Clifford G-4
Clinton F-2
Cloverdale F-3
Clymers D-4
Colfax E-3
Collegeville C-3
Columbia City C-5
Columbus G-4
Connersville F-6
Converse D-4
Cope F-4
Correct G-5
Corydon J-4
Covington E-2
Crandall J-4
Crawfordsville E-3
Cromwell C-5
Cross Plains G-5

Crothersville H-4
Crown Point B-3
Crystal H-3
Culver C-4
Cumberland F-4
Cynthiana J-1
Dale J-3
Dana E-2
Danville F-4
Darlington E-3
Darmstadt J-2
Dayton D-3
Dayville J-2
Decatur D-6
Decker H-2
Deerfield E-6
Delphi D-3
Demotte C-3
Denver C-4
Dexter J-3
Dillsboro G-6
Doans G-3
Dogwood J-4
Doolittle Mills J-3
Dover Hill H-3
Dublin F-5
Dudleytown G-4
Dugger G-2
Dunkirk E-5
Dupont G-5
Dyer B-3
  Vicinity . . . . . Pg. 109, B-5
Earl Park D-2
East Chicago B-3
  Vicinity . . . . . Pg. 109, A-6
East Gary . . . . ★
  Vicinity . . . . . Pg. 109, B-7
Eaton E-5
Eby J-2
Economy E-5
Edgewood . . . . ★
  Vicinity . . . . . Pg. 122, F-4
Edinburgh G-4
Edwardsport G-2
Effner C-2
Elberfeld J-2
Elizabeth J-4
Elizabethtown G-5
Elkhart B-5
Elletsville G-3
Ellis B-6
Elnora G-3
Elrod G-5
Elwood E-5
Eminence F-3
English H-3
Enos C-2
Erie D-4
Etna Green C-4
Evansville J-2
Everton F-6
Fairfield F-5
Fairmount D-5
Fairview Park F-2
Farmersburg F-2
Farmland E-5
Fayette E-4
Ferdinand J-3
Fiat D-6
Fishers E-4
Five Points . . . . . . ★
  Vicinity . . . . . Pg. 122, E-5
Flint B-6
Flora D-4
Foresman D-3
Foreman C-3
Fort Branch H-2
Fort Wayne C-6
Fortville E-5
Foster E-2
Fountain City E-6
Fountain Park C-3
Fowler D-3
Francesville C-3
Francisco H-2
Frankfort E-4
Franklin F-4
Freeman G-3
Fremont B-6
French Lick H-3
Friendship G-5
Galveston D-4
Garden City G-4
Garfield F-5
Garrett B-6
Gary B-3
  Vicinity . . . . . Pg. 109, B-6
Gas City D-5
Gasburg F-5
Gaston E-5
Geneva F-5
Gentryville J-3
Georgetown H-4
Georgetown D-3
Gilead C-4
Glenns Valley . . . . . ★
  Vicinity . . . . . Pg. 122, D-4
Glenwood F-5
Goodland C-3
Goshen B-5
Gosport F-3
Grandview J-3
Gravel Hill D-2
Graysville G-2
Green Oak C-4

Greencastle F-3
Greendale G-6
Greenfield F-5
Greensburg G-5
Greentown D-5
Greenville H-4
Greenwood F-4
Griffith . . . . ★
  Vicinity . . . . . Pg. 109, B-6
Guilford G-6
Hagerstown E-5
Hamilton B-4
Hamilton B-6
Hamlet B-4
Hammond B-3
  Vicinity . . . . . Pg. 109, A-5
Hanover H-5
Hardinsburg H-4
Harrisburg H-4
Hartford City D-5
Haubstadt H-2
Haysville H-3
Hazleton H-2
Hebron C-3
Heilman J-2
Henryville H-5
Heusler J-2
Highland B-3
  Vicinity . . . . . Pg. 109, B-6
Highwoods . . . . ★
  Vicinity . . . . . Pg. 122, C-3
Hillham H-3
Hillsboro E-3
Hobart B-3
  Vicinity . . . . . Pg. 109, B-7
Holland H-3
Holton G-5
Homecroft . . . . ★
  Vicinity . . . . . Pg. 122, F-4
Hope F-5
Hovey J-1
Huntertown C-5
Huntingburg H-3
Huntington D-5
Huron H-3
Hymera G-2
Indianapolis F-4
  Vicinity . . . . . Pg. 122
Ingalls E-5
Ireland H-3
Iva H-3
Jamestown E-3
Jasonville G-3
Jasper H-3
Jeffersonville J-5
  Vicinity . . . . . Pg. 130, A-3
Johnsburg J-3
Kempton E-4
Kendallville B-6
Kent C-3
Kewanna C-4
Kingman E-2
Kingsbury B-4
Kingsford Hts. B-4
Kirby G-3
Kirklin E-4
Knightstown F-5
Knightsville F-3
Knox C-4
Koutz B-3
Kokomo D-4
Kyle G-6
La Crosse C-3
La Fontaine D-5
La Grange B-5
LaPorte B-3
Laconia J-4
Ladoga E-3
Lafayette D-3
Lagro D-5
Lakeville B-4
Lanesville J-4
Lapaz B-4
Lapel E-4
Laurel F-5
Lawrenceburg G-6
Leavenworth J-3
Lebanon E-4
Leo C-6
Leroy B-3
Lewis F-2
Lewisville F-5
Liberty F-6
Ligonier B-5
Linden E-3
Linton G-3
Little York H-4
Livonia H-4
Logansport D-4
Long Beach B-3
Loogootee H-3
Losantville E-6
Lowell B-2
Lynn E-6
Lynnville J-2
Lyons G-2
Mace E-3
Mackey H-2
Madison H-5
Mahon B-3
Majenica D-5
Mansfield F-3
Marco G-3
Marengo H-4
Marion D-5

Markle D-5
Mars Hill . . . . ★
  Vicinity . . . . . Pg. 122, E-2
Marshall E-3
Marshfield D-2
Marshtown C-4
Martinsville F-3
Matthews D-5
Mauckport J-4
Maywood . . . . ★
  Vicinity . . . . . Pg. 122, E-3
Medaryville C-3
Medora H-4
Mellott E-3
Mentone C-4
Meridian Hills . . . . . ★
  Vicinity . . . . . Pg. 122, B-3
Merillville B-3
  Vicinity . . . . . Pg. 109, B-6
Merom G-2
Merriam C-5
Mexico D-4
Michigan City B-3
Mickeyville . . . . ★
  Vicinity . . . . . Pg. 122, E-2
Middlebury B-5
Middletown E-5
Milan G-5
Milford B-5
Millersburg B-5
Milligan E-3
Milltown H-4
Milport H-4
Milroy F-5
Milton F-5
Mishawaka B-4
Mitchell H-4
Modoc E-6
Monon C-3
Monroe D-6
Monroe City H-2
Monroeville C-6
Monterey E-2
Montezuma E-2
Monticello D-3
Montmorenci D-3
Montpelier D-5
Moores Hill G-5
Mooresville F-4
Morgantown F-4
Morocco C-2
Morristown F-4
Morton E-3
Mt. Ayr C-3
Mt. Carmel D-5
Mt. Etna D-5
Mt. Healthy G-4
Mt. Sterling H-6
Mt. Summit E-5
Mt. Vernon J-1
Mulberry E-3
Muncie E-5
Munster B-3
  Vicinity . . . . . Pg. 109, B-5
Munster B-3
  Vicinity . . . . . Pg. 111, K-7
N. Liberty B-4
N. Manchester C-5
N. Salem E-3
N. Vernon G-5
N. Webster C-5
Nappanee B-4
Nashville G-4
Natchez H-3
Needmore G-3
New Albany J-4
  Vicinity . . . . . Pg. 130, A-1
New Augusta . . . . . ★
  Vicinity . . . . . Pg. 122, B-2
New Bethel . . . . . . ★
  Vicinity . . . . . Pg. 122, B-4
New Carlisle B-4
New Castle E-5
New Haven C-6
New Liberty H-4
New Palestine F-5
New Pekin H-4
New Providence H-4
New Salem F-5
New Whiteland F-4
Newberry G-3
Newburgh J-2
Newport E-2
Newtown E-3
Nobelsville E-4
Nora . . . . ★
  Vicinity . . . . . Pg. 122, B-4
North Crows Nest . . . ★
  Vicinity . . . . . Pg. 122, B-3
North Judson C-3
Oakland City H-2
Oaktown G-2
Odell D-3
Odon G-3
Oldenburg G-5
Onward D-4
Oolitic G-3
Orestes E-5
Orland B-6
Orleans H-3
Osgood G-5
Ossian D-6
Otisco H-5
Otterbein D-3
Otwell H-3

Owensville H-1
Oxford D-3
Palmyra H-4
Paoli H-3
Paragon F-3
Patoka H-2
Patricksburg F-3
Patriot H-6
Pembroke C-3
Pendleton E-5
Pennville D-6
Perrysville E-2
Peru D-4
Petersburg H-2
Pierceton C-5
Pike E-4
Pimento F-2
Pittsboro E-4
Plainfield F-4
  Vicinity . . . . . Pg. 109, B-6
Plainville G-3
Plattsburg H-4
Pleasant D-6
Pleasant Mills D-6
Plum Tree D-5
Plymouth C-4
Poneto D-5
Portage B-3
Porter B-3
Portland D-6
Poseyville H-1
Prairie City F-3
Prairie Creek F-2
Prince's Lake F-4
Princeton H-2
Prospect H-3
Quaker E-5
Ravenswood . . . . . . ★
  Vicinity . . . . . Pg. 122, B-4
Redkey D-5
Reiffsburg D-6
Remington D-3
Rensselaer C-3
Reynolds D-3
Richmond F-6
Riddle J-3
Riley F-2
Rising Sun G-6
Roachdale E-3
Roann C-5
Roanoke C-5
Rochester C-4
Rockfield D-3
Rockport J-2
Rockville F-2
Rocky Ripple . . . . . . ★
  Vicinity . . . . . Pg. 122, C-3
Roland H-3
Roll J-1
Rome City B-5
Romney D-3
Roseburg F-5
Rosedale H-4
Roselawn C-3
Rossville D-4
Royal Center D-4
Rushville F-5
Salem H-4
Saltillo H-4
Sandborn G-2
Sandford F-2
Sandusky F-5
Saratoga E-6
Savah J-1
Schererville B-3
  Vicinity . . . . . Pg. 109, C-5
Schneider C-3
Scottsburg H-5
Seelyville F-2
Sellersburg H-5
Selma E-5
Servia C-5
Sexton D-3
Seymour G-4
Shadeland D-3
Shelburn G-2
Shelbyville F-5
Sheridan E-4
Shipshewana B-5
Shirley F-5
Shoals H-3
Shore Acres . . . . . . ★
  Vicinity . . . . . Pg. 122, B-4
Sidney C-5
Silver Lake C-5
Sleeth D-3
Sloan D-2
Smyrna G-5
Solsberry G-3
South Bend B-4
South Whitley C-5
Southport F-3
Southport . . . . ★
  Vicinity . . . . . Pg. 122, G-4
Speedway E-4
Spencer F-3
Spencerville C-6
Spring Hills . . . . ★
  Vicinity . . . . . Pg. 122, C-3
Springport B-3
Springville G-3
St. Joe C-6
St. John B-3
  Vicinity . . . . . Pg. 111, K-7

St. Leon G-6
Star City C-3
Staser J-2
State Line City E-2
Stearleyville F-3
Stewart D-2
Stilesville F-3
Story G-4
Sullivan F-2
Sulphur J-3
Summit B-6
Summitsville E-5
Sunman G-5
Swalls F-2
Swanington D-2
Swayzee D-5
Switz City G-3
Syracuse B-5
Tab D-2
Tampico H-4
Tell City J-3
Tennyson J-2
Terre Huate F-2
Thornhope C-3
Thorntown E-4
Tiosa C-4
Tipton E-4
Tocsin D-6
Topeka B-5
Townley C-6
Traders Point . . . . . ★
  Vicinity . . . . . Pg. 122, B-1
Trafalgar F-4
Treaty D-5
Tremont . . . . ★
  Vicinity . . . . . Pg. 122, D-1
Trinity D-6
Trinity Springs G-3
Troy J-3
Unindale D-6
Union City E-6
Upland D-5
Valentine B-5
Vallonia G-4
Valparaiso B-3
Van Buren D-5
Veedersburg E-2
Vera Cruz D-6
Vernon G-5
Versailles G-5
Vevay H-6
Vienna H-5
Vincennes H-2
W. Baden Springs . . . H-3
W. College Corner . . . F-6
W. Lebanon E-2
W. Terre Haute F-2
Wabash D-5
Wadesville J-1
Wakarusa B-4
Walkerton B-4
Wallace E-3
Walnut D-4
Walton D-4
Wanatah B-3
Warren D-5
Warsaw C-5
Washington H-2
Waterloo B-6
Waveland E-3
Webster E-6
West Lafayette D-3
West Newton . . . . . . ★
  Vicinity . . . . . Pg. 122, G-2
Westfield E-4
Westphalia G-2
Westport G-5
Westville B-3
Wheatfield C-3
Whiteland F-4
Whiting B-3
  Vicinity . . . . . Pg. 109, A-6
Whiting B-3
  Vicinity . . . . . Pg. 111, H-7
Williams Creek . . . . . ★
  Vicinity . . . . . Pg. 122, B-4
Williamsport D-2
Wilson H-4
Winamac C-4
Winchester E-6
Wingate E-3
Winona Lake C-5
Winslow H-2
Wirt H-5
Wolcott D-3
Wolcottville B-5
Woodland B-4
Woodstock . . . . ★
  Vicinity . . . . . Pg. 122, C-3
Worthington G-3
Wynnedale . . . . ★
  Vicinity . . . . . Pg. 122, C-3
Yorktown E-5
Zanesville C-5
Zionsville E-4
  Vicinity . . . . . Pg. 122, A-2
Zulu C-6

IOWA

IOWA
Page 39

Abingdon F-7
Ackley C-6
Adair E-4

Adel E-4
Afton F-4
Agency E-6
Ainsworth E-8
Akron C-1
Albia E-6
Alden C-5
Algona B-4
Allendorf B-2
Allerton F-5
Allison C-6
Alta C-3
Alta Vista B-7
Alton B-1
Altoona E-5
Amana D-8
Ames D-5
Anamosa D-9
Anderson F-2
Andrew D-10
Anita E-3
Anthon C-2
Aplington C-6
Arcadia D-3
Archer B-2
Aredale C-6
Arispe F-4
Arlington C-8
Armstrong B-4
Arnolds Park A-3
Arthur D-3
Asbury D-9
Ashton B-2
Athelstan D-7
Atkins D-8
Atlantic E-3
Attica E-6
Auburn D-3
Audubon E-3
Aurelia C-3
Avery E-6
Avoca E-3
Badger C-4
Baldwin D-9
Bancroft B-4
Barnes City E-6
Barnum C-4
Bartlett F-2
Battle Creek D-2
Baxter D-6
Bayard D-4
Beacon E-6
Beaver D-5
Bedford F-4
Beech E-6
Belle Plaine D-7
Bellevue D-9
Belmond C-5
Bennett E-9
Bettendorf E-10
Bevington E-5
Blakesburg F-7
Blencoe D-2
Bloomfield F-7
Bonaparte F-8
Boone D-5
Boyden B-2
Bradford C-6
Brayton E-3
Breda C-3
Bridgewater F-4
Brighton E-8
Britt B-5
Brooklyn D-7
Brooks F-3
Brunsville C-1
Bryant D-10
Buffalo Center B-5
Burlington F-8
Burr Oak A-8
Burt B-4
Bussey E-6
Calmar B-8
Calumet B-2
Camanche D-10
Cantril G-7
Carbon F-3
Carpenter B-6
Carroll D-3
Carson F-3
Carter Lake E-1
Carter Lake . . . . . . ★
  Vicinity . . . . . Pg. 145, D-5
Cascade D-9
Casey E-4
Cedar F-7
Cedar Falls C-7
Cedar Rapids D-8
Center Point D-8
Centerville F-6
Central City D-8
Chapin C-6
Chariton F-6
Charles City B-6
Charlotte D-10
Charter Oak D-2
Chatsworth B-1
Chautauqua . . . . . . ★
  Vicinity . . . . . Pg. 144, D-6
Chelsea D-7
Cherokee C-2
Churdan D-4
Cincinnati G-6
Clara B-6
  Vicinity . . . . . Pg. 144, C-5

Clare C-4
Clarence D-9
Clarinda F-3
Clarion C-5
Clarksville C-7
Clear Lake B-6
Clearfield F-4
Cleghorn C-2
Clinton D-10
Clutier D-7
Coggon D-8
Colesburg C-9
Colfax E-6
Collins D-6
Colo D-5
Columbia F-6
Columbus Jct. E-8
Colwell B-7
Conesville E-8
Conrad D-6
Conroy E-8
Conway F-4
Coon Rapids D-3
Cooper D-4
Coppock F-8
Coralville E-8
Corley E-2
Corning F-3
Correctionville C-2
Corwith B-5
Corydon F-6
Council Bluffs F-2
Council Bluffs F-2
  Vicinity . . . . . Pg. 144, E-6
Crescent E-1
Crescent . . . . ★
  Vicinity . . . . . Pg. 144, C-5
Cresco B-7
Creston F-4
Curlew B-4
Dakota City C-4
Dallas Center D-4
Dana D-4
Danbury D-2
Danville F-8
Davenport E-9
Davis City G-5
Dayton D-4
De Soto E-5
De Witt D-9
Decorah B-8
Dedham D-3
Defiance D-3
Delhi C-8
Delmar D-9
Deloit D-3
Delta E-7
Denison D-3
Denver C-7
Derby F-5
Des Moines E-5
Dexter E-4
Dickens B-3
Dike C-7
Dolliver B-4
Donnellson F-8
Doon B-1
Dorchester B-8
Dow City D-2
Dows C-5
Drakesville F-7
Dubuque D-9
Dumfries . . . . ★
  Vicinity . . . . . Pg. 144, G-7
Dumont C-6
Duncombe C-4
Dunkerton C-7
Dunlap D-2
Durant E-9
Dyersville D-9
Dysart D-7
Eagle Grove C-5
Earlham E-4
Earling E-3
Early C-3
Eddyville E-6
Edgewood C-8
Eldon F-7
Eldora D-6
Eldridge E-10
Elgin B-8
Elk Horn E-3
Elkader C-8
Elliott F-3
Ellsworth D-5
Emerson F-2
Emmetsburg B-4
Epworth C-9
Essex F-2
Estherville B-4
Evansdale C-7
Everly B-3
Exira E-3
Fairbank C-7
Fairfield F-8
Farley C-9
Farnhamville D-4
Farragut F-2
Fayette C-8
Fenton B-4
Floyd B-6
Fonda C-3
Fontanelle E-4
Forest City B-5

★ Denotes City only on Vicinity map. City not located on State map.

IOWA

City	Loc.	City	Loc.	City	Loc.	City	Loc.
Fort Dodge	C-4	Klemme	B-5	New Hampton	B-7	Sharpsburg	F-3
Fort Madison	F-9	Knoxville	E-6	New Haven	B-7	Sheffield	C-6
Fostoria	B-3	La Porte City	D-7	New London	F-9	Sheldon	B-2
Frankville	B-8	Lake City	C-3	New Market	F-3	Shell Rock	C-7
Fraser	D-5	Lake Mills	B-5	New Providence	D-6	Shellsburg	D-8
Fredericksburg	B-7	Lake Park	B-3	New Sharon	E-7	Shenandoah	F-3
Fremont	E-7	Lake View	D-3	New Virginia	F-5	Sibley	A-2
Froelich	B-8	Lamoni	G-4	Newburg	D-7	Sidney	F-2
Frytown	E-8	Lamont	C-8	Newkirk	B-2	Sigourney	E-7
Fulton	D-9	Lansing	B-8	Newton	E-6	Sioux Center	B-1
Garden City	D-6	Larchwood	A-1	Nichols	E-9	Sioux City	C-1
Garnavillo	C-9	Larrabee	C-2	Nora Springs	B-6	Sioux Rapids	B-3
Garner	B-5	Laurel	D-6	North English	E-7	Sloan	D-1
Garwin	C-6	Laurens	C-3	Northboro	G-3	Smithland	D-2
George	B-2	Le Claire	D-9	Northwood	B-6	Soldier	D-2
Gibson	E-7	Le Mars	C-2	Norwalk	E-5	Solon	D-8
Gilbert	D-5	Ledyard	B-4	Norway	D-7	Somers	C-4
Gilman	D-6	Lehigh	D-5	Oakland	E-3	Spencer	B-3
Gilmore City	C-4	Leighton	E-7	Ocheyedan	A-2	Spirit Lake	B-3
Gladbrook	C-6	Lenox	F-4	Odebolt	D-3	Springville	D-8
Glenwood	F-2	Leon	F-5	Oelwein	C-8	St. Ansgar	B-6
Glenwood	F-2	Lester	B-1	Ogden	D-4	St. Charles	E-5
Vicinity	Pg. 144, J-7	Lewis	E-3	Olin	D-9	St. Joseph	B-4
Glidden	D-4	Liberty Center	F-6	Onawa	D-2	St. Marys	D-5
Goldfield	C-5	Lime Springs	B-7	Onslow	D-9	Stacyville	A-6
Goodell	B-5	Linderwood	C-8	Orange City	B-2	Stanton	E-2
Gowrie	D-4	Lineville	G-5	Orient	F-4	Stanwood	D-8
Graettinger	B-4	Lisbon	D-8	Osage	B-6	State Center	D-6
Grafton	B-6	Little Rock	B-2	Osceola	E-5	Steamboat Rock	C-6
Grand Jct.	D-4	Little Sioux	D-2	Oskaloosa	E-7	Storm Lake	C-3
Grand River	F-4	Livermore	C-5	Otho	D-5	Story City	D-5
Grandview	E-9	Logan	E-2	Oto	D-2	Stout	C-7
Grant	F-3	Lohrville	C-3	Ottumwa	F-7	Strawberry Point	C-8
Green Mountain	D-6	Long Grove	D-9	Oxford	E-8	Stuart	E-4
Greene	C-6	Long Tree	E-8	Oyens	C-2	Sully	E-6
Greenfield	E-4	Lorimor	F-5	Pacific City	★	Sulphur Springs	C-3
Grimes	D-4	Lost Nation	D-9	Vicinity	Pg. 144, J-6	Sumner	C-7
Grinnell	E-7	Lovilia	F-6	Pacific Junction	F-2	Superior	B-3
Griswold	F-3	Lowden	D-9	Vicinity	Pg. 144, K-6	Sutherland	B-2
Grundy Center	C-6	Lucas	F-5	Panama	E-3	Swea City	B-4
Guernsey	E-7	Luther	D-5	Panora	E-4	Tabor	F-2
Gunder	B-8	Luxemburg	C-9	Park View	E-10	Tama	D-7
Guthrie Center	E-4	Lyman	F-3	Parkersburg	C-7	Templeton	D-3
Guttenburg	B-9	Lytton	C-3	Parnell	E-7	Terril	B-3
Hamburg	G-2	Macedonia	F-3	Paullina	B-2	Thompson	B-5
Hamilton	F-6	Macksburg	E-4	Pella	E-6	Thornton	C-6
Hamlin	E-3	Madrid	D-5	Percival	F-2	Thurman	F-2
Hampton	C-6	Malcom	E-6	Perkins	B-1	Tiffin	E-8
Hancock	E-3	Mallard	B-4	Perry	D-5	Tipton	D-9
Hanlontown	B-5	Malvern	F-2	Persia	E-2	Titonka	B-5
Harcourt	D-4	Manchester	C-8	Pierson	C-2	Toledo	D-7
Harlan	E-3	Manilla	D-3	Pilot Mound	D-5	Traer	D-7
Harper's Ferry	B-9	Manly	B-6	Pisgah	D-2	Trenton	F-8
Hartley	B-3	Manning	D-3	Plain View	E-9	Tripoli	C-7
Hartwick	D-7	Manson	C-4	Plainfield	C-7	Truesdale	C-3
Harvey	E-6	Mapleton	D-2	Plano	F-6	Truro	F-5
Havelock	C-4	Maquoketa	D-10	Pleasant Plain	F-7	Turin	D-2
Haven	D-7	Marathon	C-3	Pleasantville	E-5	Ulmer	D-3
Hawarden	B-1	Marcus	C-2	Pocahontas	C-4	Underwood	E-2
Hawkeye	B-7	Marengo	E-7	Polk City	E-5	Union	C-5
Hazleton	C-8	Marion	D-8	Pomeroy	C-4	Urbana	D-7
Hedrick	F-7	Marne	E-3	Popejoy	C-6	Urbandale	E-5
Henderson	F-2	Marquette	B-9	Portsmouth	E-3	Ute	D-2
Hepburn	F-3	Marshalltown	D-6	Postville	B-8	Vail	D-3
Hesper	B-8	Mason City	B-6	Prairie City	E-6	Valeria	E-6
Hiawatha	D-7	Massena	E-4	Preston	D-10	Van Horne	D-7
Hillsboro	F-8	Matlock	B-2	Primghar	B-2	Van Wert	F-5
Hinton	C-1	Maxwell	D-5	Prole	E-5	Varina	C-3
Holmes	C-5	May City	B-3	Pulaski	F-7	Ventura	B-5
Holstein	C-2	Maynard	C-7	Quasqueton	C-8	Victor	E-7
Honey Creek	★	McGregor	B-8	Quimby	C-2	Villisca	F-3
Vicinity	Pg. 144, A-5	McIntire	B-7	Rathbun	F-6	Vining	D-7
Hopeville	F-5	Mechanicsville	D-8	Reasnor	E-6	Vinton	D-7
Hopkinton	C-9	Mediapolis	F-9	Red Oak	F-3	W. Burlington	F-8
Hospers	B-1	Melbourne	D-6	Redding	G-4	Walford	D-8
Hubbard	C-5	Melcher	E-5	Redfield	E-4	Walker	D-8
Hudson	C-7	Melvin	B-2	Reinbeck	D-7	Wall Lake	C-2
Hull	B-2	Meriden	C-2	Rembrandt	C-3	Wallingford	B-4
Humboldt	C-4	Merrill	C-1	Remsen	C-2	Wapello	E-8
Humeston	F-5	Milford	B-3	Renwick	C-5	Washington	E-8
Huxley	D-5	Millerton	F-5	Rhodes	D-6	Washta	C-2
Iconium	F-6	Millville	C-9	Riceville	B-6	Waterloo	C-7
Ida Grove	C-2	Milo	E-5	Richland	E-7	Waukee	E-5
Imogene	F-3	Milton	G-7	Rickardsville	C-9	Waukon	B-8
Independence	C-8	Minburn	E-5	Ridgeway	B-8	Waverly	C-7
Indianola	E-5	Minden	E-2	Ringsted	A-3	Webster	C-7
Inwood	B-1	Mingo	E-6	Rippey	D-4	Webster City	C-5
Iowa Center	D-6	Missouri Valley	E-2	Rochester	E-9	Weldon	F-5
Iowa City	E-8	Mitchellville	D-5	Rock Rapids	B-2	Wellman	E-8
Iowa Falls	C-6	Mondamin	E-2	Rock Valley	B-1	Welton	D-10
Ireton	B-1	Moneta	B-3	Rockford	B-6	Wesley	B-5
Irwin	E-3	Monona	B-8	Rockwell	B-6	West Bend	B-4
Jackson Jct.	B-7	Monroe	E-6	Rockwell City	C-4	West Des Moines	D-4
Jamaica	D-4	Montezuma	E-7	Roland	C-5	West Grove	F-7
Janesville	C-7	Monticello	C-9	Rolfe	C-4	West Liberty	E-8
Jefferson	D-4	Montrose	G-8	Roselle	D-3	West Point	F-8
Jerico	B-7	Moorhead	E-2	Rossie	B-3	West Union	B-8
Jesup	C-7	Moravia	F-6	Rossville	B-8	Westfield	C-1
Jewell	D-5	Morning Sun	F-9	Royal	B-3	Weston	★
Joice	B-5	Morse	E-8	Russell	F-6	Vicinity	Pg. 144, C-7
Kalona	E-8	Moulton	G-7	Ruthven	B-3	Wheatland	D-9
Kamrar	C-5	Mount Ayr	F-4	Ryan	C-8	Whiting	D-2
Kanawha	B-4	Mount Etna	F-4	Sabula	C-10	Whittemore	B-4
Kellogg	D-6	Mount Sterling	G-8	Sac City	C-3	Wick	E-5
Kendallville	B-8	Mount Union	F-8	Sanborn	B-2	Willey	D-3
Kent	F-4	Moville	C-1	Saratoga	B-7	Williams	C-5
Keokuk	G-8	Mt. Pleasant	F-8	Schaller	C-3	Williamsburg	E-8
Keosauqua	F-8	Mt. Vernon	D-8	Schleswig	D-2	Williamson	F-5
Keota	E-8	Murray	F-4	Schley	B-7	Wilton	D-8
Keswick	D-7	Muscatine	E-9	Scranton	D-4	Winfield	F-8
Keystone	D-7	Nashua	B-7	Searsboro	E-7	Winterset	E-4
Killduff	E-6	Neola	E-2	Selma	F-7	Wiota	E-3
Kingsley	C-2	Nevada	D-5	Sergeant Bluff	C-2	Woodbine	E-2
Kirkman	E-3	Nevinville	F-4	Seymour	F-5	Woodburn	F-5
Kiron	D-3	New Albin	A-8	Shambaugh	G-3	Woodward	D-4

KANSAS

City	Loc.
Woolstock	C-5
Wyoming	D-9
Yale	E-4
Zwingle	C-9

KANSAS
Pages 40-41

City	Loc.	City	Loc.	City	Loc.	City	Loc.
Abbeyville	F-7	Colby	C-4	Haysville	G-9	McCune	H-12
Abilene	E-9	Coldwater	H-6	Hazelton	H-7	McDonald	C-3
Admire	E-10	Collyer	D-5	Healy	E-4	McFarland	D-10
Agenda	C-9	Colony	F-11	Herington	E-10	McPherson	F-8
Agra	C-6	Columbus	H-12	Hesston	F-9	Meade	H-4
Alden	F-7	Concordia	C-8	Hiawatha	C-11	Medicine Lodge	H-7
Alexander	E-6	Conway Springs	H-8	Highland	C-11	Melvern	E-11
Allen	E-10	Coolidge	F-2	Hill City	D-5	Menlo	D-4
Alma	E-10	Copeland	G-4	Hillsboro	F-9	Meriden	D-11
Almena	B-6	Cottonwood Falls	F-10	Hoisington	E-7	Merriam	★
Alta Vista	E-10	Council Grove	E-10	Holcomb	F-4	Vicinity	Pg. 125, H-2
Altamont	H-12	Countryside	★	Hollenberg	C-9	Milan	H-8
Alton	H-11	Vicinity	Pg. 125, H-2	Holton	D-11	Mildred	G-12
Altoona	G-11	Courtland	C-8	Holyrood	E-7	Milford	D-10
Americus	F-11	Cuba	C-9	Hope	E-9	Miltonvale	D-9
Andale	F-8	Cullison	G-7	Horton	C-11	Minneapolis	D-8
Andover	G-9	Culver	E-8	Howard	G-10	Minneola	G-5
Anthony	H-8	Cunningham	G-7	Hoxie	D-5	Mission	★
Arcadia	G-12	Damar	D-6	Hoyt	D-11	Vicinity	Pg. 125, H-2
Argonia	H-8	Danville	H-8	Hudson	F-7	Mission Hills	★
Arkansas City	H-9	De Soto	E-12	Hugoton	H-3	Vicinity	Pg. 125, H-3
Arlington	G-7	Dearing	H-11	Humboldt	G-12	Moline	H-10
Arma	G-13	Deerfield	F-3	Hunter	D-7	Montezuma	G-4
Ashland	H-5	Delphos	D-8	Huron	C-12	Moran	G-12
Atchison	C-12	Denison	D-11	Hutchinson	F-8	Morganville	C-9
Athol	C-7	Denton	C-12	Independence	H-11	Morland	D-5
Atlanta	H-9	Derby	G-9	Ingalls	G-4	Morrill	C-11
Attica	H-7	Dexter	H-10	Inman	F-8	Morrowville	C-9
Atwood	C-4	Dighton	E-4	Iola	G-11	Moscow	G-3
Augusta	G-9	Dodge City	G-5	Isabel	G-7	Mound City	F-12
Axtell	C-10	Douglass	G-9	Jamestown	C-8	Mound Valley	H-11
Baldwin City	E-12	Downs	C-7	Jennings	C-5	Moundridge	F-8
Barnard	D-8	Dresden	C-5	Jetmore	F-5	Mount Hope	F-8
Barnes	C-10	Dunlap	E-10	Jewell	C-8	Mulberry	G-13
Bartlett	H-12	Dwight	E-10	Johnson City	G-3	Mullinville	G-6
Basehor	D-12	Earlton	G-12	Junction City	D-9	Mulvane	G-9
Bassett	G-11	Easton	D-12	Kanapolis	E-8	Munden	C-9
Baxter Springs	H-12	Edgerton	E-12	Kansas City	E-13	Muscotah	C-11
Bazine	E-5	Edmond	C-5	Vicinity	Pg. 124, F-2	Narka	C-9
Beattie	C-10	Edna	H-11	Kenneth	★	Nashville	G-7
Belle Plaine	H-9	Effingham	D-12	Vicinity	Pg. 125, L-3	Natoma	D-6
Belleville	C-9	El Dorado	F-9	Kensington	C-6	Neodesha	H-11
Beloit	C-8	Elbing	F-9	Kincaid	F-12	Neosho Falls	F-11
Belpre	F-6	Elgin	H-10	Kingman	G-8	Ness City	E-5
Belvue	D-11	Elk City	H-11	Kinsley	G-6	Netawaka	C-11
Benedict	G-11	Elk Falls	H-10	Kiowa	H-7	New Cambria	E-9
Bennington	D-9	Elkhart	H-2	Kirwin	C-6	New Strawn	F-11
Bentley	G-9	Ellinwood	E-7	Kismet	H-4	Newton	F-8
Benton	G-9	Ellis	D-6	La Crosse	E-6	Nickerson	F-8
Bern	C-11	Ellsworth	E-7	La Cygne	F-12	Norcatur	C-5
Beverly	D-8	Elmdale	F-10	La Harpe	G-12	North Newton	F-9
Bird City	C-3	Emmett	D-11	Lakin	F-3	Norton	C-6
Bison	E-6	Emporia	F-11	Lane	F-12	Nortonville	D-12
Blue Mound	F-12	Englewood	H-5	Langdon	G-8	Norwich	G-8
Blue Rapids	C-10	Ensign	G-4	Lansing	D-12	Oak Hill	D-9
Bluff City	H-8	Enterprise	E-9	Larned	F-7	Oakley	D-4
Bogue	D-6	Erie	G-12	Latham	H-10	Oberlin	C-5
Brewster	C-3	Esbon	C-8	Latimer	E-9	Offerle	F-6
Bronson	G-12	Eskridge	E-11	Lawrence	E-11	Ogden	D-10
Brookville	E-8	Eudora	D-12	Le Roy	F-11	Oketo	C-10
Brownell	E-6	Eureka	G-10	Leavenworth	D-12	Olathe	E-12
Bucklin	G-5	Fairview	C-11	Leawood	★	Olmitz	E-7
Buffalo	G-11	Florence	F-9	Vicinity	Pg. 125, K-3	Olpe	F-11
Buhler	F-8	Fontana	F-12	Lebanon	C-7	Olsburg	D-10
Bunker Hill	E-7	Ford	G-5	Lebo	F-11	Onaga	C-10
Burden	H-9	Formoso	C-8	Lecompton	D-12	Oneida	C-11
Burdett	F-6	Fort Scott	G-13	Lehigh	F-9	Osage City	E-11
Burlingame	E-11	Fowler	G-4	Lenexa	★	Osawatomie	F-12
Burlington	F-11	Frankfort	C-10	Vicinity	Pg. 125, J-1	Osborne	D-7
Burns	F-10	Fredonia	G-11	Lenora	C-5	Oskaloosa	D-12
Burr Oak	C-8	Freeport	H-8	Leon	G-10	Oswego	H-12
Burrton	F-8	Frontenac	H-12	Leona	C-12	Otis	E-6
Bushong	E-10	Fulton	F-13	Leonardville	D-10	Ottawa	E-12
Bushton	E-7	Galatia	E-7	Leoti	E-3	Overbrook	E-11
Byers	G-7	Galena	H-12	Lewis	F-6	Overland Park	★
Caldwell	H-8	Galesburg	H-12	Liberal	H-4	Vicinity	Pg. 125, J-2
Cambridge	H-10	Galva	F-9	Liberty	H-11	Oxford	H-9
Caney	H-11	Garden City	F-4	Lincoln	D-8	Palco	D-6
Canton	F-9	Garden Plain	G-8	Lincolnville	E-10	Palmer	C-9
Carbondale	E-11	Gardner	E-12	Lindsborg	E-8	Paola	E-12
Carlton	E-9	Garfield	F-6	Linn	C-9	Paradise	D-7
Cassoday	G-10	Garnett	F-12	Linwood	E-12	Park	D-5
Cawker City	C-7	Gaylord	C-7	Little River	E-8	Park City	F-9
Cedar	C-7	Gem	C-4	Logan	C-6	Parker	F-12
Cedar Point	F-10	Geneseo	E-8	Lone Elm	F-12	Parsons	H-11
Cedar Vale	H-10	Girard	G-12	Long Island	B-6	Pawnee Rock	F-7
Centralia	C-11	Glade	C-6	Longford	D-9	Paxico	D-10
Chanute	G-11	Glasco	D-8	Longton	H-11	Peabody	F-9
Chapman	E-10	Glen Elder	C-8	Lorraine	E-8	Perry	D-11
Chase	F-8	Goessel	F-9	Lost Springs	E-9	Peru	H-11
Chautauqua	H-10	Goodland	C-3	Louisburg	E-13	Phillipsburg	C-6
Cheney	G-8	Gorham	D-7	Louisville	D-10	Pittsburg	H-13
Cherokee	G-12	Gove	D-5	Lucas	D-7	Plains	H-4
Cherryvale	H-11	Grainfield	D-4	Luka	G-7	Plainville	D-6
Chetopa	H-12	Grandview Plaza	E-10	Luray	D-7	Pleasanton	F-13
Cimarron	G-5	Great Bend	F-7	Lyndon	E-11	Plevna	F-7
Circleville	D-11	Greeley	E-11	Lyons	F-8	Pomona	E-11
Claflin	E-7	Greenleaf	C-9	Macksville	F-7	Portis	C-7
Clay Center	D-9	Greensburg	G-6	Madison	F-10	Potwin	F-9
Clayton	C-5	Gridley	F-11	Mahaska	C-9	Powhattan	C-11
Clearwater	G-8	Grinnell	D-4	Maize	G-9	Prairie View	C-6
Clifton	C-9	Halstead	F-9	Manchester	E-9	Prairie Village	★
Climax	G-10	Hamilton	G-10	Manhattan	D-10	Vicinity	Pg. 125, H-3
Clyde	C-9	Hamlin	C-11	Mankato	C-8	Pratt	G-7
Coats	H-7	Hanover	C-10	Manter	G-3	Prescott	F-13
Coffeyville	H-11	Hanston	F-6	Maple Hill	D-11	Preston	G-7
		Hardtner	H-7	Mapleton	G-12	Pretty Prairie	G-8
		Harper	H-8	Marion	F-9	Princeton	E-12
		Harris	F-12	Marquette	E-8	Protection	H-6
		Hartford	F-11	Marysville	C-10	Quenemo	E-11
		Harveyville	E-11	Matfield Green	G-10	Quinter	D-5
		Havana	H-11	Mayetta	D-11	Ramona	E-9
		Haven	G-8	Mayfield	H-9	Randall	C-8
		Havensville	C-10	McCracken	E-6	Randolph	D-10
		Haviland	G-6			Ransom	E-5
		Hays	E-6				

★ Denotes City only on Vicinity map. City not located on State map.

172 Index

KANSAS

LOUISIANA

Rantoul E-12
Raymond F-7
Reading E-11
Redfield G-12
Republic C-8
Rexford C-4
Richfield G-3
Richmond F-12
Riley D-9
Robinson C-12
Roeland Park ★
Vicinity Pg. 125, H-2
Rolla G-2
Rose Hill G-9
Roseland H-12
Rossville D-11
Rozel F-6
Rush Center E-6
Russel E-7
Russel Springs D-4
Sabetha C-11
Salina E-8
Satanta G-3
Sawyer G-7
Scandia C-8
Schoenchen E-6
Scott City E-4
Scottsville C-8
Sedan H-10
Sedgwick G-9
Selden C-4
Seneca C-11
Severy G-10
Seward F-6
Sharon H-7
Sharon Springs D-3
Shawnee ★
Vicinity Pg. 125, H-1
Silver Lake D-11
Simpson D-8
Smith Center C-7
Smolan E-8
Solomon E-9
South Haven H-9
Spearville G-5
Spivey G-8
Spring Hill E-12
St. Francis C-3
St. John F-7
St. Marys D-11
St. Paul H-12
Stafford G-7
Stark G-12
Sterling F-8
Stockton D-6
Strong City F-10
Sublette G-4
Summerfield C-10
Sun City H-7
Sylvan Grove D-7
Sylvia F-7
Syracuse F-3
Tampa E-9
Tescott D-8
Thayer G-12
Timken E-6
Tipton D-7
Tonganoxie D-12
Topeka E-11
Toronto G-11
Towanda G-9
Tribune E-3
Troy C-12
Turon G-7
Tyro H-11
Udall H-9
Ulysses G-3
Uniontown G-12
Utica E-5
Valley Center G-9
Valley Falls D-11
Vermillion C-10
Victoria E-6
Vining C-9
Virgil F-11
WaKeeney D-6
Wakefield D-9
Waldo D-7
Waldron H-8
Wallace D-3
Walnut G-12
Walton F-9
Wamego D-10
Washington C-9
Waterville C-10
Wathena C-12
Waverly F-11
Webber C-8
Weir Scammon H-12
Wellington H-8
Wellsville E-12
Westmoreland D-10
Westphalia F-11
Wetmore C-11
Wheaton C-10
White City E-9
Whitewater G-9
Whiting C-11
Wichita G-9
Williamsburg F-12
Willowbrook F-8
Wilmore G-6
Wilsey E-9
Wilson E-7
Winchester D-12
Windom F-8
Winfield H-9
Winona D-3
Woodbine E-9
Woodston C-6
Yates Center G-11
Zenda H-7
Zurich D-6

KENTUCKY
Pages 42-43

Adairville F-6
Albany F-9
Alexandria B-10
Allen D-12
Allensville F-6
Arlington F-3
Ashland C-12
Auburn F-7
Audobon Park ★
Vicinity Pg. 130, D-3
Augusta B-10
Barbourville F-11
Bardstown D-8
Bardwell F-3
Barlow E-3
Beattyville D-11
Beaver Dam E-6
Bedford B-8
Beech Grove D-6
Bellefonte C-12
Bellevue ★
Vicinity Pg. 112, E-4
Benham E-12
Benton F-4
Berea D-10
Berry B-10
Bloomfield D-9
Bonnieville E-7
Boone D-10
Boonesboro D-10
Booneville E-11
Bowling Green E-6
Bradfordsville D-9
Brandenburg C-7
Breckinridge C-10
Bremen E-6
Broadfields ★
Vicinity Pg. 130, C-5
Brodhead E-10
Bromley A-10
Brooksville B-10
Brownsville E-7
Buckhorn E-11
Buffalo E-8
Burgin D-9
Burkesville F-8
Burnside F-10
Burton E-12
Butler B-10
Cadiz F-5
Calhoun D-6
Callaway F-11
Calvert City E-4
Campbellsburg B-8
Campbellsville E-8
Campton D-11
Caneyville E-7
Carlisle C-10
Carrollton B-9
Carrsville E-4
Carter C-11
Caseyville D-4
Catlettsburg C-12
Cave City E-8
Centertown E-6
Central City E-6
Cerulean F-5
Clairfield F-10
Clay E-5
Clay City D-10
Clearfield C-11
Clinton F-3
Cloverport D-7
Cold Spring ★
Vicinity Pg. 112, G-5
Columbia E-8
Columbus F-3
Concord B-11
Constance ★
Vicinity Pg. 112, F-1
Corbin F-10
Corydon D-5
Covington B-9
Vicinity Pg. 112, F-3
Crab Orchard E-9
Crescent Springs ★
Vicinity Pg. 112, F-2
Crestview Hills ★
Vicinity Pg. 112, G-2
Crestwood C-8
Crittenden B-10
Crofton E-5
Cumberland E-12
Cynthiana C-10
Danville D-9
Dawson Springs E-5
Dayton ★
Vicinity Pg. 112, E-4
Dexter F-4
Dixon D-5
Dover B-11
Drakesboro E-6
Druid Hills ★
Vicinity Pg. 130, B-5
Dry Ridge B-10
Dunmor E-6
Dycusburg E-4
Earlington E-5
Eddyville E-4
Edmonton F-8
Ekron D-7
Elizabethtown D-7
Elkhorn City E-13
Elkton F-6
Elsmere B-10
Eminence C-9
Erlanger ★
Vicinity Pg. 112, G-2
Eubank E-9
Evarts F-12
Fairdale C-8
Fairfield D-9
Fairview F-6
Falmouth B-10
Ferguson E-10
Flatwoods C-12
Fleming E-12
Flemingsburg C-11
Florence B-10
Fordsville D-7
Foster B-10
Fountain Run F-8
Frankfort C-9
Franklin F-6
Fredonia E-5
Freeburn D-13
Frenchburg D-11
Frogue F-9
Ft. Mitchell ★
Vicinity Pg. 112, G-3
Ft. Thomas ★
Vicinity Pg. 112, F-5
Ft. Wright ★
Vicinity Pg. 112, F-3
Fulton F-3
Gamaliel F-8
Georgetown C-10
Ghent B-9
Glasgow E-8
Golden Pond F-5
Goshen C-8
Grand Rivers E-4
Gratz C-9
Grayson C-12
Greensburg E-8
Greenup B-12
Greenville E-6
Guthrie F-6
Hanson E-5
Hardin F-4
Hardinsburg D-7
Harlan F-11
Harned D-7
Harrodsburg D-9
Hartford E-6
Hawesville D-6
Hazard E-12
Hazel F-4
Hazel Green D-11
Hellier E-12
Henderson D-5
Hickman F-3
Highland Hts. ★
Vicinity Pg. 112, G-5
Hindman E-12
Hodgenville D-8
Hopkinsville F-6
Horse Cave E-8
Hustonville E-9
Hyden E-11
Independence B-10
Indian Hills ★
Vicinity Pg. 130, B-5
Inez D-12
Irvine D-10
Irvington D-7
Island E-6
Jackson D-11
Jamestown E-9
Jeffersontown C-8
Jeffersonville D-10
Vicinity Pg. 130, A-3
Jenkins E-12
Junction City D-9
Kenton Vale ★
Vicinity Pg. 112, G-3
Kingsley ★
Vicinity Pg. 130, D-5
Kirkmansville E-6
Knob Creek D-8
Kuttawa E-4
La Fayette F-5
La Grange C-8
LaCenter E-3
Lackey E-12
Lakeside Park ★
Vicinity Pg. 112, G-3
Lakeview ★
Vicinity Pg. 112, G-3
Lancaster D-10
Lawrenceburg C-9
Leatherwood E-11
Lebanon D-9
Lebanon Jct. D-8
Lee City D-11
Leitchfield D-7
Lewisburg C-11
Lewisport D-6
Lexington D-9
Liberty E-9
Livermore D-6
Livingston E-10
Lockport C-9
London E-10
Loretto D-8
Lothair E-11
Louisa C-12
Louisville C-8
Vicinity Pg. 130
Loyall F-11
Lucas F-8
Ludlow ★
Vicinity Pg. 112, F-3
Lynch F-12
Lynnview ★
Vicinity Pg. 130, E-4
Madisonville E-5
Manchester E-10
Marion E-5
Martin D-12
Mason B-10
Mayfield F-4
Maysville B-11
McCreary D-10
McHenry E-6
McKee E-10
McRoberts E-12
Middlesboro F-10
Middletown C-8
Midway C-9
Midway F-4
Millersburg C-10
Milton B-8
Minor Lake Hts. ★
Vicinity Pg. 130, F-3
Mockingbird Valley ★
Vicinity Pg. 130, B-4
Monkeys Eyebrow E-3
Monroe E-8
Monterey C-9
Monticello F-9
Morehead C-11
Moreland D-9
Morgan B-10
Morganfield D-5
Morgantown E-7
Mortons Gap E-5
Mount Olivet B-10
Mount Sterling C-11
Mount Vernon E-10
Mount Washington C-8
Muldraugh D-8
Munfordville E-8
Murray F-4
Nebo E-5
Neon E-12
New Castle C-9
New Haven D-8
Newport A-10
Vicinity Pg. 112, F-4
Nicholasville D-9
North Middletown C-10
Nortonville E-6
Oak Grove F-5
Oakland E-7
Olive Hill C-11
Owensboro D-6
Owenton C-9
Owingsville C-10
Paducah E-4
Paintsville D-12
Paris C-10
Park City E-8
Park Hills ★
Vicinity Pg. 112, F-3
Parker Lake F-10
Parkway Village ★
Vicinity Pg. 130, D-3
Pembroke F-5
Perryville D-9
Phelps D-13
Pikeville E-13
Pine Knot F-10
Pineville F-11
Pleasureville C-9
Prestonsburg D-12
Prestonville B-8
Princeton E-5
Prospect C-8
Providence E-5
Raceland B-12
Radcliff D-7
Ravenna D-11
Reidland E-4
Renfro Valley E-10
Richmond D-10
Rockcastle F-5
Rockport E-6
Rolling Fields ★
Vicinity Pg. 130, B-5
Russell B-12
Russell Springs E-9
Russellville F-6
Sadieville C-10
Salt Lick C-11
Salyersville D-12
Sanders B-9
Sandy Hook C-12
Sardis C-11
Science Hill E-9
Scottsville F-7
Sebree D-5
Seco E-12
Sedalia F-4
Seneca Gardens ★
Vicinity Pg. 130, C-5
Sharpsburg C-11
Shelby City D-9
Shelbyville C-9
Shepardsville C-8
Shively C-8
Vicinity Pg. 130, D-1
Silver Grove ★
Vicinity Pg. 112, G-6
Simpsonville C-8
Slaughters D-5
Smithland E-4
Smiths Grove E-7
Somerset E-10
Sonora D-7
South Shore B-12
South Williamson D-13
Springfield D-9
Stamping Ground C-9
Stanford D-10
Stanton D-11
Stearns F-9
Strathmoor Village ★
Vicinity Pg. 130, D-5
Sturgis D-5
Taylorsville D-9
Tompkinsville F-8
Trenton F-6
Trimble E-9
Tyner E-11
Union B-9
Uniontown D-5
Upton E-8
Valley Station C-8
Van Lear D-12
Vanceburg B-11
Vancleve D-11
Versailles C-9
Villa Hills ★
Vicinity Pg. 112, F-2
Vine Grove D-7
Wallins Creek F-11
Walton B-10
Warfield D-13
Warsaw B-9
Washington B-11
Water Valley F-4
Waverly D-5
Wayland E-12
Webster D-7
Wellington D-11
Vicinity Pg. 130, D-5
West Beauchel ★
Vicinity Pg. 130, D-5
West Liberty D-11
West Point D-8
Wheatley B-9
Wheelwright E-12
Whitesburg E-12
Whitesville D-6
Whitley City F-10
Wickliffe E-3
Wilders ★
Vicinity Pg. 112, F-4
Willard C-12
Williamsburg F-10
Williamstown B-10
Wilmore D-9
Winchester D-10
Wingo F-4
Woodburn F-7

LOUISIANA
Page 44

Abbeville F-5
Abington B-2
Abita Springs E-8
Acme D-5
Acy E-7
Ada B-3
Addis E-6
Adeline F-6
Afton B-6
Aimwell C-5
Airline Park ★
Vicinity Pg. 137, C-4
Ajax C-3
Albany E-7
Alco D-3
Alden Bridge A-2
Alexandria D-4
Alsaita A-6
Alto B-5
Ama ★
Vicinity Pg. 137, C-2
Amelia G-7
Amite E-8
Anacoco D-3
Angie D-9
Angola D-5
Ansley B-4
Antioch A-3
Arabi F-9
Vicinity Pg. 137, C-8
Archibald B-5
Archie C-5
Arcola D-8
Armistead B-3
Arnaudville E-5
Ashland B-3
Athens A-3
Atlanta C-4
Augusta ★
Vicinity Pg. 137, F-7
Avery Island F-5
Avondale ★
Vicinity Pg. 137, D-4
Aycock A-3
Bains D-6
Baker E-6
Baldwin F-6
Ball C-4
Bancroft E-2
Barataria F-8
Basile E-4
Baskin B-5
Bastrop A-5
Batchelor D-6
Baton Rouge E-7
Bayou Cane G-7
Bayou Chicot D-5
Bayou Sorrel F-6
Bayou Vista G-6
Baywood E-7
Beaver E-4
Beekman A-5
Beggs E-5
Bell City F-3
Belle Chasse F-9
Vicinity Pg. 137, E-8
Belle Rose F-7
Bellwood C-3
Belmont C-2
Benson C-2
Bentley C-4
Benton A-2
Bernice A-4
Bertrandville F-9
Vicinity Pg. 137, G-7
Berwick F-6
Bienville B-3
Blackburn A-3
Blanchard A-2
Bogalusa D-9
Bohemia G-9
Bolinger A-2
Bonita A-5
Book D-5
Boothville G-10
Bordelonville D-5
Bosco B-5
Bossier City A-2
Bourg G-8
Boyce D-4
Braithwaite ★
Vicinity Pg. 137, E-9
Branch E-5
Breaux Bridge E-5
Bridge City ★
Vicinity Pg. 137, D-4
Broussard F-5
Brusly E-6
Bryceland B-3
Bunkie D-5
Buras G-9
Burnside F-7
Burr Ferry D-2
Bush E-9
Cade F-5
Caernarvon ★
Vicinity Pg. 137, E-9
Calhoun B-4
Calvin C-4
Cameron F-3
Campti C-3
Caney D-2
Carencro E-5
Carlisle F-9
Carville E-7
Caspiana B-2
Castor B-3
Cedar Grove ★
Vicinity Pg. 137, F-7
Center Point D-5
Centerville F-6
Chacahoula F-7
Chackbay F-7
Chalmette F-9
Vicinity Pg. 137, D-8
Chase B-5
Chataignier E-4
Chatham B-4
Chauvin G-8
Cheneyville D-5
Chestnut B-3
Chipola D-7
Chopin C-4
Choudrant B-4
Church Point E-5
Clarence C-3
Clarks B-5
Clay B-4
Clayton C-6
Clifton D-8
Clinton D-7
Cloutierville C-4
Cocodrie G-7
Colfax C-4
Collinston A-5
Colquitt A-3
Columbia B-5
Concession ★
Vicinity Pg. 137, F-8
Convent F-7
Converse C-2
Cotton Valley A-3
Cottonport D-5
Coushatta B-3
Covington E-8
Cravens D-3
Creole F-3
Creston B-3
Crowley F-4
Crown Point ★
Vicinity Pg. 137, G-6
Crowville B-6
Cullen A-3
Cut Off G-8
Cypress C-3
Dalcour F-9
Vicinity Pg. 137, F-8
Darlington D-7
Darnell A-6
Davant F-9
De Quincy E-3
De Ridder E-3
Deer Park C-6
Delacroix F-9
Delcambre F-5
Delhi A-6
Derry C-3
Des Allemands F-8
Destrehan ★
Vicinity Pg. 137, D-1
Deville D-5
Diamond G-9
Dixie Inn A-2
Dodson B-4
Donaldsonville F-7
Downsville A-4
Dry Creek E-3
Dry Prong C-4
Dubach A-4
Dubuisson E-5
Dulac G-7
Dupont D-5
Duson F-5
Duty C-5
Easlyville D-7
East End ★
Vicinity Pg. 137, B-5
Eastwood B-2
Echo D-5
Edgerly F-2
Effie D-5
Elizabeth D-4
Elm Grove B-2
Elton E-4
Empire G-9
Englishturn ★
Vicinity Pg. 137, E-8
Enon D-8
Enterprise C-5
Erath F-5
Eros B-4
Estelle ★
Vicinity Pg. 137, E-6
Estherwood F-4
Esto D-2
Ethel E-6
Eunice E-4
Eva C-5
Evangeline E-4
Evans D-3
Evelyn B-2
Evergreen D-5
Farmerville A-4
Felps D-7
Fenton E-3
Ferriday C-6
Fields E-2
Fillmore A-2
Fisher C-3
Flatwoods D-4
Flora C-3
Florien D-2
Folsom E-8
Fondale B-5
Fordoche E-5
Forest A-6
Forest Hill D-4
Fort Jesup C-3
Fort Necessity B-5
Foules C-6
Franklin F-6
Franklinton D-8
French Settlement E-7
Frenier F-8
Frogmore C-5
Frost E-7
Galbraith C-4
Galion A-5
Galliano G-8
Gandy D-2
Gardner D-4
Georgetown C-4
Gheens F-8
Gibsland B-3
Gibson G-7
Gilbert B-6
Gillis E-3
Glade C-5
Glenmora D-4
Gloster B-2
Golden Meadow G-8
Goldonna B-3
Gonzales E-7
Gordon A-3
Gorum C-3
Goudeau D-5
Grambling A-4
Grand Bayou B-3
Grand Cane B-2
Grand Chenier F-4
Grand Coteau E-5
Grand Isle G-9
Grand Lake F-3
Grangeville E-7
Grayson B-5
Greensburg D-7
Gretna F-8
Vicinity Pg. 137, D-7
Grosse Tete E-6
Gueydan F-4
Hackberry F-3
Haile A-5
Hall Summit B-3
Hamburg D-5
Hammond E-8
Hanna C-3
Harahan F-8
Vicinity Pg. 137, D-4
Harrisonburg C-5
Harvey ★
Vicinity Pg. 137, D-6
Hathaway E-4
Hayes F-4
Haynesville A-3
Hebert B-5
Henderson E-6
Hermitage E-6
Hessmer D-5
Hickory E-9
Hicks D-3
Hico A-4
Highland A-6
Hodge B-4
Holloway D-5
Holly Beach F-2
Holmwood F-3
Holton E-8
Holum B-5
Homer A-3
Hornbeck D-3
Hosston A-2
Hot Wells D-4
Houma G-7
Humphreys G-7
Hutton D-3
Ida A-2
Independence E-8
Indian Mound E-7
Indian Village F-6
Iota F-4
Iowa F-3
Ivan A-2
Jackson D-6
Jamestown B-3
Jean Lafitte F-8
Vicinity Pg. 137, F-5
Jeanerette F-6
Jefferson Hts. ★
Vicinity Pg. 137, C-4
Jena C-5
Jennings F-4
Jesuit Bend ★
Vicinity Pg. 137, G-7
Jigger B-5
Johnsons Bayou F-2
Jones A-5
Jonesboro B-4
Jonesville C-5
Kaplan F-4
Keatchie B-2
Keithville B-2
Kenner F-8
Vicinity Pg. 137, B-3
Kentwood D-8
Kilbourne A-6
Killian E-8
Kinder E-4
Kingston B-2
Kisatchie D-3
Krotz Springs E-5
Kurthwood D-3
La Place F-8
Labadieville F-7
Labarre E-6
Lacamp D-3
Lacassine F-4
Lacombe E-8
Lafayette F-5
Lafitte F-8
Lafourche F-7
Lake Arthur F-4
Lake Charles F-3
Lake End C-3
Lake Providence A-6
Lakeland E-6
Larose G-8
Larto D-5
Latanier D-4
Lawtell E-5
Le Blanc E-3
LeMoyen E-5
Leander D-4
Lebeau E-5
Lecompte D-4
Leesville D-3
Leeville G-8
Leonville E-5
Libuse D-5
Lillie A-4
Linville A-5
Lisbon A-3

★ Denotes City only on Vicinity map. City not located on State map.

LOUISIANA

MARYLAND

Lismore C-5
Live Oak D-4
  Vicinity ...... Pg. 137, G-7
Live Oak Manor ...... ★
  Vicinity ...... Pg. 137, C-3
Livingston E-7
Livonia E-6
Lockport F-8
Logansport C-2
Lone Star .... ★
  Vicinity ...... Pg. 137, D-1
Longstreet B-2
Longville E-3
Lottie E-6
Louisa F-6
Lucas B-3
Lucky B-3
Luling .... ★
  Vicinity ...... Pg. 137, D-1
Luna B-5
Lutcher F-7
Madisonville E-8
Mamou E-4
Manchac E-8
Mandeville E-8
Mangham B-5
Manifest C-5
Mansfield C-2
Many C-3
Maringouin E-6
Marion A-5
Marksville D-5
Marrero .... ★
  Vicinity ...... Pg. 137, D-6
Marsalis A-3
Martin B-3
Mathews F-8
Maurepas E-7
Maxie C-5
Mayna C-5
McDade B-2
McNary D-3
Melder D-4
Melrose C-3
Melville E-5
Mer Rouge A-5
Meraux .... ★
  Vicinity ...... Pg. 137, D-9
Mermentau F-4
Merryville E-2
Metairie F-8
  Vicinity ...... Pg. 137, C-5
Midland F-4
Midway A-2
Mill B-4
Minden A-3
Mira A-2
Mitchel C-2
Mittie D-4
Mix E-6
Monroe A-5
Montegut G-8
Monterey C-6
Montgomery C-3
Montpelier E-7
Mooringsport A-2
Moreauville D-5
Morgan City F-7
Morganza E-6
Morrow E-5
Mount Carmel C-3
Myrtle Grove .... ★
Nairn G-9
Naomi F-8
Napoleonville F-7
Natchez C-3
Natchitoches C-3
Negreet C-2
New Era D-5
New Iberia F-6
New Llano D-3
New Orleans .... ★
  Vicinity ...... Pg. 137, A-7
New Roads E-6
Newellton B-6
Newlight B-6
Noble C-2
North Hodge B-4
Norwood D-6
Oak Grove A-6
Oak Grove A-6
Oak Ridge A-5
Oakdale E-4
Oakland A-4
Oakville .... ★
  Vicinity ...... Pg. 137, G-7
Oberlin D-4
Oil City A-2
Olivier F-6
Olla C-4
Opelousas E-5
Oscar E-6
Oxford C-4
Packton C-4
Paincourtville F-7
Parks F-6
Patterson F-6
Pearl River E-9
Pecan Island F-5
Perryville A-5
Phoenix F-9
Pickering D-3
Pierre Part F-6
Pigeon F-6
Pilot Town G-10

Pine D-8
Pine Grove E-7
Pine Prairie E-4
Pineville D-4
Pitkin D-3
Plain Dealing A-2
Plaquemine E-6
Pleasant Hill C-2
Pointe a La Hache ... G-9
Pollock C-4
Ponchatoula E-8
Port Allen E-6
Port Barre E-5
Port Sulphur G-9
Port Vincent E-7
Powhatan C-3
Poydras .... ★
  Vicinity ...... Pg. 137, E-10
Provencal C-3
Quitman B-4
Raceland F-7
Ragley E-3
Ramah E-6
Rayne F-5
Rayville A-5
Readhimer B-3
Reddell E-4
Reeves E-4
Reggio F-9
Reserve F-8
Richmond B-6
Richwood B-5
Ridgecrest C-6
Ringgold B-3
Riverton B-5
Robeline C-3
Robert E-8
Rocky Mountain A-2
Rodessa A-1
Rosedale E-6
Rosefield C-5
Rosepine D-3
Ruddock F-8
Ruston B-4
Sailes B-3
Saint Bernard .... ★
  Vicinity ...... Pg. 137, E-10
Saint Clair .... ★
  Vicinity ...... Pg. 137, E-8
Saint Francisville .. E-6
Saint Gabriel E-7
Saint Joseph B-6
Saint Martinville ... F-6
Saint Rose .... ★
  Vicinity ...... Pg. 137, D-1
Saline B-3
Sarepta A-3
Scarsdale .... ★
  Vicinity ...... Pg. 137, E-8
Scott F-5
Shaw D-6
Sheridan D-9
Shongaloo A-3
Shreveport B-2
Sibley A-3
Sicily Island C-5
Sieper D-4
Sikes B-4
Simmesport D-5
Simpson D-3
Singer E-3
Slagle D-3
Slaughter E-6
Slidell E-9
Slocum D-6
Somerset B-6
Sondheimer A-6
Sorrento E-7
Spearsville A-4
Spencer A-5
Spokane C-6
Spring Ridge B-2
Springfield E-7
Springhill A-2
Stanley B-2
Starks F-2
Start B-5
State Line D-9
Stella .... ★
  Vicinity ...... Pg. 137, F-8
Sterlington A-5
Stonewall B-2
Sugartown E-3
Sulphur F-3
Summerfield A-3
Sun E-8
Sunset E-5
Supreme F-7
Talisheek E-9
Tallulah B-6
Tangipahoa D-8
Tannehill B-4
Taylortown B-2
Terry A-6
Tete E-6
Thibodaux F-7
Tidewater G-9
Tioga D-4
Toomey F-2
Toro D-2
Transylvania A-6
Triumph G-10
Truxno A-4
Tullos C-5
Turkey Creek D-4

Union F-7
Union Hill D-4
Urania C-4
Vacherie F-7
Varnado D-9
Venice G-10
Verda C-4
Vidalia C-6
Vienna A-4
Ville Platte E-5
Vinton F-2
Violet F-9
Vivian A-2
Vixen B-5
Waggaman .... ★
  Vicinity ...... Pg. 137, D-3
Wakefield D-6
Waldheim E-8
Walters C-5
Warnerton D-9
Washington E-5
Waterproof C-6
Watson E-7
Waverly B-6
Weeks F-4
Welsh F-4
Weston B-4
Westwego .... ★
  Vicinity ...... Pg. 137, E-4
Weyanoke D-6
White Castle E-6
Whitehall C-5
Williana C-4
Wills Point .... ★
  Vicinity ...... Pg. 137, G-8
Willswood .... ★
  Vicinity ...... Pg. 137, D-3
Wilmer D-8
Wilson D-6
Winnfield C-4
Winnsboro B-5
Woodworth D-4
Worden D-6
Wye D-4
Youngsville F-5
Yscloskey F-9
Zenoria C-4
Zwolle C-2

MAINE
Page 45

Acton J-2
Addison F-6
Albion G-3
Alexander E-6
Allagash B-4
Andover G-2
Anson F-3
Appleton G-4
Ashland C-4
Athens F-3
Auburn H-3
Augusta G-3
Avon G-2
Bailey Island H-3
Balleyville E-6
Bangor F-5
Bar Harbor G-5
Baring E-6
Bath H-3
Beddington F-5
Belfast G-4
Belgrade G-3
Benton G-3
Berwick J-2
Bethel G-2
Biddeford J-3
Bigelow F-2
Bingham F-3
Blaine C-5
Blanchard F-3
Blue Hill G-4
Boothbay H-4
Boothbay Harbor H-4
Bradford F-4
Bradley F-4
Brewer F-5
Bridgewater C-5
Bridgton H-2
Brighton F-3
Bristol H-4
Brooks G-4
Brownfield H-2
Brownville E-4
Brownville Jct. E-4
Brunswick H-3
Buckfield G-3
Bucks Harbor F-6
Bucksport G-5
Burlington E-5
Burnham G-4
Buxton J-2
Byron G-2
Calais E-6
Cambridge F-3
Camden G-4
Canton G-2
Cape Elizabeth J-3
Cape Porpoise J-2
Caratunk E-3
Caribou B-5
Carmel F-4
Carrabassett F-2

Carroll E-5
Cary D-5
Casco H-2
Castine G-4
Charleston F-4
Cherryfield G-6
Chester E-5
Chisolm G-2
Clayton Lake C-3
Clinton G-3
Coburn Gore E-2
Colby E-6
Columbia G-6
Conner B-5
Cooper F-6
Corea G-6
Corinna F-4
Cornish H-1
Costigan F-5
Crawford F-6
Crouseville B-5
Cumberland Center ... H-2
Cutler F-7
Daigle B-4
Dallas F-2
Damariscotta H-4
Danforth D-5
Deblois F-5
Dedham F-4
Deer Isle G-5
Dennistown E-2
Dennysville F-6
Dickey B-4
Dixfield G-2
Dixmont G-4
Dover Foxcroft E-4
Durham H-3
Eagle Lake B-4
East Hampden F-4
East Machias F-6
East Millinocket E-4
East Sumner G-2
East Wilton G-3
Eastbrook F-5
Easton C-5
Eastport F-7
Eaton E-6
Eddington F-5
Ellsworth G-5
Estcourt Sta. A-4
Eustis F-2
Fairfield G-3
Farmingdale G-3
Farmington G-2
Fort Fairfield B-5
Fort Kent A-4
Franklin G-5
Freeport H-3
Frenchville A-4
Friendship H-3
Frye G-2
Fryeburg H-2
Gardiner G-3
Gilead G-2
Glenburn Center F-4
Gorham J-2
Gouldsboro G-5
Grand Isle A-5
Grand Lake Stream ... E-5
Gray H-3
Greenville E-3
Grindstone D-4
Grove F-6
Guerette B-4
Guilford F-3
Hallowell G-3
Hamlin B-5
Hampden F-4
Hancock G-5
Hanover G-2
Harrington F-5
Harrison H-2
Hartford Center G-2
Hartland F-3
Haven G-4
Haynesville D-5
Hersey D-5
Hinckley G-3
Hiram H-2
Hogdon C-5
Houghton F-2
Houlton D-5
Howland E-4
Island Falls D-5
Jackman E-2
Jay G-3
Jefferson H-4
Jemtland B-5
Jonesboro F-6
Jonesport G-6
Keegan A-5
Kenduskeag F-4
Kennebago Lake F-2
Kennebunk J-2
Kennebunkport J-3
Kingfield F-2
Kingman E-5
Kingsbury F-3
Kittery K-2
Kittery Point K-2
Knowles Corner D-4
Kokadjo E-4
Lagrange F-4
Lake Parlin E-2
Lambert Lake E-6

Larone G-3
Lee E-5
Lewiston G-3
Liberty G-4
Lille A-5
Lily Bay E-3
Limerick J-2
Limestone B-5
Limington J-2
Lincoln E-5
Lincolnville G-4
Linneus D-5
Lisbon H-3
Lisbon Falls H-3
Littleton C-5
Livermore Falls G-3
Long Pond E-3
Lovell H-2
Lubec F-7
Ludlow D-5
Lynchville G-2
Machias F-6
Macwahoc D-5
Madawaska A-4
Madison F-3
Madrid F-2
Manchester G-3
Mapleton B-5
Marion F-6
Mars Hill C-5
Masardis C-4
Mattawamkeag D-4
Mayfield F-3
Medford E-4
Medway E-4
Mexico G-2
Milbridge G-6
Milford F-5
Millinocket D-4
Milo E-4
Molunkus E-5
Monarda D-5
Monroe G-4
Monson E-3
Monticello C-5
Moose River E-2
Morrill G-4
Moscow F-3
Naples H-2
New Gloucester H-3
Newcastle H-4
Newfield J-2
Newport F-4
Newry G-2
Nobleboro G-3
Norcross E-4
Norridgewock G-3
North Amity D-6
North Anson F-2
North Berwick J-2
North Lovell H-2
North Lyndon B-5
Northeast Carry D-3
Northeast Harbor G-5
Northfield F-6
Norway H-2
Oakland G-3
Ogunquit J-2
Old Orchard Beach ... J-2
Old Town F-5
Oquossoc F-2
Orient D-5
Orland G-4
Orono F-5
Orrington F-4
Oudette B-4
Oxbow C-4
Oxford G-2
Palmyra F-3
Paris G-2
Parkman F-3
Patten D-4
Perham B-5
Perry F-7
Peru G-2
Phippsburg H-3
Pittsfield F-4
Pittston G-3
Poland H-2
Portage B-4
Portland J-3
Presque Isle B-5
Princeton E-6
Quimby B-4
Randolph G-3
Rangeley F-2
Raymond H-2
Readfield G-3
Red Beach E-7
Reed D-5
Richmond H-3
Ripley F-3
Ripogenus Dam D-4
Robbinston E-7
Robinsons C-5
Rockland H-4
Rockport H-4
Rockwood E-3
Rome G-3
Roxbury G-2
Rumford G-2
Sabattus H-3
Saco J-3
Saint Albans F-3
Saint David A-5

Saint Francis B-4
Saint George G-4
Saint John B-4
Salem F-2
Sanford J-2
Sangerville F-4
Saponac E-5
Scarborough J-2
Seal Harbor G-5
Searsmont G-4
Searsport G-4
Sebago H-2
Sebec Lake E-3
Seboeis E-4
Seboomook D-3
Sedgewick G-4
Selden D-5
Sheridan B-4
Sherman D-5
Sherman Mills D-5
Sherman Sta. D-4
Shin Pond D-4
Shirley Mills E-3
Sidney G-3
Skowhegan F-3
Smyrna Mills C-5
Soldier Pond B-4
Solon F-3
South Arm F-2
South Bancroft D-5
South China G-4
South Hope G-4
South Paris H-2
South Portland J-3
Southwest Harbor G-5
Springfield E-5
Springvale J-2
Squa Pan C-4
Stacyville D-4
Standish J-2
Starboard F-6
Stetson F-4
Steuben G-6
Stockton Springs G-4
Stonington G-5
Stow H-2
Stratton F-2
Strong G-2
Sweden H-2
The Forks E-2
Thomaston H-4
Topsfield E-6
Topsham H-3
Tremont G-5
Turner H-2
Union G-3
Unity G-4
Upton G-2
Van Buren A-5
Vanceboro E-6
Vienna G-3
Vinalhaven G-4
Waite E-6
Waldoboro H-4
Waltham F-5
Warren H-4
Washburn B-5
Washington G-3
Waterboro J-2
Waterford H-2
Waterville G-3
Wells J-2
Wesley F-6
West Enfield E-5
West Forks E-2
West Newfield J-2
West Paris G-2
Westbrook J-3
Weston D-5
Whiting F-6
Williamantic E-3
Wilsons Mills F-1
Wilton G-2
Winn E-5
Winslow G-3
Winter Harbor G-5
Winterport G-4
Winterville B-4
Winthrop G-3
Wiscasset H-3
Woodland E-7
Woolwich H-3
Wytopitlock D-5
Yarmouth H-3
York Beach K-2
York Village K-2

MARYLAND
Page 46-47

Aberdeen B-12
Accident B-1
Accokeek F-9
Airy F-12
Allanwood .... ★
  Vicinity ...... Pg. 159, B-5
Allanwood .... ★
  Vicinity ...... Pg. 159, B-5
Allview Estates ..... ★
  Vicinity ...... Pg. 101, G-1
Allview Estates ..... ★
  Vicinity ...... Pg. 101, G-1
Altamont B-1

Ammendale .... ★
  Vicinity ...... Pg. 159, C-7
Ammendale .... ★
  Vicinity ...... Pg. 159, C-7
Andersontown E-13
Andrews G-12
Annapolis D-11
Annapolis Junction .. ★
  Vicinity ...... Pg. 101, H-2
Annapolis Junction .. ★
  Vicinity ...... Pg. 101, H-2
Arbutus .... ★
  Vicinity ...... Pg. 101, E-3
Arbutus .... ★
  Vicinity ...... Pg. 101, E-3
Armiger .... ★
  Vicinity ...... Pg. 101, H-6
Armiger .... ★
  Vicinity ...... Pg. 101, H-6
Arnold D-10
Arnold .... ★
  Vicinity ...... Pg. 101, K-6
Arnold .... ★
  Vicinity ...... Pg. 101, K-6
Ashton .... ★
  Vicinity ...... Pg. 159, A-5
Ashton .... ★
  Vicinity ...... Pg. 159, A-5
Aspen Hill D-9
Avenue G-10
Ballard .... ★
  Vicinity ...... Pg. 159, J-7
Baltimore C-10
Barclay D-13
Barnesville C-7
Bay Ridge E-11
Bayard E-10
Bayside Beach .... ★
  Vicinity ...... Pg. 101, H-7
Bayview B-12
Bel Air B-11
Belltown .... ★
Beltsville D-9
Beltsville .... ★
  Vicinity ...... Pg. 159, C-6
Benfield .... ★
  Vicinity ...... Pg. 101, J-4
Berlin G-15
Bethesda D-8
Bethesda .... ★
  Vicinity ...... Pg. 159, E-4
Betterton C-12
Bladenburg .... ★
  Vicinity ...... Pg. 159, F-6
Bloomsbury .... ★
  Vicinity ...... Pg. 101, E-3
Boonsboro B-7
Bowie D-10
Braddock Hts. C-7
Brandywine F-9
Brinklow .... ★
  Vicinity ...... Pg. 159, A-5
Bristol E-10
Brooklandville ...... ★
  Vicinity ...... Pg. 101, B-4
Brooklyn .... ★
  Vicinity ...... Pg. 101, F-5
Brookview F-13
Broomes Island G-10
Brownstown .... ★
  Vicinity ...... Pg. 159, A-1
Brunswick C-7
Bryans Road F-8
Buckeystown C-7
Bucktown G-12
Burkittsville C-7
Burleytown .... ★
  Vicinity ...... Pg. 101, G-4
Burtonville .... ★
  Vicinity ...... Pg. 159, B-6
Butler B-10
Cabin John .... ★
  Vicinity ...... Pg. 159, E-2
California G-11
Cambridge F-12
Camp Springs .... ★
  Vicinity ...... Pg. 159, J-7
Cape St. Claire D-11
Capitol Hts. .... ★
  Vicinity ...... Pg. 159, G-7
Carderock .... ★
  Vicinity ...... Pg. 101, D-7
Carney .... ★
  Vicinity ...... Pg. 101, B-6
Cascade A-7
Catonsville C-10
Catonsville .... ★
  Vicinity ...... Pg. 101, E-3
Cavetown B-7
Cayots B-13
Cecilton C-12
Centreville D-12
Chaptico G-9
Charlestown B-12
Charlotte Hall F-9
Chattolanee .... ★
  Vicinity ...... Pg. 101, B-3
Chesapeake B-13
Chesapeake Beach F-10
Chestertown C-12
Cheverly .... ★
  Vicinity ...... Pg. 159, F-7

Chevy Chase .... ★
  Vicinity ...... Pg. 159, E-4
Church Creek F-12
Church Hill D-12
Clear Spring B-6
Cliffs City D-12
Clinton E-9
Clinton .... ★
  Vicinity ...... Pg. 159, J-7
Clinton Hts. .... ★
  Vicinity ...... Pg. 159, J-7
Cobb Island G-9
Cockeysville B-10
Colesville .... ★
  Vicinity ...... Pg. 159, C-5
College Park .... ★
  Vicinity ...... Pg. 159, D-6
College Pk. D-9
Colmar Manor .... ★
  Vicinity ...... Pg. 159, F-6
Columbia C-9
Columbus Hills ...... ★
  Vicinity ...... Pg. 101, E-1
Colverton .... ★
  Vicinity ...... Pg. 159, C-6
Conways .... ★
  Vicinity ...... Pg. 101, K-2
Cooksville C-9
Corriganville A-3
Cove Point G-11
Cresaptown B-3
Crisfield J-13
Crofton D-10
Cronhardt .... ★
  Vicinity ...... Pg. 101, A-3
Cropley .... ★
Crownsville D-10
Crownsville .... ★
  Vicinity ...... Pg. 101, K-5
Cub Hill .... ★
  Vicinity ...... Pg. 101, B-6
Cumberland B-3
Damascus C-8
Daniels .... ★
  Vicinity ...... Pg. 101, D-1
Dares Beach F-11
Darnestown .... ★
  Vicinity ...... Pg. 159, B-1
Deale E-10
Deer Park .... ★
  Vicinity ...... Pg. 101, B-1
Delight .... ★
  Vicinity ...... Pg. 101, A-2
Delman G-13
Denton E-13
Derwood .... ★
  Vicinity ...... Pg. 159, B-3
District Heights .... ★
  Vicinity ...... Pg. 159, G-6
Doncaster F-8
Dorrs Corner .... ★
  Vicinity ...... Pg. 101, J-4
Dorsey .... ★
  Vicinity ...... Pg. 101, G-2
Drawbridge G-13
Drum Point G-11
Dublin A-11
Dundalk C-10
Dundalk .... ★
  Vicinity ...... Pg. 101, E-6
Dunkirk F-10
Eagle Harbor F-10
East Springbrook .... ★
  Vicinity ...... Pg. 159, C-6
Easton E-12
Edgemere C-11
Edgemere .... ★
  Vicinity ...... Pg. 101, F-7
Edgewood C-11
Edmonston .... ★
  Vicinity ...... Pg. 162, E-6
Eldersburg C-9
Eldorado F-13
Elkridge .... ★
  Vicinity ...... Pg. 101, F-3
Elkton B-13
Ellicott City C-9
Ellicott City .... ★
  Vicinity ...... Pg. 101, E-2
Elliott G-12
Emmitsburg A-8
Emory Grove .... ★
  Vicinity ...... Pg. 159, A-2
Essex .... ★
  Vicinity ...... Pg. 101, D-7
Fair Hill A-12
Fairknoll .... ★
  Vicinity ...... Pg. 159, B-5
Fairland .... ★
  Vicinity ...... Pg. 159, C-6
Fairmount Heights ... ★
  Vicinity ...... Pg. 159, F-6
Fairview .... ★
  Vicinity ...... Pg. 101, G-6
Fallston B-11
Federalsburg E-13
Ferndale .... ★
  Vicinity ...... Pg. 101, G-4
Fishtown B-13
Foremans Corner ..... ★
  Vicinity ...... Pg. 101, G-5
Forest Hts. .... ★
  Vicinity ...... Pg. 159, H-5
Forestville .... ★
  Vicinity ...... Pg. 159, H-7

★ Denotes City only on Vicinity map. City not located on State map.

MARYLAND

MIICHIGAN

Fort Foot Village . . . . ★
  Vicinity . . . . Pg. 159, J-5
Fort Howard . . . . ★
  Vicinity . . . . Pg. 101, F-7
Fountain Head A-7
Frederick C-8
Friendly . . . . ★
  Vicinity . . . . Pg. 159, K-5
Friendship Heights . . . . ★
  Vicinity . . . . Pg. 159, E-4
Friendsville A-1
Frostburg B-3
Fruitland G-14
Fullerton . . . . ★
  Vicinity . . . . Pg. 101, C-6
Fulton . . . . ★
  Vicinity . . . . Pg. 159, A-7
Gaithersburg D-8
Galena C-12
Gambrills . . . . ★
  Vicinity . . . . Pg. 101, J-4
Garrison . . . . ★
  Vicinity . . . . Pg. 101, B-2
Georgetown . . . . ★
  Vicinity . . . . Pg. 101, H-2
Germantown D-8
Germantown . . . . ★
  Vicinity . . . . Pg. 101, B-7
Glen Burnie D-10
Glen Burnie . . . . ★
  Vicinity . . . . Pg. 101, G-4
Glen Echo . . . . ★
  Vicinity . . . . Pg. 159, E-3
Glen Hills . . . . ★
  Vicinity . . . . Pg. 159, B-2
Glenmont . . . . ★
  Vicinity . . . . Pg. 159, C-4
Golden Beach F-10
Goldsboro D-13
Grantie . . . . ★
  Vicinity . . . . Pg. 101, C-1
Grantsville A-2
Grasonville E-11
Gray Manor . . . . ★
  Vicinity . . . . Pg. 101, E-6
Green Haven . . . . ★
  Vicinity . . . . Pg. 101, H-6
Green Hill G-13
Green Valley C-8
Greenbelt D-9
Greensboro D-13
Guilford . . . . ★
  Vicinity . . . . Pg. 101, G-1
Hagerstown B-7
Halethorpe . . . . ★
  Vicinity . . . . Pg. 101, F-3
Halfway B-6
Hammond Park . . . . ★
  Vicinity . . . . Pg. 159, A-7
Hampstead B-9
Hampton . . . . ★
  Vicinity . . . . Pg. 101, A-5
Hancock A-5
Hanover . . . . ★
  Vicinity . . . . Pg. 101, G-3
Harkins A-11
Harmans . . . . ★
  Vicinity . . . . Pg. 101, G-3
Harmony E-13
Harrisonville . . . . ★
  Vicinity . . . . Pg. 101, B-1
Harundale . . . . ★
  Vicinity . . . . Pg. 101, H-5
Harwood . . . . ★
  Vicinity . . . . Pg. 101, G-3
Hebbville . . . . ★
  Vicinity . . . . Pg. 101, C-1
Hebron G-13
Hereford B-10
Hernwood . . . . ★
  Vicinity . . . . Pg. 101, C-1
Herwood Heights . . . . ★
  Vicinity . . . . Pg. 101, B-1
Hillondale . . . . ★
  Vicinity . . . . Pg. 159, D-5
Hillsboro E-12
Holbrook . . . . ★
  Vicinity . . . . Pg. 101, B-1
Holywood Park . . . . ★
  Vicinity . . . . Pg. 159, C-5
Honga G-11
Hoyes B-1
Hunting Hill . . . . ★
  Vicinity . . . . Pg. 159, B-2
Hurlock F-13
Hyattsville . . . . ★
  Vicinity . . . . Pg. 159, E-6
Ilchester . . . . ★
  Vicinity . . . . Pg. 101, E-2
Inverness . . . . ★
  Vicinity . . . . Pg. 101, E-7
Jacobsville . . . . ★
  Vicinity . . . . Pg. 101, H-6
Jarrettsville B-11
Jessup . . . . ★
  Vicinity . . . . Pg. 101, G-2
Jonestown . . . . ★
  Vicinity . . . . Pg. 101, F-7
Joppatowne C-11
Josenhans Corner . . . . ★
  Vicinity . . . . Pg. 101, D-7
Joyce . . . . ★
  Vicinity . . . . Pg. 101, K-6
Kennedyville C-12

Kensington . . . . ★
  Vicinity . . . . Pg. 159, D-4
Kitzmiller C-2
LaPlata F-9
LaVale B-3
Lake Shore D-11
Lake Shore . . . . ★
  Vicinity . . . . Pg. 101, J-6
Landover Hills . . . . ★
  Vicinity . . . . Pg. 159, F-7
Lansdowne . . . . ★
  Vicinity . . . . Pg. 101, E-4
Largo D-9
Laurel D-9
Laurel . . . . ★
  Vicinity . . . . Pg. 101, J-1
Layhill . . . . ★
  Vicinity . . . . Pg. 159, B-5
Laytonsville C-8
Leonardtown G-10
Lexington Pk. G-11
Linthicum . . . . ★
  Vicinity . . . . Pg. 101, F-4
Lipins Corner . . . . ★
  Vicinity . . . . Pg. 101, H-5
Lochearn . . . . ★
  Vicinity . . . . Pg. 101, C-3
Lonaconing B-2
Long Beach G-11
Longridge G-14
Longwoods E-12
Luke B-2
Lutherville B-10
Lutherville . . . . ★
  Vicinity . . . . Pg. 101, B-5
Lynch C-12
Macey's Cor. . . . . ★
  Vicinity . . . . Pg. 101, J-6
Mago Vista Beach . . . . ★
  Vicinity . . . . Pg. 101, J-6
Manchester D-2
Marbury F-8
Marion H-13
Marlow Hts. . . . . ★
  Vicinity . . . . Pg. 159, H-6
Marston B-8
Maryland City . . . . ★
  Vicinity . . . . Pg. 101, J-1
Mayfield . . . . ★
  Vicinity . . . . Pg. 101, J-3
Mayo E-11
McHenry B-1
McPherson . . . . ★
  Vicinity . . . . Pg. 101, G-4
Meadowood . . . . ★
  Vicinity . . . . Pg. 159, C-5
Melrose A-9
Middle River . . . . ★
  Vicinity . . . . Pg. 101, D-7
Middletown B-7
Midland B-3
Milford . . . . ★
  Vicinity . . . . Pg. 101, C-3
Millersville . . . . ★
  Vicinity . . . . Pg. 101, K-4
Millington C-13
Millstone A-5
Mitchells Range . . . . ★
  Vicinity . . . . Pg. 159, B-1
Monrose . . . . ★
  Vicinity . . . . Pg. 159, C-3
Montgomery Village D-8
Montgomery Village . . . . . . ★
  Vicinity . . . . Pg. 159, A-2
Morganza G-10
Morningside . . . . ★
  Vicinity . . . . Pg. 159, H-7
Mt. Airy C-8
Mt. Pleasant B-9
Mt. Rainier . . . . ★
  Vicinity . . . . Pg. 159, F-6
Mt. Wilson . . . . ★
  Vicinity . . . . Pg. 101, B-2
Mtn. Lake Park C-1
Myersville B-7
Necker . . . . ★
  Vicinity . . . . Pg. 101, B-7
New Carrollton . . . . ★
  Vicinity . . . . Pg. 159, E-7
New Market C-8
Newburg G-9
Newport G-9
Newtown C-11
Norbeck Estates . . . . ★
  Vicinity . . . . Pg. 159, A-4
North Beach E-10
North East B-12
North Point . . . . ★
  Vicinity . . . . Pg. 101, E-7
Oakland C-1
Oakland C-9
Oakland Mills . . . . ★
  Vicinity . . . . Pg. 101, F-1
Oaklawn . . . . ★
  Vicinity . . . . Pg. 159, J-6
Oakmont . . . . ★
  Vicinity . . . . Pg. 159, D-3
Ocean City G-15
Odenton . . . . ★
  Vicinity . . . . Pg. 101, J-3
Old Salem Village . . . . ★
  Vicinity . . . . Pg. 159, B-5
Oldtown B-4
Olney D-9

Orchard Beach . . . . ★
  Vicinity . . . . Pg. 101, G-6
Oriole H-13
Overlea . . . . ★
  Vicinity . . . . Pg. 101, C-6
Owings Mills C-10
Owings Mills . . . . ★
  Vicinity . . . . Pg. 101, B-2
Oxford F-12
Oxon Hill E-9
Oxon Hill . . . . ★
  Vicinity . . . . Pg. 159, J-6
Park Hill H-11
Parkton B-10
Parkville C-10
Parkville . . . . ★
  Vicinity . . . . Pg. 101, C-6
Pasadena . . . . ★
  Vicinity . . . . Pg. 101, H-5
Perry Hall B-11
Perry Hall . . . . ★
  Vicinity . . . . Pg. 101, B-7
Pikesville C-10
Pikesville . . . . ★
  Vicinity . . . . Pg. 101, C-3
Pinehurst . . . . ★
  Vicinity . . . . Pg. 101, H-7
Piney Grove A-4
Piney Point H-11
Pittsville G-14
Pleasant Hills B-11
Plum Point F-11
Pocomoke City H-13
Point Lookout H-11
Poolesville D-7
Port Deposit B-12
Pot Spring . . . . ★
  Vicinity . . . . Pg. 101, A-5
Potomac D-8
Potomac . . . . ★
  Vicinity . . . . Pg. 159, D-2
Potomac Park B-3
Powellville G-14
Pratt A-4
Preston E-12
Price D-12
Prince Frederick F-10
Princess Anne G-13
Providence . . . . ★
  Vicinity . . . . Pg. 101, B-5
Pumphrey . . . . ★
  Vicinity . . . . Pg. 101, F-4
Putty Hill . . . . ★
  Vicinity . . . . Pg. 101, C-6
Queen Anne E-12
Queenstown D-12
Quince Orchard . . . . ★
  Vicinity . . . . Pg. 162, B-1
Randallstown C-9
Randallstown . . . . ★
  Vicinity . . . . Pg. 101, C-2
Redhouse C-11
Redland . . . . ★
  Vicinity . . . . Pg. 159, A-3
Regency Estates . . . . ★
  Vicinity . . . . Pg. 159, C-2
Reisterstown B-9
Relay . . . . ★
  Vicinity . . . . Pg. 101, F-3
Riderwood . . . . ★
  Vicinity . . . . Pg. 101, B-4
Ridge H-11
Ridgely D-12
Ridgeway . . . . ★
  Vicinity . . . . Pg. 101, H-3
Rising Sun A-12
Riva E-10
Riverdale . . . . ★
  Vicinity . . . . Pg. 159, E-6
Riverside G-8
Riviera Beach D-11
Riviera Beach . . . . ★
  Vicinity . . . . Pg. 101, G-6
Robinson . . . . ★
  Vicinity . . . . Pg. 101, J-5
Rock Hall D-11
Rockdale . . . . ★
  Vicinity . . . . Pg. 101, C-2
Rockland . . . . ★
  Vicinity . . . . Pg. 101, B-4
Rockville . . . . ★
  Vicinity . . . . Pg. 159, C-3
Rodgers Forge . . . . ★
  Vicinity . . . . Pg. 101, B-5
Roe D-12
Rosedale . . . . ★
  Vicinity . . . . Pg. 101, D-6
Rosemont C-7
Rush B-4
Ruthsburg D-12
Ruxton . . . . ★
  Vicinity . . . . Pg. 101, B-4
Salisbury G-13
Sandy Bottom C-11
Sandy Spring . . . . ★
  Vicinity . . . . Pg. 159, A-5
Scaggsville . . . . ★
  Vicinity . . . . Pg. 159, A-7
Seat Pleasant E-9
Seat Pleasant . . . . ★
  Vicinity . . . . Pg. 159, G-7
Secretary F-12
Severn D-10
Severn . . . . ★
  Vicinity . . . . Pg. 101, H-3

Severna Park D-10
Severna Park . . . . ★
  Vicinity . . . . Pg. 101, J-6
Shady Side E-11
Sharpsburg C-6
Sharptown F-13
Shore Acres . . . . ★
  Vicinity . . . . Pg. 101, K-7
Silesia . . . . ★
  Vicinity . . . . Pg. 159, K-5
Silver Spring . . . . ★
  Vicinity . . . . Pg. 159, E-5
Silver Springs D-9
Snow Hill H-14
Solley . . . . ★
  Vicinity . . . . Pg. 101, G-6
South Lawn . . . . ★
  Vicinity . . . . Pg. 159, J-5
Southgate D-10
Sparrows Point . . . . ★
  Vicinity . . . . Pg. 101, F-7
Spencerville . . . . ★
  Vicinity . . . . Pg. 159, B-6
St. Charles F-9
St. Michaels E-11
Stevenson . . . . ★
  Vicinity . . . . Pg. 101, B-3
Stockton H-14
Sudlersville C-13
Suitland E-9
Suitland . . . . ★
  Vicinity . . . . Pg. 159, H-6
Swanton B-1
Sycamore Acres . . . . ★
  Vicinity . . . . Pg. 159, A-6
Sykesville C-9
Takoma Park . . . . ★
  Vicinity . . . . Pg. 159, E-5
Taneytown B-8
Tantallon F-9
Tantallon . . . . ★
  Vicinity . . . . Pg. 159, K-5
Taylors Island F-11
Taylorsville B-8
Temple Hills . . . . ★
  Vicinity . . . . Pg. 159, H-6
Templeville D-13
The Glen . . . . ★
  Vicinity . . . . Pg. 159, C-2
Thurmont B-8
Timanium . . . . ★
  Vicinity . . . . Pg. 101, A-4
Tippett . . . . ★
  Vicinity . . . . Pg. 159, K-6
Towson C-10
Towson . . . . ★
  Vicinity . . . . Pg. 101, B-5
Travilan . . . . ★
  Vicinity . . . . Pg. 159, C-1
Truxton . . . . ★
  Vicinity . . . . Pg. 159, D-1
Turner G-10
Union Bridge B-8
University Park . . . . ★
  Vicinity . . . . Pg. 159, F-6
Upper Marlboro E-10
Veirs Mills . . . . ★
  Vicinity . . . . Pg. 159, C-4
Vienna F-13
Waldorf F-9
Walkersville B-8
Washington Grove . . . . ★
  Vicinity . . . . Pg. 159, A-3
Waterloo . . . . ★
  Vicinity . . . . Pg. 101, G-2
Waterview G-13
Wenona H-12
Wesley G-14
West Laurel . . . . ★
  Vicinity . . . . Pg. 159, B-7
Westernport B-2
Westminster B-9
Westover H-13
Wheaton . . . . ★
  Vicinity . . . . Pg. 159, C-5
White Marsh . . . . ★
  Vicinity . . . . Pg. 101, C-7
White Oak . . . . ★
  Vicinity . . . . Pg. 159, C-5
White Plains F-9
Whiteford A-11
Widgeon G-13
Willards G-15
Woodlawn . . . . ★
  Vicinity . . . . Pg. 101, D-3

MASSACHUSETTS
page 30-31

Abington D-11
Acton B-9
Acushnet F-11
Adams B-3
Agawam E-5
Amesbury A-11
Amherst C-5
Andover A-10
Arlington . . . . ★
  Vicinity . . . . Pg. 106, E-3
Ashburnham B-8
Ashfield C-4
Athol B-7
Attleboro E-10

Auburn D-8
Avon D-11
Ayer B-9
Baldwinville B-7
Barnstable F-13
Barre C-7
Becket C-3
Bedford . . . . ★
  Vicinity . . . . Pg. 106, C-1
Belchertown C-6
Bellingham E-9
Belmont . . . . ★
  Vicinity . . . . Pg. 106, E-3
Berkley F-11
Bernardston B-5
Beverly B-12
  Vicinity . . . . Pg. 106, A-7
Billerica B-10
Blackstone E-9
Blanford D-4
Bolton C-9
Boston C-11
  Vicinity . . . . . . Pg. 106-107
Bourne F-13
Boxborough C-9
Boxford B-11
Boylston C-8
Braintree D-11
  Vicinity . . . . Pg. 107, K-6
Bridgewater E-11
Brimfield D-7
Brockton E-11
Brookfield D-7
Brookline . . . . ★
  Vicinity . . . . Pg. 107, G-3
Buckland B-4
Burlington . . . . ★
  Vicinity . . . . Pg. 106, C-2
Buzzards Bay F-12
Cambridge . . . . ★
  Vicinity . . . . Pg. 106, F-4
Canton D-11
  Vicinity . . . . Pg. 107, L-3
Carlisle B-10
Carver E-12
Centerville G-13
Charlemont B-4
Charlton D-7
Chatham F-15
Chelmsford B-10
Chelsea C-11
Chelsea . . . . ★
  Vicinity . . . . Pg. 106, E-5
Cheshire B-3
Chesterfield C-4
Chicopee D-5
Chilmark H-12
Clarksburg A-3
Cliftondale . . . . ★
  Vicinity . . . . Pg. 106, D-5
Clinton C-9
Cochituate C-9
Colrain B-4
Concord C-10
Conway B-5
Cummington C-4
Dalton B-3
Danvers B-11
  Vicinity . . . . Pg. 106, A-6
Dartmouth G-11
Dedham . . . . ★
  Vicinity . . . . Pg. 107, J-3
Deerfield B-5
Dennis F-14
Dennis Port G-14
Dighton E-10
Dover . . . . ★
  Vicinity . . . . Pg. 107, J-1
Dracut B-10
Dudley E-7
Duxbury E-12
East Bridgewater E-11
East Falmouth G-13
East Longmeadow E-6
Eastham F-15
Easthampton C-4
Easton E-11
Edgartown H-13
Essex B-12
Everett . . . . ★
  Vicinity . . . . Pg. 106, E-5
Fairhaven G-12
Falmouth G-12
Fitchburg B-8
Framingham D-9
Freetown F-11
Gardner B-7
Gay Head H-12
Georgetown A-11
Gilbertville C-6
Gill B-5
Gloucester B-13
Grafton D-9
Granby D-5
Granville E-4
Great Barrington D-2
Greenfield B-5
Groton B-9
Groveland A-11
Hadley C-5
Halifax E-12
Hamilton B-12
Hampden E-6

Hanover D-12
Hardwick C-6
Harvard B-9
Harwich F-15
Hatfield C-5
Haverhill A-11
Hawley B-4
Heath B-4
Hingham D-11
  Vicinity . . . . . . Pg. 107, J-7
Holbrook D-11
Holbrook . . . . ★
  Vicinity . . . . Pg. 107, L-5
Holden C-8
Holland E-7
Holyoke D-5
Hopedale D-9
Hopkinton D-9
Hudson C-9
Hull C-11
Huntington D-4
Hyannis G-14
Ipswich B-11
Kingston E-12
Lee C-3
Leicester D-8
Lenox C-2
Leominster B-8
Leverett C-5
Lexington . . . . ★
  Vicinity . . . . Pg. 106, D-2
Leyden A-5
Lincoln C-10
Littleton B-9
Longmeadow D-5
Lowell B-10
Lunenburg B-8
Lynn C-11
  Vicinity . . . . Pg. 106, D-6
Lynnfield B-11
Lynnfield . . . . ★
  Vicinity . . . . Pg. 106, B-5
Malden . . . . ★
  Vicinity . . . . Pg. 106, D-4
Manchester B-12
Mansfield E-10
Marblehead B-12
Marion F-12
Marlborough C-9
Marshfield D-12
Mattapoisett G-12
Maynard C-9
Medfield D-10
Medford . . . . ★
  Vicinity . . . . Pg. 106, E-4
Medway D-10
Melrose . . . . ★
  Vicinity . . . . Pg. 106, D-5
Mendon D-9
Merrimac A-11
Methuen A-10
Middleborough F-11
Middlefield C-3
Middleton B-11
Milford D-9
Millbury D-8
Millers Falls B-6
Millis D-10
Milton D-11
  Vicinity . . . . Pg. 107, J-4
Monson D-6
Montague B-5
Monterey D-3
N. Attleborough E-10
Nahant C-11
Nantucket H-14
Natick D-10
Needham . . . . ★
  Vicinity . . . . Pg. 107, H-2
New Bedford G-11
New Braintree C-7
New Marlborough D-3
Newbury A-12
Newton . . . . ★
  Vicinity . . . . Pg. 106, F-2
Norfolk D-10
North Adams A-3
North Brookfield C-7
North Reading B-11
Northampton C-4
Northborough C-8
Northbridge D-9
Northfield A-6
Norton E-10
Norwood D-10
  Vicinity . . . . Pg. 107, K-2
Oak Bluffs H-13
Oakham C-7
Orange B-6
Orleans F-15
Osterville G-13
Otis D-3
Oxford D-8
Palmer D-6
Paxton C-8
Peabody B-11
Peabody . . . . ★
  Vicinity . . . . Pg. 106, B-7
Pepperell B-9
Peru C-3
Petersham B-7
Pinehurst . . . . ★
  Vicinity . . . . Pg. 106, B-1

Pittsfield B-2
Plainfield B-4
Plymouth E-12
Plympton E-12
Princeton C-8
Provincetown E-14
Quincy D-11
  Vicinity . . . . Pg. 107, J-5
Randolph D-11
  Vicinity . . . . Pg. 107, L-5
Raynham E-11
Reading B-11
  Vicinity . . . . Pg. 106, B-4
Rehoboth F-10
Revere C-11
Revere . . . . ★
  Vicinity . . . . Pg. 106, E-5
Richmond C-2
Rochester F-12
Rockland D-11
Rockport B-13
Rowley A-12
Royalston A-7
Rutland C-7
Sagamore F-13
Salem B-12
  Vicinity . . . . Pg. 106, B-7
Salisbury A-12
Sandisfield D-3
Sandwich F-13
Saugus C-11
Saugus . . . . ★
  Vicinity . . . . Pg. 106, D-5
Savoy B-4
Scituate D-12
Seekonk F-10
Sharon D-10
Sheffield D-2
Shelburne B-4
Shirley B-9
Shrewsbury C-9
So. Yarmouth G-14
Somerset F-10
Somerville . . . . ★
  Vicinity . . . . Pg. 106, E-4
South Hadley C-5
Southbridge E-7
Spencer D-7
Sterling C-8
Stockbridge C-2
Stoneham . . . . ★
  Vicinity . . . . Pg. 106, C-4
Stoughton D-11
Stow C-9
Sturbridge D-7
Sunderland C-5
Sutton D-8
Swampscott C-12
  Vicinity . . . . Pg. 106, D-5
Swansea F-10
Taunton E-10
Templeton B-7
Tewksbury B-10
Three Rivers D-6
Tisbury H-12
Topsfield B-11
Townsend B-9
Truro E-15
Tyngsborough A-10
Upton D-9
Uxbridge E-9
Vineyard Haven H-13
Wakefield C-11
  Vicinity . . . . Pg. 106, C-4
Wales D-6
Walpole D-10
  Vicinity . . . . Pg. 107, L-1
Waltham . . . . ★
  Vicinity . . . . Pg. 106, F-1
Ware C-6
Wareham F-12
Warren D-7
Warwick A-6
Washington C-3
Watertown . . . . ★
  Vicinity . . . . Pg. 106, F-2
Wayland C-10
Webster E-7
Wellesley D-10
Wellesley . . . . ★
  Vicinity . . . . Pg. 107, G-1
Wellfleet E-14
Wendell B-6
Wenham B-11
West Boylston C-8
West Brookfield D-7
West Dennis G-14
West Newbury A-11
West Springfield D-5
West Stockbridge C-2
West Tisbury H-12
Westborough D-9
Westfield D-4
Westford B-9
Westhampton C-4
Westminster B-8
Westport G-11
Westwood D-10
Westwood . . . . ★
  Vicinity . . . . Pg. 107, K-2
Weymouth D-11
  Vicinity . . . . Pg. 107, K-6
Whately C-5
Whitinsville D-8
Whitman E-11

Wilbraham D-6
Williamstown C-3
Wilmington B-10
  Vicinity . . . . Pg. 106, B-3
Winchendon A-7
Winchester . . . . ★
  Vicinity . . . . Pg. 106, D-3
Windsor B-3
Winthrop C-11
Winthrop . . . . ★
  Vicinity . . . . Pg. 106, F-6
Woburn B-10
Woburn C-10
Worcester C-7
Worthington C-5
Wrentham D-10
Yarmouth F-14

MICHIGAN
Pages 48-49

Acme F-6
Adamsville L-4
Adrian L-8
Afton E-7
Agnew J-4
Ahmeek A-2
Akron H-8
Alabaster G-8
Alanson E-7
Alaska J-5
Alba F-6
Alberta B-2
Albion L-6
Alcona F-9
Alger G-8
Algonac K-10
Allegan K-5
Allen L-6
Allen Park . . . . ★
  Vicinity . . . . Pg. 119, K-3
Allendale J-5
Allenville D-7
Allouez A-2
Alma J-7
Almena L-5
Almont K-9
Aloha E-7
Alpena F-9
Alpha D-2
Alston B-2
Alto K-6
Alverno E-7
Amador J-10
Amasa C-2
Amble H-5
Anchorville K-10
Ann Arbor L-8
  Vicinity . . . . Pg. 118, H-1
Antrim F-6
Applegate J-10
Arbutus Beach F-7
Arcadia G-4
Argentine K-7
Argyle H-9
Arnheim B-2
Arnold D-3
Arthur J-8
Ashley J-7
Ashton H-6
Assinins B-2
Athens L-6
Atlanta F-8
Atlantic Mine B-2
Attica J-9
Atwood E-6
Au Gres H-8
Au Sable G-9
Au Train C-4
Auburn H-8
Austin C-3
Averill H-7
Bad Axe H-9
Bailey J-5
Baldwin H-5
Banat D-3
Bancroft K-8
Banfield K-6
Bangor K-4
Baraga B-2
Bark River D-3
Barker Creek F-6
Barryton H-6
Barton City F-8
Batavia L-6
Bates F-6
Bath K-7
Battle Creek K-6
Bay City H-8
Bay Mills C-7
Bay Park H-8
Bay Port H-8
Bay View E-7
Beacon C-2
Bear Lake G-5
Beaverton H-7
Beechwood C-2
Belding J-6
Belleville . . . . ★
  Vicinity . . . . Pg. 118, K-4
Bellevue K-6
Bendon F-5
Bennington J-7

MICHIGAN

MINNESOTA

Benton Harbor ...L-4
Benzonia ...F-5
Bergland ...A-10
Berkley ...★
 Vicinity ...Pg. 119, D-8
Berrien Sp. ...L-4
Bessemer ...B-9
Bethel ...L-6
Beulah ...F-5
Beverly Hills ...★
 Vicinity ...Pg. 118, C-7
Big Bay ...B-3
Big Rapids ...H-6
Birch Creek ...E-3
Birch Run ...J-8
Birmingham ...★
 Vicinity ...Pg. 119, C-8
Bitley ...H-5
Black River ...F-9
Blanchard ...H-6
Blaney Park ...D-5
Blissfield ...L-8
Bloomfield Hills ...★
 Vicinity ...Pg. 118, B-7
Boyne City ...E-6
Boyne Falls ...E-7
Bradley ...K-5
Brampton ...D-3
Branch ...H-5
Bravo ...K-5
Breckenridge ...J-7
Brethren ...G-5
Brevort ...D-6
Bridgeport ...J-8
Bridgeton ...J-5
Bridgman ...L-4
Brighton ...K-8
Brimley ...C-7
Britton ...L-8
Brockway ...J-9
Brohman ...H-5
Bronson ...L-6
Brooklyn ...L-7
Brown City ...J-9
Bruce Crossing ...C-1
Brunswick ...H-5
Brutus ...E-7
Buchanan ...L-4
Buckley ...G-5
Burlington ...L-6
Burnside ...J-9
Burt ...J-8
Burton ...J-8
Byron Center ...J-5
Cadillac ...G-6
Cadmus ...L-7
Caledonia ...K-6
California ...L-6
Calumet ...A-2
Camden ...M-6
Capac ...J-9
Carbondale ...E-3
Carleton ...L-8
Carney ...E-3
Caro ...J-9
Carp Lake ...E-7
Carsonville ...J-9
Caseville ...H-9
Casnovia ...J-5
Cass City ...H-9
Cassopolis ...L-4
Cathro ...F-8
Cedar ...F-5
Cedar River ...E-3
Cedar Springs ...J-6
Cedarville ...D-8
Center Line ...★
 Vicinity ...Pg. 119, D-11
Centreville ...L-5
Ceresco ...L-6
Channing ...C-2
Charleviox Bay ...E-6
Charlotte ...K-6
Chase ...H-6
Chatham ...C-4
Cheboygan ...E-7
Chelsea ...L-7
Chesaning ...J-7
Christmas ...C-4
Cilo ...J-8
Clare ...H-6
Clarendon ...L-6
Clarion ...E-7
Clarksville ...K-6
Clawson ...★
 Vicinity ...Pg. 119, C-9
Clayton ...L-7
Cliff ...A-2
Climax ...L-5
Clinton ...L-8
Cloverdale ...K-6
Coldwater ...L-6
Coleman ...H-7
Coloma ...L-4
Colon ...L-6
Comins ...F-8
Concord ...L-7
Constantine ...L-5
Conway ...E-7
Coopersville ...J-5
Copemish ...G-5
Copper Harbor ...A-3
Cornell ...D-3
Corunna ...J-8
Covert ...K-4

Covington ...C-2
Cross Village ...E-7
Croswell ...J-10
Croton ...H-5
Crump ...H-7
Crystal Falls ...C-2
Cunard ...D-3
Curran ...F-8
Curtis ...D-6
Custer ...H-4
Dafter ...C-7
Daggett ...E-3
Dansville ...K-7
Darragh ...F-6
Davison ...J-8
Dayton ...L-4
Dearborn ...★
 Vicinity ...Pg. 118, G-7
Decatur ...L-5
Deer Park ...C-6
Deerton ...C-4
Deford ...J-9
Delano ...G-8
Delton ...K-5
Denton ...L-8
Detour Village ...D-8
Detroit ...★
 Vicinity ...Pg. 119, F-8
Devereaux ...K-7
Dewitt ...K-7
Dexter ...L-7
Dighton ...G-6
Disco ...K-9
Dixboro ...L-8
Donaldson ...C-8
Donken ...B-1
Dorr ...K-5
Douglas ...K-4
Dowagiac ...L-4
Dowling ...K-6
Drayton Plains ...★
Drummond ...D-8
Dublin ...G-5
Dundee ...L-8
Dunningvile ...K-5
Durand ...K-8
E. Grand Rapids ...J-5
E. Jordan ...E-6
Eagle Habor ...A-3
Eagle River ...A-2
East Detroit ...★
 Vicinity ...Pg. 119, E-12
East Gilead ...L-6
East Lake ...G-5
East Leroy ...L-6
East Tawas ...G-8
Eastport ...F-6
Eaton Rapids ...K-7
Eckerman ...C-7
Ecorse ...★
 Vicinity ...Pg. 119, J-9
Edenville ...H-7
Edmore ...J-6
Edwardsburg ...L-5
Elba ...J-8
Elberta ...F-5
Elk Rapids ...F-6
Elkton ...H-9
Elmer ...J-9
Elmira ...F-7
Elwell ...J-7
Emmett ...K-9
Empire ...F-5
Engadine ...D-6
Ensign ...D-4
Epoufette ...D-6
Erie ...M-8
Escanaba ...D-3
Essexville ...H-8
Estey ...H-7
Estral Beach ...L-9
Evans ...J-6
Evart ...H-6
Ewen ...C-1
Fair Haven ...K-9
Fairfield ...L-7
Fairgrove ...J-8
Fairview ...F-8
Farmington ...★
 Vicinity ...Pg. 118, D-5
Farmington Hills ...★
 Vicinity ...Pg. 118, D-5
Farwell ...H-6
Fawn River ...L-6
Fayette ...D-4
Felch ...D-3
Felch Mountain ...D-3
Fennville ...K-5
Fenton ...K-8
Ferndale ...★
 Vicinity ...Pg. 119, E-9
Ferry ...H-5
Ferrysburg ...J-4
Fibre ...D-7
Fife Lake ...G-6
Filer City ...G-4
Filion ...H-9
Filmore ...K-5
Flat Rock ...L-8
Flint ...J-8
Flushing ...J-8
Ford River ...D-4
Forest Hill ...J-7
Forest Lake ...C-4

Forester ...J-10
Forestville ...H-10
Foster City ...D-3
Fouch ...F-5
Fountain ...G-5
Fowler ...J-7
Fowlerville ...K-8
Frankenmuth ...J-8
Frankfort ...F-5
Franklin ...★
 Vicinity ...Pg. 118, C-7
Fraser ...★
 Vicinity ...Pg. 119, C-12
Frederick ...F-7
Freeland ...H-7
Freesoil ...G-5
Fremont ...H-5
Frontier ...L-7
Fruitport ...J-5
Galesburg ...K-5
Galien ...L-4
Ganges ...K-4
Garden ...D-4
Garden City ...★
 Vicinity ...Pg. 118, G-6
Garden Corners ...D-5
Gardendale ...J-10
Garfield ...J-7
Garnet ...D-6
Gaylord ...F-7
Gera ...J-8
Germfask ...C-5
Gibraltar ...L-9
Girard ...L-6
Gladstone ...D-4
Gladwin ...H-7
Glen Arbor ...F-5
Glen Haven ...F-5
Glenn ...K-4
Glennie ...F-7
Glenwood ...L-5
Gobles ...K-5
Goetzville ...D-8
Good Hart ...E-6
Goodrich ...K-8
Gould City ...D-5
Gourley ...D-3
Grand Beach ...L-4
Grand Blanc ...K-8
Grand Haven ...J-4
Grand Ledge ...K-6
Grand Marais ...C-5
Grand Rapids ...J-5
Grange ...L-5
Granite Bluff ...D-2
Grant ...J-5
Grawn ...F-6
Grayling ...F-7
Greenbush ...G-9
Greenland ...B-1
Greenville ...J-6
Gregory ...K-7
Grindstone City ...H-9
Gros Cap ...D-7
Grosse Pointe ...★
 Vicinity ...Pg. 119, F-13
Grosse Pointe Farms ...★
 Vicinity ...Pg. 119, F-13
Grosse Pointe Park ...★
 Vicinity ...Pg. 119, G-12
Grosse Pointe Shores ...L-9
 Vicinity ...Pg. 119, E-13
Grosse Pointe Woods ...★
 Vicinity ...Pg. 119, E-13
Gulliver ...D-5
Gwinn ...C-3
Hale ...G-8
Hamburg ...K-8
Hamilton ...K-5
Hamlin Lake ...G-4
Hamtramck ...★
 Vicinity ...Pg. 119, F-10
Hancock ...B-2
Harbert ...L-4
Harbor Beach ...H-10
Harbor Springs ...E-6
Hardwood ...D-3
Harper Woods ...★
 Vicinity ...Pg. 119, E-12
Harris ...D-3
Harrison ...H-7
Harrisville ...F-9
Hart ...H-4
Hartford ...L-4
Hartland ...K-8
Harvey ...C-3
Hastings ...K-6
Hawks ...E-8
Hazel Park ...★
 Vicinity ...Pg. 119, E-10
Helmer ...C-5
Hemans ...J-9
Henderson ...J-7
Hermansville ...D-3
Herron ...F-8
Hesperia ...H-5
Hessel ...D-7
Higgans Lake ...G-7
Highland Park ...★
 Vicinity ...Pg. 119, F-9
Hilliards ...K-5
Hillman ...F-8
Hillsdale ...L-7
Hockaday ...G-7
Hodunk ...L-6

Holland ...K-4
Holly ...K-8
Holt ...K-7
Holton ...J-5
Homer ...L-6
Honor ...F-5
Horton ...L-7
Houghton ...B-1
Houghton Heights ...G-7
Houghton Lake ...G-7
Howard City ...J-5
Howell ...K-8
Hubbard Lake ...F-8
Hubbell ...B-2
Hudson ...L-7
Hudsonville ...J-5
Huntington Woods ...★
 Vicinity ...Pg. 119, D-8
Huron Beach ...E-8
Huron City ...H-9
Hyde ...D-4
Idlewild ...H-5
Imlay City ...J-9
Ingalls ...E-3
Inkster ...★
 Vicinity ...Pg. 118, H-6
Interlochen ...F-5
Ionia ...J-6
Iron Mountain ...D-2
Iron River ...C-1
Irons ...G-5
Ironwood ...B-9
Isabella ...D-4
Ishpeming ...C-3
Ithaca ...J-7
Jackson ...L-7
Jamestown ...J-5
Jasper ...M-8
Jeddo ...J-10
Johannesburg ...F-7
Jones ...L-5
Jonesville ...L-7
Joppa ...L-6
Kalamazoo ...K-5
Kaleva ...G-5
Kalkaska ...F-6
Karlin ...F-5
Kawkawlin ...H-8
Kearsarge ...A-2
Kendall ...K-5
Kent City ...J-5
Kenton ...C-1
Kentwood ...J-5
Kewadin ...F-6
Keweenaw Bay ...B-2
Kibbie ...K-4
Kinde ...H-9
Kinderhook ...L-6
Kingsford ...D-2
Kingston ...J-9
Kinross ...C-7
Kiva ...C-4
L'Anse ...B-2
La Salle ...L-8
LaBranche ...D-3
Lachine ...F-8
Lacota ...K-5
Laingsburg ...K-7
Lake City ...G-6
Lake George ...H-6
Lake Leelanau ...F-5
Lake Linden ...A-2
Lake Odessa ...K-6
Lake Orion ...K-8
Lake Roland ...B-1
Lakeland ...K-8
Lakeport ...J-10
Lakeview ...J-6
Lambertville ...M-8
Langston ...J-6
Lansing ...K-7
Lapeer ...J-9
Laporte ...C-4
Lathrop ...C-4
Lathrup Village ...★
 Vicinity ...Pg. 119, D-8
Laurium ...A-2
Lawton ...L-5
Le Roy ...G-6
Leland ...F-5
Leoni ...L-7
Leonidas ...L-5
Leslie ...K-7
Levering ...E-7
Lexington ...J-10
Liberty ...L-7
Lilley ...H-5
Lincoln ...F-9
Lincoln Park ...★
 Vicinity ...Pg. 119, J-8
Lincoln Park ...★
 Vicinity ...Pg. 119, J-8
Linden ...K-8
Linwood ...H-8
Litchfield ...L-7
Little Lake ...C-4
Livonia ...★
 Vicinity ...Pg. 118, F-6
Long Lake ...G-8
Long Rapids ...F-8
Longrie ...E-3
Loomis ...H-7
Loretto ...D-3
Lowell ...J-6
Lucas ...G-6

Ludington ...G-4
Luna Pier ...M-8
Lupton ...G-8
Luzerne ...G-7
Mackinaw City ...D-7
Madison Heights ...★
 Vicinity ...Pg. 119, D-9
Mancelona ...F-6
Mandan ...A-3
Manistee ...G-4
Manistique ...D-5
Manton ...G-6
Maple Rapids ...J-7
Marcellus ...L-5
Marenisco ...B-10
Marine City ...K-10
Marion ...G-6
Marlette ...J-9
Marne ...J-5
Marquette ...C-4
Marshall ...K-5
Martin ...K-5
Marysville ...K-10
Mashek ...D-3
Mason ...K-7
Masonville ...D-4
Mass City ...B-1
Matchwood ...B-1
Matherton ...J-6
Mattawan ...K-5
Mayville ...J-9
McBain ...G-6
McFarland ...C-3
McMillan ...C-5
Meade ...K-9
Mears ...H-4
Mecosta ...H-6
Melstrand ...C-5
Melvin ...J-9
Memphis ...K-9
Mendon ...L-5
Menominee ...E-3
Meredith ...G-7
Merriman ...D-2
Merritt ...G-6
Merriweather ...A-10
Mesick ...G-5
Metz ...E-8
Michigamme ...C-3
Michigan Center ...L-7
Middleville ...K-6
Midland ...H-7
Mikado ...G-8
Milburg ...L-4
Milford ...K-8
 Vicinity ...Pg. 118, B-2
Millbrook ...H-6
Millersburg ...E-8
Millington ...J-8
Mineral Hills ...C-2
Mio ...F-8
Mohawk ...A-2
Moline ...K-5
Monroe ...L-8
Monroe Center ...F-6
Montague ...H-4
Montrose ...J-8
Moorestown ...G-6
Moran ...D-7
Morley ...H-6
Morneci ...M-7
Moscow ...L-7
Mottville ...L-5
Mount Forest ...H-8
Mount Pleasant ...H-7
Mt. Clemens ...★
 Vicinity ...Pg. 119, B-13
Mt. Morris ...J-8
Muir ...K-7
Mullett Lake ...E-7
Munger ...H-8
Munising ...C-5
Muskegon ...J-4
Muskegon Heights ...J-4
Muttonville ...K-9
Napoleon ...L-7
Nashville ...K-6
Nathan ...D-3
Naubinway ...D-6
Negaunee ...C-3
New Baltimore ...K-9
New Buffalo ...L-4
New Era ...J-5
New Greenleaf ...H-9
New Haven ...K-10
Newaygo ...J-5
Newberry ...C-6
Newport ...L-9
Niles ...L-4
Nirvana ...H-5
Nisula ...B-1
North Branch ...J-9
North Ironwood ...A-9
North Muskegon ...J-4
Northland ...D-3
Northport ...F-5
Northville ...★
 Vicinity ...Pg. 118, E-4
Norton Shores ...J-4
Norwalk ...G-5
Norway ...D-2
Novi ...★
 Vicinity ...Pg. 118, D-4
Nunica ...J-5

O'Neil ...F-6
Oak Grove ...F-7
Oak Park ...★
 Vicinity ...Pg. 119, E-8
Oakley ...J-7
Oakwood ...K-9
Ocqueoc ...E-8
Ogden Center ...M-8
Oil City ...H-7
Okemos ...K-7
Olivet ...K-6
Omena ...F-6
Onaway ...E-8
Onekama ...G-4
Onondaga ...K-7
Ontonagon ...B-1
Orchard Lake ...★
 Vicinity ...Pg. 118, B-5
Orleans ...J-6
Ortonville ...K-8
Oscoda ...G-9
Oskar ...A-2
Osseo ...L-7
Ossineke ...F-9
Otisville ...J-8
Otsego ...K-5
Otsego Lake ...F-7
Ottawa Lake ...M-8
Ovid ...J-7
Owasso ...J-8
Oxbow ...H-5
Oxford ...K-9
Ozark ...D-7
Painesdale ...B-2
Palmer ...C-3
Palmyra ...L-8
Palo ...J-6
Paradise ...C-7
Parchment ...K-5
Paris ...H-6
Parisville ...H-9
Parkdale ...G-4
Parkville ...L-5
Paulding ...C-1
Paw Paw ...L-5
Peck ...J-9
Pellston ...E-7
Pentwater ...H-4
Perkins ...D-4
Perrinton ...J-6
Perronville ...D-3
Perry ...K-7
Petersburg ...L-8
Petoskey ...E-7
Pewamo ...J-6
Phoenix ...A-2
Pickford ...D-7
Piconning ...H-8
Pierport ...G-4
Pierson ...J-6
Pigeon ...H-9
Pine River ...H-8
Pittsford ...L-7
Plainfield ...K-8
Plainwell ...K-5
Pleasant Ridge ...★
 Vicinity ...Pg. 119, D-9
Plymouth ...★
 Vicinity ...Pg. 118, F-4
Pointe Aux Barques ...H-9
Polaski ...F-8
Pontiac ...★
 Vicinity ...Pg. 118, A-7
Port Hope ...H-10
Port Huron ...K-10
Port Sanilac ...J-10
Portage ...K-5
Portland ...J-6
Posen ...E-8
Poseyville ...H-7
Potterville ...K-6
Powers ...D-3
Prescott ...G-8
Princeton ...C-3
Prudenville ...G-7
Pullman ...K-5
Quanicassee ...H-8
Quimby ...L-6
Quincy ...L-6
Quinnesec ...D-3
Raber ...D-8
Ralph ...C-3
Ramsay ...B-9
Randville ...D-3
Ransom ...M-7
Rattle Run ...K-10
Ray ...K-7
Reading ...L-6
Redford ...★
 Vicinity ...Pg. 118, F-7
Reed City ...H-6
Reese ...J-8
Remus ...H-6
Republic ...C-2
Rexton ...D-6
Rhodes ...H-7
Richland ...K-5
Richmond ...K-9
Richmondville ...H-10
Richville ...J-8
Ridgeway ...L-8
River Rouge ...★
 Vicinity ...Pg. 119, J-9
Riverdale ...J-6
Rives Junction ...K-7

Roberts Landing ...K-10
Rochester ...K-9
Rock ...D-4
Rockford ...J-6
Rockland ...B-1
Rockwood ...L-9
Rodney ...H-6
Rogers City ...E-8
Rome Center ...L-7
Romeo ...K-9
Romulus ...★
 Vicinity ...Pg. 118, J-5
Roosevelt Park ...★
Roscommon ...G-7
Rose City ...G-7
Roseburg ...J-9
Rosebush ...H-6
Roseville ...★
 Vicinity ...Pg. 119, D-12
Rothbury ...H-4
Royal Oak ...★
 Vicinity ...Pg. 119, C-9
Rudyard ...D-7
Rumely ...C-4
Ruth ...H-9
Saginaw ...J-7
Sagola ...D-2
Saline ...L-8
Samaria ...M-8
Sands ...C-3
Sandusky ...J-9
Sanford ...H-7
Sans Souci ...K-10
Saranac ...J-6
Saugatuck ...K-4
Sault Ste. Marie ...C-8
Sawyer ...L-4
Schaffer ...D-3
Schoolcraft ...L-5
Scottdale ...L-3
Scottville ...G-4
Sears ...H-6
Sebewaing ...H-9
Seney ...C-5
Sharon ...J-8
Shelby ...H-4
Shelbyville ...K-5
Shepherd ...H-7
Sherman ...G-5
Shingleton ...C-5
Shore ...E-6
Sidnaw ...C-2
Sigma ...F-6
Silver City ...A-10
Sister Lakes ...L-4
Six Lakes ...J-6
Skandia ...C-3
Skidway Lake ...G-8
Smithville ...G-6
Smyrna ...J-6
Snover ...J-9
Somerset ...L-7
Soo Junction ...C-6
South Boardman ...F-6
South Branch ...G-8
South Haven ...K-4
South Range ...B-1
Southfield ...★
 Vicinity ...Pg. 118, E-7
Southgate ...★
 Vicinity ...Pg. 119, K-8
Spratt ...F-8
Spring Lake ...J-5
Springport ...K-7
Spruce ...F-9
St. Clair ...K-10
 Vicinity ...Pg. 119, D-13
St. Clair Shores ...K-9
St. Ignace ...D-7
St. James ...D-6
St. Johns ...J-7
St. Louis ...J-7
Stager ...D-2
Stalwart ...D-7
Standish ...H-8
Stanton ...J-6
Stanwood ...H-6
Stephenson ...E-3
Sterling ...H-8
Sterling Hts. ...★
 Vicinity ...Pg. 119, B-10
Steuben ...C-5
Stevensville ...L-4
Stockbridge ...K-7
Stronach ...G-5
Strongs ...C-7
Sturgis ...L-5
Stutsmanville ...E-7
Sundell ...C-4
Sunfield ...K-6
Suttons Bay ...F-6
Swanson ...E-3
Swartz Creek ...J-8
Sylvester ...H-6
Tawas City ...G-8
Taylor ...★
 Vicinity ...Pg. 118, J-7

Tiovola ...B-1
Tipton ...L-7
Tower ...E-7
Traunik ...C-4
Traverse City ...F-5
Trenary ...C-4
Trenton ...L-9
Triangle Ranch ...C-2
Trout Creek ...C-1
Trout Lake ...D-7
Troy ...★
 Vicinity ...Pg. 119, B-9
Turner ...G-8
Tustin ...G-6
Twin Lake ...J-4
Twin Lakes ...B-2
Twining ...G-8
Ubly ...H-9
Union ...L-5
Union City ...L-6
Union Pier ...L-4
Unionville ...H-9
Utica ...★
 Vicinity ...Pg. 119, A-11
Vandalia ...L-5
Vanderbilt ...F-7
Vassar ...J-8
Vernon ...K-7
Verona ...H-9
Vicksburg ...L-5
Vienna ...F-7
Vogel Center ...G-6
Vriesland ...K-5
Vulcan ...D-3
Wacousta ...K-7
Wadhams ...J-9
Wakefield ...B-10
Waldron ...M-7
Walhalla ...G-5
Walkerville ...H-5
Wallace ...E-3
Walled Lake ...★
 Vicinity ...Pg. 118, C-4
Walton ...G-6
Warren ...K-9
 Vicinity ...Pg. 119, D-11
Washington ...K-9
Waterford ...★
 Vicinity ...Pg. 118, A-6
Waterloo ...K-7
Waters ...F-7
Watersmeet ...C-1
Watertown ...J-9
Watervliet ...L-4
Watson ...K-5
Watson ...D-3
Watton ...C-2
Waucedah ...D-3
Wayland ...K-5
Wayne ...★
 Vicinity ...Pg. 118, J-5
Webberville ...K-7
Wells ...D-4
Wellston ...G-5
West Branch ...G-7
West Olive ...J-5
Westland ...★
 Vicinity ...Pg. 118, G-5
Weston ...M-7
Wetmore ...C-4
White ...L-5
White Cloud ...J-5
White Pine ...A-10
White Rock ...H-10
Whitehall ...J-4
Whitney ...D-3
Whittemore ...G-8
Williamston ...K-7
Willis ...L-8
Windsor (Canada) ...★
 Vicinity ...Pg. 119, J-11
Winegars ...H-7
Winona ...B-2
Wisner ...H-8
Wixom ...★
 Vicinity ...Pg. 118, C-3
Wolf Lake ...G-5
Wolverine ...E-7
Wolverine Lake ...★
 Vicinity ...Pg. 118, B-4
Woodbury ...K-6
Woodhaven ...L-9
Woodland ...K-6
Wyandotte ...★
 Vicinity ...Pg. 119, K-8
Wyoming ...J-5
Yale ...J-9
Yalmer ...C-4
Ypsilanti ...L-8
 Vicinity ...Pg. 118, J-2
Yuma ...G-5
Zeeland ...J-5
Zilwaukee ...J-8

MINNESOTA
Pages 50-51

Ada ...D-2
Adams ...L-6
Adrian ...L-2
Ah-gwah-ching ...E-4
Aitkin ...F-5
Akeley ...E-4
Albany ...G-4

★ Denotes City only on Vicinity map. City not located on State map.

MINNESOTA

Albert Lea L-5
Alberta G-2
Alden L-5
Alexandria G-3
Alvarado C-1
Alwood D-5
Amboy K-5
Andover H-6
Angle Inlet A-3
Angora C-7
Annandale H-5
Anoka H-6
Appleton H-2
Arden Hills . . . . ★
  Vicinity . . . . . . Pg. 134, A-6
Argyle C-1
Arlington J-4
Ashby G-2
Askov F-7
Atwater H-4
Audubon E-2
Aurora D-7
Austin L-6
Avoca K-2
Avon G-4
Babbitt D-8
Backus E-4
Badger B-2
Bagley D-3
Ball Club D-5
Barnesville F-1
Barnum F-6
Barrett G-2
Barry G-1
Battle Lake F-3
Baudette B-4
Baxter E-4
Beardsley G-1
Beaver Bay D-9
Beaver Creek L-1
Becker H-5
Bejou D-2
Belgrade H-3
Belle Plaine J-5
Bellingham H-1
Beltrami D-1
Bemidji D-4
Bena D-4
Benedict D-4
Benson H-3
Beroun G-6
Bertha F-3
Big Falls C-5
Big Fork D-5
Big Lake H-5
Bigelow L-2
Birchdale B-5
Birchwood . . . . ★
  Vicinity . . . . . . Pg. 135, A-9
Bird Island J-4
Biwabik D-7
Blackduck D-4
Blomkest J-3
Blooming Prairie K-6
Bloomington . . . . ★
  Vicinity . . . . . . Pg. 134, F-3
Blue Earth L-5
Bluffton F-3
Bock G-5
Borup D-2
Bovey D-5
Bowstring D-5
Boy River D-5
Boyd J-2
Braham G-6
Brainerd F-4
Branch H-6
Brandon G-3
Breckenridge F-1
Brewster L-2
Britt D-7
Brook Park G-6
Brooklyn Center . . . . . . ★
  Vicinity . . . . . . Pg. 134, A-4
Brooklyn Park . . . . ★
  Vicinity . . . . . . Pg. 134, A-2
Brooks C-2
Brookston E-7
Brooten H-3
Browerville F-4
Browns Valley G-1
Brownsdale L-6
Brownsville L-8
Brownton J-4
Bruno F-7
Buffalo H-5
Buffalo Lake J-4
Buhl D-6
Burnsville . . . . ★
  Vicinity . . . . . Pg. 134, G-4
Burtrum G-4
Butterfield K-4
Buyck C-7
Byron K-7
Caledonia L-8
Callaway E-2
Cambridge H-6
Campbell F-2
Canby J-1
Cannon Falls J-6
Canyon E-7
Carlos G-3
Carlton E-7
Cass Lake D-4
Cedar Mills J-4

Centerville K-8
Ceylon L-4
Chandler K-2
Chaska J-5
Chatfield L-7
Chickamaw Beach E-4
Chisholm D-6
Clara City H-3
Claremont K-6
Clarissa F-3
Clarkfield J-2
Clarks Grove L-6
Clear Lake H-5
Clearbrook D-3
Clearwater H-5
Clements K-3
Clementson B-4
Climax D-1
Clinton H-1
Clitherall F-3
Clontarf H-3
Cloquet E-7
Cokato H-5
Cold Spring H-4
Coleraine D-6
Cologne J-5
Columbia Hts. . . . . ★
  Vicinity . . . . . . Pg. 134, A-4
Comfrey K-4
Comstock E-1
Cook C-7
Coon Rapids H-6
Correll H-2
Cosmos J-4
Cottage Grove J-6
Cotton E-7
Cottonwood J-2
Croftville D-10
Cromwell E-6
Crookston C-2
Crosby F-5
Crystal . . . . ★
  Vicinity . . . . . . Pg. 134, A-3
Currie K-2
Cushing F-4
Cuyuna F-5
Cyrus G-2
Dakota K-8
Dalton F-2
Danube J-3
Danvers H-2
Darfur K-4
Dassel H-4
Dawson H-2
De Graff H-3
Deer River D-5
Deerwood F-5
Delano H-5
Dent F-2
Detroit Lakes E-2
Dilworth E-1
Dodge Center K-6
Donaldson B-1
Donnelly G-2
Doran F-2
Dovray K-3
Duluth E-7
Dumont G-2
Dunnell L-4
Duquette F-7
Eagle Bend F-3
Eagle Lake K-5
East Bethel H-6
East Grand Forks C-1
East Gull Lake F-4
Easton L-5
Echo J-3
Eden Prairie . . . . ★
  Vicinity . . . . . . Pg. 134, E-1
Eden Valley H-4
Edgerton K-2
Edina . . . . ★
  Vicinity . . . . . . Pg. 134, E-3
Effie C-5
Elbow Lake G-2
Eldred D-1
Elgin K-7
Elizabeth F-2
Elk River H-6
Ellendale K-6
Ellsworth L-2
Elmer E-6
Elmore L-5
Elrosa G-3
Ely C-8
Emily E-5
Erhard F-2
Ericsburg B-6
Erskine D-2
Evansville G-3
Eveleth D-7
Eyota K-7
Fairfax J-4
Faribault K-6
Fairmont L-4
Falcon Heights . . . . ★
  Vicinity . . . . . . Pg. 134, C-6
Farmington J-6
Farwell G-2
Felton E-2
Fergus Falls F-2
Fertile D-2
Finland D-8
Finlayson F-6
Fisher C-1
Flom E-2

Floodwood E-6
Florence K-2
Foley G-5
Forbes D-7
Forest Lake H-6
Fort Ripley F-4
Fosston D-3
Fountain L-7
Fox Home F-2
Franklin J-3
Frazee E-3
Freeport G-4
Fridley . . . . ★
  Vicinity . . . . . . Pg. 134, A-4
Frost L-5
Fulda K-3
Funkley C-4
Garfield G-3
Garrison F-5
Garvin K-2
Gary D-2
Gatzke B-3
Gaylord J-5
Gem Lake . . . . ★
  Vicinity . . . . . . Pg. 135, A-8
Geneva L-6
Georgetown E-1
Gheen C-7
Gibbon J-4
Gilbert D-7
Gilman G-5
Glencoe J-5
Glenville L-6
Glenwood G-3
Gluek H-3
Glyndon E-1
Golden Valley . . . . ★
  Vicinity . . . . . . Pg. 134, B-2
Gonvick D-3
Good Thunder K-5
Goodhue K-7
Goodland E-6
Goodridge C-3
Goodview K-8
Graceton B-4
Graceville G-2
Granby G-6
Grand Falls C-5
Grand Marais D-9
Grand Meadow L-7
Grand Portage C-10
Grand Rapids D-5
Granite Falls J-2
Grasston G-6
Greenbush B-2
Greenfield H-5
Grey Eagle G-4
Grove City H-4
Grygla C-3
Gully D-3
Guthrie D-4
Hackensack E-4
Hallock B-1
Halma B-2
Halstad D-1
Ham Lake H-6
Hancock H-2
Hanley Falls J-3
Hanska K-4
Harding F-5
Hardwick L-1
Harmony L-7
Harris H-6
Hastings J-6
Hawley E-2
Hayfield K-7
Hayward L-6
Hazel Run J-2
Hector J-4
Heidelberg J-5
Henderson J-5
Hendricks J-1
Hendrum D-1
Henning F-3
Herman G-2
Hermantown E-7
Heron Lake L-3
Hewitt F-3
Hibbing D-6
Hill City E-5
Hills L-1
Hilltop . . . . ★
  Vicinity . . . . . . Pg. 134, A-4
Hinckley G-6
Hines C-4
Hitterdal E-2
Hoffman G-2
Hokah L-8
Holland K-2
Holloway H-2
Holt C-2
Holyoke F-7
Hope K-6
Hopkins . . . . ★
  Vicinity . . . . . Pg. 134, D-2
Houston L-8
Hovland C-10
Howard Lake H-5
Hoyt Lakes D-7
Humboldt B-1
Hutchinson J-4
Ihlen K-1
Independence H-5
Indus B-5
International Falls B-5

Inver Grove Hts. . . . . . . ★
  Vicinity . . . . . . Pg. 135, F-8
Iona K-2
Ironton F-5
Isabella D-8
Isanti H-6
Isle F-5
Ivanhoe J-2
Jackson L-4
Jacobson E-6
Janesville K-5
Jasper K-1
Jeffers K-3
Jenkins E-4
Johnson G-2
Jordan J-5
Karlstad B-2
Kasota K-5
Kasson K-7
Keewatin D-6
Kelliher C-4
Kellog K-7
Kelsey E-7
Kennedy B-1
Kensington G-2
Kent F-1
Kenyon K-6
Kerkhoven H-3
Kerrick F-7
Kettle River F-6
Kiester L-5
Kimball H-5
Kingston H-4
Knife River E-8
La Crescent L-8
La Prairie E-6
Lafayette J-4
Lake Benton K-2
Lake Bronson B-1
Lake City J-7
Lake Crystal K-4
Lake Elmo . . . . ★
  Vicinity . . . . . Pg. 135, B-10
Lake George D-3
Lake Henry H-4
Lake Lillian J-4
Lake Park E-2
Lake Shore F-4
Lake Wilson K-2
Lakefield L-3
Lakeville J-6
Lamberton K-3
Lancaster A-1
Lanesboro L-8
Laporte E-4
Larsmont E-8
Lastrup G-5
Lauderdale . . . . ★
  Vicinity . . . . . Pg. 134, B-5
Le Center K-5
LeRoy L-7
LeSueur J-5
Lengby D-3
Leonard D-3
Lester Prairie J-5
Lewiston K-8
Lilydale . . . . ★
  Vicinity . . . . . Pg. 135, D-6
Linden Grove C-6
Lindford B-5
Lindstrom H-6
Lismore L-2
Litchfield H-4
Little Canada . . . . ★
  Vicinity . . . . . Pg. 135, B-7
Little Falls G-5
Little Fork B-5
Little Rock G-5
Lockhart D-2
Loman B-5
Long Prairie G-4
Longville E-5
Lonsdale J-5
Lowry G-3
Lucan J-3
Lutsen D-9
Luverne L-2
Lyle L-6
Lynd K-2
Mable L-8
Madelia K-4
Madison H-2
Madison Lake K-5
Magnolia L-2
Mahnomen D-2
Mahtomedi . . . . ★
  Vicinity . . . . . Pg. 135, A-9
Mahtowa F-6
Malmo F-6
Manchester L-5
Mankato K-4
Mantorville K-7
Maple Lake H-5
Mapleton K-5
Mapleview L-6
Maplewood . . . . ★
  Vicinity . . . . . Pg. 135, B-8
Marcell D-5
Margie C-5
Marietta H-1
Markham D-7
Marshall J-2
McGrath F-6
McGregor F-6
McIntosh D-2

Meadowlands E-7
Medford K-6
Meire Grove G-3
Melrose G-3
Menagha E-3
Mendota . . . . ★
  Vicinity . . . . . Pg. 134, E-6
Mendota Hts. . . . . ★
  Vicinity . . . . . Pg. 135, E-7
Mentor D-2
Middle River B-2
Milaca G-5
Milan H-2
Millville K-7
Miltona G-3
Minneapolis J-5
  Vicinity . . . . Pg. 134
Minneota J-2
Minnesota Lake K-5
Minnetonka . . . . ★
  Vicinity . . . . . Pg. 134, D-1
Mizpah C-5
Montevideo H-3
Montgomery J-5
Monticello H-5
Moorhead E-1
Moose Lake F-6
Mora G-6
Morgan J-3
Morris G-2
Morton J-4
Motley F-4
Mountain Iron D-7
Mountain Lake K-3
Murdock H-3
Myrtle L-6
Nashua F-2
Nashwauk D-6
Nassau H-1
Nay-Tah-Waush D-3
Nevis E-4
New Brighton . . . . ★
  Vicinity . . . . . Pg. 134, A-5
New Hope . . . . ★
  Vicinity . . . . . Pg. 134, B-2
New London H-4
New Prague J-5
New Richland K-5
New Ulm K-4
New York Mills F-3
Newfolden B-2
Nicollet K-4
Nielsville D-1
Nimrod E-4
Nisswa F-4
Norcross G-2
North Branch H-6
North Mankato K-5
North St. Paul . . . . ★
  Vicinity . . . . . Pg. 135, B-9
Northfield J-6
Northome C-4
Northrop L-4
Norwood J-5
Noyes A-1
Oak Island A-4
Oakdale . . . . ★
  Vicinity . . . . . Pg. 135, C-9
Odessa H-1
Ogema E-2
Ogilvie G-6
Oklee C-2
Olivia J-3
Onamia G-5
Orleans A-1
Ormsby K-4
Oronoco K-7
Orr C-6
Ortonville H-2
Osage E-3
Osakis G-3
Oslo C-1
Ottertail F-3
Outing E-4
Owatonna K-6
Palisade E-6
Park Rapids E-3
Parkers Prairie F-3
Paynesville H-4
Pelican Rapids F-2
Pencer B-3
Pennock H-3
Perley E-1
Pierz G-5
Pine City G-6
Pine Island K-7
Pine River E-4
Pine Springs . . . . ★
  Vicinity . . . . Pg. 135, A-9
Pinewood D-3
Pipestone K-1
Pitt B-4
Plainview K-7
Plummer C-2
Plymouth . . . . ★
  Vicinity . . . . . Pg. 134, A-1
Ponemah C-4
Ponsford E-3
Porter J-2
Preston L-7
Princeton G-5
Prinsburg J-3
Prior Lake J-5
Proctor E-7
Quamba G-6

Randall F-4
Randolph J-6
Raudette B-4
Ray B-6
Raymond H-3
Red Lake C-3
Red Lake Falls C-2
Red Wing J-7
Redby C-4
Redwood Falls J-3
Regal H-4
Remer E-5
Renville J-3
Rice G-5
Richfield . . . . ★
  Vicinity . . . . . Pg. 134, E-4
Richmond H-4
Richville F-2
Robbinsdale . . . . ★
  Vicinity . . . . . Pg. 134, B-3
Rochester K-7
Rock Creek G-6
Roosevelt B-4
Rose Creek L-6
Roseau B-3
Roseville . . . . ★
  Vicinity . . . . . Pg. 134, B-5
Ross B-2
Rothsay F-1
Round Lake L-3
Round Prairie G-4
Royalton G-4
Rush City G-6
Rushford L-8
Russell K-2
Ruthton K-2
Rutledge F-7
Sabin E-1
Sacred Heart J-3
Warraska B-3
Saint Anthony . . . . ★
  Vicinity . . . . . Pg. 134, B-5
Saint Charles K-7
Saint Clair K-5
Saint Cloud H-5
Saint Francis H-6
Saint Hilaire C-2
Saint James K-4
Saint Joseph G-4
Saint Louis Park . . . . . . ★
  Vicinity . . . . . Pg. 134, D-2
Saint Michael H-5
Saint Paul . . . . ★
  Vicinity . . . . Pg. 135
Saint Paul Park . . . . ★
  Vicinity . . . . . Pg. 135, E-7
Saint Peter K-5
Saint Vincent A-1
Salol B-3
Sanborn K-3
Sandstone G-7
Sartell G-5
Sauk Centre G-4
Sauk Rapids G-4
Saum C-4
Sawyer F-6
Scanlon F-7
Schroeder D-9
Sebeka E-3
Sedan G-3
Shakopee J-5
Shelly D-1
Sherburn L-4
Shevlin D-3
Shoreview . . . . ★
  Vicinity . . . . . Pg. 135, A-6
Silver Bay D-9
Silver Lake J-4
Slayton K-2
Sleepy Eye K-4
Solway D-3
South International Falls . B-6
South St. Paul . . . . ★
  Vicinity . . . . . Pg. 135, E-8
Spicer H-4
Spring Grove L-8
Spring Lake D-5
Spring Valley L-7
Springfield K-4
Squaw Lake D-5
Staples F-4
Starbuck G-3
Stephen B-1
Stewartville K-7
Storden K-3
Strandquist B-2
Strathcona B-2
Sturgeon Lake F-7
Sunberg H-3
Sunfish Lake . . . . ★
  Vicinity . . . . . Pg. 135, E-7
Swan River E-6
Swanville G-4
Swatara E-5
Swift B-3
Taconite D-6
Taconite Harbor D-9
Talmoon D-5
Tamarack F-6
Taunton J-2
Taylors Falls H-7
Tenney F-1
Tenstrike D-4
Terrace H-3
Thief River Falls C-2
Togo C-6

Tommald F-5
Toopi L-7
Tower C-7
Tracy K-3
Trail C-3
Trimont L-4
Trosky K-2
Truman L-4
Turtle River D-4
Twig E-7
Twin Lakes L-5
Twin Valley D-2
Two Harbors E-8
Tyler K-2
Ulen E-2
Underwood F-2
Vadnais Hts. . . . . ★
  Vicinity . . . . . Pg. 135, A-7
Verdi K-1
Vergas F-2
Verndale F-3
Vesta J-3
Viking B-2
Villard G-3
Vining F-3
Viola K-7
Virginia D-7
Wabasha K-7
Wabasso J-3
Waconia J-5
Wadena F-3
Wahkon F-5
Waite Park H-4
Walker E-4
Walnut Grove K-3
Waltham L-6
Wanamingo K-6
Warba E-6
Warren C-1
Warroad B-3
Waseca K-6
Waskish C-4
Watertown J-5
Waterville K-5
Watkins H-4
Watson H-2
Waubun E-2
Wawina E-6
Welcome L-4
Wells L-5
West Concord K-6
West St. Paul . . . . ★
  Vicinity . . . . . Pg. 135, E-7
Westbrook K-3
Wheaton G-1
Whipholt E-4
White Bear Lake . . . . . . ★
  Vicinity . . . . . Pg. 135, A-9
White Earth E-2
Wilder L-3
Willernie . . . . ★
  Vicinity . . . . . Pg. 135, A-9
Williams B-4
Willmar H-3
Willow River F-6
Wilton D-3
Windom K-3
Winger D-2
Winnebago L-5
Winona K-8
Winthrop J-4
Winton C-8
Wirt D-5
Wolf Lake E-3
Wolverton F-1
Woodbury J-6
Woodland . . . . ★
  Vicinity . . . . . Pg. 135, D-10
Woodland D-10
Worthington L-3
Wrenshall F-7
Wyoming H-6
Zemple D-5
Zim D-7
Zimmerman H-6
Zumbro Falls K-7
Zumbrota K-7

MISSISSIPPI

MISSISSIPPI
Page 56

Abbeville B-5
Aberdeen C-6
Ackerman D-5
Alcorn G-2
Algoma B-5
Alligator C-3
Amory C-6
Anguilla E-3
Arcola D-3
Arkabutla A-4
Artesia D-6
Ashland A-5
Askew B-3
Avalon D-4
Avon D-2
Bailey F-6
Baird D-3
Baldwyn B-5
Banner B-5
Bassfield H-4
Batesville B-4
Baxterville H-5
Bay Saint Louis K-5

Bay Springs G-5
Beaumont H-6
Beauregard G-3
Becker C-6
Belden B-6
Belen B-3
Bellefontaine C-5
Belmont A-6
Belzoni D-3
Benoit D-2
Benton E-4
Bentonia E-3
Beulah C-2
Big Creek C-4
Bigbee Valley D-6
Biloxi K-6
Blue Mountain A-5
Bogue Chitto H-3
Bolton F-3
Booneville A-6
Boyle C-3
Brandon F-4
Braxton G-4
Brookhaven H-3
Brooklyn H-5
Brooksville D-6
Bruce C-4
Buckatunna G-6
Bude H-3
Burnsville A-6
Byhalia A-4
Caledonia C-6
Calhoun City C-5
Call Town J-6
Camden E-4
Canton E-4
Carlisle G-3
Carpenter G-3
Carriere J-5
Carrollton D-4
Carson H-4
Carthage E-5
Cary E-3
Cascilla C-4
Cedarbluff C-5
Centreville J-3
Charleston C-4
Chatawa J-4
Chatham E-2
Chunky F-6
Church Hill G-2
Clara G-6
Clarksdale B-3
Cleveland C-3
Cliftonville D-6
Clinton F-3
Coahoma B-3
Coffeeville C-4
Coila D-4
Coldwater A-4
Collins G-5
Collinsville E-6
Columbia H-4
Columbus C-6
Como B-4
Conehatta F-5
Corinth A-6
Courtland B-4
Crawford D-6
Crenshaw B-3
Crosby H-2
Cross Roads A-6
Crowder B-3
Crystal Springs G-3
D'Lo G-4
Daleville E-6
Darling B-3
Darlove D-3
DeKalb E-6
Decatur F-5
Dennis A-6
Derma C-5
Doddsville D-3
Dorsey B-6
Drew C-3
Dublin C-3
Duck Hill C-4
Dumas A-5
Duncan C-3
Dundee B-3
Durant D-4
Eastabuchie H-5
Ebenezer E-4
Ecru B-5
Eden E-4
Edinburg E-5
Edwards F-3
Electric Mills E-6
Elizabeth D-3
Ellisville G-5
Enid B-4
Enterprise F-6
Ethel D-5
Etta B-5
Eupora D-5
Falcon B-3
Falkner A-5
Fannin F-4
Fayette G-2
Fitler E-2
Flora F-3

★ Denotes City only on Vicinity map. City not located on State map.

MISSISSIPPI

Florence F-4
Forest F-5
Forkville F-4
Fort Adams H-2
Foxworth H-4
French Camp D-5
Friar's Pt. B-3
Fruitland Park J-5
Fulton B-6
Futheyville C-4
Gallman G-3
Gattman C-6
Gautier K-6
Georgetown G-4
Gholson E-6
Gillsburg J-3
Glen A-6
Glen Allan E-2
Glendora C-3
Gloster H-2
Golden B-6
Goodman E-4
Gore Springs C-4
Grace E-2
Grand Gulf G-2
Greenville D-2
Greenwood C-4
Grenada C-4
Gulfport K-6
Gunnison C-2
Guntown B-6
Hamilton C-6
Harperville F-5
Harriston G-2
Harrisville G-3
Hatley B-6
Hattiesburg H-5
Hazlehurst G-3
Heidelberg G-6
Helena H-6
Hermanville G-3
Hernando A-4
Hickory F-5
Hickory Flat A-5
Hilhouse C-2
Hillsboro F-5
Homewood F-5
Horn C-5
Houston C-5
Hurley J-6
Independence A-4
Indianola D-3
Inverness D-3
Isola D-3
Iuka A-6
Jackson F-4
Jayess H-4
Johnstons Station H-4
Jonestown B-3
Kewanee F-6
Kilmichael D-4
Kiln K-5
Kokomo E-5
Kosciusko E-5
Lafayette Springs B-5
Lake F-5
Lake View ★
  Vicinity Pg. 131, G-2
Lakeshore K-5
Lambert B-3
Lauderdale E-4
Laurel G-5
Lawrence F-5
LeFlore B-6
Leaf H-6
Leakesville H-6
Leland D-3
Lena E-4
Lessley H-2
Lexington D-4
Liberty H-3
Little Rock F-5
Long Beach K-5
Lorman F-2
Louin F-5
Louise E-3
Louisville D-5
Lucedale J-6
Lucien H-3
Ludlow F-4
Lula B-3
Lumberton J-5
Lyman J-5
Lyon B-3
Maben D-5
Macon E-5
Madden E-5
Madison F-4
Magee G-4
Magnolia H-3
Mantachie B-6
Mantee C-5
Marietta B-6
Marion F-6
Marks B-3
Martinsville G-3
Mathiston D-5
McAdams E-4
McCall Creek H-3

McCarley D-4
McComb H-3
McCondy C-5
McCool D-5
McHenry J-5
McLain H-6
McNeill J-5
Meadville H-3
Mendenhall G-4
Meridian F-6
Merigold C-3
Metcalfe D-2
Michigan City A-5
Mineral Wells A-4
  Vicinity Pg. 131, G-7
Minter City C-3
Mize G-5
Money C-3
Monticello H-4
Montpelier C-5
Montrose F-5
Mooreville B-6
Moorhead D-3
Morgan City D-3
Morgantown H-4
Morton F-4
Moselle H-5
Moss G-5
Moss Point K-6
Mound Bayou C-3
Mount Olive G-5
Myrtle A-5
Natchez H-2
Necaise J-5
Nesbit A-3
Neshoba E-5
Nettleton B-6
New Albany B-5
New Augusta H-5
New Hebron G-4
New Houlka C-5
New Site A-6
Newton F-5
Nicholson K-5
Nitta Yuma E-3
Noxapater E-5
Oak Vale H-4
Oakland C-4
Ocean Springs K-6
Ofahoma E-4
Okolona B-6
Olive Branch A-4
Oma G-4
Onward E-3
Osyka J-3
Oxford B-4
Pace C-2
Pachuta F-6
Paden A-6
Panther Burn D-3
Paris B-4
Parchman C-3
Pascagoula K-7
Pass Christian K-5
Paulding F-5
Paulette D-6
Pearl F-4
Pearlington K-5
Pelahatchie F-4
Perkinston J-5
Petal H-5
Pheba C-5
Philadelphia E-5
Philipp C-3
Picayune K-5
Pickens E-4
Pinkneyville J-2
Pinola G-4
Planterville B-6
Plum Point ★
  Vicinity Pg. 131, G-5
Pocahontas F-3
Pond J-2
Pontotoc B-5
Pope B-4
Poplarville J-5
Port Gibson G-2
Porterville E-6
Potts Camp A-5
Prairie C-6
Prairie Point D-6
Prentiss G-4
Preston E-6
Puckett F-4
Pulaski F-5
Purvis H-5
Quentin H-3
Quitman F-6
Raleigh G-5
Randolph B-5
Raymond F-3
Red Banks A-4
Redwood F-3
Reform F-4
Rena Lara B-2
Richland G-4
Richton H-6
Ridgecrest B-6
Ridgeland F-4
Rienzi A-6
Ripley A-5
Robinsonville A-3
Rolling Fork E-3
Rome C-3

Rosedale C-2
Roxie H-2
Ruleville C-3
Runnelstown H-6
Ruth H-4
Sallis E-4
Saltillo B-6
Sandersville G-6
Sandhill G-4
Sandy Hook H-5
Sanford H-5
Sarah B-3
Sardis B-4
Sarepta B-5
Satartia F-3
Saucier J-5
Savage A-3
Schlater D-3
Scobey C-4
Scooba E-6
Scott D-2
Sebastopol F-5
Seminary G-5
Senatobia A-4
Sessums D-6
Seypal Lake A-3
Shannon B-6
Sharon F-4
Shaw D-2
Shelby C-3
Sherard C-2
Sherman B-6
Shivers G-4
Shubuta F-6
Shuqualak D-6
Sibley H-2
Sidon D-4
Silver City E-3
Silver Creek G-4
Skene C-2
Slate Springs C-5
Slayden A-4
Sledge B-3
Smithdale H-3
Smithville B-6
Sontag G-4
Soso G-5
Southaven A-3
Star F-4
Starkville D-6
State Line H-6
Steens D-6
Stewart D-5
Stoneville D-2
Stonewall F-6
Stovall B-3
Stringer G-5
Sturgis H-3
Summit H-3
Sumner C-3
Sumrall H-5
Sunflower D-3
Suqualena F-5
Swan Lake C-3
Swiftown D-3
Sylvarena G-5
Taylor B-4
Taylorsville G-5
Tchula D-4
Terry G-3
Thaxton B-5
Thomastown E-4
Thorn D-5
Thornton D-3
Thyatira A-4
Tie Plant C-4
Tillatoba C-4
Tinsley E-3
Tiplersville A-5
Tippo D-3
Tishomingo A-6
Toccopola C-5
Tomnolen D-5
Toomsuba F-6
Trebloc C-6
Tremont B-6
Tula B-5
Tunica A-3
Tupelo B-5
Tutwiler C-3
Tylertown H-4
Union E-5
Union Church G-3
University B-4
Utica G-3
Vaiden D-4
Valley Park E-3
Van Vleet C-5
Vance C-3
Vancleave J-6
Vardaman C-5
Vaughan F-3
Verona B-5
Vicksburg F-3
Victoria A-4
Vossburg G-6
Wade J-6
Walls A-3
Walnut A-5
Walnut Grove E-5
Walthall C-5
Washington H-2
Water Valley B-4
Waterford A-5
Waveland K-5

Waynesboro G-6
Wayside D-2
Weathersby G-4
Webb C-3
Weir D-5
Wenasoga A-6
Wesson G-3
West Gulfport J-5
West Point C-6
Wheeler A-6
Whitfield F-4
Wiggins J-6
Winona D-4
Winstonville C-3
Woodland C-5
Woodville J-2
Yazoo City E-3

MISSOURI
Pages 52-53

Adair D-5
Adrian H-2
Advance K-9
Agency F-2
Albany D-2
Alexandria D-7
Allendale D-3
Alma G-4
Altamont E-3
Alton L-7
Amoret H-2
Anderson L-2
Annapolis K-8
Anniston K-10
Appleton City H-3
Arab K-9
Arbela D-6
Arbor Terrace ★
  Vicinity Pg. 152, E-5
Arbyrd M-9
Arcadia J-8
Archie H-3
Arcola J-3
Arkoe E-2
Arnold ★
  Vicinity Pg. 153, L-3
Arroll K-6
Arrow Rock G-4
Asbury K-2
Ash Grove K-3
Ashland G-6
Ashley F-7
Athens D-6
Atlanta E-5
Aullville G-3
Aurora K-3
Auxvasse G-6
Ava K-5
Avalon F-4
Avondale ★
  Vicinity Pg. 124, E-4
Bado K-6
Bakersfield L-6
Ballard H-3
Bardley L-7
Baring E-6
Barnard E-1
Battlefield K-4
Bay H-7
Beaufort H-7
Bel Nor ★
  Vicinity Pg. 152, E-4
Bel Ridge ★
  Vicinity Pg. 152, E-4
Bell City K-9
Bella Villa ★
  Vicinity Pg. 152, J-5
Bellair G-5
Belle J-6
Bellefontaine Neighbors ★
  Vicinity Pg. 152, D-6
Bellerive ★
  Vicinity Pg. 152, E-4
Belton G-2
Bem H-7
Bendavis K-5
Bennett Springs J-5
Benton K-10
Berdell Hills ★
  Vicinity Pg. 152, E-5
Berkeley ★
  Vicinity Pg. 152, E-4
Bernie L-9
Bertrand K-10
Bethany D-3
Bethel E-6
Beulah J-6
Beverly Hills ★
  Vicinity Pg. 152, E-5
Bevier E-5
Bible Grove D-6
Bigelow E-1
Bigspring G-7
Birch Tree K-7
Birmingham ★
  Vicinity Pg. 124, E-5
Bismark J-8
Bixby J-7
Black Jack ★
  Vicinity Pg. 152, C-5
Black Walnut ★
  Vicinity Pg. 152, A-3
Blackburn G-4

Blodgett K-10
Bloomfield K-9
Blue Eye L-4
Blue Springs G-3
Blue Summit ★
  Vicinity Pg. 125, D-5
Blythedale D-3
Bogard F-3
Bolckow E-2
Bolivar J-4
Bonne Terre J-8
Boonesboro G-5
Boonville G-4
Bosherton ★
  Vicinity Pg. 152, B-2
Bosworth F-4
Bourbon H-7
Bowling Green F-7
Boynton D-4
Bradleyville L-4
Branson L-4
Braymer F-3
Brazeau J-10
Breckenridge E-3
Breckenridge Hills ★
  Vicinity Pg. 152, E-3
Brentwood ★
  Vicinity Pg. 153, G-4
Briar L-8
Bridgeton ★
  Vicinity Pg. 152, D-3
Bridgeton Terrace ★
  Vicinity Pg. 152, D-3
Brighton K-4
Brimson E-4
Brinktown J-6
Bronaugh J-2
Brookfield E-4
Broseley L-9
Brownbranch L-5
Browning E-4
Brumley K-5
Bruner K-5
Brunswick F-4
Buckhorn K-9
Bucklin E-5
Buckner G-3
Buffalo J-4
Bunker J-7
Burlington Jct. D-1
Butler H-2
Caboll K-6
Cainsville D-3
Cairo F-5
California G-5
Callao E-5
Calverton Park ★
  Vicinity Pg. 152, D-4
Calwood G-6
Camdenton H-5
Cameron E-3
Campbell L-9
Canton E-7
Cape Girardeau K-9
Caplinger Mills J-3
Cardwell M-9
Carrington G-6
Carrollton F-3
Carsonville ★
  Vicinity Pg. 152, E-4
Carthage K-2
Caruthersville M-10
Cascade K-9
Cassville L-3
Catherine Place J-9
Caulfield L-6
Center F-7
Centerville J-8
Centralia F-6
Chadwick L-4
Chaffee K-10
Chain-O-Lakes ★
Chamois G-6
Champ ★
  Vicinity Pg. 152, D-2
Charlack ★
  Vicinity Pg. 152, E-4
Charleston K-10
Cherryville J-7
Chilhowee G-3
Chillicothe E-4
Chula E-4
Clarence E-6
Clarksdale E-2
Clarksville F-7
Clarkton L-9
Claycomo ★
  Vicinity Pg. 124, D-5
Clayton ★
  Vicinity Pg. 153, F-4
Clearmont D-1
Clever K-4
Clifton City G-4
Climax Springs H-4
Clinton H-3
Clyde D-2
Coal H-3
Coatsville D-5
Coldwater K-8
Cole Camp H-4
Collins J-3
Coloma F-4
Columbia G-6
  Vicinity Pg. 124, B-2
Concordia G-3
Connelsville D-5

Conway J-5
Cook Station J-7
Cool Valley ★
  Vicinity Pg. 152, D-4
Corning D-1
Corridon K-7
Couch L-7
Country Club Hills ★
  Vicinity Pg. 152, E-5
County Life Acres ★
  Vicinity Pg. 153, H-3
Craig E-1
Crane K-4
Crestwood ★
  Vicinity Pg. 153, H-3
Creve Coeur ★
  Vicinity Pg. 152, F-2
Crocker J-6
Cross Timbers H-4
Crystal Lake Park ★
Cuba H-7
Cul Du Sac ★
Curryville F-7
Cyrene F-7
Dadeville J-3
De Soto H-8
Dearborn F-2
Deerfield J-2
Defiance G-8
Dellwood ★
  Vicinity Pg. 152, D-5
Denver D-3
Des Arc K-8
Des Peres H-7
Desloge J-8
Dexter K-9
Diamond K-2
Dixon J-6
Doe Run J-8
Dongola L-8
Doniphan L-8
Doolittle J-6
Dorena L-10
Downing D-5
Drexel H-2
Drury K-5
Duenweg K-2
Duncans Bridge F-5
Dunlap J-6
Dunnegan J-4
Durham E-7
Dutchtown K-9
Eagleville D-3
East Prairie L-10
Ectonville ★
  Vicinity Pg. 124, A-5
Edgar Springs J-6
Edgerton F-2
Edina E-6
Edinburg E-3
Edmundson ★
  Vicinity Pg. 152, D-3
El Dorado Springs J-3
Eldon H-4
Eldridge J-5
Elkland J-4
Ellington K-7
Ellsinore K-8
Elm Point ★
  Vicinity Pg. 152, B-1
Elmira F-3
Elmo D-1
Elsberry F-8
Elvins J-8
Elwood E-2
Emden E-6
Eminence K-7
Emma G-4
Essex L-9
Esther J-8
Ethel E-5
Eudora J-4
Eunice K-6
Eureka H-8
Everton K-3
Ewing E-7
Excello F-5
Excelsior Springs F-2
Exeter L-3
Fagus L-9
Fair Grove K-4
Fair Play J-4
Fairdealing L-8
Fairfax D-1
Fairmont H-3
Fairview K-6
Farber F-6
Farley F-2
Farmersville E-4
Farmington J-9
Farrar J-9
Faucett F-2
Fayette F-5
Fayetteville K-3
Fenton ★
  Vicinity Pg. 153, J-2
Ferguson ★
  Vicinity Pg. 124, D-4
Ferrelview F-2
Festus H-8
Filley J-3

Fillmore E-2
Fisk L-9
Flat River J-8
Flordell Hills ★
  Vicinity Pg. 152, E-5
Florence G-4
Florida F-6
Florissant ★
  Vicinity Pg. 152, C-4
Foley G-8
Forbes E-1
Fordland K-4
Forest City E-1
Forest Green F-5
Foristell G-8
Forsyth L-4
Fortescue E-1
Fortuna H-5
Fountain Grove E-4
Frankford F-7
Frederick Town J-9
Freeburg H-6
Fremont K-7
French Village J-9
Frontenac ★
  Vicinity Pg. 153, G-3
Fulton G-6
Gainesville L-5
Galena L-3
Gallatin E-3
Galt E-4
Garden City H-3
Garwood K-8
Gatewood L-7
Gentry D-2
Gerald H-7
Gilliam F-4
Gladden J-7
Gladstone ★
  Vicinity Pg. 124, D-4
Glasgow F-5
Glen Echo Park ★
  Vicinity Pg. 152, E-4
Glenaire ★
  Vicinity Pg. 124, D-5
Glendale ★
  Vicinity Pg. 153, G-3
Glenwood D-5
Glover J-8
Golden City K-3
Goodfellow Terr. ★
  Vicinity Pg. 152, E-5
Goodman L-2
Gower F-2
Graham D-1
Grain Valley G-3
Granby K-3
Grand Pass F-4
Grandin L-8
Grandview ★
  Vicinity Pg. 125, L-4
Granger D-6
Grant City D-2
Grantwood Village ★
  Vicinity Pg. 153, H-4
Granville F-6
Grassy K-9
Gray Summit H-8
Graysville D-5
Green City D-4
Green Ridge G-4
Greencastle D-5
Greendale ★
  Vicinity Pg. 153, G-3
Greenfield K-3
Greensburg D-6
Greentop D-5
Greenville K-8
Greenwood ★
  Vicinity Pg. 124, D-2
Greer L-6
Grovespring K-5
Halfway J-4
Hallsville F-6
Halltown K-3
Hamilton E-3
Hanley Hills ★
  Vicinity Pg. 152, E-4
Hannibal E-7
Hardin F-3
Harris D-4
Harrisburg G-5
Harrisonville G-3
Hartford D-5
Hartville K-5
Hartwell H-3
Harwood J-3
Hatfield D-3
Hawk Point G-7
Hayti M-9
Hayti Heights M-10
Hazelwood ★
  Vicinity Pg. 152, C-4
Helena E-2
Hermann G-7
Hermitage J-4
Higbee F-5
High Point H-5
Higginsville G-3
Hillsboro H-8
Hillsdale ★
  Vicinity Pg. 152, E-5
Hinton G-5
Hitt D-5
Holcomb L-9

Holden G-3
Hollister L-4
Holt F-2
Holts Summit G-6
Hoover ★
  Vicinity Pg. 124, A-2
Hopkins D-2
Hornersville M-9
House Springs H-8
Houston K-6
Houston Lake ★
  Vicinity Pg. 124, D-3
Houstonia G-4
Humansville J-4
Humphreys E-4
Hunter K-8
Huntleigh ★
  Vicinity Pg. 153, G-3
Huntsdale G-5
Huntsville F-5
Hurdland E-6
Hurricane Deck H-5
Iberia H-6
Idlewild K-9
Independence G-3
  Vicinity Pg. 125, D-4
Ironton J-8
Jackson J-10
Jacksonville F-5
Jameson E-3
Jamesport E-3
Jamestown G-5
Jane L-2
Jasper K-2
Jefferson City H-5
Jenkins L-3
Jennings ★
  Vicinity Pg. 152, G-9
Jerico Springs J-3
Joplin K-2
Kahoka D-6
Kansas City G-2
  Vicinity Pg. 124-125
Kearney F-2
  Vicinity Pg. 124, A-7
Kendricktown K-3
Kennett M-9
Kerrville ★
  Vicinity Pg. 124, A-2
Keytesville E-4
Kidder E-3
Kimberling City L-4
King City E-2
Kingston F-3
Kinloch ★
  Vicinity Pg. 152, D-4
Kirksville E-5
Kirkwood ★
  Vicinity Pg. 153, G-2
Kliever G-5
Knob Noster G-3
Knox City E-6
Knoxville F-3
Koshkonong L-7
La Grange E-7
La Plata E-6
La Tour G-3
LaBelle E-6
LaMonte G-4
Laddonia F-6
Ladue ★
  Vicinity Pg. 153, G-3
Lake Lotawana G-2
Lake Saint Louis G-8
Lake Spring J-7
Lake Waukomis ★
  Vicinity Pg. 124, D-2
Lakenan F-6
Lakeshire ★
  Vicinity Pg. 153, J-4
Lamar J-3
Lancaster D-5
Lanton L-6
Lathrop F-2
Latty J-8
Lawson F-3
Leadwood J-8
Leasburg H-7
Lebanon J-5
Lee's Summit ★
  Vicinity Pg. 125, K-5
Leeper K-8
Lenox H-3
Lemons D-4
Lentner E-5
Leonard E-5
Lewistown E-7
Lexington F-3
Liberal J-2
Liberty F-2
  Vicinity Pg. 124, C-5
Licking J-6
Lilbourn L-10
Lincoln H-4
Linn H-6
Linneus E-4
Lockwood K-3
Lone Jack G-3
Long Lane J-5
Longrun L-5
Longwood G-4
Louisiana F-7
Lowry City H-3
Ludlow F-3

MISSOURI

★ Denotes City only on Vicinity map. City not located on State map.

MISSOURI

Luray . . . D-6
Macks Creek . . . J-5
Macon . . . E-5
Madison . . . F-6
Malden . . . L-9
Manchester . . . G-8
  Vicinity . . . Pg. 153, G-1
Manes . . . K-5
Mansfield . . . K-5
Maplewood . . . ★
  Vicinity . . . Pg. 153, G-4
Marais Croche . . . ★
  Vicinity . . . Pg. 152, B-3
Marble Hills . . . K-9
Marcelene . . . E-4
March . . . J-4
Margona . . . ★
  Vicinity . . . Pg. 152, E-4
Marionville . . . K-4
Marlborough . . . ★
  Vicinity . . . Pg. 153, H-4
Marshall . . . F-4
Marshfield . . . K-5
Marthasville . . . G-7
Martinsburg . . . G-6
Mary Ridge . . . ★
  Vicinity . . . Pg. 152, E-3
Maryville . . . D-1
Matthews . . . L-10
Maxville . . . ★
  Vicinity . . . Pg. 153, L-3
Maysville . . . E-2
McBaine . . . G-5
McFall . . . E-2
Melbourne . . . E-3
Memphis . . . D-5
Mendon . . . F-4
Mercer . . . D-4
Mexico . . . F-6
Miami . . . F-4
Miami Station . . . F-4
Middle Grove . . . F-6
Midway . . . G-5
Milan . . . E-4
Milford . . . J-3
Mill Grove . . . D-4
Millard . . . E-5
Miller . . . K-3
Millersburg . . . G-6
Milo . . . J-2
Mineola . . . G-7
Miner . . . K-10
Mirabile . . . F-3
Moberly . . . F-5
Mokane . . . G-6
Moline Acres . . . ★
  Vicinity . . . Pg. 152, D-5
Monett . . . K-3
Monroe City . . . F-6
Montevallo . . . J-3
Montgomery City . . . G-7
Monticello . . . E-6
Montreal . . . J-5
Montrose . . . H-3
Moody . . . L-6
Morley . . . K-10
Morrisville . . . J-4
Mound City . . . E-1
Moundville . . . J-2
Mount Moriah . . . D-3
Mount Vernon . . . K-3
Mount Zion . . . K-5
Mountain Grove . . . K-5
Mountain View . . . K-7
Murphy . . . ★
  Vicinity . . . Pg. 153, K-1
Myrtle . . . L-7
Mystic . . . E-4
Nashville . . . K-2
Naylor . . . L-8
Nebo . . . J-5
Neelyville . . . L-8
Neosho . . . L-2
Nevada . . . J-2
New Bloomfield . . . G-6
New Boston . . . E-4
New Florence . . . G-7
New Franklin . . . G-5
New Hartford . . . F-7
New Haven . . . G-7
New Hope . . . F-8
New London . . . F-7
New Madrid . . . L-10
New Market . . . F-2
New Melle . . . G-7
New Point . . . E-1
Newburg . . . J-6
Niangua . . . K-5
Nixa . . . K-4
Noel . . . L-1
Norborne . . . F-3
Normandy . . . ★
  Vicinity . . . Pg. 152, E-5
Northmoor . . . ★
  Vicinity . . . Pg. 124, D-3
Northview . . . K-4
Northwoods . . . ★
  Vicinity . . . Pg. 152, E-5
Norwood . . . K-6
  Vicinity . . . Pg. 152, E-5
Noser Mill . . . H-7
Novelty . . . E-5
Novinger . . . E-4
O'Fallon . . . G-8
Oak Grove . . . G-3

Oak Hill . . . H-7
Oakland . . . ★
  Vicinity . . . Pg. 153, H-3
Oaks . . . ★
  Vicinity . . . Pg. 124, D-3
Oakview . . . ★
  Vicinity . . . Pg. 124, D-3
Oakville . . . ★
  Vicinity . . . Pg. 153, K-4
Oakwood . . . ★
  Vicinity . . . Pg. 124, D-3
Oakwood Manor . . . ★
  Vicinity . . . Pg. 124, D-4
Oakwood Park . . . ★
  Vicinity . . . Pg. 124, D-3
Ocie . . . L-5
Odessa . . . G-3
Oermann . . . H-8
Olivette . . . ★
  Vicinity . . . Pg. 152, E-3
Olympian Village . . . H-8
Oran . . . K-10
Orchard Farm . . . H-8
  Vicinity . . . Pg. 152, A-2
Oregon . . . E-1
Orrick . . . F-3
Orrick . . . F-3
Osage Beach . . . H-5
Osceola . . . H-3
Osgood . . . E-4
Oskaloosa . . . J-2
Otto . . . H-8
Overland . . . ★
  Vicinity . . . Pg. 152, E-3
Owensville . . . H-6
Ozark . . . K-4
Pacific . . . H-8
Pagedale . . . ★
  Vicinity . . . Pg. 152, E-4
Palmyra . . . E-7
Paris . . . F-6
Parkville . . . ★
  Vicinity . . . Pg. 124, D-2
Parma . . . L-9
Pasadena Hills . . . ★
  Vicinity . . . Pg. 152, E-5
Pasadena Park . . . ★
  Vicinity . . . Pg. 152, E-4
Patton . . . J-9
Pattonsburg . . . E-2
Peace Valley . . . L-6
Peach Orchard . . . L-10
Peculiar . . . G-2
Peerless Park . . . ★
  Vicinity . . . Pg. 153, H-1
Pennsboro . . . K-3
Perrin . . . E-2
Perry . . . F-6
Perryville . . . J-9
Pevely . . . H-8
Phelps . . . K-3
Philadelphia . . . E-6
Phillipsburg . . . J-5
Piedmont . . . K-8
Pierce City . . . K-3
Pilot Grove . . . G-4
Pilot Knob . . . J-8
Pine Lawn . . . ★
  Vicinity . . . Pg. 152, E-5
Pineville . . . L-2
Plad . . . J-4
Plato . . . J-6
Platte Woods . . . ★
  Vicinity . . . Pg. 124, D-2
Plattsburg . . . F-2
Pleasant Green . . . G-5
Pleasant Valley . . . ★
  Vicinity . . . Pg. 124, D-5
Plevna . . . E-6
Pocahontas . . . J-9
Polk . . . J-4
Pollock . . . D-4
Polo . . . F-3
Pomona . . . L-6
Poplar Bluff . . . L-8
Portageville . . . L-10
Potosi . . . J-8
Prairie Hill . . . F-5
Prairie Home . . . G-5
Preston . . . J-4
Princeton . . . D-4
Protem . . . L-5
Purdin . . . E-4
Purdy . . . L-3
Puxico . . . K-9
Queen City . . . D-5
Quincy . . . J-3
Qulin . . . L-9
Racine . . . K-2
Randolph . . . ★
  Vicinity . . . Pg. 124, D-4
Ravanna . . . D-4
Ravenwood . . . D-2
Raymondville . . . K-6
Raymore . . . G-2
Raytown . . . ★
  Vicinity . . . Pg. 124, F-5
Rea . . . E-2
Redford . . . K-8
Reeds Spring . . . L-4
Regal . . . L-5
Reger . . . E-3
Renick . . . F-5
Rensselaer . . . F-7
Republic . . . K-4

Reynolds . . . K-8
Rhineland . . . G-7
Rich Hill . . . H-2
Richland . . . J-5
Richmond . . . F-3
Richmond Heights . . . ★
  Vicinity . . . Pg. 153, G-4
Ridgedale . . . L-4
Ridgeway . . . D-3
Risco . . . L-9
Riverside . . . ★
  Vicinity . . . Pg. 124, E-2
Riverton . . . L-7
Riverview . . . ★
  Vicinity . . . Pg. 152, D-6
Rock Hill . . . ★
  Vicinity . . . Pg. 153, G-3
Rock Port . . . D-1
Rockville . . . H-3
Rocky Comfort . . . L-3
Rogersville . . . K-4
Rolla . . . J-6
Romance . . . J-8
Rombauer . . . K-8
Rosati . . . H-7
Rosebud . . . H-7
Rosendale . . . E-2
Rothville . . . F-4
Round Spring . . . K-7
Rover . . . L-7
Rushville . . . F-1
Saint Ann . . . ★
  Vicinity . . . Pg. 152, D-3
Saint Charles . . . G-8
  Vicinity . . . Pg. 152, C-1
Saint Clair . . . H-8
Saint Clement . . . F-7
Saint George Village . . . ★
  Vicinity . . . Pg. 153, J-4
Saint James . . . H-6
Saint John . . . ★
  Vicinity . . . Pg. 152, E-4
Saint Joseph . . . E-2
Saint Louis . . . G-8
  Vicinity . . . Pg. 152-153
Saint Marys . . . J-9
Saint Patrick . . . E-7
Saint Robert . . . J-6
Sainte Genevieve . . . H-8
Salem . . . J-7
Saline . . . D-3
Salisbury . . . F-5
Sandy Hook . . . G-5
Santa Fe . . . F-6
Sarcoxie . . . K-3
Savannah . . . E-2
Schuermann Heights . . . ★
  Vicinity . . . Pg. 152, D-4
Scott City . . . K-10
Sedalia . . . G-4
Sedgewickville . . . J-9
Seligman . . . L-3
Senath . . . M-9
Seneca . . . L-2
Seymour . . . K-5
Shannondale . . . F-5
Shelbina . . . F-6
Shelbyville . . . E-6
Sheldon . . . J-3
Sheridan . . . D-2
Shirley . . . J-8
Shrewsbury . . . ★
  Vicinity . . . Pg. 153, H-4
Sikeston . . . K-10
Silva . . . K-8
Silver Lake . . . J-9
Simmons . . . K-6
Skidmore . . . D-1
Slater . . . F-4
Sleeper . . . J-5
Sligo . . . J-7
Smithton . . . G-4
Smithville . . . F-2
South Fork . . . L-6
South Gifford . . . E-4
South Lineville . . . D-4
Southwest City . . . L-2
Sparta . . . K-4
Spickard . . . E-4
Spokane . . . L-4
Springfield . . . K-4
Squires . . . L-5
Stanberry . . . E-2
State Line . . . M-9
Steele . . . M-9
Steelville . . . J-7
Stockton . . . J-3
Stoutsville . . . F-6
Stover . . . H-4
Strafford . . . K-4
Strasburg . . . G-3
Sturgeon . . . F-5
Sugar Creek . . . ★
  Vicinity . . . Pg. 124, F-5
Sullivan . . . H-7
Summersville . . . K-7
Sumner . . . F-4
Sunset Hills . . . ★
  Vicinity . . . Pg. 153, J-3
Sweet Springs . . . G-4
Sycamore . . . L-6
Sycamore Hills . . . ★
  Vicinity . . . Pg. 152, E-4
Tarkio . . . D-1
Tebbetts . . . G-6

Thayer . . . L-7
Theodosia . . . L-5
Thomas Hill . . . F-5
Thomasville . . . L-6
Thompson . . . F-6
Thornfield . . . L-5
Tiffin . . . J-3
Tina . . . F-4
Tindall . . . E-4
Tipton . . . G-5
Town & Country . . . ★
  Vicinity . . . Pg. 153, G-2
Townley . . . L-9
Trenton . . . E-4
Troy . . . G-8
Truesdale . . . G-7
Truxton . . . G-7
Tunas . . . J-4
Turney . . . F-2
Tuscumbia . . . H-5
Twin Oaks . . . ★
  Vicinity . . . Pg. 153, H-1
Tyrone . . . K-6
Union . . . H-7
Union Star . . . E-2
Unionville . . . D-4
Unity Village . . . ★
  Vicinity . . . Pg. 125, J-6
University City . . . ★
  Vicinity . . . Pg. 152, E-4
Uplands Park . . . ★
  Vicinity . . . Pg. 152, E-5
Urich . . . H-3
Utica . . . E-3
Valley Park . . . ★
  Vicinity . . . Pg. 153, H-1
Van Buren . . . K-8
Vandalia . . . F-7
Vanzant . . . K-6
Velda . . . ★
  Vicinity . . . Pg. 152, E-5
Velda Village Heights . . . ★
  Vicinity . . . Pg. 152, E-5
Versailles . . . H-5
Viburnum . . . J-7
Vichy . . . H-6
Vienna . . . H-6
Vinita Park . . . ★
  Vicinity . . . Pg. 152, E-4
Vulcan . . . K-8
Wainwright . . . G-6
Walnut Grove . . . K-4
Wardsville . . . H-6
Warren . . . E-6
Warrensburg . . . G-3
Warrenton . . . G-7
Warsaw . . . H-4
Warson Woods . . . ★
  Vicinity . . . Pg. 153, G-3
Washington . . . G-7
Wasola . . . L-5
Waverly . . . F-4
Wayland . . . D-6
Waynesville . . . J-6
Weatherby Lake . . . ★
  Vicinity . . . Pg. 124, D-2
Weaubleau . . . J-4
Webb City . . . K-2
Weber Hill . . . H-8
Webster Groves . . . ★
  Vicinity . . . Pg. 153, G-4
Wellston . . . ★
  Vicinity . . . Pg. 152, F-5
Wellsville . . . G-7
Wentworth . . . K-3
West Alton . . . ★
  Vicinity . . . Pg. 152, B-6
West Plains . . . L-6
Westboro . . . D-1
Weston . . . F-1
Westphalia . . . H-6
White Oak . . . L-9
Wilbur Park . . . ★
  Vicinity . . . Pg. 153, H-4
Wilcox . . . D-2
Willard . . . K-4
Williamsburg . . . G-6
Williamsville . . . K-8
Willow Springs . . . K-6
Wilson City . . . K-10
Winchester . . . ★
  Vicinity . . . Pg. 153, G-1
Windsor . . . H-4
Winfield . . . G-8
Winigan . . . E-4
Winona . . . K-7
Winston . . . E-3
Winthrop . . . F-1
Woodlawn . . . F-6
Woods Heights . . . F-3
Woodson Terr. . . . ★
  Vicinity . . . Pg. 152, D-4
Wooldridge . . . G-5
Worth . . . D-2
Wyaconda . . . D-6
Yarnell . . . ★
Yarrow . . . J-9
Yount . . . J-9
Yukon . . . K-6
Zalma . . . K-9

MONTANA
Pages 54-55

Absarokee . . . H-8
Acton . . . G-9
Alberton . . . E-2
Alder . . . H-5
Alzada . . . H-14
Amsterdam . . . G-6
Anaconda . . . G-4
Angela . . . F-12
Antelope . . . B-13
Apgar . . . B-3
Arlee . . . E-3
Ashland . . . G-12
Augusta . . . D-5
Avon . . . F-4
Babb . . . B-4
Baker . . . F-14
Ballantine . . . G-10
Basin . . . F-5
Bearcreek . . . H-8
Belfry . . . H-9
Belgrade . . . G-6
Belt . . . D-6
Biddle . . . H-13
Big Arm . . . D-3
Big Fork . . . C-3
Big Sandy . . . C-7
Big Sky . . . H-6
Big Timber . . . G-7
Bighorn . . . F-10
Billings . . . G-9
Birney . . . H-11
Black Eagle . . . D-6
Blackfoot . . . B-4
Bloomfield . . . D-13
Bonner . . . E-3
Boulder . . . F-5
Box Elder . . . C-7
Boyd . . . H-8
Bozeman . . . G-6
Bozeman Hot Springs . . . H-6
Brady . . . C-6
Bridger . . . H-9
Broadus . . . H-13
Broadview . . . G-9
Brockton . . . C-13
Brockway . . . D-12
Browning . . . B-4
Busby . . . H-11
Butte . . . G-5
Bynum . . . C-5
Cameron . . . H-6
Canyon Creek . . . E-5
Capitol . . . H-14
Carter . . . D-6
Cartersville . . . F-11
Cascade . . . E-6
Checkerboard . . . F-7
Chester . . . B-7
Chico Hot Springs . . . H-7
Chinook . . . B-8
Choteau . . . D-5
Christina . . . D-8
Churchill . . . G-6
Circle . . . D-12
Cleveland . . . C-8
Clinton . . . E-3
Clyde Park . . . G-7
Coffee Creek . . . D-7
Cohagen . . . E-11
Colstrip . . . G-11
Columbia Falls . . . B-3
Columbus . . . G-8
Conner . . . G-3
Conrad . . . C-5
Cooke City . . . H-8
Coram . . . C-3
Corvallis . . . F-3
Craig . . . E-5
Crane . . . D-14
Crow Agency . . . H-10
Culbertson . . . C-13
Custer . . . G-10
Cut Bank . . . B-5
Darby . . . G-3
Dayton . . . C-3
DeBorgia . . . D-2
Dean . . . H-8
Decker . . . H-11
Deer Lodge . . . G-4
Dell . . . J-4
Denton . . . E-7
Dillon . . . H-4
Divide . . . G-4
Dixon . . . D-3
Dodson . . . C-9
Drummond . . . F-4
Dupuyer . . . C-5
Dutton . . . D-6
East Glacier Park . . . C-4
East Helena . . . F-5
Edgar . . . H-9
Ekalaka . . . G-14
Elliston . . . F-5
Elmo . . . C-3
Emigrant . . . H-6
Ennis . . . H-5
Essex . . . C-3
Ethridge . . . B-5
Eureka . . . A-2
Fairfield . . . D-5
Fairview . . . C-14

Fallon . . . E-13
Fenchtown . . . E-3
Fishtail . . . H-8
Flatwillow . . . E-9
Flaxville . . . B-12
Florence . . . F-3
Ford . . . H-12
Forestgrove . . . E-8
Forsyth . . . F-11
Fort Belknap Agency . . . B-9
Fort Benton . . . D-7
Fort Peck . . . C-11
Fort Shaw . . . D-5
Fortine . . . B-2
Four Buttes . . . B-12
Frazer . . . C-12
Froid . . . C-13
Fromberg . . . H-9
Galen . . . F-4
Gallatin Gateway . . . H-6
Gardiner . . . H-7
Garneill . . . E-8
Garrison . . . F-4
Garyowen . . . H-10
Geraldine . . . D-7
Geyser . . . E-7
Gildford . . . B-7
Glasgow . . . C-11
Glen . . . H-4
Glendive . . . E-13
Grant . . . H-4
Grantsdale . . . F-3
Grassrange . . . E-8
Great Falls . . . D-6
Hall . . . F-4
Hamilton . . . F-3
Hammond . . . H-13
Happy's Inn . . . C-2
Hardin . . . G-10
Harlem . . . B-9
Harlowtown . . . F-8
Harrison . . . G-5
Hathaway . . . F-11
Haugan . . . D-1
Havre . . . B-8
Helena . . . F-5
Helmville . . . E-4
Heron . . . C-1
Hilger . . . E-8
Hingham . . . B-7
Hinsdale . . . B-11
Hobson . . . E-7
Homestead . . . B-13
Hot Springs . . . D-2
Hungry Horse . . . C-3
Huntley . . . G-9
Huson . . . E-3
Hysham . . . F-10
Ingomar . . . F-10
Inverness . . . B-7
Jackson . . . H-4
Jefferson City . . . F-5
Joliet . . . H-8
Joplin . . . B-7
Jordan . . . E-11
Judith Gap . . . F-7
Kalispell . . . C-3
Kiowa . . . B-4
Klein . . . F-9
Kremlin . . . B-7
Lakeside . . . C-3
Lambert . . . D-13
Lame Deer . . . G-11
Laurel . . . G-9
Laurin . . . H-5
Lavina . . . F-9
Lewistown . . . E-8
Libby . . . B-1
Lima . . . J-4
Lincoln . . . E-4
Lindsay . . . D-13
Livingston . . . G-7
Lloyd . . . C-8
Lodge Grass . . . H-10
Logan . . . G-6
Lohman . . . B-8
Lolo . . . E-3
Lolo Hot Springs . . . E-2
Loma . . . D-7
Loring . . . B-10
Lothair . . . C-6
Malta . . . C-10
Manhattan . . . G-6
Marion . . . C-2
Martin City . . . C-3
Martinsdale . . . F-7
McLeod . . . G-7
Medicine Lake . . . B-13
Melrose . . . G-4
Melstone . . . F-10
Melville . . . G-7
Miles City . . . F-12
Milltown . . . E-3
Missoula . . . E-3
Moccasin . . . E-7
Monarch . . . E-6
Montague . . . D-7
Montana City . . . F-5
Moore . . . E-8
Musselshell . . . F-9
Nashua . . . C-11
Neihart . . . E-7
Niarada . . . D-2
Norris . . . H-5
Noxon . . . C-1

Nye . . . H-8
Olney . . . B-3
Opheim . . . B-11
Opportunity . . . G-4
Oswego . . . C-12
Ovando . . . E-4
Pablo . . . D-3
Paradise . . . D-2
Park City . . . H-9
Peerless . . . B-12
Pendroy . . . C-5
Philipsburg . . . F-4
Plains . . . D-2
Plentywood . . . B-13
Plevna . . . F-14
Polebridge . . . B-3
Polson . . . D-3
Pompeys Pillar . . . G-10
Poplar . . . C-13
Port of Del Bonita . . . B-5
Port of Morgan . . . B-10
Port of Opheim . . . B-11
Port of Raymond . . . A-13
Port of Whitetail . . . A-13
Potomac . . . E-4
Powderville . . . G-13
Power . . . D-5
Pray . . . H-7
Proctor . . . C-2
Radersburg . . . F-6
Rapelje . . . G-8
Ravalli . . . D-3
Raymond . . . B-13
Raynesford . . . D-7
Red Lodge . . . H-8
Redstone . . . B-13
Reedpoint . . . G-8
Reserve . . . B-13
Rexford . . . A-2
Richey . . . D-13
Richland . . . B-11
Ringling . . . F-7
Roberts . . . H-8
Rock Springs . . . E-12
Rollins . . . C-3
Ronan . . . D-3
Rosebud . . . F-12
Roundup . . . F-9
Roy . . . E-8
Rudyard . . . B-7
Ryegate . . . F-8
Saco . . . B-10
Saint Ignatius . . . D-3
Saint Mary . . . B-4
Saint Regis . . . D-2
Saltese . . . D-1
Santa Rita . . . B-5
Savage . . . D-13
Scoby . . . B-12
Seeley Lake . . . E-3
Shawmut . . . F-8
Shelby . . . B-6
Sheridan . . . H-5
Sidney . . . D-14
Silesia . . . H-9
Silver Star . . . G-5
Simms . . . D-5
Somers . . . C-3
Springdale . . . G-7
Stanford . . . E-7
Stevensville . . . F-3
Stryker . . . B-2
Suffolk . . . E-9
Sumatra . . . F-9
Sun River . . . D-6
Sunburst . . . B-5
Superior . . . D-2
Swan Lake . . . C-3
Sweetgrass . . . B-5
Tarkio . . . C-3
Teigen . . . E-9
Terry . . . E-13
Thompson Falls . . . D-1
Three Forks . . . G-6
Toston . . . F-6
Townsend . . . F-6
Trego . . . B-2
Trout Creek . . . C-1
Troy . . . B-1
Turner . . . B-9
Twin Bridges . . . H-5
Twodot . . . F-7
Ulm . . . D-6
Valier . . . C-5
Vaughn . . . D-6
Victor . . . F-3
Vida . . . C-12
Virginia City . . . H-5
Volborg . . . G-12
Walkerville . . . G-5
Warmsprings . . . F-4
Waterloo . . . G-5
West Glacier . . . B-3
West Yellowstone . . . J-6
Westby . . . A-14
White Hall . . . G-5
White Sulphur Springs . . . F-6
Whitefish . . . B-3
Whitetail . . . B-13
Wibaux . . . E-14
Willow Creek . . . G-6
Wilsall . . . G-7
Winifred . . . D-7
Winnett . . . E-9
Winston . . . F-5

Wisdom . . . G-4
Wise River . . . G-4
Wolf Creek . . . E-5
Wolf Point . . . C-12
Worden . . . G-9
Wyola . . . H-10
Yaak . . . B-1
Zurich . . . B-9

NEBRASKA
Pages 58-59

Abie . . . F-11
Adams . . . H-12
Ainsworth . . . D-7
Albion . . . E-10
Alda . . . G-9
Alexandria . . . H-11
Allen . . . D-11
Alliance . . . D-3
Alma . . . H-8
Almeria . . . E-8
Amelia . . . D-9
Ames . . . F-12
Amherst . . . G-8
Angora . . . D-3
Anoka . . . C-9
Anselmo . . . E-7
Ansley . . . F-8
Antioch . . . D-4
Arapahoe . . . H-7
Arcadia . . . F-8
Archer . . . F-10
Arlington . . . F-12
Arnold . . . F-7
Arthur . . . E-5
Ashby . . . D-4
Ashland . . . G-12
Ashton . . . F-9
Atkinson . . . D-9
Atlanta . . . H-8
Auburn . . . H-12
Aurora . . . G-10
Axtell . . . H-8
Ayr . . . H-9
Bancroft . . . E-11
Barneston . . . J-12
Bartlett . . . E-9
Bartley . . . H-6
Bassett . . . D-8
Battle Creek . . . E-10
Bayard . . . E-3
Bazile Mills . . . D-10
Beatrice . . . H-11
Beaver City . . . H-7
Beaver Crossing . . . G-11
Beemer . . . E-11
Belden . . . D-11
Belgrade . . . F-10
Bellevue . . . G-12
Bellevue . . . G-12
  Vicinity . . . Pg. 144, G-5
Belvidere . . . H-10
Benedict . . . G-10
Benkelman . . . H-5
Bennet . . . G-12
Bertrand . . . H-7
Berwyn . . . F-8
Big Springs . . . F-4
Bingham . . . D-4
Bladen . . . H-9
Blair . . . F-12
Bloomfield . . . D-10
Blue Hill . . . H-9
Blue Springs . . . H-11
Boelus . . . G-9
Boone . . . E-10
Boystown . . . F-12
Boystown . . . F-12
  Vicinity . . . Pg. 144, E-1
Bradshaw . . . G-10
Brady . . . F-6
Brandon . . . G-4
Brewster . . . E-7
Bridgeport . . . E-3
Bristow . . . C-9
Broadwater . . . E-3
Brock . . . H-12
Broken Bow . . . F-7
Brownlee . . . D-6
Brule . . . F-4
Bruning . . . H-10
Bruno . . . F-11
Brunswick . . . D-10
Burchard . . . H-12
Burton . . . C-8
Burwell . . . E-8
Bushnell . . . F-2
Butte . . . C-9
Cairo . . . G-9
Callaway . . . F-7
Cambridge . . . H-6
Campbell . . . H-9
Capehart . . . ★
  Vicinity . . . Pg. 144, H-4
Carleton . . . H-10
Carroll . . . D-11
Carter lake . . . ★
  Vicinity . . . Pg. 144, D-4
Cedar Bluffs . . . F-12
Cedar Creek . . . ★
  Vicinity . . . Pg. 144, K-1
Cedar Rapids . . . F-9

NEBRASKA

NEW JERSEY

Center ... D-10
Central City ... G-9
Ceresco ... G-12
Chadron ... C-3
Chalco ... ★
  Vicinity ... Pg. 144, F-1
Chambers ... D-9
Champion ... G-5
Chapman ... G-9
Chappell ... F-4
Chester ... J-10
Clarks ... F-10
Clarkson ... E-11
Clatonia ... H-11
Clay Center ... H-10
Clearwater ... D-10
Clinton ... C-4
Cody ... C-6
Coleridge ... D-11
Columbus ... F-11
Comstock ... F-8
Concord ... D-11
Cook ... H-12
Cornlea ... F-10
Cortland ... H-11
Cotesfield ... F-9
Cowles ... H-9
Cozad ... G-7
Crab Orchard ... H-12
Craig ... E-12
Crawford ... C-3
Creighton ... D-10
Creston ... E-11
Crete ... H-11
Crofton ... C-10
Crookston ... C-6
Culbertson ... H-6
Cullom ... ★
  Vicinity ... Pg. 144, K-2
Curtis ... G-6
Dakota City ... D-12
Dalton ... E-3
Danbury ... H-6
Dannebrog ... F-9
Davenport ... H-10
David City ... F-11
Dawson ... J-13
Daykin ... H-11
Debolt ... ★
  Vicinity ... Pg. 144, C-3
Decatur ... E-12
Denton ... G-11
Deshler ... H-10
Dewitt ... H-11
Dickens ... G-6
Diller ... H-11
Dix ... F-2
Dodge ... E-11
Doniphan ... G-9
Dorchester ... G-11
Douglas ... H-12
DuBois ... J-12
Dunbar ... G-12
Duncan ... F-10
Dunning ... E-7
Dwight ... G-11
Eddyville ... G-7
Edgar ... H-10
Edison ... H-7
Elba ... F-9
Elgin ... E-9
Eli ... C-5
Elk Creek ... H-12
Elkhorn ... F-12
Ellsworth ... D-4
Elm Creek ... G-8
Elmwood ... G-12
Elsie ... G-5
Elsmere ... D-7
Elwood ... G-7
Elyria ... E-8
Emerson ... D-11
Emmet ... D-9
Enders ... H-5
Endicott ... J-11
Ericson ... E-9
Eustis ... G-7
Exeter ... G-10
Fairbury ... H-11
Fairfield ... H-10
Fairmont ... H-10
Falls City ... J-13
Farnam ... G-7
Farwell ... F-9
Filley ... H-11
Firth ... H-11
Fordyce ... D-11
Fort Calhoun ... ★
  Vicinity ... Pg. 144, A-3
Fort Crook ... ★
  Vicinity ... Pg. 144, H-4
Foster ... D-10
Franklin ... H-8
Fremont ... F-12
Friend ... G-10
Fullerton ... F-10
Funk ... H-8
Gandy ... F-6
Garrison ... F-11
Genoa ... F-10
Geneva ... H-10
Gering ... E-2
Gilmore ... ★
  Vicinity ... Pg. 144, H-4
Giltner ... G-9

Glenvil ... H-9
Goehner ... G-11
Gordon ... C-4
Gothenburg ... G-7
Grafton ... G-10
Grainton ... G-5
Grand Island ... G-9
Grant ... G-5
Greeley ... F-9
Greenwood ... G-12
Gresham ... G-11
Guide Rock ... J-9
Gurley ... F-3
Hadar ... E-11
Haigler ... H-4
Hallam ... H-11
Halsey ... E-7
Hamlet ... H-5
Hampton ... G-10
Harrisburg ... E-2
Harrison ... C-2
Hartington ... D-11
Harvard ... H-9
Hastings ... H-9
Hay Springs ... C-4
Hayes Center ... H-5
Hazard ... F-8
Hebron ... H-10
Hemingford ... D-3
Henderson ... G-10
Herman ... F-12
Hershey ... F-6
Hildreth ... H-8
Holdrege ... H-7
Holstein ... H-9
Hooper ... F-11
Hoskins ... E-11
Howells ... E-11
Humboldt ... J-12
Humphrey ... F-10
Huntley ... H-8
Hyannis ... D-5
Imperial ... G-5
Inavale ... J-9
Indianola ... H-6
Inman ... D-9
Irvington ... ★
  Vicinity ... Pg. 144, C-2
Ithaca ... F-11
Johnson ... H-12
Johnstown ... D-7
Juniata ... G-8
Kearney ... G-8
Kenesaw ... G-9
Kennard ... F-12
Keystone ... F-5
Kilgore ... C-6
Kimball ... F-2
La Vista ... ★
  Vicinity ... Pg. 144, F-3
Lakeside ... D-4
Laurel ... D-11
Lawrence ... H-9
Lebanon ... H-6
Leigh ... E-11
Lemoyne ... F-5
Lewellen ... F-4
Lewiston ... H-12
Lexington ... G-7
Liberty ... J-12
Lincoln ... H-11
Linwood ... F-11
Lisco ... E-4
Litchfield ... F-8
Lodgepole ... F-3
Long Pine ... D-7
Loomis ... H-7
Louisville ... G-12
Loup City ... F-8
Lyman ... D-2
Lynch ... C-9
Lyons ... E-12
Madison ... E-11
Madrid ... G-5
Magnet ... D-10
Malmo ... F-11
Marquette ... G-10
Martell ... H-11
Martinsburg ... D-11
Mason City ... F-8
Max ... H-5
Maxwell ... F-6
May ... ★
  Vicinity ... Pg. 144, F-3
Maywood ... G-6
McCook ... H-6
McCool Jct. ... G-10
McGrew ... E-2
Mead ... F-12
Meadow ... ★
  Vicinity ... Pg. 144, K-1
Melbeta ... E-2
Memphis ... G-12
Merna ... F-7
Merriman ... C-5
Milford ... G-11
Millard ... ★
  Vicinity ... Pg. 144, F-1
Miller ... G-8
Milligan ... H-10
Mills ... C-7
Minden ... H-8
Minitare ... E-2
Mitchell ... D-2

Monowi ... C-9
Moorefield ... G-6
Morrill ... D-2
Mullen ... D-6
Murray ... G-12
Naper ... C-8
Naponee ... J-8
Nashville ... ★
  Vicinity ... Pg. 144, B-3
Nebraska City ... H-12
Neligh ... E-10
Nelson ... H-10
Nenzel ... C-6
Newman Grove ... E-10
Newport ... D-8
Nickerson ... F-12
Niobrara ... C-10
Norden ... C-7
Norfolk ... E-10
North Bend ... F-11
North Loup ... F-9
North Platte ... F-6
O'Neill ... D-9
Oak ... H-10
Oakdale ... E-10
Oakland ... E-12
Obert ... D-11
Oconto ... F-7
Octavia ... F-11
Odell ... J-11
Odessa ... G-8
Ogallala ... F-5
Ohiowa ... H-10
Omaha ... F-12
  Vicinity ... Pg. 144
Ong ... H-10
Ord ... E-8
Oreapolis ... ★
  Vicinity ... Pg. 144, J-5
Orleans ... H-8
Osceola ... F-10
Oshkosh ... E-4
Osmond ... D-10
Overton ... G-8
Oxford ... H-7
Page ... D-9
Palisade ... H-5
Palmer ... F-9
Palmyra ... G-12
Panama ... H-12
Papillion ... G-12
Papillion ... G-12
  Vicinity ... Pg. 144, G-3
Parks ... H-4
Pawnee City ... J-12
Paxton ... F-5
Pender ... E-12
Petersburg ... E-10
Phillips ... G-9
Pickrell ... H-11
Pierce ... D-10
Pilger ... E-11
Plainview ... D-10
Platte Center ... F-10
Plattsmouth ... G-12
Plattsmouth ... G-12
  Vicinity ... Pg. 144, K-5
Pleasanton ... G-8
Plymouth ... H-11
Polk ... G-10
Poole ... G-8
Potter ... F-3
Prague ... F-11
Primrose ... F-9
Prosser ... G-9
Purdum ... D-7
Raeville ... E-10
Ragan ... H-8
Ralston ... ★
  Vicinity ... Pg. 144, F-2
Randolph ... D-11
Ravenna ... G-9
Raymond ... G-11
Red Cloud ... H-9
Republican City ... H-8
Reynolds ... J-11
Richfield ... ★
  Vicinity ... Pg. 144, H-2
Richland ... F-11
Rising City ... F-11
Riverdale ... G-8
Riverton ... H-9
Roca ... G-11
Rockville ... F-9
Rogers ... F-11
Rosalie ... E-12
Rose ... D-8
Roseland ... H-9
Rushville ... C-4
Ruskin ... H-9
Saint Edward ... F-10
Saint Helena ... C-11
Saint Libory ... G-9
Saint Mary ... H-12
Saint Paul ... F-9
Santee ... C-10
Sargent ... E-8
Saronville ... H-9
Schuyler ... F-11
Scotia ... F-9
Scottsbluff ... D-2
Scribner ... F-11
Seneca ... D-6
Seward ... G-11

Shelby ... F-10
Shelton ... G-8
Shickley ... H-10
Sholes ... D-11
Shubert ... H-12
Sidney ... F-3
Silver Creek ... F-10
Smithfield ... G-7
Snyder ... E-11
South Bend ... G-12
South Souix City ... D-12
Spalding ... E-9
Spencer ... C-9
Springfield ... G-12
  Vicinity ... Pg. 144, J-4
Springview ... C-8
Stamford ... H-7
Stanton ... E-11
Staplehurst ... H-11
Stapleton ... F-6
Steele City ... J-11
Steinauer ... H-12
Stockville ... G-6
Strang ... H-10
Stratton ... H-5
Stromsburg ... F-10
Stuart ... D-8
Summerfield ... J-12
Sumner ... G-8
Superior ... J-10
Surprise ... G-11
Sutherland ... F-6
Sutton ... H-10
Syracuse ... G-12
Table Rock ... H-12
Tarnov ... F-10
Taylor ... E-8
Tecumseh ... H-12
Tekamah ... E-12
Terrytown ... D-2
Thayer ... G-10
Thedford ... E-6
Thurston ... E-12
Tilden ... E-10
Tobias ... H-11
Trenton ... H-5
Trumbull ... G-9
Tryon ... E-6
Uehling ... E-12
Ulysses ... G-11
Unadilla ... G-12
Upland ... H-8
Valentine ... C-7
Valley ... F-12
Valparaiso ... G-11
Venango ... G-4
Verdel ... C-10
Verdigre ... D-10
Verdon ... J-13
Waco ... G-10
Wahoo ... G-11
Wakefield ... D-11
Wallace ... G-5
Walthill ... E-12
Wauneta ... H-5
Wausa ... D-10
Waverly ... G-12
Wayne ... D-11
Weeping Water ... G-12
Weissert ... F-8
Wellfleet ... G-6
West Point ... E-11
Western ... H-11
Westerville ... F-8
Whitman ... D-5
Whitney ... C-3
Wilber ... H-11
Wilcox ... H-8
Willow Island ... G-7
Wilsonville ... H-7
Winnebago ... D-12
Winnetoon ... D-9
Winside ... D-11
Winslow ... F-12
Wisner ... E-11
Wolbach ... F-9
Wood Lake ... C-7
Wood River ... G-8
Wymore ... J-12
Wynot ... C-10
York ... G-10

NEVADA
Pages 60-61

Adaven ... H-8
Alamo ... K-8
Arden ... M-8
Armogosa Valley ... L-6
Ash Springs ... K-8
Austin ... G-5
Babbitt ... G-3
Baker ... G-10
Battle Mountain ... D-5
Beatty ... L-6
Beowawe ... D-6
Blue Diamond ... M-8
Boulder City ... M-9
Bunkerville ... L-10
Cactus Springs ... L-7
Cal Nev Ari ... N-9
Caliente ... J-9

Carlin ... D-7
Carson City ... F-2
Carver's ... G-5
Caselton ... J-9
Charleston Park ... M-7
Cherry Creek ... E-8
Coaldale ... H-4
Cold Spring ... F-4
Contact ... B-9
Cottonwood Cove ... N-9
Crescent Valley ... D-6
Crystal Bay ... F-1
Currant ... G-8
Currie ... E-9
Dayton ... F-2
Deeth ... C-8
Denio ... A-3
Denio Junction ... A-3
Dixie Valley ... E-4
Duckwater ... G-7
Dyer ... J-4
Eagle Picher Mine ... D-3
East Ely ... F-9
East Las Vegas ... M-9
Elgin ... K-9
Elko ... D-7
Ely ... F-9
Empire ... D-2
Eureka ... F-7
Fallon ... F-3
Fernley ... F-2
Frenchman ... F-3
Gabbs ... G-4
Gardnerville ... G-1
Genoa ... G-1
Gerlach ... D-2
Glenbrook ... F-1
Glendale ... L-9
Golconda ... C-5
Gold Hill ... F-2
Gold Point ... K-5
Goldfield ... J-5
Goodsprings ... M-8
Halleck ... D-8
Hawthorne ... H-3
Hazen ... F-2
Henderson ... M-9
Hiko ... J-8
Imlay ... D-4
Incline Village ... F-1
Indian Springs ... L-8
Ione ... G-5
Jack Creek ... B-7
Jackpot ... B-9
Jarbidge ... B-8
Jean ... N-8
Jiggs ... D-8
Kimberly ... F-8
Lage's ... E-9
Lamoille ... D-8
Las Vegas ... M-8
Laughlin ... N-9
Lee ... D-8
Lee Canyon ... L-7
Lida ... K-5
Logandale ... L-9
Lovelock ... E-3
Lund ... G-9
Luning ... H-4
Major's Place ... G-9
Manhattan ... H-5
Mason ... G-2
McDermitt ... A-5
McGill ... F-9
Mercury ... M-7
Mesquite ... L-10
Midas ... C-6
Middle Gate ... F-4
Mill City ... D-4
Mina ... H-4
Minden ... G-1
Moapa ... L-9
Montello ... C-10
Mountain City ... B-7
Mt. Charleston ... M-7
Nelson ... N-9
Nixon ... E-2
North Las Vegas ... M-9
Nyala ... H-7
Oasis ... C-9
Oreana ... D-4
Orovada ... B-4
Overton ... L-9
Owyhee ... B-7
Pahrump ... M-7
Panaca ... J-9
Paradise Valley ... B-5
Pioche ... J-9
Preston ... G-8
Rachel ... J-7
Reno ... F-1
Rhyolite ... K-6
Round Mt. ... G-5
Ruby Valley ... D-8
Ruth ... F-9
Sandy ... N-8
Schurz ... G-3
Scotty's Jct. ... K-5
Searchlight ... N-8
Shantytown ... L-9
Silver City ... F-2
Silver Springs ... F-2
Silverpeak ... J-4
Sloan ... M-8

Smith ... G-2
South Lake Tahoe ... G-1
Sparks ... F-1
Stateline ... G-1
Stewart ... F-1
Stillwater ... F-3
Sulphur ... C-3
Sutcliffe ... E-1
Thousand Springs ... C-9
Tonopah ... H-5
Tuscarora ... C-7
Unionville ... D-4
Ursine ... J-10
Valmy ... D-6
Verdi ... F-1
Virginia City ... F-2
Wabuska ... F-2
Wadsworth ... E-2
Warm Springs ... H-6
Washoe ... F-1
Weed Heights ... G-2
Wellington ... G-2
Wells ... C-9
Winnemucca ... C-4
Yerington ... G-2
Zephyr Cove ... F-1

NEW HAMPSHIRE
Page 57

Albany ... E-6
Allenstown ... H-6
Alstead ... H-3
Alton ... G-6
Alton Bay ... G-6
Amherst ... J-5
Andover ... G-4
Antrim ... J-4
Ashland ... F-5
Ashuelot ... K-3
Atkinson ... J-6
Auburn ... J-6
Barnstead ... H-6
Bartlett ... E-6
Bath ... E-4
Bayside ... J-7
Bedford ... J-5
Belmont ... G-5
Bennington ... J-4
Berlin ... C-6
Bethlehem ... D-5
Boscawen ... H-5
Bow Center ... H-5
Bradford ... H-4
Brentwood ... J-6
Bretton Woods ... E-5
Bridgewater ... G-5
Bristol ... G-5
Brookfield ... G-6
Brookline ... K-5
Canaan ... G-4
Canaan Center ... F-4
Candia ... J-6
Carroll ... D-5
Cascade ... D-6
Center Conway ... E-6
Center Ossipee ... F-6
Charlestown ... H-3
Cheever ... H-3
Chester ... J-5
Chesterfield ... J-3
Chichester ... H-5
Chocorua ... F-6
Cilleyville ... G-4
Claremont ... H-3
Coburn ... G-6
Cold River ... H-3
Colebrook ... B-5
Columbia ... B-5
Concord ... H-5
Contoocook ... H-5
Conway ... E-6
Coos Junction ... C-6
Cornish City ... G-3
Cornish Flat ... G-3
Crystal ... C-6
Danbury ... G-5
Davisville ... H-5
Derry ... J-6
Derry Village ... J-6
Dixville ... B-6
Dorchester ... F-4
Dover ... H-7
Drewsville ... H-3
Dublin ... J-4
Dummer ... C-6
Durham ... H-7
East Alton ... G-6
East Barrington ... H-6
East Grafton ... G-4
East Hebron ... F-5
East Kingston ... J-6
East Lempster ... H-3
East Madison ... F-6
Easton ... E-5
Eaton Center ... F-6
Effingham Falls ... F-6
Elkins ... G-4
Epping ... J-6
Epsom ... H-6
Epsom Four Corners ... H-6
Errol ... C-6
Exeter ... J-7
Fabyan ... D-5

Farmington ... G-7
Fish Market ... G-4
Francestown ... J-4
Franconia ... D-5
Franklin ... G-5
Freedom ... F-6
Fremont ... J-6
Gerrish ... H-5
Gilford ... G-6
Gilmans Corner ... F-4
Gilmanton ... G-6
Gilsum ... J-4
Glen ... E-6
Glen House ... D-6
Glendale ... G-5
Goffs Falls ... J-5
Goffstown ... J-5
Gorham ... D-6
Goshen ... H-4
Gossville ... H-6
Grafton ... G-4
Grantham ... G-4
Greenfield ... J-4
Greenville ... K-4
Groton ... F-4
Groveton ... C-5
Guild ... G-4
Guildhall ... C-5
Hampton ... J-7
Hampton Beach ... J-7
Hancock ... J-4
Hanover ... F-3
Hanover Center ... F-4
Harts Location ... E-6
Haverhill ... E-4
Hebron ... F-4
Henniker ... H-4
Hillsborough ... H-4
Hinsdale ... J-3
Hooksett ... H-6
Hopkinton ... H-5
Hoyts Corner ... H-5
Hudson ... K-6
Jackson ... D-6
James City ... H-6
Jefferson ... D-5
Jefferson Highlands ... D-5
Keene ... J-3
Kensington ... J-7
Kidderville ... B-5
Kingston ... J-6
Laconia ... G-5
Lancaster ... D-5
Laskey Corner ... G-7
Leavitts Hill ... H-6
Lebanon ... G-4
Lincoln ... E-4
Lisbon ... E-4
Little Boars Head ... J-7
Littleton ... D-5
Loudon ... H-5
Lower Shaker Village ... G-4
Lower Village ... J-3
Lyme ... F-4
Lyme Center ... F-4
Madbury ... H-7
Madison ... F-6
Manchester ... J-5
Marlborough ... J-4
Marlow ... J-4
Martin ... J-6
Mason ... K-5
Meadows ... F-5
Meredith ... F-5
Meriden ... G-3
Merrimack ... J-5
Milan ... C-6
Milford ... J-5
Milton ... G-7
Mirror Lake ... F-6
Monroe ... D-4
Mont Vernon ... J-5
Moultonborough ... F-6
Moultonville ... F-6
Mount Sunapee ... H-4
Munsonville ... J-4
Nashua ... K-5
New Durham ... G-6
New Hampton ... G-5
New Ipswich ... K-4
New London ... H-4
New Rye ... H-6
Newbury ... H-4
Newfields ... J-7
Newington ... J-7
Newmarket ... J-7
Newport ... H-4
Newton ... J-7

Ossipee ... F-6
Otterville ... G-4
Pages Corner ... H-5
Parker ... J-5
Pearls Corner ... H-5
Pelham ... K-6
Pembroke ... H-5
Penacook ... H-5
Peterborough ... J-4
Pinardville ... J-5
Pittsburg ... B-6
Pittsfield ... H-6
Plainfield ... G-3
Plaistow ... J-6
Plymouth ... F-5
Portsmouth ... H-7
Potter Place ... G-4
Province Lake ... F-7
Randolph ... D-6
Raymond ... J-6
Redstone ... E-6
Richmond ... K-3
Rindge ... K-4
Riverton ... D-5
Rochester ... H-6
Rollinsford ... H-7
Rumney ... F-5
Rye ... J-7
Rye Beach ... J-7
Salem ... J-6
Salisbury ... H-5
Sanbornton ... G-5
Sanbornville ... G-7
Sandwich ... F-6
Seabrook Beach ... J-7
Sharon ... J-4
Shelburne ... D-6
Somersworth ... H-7
South Acworth ... H-4
South Cornish ... G-3
South Danbury ... G-5
South Stoddard ... J-4
South Weare ... J-5
Spofford ... J-3
Springfield ... G-4
Squantum ... J-4
Stark ... C-6
Stewartstown ... B-6
Stoddard ... H-4
Stratford ... C-5
Stratham ... J-7
Sunapee ... G-4
Surry ... J-3
Sutton ... H-4
Swiftwater ... E-4
Tamworth ... F-6
Temple ... J-4
Thornton ... F-5
Tilton ... G-5
Trapshire ... H-3
Troy ... J-4
Tuftonboro ... F-6
Twin Mountain ... D-5
Union ... G-6
Wakefield ... G-7
Wallis Sands ... J-7
Walpole ... J-3
Warner ... H-5
Warren ... F-4
Washington ... H-4
Weare ... J-5
Wendell ... H-4
Wentworth ... F-4
Wentworths Location ... B-6
West Campton ... F-5
West Lebanon ... F-4
West Milan ... C-6
West Ossipee ... F-6
West Rindge ... K-4
West Rumney ... F-5
West Stewartstown ... B-5
West Swanzey ... J-4
Westmoreland ... J-3
Westville ... J-6
Willey House ... E-5
Wilton ... J-4
Winchester ... J-3
Windsor ... H-4
Winnisquam ... G-5
Wolfeboro ... G-6
Wonalancet ... F-5
Woodman ... F-7
Woodsville ... E-4

NEW JERSEY
Page 62-63

Absecon ... M-6
Adelphia ... H-7
Albion ... G-4
  Vicinity ... Pg. 147, G-9
Allamuchy ... C-5
Allendale ... ★
  Vicinity ... Pg. 138, D-4
Allentown ... H-6
Alloway ... M-2
Almonesson ... ★
  Vicinity ... Pg. 147, G-8
Alpha ... E-3
Alpine ... B-6
  Vicinity ... Pg. 138, C-7
Andover ... C-5
Asbury Park ... G-8

★ Denotes City only on Vicinity map. City not located on State map.

NEW JERSEY

Ashland ....★
  Vicinity ....Pg. 147, F-9
Atlantic City N-7
Atlantic Highlands F-8
Atsion K-5
Audubon K-4
  Vicinity ....Pg. 147, E-8
Avalon P-5
Avenel ....★
  Vicinity ....Pg. 139, P-1
Baptistown F-4
Barnegat K-8
Barnegat Light K-8
Barrington ....★
  Vicinity ....Pg. 147, F-8
Bay Head H-8
Bay Point N-3
Bayonne E-8
  Vicinity ....Pg. 139, M-4
Beach Haven M-7
Beachwood J-7
Bedminster E-5
Beesley Pt. N-5
Belleplain N-4
Belleville D-7
  Vicinity ....Pg. 139, J-3
Bellmawr K-3
  Vicinity ....Pg. 147, F-8
Belmar H-8
Belvidere D-3
Bergenfield C-8
  Vicinity ....Pg. 138, F-6
Berlin K-4
  Vicinity ....Pg. 147, G-10
Bernardsville D-6
Beverly H-4
  Vicinity ....Pg. 147, B-10
Blackwood ....★
  Vicinity ....Pg. 147, G-8
Blairstown C-4
Blawenburg F-5
Bloomfield D-7
  Vicinity ....Pg. 139, J-3
Bloomingdale C-7
  Vicinity ....Pg. 138, D-1
Bloomsbury E-3
Boonton C-7
Bordentown H-5
Bound Brook F-6
Bradley Beach H-8
Branchville B-5
Bridgeboro ....★
  Vicinity ....Pg. 147, C-9
Bridgeport K-2
  Vicinity ....Pg. 147, G-4
Bridgeton M-2
Brielle H-8
Brigantine N-6
Broadway D-4
Brooklawn ....★
  Vicinity ....Pg. 147, E-7
Browns Mills J-6
Budd Lake C-5
Buena M-4
Burlington H-4
  Vicinity ....Pg. 147, B-11
Butler C-7
Buttzville D-4
Caldwell ....★
  Vicinity ....Pg. 139, H-1
Califon E-5
Camden K-3
  Vicinity ....Pg. 147, D-7
Cape May Q-4
Cape May Court House ..Q-4
Carls Corner M-3
Carneys Pt. L-1
Carteret E-6
  Vicinity ....Pg. 139, P-2
Cassville H-7
Cedar Bridge K-7
Cedar Grove J-8
  Vicinity ....Pg. 138, G-2
Cedarville N-3
Centerton M-3
  Vicinity ....Pg. 147, C-10
Chatham D-6
Chatsworth K-6
Cherry Hill J-4
  Vicinity ....Pg. 147, E-8
Chesilhurst K-4
Chester D-5
Cinnaminson J-4
  Vicinity ....Pg. 147, C-9
Clark ....★
  Vicinity ....Pg. 139, N-1
Clarksboro ....★
  Vicinity ....Pg. 147, G-5
Clarksburg H-6
Clarksville L-3
Clayton L-3
Clementon ....★
  Vicinity ....Pg. 147, G-9
Clermont P-5
Cliffside Park ....★
  Vicinity ....Pg. 139, J-8
Clifton D-8
  Vicinity ....Pg. 138, H-3
Clinton E-4
Closter ....★
  Vicinity ....Pg. 138, E-7
Coffins Corner ....★
  Vicinity ....Pg. 147, F-9
Colesville A-5

Collingswood J-3
  Vicinity ....Pg. 147, E-8
Colonia ....★
  Vicinity ....Pg. 139, P-1
Colts Neck G-7
Columbus H-5
Corbin City N-5
Cranbury G-6
Cranford ....★
  Vicinity ....Pg. 139, M-1
Cresskill B-6
  Vicinity ....Pg. 138, F-7
Crestwood Village J-7
Croton F-4
Cumberland N-4
Deacons J-5
  Vicinity ....Pg. 147, C-11
Deerfield M-3
Delair ....★
  Vicinity ....Pg. 147, D-8
Delanco ....★
  Vicinity ....Pg. 147, B-9
Delaware C-3
Denville C-6
Deptford ....★
  Vicinity ....Pg. 147, F-7
Dividing Creek N-3
Dover C-6
Dumont ....★
  Vicinity ....Pg. 138, F-6
Dunellen E-6
East Orange D-7
  Vicinity ....Pg. 139, J-3
East Rutherford ....★
  Vicinity ....Pg. 139, H-4
East Vineland M-4
Eatontown G-8
Edgewater Park J-4
Edinburg G-5
Edison F-6
Egg Harbor M-6
Elizabeth E-7
  Vicinity ....Pg. 139, M-3
Ellisburg ....★
  Vicinity ....Pg. 147, E-9
Elmer L-3
Elmwood Park ....★
  Vicinity ....Pg. 138, G-4
Elwood M-5
Emerson ....★
  Vicinity ....Pg. 138, E-6
Englewood ....★
  Vicinity ....Pg. 138, G-7
Englewood Cliffs A-6
  Vicinity ....Pg. 138, B-1
Englishtown G-7
Estell Manor N-5
Everittstown E-4
Evesboro ....★
  Vicinity ....Pg. 147, E-10
Ewingville G-5
Fair Haven G-8
  Vicinity ....Pg. 138, G-1
Fair Lawn C-8
  Vicinity ....Pg. 138, F-4
Fairmount D-5
Fairton N-3
Fairview ....★
  Vicinity ....Pg. 147, G-7
Fanwood ....★
  Vicinity ....Pg. 147, E-9
Farmingdale H-7
Flemington F-4
Florham Park D-7
Folsom L-4
  Vicinity ....Pg. 139, Q-1
Forked River K-8
Fort Dix J-6
Fort Lee D-9
Four Mile F-6
Franklin B-6
Franklin Lakes ....★
  Vicinity ....Pg. 138, D-3
Franklinville L-3
Fredon C-5
Freehold G-7
Freewood Acres H-7
Frenchtown F-4
Garfield C-8
  Vicinity ....Pg. 138, G-4
Garwood ....★
  Vicinity ....Pg. 139, M-1
Gibbsboro K-4
  Vicinity ....Pg. 147, F-9
Gibbstown ....★
  Vicinity ....Pg. 147, F-5
Gilford Park J-8
Glassboro L-3
Glen Gardner E-4
Glen Rock ....★
  Vicinity ....Pg. 138, E-4
Glendale ....★
  Vicinity ....Pg. 147, F-9
Glenwood A-6
Gloucester City K-3
  Vicinity ....Pg. 147, E-7
Gouldtown M-3
Great Meadows D-4
Green Bank K-6
Grenlock ....★
  Vicinity ....Pg. 147, G-8
Guttenberg ....★
  Vicinity ....Pg. 139, J-5

Hackensack C-8
  Vicinity ....Pg. 138, G-6
Hackettstown D-4
Haddon Heights ....★
  Vicinity ....Pg. 147, E-8
Haddonfield K-4
  Vicinity ....Pg. 147, E-8
Hainesburg C-4
Hainesport ....★
  Vicinity ....Pg. 147, D-11
Haledon C-7
  Vicinity ....Pg. 138, F-3
Hamburg B-6
Hamilton Sq. G-6
Hammonton L-5
Hampton E-4
Hanover D-6
Harmony D-3
Harrington Park ....★
  Vicinity ....Pg. 138, E-6
Harrison ....★
  Vicinity ....Pg. 139, K-4
Harrisonville L-1
Harvey Cedars L-8
Hasbrouck Hts ....★
  Vicinity ....Pg. 138, G-5
Hawthorne C-8
  Vicinity ....Pg. 138, F-3
Helmetta G-7
Hewitt A-6
  Vicinity ....Pg. 138, B-1
High Bridge E-4
Highland Park F-7
Highlands F-9
Hightstown G-6
Hillsdale B-6
Ho-Ho-Kus ....★
  Vicinity ....Pg. 138, E-4
Hoboken D-8
  Vicinity ....Pg. 139, K-5
Holmdel F-7
Hopatcong C-5
Hope C-4
Hopewell F-5
Hurdtown C-6
Irvington ....★
  Vicinity ....Pg. 139, L-2
Iselin ....★
  Vicinity ....Pg. 139, P-1
Island Hts. J-8
Jamesburg G-6
Jersey City D-8
Johnsonburg C-4
Jordentown ....★
  Vicinity ....Pg. 147, D-9
Keansburg F-8
Kearny D-8
  Vicinity ....Pg. 139, K-4
Kenilworth E-7
Keyport F-8
Kinnelon C-7
  Vicinity ....Pg. 138, D-2
Kresson ....★
  Vicinity ....Pg. 147, F-10
Lafayette B-5
Lakehurst J-7
Lakehurst ....★
  Vicinity ....Pg. 147, F-7
Lakeside B-7
Lakewood H-7
Lambertville G-4
Larisons Cor. F-4
Laurel Springs ....★
  Vicinity ....Pg. 147, G-9
Laurence Harbor F-7
Lavallette J-8
Lawnside ....★
  Vicinity ....Pg. 147, F-8
Lawrence G-5
Lebanon E-5
Lenola ....★
  Vicinity ....Pg. 147, D-9
Liberty Cor. E-6
Lincoln Park C-7
  Vicinity ....Pg. 138, F-1
Linden E-7
  Vicinity ....Pg. 139, N-2
Lindenwold K-4
  Vicinity ....Pg. 147, G-9
Linwood N-6
Little Egg Harbor M-7
Little Falls ....★
  Vicinity ....Pg. 138, G-2
Little Ferry ....★
  Vicinity ....Pg. 138, H-5
Livingston ....★
  Vicinity ....Pg. 139, J-1
Lodi ....★
  Vicinity ....Pg. 138, G-4
Long Branch G-9
Long Valley D-5
Longport N-6
Lumberton J-5
Lyndhurst ....★
  Vicinity ....Pg. 139, J-4
Madison D-6
Magnolia ....★
  Vicinity ....Pg. 147, F-8
Mahwah ....★
  Vicinity ....Pg. 138, C-4
Manahawkin L-7
Manalapan G-6
Manasquan H-8

Mantoloking J-8
Mantua ....★
  Vicinity ....Pg. 147, G-6
Manville F-6
Maple Shade J-3
Maple Shade ....★
  Vicinity ....Pg. 147, D-9
Maplewood ....★
  Vicinity ....Pg. 139, K-2
Marcella C-6
Margate City N-6
Marlboro G-7
Marlton E-4
  Vicinity ....Pg. 147, E-10
Marshallville N-5
Masonville ....★
  Vicinity ....Pg. 147, D-11
Matawan F-7
Maurice River P-4
Mays Landing M-5
Maywood ....★
  Vicinity ....Pg. 138, G-5
McAfee B-6
Medford K-5
Medford Lakes K-5
Mendham D-6
Merchantville ....★
  Vicinity ....Pg. 147, D-8
Metuchen E-7
Mickleton K-3
  Vicinity ....Pg. 147, G-6
Midland Park ....★
  Vicinity ....Pg. 138, E-4
Milford E-3
Millstone F-6
Milltown F-6
Millville N-3
Monmouth Jct. G-6
Monroe A-5
Montague A-5
Montvale ....★
  Vicinity ....Pg. 138, D-5
Montville C-7
Moonachie ....★
  Vicinity ....Pg. 147, D-10
Moorestown J-4
Morris Plains D-6
Morristown D-6
Morrisville E-3
  Vicinity ....Pg. 147, D-8
Mt. Arlington C-6
Mt. Ephraim ....★
  Vicinity ....Pg. 147, F-7
Mt. Holly J-5
  Vicinity ....Pg. 147, D-10
Mt. Laurel ....★
  Vicinity ....Pg. 147, D-10
Mt. Laurel ....★
  Vicinity ....Pg. 147, D-10
Mullica Hill L-3
National Park K-3
  Vicinity ....Pg. 147, F-6
Neptune H-8
Neshanic F-5
Netcong C-5
New Brunswick F-6
New Egypt H-6
New Gretna L-6
New Providence ....★
New Rochelle ....★
Newark D-8
  Vicinity ....Pg. 139, K-4
Newfield M-4
Newfoundland B-6
Newton B-5
North Arlington ....★
  Vicinity ....Pg. 139, J-4
North Bergen ....★
  Vicinity ....Pg. 139, J-6
North Caldwell ....★
  Vicinity ....Pg. 138, G-2
North Cape May Q-4
North Dennis P-4
North Haledon C-7
  Vicinity ....Pg. 138, F-3
North Wildwood Q-5
Northfield N-6
Northvale ....★
  Vicinity ....Pg. 138, D-7
Norwood C-9
  Vicinity ....Pg. 139, E-7
Nutley ....★
  Vicinity ....Pg. 139, H-3
Oakland ....★
  Vicinity ....Pg. 138, D-2
Oaklyn ....★
  Vicinity ....Pg. 147, E-8
Ocean City N-6
Ocean Gate J-8
Oceanport G-8
Ogdensburg B-5
Old Bridge F-7
Old Tappan C-8
  Vicinity ....Pg. 138, D-6
Oldwick E-5
Oradell ....★
  Vicinity ....Pg. 138, F-6
Orange D-7
  Vicinity ....Pg. 139, K-2
Oxford D-4
Palisades Park ....★
  Vicinity ....Pg. 138, H-6
Palmyra J-3
  Vicinity ....Pg. 147, C-8

Paramus C-8
  Vicinity ....Pg. 138, F-5
Park Ridge ....★
  Vicinity ....Pg. 138, D-5
Parsippany-Troy Hills ...D-6
Passaic C-7
  Vicinity ....Pg. 138, H-4
Paterson C-7
Paterson B-6
  Vicinity ....Pg. 138, F-3
Paulsboro K-2
Peapack E-5
Pemberton J-5
Pennington G-5
Penns Grove L-2
Pennsauken ....★
  Vicinity ....Pg. 147, D-8
Pennsville L-1
Penny Pot M-5
Pequannock ....★
  Vicinity ....Pg. 138, F-1
Perth Amboy F-7
  Vicinity ....Pg. 139, Q-2
Phillipsburg E-3
Pine Beach ....★
  Vicinity ....Pg. 138, H-1
Pine Hill K-4
Pitman L-3
Pittstown E-4
Plainfield E-6
Plainsboro G-6
Pleasantville N-6
Pole Tavern L-3
Pomona M-6
Pompton Lakes ....★
  Vicinity ....Pg. 138, D-1
Pompton Plains B-6
Port Elizabeth N-4
Port Norris P-4
Port Reading ....★
  Vicinity ....Pg. 139, Q-2
Port Republic M-6
Princeton G-5
Princeton Jct. G-6
Prospect Park C-8
Pt. Pleasant H-8
Pt. Pleasant Beach H-8
Quinton M-2
Rahway E-7
  Vicinity ....Pg. 139, N-2
Ramsey B-6
Rancocas ....★
  Vicinity ....Pg. 147, C-10
Raritan E-5
Readington E-5
Reaville F-5
Red Bank G-8
Red Lion K-5
Repaupo ....★
  Vicinity ....Pg. 147, F-6
Ridgefield ....★
  Vicinity ....Pg. 147, G-5
Ridgefield Park ....★
  Vicinity ....Pg. 138, G-6
Ridgewood C-8
  Vicinity ....Pg. 138, E-4
Ringwood B-7
  Vicinity ....Pg. 138, B-2
Rio Grande Q-4
River Vale ....★
  Vicinity ....Pg. 138, E-6
Riverdale C-7
Riverside J-4
  Vicinity ....Pg. 147, C-9
Riverton ....★
  Vicinity ....Pg. 147, C-9
Robertsville G-7
Rock Leigh ....★
  Vicinity ....Pg. 138, E-7
Rockaway C-6
Rocky Hill F-5
Roosevelt H-6
Roseland ....★
  Vicinity ....Pg. 139, H-1
Roselle ....★
  Vicinity ....Pg. 139, M-2
Roselle Park ....★
  Vicinity ....Pg. 139, M-2
Ross Cor. B-5
Rumson G-8
Runnemede K-3
  Vicinity ....Pg. 147, F-8
Rutherford ....★
  Vicinity ....Pg. 139, H-4
Saddle Brook ....★
  Vicinity ....Pg. 138, G-5
Saddle River ....★
  Vicinity ....Pg. 138, D-4
Salem M-1
Sayreville F-7
Sea Isle City P-5
Seabrook M-3
Seaside Heights J-8
Seaside Pk. J-8
Seaville P-5
Secaucus ....★
  Vicinity ....Pg. 139, J-5
Sewaren ....★
  Vicinity ....Pg. 139, P-2
Sharptown L-2
Shiloh M-2
Ship Bottom L-8

Shrewsbury G-8
Silverton J-8
Smithburg H-7
Smithville M-6
Somerdale F-4
Somers Pt. N-6
Somerville F-5
South Amboy F-7
South Brunswick G-6
South Dennis P-5
South Orange ....★
  Vicinity ....Pg. 139, K-2
South Plainfield E-6
South River F-7
South Toms River J-7
Sparta C-5
Speedwell K-6
Spotswood ....★
Spring Lakes Heights H-8
Spring Mills E-3
Springdale B-5
  Vicinity ....Pg. 147, E-9
Springfield ....★
  Vicinity ....Pg. 139, L-1
Stanhope C-5
  Vicinity ....Pg. 147, D-9
Stockholm B-6
Stockton F-4
Stone Harbor Q-5
Stratford K-4
  Vicinity ....Pg. 147, F-8
Summit D-7
Surf City L-8
Sussex A-5
Swedesboro K-2
Tabernacle K-5
Tansboro ....★
  Vicinity ....Pg. 147, G-10
Taunton Lake ....★
  Vicinity ....Pg. 147, F-11
Tenafly C-9
  Vicinity ....Pg. 138, F-7
Tinton Falls G-8
Toms River J-7
Totowa C-7
Totowa C-7
  Vicinity ....Pg. 138, G-3
Trenton G-5
Tuckerton L-7
Tuttles Cor. B-5
Union Beach F-8
  Vicinity ....Pg. 139, L-2
Union City D-8
  Vicinity ....Pg. 139, K-5
Upper Saddle River ....★
  Vicinity ....Pg. 138, C-4
Ventnor City N-6
Vernon B-6
Villas Q-4
Vineland M-4
Waldwick ....★
  Vicinity ....Pg. 138, D-4
Wanaque B-7
  Vicinity ....Pg. 138, D-1
Waretown K-8
Warren E-6
Warren Grove K-7
Washington D-4
Washington Crossing F-4
Watchung E-6
Wayne ....★
  Vicinity ....Pg. 138, F-2
Weehawken ....★
  Vicinity ....Pg. 139, K-5
Welchville L-2
Wells Mills K-7
Wenonah K-3
  Vicinity ....Pg. 147, G-6
West Berlin ....★
  Vicinity ....Pg. 147, G-9
West Caldwell ....★
  Vicinity ....Pg. 138, H-1
West Cape May Q-4
West Long Branch G-8
  Vicinity ....Pg. 147, E-8
West Milford B-6
West New York ....★
  Vicinity ....Pg. 139, J-6
West Orange ....★
  Vicinity ....Pg. 139, J-2
West Paterson ....★
  Vicinity ....Pg. 138, G-3
West Portal E-4
Westfield E-6
Westville ....★
  Vicinity ....Pg. 147, F-7
Westwood C-8
  Vicinity ....Pg. 138, E-6
Weymouth M-6
Wharton C-6
White Horse H-5
Whitehouse E-5
Whitesboro Q-4
Whitesville H-7
Wildwood Q-5
Wildwood Crest Q-5
Williamstown L-4
Willingboro ....★
  Vicinity ....Pg. 147, C-10
Winslow L-4
Wood Ridge ....★
  Vicinity ....Pg. 138, H-5
Woodbine P-4

Woodbridge C-6
  Vicinity ....Pg. 139, P-2
Woodbury K-3
  Vicinity ....Pg. 147, F-7
Woodbury Heights K-3
  Vicinity ....Pg. 147, F-7
Woodcliff Lake ....★
  Vicinity ....Pg. 138, D-5
Woodlynne ....★
  Vicinity ....Pg. 147, E-7
Woods Tavern F-5
Woodstown L-2
Woodsville G-4
Wrightstown J-6
  Vicinity ....Pg. 138, D-9
Yardville H-5

NEW MEXICO
Pages 64-65

Abbott D-8
Abeytas H-4
Abiquiu E-5
Abo H-5
Alameda F-4
Alamo H-3
Alamogordo K-5
Albuquerque G-4
Alcalde E-5
Algodones F-4
Alma K-1
Alto K-6
Ambrosia Lake F-3
Amistad E-10
Anapra M-5
Ancho J-6
Angus J-6
Animas M-1
Antelope Wells N-2
Apache Creek J-1
Aqua Fria F-5
Arabela J-7
Aragon J-1
Arch H-10
Archuleta D-3
Armijo G-4
Arrey L-3
Arroyo Hondo D-6
Arroyo Seco D-6
Artesia K-8
Atoka L-8
Aztec D-2
Bayard L-2
Beklabito D-1
Belen G-4
Bellview G-10
Bent K-6
Berino M-5
Bernal F-7
Bernalillo F-4
Bernardo H-4
Bingham J-5
Black Lake D-7
Black River Village M-9
Black Rock G-1
Blanco D-3
Blanco Trading Post D-3
Bloomfield D-2
Bluewater F-2
Brazos D-5
Broadview G-10
Buckhorn K-1
Bueyeros E-9
Caballo K-4
Canjilon D-5
Canon F-4
Canon Plaza D-5
Capitan J-6
Caprock J-9
Capulin C-8
Carlsbad L-8
Carlsbad Caverns M-8
Carrizozo J-6
Causey J-10
Cebolla D-4
Cebolleta F-3
Cebolletita F-3
Cedar Crest G-5
Cedar Hill C-2
Cedarvale H-6
Central L-2
Cerro C-6
Chacon E-6
Chama C-5
Chamberino M-4
Chamizal H-4
Chaparral M-5
Chilili G-5
Chimayo E-6
Cimarron D-7
Claunch H-6
Clayton D-10
Cleveland E-6
Cliff L-1
Clines Corners G-6
Cloudcroft K-6
Clovis H-10
Cochiti Lake F-5
Columbus M-3
Conchas F-8
Corona H-6
Cotton City M-1
Counselors E-3

Coyote E-4
Coyote Canyon F-1
Crossroads J-10
Crownpoint F-2
Cruzville J-1
Crystal E-4
Cuba E-4
Cuchillo K-3
Cuervo G-8
Cundiyo E-6
Datil H-3
Deming M-3
Derry L-3
Des Moines C-9
Dexter K-8
Dilia F-7
Dona Ana L-4
Dora H-10
Dulce C-4
Dunken L-7
Duran H-7
Dwyer L-3
Eagle Nest D-6
Edgewood G-5
El Morro G-2
El Porvenir E-6
El Rito D-5
El Vado D-5
Elephant Butte K-4
Elida H-9
Elk K-7
Elk Silver K-6
Elkins J-9
Embudo D-6
Encino G-6
Endee F-10
Engle K-4
Ensenada D-5
Escobosa G-5
Escondida H-4
Espanola E-5
Estancia G-5
Eunice L-10
Fairacres M-4
Farley D-8
Farmington D-2
Fence Lake G-1
Flora Vista D-2
Floyd H-10
Folsom C-9
Forrest G-9
Fort Stanton J-6
Fort Sumner H-8
Fort Wingate F-1
Frijoles E-5
Gage M-2
Galisteo F-5
Gallina E-4
Gallinas E-6
Gallup F-1
Gamerco F-1
Garfield L-3
Gladstone D-9
Glenrio F-10
Glenwood K-1
Golden F-5
Grady G-10
Gran Quivira H-5
Grants G-3
Greenfield K-8
Grenville C-9
Guadalupita E-6
Hachita M-2
Hagerman K-8
Hanover L-2
Hatch L-4
Hayden E-10
Hernandez E-5
High Rolls K-6
Hilburn City K-10
Hill L-3
Hillsboro K-3
Hobbs L-10
Holman E-6
Hondo K-7
Hope K-7
House G-9
Humble City K-10
Hurley L-2
Jal M-10
Jarales G-4
Jemez Springs E-4
Jicarilla J-6
Kenna J-9
Kingston L-3
Kirtland D-1
Knowles K-10
La Cienega F-5
La Cueva E-6
La Jara E-4
La Joya H-4
La Luz K-6
La Madera E-5
La Mesa M-4
La Plata C-2
La Puente D-4
La Union M-4
Laborcita K-6
Laguna G-3
Lake Arthur K-8
Lake Valley L-3
Lamy F-5
Las Cruces M-5
Las Nutrias H-4

★ Denotes City only on Vicinity map. City not located on State map.

NEW MEXICO   NEW YORK

Las Palomas ... K-3
Las Vegas ... F-7
Ledoux ... E-6
Lemitar ... H-4
Lincoln ... J-7
Lindrith ... D-4
Lingo ... J-10
Loco Hills ... L-9
Logan ... F-10
Lordsburg ... M-1
Los Alamos ... E-5
Los Cerrillos ... F-5
Los Chavez ... G-4
Los Lunas ... G-4
Los Ojos ... D-4
Los Padillas ... G-4
Loving ... M-9
Lovington ... K-10
Luis Lopez ... J-4
Lumberton ... C-4
Luna ... J-1
Madrid ... F-5
Magdalena ... H-4
Malaga ... M-9
Maljamar ... K-9
Manuelito ... F-1
Manzano ... G-5
Maxwell ... D-8
Mayhill ... K-7
McAlister ... G-9
McCartys ... G-3
McDonald ... K-10
Melrose ... H-9
Mentmore ... F-1
Mesa ... J-8
Mescalero ... K-6
Mesilla ... M-4
Mesita ... G-3
Mesquite ... M-5
Mexican Springs ... E-1
Miami ... D-7
Milan ... F-3
Mills ... E-8
Milnesand ... J-10
Mimbres ... L-2
Mineral Hill ... F-6
Mogollon ... K-1
Monero ... C-4
Montezuma ... F-6
Monticello ... K-3
Montoya ... G-9
Monument ... L-10
Mora ... E-6
Moriarty ... G-5
Mosquero ... E-9
Mountainair ... H-5
Mt. Dora ... D-9
Mule Creek ... K-1
Nachitti ... E-1
Nadine ... L-10
Nageezi ... E-3
Nara Visa ... E-10
Navajo ... E-1
Newcomb ... E-1
Newkirk ... F-8
Ocate ... E-7
Oil Center ... L-10
Ojo Caliente ... D-5
Ojo Feliz ... E-7
Old Horse Springs ... J-2
Omega ... H-2
Organ ... L-5
Orogrande ... L-6
Oscuro ... J-5
Paguate ... G-3
Pastura ... G-7
Pecos ... F-6
Pena Blanca ... F-5
Penasco ... E-6
Pep ... J-10
Pescado ... G-1
Picacho ... K-7
Pie Town ... H-2
Pine Lodge ... J-7
Pinon ... L-7
Pinos Altos ... L-2
Placita ... K-3
Placitas ... F-5
Pleasant Hill ... G-10
Pleasanton ... K-1
Pojoaque ... E-6
Portales ... H-10
Prewitt ... F-2
Pueblo ... F-6
Pueblo Bonito ... E-2
Puerto De Luna ... G-8
Punta ... G-5
Quay ... G-9
Quemado ... H-2
Questa ... D-6
Radium Springs ... L-4
Ragland ... G-9
Rainsville ... E-7
Ramah ... G-2
Ramon ... H-7
Ranchos De Taos ... D-6
Ranchvale ... H-10
Raton ... C-8
Rayado ... D-7
Red Hill ... H-1
Red River ... D-6
Red Rock ... L-1
Regina ... E-4
Reserve ... J-1
Rincon ... L-4

Rinconada ... E-6
Riverside ... K-8
Rociada ... E-6
Rodeo ... M-1
Rogers ... H-10
Romeroville ... F-7
Roswell ... J-8
Rowe ... F-6
Roy ... E-8
Ruidoso ... K-6
Ruidoso Downs ... K-6
Rutheron ... D-4
Sabinal ... H-4
Sacramento ... L-6
Saint Vrain ... H-10
Salem ... L-3
Salt Lake ... H-1
San Acacia ... H-4
San Antonio ... J-4
San Antonio ... F-5
San Fidel ... G-3
San Ignacio ... E-6
San Jon ... F-10
San Juan ... L-3
San Lorenzo ... L-3
San Mateo ... G-3
San Miguel ... M-4
San Miguel ... F-6
San Patricio ... J-7
San Rafael ... G-2
San Ysidro ... F-4
Santa Cruz ... E-5
Santa Fe ... F-5
Santa Rita ... L-2
Santa Rosa ... E-7
Sapello ... E-7
Sedan ... D-10
Sena ... F-7
Seneca ... D-10
Separ ... M-1
Seven Rivers ... L-8
Shadybrook ... D-6
Sheep Springs ... E-1
Shiprock ... D-1
Silver City ... L-2
Socorro ... H-4
Solano ... E-9
Springer ... D-8
Standing Rock ... E-1
Stanley ... F-6
Sunset ... K-7
Sunshine ... M-3
Taiban ... H-9
Tajique ... G-5
Talpa ... D-6
Taos ... D-6
Tatum ... K-10
Terrero ... E-6
Tesuque ... E-6
Thoreau ... F-2
Three Rivers ... K-5
Tierra Amarilla ... D-5
Tierra Monte ... E-6
Tijeras ... G-5
Tinnie ... K-7
Tohatchi ... E-1
Tolar ... H-9
Tome ... G-4
Torreon ... D-6
Tres Piedras ... D-6
Tres Ritos ... E-6
Truchas ... E-6
Trujillo ... F-8
Truth or Consequences ... K-4
Tucumcari ... F-9
Tularosa ... K-5
Turley ... D-2
Turn ... G-4
Tyrone ... L-2
Ute Park ... D-7
Vado ... M-5
Valencia ... G-4
Vallecitos ... D-5
Vallecitos ... N-6
Valmora ... E-7
Variadero ... F-8
Vaughn ... G-7
Veguita ... H-4
Velarde ... E-5
Villanueva ... F-6
Virden ... L-1
Wagon Mound ... E-8
Watrous ... E-7
Weed ... L-7
Wheatland ... G-10
White Horse ... E-3
White Oaks ... J-6
White Rock ... E-5
White Sands Missile Range ... F-5
Whites City ... M-8
Whitewater ... F-1
Willard ... G-6
Williamsburg ... K-3
Winston ... K-3
Yeso ... H-8
Youngsville ... E-5

NEW YORK
Pages 66-69

Adams ... F-12
Addison ... N-8
Afton ... M-13

Airmont ... ★
  Vicinity ... Pg. 138, B-4
Akron ... J-5
Albany ... K-18
Albertson ... ★
  Vicinity ... Pg. 141, L-13
Albion ... H-6
Alden ... K-5
Alexander ... K-5
Alexandria Bay ... D-12
Alfred ... M-7
Allegany ... N-5
Almond ... M-7
Altamont ... K-18
Altmar ... G-12
Amagansett ... C-9
Amenia ... O-19
Ames ... K-16
  Vicinity ... Pg. 141, N-16
Amsterdam ... J-18
Andes ... M-16
Andover ... N-7
Angelica ... M-6
Angola ... L-3
Angola-on-the-Lake ... L-3
Antwerp ... D-13
Apalachin ... N-12
Arcade ... L-5
Archville ... ★
  Vicinity ... Pg. 138, B-8
Ardsley ... ★
  Vicinity ... Pg. 138, D-9
Argyle ... H-20
Arkport ... M-7
Arlington ... O-19
Armonk ... ★
  Vicinity ... Pg. 140, C-11
Astoria ... ★
  Vicinity ... Pg. 139, K-8
Athens ... M-19
Atlantic Beach ... E-4
  Vicinity ... Pg. 141, Q-11
Attica ... A-5
Atwell ... G-15
Auburn ... K-10
Aurora ... K-10
Avoca ... M-8
Avon ... K-7
Babylon ... E-5
  Vicinity ... Pg. 141, N-18
Bainbridge ... M-13
Baldwin ... E-4
  Vicinity ... Pg. 141, P-13
Baldwinsville ... J-11
Ballston Spa ... J-18
Ballville ... A-3
Balmville ... ★
  Vicinity ... Pg. 138, B-6
Bardonia ... ★
  Vicinity ... Pg. 138, A-9
Barker ... H-5
Barneveld ... H-14
Batavia ... J-6
Bath ... M-8
Bay Park ... ★
  Vicinity ... Pg. 141, P-12
Bay Ridge ... ★
  Vicinity ... Pg. 139, M-6
Bay Shore ... E-6
  Vicinity ... Pg. 141, M-19
Bayberry ... J-11
Bayside ... ★
  Vicinity ... Pg. 139, K-10
Bayville ... D-5
  Vicinity ... Pg. 141, H-14
Beacon ... A-3
Bedford ... B-4
  Vicinity ... Pg. 140, B-13
Bedford Hills ... ★
  Vicinity ... Pg. 140, A-11
Belle Rose ... ★
  Vicinity ... Pg. 141, M-11
Bellmore ... E-4
  Vicinity ... Pg. 141, N-15
Belmont ... N-6
Bemus Pt. ... N-2
Benson Hurst ... ★
  Vicinity ... Pg. 139, M-7
Bergen ... J-6
Bethpage ... D-5
  Vicinity ... Pg. 141, M-15
Big Flats ... N-9
Binghamton ... N-12
Black River ... E-13
Blasdell ... K-4
  Vicinity ... Pg. 105, G-4
Blauvelt ... ★
  Vicinity ... Pg. 138, C-7
Bloomingburgh ... A-2
Bloomingdale ... C-18
Bloomington ... N-18
Bolivar ... N-6
Boonville ... G-14
Bovsen Bay ... J-11
Brasher Falls ... B-16
Brentwood ... D-6
Brewerton ... J-11
Brewster ... B-4
Briarcliff Manor ... C-4
Bridgehampton ... C-9
Bridgewater ... K-14
Brightwaters ... ★
  Vicinity ... Pg. 141, M-19
Broadalbin ... J-18
Brockport ... J-6

Brocton ... M-2
Bronx ... ★
  Vicinity ... Pg. 138, G-8
Bronxville ... ★
  Vicinity ... Pg. 138, F-9
Brooklyn ... ★
  Vicinity ... Pg. 139, L-6
Brownville ... E-12
Brushton ... B-16
Buchanan ... B-3
Buffalo ... K-4
  Vicinity ... Pg. 105
Burdett ... M-10
Burke ... B-17
Cairo ... M-18
Caledonia ... K-7
Calverton ... D-7
Cambridge ... J-20
Camden ... H-13
Camillus ... J-11
Canajoharie ... K-16
Canandaigua ... K-8
Canarisie ... ★
  Vicinity ... Pg. 139, M-8
Canaseraga ... M-7
Canastota ... J-13
Candor ... M-11
Canisteo ... M-7
Canton ... C-14
Cape Vincent ... E-11
Carle Place ... ★
  Vicinity ... Pg. 141, M-13
Carthage ... E-13
Cassadaga ... M-2
Castile ... L-6
Castleton Corners ... ★
  Vicinity ... Pg. 139, N-4
Castleton-on-Hudson ... L-18
Castorland ... F-13
Cato ... J-10
Catskill ... M-19
Cattaraugus ... M-4
Cayuga ... K-10
Cayuga Hts ... L-11
Cazenovia ... K-13
Cedarhurst ... ★
  Vicinity ... Pg. 141, P-11
Celoron ... N-2
Center Itsip ... ★
  Vicinity ... Pg. 141, K-20
Center Moriches ... D-7
Centereach ... D-6
Central Nyack ... ★
  Vicinity ... Pg. 138, B-7
Central Square ... H-12
Central Valley ... B-3
Champlain ... A-19
Chappaqua ... ★
  Vicinity ... Pg. 138, A-9
Chateaugay ... A-17
Chatham ... M-19
Chaumont ... E-12
Chelsea ... ★
  Vicinity ... Pg. 139, N-3
Cherry Creek ... M-3
Cherry Valley ... K-16
Chester ... B-2
Chittenango ... J-13
Churchville ... J-7
Clarence Center ... J-4
Claverack ... M-19
Clayton ... D-12
Clayville ... J-14
Cleveland ... H-13
Clifton Knolls ... K-18
Clifton Springs ... K-9
Clinton ... J-14
Clintondale ... O-18
Clyde ... J-10
Cobleskill ... K-17
Cohocton ... M-8
Cohoes ... K-19
Cold Brook ... H-15
Cold Spring ... J-11
Coldspring Harbor ... ★
  Vicinity ... Pg. 141, J-15
College Point ... ★
  Vicinity ... Pg. 139, J-9
Colonie ... K-18
Commack ... ★
  Vicinity ... Pg. 141, K-12
Coney Island ... ★
  Vicinity ... Pg. 139, P-10
Constableville ... G-14
Constantia ... H-12
Cooperstown ... K-15
Copenhagen ... F-13
Copiague ... ★
  Vicinity ... Pg. 141, N-17
Coram ... D-6
Corfu ... K-5
Corinth ... H-18
Corning ... N-9
Cornwall-on-Hudson ... A-3
Cortland ... L-11
County Knolls ... J-18
Coxsackie ... M-19
Croghan ... F-14
Croton-on-Hudson ... B-3
Cuba ... N-6
Cutchogue ... C-8
Dannemora ... B-18
Dansville ... L-7
DeRuyter ... K-13
DeWitt ... J-11

Deer Park ... D-5
  Vicinity ... Pg. 141, L-18
Deferiet ... E-13
Delanson ... K-17
Delevan ... L-5
Delhi ... M-15
Delmar ... L-18
Depew ... K-4
  Vicinity ... Pg. 105, E-6
Deposit ... N-14
Dexter ... E-12
Dobbs Ferry ... C-3
Dolgeville ... J-16
Dongan Hills ... ★
  Vicinity ... Pg. 139, N-4
Dover Plains ... O-19
Dresden ... L-9
Dryden ... L-11
Dundee ... L-9
Dunkirk ... M-2
Earlville ... K-13
East Aurora ... K-4
East Bloomfield ... K-8
East Glenville ... J-18
East Hampton ... C-9
East Hills ... ★
  Vicinity ... Pg. 141, K-13
East Ilsip ... ★
  Vicinity ... Pg. 141, M-20
East Irvington ... ★
  Vicinity ... Pg. 138, C-9
East Meadow ... D-4
  Vicinity ... Pg. 141, N-14
East New York ... ★
  Vicinity ... Pg. 139, L-8
East Northport ... ★
  Vicinity ... Pg. 141, J-17
East Quogue ... C-8
East Randolph ... N-3
East Rochester ... J-8
East Rockaway ... ★
  Vicinity ... Pg. 141, P-12
East View ... ★
  Vicinity ... Pg. 138, C-9
Eastchester ... ★
  Vicinity ... Pg. 138, E-9
Eatons Neck ... C-7
Eden ... L-4
Edgemere ... ★
  Vicinity ... Pg. 139, N-10
Edwards ... D-14
Elba ... J-6
Elbridge ... J-11
Ellenville ... O-17
Ellicottville ... M-4
Ellisburg ... F-12
Elma ... K-4
  Vicinity ... Pg. 105, F-7
Elmira Hts ... N-10
Elmont ... ★
  Vicinity ... Pg. 141, N-12
Elwood ... ★
  Vicinity ... Pg. 141, J-17
Endicott ... N-12
Endwell ... N-12
Esperance ... K-17
Evans Mills ... E-12
Fabius ... K-12
Fair Harbor ... ★
  Vicinity ... Pg. 141, P-20
Fair Haven ... H-10
Fairport ... J-8
Falconer ... N-3
Far Rockaway ... ★
  Vicinity ... Pg. 139, N-19
Farmingdale ... E-4
  Vicinity ... Pg. 141, M-16
Farnham ... L-3
Fayetteville ... J-12
Fernwood ... H-19
Fillmore ... M-6
Firthcliffe ... A-3
Fishkill ... A-3
Flatbush ... ★
  Vicinity ... Pg. 139, M-7
Fleischmanns ... N-17
Florida ... B-2
Flower Hill ... ★
  Vicinity ... Pg. 141, K-12
Flushing ... ★
  Vicinity ... Pg. 139, K-9
Fonda ... J-17
Forest Hills ... ★
  Vicinity ... Pg. 139, K-9
Forestville ... M-3
Fort Ann ... G-19
Fort Edward ... H-19
Fort Johnson ... J-17
Fort Plain ... K-16
Fort Salonga ... C-7
Frankfort ... J-15
Franklin ... M-15
Franklin Square ... ★
  Vicinity ... Pg. 141, N-12
Franklinville ... M-5
Freeport ... E-4
  Vicinity ... Pg. 141, P-14
Frewsburg ... N-3
Friendship ... N-6
Fulton ... H-11
Fultonville ... K-17
Gainesville ... L-6

Galway ... J-18
Gang Mills ... N-9
Garden City Park ... ★
  Vicinity ... Pg. 141, M-12
Geneseo ... K-7
Geneva ... K-9
Gilbertsville ... L-14
Glasco ... N-18
Glen Cove ... D-4
  Vicinity ... Pg. 141, P-13
Glen Park ... E-12
Glenham ... A-3
Glens Falls ... H-19
Glenville ... ★
  Vicinity ... Pg. 138, C-9
Glenwood Landing ... ★
  Vicinity ... Pg. 141, L-14
Gloversville ... J-17
Goldens Bridge ... B-4
Goshen ... B-2
Gouverneur ... D-14
Gowanda ... M-3
Grand View ... ★
  Vicinity ... Pg. 138, C-8
Granville ... G-20
Great Kills ... ★
  Vicinity ... Pg. 139, P-4
Great Neck ... D-4
  Vicinity ... Pg. 141, K-11
Greece ... J-7
Green Island ... K-19
Green Lawn ... ★
  Vicinity ... Pg. 141, J-7
Green Lawn ... ★
  Vicinity ... Pg. 141, J-7
Greene ... M-13
Greenport ... C-9
Greenvale ... ★
  Vicinity ... Pg. 141, K-13
Greenville ... ★
  Vicinity ... Pg. 138, D-9
Greenwich ... J-20
Greenwood Lake ... B-2
Groton ... L-11
Hadley ... H-19
Hagaman ... J-18
Halesite ... ★
  Vicinity ... Pg. 141, H-16
Hamburg ... K-4
  Vicinity ... Pg. 105, J-5
Hamilton ... K-14
Hammond ... C-13
Hammondsport ... M-8
Hampton Bays ... D-8
Hancock ... O-15
Hannibal ... H-10
Harriman ... B-2
Harrison ... C-4
  Vicinity ... Pg. 140, C-11
Harrisville ... E-14
Hartsdale ... ★
  Vicinity ... Pg. 138, D-10
Hastings-On-Hudson ... ★
  Vicinity ... Pg. 138, D-8
Hauppage ... ★
  Vicinity ... Pg. 141, K-20
Haverstraw ... B-3
Haviland ... O-19
Hawthorne ... ★
  Vicinity ... Pg. 138, B-9
Hempstead ... E-4
Herkimer ... J-15
Hermon ... C-14
Herrings ... E-13
Heuvelton ... C-14
Hewlett ... ★
  Vicinity ... Pg. 141, P-12
Hicksville ... D-5
Highland ... O-18
Highland Falls ... B-3
Highland Mills ... B-3
Hillburn ... C-2
  Vicinity ... Pg. 138, B-3
Hillcrest ... ★
  Vicinity ... Pg. 138, B-5
Hillside Lake ... P-19
Hilton ... H-7
Hobart ... N-17
Holbrook ... D-6
Holcomb ... K-8
Holland ... L-5
Holland Patent ... H-14
Holley ... J-6
Homer ... L-11
Honeoye Falls ... J-8
Hoosick Falls ... J-20
Hornell ... M-7
Horseheads ... N-10
Houghton ... M-6
Hudson ... M-19
Hudson Falls ... H-19
Hugenot ... ★
  Vicinity ... Pg. 139, Q-2
Hugenot Park ... ★
  Vicinity ... Pg. 139, Q-3
Hunter ... M-17
Huntington ... D-5
  Vicinity ... Pg. 141, J-16
Huntington Sta. ... D-5
  Vicinity ... Pg. 141, K-11
Hurley ... O-18
Hyde Park ... O-18
Ilion ... J-15
Interlaken ... L-10

Inwood ... ★
  Vicinity ... Pg. 141, Q-11
Irvington ... ★
  Vicinity ... Pg. 138, C-8
Iselin ... ★
  Vicinity ... Pg. 139, P-1
Island Park ... ★
  Vicinity ... Pg. 141, P-13
Islip ... D-6
  Vicinity ... Pg. 141, M-20
Islip Terrace ... ★
  Vicinity ... Pg. 141, L-20
Ithaca ... M-11
Jackson Hts. ... ★
  Vicinity ... Pg. 139, K-8
Jamaica ... ★
  Vicinity ... Pg. 141, L-16
Jamesport ... C-8
Jamestown ... N-3
Jefferson Hts ... M-18
Jefferson Valley ... B-4
Jeffersonville ... O-15
Jericho ... D-5
Johnson City ... N-12
Johnstown ... J-17
Jordan ... J-11
Keeseville ... C-19
Kenmore ... K-3
  Vicinity ... Pg. 105, C-4
Kerhonkson ... O-17
Keuka Park ... L-9
Kinderhook ... M-19
Kings Park ... ★
  Vicinity ... Pg. 141, J-19
Kings Point ... ★
  Vicinity ... Pg. 139, H-10
Kiryas Joel ... B-2
Kingston ... N-18
Lackawanna ... K-4
  Vicinity ... Pg. 105, G-4
Lacona ... G-12
Ladentown ... ★
  Vicinity ... Pg. 138, A-5
Lake Carmel ... A-4
Lake Erie Beach ... L-3
Lake George ... G-19
Lake Luzerne ... H-18
Lake Placid ... D-18
Lake Ronkonkoma ... D-6
Lakewood ... N-2
Lancaster ... K-4
  Vicinity ... Pg. 105, E-7
Lansing ... L-11
Larchmont ... ★
  Vicinity ... Pg. 140, B-11
Latham ... K-18
Lattingtown ... ★
  Vicinity ... Pg. 141, J-12
Laurens ... L-15
LeRoy ... K-6
Leicester ... K-6
Levittown ... ★
  Vicinity ... Pg. 141, M-15
Lewiston ... J-3
Liberty ... O-16
Lido Beach ... ★
  Vicinity ... Pg. 141, Q-13
Lima ... K-7
Limestone ... N-4
Lincoln Park ... N-18
Lindenhurst ... E-5
  Vicinity ... Pg. 141, N-17
Lisle ... M-12
Little Falls ... J-16
Little Valley ... M-4
Liverpool ... J-11
Livingston Manor ... O-16
Livonia ... K-7
Lloyd Harbor ... D-5
  Vicinity ... Pg. 141, H-15
Lockport ... J-4
Lodi ... L-10
Long Beach ... E-4
  Vicinity ... Pg. 141, Q-12
Long Island ... ★
  Vicinity ... Pg. 139, K-7
Lorenz Pk ... M-19
Lowville ... F-14
Lynbrook ... ★
  Vicinity ... Pg. 141, P-11
Lyndonville ... H-5
Lyons ... J-9
Lyons Falls ... G-14
Macedon ... J-8
Machias ... M-5
Madison ... K-14
Mahopac ... B-4
Malone ... B-17
Mamaroneck ... C-4
  Vicinity ... Pg. 140, G-11
Manchester ... J-8
Manhattan ... ★
  Vicinity ... Pg. 139, J-7
Manlius ... J-12
Mannsville ... F-12
Manorhaven ... ★
  Vicinity ... Pg. 141, K-11
Marathon ... M-12
Marcellus ... J-11
Margaretville ... N-16
Marlboro ... P-18

Massapequa ... E-5
  Vicinity ... Pg. 141, N-15
Massena ... B-15
Mastic ... D-7
Mastic Beach ... D-7
Mattituck ... C-8
Mattydale ... J-11
Maybrook ... A-2
Mayfield ... M-2
Mayville ... M-2
McGraw ... L-12
Mechanicville ... K-19
Medford ... D-6
Medina ... J-5
Melville ... ★
  Vicinity ... Pg. 141, L-16
Menands ... K-19
Meridian ... J-11
Merrick ... ★
  Vicinity ... Pg. 141, P-14
Merriewold Lake ... ★
Mexico ... H-11
Middle Hope ... P-18
Middleburgh ... L-17
Middleport ... J-5
Middletown ... A-2
Middleville ... J-15
Milburn ... ★
  Vicinity ... Pg. 139, K-1
Milford ... L-15
Millbrook ... O-19
Millerton ... N-19
Millport ... M-10
Milton ... O-18
Minetto ... H-11
Mineville ... E-19
Minoa ... J-12
Mohawk ... J-15
Monroe ... B-2
Monsey ... C-3
  Vicinity ... Pg. 138, B-5
Montauk ... C-10
Montgomery ... A-2
Monticello ... P-16
Montour Falls ... M-10
Mooers ... A-19
Moravia ... L-11
Morris ... L-15
Morristown ... C-13
Morrisville ... K-13
Mount Ivy ... ★
  Vicinity ... Pg. 138, A-6
Mount Kisco ... B-4
  Vicinity ... Pg. 140, B-11
Mount Morris ... L-7
Mount Vernon ... D-4
  Vicinity ... Pg. 138, F-9
  Vicinity ... Pg. 105, H-4
Munnsville ... J-13
Munsey Park ... ★
  Vicinity ... Pg. 141, L-13
Nanuet ... ★
  Vicinity ... Pg. 138, A-6
Napanoch ... O-17
Naples ... L-8
Nassau ... L-19
Nassau Shores ... ★
  Vicinity ... Pg. 141, O-16
Nelliston ... J-16
New Berlin ... L-14
New Brighton ... ★
  Vicinity ... Pg. 139, M-5
New Cassel ... ★
  Vicinity ... Pg. 141, L-14
New Drop ... ★
  Vicinity ... Pg. 139, P-4
New Drop Beach ... ★
  Vicinity ... Pg. 139, P-4
New Hartford ... J-14
New Hyde Park ... ★
  Vicinity ... Pg. 141, M-12
New Paltz ... O-18
New Rochelle ... D-4
  Vicinity ... Pg. 138, F-10
New Suffolk ... C-8
New York City ... E-3
  Vicinity ... Pg. 138-141
  Vicinity ... Pg. 105
New York Mills ... J-14
Newark ... J-9
Newark Valley ... M-12
Newburgh ... P-18
Newburgh ... A-3
Newfane ... H-5
Newport ... H-15
Niagara Falls (Canada) ... J-2
  Vicinity ... Pg. 105, A-1
Niagara Falls (U.S.) ... J-3
  Vicinity ... Pg. 105, A-2
Nichols ... N-11
Norfolk ... B-15
North Collins ... L-3
North Haven ... C-9
North Hornell ... M-7
North Sea ... C-9
North Syracuse ... J-12
North Tareytown ... ★
  Vicinity ... Pg. 138, B-8
North Tonawanda ... J-4
Northport ... ★
  Vicinity ... Pg. 141, H-17
Northville ... H-17
Norwich ... L-13
Norwood ... B-15
Noyack ... C-9

★ Denotes City only on Vicinity map. City not located on State map.

NEW YORK

Nunda L-6
Nyack C-3
  Vicinity . . . . . Pg. 138, B-7
Oak Beach . . . . ★
  Vicinity . . . . . Pg. 141, P-19
Oakfield J-5
Ocean Beach E-6
  Vicinity . . . . . Pg. 141, P-20
Oceanside . . . . ★
  Vicinity . . . . . Pg. 141, P-19
Odessa M-10
Ogdensburg B-13
Olcott H-4
Old Forge G-14
Olean N-5
Oneida J-13
Oneida Castle J-13
Oneonta M-15
Orange Lake A-3
Orangeburg . . . . ★
  Vicinity . . . . . Pg. 138, C-7
Orchard Park K-4
  Vicinity . . . . . Pg. 105, C-4
Oriskany J-14
Oriskany Falls J-14
Ossining C-4
Otego M-14
Otisville A-1
Ovid L-10
Owego N-11
Oxford M-13
Oyster Bay . . . . ★
  Vicinity . . . . . Pg. 141, J-14
Ozone Park . . . . ★
  Vicinity . . . . . Pg. 139, L-9
Painted Post N-9
Palatine Bridge K-16
Palisades . . . . ★
  Vicinity . . . . . Pg. 138, D-8
Palmyra J-9
Panama N-2
Parish H-12
Patchogue D-6
Pawling A-4
Pearl River C-3
  Vicinity . . . . . Pg. 138, C-6
  Vicinity . . . . . Pg. 105, C-6
Peconic C-8
Peekskill B-3
Pelham . . . . ★
  Vicinity . . . . . Pg. 138, G-9
Pelham Manor . . . . ★
  Vicinity . . . . . Pg. 138, G-10
Penn Yan L-9
Perry L-6
Perrysburg M-3
Peru C-19
Phelps K-9
Philadelphia E-13
Philmont M-19
Phoenix H-11
Piermont . . . . ★
  Vicinity . . . . . Pg. 138, C-8
Pike L-6
Pine Bush P-17
Pine Hill N-17
Pine Plains N-19
Pittsford J-8
Plainview D-5
  Vicinity . . . . . Pg. 141, L-16
Plattsburgh B-19
Pleasantville C-4
Pocantico Hills . . . . . ★
  Vicinity . . . . . Pg. 138, B-9
Poestenkill K-20
Poland H-15
Pomona B-3
Port Byron J-10
Port Dickinson N-13
Port Ewen N-18
Port Henry E-19
Port Jefferson C-6
Port Jervis B-1
Port Leyden G-14
Port Richmond . . . . . . ★
  Vicinity . . . . . Pg. 139, M-3
Port Washington . . . . . ★
  Vicinity . . . . . Pg. 141, K-12
Portville N-5
Potsdam B-15
Poughkeepsie O-19
Pound Ridge . . . . ★
  Vicinity . . . . . Pg. 140, B-13
Prospect H-14
Pulaski G-12
Queens . . . . ★
  Vicinity . . . . . Pg. 139, K-10
Queens Village . . . . . . ★
  Vicinity . . . . . Pg. 139, K-10
Quogue D-8
Ramapo . . . . ★
  Vicinity . . . . . Pg. 138, B-3
Randolph N-3
Ransomville J-4
Ravena L-18
Red Creek H-10
Red Hook N-19
Red Oaks Mill O-19
Remsen H-15
Rensselaer L-19
Rensselaer Falls C-14
Rhinebeck N-19
Richburg N-6
Richfield Springs K-15
Richmond Hill . . . . . . ★
  Vicinity . . . . . Pg. 139, L-9
Richmondville L-17
Richville C-14
Ridge D-7

Riverdale . . . . ★
  Vicinity . . . . . Pg. 138, C-8
Riverhead D-8
Riverside N-9
Rochester J-7
Rockville Centre . . . . . ★
  Vicinity . . . . . Pg. 141, P-12
Rocky Pt. C-7
Roessleville K-18
Rome J-13
Roosevelt . . . . ★
  Vicinity . . . . . Pg. 141, N-14
Roselyn Hts. . . . . ★
  Vicinity . . . . . Pg. 141, L-12
Rosendale O-18
Rossville . . . . ★
  Vicinity . . . . . Pg. 139, P-3
Round Lake J-19
Rouses Point A-19
Ruby N-18
Rushville K-9
Rye C-4
  Vicinity . . . . . Pg. 140, G-12
Rye Brook C-4
Sackets Harbor F-12
Sag Harbor C-9
Saint James . . . . ★
  Vicinity . . . . . Pg. 141, J-20
Saint Johnsville L-16
Saint Lawrence Park . . . D-12
Salamanca N-4
Salem H-20
San Remo . . . . ★
  Vicinity . . . . . Pg. 141, J-19
Sand Ridge J-11
Sands Point . . . . ★
  Vicinity . . . . . Pg. 141, J-11
Sandy Creek G-12
Saranac Lake D-18
Saratoga Springs J-18
Saugerties N-18
Savona M-9
Sayville D-6
Scarsdale C-4
  Vicinity . . . . . Pg. 138, E-9
Schaghticoke J-19
Schenectady K-18
Schenevus L-15
Schoharie L-17
Schuylerville J-19
Scotch Town A-2
Scotia K-18
Scottsville J-7
Sea Cliff . . . . ★
  Vicinity . . . . . Pg. 141, J-13
Seaford . . . . ★
  Vicinity . . . . . Pg. 141, N-15
Selden D-6
Seneca Falls K-10
Sharon Springs K-16
Shelter Island C-9
Sherburne L-14
Sherman N-1
Sherrill J-13
Shirley D-7
Shortsville K-8
Sidney M-14
Silver Creek L-3
Silver Springs L-6
Sinclairville M-2
Skaneateles K-11
Sloatsburg C-2
  Vicinity . . . . . Pg. 138, A-3
Smithtown D-6
  Vicinity . . . . . Pg. 141, J-20
Smyrna L-13
Sodus H-9
Sodus Point H-9
Solvay J-11
Sound Beach C-6
South Corning N-9
South Fallsburg O-16
South Glens Falls H-19
South Nyack . . . . ★
  Vicinity . . . . . Pg. 138, C-8
Southampton D-9
Southold C-8
Southport N-10
Sparkill . . . . ★
  Vicinity . . . . . Pg. 138, D-7
Speculator G-17
Spencer N-11
Spencerport J-7
Spring Valley C-3
  Vicinity . . . . . Pg. 138, B-5
Springfield Gdns. . . . . ★
  Vicinity . . . . . Pg. 139, L-10
Springs C-9
Springville L-4
Stamford M-16
Stannards N-6
Star Lake D-15
Staten Island . . . . . . ★
  Vicinity . . . . . Pg. 139, O-5
Stillwater J-19
Stony Brook C-6
Stony Pt. C-3
Stottville M-19
Suffern C-3
  Vicinity . . . . . Pg. 138, B-3
Sylvan Beach J-13
Syosset . . . . ★
  Vicinity . . . . . Pg. 141, K-15
Syracuse J-11
Tall Man . . . . ★
  Vicinity . . . . . Pg. 138, B-4
Tannersville M-18
Tappan . . . . ★
  Vicinity . . . . . Pg. 138, D-7

Tarrytown C-4
  Vicinity . . . . . Pg. 138, C-8
Theresa D-13
Thomaston . . . . ★
  Vicinity . . . . . Pg. 141, L-11
Thornwood . . . . ★
  Vicinity . . . . . Pg. 138, B-10
Ticonderoga F-19
Tillson O-18
Tivoli N-18
Tonawanda J-4
  Vicinity . . . . . Pg. 105, C-4
Town Line K-5
Tribes Hill J-17
Troy K-19
Trumansburg L-10
Trumbull . . . . ★
  Vicinity . . . . . Pg. 140, A-3
Tuckahoe D-8
Tully K-12
Tupper Lake D-17
Turin F-14
Tuxedo Park B-2
  Vicinity . . . . . Pg. 138, A-3
Unadilla M-14
Union Springs K-10
Union Vale . . . . ★
  Vicinity . . . . . Pg. 141, N-13
Unionville B-15
Upper Nyack . . . . ★
  Vicinity . . . . . Pg. 138, B-7
Utica J-15
Valatie L-19
Valhalla . . . . ★
  Vicinity . . . . . Pg. 138, C-10
Valley Cottage . . . . . . ★
  Vicinity . . . . . Pg. 138, B-7
Valley Falls J-20
Valley Stream E-4
  Vicinity . . . . . Pg. 141, P-11
Van Etten N-11
Vernon J-14
Verona J-12
Victor K-8
Victory J-10
Village of the Branch . . ★
  Vicinity . . . . . Pg. 141, J-20
Viola . . . . ★
  Vicinity . . . . . Pg. 138, B-5
Vista . . . . ★
  Vicinity . . . . . Pg. 140, B-14
Voorheesville L-18
Waddington B-14
Wading River C-7
Walden A-2
Wallkill A-2
Walton N-15
Walton Park B-2
Wampsville J-13
Wantagh . . . . ★
  Vicinity . . . . . Pg. 141, N-15
Wappinger Falls A-3
Warrensburg G-19
Warsaw K-6
Warwick B-2
Washingtonville A-2
Waterford K-19
Waterloo K-9
Watertown E-13
Watervliet K-19
Waterville K-14
Watkins Glen M-10
Waverly N-11
Wayland L-7
Webster J-8
Weedsport J-10
Wellsburg N-10
Wellsville N-6
West Babylon . . . . ★
  Vicinity . . . . . Pg. 141, N-18
West Carthage F-13
West End L-15
West Nyack . . . . ★
  Vicinity . . . . . Pg. 138, B-6
West Plattsburgh B-19
West Point B-3
West Sand Lake L-19
West Winfield K-15
Westbury . . . . ★
  Vicinity . . . . . Pg. 141, M-13
Westfield M-2
Westhampton D-8
Westmere K-17
Westons Mills N-5
Westport D-19
White Plains . . . . ★
  Vicinity . . . . . Pg. 138, D-10
Whitehall G-20
Whitesboro J-14
Whitney Point M-12
Willard L-10
Williamsville K-4
  Vicinity . . . . . Pg. 105, D-6
Williston Park . . . . . . ★
  Vicinity . . . . . Pg. 141, L-13
Willow Brook . . . . ★
  Vicinity . . . . . Pg. 139, N-4
Wilson H-4
Windsor N-13
Winthrop B-16
Witherbee E-19
Wolcott H-10
Woodbury . . . . ★
  Vicinity . . . . . Pg. 141, K-15
Woodhull N-8
Woodridge O-17
Woodstock N-18
Wyandanch . . . . ★
  Vicinity . . . . . Pg. 141, L-17
Wyoming K-6

Yonkers D-3
  Vicinity . . . . . Pg. 138, F-8
Yorkshire L-5
Yorktown Hts B-4
Yorkville J-13
Youngstown H-3
Zena N-18

NORTH CAROLINA
Pages 70-71

Abbotsburg E-10
Aberdeen D-8
Acre C-12
Ahoskie A-12
Albemarle D-7
Allen D-7
Allenton E-9
Andrews D-2
Arapahoe D-12
Archdale B-10
Arcola B-10
Arlington B-6
Asheboro C-8
Asheville C-4
Ashland B-12
Askin C-12
Aurora D-12
Avery Creek D-4
Avon C-14
Ayden C-11
Badin D-7
Bagley B-11
Bald Creek C-4
Baldwin B-5
Bandana B-4
Banner Elk B-5
Barco A-13
Bat Cave D-4
Battleboro B-11
Bear Creek C-9
Beaufort D-13
Belgrade D-11
Belhaven D-6
Belmont C-9
Benson C-9
Bertha A-13
Bessemer City D-6
Bethel B-11
Bethel Hill A-9
Beulaville D-11
Biscoe D-8
Black Mtn. C-4
Bladenboro E-9
Blowing Rock B-5
Bolton E-10
Boone B-5
Bottom A-6
Bowdens D-10
Brasstown D-2
Brevard D-4
Bridgeton D-12
Bridgewater C-5
Brookford B-6
Brooks Cross Roads B-6
Brooksdale B-9
Browns Summit B-8
Brunswick F-10
Bryson City D-2
Bulade A-9
Bullock A-9
Bunn B-10
Burch B-6
Burgaw E-11
Burlington B-8
Burnsville B-4
Buxton C-14
Calypso D-10
Camden A-13
Cameron D-9
Candor D-8
Canto C-3
Canton D-3
Carolina Beach F-11
Carr B-8
Carrboro B-9
Cary B-9
Casville B-9
Cedar Creek D-10
Celo B-4
Centerville B-10
Chadbourn F-10
Chapel Hill C-9
Charlotte D-7
Cherokee D-3
Cherryville D-6
China Grove C-7
Chinquapin D-11
Chocowinity C-12
Churchland C-7
Cid C-7
Clemmons B-7
Clinton D-10
Coinjock A-13
Colerain B-12
College B-8
Columbia B-13
Columbus D-5
Comfort D-11
Concord D-7
Conover C-6
Conway A-12
Corapeake A-12
Cornelius D-6
Council E-10
Cove Creek C-3
Creedmoor B-10
Creswell B-13

Culberson D-1
Currie E-10
Dalton B-7
Darden B-12
Davidson C-6
Deep Gap B-5
Del Mar Beach E-12
Delway E-10
Dillsboro D-3
Dobson B-7
Dortches B-10
Dudley D-10
Dunn D-9
Durham B-9
East Flat Rock D-4
East Lake B-13
East Laport D-3
Eastwood D-8
Eden A-8
Edenhouse B-12
Edenton B-12
Edneyville D-4
Edward C-12
Ela D-3
Eldorado C-7
Elizabeth City A-13
Elizabethtown E-10
Elk Park B-4
Elkin B-6
Emery D-8
Enfield B-11
Englehard C-13
Erwin D-9
Essex B-10
Ether C-8
Evergreen E-9
Fair Bluff E-9
Fairmont E-9
Faison D-10
Farmville C-11
Fayetteville D-9
Flat Rock D-4
Fletcher D-4
Folkston E-11
Fontana Village D-2
Forest City D-5
Fountain C-11
Franklin D-2
Freeman E-10
Fremont C-10
Frisco C-14
Fuquay-Varina C-9
Garysburg A-11
Gastonia D-6
Gates A-12
Gilkey D-5
Glade Valley B-6
Glenview B-10
Glenwood C-5
Gneiss D-3
Godwin D-9
Gold Rock B-11
Goldsboro C-10
Goldston C-8
Gordonton B-9
Graingers C-11
Grandy A-13
Granite Falls C-5
Granite Quarry C-7
Grantham D-10
Greensboro B-8
Greenville C-11
Grifton C-11
Grissettown F-10
Guilford B-8
Halifax A-11
Hamlet D-8
Hampstead E-11
Harbinger B-14
Harmony B-6
Harrells E-10
Harrisburg D-7
Hatteras C-14
Hazelwood D-3
Heartsease B-11
Henderson B-10
Hendersonville D-4
Henrietta D-5
Hertford B-12
Hester B-9
Hickory C-6
High Hampton D-3
High Point B-7
Hightowers B-9
Hill Crest D-8
Hillsborough B-9
Hiwassee D-2
Hoffman D-8
Holly Ridge E-11
Hollyville (Cash Corner) . D-12
Hope Mills D-9
House C-11
Hubert D-11
Hudson C-5
Ingleside B-10
Jackson A-11
Jacksonville D-11
Jamesville B-12
Jarvisburg A-13
Jason C-11
Johns E-9
Jonas Ridge C-5
Jonesville B-6
Julian B-8
Justice B-10

Kannapolis C-7
Keener E-10
Kelley E-10
Kenansville D-11
Kenly C-10
Kernersville B-7
Kilkenny F-10
King B-7
Kings Mountain D-5
Kinston D-11
Kittrell B-10
Kuhns D-7
Kure Beach F-11
La Grange D-11
Lake Landing C-13
Lakeview D-9
Landis C-7
Lauada D-2
Laurinburg E-9
Lawrence B-11
Leasburg A-9
Leechville C-13
Lemon Springs C-8
Lenoir C-5
Level Cross B-8
Lewis A-9
Lexington C-7
Liberia B-10
Liberty B-8
Lilesville D-8
Lillington C-9
Lincolnton D-5
Linwood C-7
Lizzie C-11
Logan D-5
Long Beach F-10
Longview C-5
Louisburg B-10
Lucama C-11
Luck B-4
Lumber Bridge D-9
Lumberton E-9
Maco E-10
Madison B-7
Magnolia D-10
Maiden C-6
Mamie B-13
Manns Harbor B-13
Manteo B-14
Maple Hill D-11
Marble D-2
Marion C-5
Mars Hill C-4
Marshall C-3
Marshville D-7
Marston D-8
Matthews E-9
Maxton E-9
Mayodan B-8
Maysville D-11
Mesic C-12
Micro C-10
Middleburg B-10
Midway B-12
Midway Park E-11
Mineola C-11
Mint Hill D-7
Mocksville C-7
Moncure C-9
Monroe D-7
Monticello B-8
Mooresville C-6
Morehead City D-12
Morgans Corner A-13
Morganton C-5
Mount Airy A-7
Mount Gilead D-7
Mount Holly D-6
Mount Mourne C-6
Mount Olive D-11
Mountain Home D-4
Mulberry B-6
Murfreesboro A-12
Nags Head B-14
Nakina F-10
Nantahala D-2
Nashville B-11
New Bern D-12
New Holland C-13
New Salem D-7
Newport D-12
Newton C-6
Newton Grove D-10
Norlina A-10
Norman D-8
North Wilkesboro B-6
Northside B-9
Oak Grove B-9
Oakboro D-7
Ocracoke D-14
Old Dock F-10
Old Fort C-4
Olivia D-9
Osceola B-8
Oswalt C-6
Oteen C-4
Otto D-3
Oxford B-9
Pantego C-12
Patterson B-5
Peachtree D-2
Pembroke E-9
Penderlea E-10
Picks B-7
Pilot Mountain B-7

Pine Ridge A-6
Pinebluff D-8
Pineola B-5
Pinetops B-11
Pineville D-6
Pinnacle B-7
Pireway F-10
Pittsboro C-9
Pleasant Hill A-11
Plymouth B-12
Point Harbor B-13
Polkton D-7
Pollocksville D-11
Portsmouth D-13
Postell D-1
Powells Point B-14
Raeford D-9
Rainbow Springs D-2
Raleigh C-9
Randleman C-8
Ranger D-1
Ransomville C-12
Rapids A-11
Red Hill B-4
Red Springs E-9
Reidsville B-8
Rheasville A-11
Rich Square B-11
Roanoke A-11
Robbinsville D-2
Robersonville B-11
Rockingham D-8
Rocky Mount B-11
Rodanthe B-14
Roduco B-12
Roper B-12
Rose Hill D-10
Roseboro D-10
Roseneath B-11
Rougemont B-9
Rowan E-10
Rowland E-9
Roxboro A-9
Ruth D-5
Rutherfordton D-4
Saint Pauls E-9
Salemburg D-10
Salisbury C-7
Salvo B-14
Sanford C-9
Schley B-9
Scotland Neck B-11
Scott's Hill E-11
Scranton C-13
Seabreeze F-11
Seagrove C-8
Selma C-10
Shallotte F-10
Sharpsburg B-11
Shelby D-5
Siler City C-8
Sioux B-4
Skyland C-4
Smith F-10
Smithfield C-10
Snow Hill C-11
Southern Pines D-9
Southport F-10
Sparta A-6
Spencer C-7
Spindale D-5
Spivey's Corner D-10
Spout Springs D-9
Spring Hill B-11
Spring Lake D-9
Spruce Pine C-5
Stanhope B-10
Stanleyville B-7
State Road B-6
Statesville C-6
Steeds C-8
Stocksville C-4
Stokes C-12
Stony Point C-6
Stovall A-10
Stratford A-6
Sunbury A-12
Supply F-10
Surf City E-11
Surl B-9
Swann C-9
Swannanoa C-4
Swansboro E-12
Swiss C-4
Sylva D-3
Tabor City E-9
Tapoco D-2
Tar Heel D-9
Tarboro B-11
Taylorsville C-6
Teachey D-10
Thomasville C-7
Tillery B-11
Tin City E-10
Tobaccoville B-7
Toluca C-5
Topsail Beach E-12
Topton D-2
Tramway C-9
Trent Woods D-12
Trenton D-11
Trust C-3
Tryon D-4
Turnersburg C-6
Tuxedo D-4

Twin Oaks A-6
Ulah C-8
Unaka D-2
Uwharrie C-8
Valdese C-5
Vanceboro C-11
Vander D-9
Violet D-1
Wadesboro E-7
Wadeville D-7
Wagram D-9
Wake Forest B-10
Wallace E-11
Wallburg B-7
Walnut C-4
Walnut Creek C-11
Wanchese B-14
Wards Corner E-10
Warsaw D-10
Waves B-14
Waynesville D-3
Weldon A-11
Wendell C-10
Wesser D-2
West Onslow Beach E-12
Westminster D-5
Whalebone B-14
White Lake E-10
White Oak E-10
Whiteville F-10
Wilbar B-6
Wilkesboro B-6
Willard E-10
Williamsburg B-8
Williamston B-12
Wilmar C-12
Wilmington F-11
Wilmington Beach F-11
Wilson C-11
Windsor B-12
Wingate D-7
Winnabow F-10
Winston-Salem B-7
Winterville C-11
Winton A-10
Wise A-10
Wise Fork D-11
Woodland A-12
Woodley B-13
Wrightsville Beach F-11
Yadkinville B-7
Yancyville A-8
Yeatesville C-12
Youngsville B-10
Zebulon B-10

NORTH DAKOTA
Pages 72-73

Abercrombie G-10
Adams C-9
Alamo B-2
Alexander C-2
Alice F-9
Almont F-5
Alsen B-8
Ambrose A-3
Amenia F-10
Amidon F-2
Anamoose D-6
Aneta D-9
Antler A-5
Ardoch C-9
Arena E-6
Argusville E-10
Arnegard C-2
Arthur E-9
Ashley G-7
Ayr E-9
Balfour D-6
Balta C-6
Bantry C-6
Barney G-10
Barton B-6
Bathgate B-9
Battleview B-3
Beach E-1
Belcourt B-7
Belfield E-2
Benedict D-5
Bergen C-6
Berlin G-8
Berthold C-5
Berwick C-6
Beulah E-4
Binford D-8
Bisbee B-7
Bismarck F-5
Bottineau B-6
Bowbells B-4
Bowdon D-7
Bowman G-2
Braddock F-6
Breien F-5
Bremen D-7
Brinsmade C-7
Brocket C-8
Bucyrus G-3
Buffalo F-9
Burlington C-5
Butte D-6
Buxton E-10
Calio B-8
Calvin B-8

★ Denotes City only on Vicinity map. City not located on State map.

NORTH DAKOTA

OHIO

Cando ... C-7
Carbury ... B-6
Carpio ... B-4
Carrington ... E-8
Carson ... F-4
Casselton ... F-9
Cathay ... D-7
Cavalier ... B-9
Cayuga ... G-9
Center ... E-5
Charlson ... C-3
Chaseley ... E-7
Churchs Ferry ... C-7
Cleveland ... F-7
Clifford ... E-10
Colehabor ... D-5
Colfax ... G-10
Columbus ... A-3
Conway ... C-9
Cooperstown ... E-9
Courtenay ... E-8
Crary ... D-8
Crosby ... A-2
Crystal ... B-9
Davenport ... F-9
Dawson ... F-6
Dazey ... E-9
Deering ... C-5
Des Lacs ... C-4
Devils Lake ... C-8
Dickey ... G-8
Dickinson ... E-3
Dodge ... E-4
Donnybrook ... B-4
Douglas ... D-5
Drake ... D-6
Drayton ... C-10
Driscoll ... F-6
Dunn Center ... D-3
Dunseith ... B-7
Dwight ... G-10
Edgeley ... G-8
Edinburg ... C-9
Edmore ... C-8
Egeland ... B-8
Elgin ... F-4
Ellendale ... G-8
Elliott ... G-9
Emerado ... D-9
Enderlin ... F-9
Epping ... C-2
Esmond ... C-7
Fairdale ... C-8
Fairfield ... E-3
Fargo ... F-10
Farimont ... H-10
Fessenden ... D-7
Fingal ... F-9
Finley ... E-9
Flasher ... F-5
Flaxton ... B-4
Flora ... D-7
Forbes ... G-7
Fordville ... C-9
Forest River ... C-9
Forman ... G-9
Fort Ransom ... G-9
Fort Yates ... G-5
Fortuna ... A-2
Freda ... G-5
Fredonia ... G-7
Fullerton ... G-8
Gackle ... F-7
Galesburg ... E-9
Gardena ... B-6
Garrison ... D-5
Gascoyne ... G-2
Gilby ... C-9
Gladstone ... E-3
Glen Ullin ... F-4
Glenburn ... B-5
Glenfield ... E-8
Golden Valley ... E-4
Golva ... E-1
Goodrich ... D-6
Grafton ... C-9
Grand Forks ... D-10
Grandin ... E-10
Grano ... B-4
Granville ... C-6
Grassy Butte ... D-3
Great Bend ... G-10
Grenora ... B-2
Gwinner ... G-9
Hague ... G-6
Haley ... G-2
Halliday ... D-4
Hamberg ... D-7
Hampden ... C-8
Hankinson ... H-10
Hanks ... B-2
Hannaford ... E-9
Hannah ... B-8
Harlow ... C-7
Harvey ... D-7
Harwood ... F-10
Hatton ... D-9
Havana ... H-9
Haynes ... G-3
Hazelton ... F-6
Hazen ... E-4
Hebron ... E-4
Heimdal ... D-7
Hensel ... B-9
Hettinger ... G-3

Hillsboro ... E-10
Hoople ... C-9
Hope ... E-9
Hunter ... E-9
Hurdsfield ... E-6
Inkster ... C-9
Jamestown ... F-8
Joliette ... B-10
Jud ... F-8
Karlsruhe ... C-6
Kathryn ... F-9
Kenmare ... B-4
Kensal ... E-8
Kief ... D-6
Killdeer ... D-3
Kindred ... F-10
Knox ... C-7
Kramer ... B-6
Kulm ... G-8
La Moure ... G-8
Lakota ... D-8
Landa ... B-5
Langdon ... B-8
Lansford ... B-5
Larimore ... D-9
Larson ... A-3
Lawton ... C-8
Leal ... E-8
Leeds ... C-7
Lehr ... G-7
Leith ... F-5
Leonard ... F-9
Lidgerwood ... G-9
Lignite ... A-4
Lincoln ... F-5
Linton ... G-6
Lisbon ... G-9
Litchville ... F-8
Loma ... B-8
Loraine ... B-5
Ludden ... H-9
Maddock ... D-7
Makoti ... C-4
Mandan ... F-5
Manfred ... D-7
Manning ... D-3
Mantador ... G-10
Manvel ... D-9
Marion ... F-8
Marmarth ... F-2
Marshall ... E-4
Martin ... D-6
Max ... D-5
Maxbass ... B-5
Mayville ... E-9
Maza ... C-7
McClusky ... D-6
McHenry ... D-8
McVille ... D-9
Medina ... F-7
Medora ... E-2
Melville ... E-8
Mercer ... D-5
Merricourt ... G-7
Michigan ... D-9
Milnor ... G-9
Milton ... B-9
Minnewaukan ... D-7
Minot ... C-5
Minto ... C-9
Mohall ... B-5
Monango ... G-8
Montpelier ... F-8
Mooreton ... G-10
Mott ... F-3
Mountain ... B-9
Munich ... B-8
Mylo ... B-7
Napoleon ... F-7
Neche ... B-9
Nekoma ... B-8
New England ... F-3
New Leipzig ... F-4
New Rockford ... D-8
New Salem ... F-5
New Town ... C-4
Newburg ... B-6
Nome ... F-9
Noonan ... A-3
Northwood ... D-9
Oakes ... G-9
Oberon ... D-7
Omemee ... B-6
Oriska ... F-9
Osnabrock ... B-8
Overly ... B-6
Page ... E-9
Palermo ... B-4
Park River ... C-9
Parshall ... C-4
Pekin ... D-8
Pembina ... B-9
Perth ... B-7
Petersburg ... D-9
Pettibone ... E-7
Pick City ... D-4
Pillsbury ... E-9
Pingree ... E-8
Pisek ... C-9
Plaza ... C-4
Portal ... A-3
Portland ... E-10
Powers Lake ... B-3
Prairie Rose ... F-10
Raleigh ... G-5

Rawson ... C-2
Ray ... B-3
Reeder ... G-3
Regan ... E-6
Regent ... F-3
Rhame ... G-2
Richardton ... F-4
Riverdale ... D-5
Riverside ... F-10
Robinson ... E-7
Rock Lake ... B-7
Rogers ... E-9
Rolette ... B-7
Rolla ... B-7
Ross ... C-4
Rugby ... C-7
Ruso ... D-5
Rutland ... H-9
Ryder ... C-4
Saint Thomas ... B-10
Sanborn ... F-8
Sarles ... B-8
Sawyer ... C-5
Scranton ... G-2
Selfridge ... G-5
Sentinel Butte ... E-2
Sharon ... D-9
Sheilds ... G-4
Sheldon ... F-9
Sherwood ... A-4
Sheyenne ... D-8
Sibley ... E-9
Solen ... G-5
Souris ... B-6
South Heart ... E-3
Spiritwood ... F-8
Spiritwood Lake ... F-8
Spring Brook ... C-2
Stanley ... C-3
Stanton ... E-5
Starkweather ... C-8
Steele ... E-6
Strasburg ... G-6
Streeter ... F-7
Surrey ... C-5
Sydney ... F-8
Sykeston ... E-7
Tappen ... F-7
Thompson ... D-10
Tioga ... B-3
Tolley ... B-4
Tolna ... D-8
Tower City ... F-9
Towner ... C-6
Turtle Lake ... D-5
Tuttle ... E-6
Underwood ... D-5
Upham ... B-6
Valley City ... F-9
Velva ... C-5
Venturia ... G-7
Verendrye ... C-6
Verona ... G-9
Voltaire ... C-6
Wahpeton ... G-10
Walcott ... G-10
Wales ... B-8
Walhalla ... B-8
Walseth ... B-5
Warwick ... D-8
Washburn ... E-5
Watford City ... C-3
Wellsburg ... D-7
West Fargo ... F-10
Westfeild ... G-6
Westhope ... B-5
Wheelock ... B-3
White Earth ... B-3
Wildrose ... B-3
Williston ... C-2
Willow City ... B-6
Wilton ... E-5
Wimbledon ... E-8
Wing ... E-6
Wishek ... G-7
Wolford ... C-7
Woodworth ... E-7
Wyndmere ... G-9
York ... C-7
Ypsilanti ... F-8
Zap ... E-4
Zeeland ... G-6

OHIO
Pages 74-75

Abbeyville ... ★
  Vicinity ... Pg. 113, J-1
Aberdeen ... N-3
Ada ... G-3
Addyston ... M-1
Adena ... J-9
Africa ... ★
  Vicinity ... Pg. 153, A-4
Akron ... E-8
Albany ... M-7
Alexandria ... J-5
Alger ... H-3
Alliance ... F-9
Alton ... ★
  Vicinity ... Pg. 153, F-1
Amanda ... L-5
Amberley ... ★
  Vicinity ... Pg. 112, C-5

Amberley ... ★
  Vicinity ... Pg. 112, C-5
Amelia ... M-2
Amesville ... L-7
Amherst ... F-6
Amlin ... ★
  Vicinity ... Pg. 153, D-1
Amsterdam ... H-9
Andover ... E-10
Anna ... J-2
Ansonia ... J-1
Antwerp ... F-1
Apple Creek ... H-7
Arcadia ... F-4
Arcanum ... K-1
Archbold ... E-2
Arlington ... G-3
Ashland ... G-6
Ashley ... H-5
Ashtabula ... D-9
Ashville ... K-5
Athalia ... O-6
Athens ... M-7
Attica ... G-5
Aurora ... F-8
Avon Lake ... E-7
Bainbridge ... M-4
Baltic ... H-8
Baltimore ... K-6
Barberton ... G-8
Barnesville ... K-9
Barnsburg ... ★
  Vicinity ... Pg. 112, B-2
Batavia ... M-2
Bath ... ★
  Vicinity ... Pg. 113, K-4
Bath Ctr. ... ★
  Vicinity ... Pg. 113, K-4
Bay View ... E-5
Beach City ... H-8
Beallsville ... K-9
Beavercreek ... K-2
Beaverdam ... G-3
Bedford ... ★
  Vicinity ... Pg. 113, E-6
Bedford Heights ... ★
  Vicinity ... Pg. 113, E-6
Beechwood ... ★
  Vicinity ... Pg. 113, C-6
Beloit ... F-9
Bellaire ... K-10
Bellbrook ... L-2
Belle Center ... H-3
Belle Valley ... K-8
Bellefontaine ... H-3
Bellevue ... F-5
Bellville ... H-6
Belmont ... J-9
Belpre ... M-8
Belvis ... ★
  Vicinity ... Pg. 112, A-2
Bennetts Corner ... ★
  Vicinity ... Pg. 113, F-2
Berea ... ★
  Vicinity ... Pg. 113, F-1
Bergholz ... H-9
Berlin Heights ... F-6
Bethel ... N-2
Bethseda ... J-9
Bettsville ... F-4
Beverly ... L-8
Bexley ... J-5
Bexley ... J-5
  Vicinity ... Pg. 153, F-5
Black Lick ... ★
  Vicinity ... Pg. 153, E-7
Blanchester ... M-3
Bloomdale ... F-4
Bloomingburg ... L-4
Bloomville ... G-5
Blue Ash ... ★
  Vicinity ... Pg. 113, B-6
Bluffton ... G-3
Bolivar ... H-8
Botkins ... H-2
Botzum ... ★
  Vicinity ... Pg. 113, K-5
Bowersville ... L-3
Bowling Green ... F-3
Bradford ... J-2
Bradner ... F-4
Brecksville ... ★
  Vicinity ... Pg. 113, F-4
Bremen ... K-6
Brewster ... H-8
Brice ... ★
  Vicinity ... Pg. 153, G-7
Bridgetown ... ★
  Vicinity ... Pg. 112, D-1
Briggsdale ... ★
  Vicinity ... Pg. 153, G-3
Brilliant ... J-10
Broadview Heights ... ★
  Vicinity ... Pg. 113, G-4
Brook Park ... ★
  Vicinity ... Pg. 113, E-2
Brooklyn ... ★
  Vicinity ... Pg. 113, D-3
Brunswick ... F-7
  Vicinity ... Pg. 113, J-2
Bryan ... E-2
Buchtel ... L-7
Bucyrus ... G-5
Burton ... E-9
Butler ... H-6

Byesville ... K-8
Cadiz ... J-9
Cairo ... G-2
Caldwell ... K-8
Caledonia ... H-5
Cambridge ... J-8
Camden ... L-1
Campbell ... F-10
Canal Fulton ... G-8
Canal Winchester ... K-5
Canal Winchester ... K-5
  Vicinity ... Pg. 153, J-7
Canal Winchester ... K-5
  Vicinity ... Pg. 116, J-7
Canfield ... G-9
Canton ... G-8
Cardington ... H-5
Carey ... G-4
Carroll ... K-5
Carrollton ... H-9
Castalia ... F-5
Cedarville ... K-3
Celina ... H-1
Center Village ... ★
  Vicinity ... Pg. 116, B-3
Centerburg ... J-5
Centerville ... L-2
Chardon ... E-9
Chauncey ... L-7
Chesapeake ... O-6
Chesterhill ... L-7
Cheviot ... M-1
  Vicinity ... Pg. 112, D-2
Chillicothe ... L-5
Christiansburg ... J-3
Cincinnati ... M-2
  Vicinity ... Pg. 112, H-2
Circleville ... K-5
Clarington ... K-9
Clarksville ... L-3
Cleveland ... E-7
  Vicinity ... Pg. 113, C-5
Cleveland Heights ... E-8
  Vicinity ... Pg. 113, C-6
Cleves ... L-1
  Vicinity ... Pg. 112, C-1
Clyde ... F-5
Coal Grove ... O-6
Coalton ... M-6
Coldwater ... H-1
Columbiana ... G-10
Columbus ... J-4
Columbus ... J-4
  Vicinity ... Pg. 116, E-4
Columbus Grove ... G-2
Commercial Point ... ★
  Vicinity ... Pg. 116, K-3
Conneaut ... D-10
Continental ... F-2
Convoy ... G-1
Coolville ... M-7
Corning ... L-7
Cortland ... F-10
Coshocton ... J-7
Covington ... J-2
Craig Beach ... G-9
Crestline ... H-5
Cridersville ... H-2
Crooksville ... K-7
Crown City ... O-6
Cuyahoga Falls ... F-8
  Vicinity ... Pg. 113, K-7
Cygnet ... F-3
Dalton ... G-8
Danville ... H-6
Darbydale ... K-4
Darbydale ... K-4
  Vicinity ... Pg. 116, J-1
Dayton ... K-2
  Vicinity ... Pg. 113, K-3
De Graff ... J-3
Delaware ... J-4
Delphos ... G-2
Delta ... E-3
Dennison ... H-9
Derby ... ★
  Vicinity ... Pg. 116, K-1
Deshler ... F-3
Dover ... H-8
Dresden ... J-7
Dublin ... J-4
Dublin ... J-4
  Vicinity ... Pg. 116, C-2
Dunkirk ... G-3
Dunlap ... ★
  Vicinity ... Pg. 112, A-1
Duvall ... ★
  Vicinity ... Pg. 116, K-5
E. Canton ... G-8
E. Cleveland ... E-8
  Vicinity ... Pg. 113, B-5
E. Liverpool ... H-10
E. Palestine ... G-10
E. Sparta ... H-8
Eastlake ... E-8
Eaton ... K-1
Edgerton ... E-1
Edgewater Park ... ★
  Vicinity ... Pg. 116, G-6
Edison ... H-5
Eldorado ... K-1
Elmore ... F-4
Elmwood Place ... ★
  Vicinity ... Pg. 112, C-4
Elyria ... F-7

Emery ... ★
  Vicinity ... Pg. 113, D-6
Englewood ... K-2
Eon ... N-3
Euclid ... E-8
  Vicinity ... Pg. 113, A-6
Evendale ... ★
  Vicinity ... Pg. 112, B-5
Everett ... ★
  Vicinity ... Pg. 113, J-5
Fairfax ... ★
  Vicinity ... Pg. 112, D-6
Fairfield ... L-1
Fairlawn ... F-8
Fairport Harbor ... D-9
Fairview Park ... ★
  Vicinity ... Pg. 113, D-1
Fayette ... E-2
Felicity ... N-2
Findlay ... G-3
Flint ... ★
  Vicinity ... Pg. 116, C-4
Flushing ... J-9
Forest ... G-4
Forest Park ... M-1
  Vicinity ... Pg. 112, A-3
Fostoria ... F-4
Frankfort ... L-4
Franklin ... L-2
Frazeysburg ... J-7
Fredericksburg ... H-7
Fredericktown ... H-6
Freeport ... J-8
Fremont ... F-5
Ft. Jennings ... G-2
Ft. Loramie ... J-2
Ft. Recovery ... H-1
Ft. Shawnee ... H-2
Gahanna ... J-5
Gahanna ... J-5
  Vicinity ... Pg. 116, E-6
Galena ... ★
  Vicinity ... Pg. 116, A-6
Galion ... H-5
Gallipolis ... N-7
Galloway ... ★
  Vicinity ... Pg. 116, G-2
Gambier ... J-9
Garfield Hts. ... F-8
  Vicinity ... Pg. 113, D-5
Garrettsville ... F-9
Geneva ... D-9
Geneva-on-the-Lake ... D-9
Genoa ... E-4
Georgetown ... N-3
Georgeville ... ★
  Vicinity ... Pg. 116, H-1
Germantown ... L-1
Gettysburg ... J-1
Ghent ... ★
  Vicinity ... Pg. 113, K-4
Gibsonburg ... F-4
Girard ... F-10
Glandorf ... G-2
Glendale ... ★
  Vicinity ... Pg. 112, A-4
Glouster ... L-7
Gnaddenhutten ... J-8
Golf Manor ... ★
  Vicinity ... Pg. 112, C-5
Gould Park ... ★
  Vicinity ... Pg. 112, B-4
Grafton ... F-7
Grand Rapids ... F-3
Grandview Heights ... ★
  Vicinity ... Pg. 116, F-4
Granger ... ★
  Vicinity ... Pg. 113, K-3
Granville ... J-6
Gratis ... L-1
Green Springs ... F-5
Greenfield ... L-4
Greenhills ... ★
  Vicinity ... Pg. 112, A-3
Greenville ... J-1
Greenwich ... G-6
Grove City ... K-4
Grove City ... K-4
  Vicinity ... Pg. 116, H-3
Groveport ... K-5
Groveport ... K-5
  Vicinity ... Pg. 112, C-6
Hamden ... M-6
Hamersville ... N-3
Hamilton ... L-1
Hanover ... J-6
Hanoverton ... G-9
Hariem ... ★
  Vicinity ... Pg. 116, B-6
Harrisburg ... ★
  Vicinity ... Pg. 116, K-1
Harrison ... M-1
Harrod ... H-3
Hartville ... G-8
Hayden ... ★
  Vicinity ... Pg. 112, D-4
Hayesville ... G-7
Heath ... K-6
Hebron ... K-6
Hicksville ... F-1
Higginsport ... N-3
Hilliard ... J-4
Hilliard ... J-4
  Vicinity ... Pg. 116, E-1

Hillsboro ... M-3
Hinckley ... ★
  Vicinity ... Pg. 113, H-2
Hiram ... F-9
Holgate ... F-2
Holland ... E-3
Hopedale ... J-9
Hubbard ... F-10
Huber Hts. ... K-2
Huber Ridge ... ★
  Vicinity ... Pg. 116, C-6
Hudson ... ★
  Vicinity ... Pg. 113, H-7
Huron ... F-6
Hyatts ... ★
  Vicinity ... Pg. 116, A-3
Independence ... ★
  Vicinity ... Pg. 113, F-4
Ironton ... O-6
Jackson ... M-5
Jackson Center ... H-3
Jacksonville ... L-7
Jamestown ... L-3
Jefferson ... E-9
Jeffersonville ... L-4
Jerome ... ★
  Vicinity ... Pg. 116, B-1
Jeromesville ... G-7
Jewett ... J-9
Johnstown ... J-5
Junction City ... K-6
Kalida ... G-2
Kellys Island ... E-6
Kent ... F-8
Kenton ... H-3
Kettering ... K-2
Kileville ... ★
  Vicinity ... Pg. 116, C-1
Killbuck ... H-7
Kingston ... L-5
Kirkersville ... K-6
Kirtland Hills ... E-9
Lagrange ... F-7
Lakemore ... G-8
Lakeview ... H-3
Lakewood ... E-7
  Vicinity ... Pg. 113, C-1
Lancaster ... K-6
Laurelville ... L-5
Lebanon ... L-2
Leesburg ... L-4
Leetonia ... G-10
Leipsic ... G-3
Lewis Center ... ★
  Vicinity ... Pg. 116, A-4
Lewisburg ... K-1
Lexington ... H-6
Liberty Center ... E-2
Lima ... G-2
Lincoln Heights ... ★
  Vicinity ... Pg. 112, B-4
Lindsey ... F-4
Linworth ... ★
  Vicinity ... Pg. 116, C-3
Lisbon ... G-10
Lithopolis ... K-5
  Vicinity ... Pg. 116, K-7
Lockbourn ... ★
  Vicinity ... Pg. 116, K-4
Lockland ... ★
  Vicinity ... Pg. 112, B-4
Lodi ... F-7
Logan ... L-6
London ... K-4
Lorain ... E-6
Lordstown ... F-9
Loudonville ... H-6
Louisville ... G-9
Loveland ... M-2
Lowell ... L-8
Lowellville ... G-10
Luckey ... F-4
Lynchburg ... M-3
Lyndhurst ... ★
  Vicinity ... Pg. 113, B-7
Lyons ... E-2
Macedonia ... F-8
  Vicinity ... Pg. 113, G-6
Madeira ... M-2
  Vicinity ... Pg. 112, C-6
Madison ... E-9
Magnolia ... H-8
Malta ... L-8
Malvern ... H-9
Manchester ... N-3
Mansfield ... H-6
Maple Hts. ... ★
  Vicinity ... Pg. 113, E-5
Marble Cliff ... ★
  Vicinity ... Pg. 116, F-3
Marblehead ... E-5
Marietta ... L-8
Marimet ... ★
  Vicinity ... Pg. 112, D-5
Marion ... H-4
Martins Ferry ... J-10
Martinsville ... L-3
Marysville ... J-4
Mason ... L-2
Massillon ... G-8
Maumee ... E-3
Mayfield Hts ... ★
McArthur ... M-6

McClure ... F-3
McConnelsville ... L-7
McGuffey ... H-3
Mechanicsburg ... J-4
Medina ... F-7
  Vicinity ... Pg. 113, K-1
Mentor ... E-8
Mentor-on-the-Lake ... E-8
Metamora ... E-3
Miamisburg ... L-2
Middle Point ... G-2
Middleburg Hts ... ★
  Vicinity ... Pg. 113, F-2
Middleport ... M-7
Middletown ... L-1
Midvale ... H-8
Midway ... K-4
Milan ... F-5
Milford ... M-2
Milford Center ... J-4
Millersburg ... H-7
Millersport ... K-6
Millville ... L-1
Mineral City ... H-8
Minerva ... G-9
Minerva Park ... J-5
  Vicinity ... Pg. 116, D-4
Mingo Junction ... J-10
Minster ... H-2
Monroe ... L-2
Monroeville ... F-5
Montpelier ... E-1
Moraine ... K-2
Moreland Hills ... ★
  Vicinity ... Pg. 113, D-7
Morrow ... L-2
Mt. Air ... ★
  Vicinity ... Pg. 116, B-3
Mt. Blanchard ... G-4
Mt. Gilead ... H-5
Mt. Healthy ... ★
  Vicinity ... Pg. 112, B-3
Mt. Orab ... M-3
Mt. Sterling ... K-4
Mt. Vernon ... H-6
Mt. Victory ... H-4
Mudsock ... ★
  Vicinity ... Pg. 116, E-1
Murray City ... L-7
N. Baltimore ... F-3
N. Bend ... M-1
N. Canton ... G-8
N. College Hill ... ★
  Vicinity ... Pg. 112, C-3
N. Fairfield ... F-6
N. Kingsville ... D-10
N. Lewisburg ... J-4
N. Olmsted ... F-7
N. Ridgeville ... F-7
N. Royalton ... F-7
Napoleon ... F-2
Navarre ... H-8
Nelsonville ... L-6
Nevada ... G-5
New Albany ... ★
  Vicinity ... Pg. 116, C-7
New Boston ... N-5
New Bremen ... H-2
New Carlisle ... K-3
New Concord ... K-7
New Holland ... L-4
New Knoxville ... H-2
New Lebanon ... K-1
New Lexington ... L-7
New London ... G-6
New Madison ... K-1
New Maramoras ... L-9
New Miami ... L-1
New Middletown ... G-10
New Paris ... K-1
New Philadelphia ... H-8
New Richmond ... N-2
New Rome ... ★
  Vicinity ... Pg. 116, F-2
New Straitsville ... L-7
New Vienna ... L-3
New Washington ... G-5
New Waterford ... G-10
Newark ... J-6
Newcomerstown ... J-8
Newton ... M-2
Newton Falls ... F-9
Niles ... F-10
Northwood ... E-4
Norton ... G-8
Norwalk ... F-6
Norwood ... ★
  Vicinity ... Pg. 112, D-4
Oak Harbor ... E-5
Oak Hill ... N-6
Oakwood ... F-2
Oakwood ... K-2
Oberlin ... F-6
Obetz ... K-5
Obetz ... K-5
  Vicinity ... Pg. 116, H-5
Ohio City ... G-1
Ontario ... H-6
Orange ... ★
  Vicinity ... Pg. 113, D-7
Orangeville ... F-10
Oregon ... E-4

★ Denotes City only on Vicinity map. City not located on State map.

Orient .... ★
Vicinity .... Pg. 116, K-2
Orrville G-7
Orwell E-9
Ottawa G-3
Ottawa Hills E-3
Ottoville G-2
Otway N-4
Owensville M-2
Oxford L-1
Painesville E-9
Pandora G-3
Parma F-8
Vicinity .... Pg. 113, E-3
Parma Hts F-8
Vicinity .... Pg. 113, E-2
Pataskala K-6
Paulding F-1
Payne G-1
Pemberville F-4
Peninsula F-8
Vicinity .... Pg. 113, J-5
Pepper Pike .... ★
Vicinity .... Pg. 113, C-7
Perry E-9
Perrysburg E-4
Perrysville H-6
Philo K-7
Pickerington K-5
Piketon M-5
Pioneer E-2
Piqua J-2
Plain City J-4
Pleasant Corners .... ★
Vicinity .... Pg. 116, J-2
Pleasant Hill J-2
Pleasantville K-6
Plymouth G-6
Poland G-10
Pomeroy M-7
Port Clinton E-5
Port Washington J-8
Portsmouth N-5
Powell .... ★
Vicinity .... Pg. 116, B-3
Powhatan Point K-9
Proctorville O-6
Prospect H-4
Put-in-Bay E-5
Quaker City K-8
Quincy J-3
Racine M-7
Rathbone .... ★
Vicinity .... Pg. 116, A-2
Ravenna F-9
Reading M-2
Vicinity .... Pg. 112, B-5
Reese .... ★
Vicinity .... Pg. 116, H-5
Remsen Corners .... ★
Vicinity .... Pg. 113, K-3
Republic F-5
Reynoldsburg K-5
Reynoldsburg .... ★
Vicinity .... Pg. 116, F-7
Richfield .... ★
Vicinity .... Pg. 113, H-5
Richmond H-9
Richmond Hts .... ★
Vicinity .... Pg. 113, A-6
Rio Grande N-6
Ripley N-3
Rising Sun F-4
Rittman G-7
Riverlea .... ★
Vicinity .... Pg. 116, D-4
Roaming Shores E-10
Rock Creek E-9
Rockford H-1
Rocky River .... ★
Vicinity .... Pg. 113, C-1
Rome N-4
Roseville K-7
Rossford E-4
Rushsylvania H-3
Russells Point H-3
Rutland M-7
Sabina L-3
Sagamore Hills .... ★
Vicinity .... Pg. 113, G-5
Saint Bernard .... ★
Vicinity .... Pg. 112, D-4
Saint Clairsville J-9
Saint Henry H-1
Saint Marys H-2
Saint Paris J-3
Salem G-9
Salineville H-9
San Margherita .... ★
Vicinity .... Pg. 116, F-2
Sandusky E-6
Sarahsville K-8
Sardinia N-3
Scio H-9
Seaman N-4
Sebring G-9
Senecaville K-8
Seven Hills .... ★
Vicinity .... Pg. 113, E-4
Seven Mile L-1
Seville G-7
Shadeville .... ★
Vicinity .... Pg. 116, J-4
Shadyside K-9

Shaker Hts F-8
Vicinity .... Pg. 113, C-6
Sharonville .... ★
Vicinity .... Pg. 112, A-5
Shawnee L-7
Shawnee Hills .... ★
Vicinity .... Pg. 116, B-1
Sheffield Lake E-6
Shelby G-6
Sherwood F-1
Shiloh G-6
Shreve H-7
Sidney J-2
Silverton .... ★
Vicinity .... Pg. 112, C-5
Sinking Springs N-4
Smithfield J-10
Solon .... ★
Vicinity .... Pg. 113, E-7
Somerset K-6
South Bloomfield K-5
South Charleston K-3
South Euclid .... ★
Vicinity .... Pg. 113, B-6
South Lebanon L-2
South Point O-6
South Russell F-9
Inset Map
South Webster N-5
South Zanesville K-7
Spencer F-7
Spencerville H-2
Spring Valley L-3
Springboro L-2
Springdale .... ★
Vicinity .... Pg. 112, A-4
Springfield K-3
Stockport L-7
Stoutsville L-5
Stow F-8
Vicinity .... Pg. 113, K-7
Strasburg H-8
Streetsboro F-9
Strongsville F-7
Vicinity .... Pg. 113, G-1
Struthers G-10
Stryker E-2
Stuebenville H-10
Sugar Grove L-6
Sugarcreek H-8
Sunbury J-5
Swanton E-3
Sycamore G-4
Sylvania E-3
Syracruse M-7
Tallmadge G-8
Terrace Park M-2
Thornville K-6
Tiffin G-5
Tiltonsville J-10
Tipp City K-2
Toledo E-4
Toronto H-10
Trenton L-1
Trimble L-7
Trotwood K-2
Troy J-2
Tuscarawas H-8
Twinsburg .... ★
Vicinity .... Pg. 113, G-7
Uhrichsville J-8
Union K-2
Union City J-1
University Hts .... ★
Vicinity .... Pg. 113, C-6
Upper Arlington K-4
Upper Arlington .... ★
Vicinity .... Pg. 116, E-3
Upper Sandusky G-4
Urbana J-3
Urbancrest K-4
Urbancrest .... ★
Vicinity .... Pg. 116, H-3
Utica J-6
Valley View .... ★
Vicinity .... Pg. 113, E-5
Valleyview .... ★
Vicinity .... Pg. 116, F-2
Van Wert G-1
Vandalia K-2
Vermilion F-6
Versailles J-2
Vinton M-6
Wadsworth G-7
Wakeman F-6
Walbridge E-4
Wapokoneta H-2
Warren F-10
Warrensville Hts .... ★
Vicinity .... Pg. 113, D-6
Warsaw J-7
Washington C.H. L-4
Washingtonville G-10
Waterloo .... ★
Vicinity .... Pg. 116, J-7
Waterville E-3
Wauseon E-2
Waverly M-5
Wayne F-4
Waynesburg G-9
Waynesfield H-3
Waynesville L-3
Wellington F-6
Wellston M-6
Wellsville H-10

West Alexandria K-1
West Carrollton K-2
West Farmington F-9
West Jefferson K-4
West Lafayette J-8
West Liberty J-3
West Mansfield H-4
West Milton K-2
West Richfield .... ★
Vicinity .... Pg. 113, H-4
West Salem G-7
West Union N-4
West Unity E-2
Westerville J-5
Westerville .... ★
Vicinity .... Pg. 116, C-5
Westfield Center G-7
Weston F-3
Whitehall K-5
Whitehall .... ★
Vicinity .... Pg. 116, F-6
Whitehouse E-3
Wickliffe .... ★
Vicinity .... Pg. 113, A-7
Wilkesville M-6
Willard G-5
Williamsburg M-2
Williamsport L-4
Willoughby E-8
Willoughby Hills E-8
Willowick E-8
Willshire H-1
Wilmington L-3
Winchester N-3
Windham F-9
Wintersville H-10
Woodlawn .... ★
Vicinity .... Pg. 112, B-4
Woodsfield K-9
Woodville F-4
Wooster G-7
Worthington J-5
Worthington .... ★
Vicinity .... Pg. 116, C-4
Wyoming .... ★
Vicinity .... Pg. 112, B-4
Xenia L-3
Yellow Springs K-3
Yorkville J-10
Youngstown F-9
Zanesville K-7

OKLAHOMA
Pages 76-77

Achille J-11
Acme G-8
Ada G-10
Adair C-13
Addington H-9
Afton C-13
Agawam G-9
Agra E-10
Ahloso G-11
Albany H-11
Albert F-8
Albion G-13
Alcorn C-9
Alderson G-12
Aledo E-7
Alex F-9
Alfalfa G-8
Aline C-8
Allen G-11
Alpers G-9
Altus F-7
Alva C-7
Amber F-9
Ames D-8
Amorita B-8
Anadarko F-8
Angora E-6
Antioch H-9
Apache F-8
Apperson C-10
Apple H-12
Aqua Park E-13
Arapaho E-7
Arcadia E-9
Vicinity .... Pg. 143, A-7
Ardmore H-10
Arnett D-6
Arpelar F-12
Asher F-10
Ashland G-11
Atoka H-11
Atwood F-11
Avant C-11
Avard C-7
Avery E-10
Aydelotte E-10
Babbs F-7
Bache G-12
Bado D-7
Bald Hill E-12
Balko B-5
Barnsdall C-11
Barr D-8
Bartlesville C-11
Battiest G-13
Baum H-10
Bearden F-11
Beckett (Survey) .... ★
Beggs E-11

Bellvue E-11
Belva C-7
Bengal G-13
Bennington H-11
Bernice C-13
Bessie F-7
Bethany .... ★
Vicinity .... Pg. 143, D-2
Bethel H-13
Bethel Acres F-10
Big Cabin C-13
Big Cedar G-13
Bigheart C-11
Billings C-9
Binger F-8
Bison D-9
Bixby D-12
Blackburn D-11
Blackwell C-10
Blair G-6
Blanchard F-9
Blocker F-12
Blue H-11
Boise City C-2
Boley E-11
Bomar J-10
Boswell H-11
Bowlegs F-11
Box E-13
Boyd C-4
Boynton E-12
Brace C-7
Braggs E-12
Braman C-9
Bray G-9
Briartown F-13
Bridgeport E-8
Brinkman F-6
Bristow E-11
Bromide H-11
Brooksville F-10
Brown H-11
Brushy E-13
Bryan's Corner C-4
Bryant F-11
Buffalo C-6
Bugtussle F-12
Bunch E-13
Burbank C-10
Burlington C-8
Burmah E-7
Burns Flat F-7
Butler E-7
Byars G-10
Byng G-10
Byron C-8
Cabiniss F-11
Cache G-8
Caddo H-11
Calera H-11
Calvin F-11
Camargo D-7
Canadian F-12
Canadian Club City F-9
Caney H-11
Canton D-8
Capron C-8
Carleton D-8
Carmen C-8
Carnegie F-8
Carney E-10
Carrier C-8
Carter F-6
Cartwright J-10
Cashion E-9
Castle E-11
Caston F-13
Catesby D-6
Catoosa D-12
Cedar Springs D-8
Cement F-8
Centrahoma G-11
Centralia C-12
Ceres D-10
Cestos D-7
Chandler E-10
Chattanooga G-7
Checotah E-12
Chelsea D-12
Cherokee C-8
Chester D-7
Cheyenne E-6
Chickasha F-8
Childers C-12
Chilocco B-10
Chisney F-10
Chloeta C-13
Chockie G-11
Choska E-12
Chouteau D-12
Cimmarron City E-9
Claremore D-12
Clayton G-12
Clemscott H-9
Cleo Springs D-8
Cleveland D-11
Clinton E-7
Cloud Chief F-7
Coalgate G-11
Cogar F-8
Colbert J-11
Cole F-9
Coleman H-11
Collinsville D-12

Colony F-8
Comanche H-9
Commerce B-13
Connerville G-11
Cookietown H-8
Cookson E-13
Cooperton G-7
Cora C-7
Cordell F-7
Corinne H-13
Corn E-7
Cornish H-9
Corum H-8
Council Hill E-12
Courtney H-9
Covington D-9
Cowden F-8
Coweta D-12
Cowlington F-13
Coyle D-10
Crawford E-6
Crekola E-12
Crescent D-9
Creta E-7
Criner F-9
Cromwell F-11
Crowder F-12
Curtis D-10
Cushing E-10
Custer City E-7
Cyril G-8
Dacoma C-8
Daisy G-12
Dale F-10
Darwin H-12
Davenport E-10
Davidson H-7
Davis G-10
Deer Creek C-9
Del City .... ★
Vicinity .... Pg. 143, F-5
Delaware C-12
Dempsey E-6
Denman F-13
Depew E-11
Devol H-7
Dewey C-12
Dibble F-9
Dickson H-10
Dill City F-7
Dillworth B-10
Dougherty G-10
Douglas D-9
Dover D-9
Doxey E-7
Drake H-10
Driftwood C-8
Drummond D-8
Drumright D-11
Duke F-7
Dunbar G-12
Duncan H-9
Durant H-11
Durham E-6
Durwood H-11
Dustin F-11
Eagle City D-8
Eakly F-8
Earlsboro F-10
Eason F-7
Eddy C-9
Edith C-7
Edmond E-9
Vicinity .... Pg. 143, A-5
El Reno E-8
Eldon D-13
Eldorado G-6
Elgin G-8
Elk City E-6
Elmer G-7
Elmore City G-9
Elmwood B-4
Emet H-10
Empire City H-9
Enid D-9
Enterprise F-12
Erick E-6
Eubanks F-13
Eufaula F-12
Eva C-3
Fair Oaks D-12
Fairfax C-10
Fairland C-13
Fairmont D-9
Fairview D-8
Fallis E-10
Fallon F-13
Fanshawe F-13
Fargo D-6
Farris H-12
Faxon G-8
Fay E-7
Featherston F-12
Felt C-2
Fewell G-13
Fillmore H-11
Finley G-12
Fittstown G-10
Fitzhugh G-10
Fleetwood H-9
Fletcher G-8
Floris B-5
Folsom H-12
Foraker C-11

Forest Park .... ★
Vicinity .... Pg. 143, D-5
Forgan B-5
Fort Arbuckle G-9
Fort Cobb F-8
Fort Gibson E-13
Fort Supply C-6
Fort Towson H-13
Forty One E-7
Foss E-7
Fowler E-10
Fox H-9
Foyil C-12
Francis G-10
Frederick G-7
Freedom C-7
Gage D-6
Gans F-13
Gansel D-9
Garber D-9
Garvin H-13
Gate C-6
Gay H-12
Geary E-8
Gene Autry H-10
Gerty G-11
Gibbon B-8
Gideon D-13
Glencoe D-10
Glenpool D-11
Glover H-13
Goldsby F-9
Goltry D-8
Goodland H-12
Goodwell C-3
Goodwin D-6
Gore E-13
Gotebo F-7
Gould G-6
Gowan G-12
Gracemont F-8
Grady H-9
Grainola B-11
Grandfield H-7
Granite F-6
Grant H-12
Gray C-4
Grayson E-12
Green D-13
Greenfield E-8
Griggs C-3
Grove C-13
Guthrie E-9
Guymon C-3
Haileyville G-12
Hall Park F-9
Hammon E-6
Harden City G-10
Hardesty C-4
Hardy B-10
Harmon D-6
Harrah E-10
Hartshorne G-12
Haskell E-12
Hastings H-8
Hayward D-9
Haywood G-11
Hayworth J-13
Headrick G-7
Healdton H-9
Heavener G-13
Hectorville E-12
Helena C-8
Hennepin G-9
Hennessey D-9
Henryetta E-11
Hickory G-10
Higgins G-12
Hillsdale C-8
Hinton E-8
Hitchcock D-8
Hitchita E-12
Hobart F-7
Hodgen G-13
Hoffman F-12
Holdenville F-11
Hollis G-6
Hollister H-7
Hollow F-12
Homestead D-8
Hominy D-11
Honobia G-13
Hooker B-4
Hoot Owl D-13
Hopeton C-7
Hough B-3
Howe G-13
Hucmac D-7
Hugo H-12
Hulah B-11
Hulbert D-13
Hulen G-8
Humphreys G-7
Hunter C-9
Huskey H-12
Hydro E-8
Idabel H-13
Indiahoma G-7
Indianola F-12
Ingersoll C-8
Inola D-12
Isabella D-8
Jay C-13
Jefferson C-9

Jenks D-11
Jennings D-11
Jesse G-11
Jet C-8
Joy G-10
Kansas D-13
Karma J-11
Karns E-8
Kellyville E-11
Kendrick E-10
Kent H-12
Kenton B-2
Keota F-13
Keyes C-3
Kiamichi G-12
Kildare C-10
Kingfisher D-8
Kingston H-10
Kinta F-13
Kiowa G-11
Knowles C-5
Konawa F-11
Kosoma H-12
Kremlin D-9
Kusa E-12
Lacey D-8
Lahoma D-8
Lake Valley F-7
Lamar F-11
Lambert C-8
Lamont C-9
Lane H-11
Langston E-10
Latta G-10
Laverne C-6
Lawton G-8
Leach D-13
Lebanon H-10
Leedey E-6
Lehigh G-11
Lela D-10
Lenapah C-12
Leon H-9
Leonard E-12
Lequire F-13
Letitia G-8
Lewisville E-10
Lexington F-10
Lima F-10
Lincoln G-6
Lindsay G-9
Little Axe F-10
Little City H-10
Loco H-9
Locust Grove D-12
Lone Grove H-9
Lone Wolf F-7
Longdale D-8
Lookeba F-8
Lookout B-7
Lovedale E-7
Loveland H-7
Lovell D-9
Loyal D-8
Lucien D-9
Lugert F-7
Lula G-11
Luther E-10
Lyman C-10
Lyons E-13
Macomb F-10
Madill H-10
Manchester B-9
Mangum F-6
Manitou G-7
Mannsville H-10
Maramac D-10
Marietta H-10
Marland D-9
Marlow G-9
Marshall D-9
Martha F-7
Mason E-11
Maud F-10
May C-6
Mayfield F-6
Maysville G-9
Mazie D-12
McAlester F-12
McBride H-11
McCurtain F-13
McLoud E-10
McQueen G-6
McWillie C-8
Mead H-11
Medford C-9
Meeker E-10
Meers G-8
Meno D-8
Meridian E-10
Messer F-12
Miami C-13
Middleberg F-9
Milburn H-11
Milfay E-11
Mill Creek G-10
Millerton H-13
Milo H-9
Milton F-13
Minco F-9
Mocane B-5
Moore .... ★
Vicinity .... Pg. 143, H-5
Mooreland C-7
Morris E-12

Morrison D-10
Mounds E-11
Mountain View F-7
Moyers H-12
Mulhall D-9
Muskogee E-12
Mustang F-9
Mutual D-7
Narcissa C-13
Nardin C-9
Nash C-8
Nashoba G-13
Navina E-9
Nebo H-10
New Alluwe C-12
New Eucha D-13
New Prue D-11
New Ringold H-13
New Tulsa D-12
New Woodville H-10
Newcastle F-9
Vicinity .... Pg. 143, J-2
Newkirk C-10
Nichols Hills .... ★
Vicinity .... Pg. 143, C-4
Nida H-11
Ninnekah F-9
Noble F-10
Norge F-8
Norman F-9
Vicinity .... Pg. 143, K-5
North Miami B-13
Nowata C-12
Numa C-9
Oakland H-10
Oaks D-13
Oakwood D-7
Ochelata C-12
Octavia G-13
Oilton D-11
Okeene D-8
Okemah F-11
Okesa C-11
Okfuskee E-11
Oklahoma City E-9
Vicinity .... Pg. 143
Okmulgee E-12
Oleta H-12
Olney G-11
Olustee G-6
Omega E-8
Onapa F-12
Oneta D-12
Oologah C-12
Optima C-4
Ord H-12
Orienta D-8
Orion D-7
Orlando D-9
Osage D-11
Ottawa C-13
Overbrook H-10
Owasso D-12
Owen B-11
Ozark G-7
Paden E-11
Panama F-13
Panola F-12
Paoli G-10
Patton C-13
Pauls Valley G-10
Pawhuska C-11
Pawnee D-10
Payne G-9
Pearson E-11
Pearsonia C-11
Peggs D-13
Peoria B-13
Perkins E-10
Perry D-10
Pershing C-11
Petersburg H-9
Pharoah F-11
Phillips G-11
Picher B-13
Pierce F-12
Pink F-10
Pittsburg G-12
Plainview C-7
Platter H-11
Poccasset F-8
Ponca City C-10
Pond Creek C-9
Pontotoc G-11
Pooleville G-9
Porter E-12
Porum F-13
Poteau F-13
Prague E-10
Preston E-11
Pryor D-12
Pumpkin Center G-8
Purcell G-9
Purdy G-9
Putnam E-7
Pyramid Corners C-12
Quapaw B-13
Quay D-10
Quinlan C-7
Quinton F-12
Ralston C-10
Ramona C-11
Randlett H-8
Rankin E-6

★ Denotes City only on Vicinity map. City not located on State map.

OKLAHOMA

Ratliff City ... G-9
Rattan ... H-12
Rayia ... H-10
Reagan ... H-10
Red Bird ... E-12
Red Oak ... F-13
Red Rock ... D-10
Redden ... G-12
Reed ... F-6
Remus ... F-10
Renfrow ... B-9
Retrop ... F-7
Reydon ... E-6
Rhea ... E-7
Richards Spur ... G-8
Ringling ... H-9
Ringold ... H-12
Ringwood ... D-8
Roberta ... H-11
Rocky ... F-7
Roff ... G-10
Roll ... E-6
Roosevelt ... G-7
Rose ... D-13
Rosedale ... G-10
Rosston ... C-6
Rubottom ... H-9
Rush Springs ... G-9
Ryan ... H-9
Saddle Mountain ... G-7
Saint Louis ... F-10
Salem ... F-12
Salina ... D-13
Sallisaw ... E-13
Salt Fork ... C-9
Sand Springs ... D-11
Sapulpa ... D-11
Sasakwa ... F-10
Sayre ... F-6
Scraper ... D-13
Scullin ... G-10
Seiling ... D-7
Selman ... C-6
Seminole ... F-11
Sentinel ... F-7
Shamrock ... E-11
Sharon ... D-6
Shattuck ... D-6
Shawnee ... F-10
Shidler ... C-11
Skedee ... D-10
Skiatook ... D-11
Slapout ... C-6
Slaughterville ... F-10
Slick ... E-11
Smithville ... G-13
Snow ... G-12
Snyder ... G-7
Soper ... H-12
South Coffeyville ... C-12
Southard ... D-8
Sparks ... E-10
Spear ... H-12
Spencer ... ★
  Vicinity ... Pg. 143, D-6
Sperry ... D-11
Spiro ... F-13
Springer ... H-10
Stanley ... G-12
Steadman ... G-11
Stecker ... F-8
Sterling ... G-8
Stidham ... F-12
Stigler ... F-13
Stillwater ... D-10
Stilwell ... E-13
Stonewall ... G-11
Stratford ... G-10
Stringtown ... G-11
Stroud ... E-11
Stuart ... G-11
Sturgis ... B-3
Sugden ... H-9
Sulphur ... G-10
Summerfield ... G-13
Summit ... E-12
Sumner ... D-10
Sumpter ... C-10
Surrey Hills ... B-3
Sweetwater ... E-6
Sylvian ... F-11
Tabler ... F-9
Taft ... E-12
Tahlequah ... E-13
Talala ... C-12
Talihina ... G-13
Tallant ... C-11
Taloga ... D-7
Tangier ... C-6
Tatums ... H-8
Taylor ... H-8
Tecumseh ... F-10
Tegarden ... C-7
Temple ... H-8
Terlton ... D-11
Terral ... H-9
Texola ... F-6
The Village ... ★
  Vicinity ... Pg. 143, C-3
Thomas ... E-7
Three Sands ... C-10
Tiawah ... D-12
Tipton ... G-7
Tonkawa ... C-10

Trail ... D-7
Tribbey ... F-10
Trousdale ... F-10
Troy ... H-10
Tryon ... E-10
Tullahassee ... E-12
Tulsa ... D-11
Tupelo ... G-11
Turpin ... C-4
Tushka ... H-11
Tuskahoma ... G-13
Tuttle ... F-9
Tyrone ... B-4
Unger ... H-12
Union City ... F-8
Utica ... H-11
Valley Brook ... ★
  Vicinity ... Pg. 133, F-5
Valliant ... H-13
Vanoss ... G-9
Velma ... G-9
Vera ... C-12
Verdigris ... D-12
Vernon ... F-11
Vian ... E-13
Vici ... D-7
Vinita ... C-12
Vinson ... F-6
Wade ... H-11
Wadena ... D-12
Wagoner ... D-12
Wakita ... C-9
Wanette ... F-10
Wapanucka ... H-11
Warner ... E-12
Warr Acres ... ★
  Vicinity ... Pg. 143, C-2
Warren ... G-7
Warwick ... E-10
Waters ... H-8
Watonga ... E-8
Watova ... C-12
Watson ... G-13
Waukomis ... D-8
Waurika ... H-9
Wayne ... F-10
Waynoka ... C-7
Weatherford ... E-7
Webb City ... C-10
Webbers Falls ... E-12
Welch ... C-13
Weleetka ... F-11
Wellston ... E-10
Welty ... E-11
Westport ... F-11
Wetumka ... F-11
Wewoka ... F-11
Wheeless ... C-2
White Bead ... G-9
White Oak ... C-12
Whitefield ... F-12
Whitesboro ... G-13
Willis ... J-10
Willow ... F-6
Wilson ... H-9
Wolco ... C-11
Woodford ... H-10
Woodlawn Park ... ★
  Vicinity ... Pg. 143, D-2
Woodward ... D-7
Wyandotte ... C-13
Wynnewood ... G-10
Wynona ... C-11
Yale ... D-10
Yeager ... F-11
Yewed ... C-8
Yost ... D-10
Yuba ... J-11
Yukon ... F-9
Zeb ... E-13
Zena ... C-13

OREGON
Pages 78-79

Adair Village ... D-3
Adams ... C-9
Adel ... J-7
Adrian ... G-11
Agness ... H-1
Albany ... D-3
Algoma ... J-5
Alicel ... C-10
Allegany ... F-2
Alpine ... E-3
Alsea ... E-3
Amity ... C-3
Andrews ... J-9
Antelope ... D-6
Applegate ... J-2
Arlington ... C-7
Arock ... H-10
Ashland ... J-3
Ashwood ... D-6
Astoria ... A-3
Athena ... C-9
Aurora ... C-4
Austin ... E-9
Azalea ... H-3
Baker ... E-10
Bandon ... F-1
Banks ... B-3
Barlow ... C-4
Bay City ... B-2

Beatty ... J-5
Beaver ... C-2
Beaverton ... ★
  Vicinity ... Pg. 150, E-2
Belknap Springs ... E-4
Bend ... F-5
Biggs ... C-6
Birkenfeld ... B-3
Blalock ... C-7
Blodgett ... D-2
Blue River ... E-4
Bly ... J-5
Boardman ... B-8
Bonanza ... J-5
Bonneville ... C-5
Boring ... C-5
Breitenbush Springs ... D-5
Bridge ... G-2
Bridgeport ... E-10
Brightwood ... C-5
Broadbent ... G-2
Brogan ... F-10
Brookings ... J-1
Brooks ... D-4
Brothers ... F-6
Brownsville ... E-4
Burns ... G-8
Burns Jct. ... J-9
Butte Falls ... H-4
Buxton ... B-3
Camas Valley ... G-2
Camp Sherman ... E-5
Canby ... C-4
Cannon Beach ... B-2
Canyon City ... E-9
Canyonville ... H-2
Carlton ... C-3
Cascade Locks ... C-5
Cascadia ... E-4
Cave Junction ... J-2
Cecil ... C-7
Central Point ... J-3
Charleston ... G-1
Chemult ... G-5
Cheshire ... E-3
Chiloquin ... H-5
Christmas Valley ... G-6
Clackamas ... ★
  Vicinity ... Pg. 150, G-6
Clatskanie ... A-3
Cloverdale ... C-2
Coburg ... E-3
Colton ... C-4
Columbia City ... B-3
Condon ... D-7
Coos Bay ... F-1
Coquille ... G-2
Corvallis ... D-2
Cottage Grove ... F-3
Council Crest ... ★
  Vicinity ... Pg. 150, E-4
Cove ... D-10
Crabtree ... D-4
Crane ... G-9
Crawfordsville ... E-4
Crescent ... G-5
Crescent Lake ... G-4
Creswell ... F-3
Culp Creek ... F-3
Culver ... E-5
Curtin ... F-3
Cushman ... E-2
Dairy ... J-5
Dallas ... D-3
Days Creek ... H-3
Dayton ... C-3
Dayville ... E-8
Dee ... C-5
Deer Island ... B-3
Denmark ... G-1
Depoe Bay ... D-2
Detroit ... D-4
Dexter ... F-3
Diamond ... H-9
Diamond Lake ... G-4
Dillard ... G-2
Disston ... F-4
Donald ... C-4
Dorena ... F-4
Drain ... F-3
Drew ... H-3
Drewsey ... F-9
Dufur ... C-6
Dunes City ... F-2
Durkee ... E-10
Eagle Creek ... C-4
Eagle Point ... J-3
Eastside ... G-2
Echo ... C-8
Eddyville ... D-3
Elgin ... C-10
Elk City ... D-2
Elkton ... F-2
Elmira ... E-3
Enterprise ... C-11
Estacada ... C-5
Eugene ... F-3
Falls City ... D-3
Falls Creek ... F-4
Fields ... J-8
Flora ... B-11
Florence ... E-2
Forest Grove ... C-3
Fort Klamath ... H-4
Fort Rock ... G-6

Fossil ... D-7
Fox ... E-8
Frenchglen ... H-8
Friend ... C-6
Gales Creek ... B-3
Gardiner ... F-2
Garibaldi ... B-2
Gaston ... C-3
Gates ... D-4
Gaylord ... H-2
Gearhart ... A-2
Gervais ... C-4
Gibbon ... C-9
Gilchrist ... G-5
Gladstone ... ★
  Vicinity ... Pg. 150, G-6
Glenada ... E-2
Glendale ... H-2
Gleneden Beach ... D-2
Glenwood ... B-3
Glide ... G-3
Goble ... B-4
Gold Beach ... H-1
Gold Hill ... H-3
Goshen ... F-3
Government Camp ... C-5
Grand Ronde ... C-3
Grangeville ... B-12
Granite ... D-9
Grants Pass ... H-2
Grass Valley ... C-6
Gravelford ... G-2
Greenhorn ... E-9
Gresham ... C-4
Haines ... D-10
Halfway ... D-11
Halsey ... E-3
Hamilton ... D-8
Hammond ... A-2
Hampton ... G-6
Harbor ... J-1
Hardman ... D-7
Harlan ... D-2
Harper ... F-10
Harrisburg ... E-3
Hebo ... C-2
Helix ... B-9
Heppner ... C-8
Hereford ... E-9
Hermiston ... B-8
Hillsboro ... C-3
Hillsdale ... ★
  Vicinity ... Pg. 150, E-4
Hines ... G-9
Holley ... E-4
Homestead ... D-11
Hood River ... B-5
Horton Blachly ... E-3
Hoskins ... D-3
Hubbard ... C-4
Huntington ... E-10
Idanha ... D-4
Ideyld Park ... G-3
Imbler ... C-10
Imnaha ... C-11
Independence ... D-3
Ione ... C-8
Ironside ... E-10
Irrigon ... B-8
Island City ... C-10
Jacksonville ... J-3
Jamieson ... F-10
Jasper ... F-3
Jefferson ... D-4
Jewell ... B-3
John Day ... E-9
Jordan Valley ... H-10
Joseph ... D-11
Junction City ... E-3
Juntura ... G-9
Kamela ... C-9
Keizer ... ★
Keno ... J-4
Kent ... D-6
Kerby ... J-2
Kernville ... D-2
Kimberly ... D-7
King City ... ★
  Vicinity ... Pg. 150, D-2
Kings Valley ... D-3
Kinzua ... D-7
Klamath Agency ... H-4
Klamath Falls ... J-4
La Grande ... D-9
LaPine ... G-5
Lacomb ... D-4
Lafayette ... C-3
Lake Grove ... ★
  Vicinity ... Pg. 150, G-4
Lakecreek ... J-3
Lakeside ... F-1
Lakeview ... J-7
Langlois ... G-1
Lawen ... G-9
Leaburg ... E-4
Lebanon ... E-3
Lexington ... C-7
Lincoln Beach ... D-2
Lincoln City ... D-2
Lonerock ... D-7
Long Creek ... E-8
Lorane ... F-3
Lostine ... C-11
Lowell ... F-4

Lyons ... D-4
Mabel ... E-4
Madras ... E-6
Malin ... K-5
Manning ... B-4
Manzanita ... B-2
Mapleton ... E-2
Marcola ... E-4
Marion ... D-4
Maupin ... C-6
Mayville ... D-7
McCredie Springs ... F-4
McKenzie Bridge ... E-5
McMinnville ... C-3
McNary ... B-8
Meacham ... C-9
Medford ... J-3
Medical Springs ... D-10
Merlin ... H-2
Merrill ... K-5
Metolius ... E-6
Metzger ... ★
  Vicinity ... Pg. 150, F-2
Midland ... J-5
Mikkalo ... C-7
Mill City ... D-4
Millersburg ... D-3
Millican ... F-6
Milo ... H-3
Milton Freewater ... B-10
Milwaukie ... ★
  Vicinity ... Pg. 150, F-5
Minam ... C-10
Mission ... C-9
Mist ... B-3
Mitchell ... E-7
Mohawk ... E-4
Mohler ... B-2
Molalla ... C-4
Monmouth ... D-3
Monroe ... E-3
Monument ... D-8
Moro ... C-6
Mosier ... C-6
Mount Hood ... C-5
Mount Vernon ... E-8
Mt. Angel ... C-4
Mulino ... C-4
Multnomah ... ★
  Vicinity ... Pg. 150, E-3
Murphy ... J-2
Myrtle Creek ... G-3
Myrtle Point ... G-1
Nehalem ... B-3
Neskowin ... C-2
Netarts ... C-2
New Bridge ... E-11
New Princeton ... G-9
Newberg ... C-3
Newport ... D-2
North Bend ... F-2
North Plains ... B-4
North Powder ... D-10
Norway ... G-2
Noti ... E-3
Nyssa ... F-11
O'Brien ... J-2
Oak Grove ... ★
  Vicinity ... Pg. 150, G-5
Oakland ... G-3
Oakridge ... F-4
Oceanside ... C-2
Odell ... C-5
Olene ... J-5
Ontario ... F-11
Ophir ... H-1
Oregon City ... C-4
Otis ... C-2
Otter Rock ... D-2
Owyhee ... F-11
Pacific City ... C-2
Paisley ... H-6
Parkdale ... C-5
Paulina ... F-7
Pendleton ... C-8
Philomath ... D-3
Phoenix ... J-3
Pilot Rock ... C-9
Pinehurst ... J-4
Pistol River ... J-1
Pleasant Hill ... F-4
Pleasant Valley ... E-10
Plush ... J-7
Port Orford ... H-1
Portland ... C-4
  Vicinity ... Pg. 150
Post ... E-7
Powell Butte ... E-6
Powers ... H-2
Prairie City ... E-9
Prescott ... B-4
Prineville ... E-6
Prospect ... H-4
Rainier ... B-4
Raleigh Hills ... ★
  Vicinity ... Pg. 150, E-3
Redmond ... E-5
Reedsport ... F-2
Remote ... G-2
Rhododendron ... C-5
Richland ... E-11
Riddle ... G-2
Riley ... G-8
Ritter ... D-8
Riverton ... G-1

Rockaway ... B-2
Rogue River ... H-3
Rome ... H-10
Roseburg ... G-3
Rufus ... C-7
Saginaw ... F-3
Saint Helens ... B-4
Saint Paul ... C-4
Salem ... D-3
Sandy ... C-5
Scappoose ... B-3
Scio ... D-4
Scottsburg ... F-2
Seal Rock ... D-2
Seaside ... A-2
Selma ... J-2
Seneca ... F-8
Shady Cove ... H-3
Shaniko ... D-6
Sheaville ... H-11
Shedd ... E-3
Sheridan ... C-3
Sherwood ... E-3
Siletz ... D-2
Siltcoos ... F-2
Silver Lake ... G-5
Silverton ... D-4
Sisters ... E-5
Sitkum ... G-2
Sixes ... G-1
Skipanon ... A-2
Sodaville ... E-4
South Beach ... D-2
Sprague River ... J-5
Spray ... D-7
Springfield ... E-4
Stanfield ... B-8
Stayton ... D-4
Sublimity ... D-4
Summer Lake ... H-6
Summerville ... C-10
Sumner ... G-1
Sumpter ... E-9
Sunriver ... F-5
Sutherlin ... G-3
Sweethome ... E-4
Swisshome ... E-2
Talent ... J-3
Tangent ... D-3
Telocaset ... D-10
Tenmile ... G-2
Terrebonne ... E-5
The Dalles ... C-6
Tidewater ... E-2
Tiernan ... E-2
Tigard ... C-4
  Vicinity ... Pg. 150, F-2
Tillamook ... C-3
Tiller ... H-3
Timber ... B-3
Toledo ... D-2
Trail ... H-4
Troutdale ... C-5
Troy ... B-10
Tualatin ... C-4
Turner ... D-3
Tygh Valley ... C-6
Ukiah ... D-8
Umapine ... B-9
Umatilla ... B-8
Umpqua ... G-2
Union ... D-10
Union Creek ... H-3
Unity ... E-10
Vale ... F-10
Valley Falls ... J-6
Valsetz ... D-3
Veneta ... E-3
Vernonia ... B-3
Vida ... E-4
Waldport ... E-2
Walker ... F-4
Wallowa ... C-10
Walterville ... E-4
Walton ... E-3
Wamic ... C-6
Warm Springs ... D-5
Warren ... A-2
Warrenton ... A-2
Wasco ... C-7
Waterloo ... E-4
Wedderburn ... H-1
Wemme ... C-5
West Fir ... F-4
West Linn ... C-4
West Slope ... ★
  Vicinity ... Pg. 150, D-2
West Stayton ... D-3
Westfall ... F-10
Weston ... B-9
Westport ... A-3
Wheeler ... B-2
White City ... J-3
Whitney ... E-9
Wilbur ... G-3
Wilderville ... J-2
Williamina ... C-3
Williams ... J-2
Willow Creek ... F-10
Wilsonville ... C-4
Winchester ... G-2
Winchester Bay ... F-1
Winston ... G-3
Wolfcreek ... H-2
Wonder ... J-2

PENNSYLVANIA
Pages 80-81

Abington ... ★
  Vicinity ... Pg. 147, A-7
Adamstown ... H-11
Addison ... K-4
Akron ... H-11
Alba ... C-9
Albion ... C-1
Alburtis ... G-12
Aliquippa ... G-2
Allentown ... G-13
Altoona ... G-6
Ambler ... H-13
Ambridge ... G-2
Andalusia ... ★
  Vicinity ... Pg. 147, B-9
Archbald ... D-12
Ardmore ... ★
  Vicinity ... Pg. 146, C-5
Arendtsville ... J-8
Armagh ... G-4
Ashley ... E-11
Ashville ... G-5
Aston Mills ... ★
  Vicinity ... Pg. 146, E-3
Athens ... C-10
Audubon ... ★
  Vicinity ... Pg. 146, A-1
Austin ... D-7
Avalon ... ★
  Vicinity ... Pg. 149, B-1
Avis ... E-8
Avondale ... G-3
Baden ... G-2
Baldwin ... ★
  Vicinity ... Pg. 149, F-5
Bally ... H-12
Bangor ... F-13
Barnesboro ... G-5
Barren Hill ... ★
  Vicinity ... Pg. 146, B-5
Bath ... G-13
Battle's Cor. ... ★
  Vicinity ... Pg. 146, D-3
Beaver ... G-1
Beaver Falls ... F-1
Beavertown ... F-9
Bedford ... J-6
Beech Creek ... E-8
Belle Vernon ... J-2
Bellefonte ... F-7
Bellevue ... ★
  Vicinity ... Pg. 149, B-2
Bellwood ... G-6
Ben Avon ... ★
  Vicinity ... Pg. 149, A-1
Bendersville ... J-8
Benson ... H-5
Benton ... E-10
Berlin ... J-4
Berrysburg ... G-9
Berwick ... F-11
Bessemer ... F-1
Bethayres ... ★
  Vicinity ... Pg. 147, A-8
Bethel Park ... H-2
Bethlehem ... G-13
Big Beaver ... G-1
Big Run ... F-5
Birdsboro ... H-12
Black Horse ... ★
  Vicinity ... Pg. 146, E-3
Blain ... H-7
Blairsville ... G-4
Blakely ... D-12
Blooming Valley ... C-2
Bloomsburg ... F-10
Blossburg ... C-9
Bolivar ... H-4
Booth Cors. ... ★
  Vicinity ... Pg. 146, F-2
Boothwyn ... ★
  Vicinity ... Pg. 146, F-3
Boswell ... H-4
Bowmanstown ... F-12
Boyertown ... H-12
Brackenridge ... G-3
Bradford ... C-5
Brentwood ... ★
  Vicinity ... Pg. 149, F-4
Briar Creek ... F-11
Bridgeport ... ★
  Vicinity ... Pg. 146, A-4
Bridgeville ... H-2
Bristol ... J-14
  Vicinity ... Pg. 147, B-10
Broad Top City ... H-6
Brockway ... E-5
Brookhaven ... J-13
Brookville ... E-4
Broomall ... ★
  Vicinity ... Pg. 146, D-4
Brownstown ... H-5
Brownsville ... J-2

Bruin ... E-3
Bryn Athyn ... ★
  Vicinity ... Pg. 147, A-8
Bryn Mawr ... ★
  Vicinity ... Pg. 146, C-4
Burgettstown ... H-1
Burlington ... C-10
Burnham ... G-8
Butler ... F-2
California ... J-2
Callensburg ... E-3
Callery ... F-2
Cambridge Springs ... C-2
Canonsburg ... H-2
Canton ... D-9
Carbondale ... D-12
Carlisle ... H-9
Carmichaels ... J-2
Carnegie ... G-2
Carroll Valley ... K-8
Carrolltown ... G-5
Cassandra ... H-5
Castle Shannon ... ★
  Vicinity ... Pg. 149, F-3
Catasauqua ... G-12
Catawissa ... F-10
Centerville ... J-2
Centerville ... C-3
Central City ... J-5
Centre Hall ... F-7
Chadds Ford ... ★
  Vicinity ... Pg. 146, E-1
Chalfont ... H-13
Chambersburg ... H-7
Charleroi ... H-2
Charlestown ... ★
  Vicinity ... Pg. 146, A-1
Chelsea ... ★
  Vicinity ... Pg. 146, F-2
Cheltenham ... ★
  Vicinity ... Pg. 147, B-7
Cherry Tree ... G-5
Chester ... J-13
  Vicinity ... Pg. 146, F-4
Chester Heights ... J-12
Chester Hill ... F-6
Cheyney ... ★
  Vicinity ... Pg. 146, D-2
Chicora ... F-3
Clairton ... H-2
Clarendon ... C-4
Clarion ... E-4
Clarks Summit ... D-12
Clearfield ... F-6
Cleona ... H-10
Clifton Heights ... ★
  Vicinity ... Pg. 146, E-5
Clintonville ... E-3
Clymer ... G-4
Coalport ... G-5
Coatesville ... J-12
Cochranton ... D-2
Cokeburg ... H-2
Collegeville ... H-13
Colling Dale ... ★
  Vicinity ... Pg. 146, E-5
Columbia ... J-10
Concordville ... ★
  Vicinity ... Pg. 146, E-2
Conneautville ... C-1
Connellsville ... J-3
Connoquenessing ... F-2
Conshohocken ... J-13
  Vicinity ... Pg. 146, B-4
Conway ... G-2
Conyngham ... F-11
Coopersburg ... G-13
Cooperstown ... D-3
Coraopolis ... G-2
Cornwall ... H-10
Cornwells Hts. ... ★
  Vicinity ... Pg. 147, B-9
Corry ... C-3
Corsica ... E-4
Coudersport ... C-7
Crafton ... ★
  Vicinity ... Pg. 149, D-2
Cranesville ... C-1
Creekside ... G-4
Cresson ... G-5
Cressona ... G-11
Croydon ... ★
  Vicinity ... Pg. 147, B-10
Crozierville ... ★
  Vicinity ... Pg. 146, E-3
Curwensville ... F-6
Dalesford ... ★
  Vicinity ... Pg. 146, B-2
Dallastown ... J-10
Dalton ... D-12
Danville ... F-10
Darby ... J-13
  Vicinity ... Pg. 146, E-5
Darling ... ★
  Vicinity ... Pg. 146, E-2
Darlington Cors. ... ★
  Vicinity ... Pg. 146, D-1
Dauphin ... H-9
Dayton ... F-4
Delaware Water Gap ... K-11
Delta ... K-11
Denver ... H-11
Derry ... H-4
Devon ... ★
  Vicinity ... Pg. 146, D-3

★ Denotes City only on Vicinity map. City not located on State map.

PENNSYLVANIA

Devoult .... ★
  Vicinity ... Pg. 146, B-1
Dickson City ... D-12
Dillsburg ... J-9
Dilworthton ... ★
  Vicinity ... Pg. 146, E-1
Donegal ... J-4
Donora ... H-2
Dormont ... H-2
  Vicinity ... Pg. 149, E-2
Dover ... J-9
Downingtown ... J-12
Doylestown ... H-13
Drexel Hill ... ★
  Vicinity ... Pg. 146, E-5
Driftwood ... E-6
DuBois ... E-5
Duboistown ... E-9
Dudley ... H-6
Dunbar ... J-3
Duncannon ... H-9
Duncansville ... H-6
Dunmore ... D-12
Dushore ... D-10
Eagles Mere ... D-10
Eagleville ... ★
  Vicinity ... Pg. 146, A-3
East Berlin ... J-9
East Brady ... F-3
East Butler ... F-3
East Greenville ... H-12
East Lansdowne ... ★
  Vicinity ... Pg. 146, D-5
East Stroudsburg ... F-13
East Washington ... H-2
Easton ... G-13
Eau Claire ... E-3
Ebensburg ... G-5
Economy ... G-2
Eddystone ... ★
  Vicinity ... Pg. 146, F-4
Edge Hill ... ★
  Vicinity ... Pg. 147, A-6
Edgely ... ★
  Vicinity ... Pg. 147, A-11
Edgemont ... ★
  Vicinity ... Pg. 146, D-3
Edinboro ... C-2
Edwardsville ... E-11
Elam ... ★
  Vicinity ... Pg. 146, F-1
Eldred ... C-6
Elizabethtown ... H-10
Elizabethville ... G-10
Elkins Park ... ★
  Vicinity ... Pg. 147, B-7
Elkland ... C-8
Ellport ... F-2
Ellwood City ... F-2
Elwyn ... ★
  Vicinity ... Pg. 146, E-3
Emlenton ... E-3
Emmaus ... G-12
Emporium ... D-6
Ephrata ... H-11
Erie ... B-2
Etna ... ★
  Vicinity ... Pg. 149, B-5
Evans City ... F-2
Everett ... J-6
Everson ... J-3
Factoryville ... D-12
Fairchance ... J-3
Fairfield ... K-8
Fairview ... B-2
Falls Creek ... E-5
Farrell ... E-1
Faust Cor. ... ★
  Vicinity ... Pg. 146, A-2
Fawn Grove ... K-10
Feasterville ... ★
  Vicinity ... Pg. 147, A-9
Fitzwatertown ... ★
  Vicinity ... Pg. 147, A-7
Five Points ... ★
  Vicinity ... Pg. 147, A-6
Fleetwood ... G-12
Flemington ... E-8
Florida Park ... ★
  Vicinity ... Pg. 146, D-3
Ford City ... F-3
Ford Cliff ... F-3
Forest City ... D-12
Forksville ... D-10
Fort Washington ... ★
  Vicinity ... Pg. 146, A-6
Forty Fort ... E-12
Fountain Hill ... G-13
Frackville ... F-11
Franklin ... D-3
Franklin Park ... G-2
Freeburg ... G-9
Freeland ... F-12
Freemansburg ... G-13
Freeport ... G-3
Galeton ... C-8
Gallitzin ... G-5
Garden City ... ★
  Vicinity ... Pg. 146, F-4
Garrett ... J-4
Geistown ... H-5
General Greene ... ★
  Vicinity ... Pg. 146, C-1
Gettysburg ... K-9
Girard ... B-2

Gladwyne ... ★
  Vicinity ... Pg. 146, C-5
Glen Campbell ... F-5
Glen Hope ... F-6
Glen Mills ... ★
  Vicinity ... Pg. 146, E-2
Glen Riddle ... ★
  Vicinity ... Pg. 146, E-3
Glen Rock ... K-10
Glenolden ... ★
  Vicinity ... Pg. 146, E-5
Glenside ... ★
  Vicinity ... Pg. 147, B-7
Gordon ... G-11
Goshenville ... ★
  Vicinity ... Pg. 146, C-1
Gradyville ... ★
  Vicinity ... Pg. 146, D-2
Grampian ... F-5
Gratz ... G-10
Great Bend ... C-12
Greencastle ... K-7
Greensboro ... K-2
Greensburg ... H-3
Greentree ... ★
  Vicinity ... Pg. 149, E-2
Greenville ... D-1
Grenloch ... ★
  Vicinity ... Pg. 146, C-1
Grove City ... E-2
Gulph Mills ... ★
  Vicinity ... Pg. 146, B-4
Halifax ... G-9
Hallstead ... C-12
Hamburg ... G-11
Hanover ... K-9
Harmony ... F-2
Harrisburg ... H-9
Harrisville ... E-2
Harveys Lake ... D-11
Hastings ... G-5
Hatboro ... H-13
Haverford ... ★
  Vicinity ... Pg. 146, C-5
Havertown ... ★
  Vicinity ... Pg. 146, D-4
Hawley ... D-13
Hawthorn ... F-4
Hazleton ... F-11
Heidelberg ... ★
  Vicinity ... Pg. 149, E-1
Herndon ... G-9
Hershey ... H-10
Holidaysburg ... H-6
Homer City ... G-4
Homestead ... ★
  Vicinity ... Pg. 149, E-6
Honesdale ... D-13
Honey Brook ... J-12
Hooversville ... H-5
Hop Bottom ... C-12
Hopewell ... H-6
Houston ... H-2
Houtzdale ... F-6
Howeville ... ★
  Vicinity ... Pg. 146, B-2
Hughesville ... E-10
Hummelstown ... H-10
Huntingdon ... G-7
Hydetown ... C-3
Hyndman ... K-5
Indian Lake ... J-5
Indiana ... G-4
Industry ... G-1
Ingram ... ★
  Vicinity ... Pg. 149, D-1
Irvona ... F-5
Ithan ... ★
  Vicinity ... Pg. 146, C-4
Jackson Center ... E-2
Jacobus ... J-10
Jamestown ... D-1
Jeanette ... H-3
Jeddo ... F-12
Jefferson ... H-2
Jeffersonville ... ★
  Vicinity ... Pg. 146, A-4
Jennerstown ... H-4
Jermyn ... D-12
Jersey Shore ... E-9
Jim Thorpe ... F-12
Johnson's Cors. ... ★
  Vicinity ... Pg. 146, F-1
Johnsonburg ... D-5
Johnstown ... H-5
Jonestown ... H-10
Kane ... C-5
Karns City ... F-3
Kennett Square ... J-12
Kimberton ... ★
  Vicinity ... Pg. 146, A-1
King of Prussia ... ★
  Vicinity ... Pg. 146, B-3
Kingston ... E-12
Kistler ... H-7
Kittanning ... F-3
Knox ... E-3
Knoxville ... C-8
Kulpmont ... F-10
Kutztown ... G-11
Lake City ... B-2
Lake Pine ... ★
  Vicinity ... Pg. 147, F-11
Lancaster ... J-11
Landisburg ... H-8

Lanesboro ... C-12
Langhorne ... H-14
Lansdale ... H-13
Lansdowne ... ★
  Vicinity ... Pg. 146, D-5
Lansford ... F-12
Laporte ... D-10
Latrobe ... H-4
Laureldale ... H-12
Le Raysville ... C-11
Lebanon ... H-10
Leesport ... G-11
Lehighton ... F-12
Lemoyne ... H-9
Lenni ... ★
  Vicinity ... Pg. 146, E-3
Leopard ... ★
  Vicinity ... Pg. 146, C-3
Levittown ... H-14
Lewisburg ... F-9
Lewistown ... G-8
Liberty ... D-9
Ligonier ... H-4
Lilly ... H-5
Lima ... ★
  Vicinity ... Pg. 146, E-3
Lincoln ... H-11
Linesville ... C-1
Linwood ... ★
  Vicinity ... Pg. 146, F-3
Lititz ... J-11
Little Meadows ... C-11
Littlestown ... K-9
Liverpool ... H-9
Llanerch ... ★
  Vicinity ... Pg. 146, D-5
Lock Haven ... E-8
Locksley ... ★
  Vicinity ... Pg. 146, D-2
Loganton ... E-8
Loretto ... G-5
Lower Burrell ... G-3
Lumber City ... F-5
Lykens ... G-10
Macungie ... G-12
Mahanoy City ... F-11
Manchester ... J-10
Manheim ... J-11
Manns Choice ... J-5
Manoa ... ★
  Vicinity ... Pg. 146, D-4
Mansfield ... C-9
Marcus Hook ... K-13
  Vicinity ... Pg. 146, F-3
Marianna ... J-2
Marietta ... J-10
Marion Center ... F-4
Markham ... ★
  Vicinity ... Pg. 146, E-2
Marklesburg ... H-6
Marpel ... ★
  Vicinity ... Pg. 146, D-4
Mars ... G-2
Martinsburg ... H-6
Marysville ... H-9
Masontown ... J-2
Matamoras ... D-14
McKean ... B-2
McKeesport ... H-2
McSherrytown ... K-9
McVeytown ... G-7
Mckee's Rocks ... ★
  Vicinity ... Pg. 149, C-2
Meadville ... D-2
Mechanicsburg ... H-9
Media ... J-13
  Vicinity ... Pg. 146, E-3
Melrose Park ... ★
  Vicinity ... Pg. 147, B-7
Mercer ... E-2
Mercersburg ... K-7
Meshoppen ... D-11
Meyersdale ... K-4
Middleburg ... G-9
Middletown ... H-10
  Vicinity ... Pg. 147, A-10
Midland ... G-1
Mifflinburg ... F-9
Mifflintown ... G-8
Milbourne ... ★
  Vicinity ... Pg. 146, D-5
Milesburg ... F-7
Milford ... E-14
Mill Creek ... H-7
Mill Hall ... E-8
Mill Village ... C-2
Millersburg ... G-9
Millerstown ... G-9
Millersville ... J-10
Millheim ... F-8
Milltown ... ★
  Vicinity ... Pg. 146, D-1
Milton ... F-9
Minersville ... G-11
Mohnton ... H-11
Monaca ... G-2
Monessen ... H-2
Monroe ... ★
  Vicinity ... Pg. 146, C-5
Monroeville ... G-3
Mont Alto ... K-8
Mont Clare ... ★
  Vicinity ... Pg. 146, A-2
Montoursville ... E-9
Montrose ... C-12
Moosic ... D-12

Morrisville ... H-14
Morton ... ★
  Vicinity ... Pg. 146, E-4
Moscow ... E-12
Mountville ... J-10
Mt. Carmel ... F-10
Mt. Holly Springs ... J-9
Mt. Jewett ... C-5
Mt. Joy ... J-10
Mt. Lebanon ... ★
  Vicinity ... Pg. 149, F-2
Mt. Oliver ... ★
  Vicinity ... Pg. 149, E-4
Mt. Pleasant ... H-3
Mt. Pocono ... E-13
Mt. Union ... H-7
Mt. Wolf ... J-10
Murrysville ... G-3
Myerstown ... H-11
Nanticoke ... E-11
Nanty-Glo ... G-5
Narberth ... J-13
  Vicinity ... Pg. 146, D-5
Nazareth ... G-13
Nescopeck ... F-11
New Albany ... D-10
New Alexandra ... H-3
New Beaver ... F-1
New Berlin ... F-9
New Bethlehem ... F-4
New Brighton ... F-1
New Buffalo ... G-9
New Castle ... F-1
New Centerville ... J-4
  Vicinity ... Pg. 146, B-3
New Cumberland ... H-9
New Eagle ... H-2
New Florence ... H-4
New Freedom ... K-10
New Holland ... J-11
New Kensington ... G-3
New Lebanon ... D-2
New Milford ... C-12
New Oxford ... J-9
New Paris ... J-5
New Philadelphia ... G-11
New Salem ... J-2
New Stanton ... H-3
New Wilmington ... E-1
Newburg ... F-5
Newburg ... J-8
Newport ... G-9
Newportville ... ★
  Vicinity ... Pg. 147, A-10
Newry ... H-6
Newton Square ... ★
  Vicinity ... Pg. 146, D-3
Newville ... H-8
Nicholson ... D-12
Norristown ... J-13
  Vicinity ... Pg. 146, A-4
North Apollo ... G-3
North Belle Vernon ... H-3
North East ... B-3
North Wales ... H-13
North York ... J-10
Northampton ... G-12
Northumberland ... F-10
Norwood ... ★
  Vicinity ... Pg. 146, E-5
Nuangola ... E-11
Oakford ... ★
  Vicinity ... Pg. 147, A-9
Oakland ... C-12
Oakmont ... G-3
  Vicinity ... Pg. 146, D-4
Oaks ... ★
  Vicinity ... Pg. 146, A-3
Ogden ... ★
  Vicinity ... Pg. 146, F-2
Ogontz ... ★
  Vicinity ... Pg. 147, B-7
Ohiopyle ... J-3
Oil City ... D-3
Old Forge ... D-12
Olyphant ... D-12
Orangeville ... E-10
Orbisonia ... H-7
Orrstown ... J-8
Orwigsburg ... G-11
Osceola Mills ... F-6
Oswayo ... C-7
Oxford ... K-11
Painters Crossroads ... ★
  Vicinity ... Pg. 146, E-1
Palmerton ... F-12
Palmyra ... H-10
Paoli ... ★
  Vicinity ... Pg. 146, C-2
Parker ... E-3
Parkesburg ... J-11
Parkside ... ★
  Vicinity ... Pg. 146, E-1
Patton ... G-6
Paxtang ... ★
  Vicinity ... Pg. 146, B-2
Pen Argyl ... F-13
Penn Valley ... ★
  Vicinity ... Pg. 146, C-5
Penn Wynne ... ★
  Vicinity ... Pg. 146, D-5
Pennsburg ... H-13
Perkasie ... H-13
Perkiomer ... ★
  Vicinity ... Pg. 146, A-2
Petersburg ... G-7

Petrolia ... F-3
Philadelphia ... J-13
  Vicinity ... Pg. 136-137
Philipsburg ... F-6
Philmont ... ★
  Vicinity ... Pg. 147, A-8
Phoenixville ... H-12
Pickering ... ★
  Vicinity ... Pg. 146, A-2
Picture Rocks ... E-10
Pillow ... G-9
Pine Grove ... G-10
Pittsburgh ... G-2
  Vicinity ... Pg. 149
Pittston ... E-12
Planebrook ... ★
  Vicinity ... Pg. 146, B-1
Platea ... B-2
Pleasantville ... D-3
Pleasantville ... H-5
Plum ... G-3
Plumville ... F-4
Plymouth Meeting ... ★
  Vicinity ... Pg. 146, A-5
Point Marion ... K-2
Polk ... D-2
Port Allegany ... C-6
Port Carbon ... G-11
Port Kennedy ... ★
  Vicinity ... Pg. 146, A-3
Port Matilda ... F-7
Port Royal ... G-8
Portage ... H-5
Portersville ... F-2
Portland ... F-13
Pottstown ... H-12
Pottsville ... G-11
Prospect Park ... ★
  Vicinity ... Pg. 146, E-4
Punxsutawney ... F-4
Quakertown ... G-13
Quarryville ... J-11
Radnor ... ★
  Vicinity ... Pg. 146, C-4
Rainsburg ... J-5
Ramey ... F-6
Reading ... H-12
Red Hill ... H-13
Red Lion ... J-10
Renovo ... E-7
Reynoldsville ... E-5
Rices Landing ... J-2
Richland ... H-11
Richlandtown ... G-13
Ridgway ... D-5
Ridley Park ... ★
  Vicinity ... Pg. 146, E-4
Rimersburg ... E-3
Ringtown ... F-11
Riverside ... F-10
Roaring Spring ... H-6
Robesonia ... H-11
Rockdale ... ★
  Vicinity ... Pg. 146, E-3
Rockledge ... ★
  Vicinity ... Pg. 147, B-7
Rockwood ... J-4
Rocky Hill ... ★
  Vicinity ... Pg. 146, D-1
Rome ... C-11
Rose Tree ... ★
  Vicinity ... Pg. 146, D-3
Rose Valley ... ★
  Vicinity ... Pg. 146, E-3
Roseto ... F-13
Roseville ... C-9
Roslyn ... ★
  Vicinity ... Pg. 147, A-7
Rosslyn Farms ... ★
  Vicinity ... Pg. 149, D-1
Rouseville ... D-3
Royersford ... H-12
Rural Valley ... F-4
Rutledge ... ★
  Vicinity ... Pg. 147, A-9
Saegertown ... C-2
Saint Clair ... G-11
  Vicinity ... Pg. 146, E-4
Saint Davids ... ★
  Vicinity ... Pg. 146, C-4
Saint Marys ... D-5
Saint Petersburg ... E-3
Salisbury ... K-4
Salladasburg ... E-9
Saltillo ... H-7
Saltsburg ... G-3
Sandy Lake ... D-2
Sankertown ... G-5
Saxonburg ... F-3
Saxton ... H-6
Sayre ... C-10
Scalp Level ... H-5
Schuylkill Haven ... G-11
Scottdale ... H-3
Scranton ... D-12
Selinsgrove ... G-9
Sellersville ... H-13
Seward ... H-4
Shade Gap ... H-7
Shamokin ... F-10
Shamokin Dam ... F-9
Sharon ... E-1
Sharon Hill ... ★
  Vicinity ... Pg. 146, E-5
Sharpsburg ... ★
  Vicinity ... Pg. 149, B-5

Shenandoah ... F-11
Shickshinny ... E-11
Shillington ... H-11
Shinglehouse ... C-6
Shippensburg ... J-8
Shippenville ... E-3
Shirleysburg ... H-7
Shrewsbury ... K-10
Slatington ... F-12
Sligo ... E-3
Slippery Rock ... E-2
Smethport ... C-6
Smithfield ... K-3
Snow Shoe ... F-7
Somerset ... J-4
Souderton ... H-13
South Bethlehem ... F-4
South Coatesville ... J-12
South Connellsville ... J-3
South Fork ... H-5
South Renovo ... E-7
South Waverly ... B-10
South Williamsport ... E-9
Spangler ... G-5
Spartanburg ... C-3
Spring City ... H-12
Spring Grove ... J-9
Springboro ... C-1
State College ... F-7
Stillwater ... E-10
Stoneboro ... D-2
Stoystown ... J-4
Strasburg ... J-11
Strattanville ... E-4
Strausstown ... G-11
Stroudsburg ... F-13
Sugar Grove ... B-4
Sugarcreek ... D-3
Sugartown ... ★
  Vicinity ... Pg. 146, C-2
Summerhill ... H-5
Summerville ... E-4
Summit Hill ... F-12
Sunbury ... F-10
Susquehanna ... C-12
Swarthmore ... ★
  Vicinity ... Pg. 146, E-4
Swedeland ... ★
  Vicinity ... Pg. 146, B-4
Swedesburg ... ★
  Vicinity ... Pg. 146, A-4
Sycamore Mills ... ★
  Vicinity ... Pg. 146, D-3
Sykesville ... F-5
Sylvania ... B-9
Tamaqua ... F-12
Tanguy ... ★
  Vicinity ... Pg. 146, D-2
Tatamy ... G-13
Taylor ... D-12
Telford ... H-13
Temple ... H-12
Terre Hill ... H-11
Thompsontown ... G-9
Thornburg ... ★
  Vicinity ... Pg. 149, D-1
Thornton ... ★
  Vicinity ... Pg. 146, E-1
Three Springs ... H-7
Tidioute ... C-4
Tiona ... C-4
Tionesta ... D-3
Titusville ... D-3
Topton ... G-12
Towanda ... C-10
Tower City ... G-10
Townville ... C-3
Trainer ... ★
  Vicinity ... Pg. 146, F-3
Trappe ... H-12
Tremont ... G-10
Trevose ... ★
  Vicinity ... Pg. 147, A-9
Trooper ... ★
  Vicinity ... Pg. 146, A-3
Troutville ... F-5
Troy ... C-10
Tullytown ... H-14
Tunkhannock ... D-11
Twin Oaks ... ★
  Vicinity ... Pg. 146, F-3
Tyrone ... G-6
Union City ... C-3
Union Dale ... C-11
Uniontown ... J-3
Upper Darby ... ★
  Vicinity ... Pg. 146, D-5
Ursina ... K-4
Valley Forge ... ★
  Vicinity ... Pg. 146, B-2
Valleystore ... ★
  Vicinity ... Pg. 146, B-2
Vandergrift ... G-3
Venango ... C-2
Village Green ... ★
  Vicinity ... Pg. 146, F-3
Villanova ... ★
  Vicinity ... Pg. 146, C-4
Walnutport ... G-12
Wampum ... F-1
Ward ... ★
  Vicinity ... Pg. 146, C-2
Warren ... B-4
Washington ... H-2

Waterford ... C-2
Watsontown ... E-9
Wattsburg ... B-3
Waymart ... D-13
Wayne ... ★
  Vicinity ... Pg. 146, C-3
Waynesboro ... K-8
Waynesburg ... J-2
Weatherly ... F-12
Wellersburg ... K-5
Wellsboro ... C-8
Wellsville ... J-9
Wesleyville ... B-2
West Brownsville ... H-2
West Chester ... J-12
West Coshohocken ... ★
  Vicinity ... Pg. 146, B-4
West Easton ... G-13
West Grove ... K-12
West Hazleton ... F-11
West Homestead ... ★
  Vicinity ... Pg. 149, E-5
West Kittanning ... F-3
West Liberty ... F-2
West Middlesex ... E-1
West Mifflin ... G-3
  Vicinity ... Pg. 149, G-5
West Newton ... H-3
West Pittston ... E-12
West Reading ... H-11
West View ... ★
  Vicinity ... Pg. 149, A-2
West York ... J-10
Westfield ... C-8
Westmont ... H-5
Westover ... G-5
Wheatland ... E-1
White Haven ... E-12
White Horse ... ★
  Vicinity ... Pg. 146, C-2
White Marsh ... ★
  Vicinity ... Pg. 146, A-6
White Oak ... H-3
Whitehall ... G-12
  Vicinity ... Pg. 149, G-4
Wilkes-Barre ... E-12
Wilkinsburg ... G-3
Williams Cors. ... ★
  Vicinity ... Pg. 146, A-4
Williams Cors. ... ★
  Vicinity ... Pg. 146, A-4
Williamsburg ... G-6
Williamsport ... E-9
Williamstown ... G-10
Willow Grove ... ★
  Vicinity ... Pg. 147, A-7
Wilson ... ★
  Vicinity ... Pg. 146, D-3
Wilsons Cors. ... ★
  Vicinity ... Pg. 146, A-1
Wind Gap ... F-13
Winterstown ... K-10
Womelsdorf ... H-11
Woodbury ... H-6
Worthington ... F-3
Wrightsville ... J-10
Wyalusing ... D-11
Wynnewood ... ★
  Vicinity ... Pg. 146, C-5
Wyola ... ★
  Vicinity ... Pg. 146, C-3
Wyomissing ... H-11
Yardley ... H-14
Yeadon ... J-13
York ... J-10
York Springs ... J-9
Youngsville ... C-4
Youngwood ... H-3
Zelienople ... F-2

RHODE ISLAND — Page 31

Ashton ... E-8
Auburn ... F-9
Barrington ... F-10
Berkeley ... E-9
Bristol ... G-10
Carolina ... H-9
Charlestown ... H-9
Chepachet ... E-8
Clayville ... F-8
Cranston ... F-9
East Greenwich ... G-9
East Providence ... F-10
Esmond ... E-9
Exeter ... F-9
Fiskeville ... F-9
Foster Center ... E-8
Glocester ... E-8
Harmony ... E-9
Harrisville ... E-9
Homestead ... G-10
Hope ... F-9
Hope Valley ... G-8
Jamestown ... G-10
Lippitt ... F-9
Little Compton ... H-11
Mapleville ... E-9
Middletown ... G-10
N. Tiverton ... G-10
Narragansett Pier ... H-9
Nasonville ... E-9
Newport ... G-10
No. Foster ... F-8
Nooseneck ... G-9
North Scituate ... F-9
Pascoag ... E-8
Pawtucket ... F-10
Portsmouth ... G-10
Providence ... F-10
Slatersville ... E-9
Usquepaug ... G-9
Vernon ... F-8
Wakefield ... H-9
Warren ... F-10
Warwick ... G-10
Washington ... F-9
Westerly ... H-8
West Greenwich ... G-8
Wickford ... G-9
Wood River Jct. ... H-8
Woodville ... H-8
Woonsocket ... E-9

SOUTH CAROLINA

SOUTH CAROLINA — Pages 70-71

Abbeville ... F-4
Adams Run ... J-7
Aiken ... G-5
Allendale ... H-6
Almeda ... J-6
Anderson ... F-4
Andrews ... G-9
Antreville ... F-4
Appleton ... H-6
Awendaw ... H-8
Aynor ... F-9
Ballentine ... F-6
Bamberg ... H-6
Barnwell ... H-6
Batesburg ... G-5
Bayboro ... F-9
Belton ... E-4
Bennettsville ... D-6
Bethany ... E-3
Bethune ... F-7
Bishopville ... F-7
Blacksburg ... D-5
Blackville ... H-6
Blenheim ... D-8
Bonneau ... H-7
Boykin ... F-7
Bradley ... F-4
Branchville ... H-6
Brownsville ... E-6
Buffalo ... E-5
Bullock Creek ... D-5
Cades ... G-8
Cainhoy ... H-8
Calhoun Falls ... F-4
Camden ... F-7
Canadys ... H-7
Carlisle ... E-6
Cassatt ... F-7
Cayce ... F-6
Centenary ... F-9
Central ... E-3
Chappells ... F-5
Charleston ... J-8
Chelsea ... K-7
Cheraw ... E-8
Chesnee ... D-5
Chester ... E-6
Chesterfield ... E-8
Clarkshill ... G-5
Clemson ... E-3
Cleveland ... D-4
Clinton ... E-5
Clio ... E-8
Clover ... D-5
Columbia ... F-6
Conway ... F-9
Cool Spring ... F-9
Cresent Beach ... G-10
Cross ... H-7
Cross Hill ... F-5
Cross Keys ... E-5
Dalzell ... F-7
Darlington ... E-7
De Kalb ... F-7
Debidue Beach ... H-9
Denmark ... H-6
Dillon ... E-8
Dovesville ... E-8
Due West ... F-4
Edgefield ... G-5
Edgemoor ... E-6
Edisto Beach ... J-8
Edisto Island ... J-7
Effingham ... F-8
Ehrhardt ... H-6
Elgin ... F-7
Enoree ... E-5
Estill ... H-6
Eureka ... G-5
Evergreen ... F-8
Fair Bluff ... F-9
Fairfax ... J-6
Filbert ... D-6
Florence ... F-8
Floydale ... F-9
Folly Beach ... J-8

★ Denotes City only on Vicinity map. City not located on State map.

SOUTH CAROLINA

Forest Beach K-7
Foreston G-7
Fork F-9
Fork Shoals E-4
Fort Mill D-6
Fountain Inn E-5
Frogmore K-7
Furman J-6
Gaffney D-5
Galivants Ferry F-9
Garden City G-9
Gardens Corner J-7
Garnett J-6
Georgetown H-7
Givhans H-7
Goose Creek H-8
Gourdin G-8
Gownesyville D-4
Grays J-6
Great Falls E-6
Greeleyville G-8
Green Pond J-7
Green Sea F-9
Greenville E-4
Greenwood E-4
Greer E-4
Hampton J-6
Hanahan H-8
Hannah F-8
Hardeeville K-6
Hartsville F-7
Hemingway G-8
Hickory Grove F-9
Hickory Grove D-5
Hilda H-6
Hilton Head Island ...K-7
Holly Hill H-7
Honea Path F-4
Horrell Hill F-6
Indiantown G-8
Inman D-4
Islandton H-7
Isle of Palms J-8
Iva F-4
Jackson H-5
Jacksonboro J-7
James Island J-8
Jamestown H-8
Jefferson E-7
Jenkinsville F-6
Joanna F-5
Johnston G-5
Jonesville E-5
Kershaw E-7
Kingsburg F-9
Kingstree G-8
Kitchings Mill G-5
Kline H-6
Lake City G-8
Lamar F-7
Lancaster E-6
Landrum D-4
Lane G-8
Latta F-8
Laurens F-4
Leeds E-5
Lena J-6
Lesslie E-6
Lewis E-6
Lexington F-6
Liberty E-4
Litchfield Beach G-9
Little River F-10
Lockhart E-5
Lodge H-6
Loris F-9
Manning G-8
Manville F-7
Marietta D-4
Marion F-9
Martin H-5
Mauldin E-4
Mayesville F-7
McBee E-7
McColl E-8
McConnells E-6
McCormick G-4
Moncks Corner H-8
Mount Pleasant J-8
Mountville F-5
Mt. Carmel F-3
Mullins F-9
Myrtle Beach G-10
New Ellenton H-5
New Prospect D-5
Newberry F-5
Nichols F-9
Nine Times E-3
Ninety Six F-5
Nixonville F-9
North G-6
North Augusta G-5
North Charleston J-8
Oatland G-9
Oats F-8
Olanta F-8
Olar H-6
Orangeburg G-6
Outland G-9
Owdoms G-5
Pacolet E-5
Pageland E-7
Pamplico F-8
Parksville G-5
Patrick E-7

Pauline E-5
Pawleys Island G-9
Pelion G-6
Pendleton E-3
Pickens E-4
Pineland J-6
Pineville G-8
Pinewood G-7
Plum Branch G-4
Pontiac F-6
Prosperity F-6
Pumpkintown E-4
Rantowles J-8
Rhems G-8
Richburg E-6
Ridgeland J-6
Ridgeway F-6
Rock Hill E-6
Rockton F-6
Rockville J-8
Rocky Bottom E-3
Ruby E-7
Salters G-8
Saluda F-5
Sampit H-9
Sandy Run G-6
Santee G-7
Sardinia G-8
Sardis F-8
Scranton F-8
Seneca E-3
Sharon E-6
Simpson F-6
Simpsonville E-4
Smallwood F-6
Smoaks H-7
Society Hill E-8
Spartanburg E-5
Springfield G-6
St. George H-7
St. Matthews G-7
St. Stephen G-8
Starr F-4
Stateburg F-7
Steedman G-6
Stoney Hill F-5
Stuckey G-9
Sullivans Island J-8
Summerton G-7
Summerville H-7
Sumter G-7
Surfside Beach G-9
Switzerland K-6
Sycamore H-6
Tamassee E-3
Tatum E-8
Taylor E-4
Tillman J-6
Timmonsville F-8
Tradesville E-7
Travelers Rest E-4
Trenton G-5
Ulmer H-6
Union E-5
Varnville J-6
Wagener G-6
Walhalla E-3
Walterboro J-7
Ward G-5
Ware Shoals F-4
Wateree G-7
Wells H-7
Westminster E-3
Westville E-7
Whitehall J-8
Whitmire E-5
Willington F-4
Williston H-5
Winnsboro F-6
Woodruff E-5
Yauhannah G-9
Yemassee J-7
Yonges Island J-8
York D-6

SOUTH DAKOTA
Pages 82-83

Aberdeen D-8
Agar E-7
Akaska D-7
Albee E-11
Alcester J-11
Alexandria H-9
Alpena G-9
Altamont E-11
Andover D-10
Arlington F-11
Armour H-9
Artas C-7
Artesian G-9
Ashton E-9
Astoria F-11
Aurora G-11
Badger F-10
Bancroft F-10
Batesland H-4
Belle Fourche E-2
Belvidere G-5
Beresford J-11
Bison D-4
Blunt F-7
Bonesteel J-8
Bowdle D-7

Bradley E-10
Brandon H-11
Brandt F-11
Brentford F-8
Bristol D-10
Britton C-10
Broadland F-9
Brookings F-11
Bruce F-11
Bryant F-10
Buffalo C-3
Buffalo Gap G-2
Burke J-8
Bushnell F-11
Butler D-10
Camp Crook C-2
Canova G-10
Canton H-11
Carthage G-10
Castle Rock D-3
Cavour F-9
Centerville J-10
Central City F-2
Chamberlain G-8
Chelsea E-8
Claire City C-10
Clark E-10
Clear Lake F-11
Colman G-11
Colton G-11
Columbia D-9
Conde E-9
Corona D-11
Corsica H-9
Cottonwood G-4
Cresbard E-8
Crooks H-11
Custer G-2
Dallas H-7
Dante J-9
De Smet F-10
Deadwood F-2
Dell Rapids G-11
Delmont H-9
Dimock H-9
Doland E-9
Dolton H-10
Draper G-6
Dupree E-5
Eagle Butte E-5
Eden D-10
Edgemont H-2
Elk Point K-11
Elm Springs F-3
Emery H-10
Enning E-4
Erwin F-10
Estelline F-10
Ethan H-10
Eureka D-7
Fairburn G-3
Fairfax J-8
Fairpoint E-3
Fairview J-11
Faith E-4
Farmer G-10
Farmingdale F-3
Faulkton E-8
Flandreau G-11
Florence E-9
Fort Pierre F-6
Fort Thompson G-7
Frankfort E-8
Frederick D-8
Freeman H-10
Fruitdale E-2
Fulton H-9
Gann Valley G-8
Garden City E-10
Garretson H-11
Gary F-11
Gayville J-10
Geddes H-8
Gettysburg E-7
Glad Valley D-5
Glenham D-7
Goodwin E-11
Greenwood H-9
Gregory H-7
Grenville D-10
Groton D-9
Hammer C-10
Harrisburg H-11
Harrold F-7
Hayti F-10
Hecla C-9
Hermosa G-3
Hereid C-7
Herrick J-7
Highmore F-7
Hill City G-2
Hillsview C-8
Hitchcock F-9
Hosmer D-7
Hot Springs H-2
Houghton D-9
Hoven D-7
Howard G-10
Howes E-4
Huron F-9
Interior G-4
Ipswich D-8
Irene J-10
Iroquois F-10
Isabel D-5

Java D-7
Jefferson K-11
Kadoka G-5
Kennebec G-7
Keystone G-2
Kimball G-8
Kranzburg E-11
Kyle H-4
La Bolt E-11
La Plant D-6
Lake Andes J-8
Lake City D-10
Lake Preston F-10
Lane G-9
Langford D-10
Lead F-2
Lebanon E-7
Lemmon C-4
Lennox H-11
Leola D-8
Letcher G-9
Lily E-10
Little Eagle C-6
Lodgepole C-4
Long Lake C-8
Long Valley H-5
Lowry D-7
Loyalton D-8
Ludlow C-3
Madison G-11
Marion H-10
Martin H-4
Marty H-9
Marvin E-11
Maurine D-4
McIntosh C-5
McLaughlin C-6
Meadow D-4
Mellette E-9
Menno H-10
Miller F-8
Mission H-6
Mitchell H-9
Mobridge D-6
Monroe H-10
Montrose H-10
Morristown C-5
Mound City C-7
Mount Vernon H-9
Mud Butte D-3
Murdo G-6
Naples E-10
New Effington C-11
Newell E-2
Nisland E-2
North Sioux City K-11
Northville E-8
Nunda G-11
Oacoma G-7
Oelrichs H-2
Oglala H-3
Okreek H-6
Oldham G-10
Olivet H-9
Onaka D-8
Onida E-7
Orient E-8
Ortley D-10
Parker H-10
Parkston H-9
Parmelee H-5
Philip G-5
Pierpont D-10
Pierre F-6
Pine Ridge H-3
Plainview E-4
Plankinton G-9
Platte H-8
Pollock C-7
Prairie City C-3
Presho G-6
Pringle G-2
Provo H-2
Pukwana G-8
Quinn G-4
Ramona G-10
Rapid City F-3
Ravinia J-9
Raymond E-9
Redfield E-8
Redig D-2
Ree Heights F-8
Reliance G-7
Reva C-3
Revillo E-11
Ridgeview E-6
Rockerville F-2
Rockham E-8
Roscoe D-8
Rosebud H-5
Roslyn D-10
Roswell G-9
Saint Charles J-8
Saint Francis H-5
Saint Lawrence F-8
Salem H-10
Scenic G-3
Scotland J-10
Selby D-7
Seneca E-7
Shadehill C-4
Sherman G-11
Sioux Falls H-11

Sisseton D-11
Sorum D-3
South Shore E-10
Spearfish E-2
Springfield J-9
Stephan F-8
Stickney H-9
Stockholm E-11
Stoneville E-4
Stratford D-9
Sturgis F-2
Summit D-11
Tabor J-10
Tea H-11
Timber Lake D-6
Tolstoy D-7
Toronto F-11
Trail City D-6
Trent G-11
Tripp J-9
Tulare E-9
Turton E-9
Tyndall J-9
Union Center E-4
Veblen C-10
Verdon E-9
Vermillion J-10
Viborg H-10
Vienna F-10
Vilas G-10
Vivian G-6
Wagner J-9
Wakonda J-10
Wall G-4
Wallace E-10
Ward G-11
Wasta F-4
Watertown E-10
Waubay D-10
Webster D-10
Wessington F-8
Wessington Springs ...G-8
Westport D-9
Wetonka D-8
Wewala J-7
White F-11
White Butte C-4
White Lake G-8
White River H-6
Whitewood E-2
Willow Lake F-10
Wilmot D-11
Winner H-6
Wood H-6
Woonsocket G-9
Worthing H-11
Yale F-9
Yankton J-10
Zeona D-3

TENNESSEE
Page 42

Adams F-6
Adamsville J-4
Aetna H-5
Alamo H-3
Alcoa H-11
Alexandria G-8
Algood G-8
Allardt G-9
Allens H-3
Allisona H-7
Allred G-9
Alpine G-9
Altamont H-8
Alto J-7
Antioch ....★
  Vicinity ...Pg. 136, F-7
Arlington J-2
  Vicinity ...Pg. 131, A-10
Arrington H-7
Arthur F-11
Ashland City G-6
Ashport H-2
Athens H-10
Atoka J-2
Atwood G-4
Avondale ....★
  Vicinity ...Pg. 136, A-9
Bailey ....★
  Vicinity ...Pg. 131, F-9
Banner Hill G-13
Bartlett J-2
  Vicinity ...Pg. 131, C-7
Beacon ....★
  Vicinity ...Pg. 136, G-6
Bean Station G-12
Beardstown H-5
Beersheba Springs H-8
Belfast H-7
Bell Buckle H-7
Belle Meade ....★
Belle Meade ....★
  Vicinity ...Pg. 136, E-4
Bellevue ....★
  Vicinity ...Pg. 136, F-2
Bells H-3
Belvidere J-7
Benjestown ....★
  Vicinity ...Pg. 131, B-7
Benton J-10
Berry Hill ....★
  Vicinity ...Pg. 136, E-6

Bethel Sprgs. J-4
Big Sandy G-4
Big Spring J-9
Birchwood J-9
Blaine G-11
Bluff City F-13
Bogota G-3
Bolivar J-3
Bolton ....★
  Vicinity ...Pg. 131, A-9
Bon Air G-9
Braden H-2
Bradford G-4
Brattontown F-8
Brentwood G-7
Brentwood ....★
  Vicinity ...Pg. 136, G-5
Briceville G-10
Brighton H-2
Bristol F-13
Brooklin ....★
  Vicinity ...Pg. 136, G-6
Brownsville H-3
Bruceton G-4
Brunswick ....★
  Vicinity ...Pg. 131, B-8
Bulls Gap G-12
Bumpus Mills F-5
Burlison H-2
Burns G-6
Busby J-5
Byrdstown F-9
Calhoun J-9
Camden G-4
Camelot F-12
Capleville ....★
  Vicinity ...Pg. 131, G-6
Carlisle G-5
Carthage G-8
Caryville G-10
Cash Point J-6
Cedar Hill F-6
Celina F-9
Center Point J-6
Centertown H-8
Centerville H-6
Central G-3
Chapel Hill H-7
Charleston J-9
Charlotte G-5
Chattanooga J-9
Church Hill F-12
Clarksburg H-4
Clarksville F-5
Cleveland J-9
Clifton J-5
Clinton G-10
Coalmont H-8
Collegedale J-9
Collierville ....★
  Vicinity ...Pg. 131, F-10
Collinwood J-5
Columbia H-6
Cookeville G-8
Copperhill J-10
Cordova ....★
  Vicinity ...Pg. 131, D-8
Cornersville H-6
Cosby H-11
Covington H-2
Crab Orchard H-9
Cross Plains F-6
Crossville H-9
Culleoka H-6
Cumberland City G-5
Cumberland Furnace ...G-5
Cumberland Gap F-11
Dancyville H-3
Dandridge G-11
Darden H-4
Dayton H-9
Decatur H-9
Decaturville H-5
Decherd J-8
Deerfield H-8
Dibrell H-8
Dickson G-5
Dixon Springs G-8
Donelson ....★
Donelson ....★
  Vicinity ...Pg. 136, C-6
Dover F-5
Dowalltown G-8
Doyle H-8
Dresden G-4
Ducktown J-10
Dunlap H-8
Dyer G-3
Dyersburg G-3
Eads ....★
  Vicinity ...Pg. 131, C-10
Eagan F-11
East Ridge J-9
Eastview J-4
Egypt ....★
  Vicinity ...Pg. 131, B-6
Elizabethton G-13
Elkton J-6
Ellandale ....★
  Vicinity ...Pg. 131, B-7
Elmore Park ....★
  Vicinity ...Pg. 131, C-7
Elora J-7
Elza ....★

Englewood J-10
Erin G-5
Erwin G-13
Estill Springs J-7
Ethridge J-6
Etowah J-10
Evensville H-9
Fairview G-6
Farmington H-6
Fayetteville J-6
Finley G-3
Fisherville ....★
  Vicinity ...Pg. 131, D-10
Flat Woods H-5
Flatcreek J-7
Flynns Lick G-8
Forbus F-9
Forest Hill ....★
  Vicinity ...Pg. 131, F-8
Forest Hills ....★
  Vicinity ...Pg. 136, F-4
Foster Corners ....★
  Vicinity ...Pg. 136, F-8
Franklin H-6
Friendship G-3
Fruitvale H-3
Gadsden H-3
Gainesboro G-8
Gallatin G-7
Gates H-3
Gatlinburg H-11
Germantown ....★
  Vicinity ...Pg. 136, B-4
Germantown J-2
  Vicinity ...Pg. 131, C-8
Gibson H-4
Gildfield ....★
  Vicinity ...Pg. 131, A-8
Gilt Edge H-2
Gleason G-4
Goodlettsville G-7
Goodlettsville ....★
  Vicinity ...Pg. 136, A-6
Goodspring J-6
Gordonsville G-7
Gower ....★
  Vicinity ...Pg. 136, C-3
Grand Junction J-3
Grandview H-9
Gray G-13
Graysville H-9
Green Hill ....★
  Vicinity ...Pg. 136, C-9
Greenback H-10
Greenbrier G-6
Greeneville G-12
Greenfield G-4
Grimsley G-9
Habersham F-10
Haletown J-8
Halls G-3
Halls Crossroads G-11
Hampshire H-5
Hampton G-13
Hanging Limb G-9
Harriman H-10
Harrogate F-11
Hartsville G-7
Henderson H-4
Hendersonville G-7
Hendersonville ....★
  Vicinity ...Pg. 136, A-8
Henning H-2
Henry G-4
Hermitage Hills ......★
  Vicinity ...Pg. 136, C-8
Hickory Valley J-3
Highland J-5
Hohenwald H-5
Hopewell ....★
  Vicinity ...Pg. 136, C-8
Hornsby J-3
Humboldt H-3
Hunter G-13
Huntingdon G-4
Huntland J-7
Huntsville G-10
India G-4
Inglewood ....★
Inglewood ....★
  Vicinity ...Pg. 136, C-6
Iron City J-5
Isham F-10
Ivydell G-10
Jacksboro G-10
Jackson H-3
Jamestown G-9
Jasper J-8
Jefferson City G-11
Jellico F-10
Joelton G-6
Joelton ....★
  Vicinity ...Pg. 136, A-4
Johnson City G-13
Jonesboro G-12
Keeling H-2
Kelso J-7
Kenton G-3
Kimbro ....★
  Vicinity ...Pg. 136, G-8
Kingsport F-13
Kingston H-10
Kirkland H-7
Knoxville H-10
Kodak H-11

Kyles Ford F-12
La Vergne G-7
La Vergne G-7
  Vicinity ...Pg. 136, G-9
LaFollette G-10
Laager J-8
Lafayette F-8
Lake City G-10
Lake Mont H-10
Lakesite J-9
Lancing G-9
Lascassas H-7
Latham G-4
Lawrenceburg J-5
Leach G-4
Lebanon G-7
Leipers Fork H-6
Lenoir City H-10
Lenow ....★
  Vicinity ...Pg. 131, C-9
Lewisburg H-6
Lexington H-4
Liberty G-8
Lickton ....★
  Vicinity ...Pg. 136, A-5
Linden H-5
Little Creek ....★
  Vicinity ...Pg. 136, B-5
Livingston G-9
Lobelville H-5
Locke J-2
Loretto J-5
Loudon H-10
Lucy ....★
  Vicinity ...Pg. 131, A-6
Luttrell G-11
Lutts J-5
Lyles H-6
Lynchburg J-7
Lynnville H-6
Madisonville H-10
Malesus H-3
Manchester H-7
Marrowbone ....★
  Vicinity ...Pg. 136, C-1
Martin G-4
Maryville H-10
Mascot G-11
Mason H-2
Maury City H-3
Mayland G-8
Maynardville G-10
McBurg J-6
McEwen G-5
McKenzie G-4
McMinnville H-8
Medina H-3
Medon H-3
Memphis J-1
  Vicinity ...Pg. 131
Mercer H-3
Michie J-4
Middleton J-3
Midtown H-10
Milan H-4
Milledgeville J-4
Milligan College G-13
Millington J-2
Minor Hill J-6
Miston G-3
Monteagle J-8
Monterey G-9
Morgantown H-9
Morris Chapel J-4
Morrison H-7
Morristown G-11
Moscow J-3
Mosheim G-12
Moss F-8
Mound City ....★
Mount Carmel F-12
Mount Crest H-9
Mount Juliet G-7
Mount Juliet ....★
  Vicinity ...Pg. 136, C-10
Mount Olive H-11
Mount Pleasant H-6
Mount Vernon J-10
Mount Zion ....★
  Vicinity ...Pg. 136, A-2
Mountain City F-14
Munford H-2
Murfreesboro H-7
Nashville G-6
Nashville G-6
  Vicinity ...Pg. 136
New Hope K-8
New Johnsonville G-5
New Market G-11
New River G-10
New Tazwell G-11
New Town J-6
Newbern G-3
Newport G-12
Niota H-10
Nixon J-4
Nobles J-6
Norris G-10
Nunnelly H-5
Oak Hill ....★
  Vicinity ...Pg. 136, F-6
Oak Ridge H-10
Oakdale G-9
Oakland J-2

TENNESSEE

★ Denotes City only on Vicinity map. City not located on State map.

TENNESSEE

TEXAS

Oakville . . . . ★
Vicinity . . . . . . Pg. 131, F-5
Oakwood F-5
Obion G-3
Ocoee J-9
Oglesby . . . . ★
Vicinity . . . . . . Pg. 136, G-6
Old Hickory . . . . ★
Vicinity . . . . . . Pg. 136, B-8
Olivehill J-4
Oliver Springs G-10
Oneida F-10
Palmer J-8
Palmyra F-5
Parago Mill . . . . ★
Vicinity . . . . . . Pg. 136, F-7
Paris G-4
Parrottsville G-12
Parsons H-4
Pasquo . . . . ★
Vicinity . . . . . . Pg. 136, F-3
Peakland H-9
Pegram G-6
Pelham J-8
Petersburg J-7
Philadelphia H-10
Pigeon Forge H-11
Pikeville H-9
Pinewood H-5
Pinson H-4
Pisgah . . . . ★
Vicinity . . . . . . Pg. 131, D-10
Pleasant Hill G-8
Pleasant View G-6
Portland F-7
Providence G-7
Providence . . . . ★
Vicinity . . . . . . Pg. 136, F-7
Pulaski J-6
Puncheon Camp G-11
Puryear F-4
Quebeck H-8
Raleigh J-2
Vicinity . . . . . . Pg. 131, B-6
Ramer J-4
Ramsey . . . . ★
Vicinity . . . . . . Pg. 131, A-4
Raus J-7
Rayon City . . . . ★
Vicinity . . . . . . Pg. 136, B-7
Red Bank J-9
Red Boiling Springs F-8
Riceville J-10
Richland . . . . ★
Vicinity . . . . . . Pg. 136, D-3
Rickman G-8
Ridgely G-3
Ridgetop G-6
Ridley H-6
Ripley H-2
Rives G-3
Roan Mountain G-13
Robbins G-9
Rockwood H-9
Rocky Fork G-12
Rogersville G-12
Rossville J-2
Rural Hill . . . . ★
Vicinity . . . . . . Pg. 136, F-8
Russellville G-12
Rutherford G-3
Rutledge G-11
Sadlersville F-6
Saint Bethlehem F-5
Saint Joseph J-5
Sale Creek J-9
Saltillo J-4
Sandy Hook H-6
Sardis H-4
Saundersville . . . . ★
Vicinity . . . . . . Pg. 136, A-9
Savannah H-4
Scotts Hill H-4
Selmer J-4
Seven Points . . . . ★
Vicinity . . . . . . Pg. 136, E-9
Seven Points . . . . ★
Vicinity . . . . . . Pg. 136, E-9
Sevierville H-11
Sewanee J-8
Shacklett G-6
Shady Valley F-13
Sharon G-3
Shelby Farms . . . . ★
Vicinity . . . . . . Pg. 131, D-7
Shelbyville H-7
Shooks Gap H-11
Shop Springs G-7
Signal Mtn. J-8
Siloam F-7
Silver Point G-8
Skiem J-6
Smartt H-8
Smith Springs . . . . ★
Vicinity . . . . . . Pg. 136, F-8
Smithville G-8
Smyrna G-7
Sneedville F-11
Soddy-Daisy J-9
Somerville J-2
South Carthage G-8
South Dyersburg G-3
South Fulton F-3
South Pittsburg J-8
Sparta H-8

Spencer H-8
Spring City H-9
Spring Creek H-4
Spring Hill H-6
Spring Lake . . . . ★
Vicinity . . . . . . Pg. 131, B-7
Springfield F-6
Stanton H-2
Sullivan Gdn. F-12
Summertown J-5
Sunbright G-10
Surgoinsville F-12
Sweetwater H-10
Sycamore . . . . ★
Vicinity . . . . . . Pg. 136, A-1
Taft J-6
Tarpley J-6
Tazewell F-11
Tellico Plains J-10
Tennessee Ridge G-5
Timberlake H-4
Tiptonville F-3
Toone J-3
Tracy City J-8
Trenton G-3
Trezevant G-4
Triune H-7
Troy G-3
Tullahoma J-7
Tusculum G-13
Tusculum G-13
Vicinity . . . . . . Pg. 136, F-6
Una . . . . ★
Vicinity . . . . . . Pg. 136, F-7
Unicoi G-13
Union City G-3
Union Grove J-9
Union Hill . . . . ★
Vicinity . . . . . . Pg. 136, A-5
Vaughlans Gap . . . . ★
Vicinity . . . . . . Pg. 136, F-4
Victoria J-8
Viola H-8
Violet J-10
Vonore H-10
Waco J-9
Walden J-9
Walkertown J-4
Walling H-8
Wartburg G-10
Wartrace H-7
Watertown G-8
Waverly G-5
Waynesboro J-5
Webber City J-5
West Meade . . . . ★
Vicinity . . . . . . Pg. 136, E-4
West Shiloh J-4
Westmoreland F-7
White Bluff G-6
White House F-7
White Pine G-12
Whites Creek . . . . ★
Vicinity . . . . . . Pg. 136, B-4
Whitesburg G-12
Whiteville J-3
Whitwell J-8
Wilder G-9
Willette G-8
Williston J-2
Winchester J-7
Winfield F-10
Woodbury H-8
Woodland Mills F-3
Woodstock . . . . ★
Vicinity . . . . . . Pg. 131, B-5
Wrencoe . . . . ★
Vicinity . . . . . . Pg. 136, G-7
Wyanoke . . . . ★
Vicinity . . . . . . Pg. 131, E-1
Wynnburg G-3

TEXAS
Pages 94-98

Abernathy E-7
Abilene G-10
Acala J-2
Ackerly G-7
Acme D-10
Adamsville J-12
Addicks L-15
Vicinity . . . . . . Pg. 120, D-2
Addison . . . . ★
Vicinity . . . . . . Pg. 115, A-9
Adrian C-7
Agua Dulce P-12
Aiken E-8
Alamo Heights L-11
Vicinity . . . . . . Pg. 154, D-5
Alanreed C-9
Alba F-15
Albany G-10
Aldine . . . . ★
Vicinity . . . . . . Pg. 120, D-2
Aledo F-12
Alexander H-12
Alfred P-12
Algoa M-16
Alice P-12
Allamoore J-3
Allen F-14
Alleyton L-14
Allison B-10
Allred F-6

Almeda . . . . ★
Vicinity . . . . . . Pg. 120, F-5
Alpine K-5
Altair M-14
Alto H-16
Alvarado G-13
Alvin M-16
Alvord E-12
Amarillo C-7
Ambrose E-14
Ames L-16
Amherst E-7
Anderson K-15
Andice K-12
Andrews G-6
Angleton M-16
Anna E-14
Annona E-16
Anson G-10
Antelope F-12
Anthony H-2
Anton E-7
Apple Springs J-16
Aquilla H-13
Aransas Pass P-13
Archer City E-11
Argyle F-13
Arlington . . . . ★
Vicinity . . . . . . Pg. 114, D-5
Arp G-16
Artesia Wells P-10
Arthur City E-15
Asherton N-10
Ashtola C-8
Aspermont F-9
Athens G-15
Atlanta F-17
Aubrey E-13
Austin L-13
Austonio J-15
Austwell N-14
Avery F-16
Avinger F-17
Avoca G-10
Azle G-13
Bacliff M-16
Bagwell E-16
Baird G-10
Bakersfield K-7
Balch Springs . . . . ★
Vicinity . . . . . . Pg. 115, E-11
Ballinger H-10
Balmorhea J-5
Bandera L-11
Bangs H-11
Barclay J-13
Bardwell H-14
Barksdale L-10
Barnhart J-8
Barrett L-16
Barrett . . . . ★
Vicinity . . . . . . Pg. 121, B-9
Barry H-14
Barstow J-5
Bartlett K-13
Bassett F-16
Bastrop L-13
Batesville N-10
Batson L-16
Bay City M-15
Baytown L-16
Vicinity . . . . . . Pg. 121, D-10
Beasley M-15
Beaumont L-17
Beckville G-17
Bedias K-15
Bee Cave L-12
Beeville N-12
Belfalls J-13
Bellaire . . . . ★
Vicinity . . . . . . Pg. 120, E-4
Bellevue E-12
Bellmead H-13
Bells E-14
Bellville L-14
Belmont M-13
Belton J-13
Ben G-15
Ben Arnold J-14
Ben Bolt P-12
Benavides Q-11
Benbrook G-13
Benchley K-14
Benjamin F-10
Bertram K-12
Bettie G-16
Big Lake J-7
Big Sandy G-16
Big Spring H-8
Big Wells N-10
Bigfoot M-11
Birthright F-15
Bishop Q-12
Bivins F-17
Black D-7
Blackwell H-9
Blanco L-11
Blanket H-11
Bleakwood K-18
Bledsoe E-5
Blessing N-15
Blewett M-9
Blooming Grove H-14
Bloomington N-13
Blossom E-15

Blue Mound . . . . ★
Vicinity . . . . . . Pg. 114, C-3
Blue Ridge F-14
Bluegrove E-12
Bluff Dale G-12
Bluffton K-11
Boca Chica S-13
Boerne L-11
Bogata F-15
Boling M-14
Bomarton F-10
Bon Wier K-18
Bonham E-14
Booker A-9
Boonsville F-12
Borger B-8
Boston F-17
Bovina D-6
Bowie E-12
Boxelder F-16
Boyd F-13
Boys Ranch Tacosa B-7
Brackettville M-9
Bradshaw H-10
Brady J-10
Brandon H-14
Brashear F-15
Brazoria M-15
Breckenridge G-11
Bremond J-14
Brenham L-14
Brice D-9
Bridge City L-18
Bridgeport F-12
Briggs K-12
Briscoe B-9
Broaddus J-17
Bronco F-6
Bronson J-17
Bronte H-9
Brookeland J-17
Brookesmith H-11
Brookshire L-15
Brookside Village . . . . ★
Vicinity . . . . . . Pg. 120, F-6
Brownfield F-7
Brownsboro G-15
Brownsville S-13
Brownwood H-11
Brundage N-10
Bruni Q-11
Bryan K-14
Bryson F-12
Buchanan Dam K-12
Buckholts L-12
Buda L-12
Buffalo J-15
Buffalo Gap G-10
Bula E-6
Bulcher E-13
Bullard G-16
Buna K-17
Bunavista B-8
Bunker Hill . . . . ★
Vicinity . . . . . . Pg. 120, D-3
Burkburnett E-11
Burke J-16
Burkett H-10
Burkeville J-18
Burleson G-13
Vicinity . . . . . . Pg. 114, G-3
Burlington J-14
Burnet K-12
Burton L-14
Bushland C-7
Bustamanete R-11
Butler K-13
Byers E-12
Bynum H-14
Cactus A-7
Caddo G-11
Caddo Mills F-15
Caldwell K-14
Calf Creek J-10
Call K-18
Calliham N-12
Calvert J-14
Camden K-16
Cameron K-14
Camilla K-16
Camp Verde L-11
Camp Wood L-10
Campbell F-15
Campbellton N-12
Canadian B-9
Canton G-15
Canutillo H-1
Canyon C-7
Caps G-10
Carbon G-11
Carlos K-15
Carlsbad H-9
Carlton H-12
Carmine L-14
Carmona J-16
Carrizo Springs N-10
Carrollton G-13
Vicinity . . . . . . Pg. 115, A-8
Carta Valley L-9
Carthage H-17
Cash F-14
Castle Hills J-10
Castroville M-11
Cat Spring L-14
Catarina N-10

Cayuga H-15
Cedar Creek L-13
Cedar Hill . . . . ★
Vicinity . . . . . . Pg. 115, F-7
Cedar Park K-12
Celeste F-14
Celina F-14
Center H-17
Centerville J-15
Chandler G-15
Channelview L-16
Vicinity . . . . . . Pg. 121, D-8
Channing B-7
Chapman H-16
Chapman Ranch P-13
Chappell Hill L-15
Charco N-13
Charlotte N-11
Cherokee J-11
Cherry Spring K-11
Chester J-17
Chico F-12
Childress D-9
Chillicothe D-10
Chilton J-13
China L-17
Chireno J-17
Chisos Basin M-5
Chriesman K-14
Christine N-11
Christoval J-9
Circle Back E-6
Cisco G-11
Cistern L-13
Clairemont F-9
Clairette H-12
Clarendon C-9
Clarksville E-16
Claude C-8
Clayton H-17
Clear Lake Shore . . . . ★
Vicinity . . . . . . Pg. 121, G-9
Cleburne G-13
Cleveland K-16
Clifton H-13
Clint H-1
Clodine . . . . ★
Vicinity . . . . . . Pg. 120, D-2
Cloverleaf . . . . ★
Vicinity . . . . . . Pg. 121, D-8
Clute M-16
Clyde G-10
Coahoma G-8
Cockrell Hill . . . . ★
Vicinity . . . . . . Pg. 115, D-8
Coffey City H-15
Coldspring K-16
Coleman H-10
College Station K-14
Colleyville . . . . ★
Vicinity . . . . . . Pg. 114, B-5
Collinsville F-13
Colmesneil K-17
Colorado City G-9
Columbus L-14
Comanche H-11
Combes R-12
Comfort L-11
Commerce F-15
Como F-15
Comstock L-8
Concan M-10
Concepcion Q-12
Concord H-16
Conroe K-16
Converse L-11
Conway C-8
Cooks Point K-14
Cookville F-16
Coolidge H-14
Cooper F-15
Coppell . . . . ★
Vicinity . . . . . . Pg. 115, A-7
Copperas Cove J-12
Cornudas H-3
Corpus Christi P-13
Corrigan J-16
Corsicana H-14
Coryell City J-13
Cost M-13
Cotton Center E-7
Cottonwood K-15
Cottonwood H-11
Cotulla N-10
Country Campus K-16
Coy City N-12
Coyanosa J-5
Crabbs Praire K-15
Crandall G-14
Crane J-6
Cranfills Gap H-13
Crawford J-13
Cresson G-13
Crews H-10
Crockett J-15
Crosby L-15
Crosby . . . . ★
Vicinity . . . . . . Pg. 121, B-9
Crosbyton E-8
Cross K-15
Cross Cut H-11
Cross Plains H-11
Cross Roads H-15
Crow G-16
Crowell E-10

Crowley G-13
Vicinity . . . . . . Pg. 114, F-3
Crystal City N-10
Cuero M-13
Cumby F-14
Cushing H-16
Cut & Shoot K-15
Cypress . . . . ★
Vicinity . . . . . . Pg. 120, A-1
Cypress Mill K-12
D'Hanis M-10
Dabney M-9
Dacosta N-14
Daingerfield F-16
Daisetta K-16
Dalhart B-7
Dalingworth Gardens . . . . ★
Vicinity . . . . . . Pg. 114, E-5
Dallas G-14
Vicinity . . . . . . Pg. 115
Damon M-15
Danbury M-15
Danevang M-15
Darrouzett A-9
Dawn C-7
Dawson H-14
Dayton L-16
Vicinity . . . . . . Pg. 121, A-11
De Berry G-17
De Kalb F-16
De Leon H-11
De Wees M-12
Deanville K-14
Decatur F-13
Deer Park . . . . ★
Vicinity . . . . . . Pg. 121, E-8
Del Rio M-8
Del Valle L-13
Dell City H-3
Denison E-14
Denton F-13
Denver City F-6
Deport F-15
Derby N-11
Desdemona H-12
Devers L-16
Devine M-11
Dew H-15
Dewalt . . . . ★
Vicinity . . . . . . Pg. 120, G-3
Deweyville K-18
Diana G-16
Diboll J-16
Dickens E-9
Dickinson L-15
Dilley N-11
Dime Box K-14
Dimmitt D-7
Dinero P-12
Divot N-11
Dobbin K-15
Dodd City E-15
Donie H-15
Donna S-12
Doole J-10
Doss K-11
Doucette K-17
Dougherty E-8
Douglass H-16
Douglassville F-17
Dozier C-9
Draw F-8
Dripping Springs L-12
Driscoll P-12
Dryden L-7
Dublin H-12
Dumas B-7
Dumont E-9
Duncanville . . . . ★
Vicinity . . . . . . Pg. 115, F-7
Dundee E-11
Dunlay M-11
Dunn G-9
Dyersdale . . . . ★
Vicinity . . . . . . Pg. 121, B-7
Eagle Lake M-14
Eagle Pass N-9
Early H-11
Earth D-7
Vicinity . . . . . . Pg. 120, G-4
East Columbia M-15
Easterly J-14
Eastland G-11
Easton G-16
Ecleto M-13
Edcouch R-12
Eddy J-13
Eden J-10
Edgecliff . . . . ★
Vicinity . . . . . . Pg. 114, E-3
Edinburg R-12
Edmonson D-7
Edna M-14
Edom G-15
Edroy P-13
Egypt M-14
El Campo M-14
El Lago . . . . ★
Vicinity . . . . . . Pg. 121, D-7
El Paso H-2
El Sauz R-10
Elbert F-11
Eldorado K-9
Electra E-11
Elgin L-13

Elkhart H-15
Ellinger L-14
Elmendorf M-12
Vicinity . . . . . . Pg. 154, J-7
Elmo G-15
Elsa R-12
Elysian Fields G-17
Emory F-14
Encinal P-10
Encino Q-12
Energy H-12
Enloe F-15
Ennis G-14
Enochs E-6
Escobas Q-11
Estelline D-9
Etoile J-17
Etter B-7
Euless . . . . ★
Vicinity . . . . . . Pg. 114, C-6
Eureka H-14
Eustace F-14
Evadale K-17
Evant J-12
Evergreen K-16
Everman . . . . ★
Vicinity . . . . . . Pg. 114, F-3
Fabens H-1
Fairbanks . . . . ★
Vicinity . . . . . . Pg. 120, C-3
Fairfield H-15
Fairlie F-15
Fairview F-14
Fairview G-8
Fairy H-12
Falcon R-11
Falfurrias Q-12
Falls City N-12
Fannett L-17
Fannin N-13
Farmers Branch . . . . ★
Vicinity . . . . . . Pg. 115, B-8
Farmersville F-14
Farrar J-14
Farwell D-6
Fayetteville L-14
Fedor K-13
Fentress L-13
Ferris G-14
Vicinity . . . . . . Pg. 115, G-10
Fieldton E-7
Fink E-14
Finney E-9
Flatonia M-13
Flomot D-8
Florence J-12
Floresville M-12
Flower Mound . . . . ★
Vicinity . . . . . . Pg. 114, A-6
Floydada E-8
Fluvanna F-8
Follett A-10
Forest J-16
Forest Hill . . . . ★
Vicinity . . . . . . Pg. 114, E-4
Forestburg F-13
Forney G-14
Fort Clark Springs M-9
Fort Davis K-5
Fort Gates J-12
Fort Griffin G-10
Fort Hancock J-2
Fort McKavett K-10
Fort Stockton J-6
Fort Worth G-13
Vicinity . . . . . . Pg. 114
Fostoria K-16
Fowlerton N-11
Frame Switch K-13
Francitas N-14
Frankel City G-6
Franklin J-14
Frankston H-15
Fransworth A-9
Fred K-17
Fredericksburg L-11
Fredonia K-11
Freeport N-16
Freer P-11
Fresno . . . . ★
Vicinity . . . . . . Pg. 120, G-4
Friday J-17
Friendswood . . . . ★
Vicinity . . . . . . Pg. 121, G-6
Frio Town M-10
Friona D-6
Frisco F-13
Fritch B-8
Frost H-14
Fruitland F-12
Fruitvale G-15
Fullbright F-16
Fulton P-13
Funston G-10
Gail F-8
Gainesville F-13
Galena Park . . . . ★
Vicinity . . . . . . Pg. 121, D-7
Galveston M-16
Ganado M-14
Garden City H-8
Garden Valley G-15
Gardendale H-7
Garland G-14
Vicinity . . . . . . Pg. 115, B-10

Garrison H-17
Garwood M-14
Gary H-17
Gatesville J-12
Gause K-14
Geneva J-17
George West N-12
Georgetown K-13
Geronimo L-12
Giddings L-13
Gilchrist L-17
Gillett N-12
Gilliland E-10
Gilmer G-16
Girard F-9
Girvin J-7
Gladewater G-16
Glazier B-9
Glen Cove H-10
Glen Flora M-15
Glen Rose H-13
Glenn E-9
Glenn Heights . . . . ★
Vicinity . . . . . . Pg. 115, G-8
Glenrio C-6
Glenwood G-16
Glidden L-14
Gober F-15
Godley G-13
Goldsboro H-10
Goldthwaite J-11
Goliad N-13
Gonzales M-13
Goodland E-6
Goodlett D-10
Goodnight C-8
Goodrich K-16
Gordon G-12
Gordonville E-13
Goree F-10
Gorman H-11
Gouldbusk J-10
Graford F-12
Graham F-11
Granbury G-12
Grand Prairie . . . . ★
Vicinity . . . . . . Pg. 115, D-6
Grand Saline G-15
Grandfalls J-6
Granger K-13
Grapeland J-15
Grapevine . . . . ★
Vicinity . . . . . . Pg. 114, B-6
Grassland F-8
Grayback E-11
Greenville F-15
Grit K-10
Groesbeck J-14
Groom C-8
Groves L-17
Groveton J-16
Gruver A-8
Gun Barrel City G-14
Gustine H-12
Guthrie E-9
Guy M-15
Hagansport F-15
Hale Center E-7
Halletsville M-14
Hallsville G-16
Haltom City . . . . ★
Vicinity . . . . . . Pg. 114, C-3
Hamilton H-12
Hamlin G-9
Hamshire L-17
Happy C-7
Hardin L-16
Hargill R-12
Harker Heights J-13
Harleton G-16
Harlingen S-13
Harper L-10
Harrold E-11
Hart D-6
Hartley B-7
Harwood M-13
Haskell F-10
Haslet . . . . ★
Vicinity . . . . . . Pg. 114, A-3
Hatchel H-10
Hawkins G-16
Hawley G-10
Hearne K-14
Hebbronville Q-11
Hebron . . . . ★
Vicinity . . . . . . Pg. 115, A-8
Hedley C-9
Hedwig Village . . . . ★
Vicinity . . . . . . Pg. 120, D-3
Helena N-13
Hemleigh G-9
Hemphill J-18
Hempstead L-14
Henderson G-16
Henrietta E-12
Hereford C-6
Hext K-10
Hico H-12
Hidalgo S-12
Higgins B-10
Highbank J-14
Highland Park . . . . ★
Vicinity . . . . . . Pg. 115, C-9
Highlands L-16

★ Denotes City only on Vicinity map. City not located on State map.

City	Ref	City	Ref
Highlands	★	Kingsland	K-11
Vicinity	Pg. 121, C-9	Kingston	F-14
Hillister	K-17	Kingsville	Q-12
Hillsboro	H-13	Kinwood	★
Hillshire Village	★	Vicinity	Pg. 120, B-6
Vicinity	Pg. 120, C-4	Kirbyville	K-17
Hilltop Lakes	J-14	Kirkland	D-9
Hindes	N-11	Kirvin	H-14
Hitchcock	M-16	Kleburg	★
Hobson	N-12	Vicinity	Pg. 115, E-11
Hochheim	M-13	Knickerbocker	J-9
Hockley	L-15	Knippa	M-10
Holland	K-13	Knott	G-7
Holliday	E-11	Knox City	F-10
Hondo	M-11	Kopperl	H-13
Honey Grove	E-15	Kosse	J-14
Horizon City	H-1	Kountze	K-17
Houston	L-15	Kress	D-7
Howe	F-14	Krum	F-13
Hubbard	H-14	Kyle	L-12
Huckabay	G-12	La Gloria	R-11
Hudson	J-16	La Grange	L-13
Hughes Springs	F-16	La Grulla	R-11
Hull	★	La Joya	R-11
Vicinity	Pg. 121, A-6	La Marque	M-16
Humble	L-16	La Paloma	S-13
Vicinity	Pg. 121, A-6	La Porte	★
Hunt	L-10	Vicinity	Pg. 121, E-9
Hunters Creek	★	La Pryor	N-10
Vicinity	Pg. 120, D-4	La Reforma	R-12
Huntington	J-17	La Vernia	M-12
Huntsville	K-15	La Villa	R-12
Hurlwood	E-7	La Ward	N-14
Hurst	★	Ladonia	F-15
Vicinity	Pg. 114, C-5	Lago Vista	K-12
Hutchins	G-14	Laguna Park	H-13
Vicinity	Pg. 115, E-10	Lake Hills	M-11
Hutto	K-13	Lake Jackson	M-15
Hye	L-11	Lake Worth	★
Idalou	E-7	Vicinity	Pg. 114, C-2
Imperial	J-6	Lakeport	G-16
Inadal	G-9	Lakeside	★
Independence	L-14	Vicinity	Pg. 114, C-1
Indian Gap	J-12	Lakeside Village	H-13
Industry	L-14	Lakeview	D-9
Inez	N-14	Lamesa	G-7
Ingleside	P-13	Lamkin	H-12
Ingram	L-11	Lampasas	J-12
Iola	K-15	Lancaster	G-14
Iowa Park	E-11	Vicinity	Pg. 115, F-9
Ira	G-8	Lane City	M-15
Iraan	K-7	Langtry	L-7
Iredell	H-12	Laredo	Q-10
Ireland	J-12	Lariat	D-6
Irving	G-13	Lark	C-8
Vicinity	Pg. 115, C-7	Larue	H-15
Italy	G-13	Lasara	R-12
Itasca	H-13	Latexo	J-15
Jacinto City	★	Lavon	F-14
Vicinity	Pg. 121, D-7	Lawn	H-10
Jacksboro	F-12	LeFors	C-9
Jacksonville	H-15	League City	L-15
Jamestown	J-18	Leakey	L-10
Jarrell	K-13	Leander	K-12
Jasper	J-17	Leesburg	F-16
Jayton	F-9	Leesville	M-13
Jean	F-11	Leggett	K-16
Jefferson	G-17	Lehman	E-6
Jermyn	F-12	Leigh	G-17
Jersey Village	★	Lela	C-9
Vicinity	Pg. 120, B-3	Lelia Lake	C-9
Jewett	J-14	Leming	M-12
Joaquin	H-17	Lenorah	G-7
Johnson City	L-11	Leon Springs	L-11
Johntown	F-16	Leon Valley	L-11
Jolly	E-12	Vicinity	Pg. 154, C-2
Jollyville	K-12	Leona	J-15
Jones Creek	M-15	Leonard	F-14
Jonesboro	H-12	Levelland	E-7
Jonestown	K-12	Lewisville	F-13
Joshua	G-13	Vicinity	Pg. 115, A-6
Jourdanton	N-11	Lexington	K-13
Joy	F-14	Liberty	L-16
Junction	K-10	Liberty Hill	K-12
Juno	L-8	Libscomb	A-9
Justiceburg	F-8	Lincoln	L-13
Justin	F-13	Lincoln City	★
Kalgary	F-8	Vicinity	Pg. 120, C-5
Kamay	E-11	Linden	F-17
Kanawha	E-16	Lindsay	E-13
Karnack	G-17	Lingleville	H-12
Karnes City	N-12	Littlefield	E-7
Katemcy	K-10	Liverpool	M-16
Katy	L-15	Livingston	K-16
Kaufman	G-14	Llano	K-11
Keene	G-13	Lobo	J-3
Keller	★	Lockett	E-10
Vicinity	Pg. 114, B-4	Lockhart	L-13
Kellerville	C-9	Lockney	E-8
Vicinity	Pg. 121, G-9	Lodi	F-17
Kemp	G-14	Loma Alta	L-8
Kempner	J-12	Lomax	H-8
Kendleton	M-15	Lometa	J-11
Kenedy	N-12	London	K-10
Kennard	J-16	Lone Star	F-16
Kennedale	★	Long Branch	H-16
Vicinity	Pg. 114, E-4	Long Mott	N-14
Kenney	L-14	Longview	G-16
Kent	J-4	Longworth	G-9
Kerens	H-14	Loop	F-7
Kermit	H-5	Lopeno	R-11
Kerrville	L-11	Loraine	G-8
Kilgore	G-16	Lorena	J-13
Killeen	J-13	Lorenzo	E-8
Kings Mill	C-8	Los Angeles	N-11

City	Ref	City	Ref
Los Fresnos	S-12	Monthalia	M-13
Lott	J-13	Moody	J-13
Louise	M-14	Moore	M-11
Lovelady	J-15	Mooring	K-14
Loving	F-11	Moran	G-11
Loyal Valley	K-11	Morgan	H-13
Lubbock	F-8	Morgan Mill	G-12
Luckenbach	L-11	Morgans Point	★
Lueders	G-10	Vicinity	Pg. 121, E-10
Lufkin	J-16	Morse	B-8
Luling	L-13	Morton	E-6
Lumberton	K-17	Morton Valley	G-11
Lutie	C-9	Moscow	J-16
Lydia	F-16	Moss Hill	K-16
Lyford	R-13	Moulton	M-13
Lyons	K-14	Mount Calm	H-13
Lytle	M-11	Mount Sylvan	G-15
Mabank	G-15	Mount Vernon	F-16
Madisonville	J-15	Mountain Home	L-10
Magnolia	M-15	Mt. Enterprise	H-16
Malakoff	H-15	Mt. Pleasant	F-16
Malta	F-16	Muenster	E-13
Mankins	E-11	Muldoon	L-14
Mansfield	G-13	Muleshoe	D-6
Vicinity	Pg. 114, F-5	Mullin	J-11
Maple	E-6	Mumford	K-14
Marathon	K-5	Munday	F-10
Marble Falls	K-12	Murchison	G-15
Marfa	K-4	Murphy	★
Marietta	F-17	Vicinity	Pg. 115, A-11
Marion	M-12	Myrtle Springs	G-15
Markham	M-15	N. Richland Hills	★
Marlin	J-14	Vicinity	Pg. 114, C-4
Marquez	J-15	Nacogdoches	H-16
Marshall	G-16	Nada	M-14
Mart	J-14	Naples	F-16
Martindale	L-13	Nash	F-17
Martinez	M-12	Natalia	M-11
Vicinity	Pg. 154, E-7	Navasota	K-15
Martinsville	H-17	Nazareth	D-7
Maryneal	G-9	Neches	H-15
Mason	K-11	Nederland	K-17
Masterson	B-7	Needmore	E-6
Matador	E-8	Needville	M-15
Matagorda	N-15	Nelsonville	L-14
Mathis	P-12	New Baden	J-14
Maud	F-17	New Boston	F-17
Mauriceville	L-17	New Braunfels	L-12
Maxwell	L-12	New Caney	L-16
May	H-11	New Deal	E-7
Maydelle	H-16	New Gulf	M-15
Maypearl	G-13	New Home	F-7
McAdoo	E-8	New London	G-16
McAllen	S-12	Vicinity	Pg. 115, A-10
McCamey	J-7	New Summerfield	H-16
McCaulley	G-9	New Ulm	L-14
McDade	L-13	New Waverly	K-15
McFaddin	N-13	Newark	★
McGregor	J-13	Vicinity	Pg. 114, A-1
McKinney	F-14	Newcastle	F-11
McLean	C-9	Newlin	D-9
McLeod	F-17	Newman	H-2
McMahan	L-13	Newsome	F-16
McNary	J-2	Newton	K-18
McQueeney	L-12	Nixon	M-13
Meadow	F-7	Nocona	E-12
Medicine Mound	D-10	Nolan	G-9
Medina	L-11	Nolanville	J-13
Megargel	F-11	Nome	K-16
Melissa	F-14	Noodle	G-10
Melrose	H-17	Nordheim	N-13
Melvin	J-10	Normandy	N-9
Memphis	D-9	Normangee	J-15
Menard	K-10	Normanna	N-13
Mendoza	L-13	North Houston	★
Mentone	H-5	Vicinity	Pg. 120, B-4
Mercedes	S-12	North Zulch	K-14
Meridian	H-13	Northcrest	H-13
Merkel	G-9	Northfield	D-9
Mertzon	J-8	Norton	H-9
Mesquite	G-14	Notrees	H-6
Vicinity	Pg. 115, C-11	Novice	H-10
Mexia	H-14	Nuevo Laredo	P-10
Miami	B-9	Nursery	N-13
Mico	M-11	O'Brien	F-10
Midland	H-7	O'Donnell	F-7
Midlothian	G-13	Oak Hill	L-12
Midway	K-15	Oakalla	J-12
Milam	J-18	Oakland	M-14
Milano	K-14	Oakwood	H-15
Miles	H-9	Odem	P-13
Milford	G-13	Odessa	H-7
Millersview	J-10	Oglesby	H-13
Millett	N-11	Oilton	Q-11
Millican	K-14	Oklaunion	E-11
Mineola	G-15	Old Boston	F-17
Mineral	N-12	Old Center	H-17
Mineral Wells	G-12	Old Glory	F-9
Mingus	G-12	Old Ocean	M-15
Mirando City	Q-11	Olden	G-11
Mission	S-12	Oldenburg	L-14
Missouri City	★	Olivia	N-14
Vicinity	Pg. 120, F-3	Olmito	S-13
Mobeetie	C-9	Olney	F-11
Moline	J-12	Olton	E-7
Monahans	H-6	Omaha	F-16
Monkstown	E-15	Orange	L-18
Monroe	L-17	Orange Grove	P-12
Mont Belvieu	L-16	Ore City	F-16
Montague	E-12	Orla	H-5
Montalba	H-15	Osceola	H-13
Monte Alto	R-12	Ottine	M-13
Montgomery	K-15	Ovalo	H-10
		Overton	G-16

City	Ref	City	Ref
Ovilla	★	Raywood	L-17
Vicinity	Pg. 115, G-8	Reagan	J-14
Ozona	K-8	Realitos	Q-11
Paducah	E-9	Red Oak	G-13
Paige	L-13	Red Oak	★
Paint Rock	J-10	Vicinity	Pg. 115, G-8
Painview	D-7	Red Springs	E-10
Palacios	N-14	Redford	M-4
Palestine	H-15	Reese Vill.	E-7
Palmer	G-14	Refugio	P-13
Palo Pinto	G-12	Reklaw	H-16
Pampa	B-8	Reno	E-15
Pandora	M-13	Retta	★
Panhandle	C-8	Vicinity	Pg. 114, G-4
Panna Maria	M-12	Rhome	F-13
Panola	G-17	Ricardo	Q-12
Paradise	F-13	Rice	H-14
Paris	E-15	Richardson	F-13
Parnell	D-9	Vicinity	Pg. 115, A-9
Pasadena	L-16	Richland	H-14
Patricia	G-7	Richland Hills	★
Patroon	H-17	Vicinity	Pg. 114, C-4
Pattonville	E-16	Richland Springs	J-11
Pawnee	N-12	Richmond	L-15
Paxton	H-17	Richwood	M-16
Pearland	★	Ridge	J-14
Vicinity	Pg. 121, G-6	Riesel	J-13
Pearsall	N-11	Ringgold	E-12
Pecos	J-5	Rio Grande City	R-11
Peggy	N-12	Rio Vista	H-13
Penwell	H-6	Riomendina	M-11
Perrin	F-12	Rios	Q-12
Perry	J-13	Rising Star	H-11
Perryton	A-9	River Oaks	★
Petersburg	E-8	Vicinity	Pg. 114, D-3
Petrolia	E-12	Riverside	K-15
Pettus	N-12	Riviera	Q-12
Petty	E-15	Roans Prairie	K-15
Pflugerville	K-13	Robbins	J-15
Phalba	G-15	Robert Lee	H-9
Pharr	S-12	Robinson	H-13
Phillips	B-7	Robstown	P-12
Pilot Point	F-13	Roby	G-9
Pine Mills	G-16	Rochelle	J-11
Pinehurst	★	Rochester	F-10
Pineland	J-17	Rock Island	M-14
Pioneer	H-11	Rockdale	K-14
Pipecreek	L-11	Rockland	J-17
Pittsburg	F-16	Rockport	P-13
Placedo	N-14	Rocksprings	L-9
Plains	F-6	Rockwood	J-10
Plano	F-14	Roganville	K-17
Vicinity	Pg. 115, A-10	Rogers	K-13
Plantersville	K-15	Roma	R-10
Plata	L-4	Romayor	K-16
Pleasanton	N-12	Roosevelt	K-9
Point Comfort	N-14	Ropesville	F-7
Pollok	J-16	Roscoe	G-9
Ponder	F-13	Rosebud	J-14
Ponta	H-16	Rosenberg	M-15
Pontotoc	K-11	Rosevine	J-17
Poolville	F-12	Rosser	G-14
Port "O" Connor	N-14	Rotan	G-9
Port Aransas	P-13	Round Mountain	K-12
Port Arthur	L-17	Round Rock	K-13
Port Bolivar	L-17	Round Top	L-14
Port Isabel	S-13	Rowena	H-9
Port Lavaca	N-14	Roxton	E-15
Port Mansfield	R-13	Royalty	J-6
Port Neches	L-17	Rule	F-10
Porter	K-16	Runge	M-12
Portland	P-13	Rusk	H-16
Posey	F-8	Rye	K-16
Post	F-8	Sabinal	M-10
Poteet	N-11	Sacul	H-16
Poth	M-12	Sadler	E-14
Pottsboro	E-14	Sagerton	F-10
Pottsville	H-12	Saginaw	G-13
Powderly	E-15	Vicinity	Pg. 114, C-2
Powell	H-14	Saint Hedwig	M-12
Poynor	H-15	Saint Jo	E-13
Prairie Dell	K-13	Salado	J-13
Prairie Hill	H-14	Salt Falt	H-3
Prairie Lea	L-13	Samnorwood	C-9
Prairie View	L-15	San Angelo	J-9
Premont	Q-12	San Antonio	M-12
Presidio	L-4	Vicinity	Pg. 154
Priddy	H-11	San Augustine	H-17
Princeton	F-14	San Benito	S-13
Pritchett	G-16	San Diego	P-12
Proctor	H-12	San Elizario	H-1
Prosper	F-14	San Felipe	L-14
Purmela	J-12	San Gabriel	K-13
Putnam	G-11	San Isidro	R-11
Pyote	H-5	San Juan	R-12
Quail	C-9	San Marcos	L-12
Quanah	D-10	San Patricio	P-12
Queen City	F-17	San Perlita	R-13
Quemado	N-9	San Saba	J-11
Quinlan	G-15	San Ygnacio	Q-10
Quitaque	D-8	Sanderson	L-6
Quitman	G-15	Sandia	P-12
		Sanford	B-8
		Sansom Park	★
		Vicinity	Pg. 114, C-2
		Santa Anna	H-11
		Santa Elena	R-12
		Santa Fe	L-15
		Santa Maria	S-12
		Santa Rosa	S-12
		Saragosa	J-5
		Saratoga	K-17
		Sarita	Q-12

City	Ref	City	Ref
Satsuma	★	Swenson	F-9
Vicinity	Pg. 120, B-2	Taft	P-13
Savoy	E-14	Tahoka	F-7
Schertz	M-12	Talco	F-16
Schulenburg	L-14	Talpa	H-10
Scotland	E-11	Tankersley	J-9
Scottsville	G-17	Tarpley	M-10
Scranton	G-11	Tarzan	G-7
Seabrook	L-16	Tatum	G-17
Vicinity	Pg. 121, G-10	Taylor	K-13
Seadrift	N-14	Taylor Lake Village	★
Seagoville	★	Vicinity	Pg. 121, F-9
Seagraves	F-6	Teague	H-14
Sealy	L-14	Telegraph	K-9
Sebastian	R-13	Telephone	E-15
Sebastopol	K-16	Telferner	N-14
Segovia	K-10	Tell	D-9
Seguin	M-12	Temple	J-13
Seminole	G-6	Tenaha	H-17
Seven Points	G-14	Tennessee Colony	H-15
Seymour	E-11	Tennyson	H-9
Shafter	L-4	Terlingua	M-5
Shallowater	E-7	Terrell	G-14
Shamrock	C-9	Texarkana	F-17
Shannon	F-12	Texas City	M-16
Sheffield	K-7	Texhoma	A-8
Shelbyville	H-17	Texico	D-6
Sheldon	L-16	Texline	A-6
Vicinity	Pg. 121, C-8	Thackerville	E-13
Sheridan	M-14	Thalia	E-10
Sherman	F-14	The Grove	J-13
Sherwood	J-9	The Woodlands	L-15
Shiner	M-13	Thomaston	M-13
Shiro	K-15	Thorndale	K-13
Shoreacres	★	Thornton	J-14
Vicinity	Pg. 121, F-10	Thorp Spring	G-12
Sidney	H-11	Thrall	K-13
Sierra Blanca	J-3	Three Rivers	N-12
Silsbee	K-17	Throckmorton	F-10
Silver	H-9	Tilden	N-11
Silverton	D-8	Timpson	H-17
Simms	F-16	Tioga	F-13
Singleton	K-15	Tira	F-15
Sinton	P-13	Tivoli	N-14
Sisterdale	L-11	Toco	E-15
Sivells Bend	E-13	Tolar	G-12
Skellytown	B-8	Tomball	K-15
Skidmore	P-12	Tool	H-14
Slaton	F-8	Topsey	J-12
Slidell	F-13	Tornillo	H-1
Slocum	H-16	Toyah	J-5
Smada	★	Trammells	★
Vicinity	Pg. 120, F-3	Vicinity	Pg. 120, G-4
Smiley	M-13	Trent	G-10
Smyer	E-7	Trenton	F-14
Snook	K-14	Trickham	H-11
Snyder	G-8	Trinidad	H-15
Socorro	H-1	Trinity	J-15
Somerset	M-11	Troup	H-16
Somerville	K-14	Troy	J-13
Sonora	K-9	Tucker	H-16
Sour Lake	L-17	Tuleta	N-13
South Bend	F-11	Tulia	D-7
South Houston	★	Turkey	D-9
Vicinity	Pg. 121, E-7	Turnertown	H-16
South Padre Island	S-13	Tuscola	H-10
South Plains	D-8	Twin Sisters	L-12
Southlake	★	Twitty	C-9
Vicinity	Pg. 114, B-5	Tye	G-10
Southland	F-7	Tyler	G-16
Spade	E-7	Tynan	P-12
Spanish Fort	E-12	Umbarger	C-7
Speaks	M-14	Unity	E-15
Spearman	B-8	Universal City	M-12
Spicewood	K-12	Utopia	M-10
Splendora	L-16	Uvalde	M-10
Spofford	M-9	Valentine	K-4
Spring	L-15	Valera	H-10
Spring Branch	L-11	Valley Mills	H-13
Spring Valley	★	Valley Spring	K-11
Vicinity	Pg. 120, C-3	Valley View	F-13
Springlake	D-7	Van	G-15
Springtown	F-12	Van Alstyne	F-14
Spur	F-9	Van Horn	J-3
Spurger	K-17	Van Vleck	M-15
Stafford	M-15	Vancourt	J-9
Vicinity	Pg. 120, F-3	Vanderbilt	N-14
Stamford	F-10	Vanderpool	L-10
Stanton	H-7	Vashti	E-12
Star	J-12	Vealmoor	G-8
Stephenville	H-12	Vega	C-7
Sterling City	H-8	Venus	G-13
Stinnett	B-8	Vera	E-10
Stockdale	M-12	Vernon	E-11
Stoneburg	E-12	Victoria	N-13
Stoneham	K-15	Vidor	L-17
Stonewall	L-11	Village Mills	K-17
Stowell	L-16	Vincent	G-8
Stratford	A-7	Voca	J-11
Strawn	G-11	Voss	H-10
Streetman	H-14	Votaw	K-16
Study Butte	M-5	Waco	H-13
Sudan	E-7	Wadsworth	N-15
Sugar Land	L-15	Waelder	L-13
Vicinity	Pg. 120, F-2	Waka	A-9
Sullivan City	S-11	Wake Village	E-17
Sulphur Sprs.	F-15	Waldeck	L-14
Summerfield	D-6	Wall	L-15
Sumner	E-15	Waller	L-15
Sundown	F-6	Wallis	L-14
Sunray	B-8	Walnut Sprs.	H-12
Sunset	F-13	Warda	L-13
Sutherland Springs	M-12	Warren	K-17
Sweeny	M-15	Washington	K-15
Sweetwater	G-9		
Swenson	F-9		

★ Denotes City only on Vicinity map. City not located on State map.

TEXAS

Waskom G-17
Water Valley H-9
Watson K-12
Watsonville .... ★
  Vicinity ...... Pg. 114, F-5
Waxahachie G-14
Wayside D-8
Weatherford G-12
Weaver F-15
Webster M-16
  Vicinity ...... Pg. 121, G-8
Weches J-16
Weesatche N-13
Weimar L-14
Weinort F-10
Welch F-7
Wellington D-9
Wellman F-7
Wells J-16
Weslaco S-12
West H-13
West Columbia M-15
West Orange K-17
West Point L-13
Westbrook G-8
Westfield L-15
Westhoff M-13
Westlake .... ★
  Vicinity ...... Pg. 114, A-4
Westover F-11
Westworth .... ★
  Vicinity ...... Pg. 114, D-2
Wharton M-15
Wheeler G-15
Wheeler C-9
Wheelock K-14
White Deer C-8
Whiteface E-6
Whiteflat E-9
Whitehouse G-15
Whitesboro E-13
Whitewright F-14
Whitharral E-7
Whitney H-13
Whittsett N-12
Wichita Falls E-12
Wickett H-5
Wiergate J-18
Wildorado C-7
Wildwood K-17
Wilkinson F-16
Willow City K-11
Wills Point G-15
Wilmer .... ★
  Vicinity ...... Pg. 115, F-10
Wilson F-8
Wimberly L-12
Winchell J-11
Windhorst E-12
Windom F-15
Winfield F-16
Wingate H-9
Wink H-5
Winnie L-17
Winnsboro F-15
Winona H-16
Winters H-9
Wolfe City F-15
Wolfforth F-7
Woodlake J-16
Woodland Hills .... ★
  Vicinity ...... Pg. 115, G-8
Woodlawn G-17
Woodsboro P-13
Woodson F-11
Woodville K-17
Woodward N-10
Wortham H-14
Yoakum M-13
Yorktown M-13
Zavalla J-17
Zephyr H-11
Zorn L-12

UTAH
Pages 84-85

Abraham H-4
Adamsville K-4
Alpine F-5
Alta F-6
Altamont F-8
Alton L-4
American Fork F-5
Aneth M-9
Angle K-5
Annabella J-5
Antimony K-5
Arcadia F-8
Aurora J-5
Austin J-5
Axtell H-5
  Vicinity ...... Pg. 160, E-2
Bear River City ... D-5
Beaver K-4
Benjamin F-5
Bennion .... ★
  Vicinity ...... Pg. 160, F-5
Beryl K-2
Bicknell K-5
Birdseye G-6
Black Rock J-4
Blanding L-9
Blue Cr. C-4

Bluebell F-8
Bluff L-9
Bluffdale F-5
  Vicinity ...... Pg. 160, G-5
Bonanza G-9
Boneta F-7
Boulder K-6
Bountiful E-5
Brian Head L-4
Bridgeland F-8
Brigham City D-5
Bryce Canyon L-4
Burmester E-4
Burrville J-5
Cannonville L-4
Carbonville G-7
Castle Dale H-7
Castle Rock E-6
Cave C-5
Cedar City L-3
Cedar Cr. C-3
Cedar Fort F-5
Cedar Springs D-4
Center Cr. F-6
Centerfield H-5
Centerville E-5
Central J-5
Central L-2
Charleston F-6
Chester H-5
Circleville K-4
Cisco J-9
Clarkston C-5
Clawson H-6
Clear Creek C-3
Clearcreek G-6
Clearfield E-5
Cleveland H-7
Clinton D-5
Clover F-4
Coalville E-6
Colton G-7
Copperton .... ★
  Vicinity ...... Pg. 160, G-2
Corinne D-5
Cornish C-5
Cottonwood .... ★
  Vicinity ...... Pg. 160, F-7
Cove Fort J-4
Crescent Jct. J-8
Croydon E-6
Delle E-4
Delta H-4
Deseret H-4
Desert Mound L-3
Dividend F-5
Draper F-5
  Vicinity ...... Pg. 160, H-6
Duchesne F-8
Dugway H-4
East Carbon City .. H-8
Eastland L-9
Echo E-6
Elberta F-5
Elmo H-7
Elsinore J-5
Emery J-6
Enoch L-3
Enterprise L-3
Ephraim H-6
Escalante L-5
Etna D-2
Eureka F-5
Fairfield F-5
Fairview H-6
Farmington E-5
Faust F-4
Fayette H-5
Ferron H-6
Fillmore H-4
Fish Sprs. G-3
Flowell H-4
Fort Duchesne F-8
Fountain Green H-5
Francis F-6
Freedom H-5
Fremont J-6
Fremont Jct. J-6
Fruit Hts. E-5
Fruitland F-7
Fry Canyon L-8
Gandy G-2
Garden City D-5
Garrison H-2
Geneva F-5
Genola G-5
Glendale L-4
Glenwood J-5
Goshen G-5
Granger .... ★
  Vicinity ...... Pg. 160, D-4
Granite .... ★
  Vicinity ...... Pg. 160, G-5
Grantsville E-4
Green Lake E-9
Green River H-8
Greenville K-4
Greenwich J-5
Greenwood G-5
Grouse Cr. C-2
Gunlock L-2
Gunnison H-5
Gusher F-8
Hamilton Fort L-3

Hanksville K-7
Hanna F-7
Harrisville D-5
Hatch L-4
Hatton J-4
Heber City F-6
Helper G-7
Henefer E-6
Henrieville L-5
Herriman .... ★
  Vicinity ...... Pg. 151, J-4
Hiawatha H-6
Hinckley H-4
Holden H-5
  Vicinity ...... Pg. 151, E-3
Honeyville D-4
Hot Springs D-5
Howell C-4
Hoytsville E-6
Huntington H-7
Huntsville D-6
Hurricane M-3
Hyde Park C-5
Hyrum D-5
Indianola F-8
Ioka F-8
Iron Sprs. L-3
Ivins M-2
Jensen F-9
Jericho G-5
Joseph J-4
Junction K-4
Kamas F-6
Kanab M-4
Kanarraville L-3
Kanosh J-4
Kaysville E-5
Kearns .... ★
  Vicinity ...... Pg. 151, E-3
Kelton D-4
Kenilworth G-7
Kimball Jct. E-6
Kingston K-5
Knolls E-3
Koosharem J-5
La Sal K-9
La Sal Jct. K-9
La Verkin L-3
Lake Pt. Jct. E-4
Lake Shore F-5
Lake View F-5
Laketown C-6
Lapoint F-8
Leamington H-5
Leeds L-3
Leeton F-8
Lehi F-5
Leota F-9
Levan G-5
Lewiston C-5
Loa J-6
Logan D-5
Long Valley Jct. .. L-4
Low E-3
Lucin D-2
Lund K-3
Lyman J-6
Lynndyl G-4
Maeser F-9
Magna .... ★
  Vicinity ...... Pg. 151, E-2
Manderfield J-4
Manila E-8
Manti H-6
Mantua D-5
Mapleton F-6
Marion E-6
Marysvale J-4
Mayfield H-6
Meadow J-4
Meadowville C-6
Mendon D-5
Mexican Hat M-8
Midvale E-5
  Vicinity ...... Pg. 151, F-6
Midway F-6
Milburn G-6
Milford J-3
Mills H-5
Minersville K-3
Moab J-9
Modena K-2
Molen H-6
Mona G-5
Monarch F-8
Monroe J-5
Montezuma Creek ... M-9
Monticello K-9
Moore H-6
Morgan E-5
Moroni H-5
Mountain Home F-7
Mt. Carmel L-4
Mt. Carmel Jct. ... L-4
Mt. Emmons F-7
Mt. Pleasant G-6
Murray E-5
  Vicinity ...... Pg. 151, E-6
Myton F-8
N. Logan C-6
N. Salt Lake E-5
Naples F-9
Neola F-8
Nephi G-5
New Harmony L-3

Newcastle L-2
Newton C-5
Oak City H-5
Oakley E-6
Oasis H-4
Ogden D-5
Orangeville H-6
Orderville L-4
Orem F-6
Ouray F-9
Panguitch K-4
Paradise D-5
Paragonah K-4
Park City E-6
Park Valley C-3
Parowan K-4
Payson G-5
Peoa E-6
Perry Willard D-5
Pigeon Hollow Jct. . H-6
Pine Valley L-2
Pintura L-3
Plain City D-5
Pleasant Grove F-6
Pleasant View D-5
Plymouth C-5
Portage C-5
Porterville E-6
Price G-7
Providence D-5
Provo F-6
Randolph D-6
Redmond H-5
Richfield J-5
Richmond C-5
Riverdale D-5
Riverton .... ★
  Vicinity ...... Pg. 151, H-5
Rockville M-3
Roosevelt F-8
Rosette C-3
Rowley Jct. E-5
Roy E-5
Ruby's Inn L-4
Saint George M-3
Saint John Sta. ... F-4
Salem G-5
Salina H-5
Salt Lake City E-5
  Vicinity ...... Pg. 151
Sandy F-5
  Vicinity ...... Pg. 151, H-5
Santa Clara M-2
Santaquin G-5
Scipio H-5
Scofield G-6
Sevier J-4
Shivwits M-2
Sigurd J-5
Silver City G-5
Smithfield C-5
Smyths C-4
Snowville C-4
Soldier Summit G-7
South Jordan F-5
  Vicinity ...... Pg. 151, H-5
South Ogden D-5
South Salt Lake ... ★
  Vicinity ...... Pg. 151, D-6
Spanish Fork F-6
Spring City H-6
Spring Lake G-5
Springdale M-3
Springville F-6
Sterling H-6
Stockton F-4
Summit K-3
Summit Pt. K-9
Sunnyside G-8
Sunset E-5
Sutherland H-4
Syracuse E-5
Tabiona F-7
Talmage F-7
Taylors .... ★
  Vicinity ...... Pg. 151, E-5
Teasdale K-6
Terrace D-6
Thistle G-6
Thompson H-9
Tooele F-4
Toquerville L-3
Torrey K-6
Trementon D-5
Tropic L-4
Trout Cr. G-2
Tucker G-7
  Vicinity ...... Pg. 151, E-5
Upalco F-8
Uvada L-2
Venice J-5
Vernal F-9
Vernon F-4
Veyo L-2
Virgin M-3
W. Valley City .... ★
Wahsatch D-6
Wales H-5
Wanship E-6
Washington M-3
Washington Terrace . D-5
Wellington G-7
Wellsville D-5
Wendover E-2

West Jordan F-5
  Vicinity ...... Pg. 151, F-5
West Point D-4
Whiterocks F-8
Widtsoe Jct. K-5
Woodruff D-6
Woods Cross E-5
Woodside H-8
Zane K-2

VERMONT
Page 57

Addison E-1
Albany C-3
Alburg B-1
Arlington J-1
Ascutney G-3
Averill B-5
Bakersfield B-2
Barnard F-3
Barnet D-4
Barre E-3
Barton C-4
Bellows Falls H-3
Bennington J-1
Bethel F-3
Bloomfield C-5
Bomoseen G-1
Bondville H-2
Bradford E-4
Brandon F-2
Brattleboro J-3
Bridgewater Cors. . G-3
Bridport E-1
Bristol E-1
Broadford Cen. E-3
Brunswick Sprs. ... C-5
Burlington D-1
Cambridge C-1
Cambridgeport H-3
Canaan B-5
Castleton G-1
Charlotte D-1
Chelsea E-3
Chester H-3
Chester Depot H-3
Chimney Cor. C-2
Concord D-4
Cornwall E-1
Danby G-2
Dorset H-1
E. Barnet D-4
E. Berkshire B-2
E. Braintree E-3
E. Brookfield E-3
E. Burke C-4
E. Calais D-3
E. Dorset H-2
E. Fairfield C-2
E. Granville E-2
E. Hardwick D-3
E. Haven C-4
Eden C-3
Eden Mills C-3
Enosburg Falls B-2
Essex Jct. D-2
Fair Haven G-1
Fairfax C-2
Ferrisburg E-1
Franklin B-2
Gassetts H-3
Gaysville F-3
Glover C-4
Grafton H-3
Grand Isle C-1
Groton E-4
Guilford J-3
Hancock F-2
Hardwick D-3
Heartwellville J-2
Hinesburg D-2
Holland B-4
Hubbardton F-1
Hyde Park C-3
Irasburg B-3
Irasville E-2
Island Pond C-4
Jacksonville J-2
Jamaica H-2
Jay B-3
Jeffersonville C-2
Johnson C-3
Lake Elmore C-3
Leicester F-2
Londonderry H-2
Lowell B-3
Ludlow G-2
Lunenberg D-5
Lyndon D-4
Lyndonville D-4
Maidstone C-5
Manchester H-2
Manchester Cen. ... H-2
Marlboro J-2
Marshfield D-3
Middlebury E-1
Middletown Sprs. .. G-1
Mill Village E-3
Montgomery Cen. ... B-3
Montpelier D-3
Morgan Cen. B-4
Morrisville C-3

New Haven E-1
New Haven Jct. E-1
Newbury E-4
Newfane J-2
Newport D-4
North Concord D-4
North Dorset H-2
North Hero C-1
North Hyde Park ... C-3
North Rupert H-1
Northfield E-2
Norton B-4
Norwich E-4
Orleans B-4
Orwell F-1
Passumpsic D-4
Pawlet H-1
Pittsfield F-2
Pittsford F-2
Pittsford Mills ... F-2
Plainfield D-3
Plymouth C-2
Plymouth Union G-2
Pompanoosuc F-3
Post Mills F-3
Poultney G-1
Pownal J-1
Pownal Cen. J-1
Putney J-3
Quechee G-3
Randolph F-2
Richford B-2
Richmond D-2
Ripton E-2
Robinson F-2
Rochester F-2
Roxbury F-2
Royalton F-2
Rutland G-2
Saint Albans B-2
Saint George D-2
Saint Johnsbury ... D-4
Searsburg J-2
Shafsbury J-1
Shafsbury Cen. J-1
Shelburne D-1
Sherburne Cen. G-2
Shoreham F-1
Simonsville H-2
South Burlington .. D-1
South Dorset H-1
South Hinesburg ... D-2
South Royalton F-3
South Ryegate E-4
South Shafsbury ... J-1
South Starksboro .. E-2
South Walden D-3
South Wallingford . G-2
Springfield H-3
Starksboro E-2
Stockbridge F-2
Sudbury F-1
Sunderland H-1
Swanton B-1
Ticonderoga F-1
Townshend H-2
Troy B-3
Tunbridge E-3
Tyson G-2
Underhill Flats ... D-2
Union Village F-3
Vergennes E-1
Vershire E-3
Waits River E-3
Waitsfield E-2
Wallingford G-2
Waltham E-1
Wardsboro J-2
Warren E-2
Washington E-3
Waterbury D-2
Waterbury Ctr. D-3
Websterville E-3
Wells G-1
West Addison E-1
West Braintree E-3
West Bridgewater .. G-2
West Burke C-4
West Danville D-3
West Dover J-2
West Fairlee F-3
West Groton E-3
West Hartford F-3
West Rutland G-1
West Topsham E-3
West Wardsboro J-2
Westfield B-3
White River Jct. .. G-3
Whiting F-1
Wilmington J-2
Windsor G-3
Wolcott C-3
Woodbury D-3
Woodford J-1
Woodstock G-3
Worcester D-3

VIRGINIA
Page 86-87

Abingdon J-3
Accomac G-12
Achilles H-11
Adner G-11

VIRGINIA

Afton F-8
Alberta H-9
Alexandria D-10
Altavista H-7
Amelia G-9
Amherst G-7
Amissville E-9
Amonate H-4
Annandale .... ★
  Vicinity ...... Pg. 162, H-2
Appalachia H-2
Appomattox G-8
Ark G-11
Arlington .... ★
  Vicinity ...... Pg. 162, E-10
Arvonia G-8
Ash Grove .... ★
  Vicinity ...... Pg. 162, E-1
Ashland G-10
Atkins H-4
Augusta Springs ... F-7
Austinville H-5
Axton J-6
Bacons Castle H-11
Bailey's Crossroads . ★
  Vicinity ...... Pg. 162, G-3
Ballsville G-9
Banco E-9
Bandy H-4
Barhamsville G-11
Bassett J-6
Bassett Forks J-6
Bastian H-4
Bavon G-11
Bayview H-12
Bedford G-7
Belle Haven G-12
Belleview .... ★
  Vicinity ...... Pg. 162, E-1
Bells Crossroads .. F-9
Bensley G-10
Bent Creek G-8
Bentonville E-9
Bergton E-8
Berryville D-9
Beverly Forest .... ★
  Vicinity ...... Pg. 162, J-2
Big Island G-7
Big Stone Gap H-2
Birchleaf H-3
Bishop H-4
Blacksburg H-5
Blackstone H-9
Blackwater J-2
Blairs J-7
Bland H-5
Bluefield H-4
Bluemont D-9
Blue Ridge G-6
Bon Air G-9
Boones Mill H-6
Boswells Tavern ... F-9
Bowling Green F-10
Boyce D-9
Boydton J-8
Boykins J-10
Branchville J-10
Brandy Station E-9
Bremo Bluff G-9
Bridgewater F-7
Brightwood E-9
Bristol J-3
Broadford H-4
Broadway E-8
Brodnax J-9
Brookneal H-7
Brownsburg F-7
Brunswick J-9
Buchanan G-7
Buckingham G-8
Bucknell Manor .... ★
  Vicinity ...... Pg. 162, J-4
Buena Vista G-7
Burgess F-11
Burke .... ★
  Vicinity ...... Pg. 162, J-1
Burkeville H-9
Burn Chimney H-6
Burrowsville H-10
Callaghan G-6
Callands H-7
Callao F-11
Calverton E-10
Cana H-5
Cape Charles G-12
Capron J-10
Carmel Church F-10
Carson H-10
Cartersville G-9
Castlewoods H-3
Catalpa E-9
Catlett E-10
Cave Spring H-6
Cedar Bluff H-4
Central Garage G-10
Chapel Acres ...... ★
  Vicinity ...... Pg. 162, K-1
Charles City G-10
Charlotte Court House . H-8
Charlottesville ... F-8
Chase City J-8
Chatham J-7
Cheriton G-12

Chesapeake J-12
Chester G-10
Chilhowie H-4
Chincoteague F-13
Christiansburg H-6
Chula G-9
Clarksville J-8
Claudville J-6
Clear Brook D-9
Clifford G-7
Clifton Forge F-6
Clinchco H-3
Clinchport J-2
Clintwood H-3
Clover H-8
Cluster Springs ... J-8
Cochran H-9
Cody H-8
Coeburn H-3
Colleen G-8
Collierstown J-6
Collinsville J-6
Colonial Beach F-10
Colonial Heights .. H-10
Concord G-7
Copper Hill H-6
Courtland J-10
Covesville G-8
Covington G-6
Craigsville F-7
Crewe H-9
Cross Junction C-9
Crows G-6
Crozet F-8
Cuckoo F-9
Cullen H-8
Culpeper E-9
Cumberland G-8
Dale E-9
Dale City E-10
Damascus J-3
Danieltown H-9
Dante H-3
Danville J-7
Davenport H-3
Dawn F-10
Dayton E-8
Deerfield F-7
Deltaville G-11
De Witt H-9
Dickensonville H-3
Dillwyn G-8
Dinwiddie H-9
Disputanta H-10
Dixie J-8
Doswell F-10
Dot J-2
Drakes Branch H-8
Draper H-5
Drewryville J-10
Dryden J-2
Dublin H-5
Dugspur H-5
Dumfries E-10
Dungannon H-3
Eagle Rock G-6
Earls G-6
Earnham F-11
Eastville G-12
Edgerton J-9
Edinburg E-8
Elberon H-11
Elkton E-8
Elliston H-6
Elon G-7
Emporia J-10
Esmont G-8
Evington H-7
Ewing J-1
Exmore G-12
Fairfax .... ★
  Vicinity ...... Pg. 162, G-1
Fairfield F-7
Falling Spring F-6
Falls Church ...... ★
  Vicinity ...... Pg. 162, G-2
Falmouth E-10
Fancy Gap J-5
Farmville G-8
Ferrum J-6
Fieldale J-6
Fincastle G-6
Finchley J-8
Fishersville F-8
Flint Hill E-9
Floyd H-6
Forest G-7
Forestville E-8
Fork Union G-9
Fort Blackmore H-3
Franconia .... ★
  Vicinity ...... Pg. 162, J-3
Franklin J-11
Fredericksburg E-9
Fries J-5
Front D-9
Fulks Run E-8
Galax J-5
Gate City J-2
Georges Tavern H-9
Gladehill H-6
Glade Spring H-4
Glasgow G-7
Gloucester G-11
Gloucester Point .. H-11

★ Denotes City only on Vicinity map. City not located on State map.

VIRGINIA   WEST VIRGINIA

Golansville ... F-10
Goochland ... G-9
Gordonsville ... F-9
Gore ... D-8
Goshen ... F-7
Great Falls ... ★
  Vicinity ... Pg. 162, D-1
Green Bay ... H-9
Greenway ... ★
  Vicinity ... Pg. 162, E-1
Gretna ... H-7
Grottoes ... F-8
Groveton ... ★
  Vicinity ... Pg. 162, J-4
Grundy ... H-3
Guilford ... G-12
Gum Spring ... G-9
Gwynn ... G-11
Hague ... F-11
Halifax ... J-8
Hampton ... H-11
  Vicinity ... Pg. 142, B-5
Hanover ... G-10
Harrisonburg ... E-8
Hartwood ... E-10
Hayfield ... D-9
Haynesville ... F-11
Healings Springs ... F-6
Hermitage ... H-7
Herndon ... D-10
Hickory ... J-11
Hightown ... E-7
Hillsboro ... D-9
Hillsville ... H-5
Hollins ... G-6
Homeville ... H-10
Honaker ... H-3
Hopewell ... G-10
Howardsville ... G-8
Independence ... J-4
Iron Gate ... G-7
Irvington ... G-11
Ivanhoe ... J-5
Ivor ... H-11
Jamestown ... H-11
Jarratt ... J-10
Jetersville ... G-9
Jewell Ridge ... H-4
Johnsontown ... G-12
Jonesville ... J-2
Jordan Mines ... G-6
Keene ... F-8
Keene Mill Heights ... ★
  Vicinity ... Pg. 162, J-4
Keller ... G-12
Kenbridge ... H-9
Kenmore ... ★
  Vicinity ... Pg. 162, E-1
Keysville ... H-8
Kilmarnock ... G-11
King George ... F-10
Kings Park ... ★
  Vicinity ... Pg. 162, H-1
Kiptopeke ... H-12
Konnarock ... J-4
Lacey Spring ... E-8
La Crosse ... J-9
Ladysmith ... F-10
Lancaster ... G-11
Langley ... ★
  Vicinity ... Pg. 162, E-2
Laurel Fork ... J-5
Lawrenceville ... J-9
Lebanon ... H-3
Leesburg ... D-10
Leesville ... H-7
Lerty ... F-10
Lexington ... G-7
Lightfoot ... G-11
Lignum ... E-9
Littleton ... H-10
Lively ... G-11
Locust ... E-9
Long Island ... H-7
Louisa ... F-9
Lovettsville ... D-9
Low Moor ... G-6
Lucketts ... D-9
Lunenburg ... H-9
Luray ... E-8
Lyells ... F-11
Lynchburg ... G-7
Madison ... E-9
Madison Heights ... G-7
Madison Mills ... F-9
Manakin ... G-9
Manassas ... E-9
Manassas Park ... E-10
Manquin ... G-10
Mappsville ... F-12
Marion ... H-4
Markham ... D-9
Marshal ... D-9
Martinsville ... J-6
Massies Mill ... G-7
Mathews ... H-11
Matoaca ... H-10
Maurertown ... D-8
Mauzy ... E-8
McDowell ... E-7
McGaheysville ... E-8
McKenney ... H-9
McLean ... ★
  Vicinity ... Pg. 149, E-3
McLean Hamlet ... ★
  Vicinity ... Pg. 149, E-2
Meadows of Dan ... H-6
Mechanicsville ... G-10
Meherrin ... H-8
Melfa ... G-12

Middleburg ... D-10
Middletown ... D-8
Midland ... E-9
Milford ... F-10
Millboro ... F-7
Millboro Springs ... F-6
Millers Tavern ... F-11
Mineral ... F-9
Moneta ... H-7
Monroe ... G-7
Montebello ... F-7
Monterey ... E-7
Montpelier ... F-10
Montross ... F-10
Morrisville ... E-10
Moseley ... G-9
Mt. Airy ... H-7
Mt. Jackson ... E-8
Mt. Olive ... D-8
Mt. Rush ... G-8
Mt. Sidney ... F-7
Mustoe ... F-7
Narrows ... G-5
Naruna ... H-8
Nassawadox ... G-12
Natural Bridge ... G-7
Nellysford ... F-8
Nelsonia ... G-13
New Baltimore ... E-9
Newbern ... H-5
New Castle ... G-6
New Kent ... G-10
New Market ... E-8
Newport ... G-6
Newport News ... H-11
  Vicinity ... Pg. 142, A-1
New Post ... F-10
Nickelsville ... J-3
Nora ... H-3
Norfolk ... H-12
  Vicinity ... Pg. 142
North Garden ... F-8
Norton ... H-2
Nottoway ... H-9
Nuttsville ... G-11
Oak Hall ... F-12
Oak Wood ... H-3
  Vicinity ... Pg. 149, K-3
Oakville ... G-8
Oilville ... G-9
Onancock ... G-12
Opal ... E-9
Orange ... E-9
Paint Bank ... G-6
Painter ... G-12
Palmer Springs ... J-9
Palmyra ... F-9
Paris ... D-9
Parksley ... G-12
Patrick Springs ... J-5
Pearisburg ... H-5
Pembroke ... H-5
Pendaw ... ★
  Vicinity ... Pg. 149, J-4
Penhook ... H-7
Pennington Gap ... H-2
Penn Laird ... F-8
Petersburg ... H-10
Pimmit Hills ... ★
  Vicinity ... Pg. 149, F-2
Piney River ... G-7
Pocahontas ... H-4
Pohick Estates ... ★
  Vicinity ... Pg. 149, K-1
Poplar Camp ... H-5
Poplar Hill ... H-5
Poquoson ... H-11
  Vicinity ... Pg. 142, A-1
Port Republic ... F-8
Port Royal ... F-10
Portsmouth ... H-11
  Vicinity ... Pg. 142, H-3
Post Oak ... F-9
Pound ... H-2
Prospect Hill ... ★
  Vicinity ... Pg. 149, E-1
Providence Forge ... G-10
Prince George ... H-10
Princess Anne ... J-12
Pulaski ... H-5
Pungoteague ... G-12
Purcellville ... D-9
Purdy ... H-10
Quantico ... E-10
Quinby ... G-12
Radford ... H-5
Raven ... H-3
Rawley Springs ... E-8
Red Ash ... H-3
Red Oak ... J-8
Rehoboth ... H-8
Remington ... E-9
Renan ... H-7
Reston ... D-10
Rice ... H-9
Richlands ... H-3
Richmond ... G-10
Ridgeway ... J-6
Rileyville ... E-8
Riner ... H-6
Rixeyville ... E-9
Roanoke ... H-6
Rochelle ... E-9
Rockbridge Baths ... F-7
Rockville ... G-9
Rocky Gap ... H-5
Rocky Mount ... H-6
Rose Hill ... J-1
Roseland ... G-7
Round Hill ... D-9

Roxbury ... G-10
Royal ... D-9
Ruckersville ... F-9
Rural Retreat ... H-4
St. Paul ... H-3
St. Stephens Church ... G-11
Salem ... G-6
  Vicinity ... Pg. 142, H-7
Saltville ... H-4
Saxix ... F-12
Scotland ... H-11
Scottsville ... G-8
Sebrell ... J-10
Shadewell ... F-8
Shady Oak ... ★
  Vicinity ... Pg. 149, D-1
Shipman ... F-8
Shenandoah ... E-8
Sheppards ... G-8
Sinking Creek ... G-6
Skippers ... J-10
Snell ... F-10
S. Boston ... J-8
South Hill ... J-9
Spencer ... J-6
Sperryville ... E-9
Spotsylvania ... F-9
Springfield ... ★
  Vicinity ... Pg. 149, J-2
Spring Grove ... H-11
Spring Hill ... ★
  Vicinity ... Pg. 149, E-1
Sprouses Corner ... G-8
Stacy ... G-3
Stafford ... E-10
Stanardsville ... F-8
Stanley ... E-8
Stanleytown ... J-6
Staunton ... F-7
Steeles ... F-7
Stephens City ... D-9
Stevensburg ... E-9
Stevensville ... G-11
Stewartsville ... H-6
Stony Creek ... H-10
Strasburg ... D-8
Stuart ... J-6
Sturats Draft ... F-8
Studley ... G-10
Suffolk ... J-11
  Vicinity ... Pg. 142, J-1
Sugar Grove ... J-4
Sunbright ... J-2
Surry ... H-11
Sussex ... H-10
Sweet Chalybeate ... G-6
Sydnorsville ... H-6
Sylvatus ... H-5
Syria ... E-8
Talleysville ... G-10
Tappahannock ... F-10
Tasley ... G-12
Tavern ... F-7
Tazewell ... H-4
Templeman ... F-11
The Falls ... H-9
Thornburg ... F-10
Timberville ... E-8
Trenholm ... G-9
Triangle ... E-10
Troutville ... G-6
Turbeville ... J-8
Unionville ... F-9
Upperville ... D-9
Urbanna ... G-11
Vanderpool ... E-7
Vansant ... H-3
Vera ... G-8
Verona ... F-7
Victoria ... H-9
Vienna ... H-11
  Vicinity ... Pg. 149, F-1
Village ... F-11
Villboro ... F-10
Vinton ... H-6
Virgilina ... J-8
Virginia Beach ... H-12
  Vicinity ... Pg. 142, E-7
Va. Mineral Springs ... G-6
Volens ... H-8
Wachapreague ... G-12
Wakefield ... H-10
Warm Springs ... F-7
Warrenton ... E-9
Warsaw ... F-11
Washington ... E-9
Waverly ... H-10
Waynesboro ... F-8
Waynewood ... ★
  Vicinity ... Pg. 149, G-8
Weber City ... J-3
Wellington ... ★
  Vicinity ... Pg. 149, K-4
West Augusta ... F-7
W. Point ... G-11
Whaleyville ... J-11
White Marsh ... H-11
Wilderness ... E-9
Williamsburg ... H-11
Williamsville ... F-7
Willis ... H-6
Willis Wharf ... G-12
Wilsons ... H-9
Winchester ... D-9
Windsor ... H-11
Windsor Estates ... ★
  Vicinity ... Pg. 149, J-8
Wingina ... G-8
Wintergreen ... F-8
Winterpock ... G-10

Wise ... H-3
Woodbridge ... E-10
Woodlawn ... J-5
Woods Mill ... G-8
Woodstock ... D-8
Woodville ... E-9
Wylie ... H-5
Wylliesburg ... H-8
Wytheville ... H-4
Yorktown ... H-11
Zion X-Roads ... F-9
Zuni ... H-11

WASHINGTON
Pages 88-89

Aberdeen ... F-3
Acme ... B-6
Addy ... B-13
Airway Heights ... D-14
Albion ... F-14
Alderwood Maner ... ★
  Vicinity ... Pg. 157, A-4
Algona ... E-6
Almira ... D-11
Altoona ... H-3
Anacortes ... B-5
Anatone ... H-14
Arlington ... C-6
Asotin ... G-14
Auburn ... E-6
Battle Ground ... J-5
Bellevue ... D-6
  Vicinity ... Pg. 157, E-6
Bellingham ... A-5
Benton City ... H-10
Bickleton ... H-9
Bingen ... J-7
Black Diamond ... E-6
Blaine ... A-5
Bonney Lake ... F-6
Bossburg ... B-13
Bothell ... D-6
  Vicinity ... Pg. 157, B-5
Boundary ... A-13
Bremerton ... D-5
Brewster ... C-10
Bridgeport ... C-10
Brier ... D-16
  Vicinity ... Pg. 157, A-4
Buckley ... E-6
Bucoda ... F-5
Burien ... ★
  Vicinity ... Pg. 157, H-3
Burlington ... B-6
Byrne Mawr ... ★
  Vicinity ... Pg. 157, H-5
Camas ... J-5
Carbonado ... F-6
Carnation ... D-6
Cashmere ... D-9
Castle Rock ... H-4
Cathlamet ... G-3
Centralia ... G-5
Chehalis ... G-5
Chelan ... C-9
Cheney ... E-14
Chewelah ... C-13
Clarkston ... G-14
Clayton ... C-13
Cle Elum ... E-8
Coalfield ... ★
  Vicinity ... Pg. 157, H-6
Coles Corner ... D-8
Colfax ... F-14
College Place ... H-12
Colton ... G-14
Colville ... B-13
Conconully ... B-10
Concrete ... B-7
Connell ... G-12
Copalis Beach ... E-2
Cosmopolis ... F-3
Coulee City ... D-11
Coulee Dam ... C-11
Coupeville ... C-6
Crescent Bar ... E-9
Creston ... D-12
Cusick ... C-14
Danville ... A-12
Darrington ... C-7
Davenport ... D-13
Dayton ... H-13
Deer Park ... C-14
Deming ... A-6
Des Moines ... E-6
  Vicinity ... Pg. 157, K-3
Disautel ... C-11
Discovery Bay ... C-5
Dodge ... G-13
Duluth ... J-5
Dusty ... F-13
Duvall ... D-6
East Wenatchee ... D-9
Eastgate ... ★
  Vicinity ... Pg. 157, F-6
Eatonville ... F-6
Edwall ... E-13
Elbe ... F-6
Eldon ... D-4
Electric City ... D-11
Ellensburg ... F-9
Elma ... F-4
Elmer City ... C-11
Endicott ... F-13
Entiat ... D-9

Enumclaw ... E-6
Ephrata ... E-10
Eureka ... H-12
Everett ... C-6
Everson ... A-6
Fairfield ... E-14
Fairholm ... C-3
Farmington ... F-15
Ferndale ... A-5
Fircrest ... E-5
Forks ... C-2
Friday Harbor ... B-5
Garfield ... F-14
Gifford ... C-13
Gig Harbor ... E-5
Glenoma ... G-6
Gold Bar ... D-7
Goldendale ... J-8
Grand Coulee ... D-11
Grandview ... H-9
Granger ... G-9
Granite Falls ... C-6
Greenwater ... F-7
Hamilton ... B-6
Harrah ... G-9
Harrington ... E-12
Hartline ... D-11
Hatton ... G-11
Hoodsport ... E-4
Hoquiam ... F-3
Humptulips ... E-3
Husum ... J-7
Hyak ... E-7
Ilwaco ... G-3
Index ... D-7
Ione ... B-14
Issaquah ... E-6
Joyce ... C-3
Juanita ... ★
  Vicinity ... Pg. 157, C-4
Kahlotus ... G-12
Kalama ... H-5
Keller ... C-12
Kelso ... H-5
Kenmoore ... ★
  Vicinity ... Pg. 157, B-4
Kennewick ... H-11
Kent ... E-6
  Vicinity ... Pg. 157, J-4
Kettle Falls ... B-13
Kingston ... D-5
  Vicinity ... Pg. 157, A-1
Kirkland ... D-6
  Vicinity ... Pg. 157, D-5
Kittitas ... F-9
Klaus ... G-5
Klickitat ... J-7
Krupp ... E-11
La Center ... J-5
La Conner ... B-5
La Crosse ... F-13
La Push ... C-2
Lacey ... F-5
Lake Stevens ... C-6
Lamont ... E-13
Langley ... C-5
Latah ... E-14
Leavenworth ... D-9
Lebam ... G-3
Lind ... F-12
Littlerock ... F-4
Long Beach ... G-3
Longview ... H-4
Lyman ... B-6
Lynden ... A-5
Lynnwood ... D-6
  Vicinity ... Pg. 157, A-3
Mabton ... H-9
Malone ... F-4
Maltby ... ★
  Vicinity ... Pg. 157, A-6
Mansfield ... D-10
Manson ... D-9
Maplewood ... ★
  Vicinity ... Pg. 157, H-5
Marcus ... B-13
Marysville ... C-6
Mattawa ... G-10
McCleary ... F-4
Medical Lake ... E-13
Megler ... H-3
Menlo ... G-3
Mercer Island ... D-5
  Vicinity ... Pg. 157, F-4
Mesa ... G-11
Metaline ... A-14
Metaline Falls ... A-14
Methow ... C-9
Millwood ... D-14
Monroe ... D-6
Montesano ... F-3
Morton ... G-6
Moses Lake ... F-11
Mossyrock ... G-5
Mount Baker ... A-7
Mount Vernon ... B-5
Mountlake Terrace ... ★
  Vicinity ... Pg. 157, A-3
Moxee City ... G-9
Mukilteo ... D-6
Naches ... F-8
Napavine ... G-4
Naselle ... G-3
Neah Bay ... B-2
Neilton ... E-3

Newcastle ... ★
  Vicinity ... Pg. 157, G-5
Newport ... C-14
Normandy Park ... ★
  Vicinity ... Pg. 157, J-2
North Bend ... E-7
North Bonneville ... J-6
Northport ... A-13
Oak Harbor ... C-5
Oakesdale ... F-14
Oakville ... F-4
Ocean Park ... G-3
Ocean Shores ... F-2
Odessa ... E-12
Okanogan ... C-10
Olympia ... F-5
Omak ... B-10
Orchards ... J-5
Orient ... A-13
Oroville ... A-10
Orting ... F-6
Othello ... F-11
Ozette ... C-2
Pacific ... E-6
Pacific Beach ... E-2
Packwood ... G-7
Palouse ... F-14
Pasco ... H-11
Pateros ... C-10
Pe Ell ... G-4
Pomeroy ... G-14
Port Angeles ... C-4
Port Gamble ... D-5
Port Orchard ... E-5
Port Townsend ... C-5
Poulsbo ... D-5
Prescott ... H-12
Prosser ... H-10
Pullman ... G-14
Puyallup ... F-5
Queets ... E-3
Quincy ... E-10
Rainier ... F-5
Randle ... G-6
Raymond ... G-3
Redmond ... D-6
  Vicinity ... Pg. 157, H-4
Renton ... E-6
  Vicinity ... Pg. 157, J-4
Republic ... B-12
Richland ... H-11
Richland Highlands ... ★
  Vicinity ... Pg. 157, B-3
Richmond Beach ... ★
  Vicinity ... Pg. 157, B-3
Ridgefield ... J-5
Rimrock ... G-7
Ritzville ... F-12
Riverside ... B-10
Rochester ... F-4
Rock Island ... E-9
Rockford ... E-14
Rockport ... B-7
Rollingbay ... ★
  Vicinity ... Pg. 157, D-1
Roosevelt ... J-9
Rosalia ... E-14
Rosburg ... H-3
Roslyn ... E-8
Roy ... F-5
Royal City ... F-10
Ryderwood ... G-4
Salmon La Sac ... D-7
Sappho ... C-3
Seattle ... D-5
  Vicinity ... Pg. 157
Sedro Woolley ... B-6
Selah ... G-9
Sequim ... C-4
Shelton ... E-4
Silver Creek ... G-5
Skykomish ... D-7
Snohomish ... D-6
Snoqualmie ... E-7
Soap Lake ... E-10
South Bend ... G-3
South Cle Elum ... E-8
South Prairie ... F-6
Spangle ... E-14
Spokane ... D-14
Sprague ... E-13
Springdale ... C-13
St. John ... F-14
Stanwood ... C-6
Starbuck ... G-13
Steilacoom ... E-5
Stella ... H-4
Steptoe ... F-14
Stevenson ... J-6
Sultan ... D-6
Sumas ... A-6
Sumner ... E-6
Sunnyside ... H-9
Tacoma ... E-5
Taholah ... E-2
Tekoa ... E-14
Telma ... D-8
Tenino ... F-5
Tieton ... G-8
Toledo ... G-5
Tonasket ... B-10
Toppenish ... H-9
Trout Lake ... H-7
Tukwila ... ★
  Vicinity ... Pg. 157, H-4

Twisp ... C-9
Union ... E-4
Union Gap ... G-9
Uniontown ... G-14
Vader ... G-4
Vancouver ... F-9
  Vicinity ... Pg. 150, A-5
Vantage ... F-9
Vashon Island ... ★
  Vicinity ... Pg. 159, K-1
Vashon Heights ... ★
  Vicinity ... Pg. 159, G-1
Waitsburg ... H-13
Walla Walla ... H-12
Wallula ... H-11
Wapato ... G-9
Warden ... F-11
Washougal ... J-5
Washtucna ... G-12
Waterville ... D-9
Wauconda ... B-11
Waverly ... E-14
Wenatchee ... E-9
Wenatchee Heights ... ★
West Richland ... H-11
Westport ... F-2
White Salmon ... J-7
White Swan ... G-9
Wickersham ... B-6
Wilbur ... D-12
Wilkeson ... ★
Wilson Creek ... E-11
Winlock ... G-4
Winslow ... D-5
Winthrop ... B-9
Wishram Heights ... J-8
Withrow ... D-10
Woodinville ... ★
  Vicinity ... Pg. 159, B-6
Woodland ... J-5
Yacolt ... J-5
Yakima ... G-9
Yelm ... F-5
Zillah ... G-9

WEST VIRGINIA
Page 86-87

Adrian ... D-6
Alderson ... G-5
Alma ... C-5
Ansted ... F-5
Arbovale ... E-6
Arnett ... F-4
Arnoldsburg ... D-4
Athens ... G-5
Baker ... D-8
Ballard ... G-5
Barboursville ... E-3
Barrackville ... C-6
Barrett ... F-4
Beatrice ... C-5
Beckley ... G-5
Belington ... D-6
Belle ... E-4
Berkeley Springs ... C-8
Bethany ... B-6
Bethlehem ... B-5
Beverly ... D-6
Bigbend ... D-4
Big Creek ... F-3
Bim ... F-4
Birch River ... E-5
Bismark ... D-7
Blacksville ... C-6
Blair ... F-4
Bluefield ... H-4
Boyer ... E-6
Bradshaw ... G-3
Brandywine ... E-7
Bridgeport ... D-6
Brooks ... F-5
Buckhannon ... D-6
Buffalo ... E-3
Burnsville ... E-5
Burton ... C-6
Cabins ... D-7
Calvin ... E-5
Camden ... D-5
Cameron ... C-5
Canfield ... D-5
Chapmanville ... F-3
Charleston ... E-4
Charles Town ... D-9
Charmco ... F-5
Chattaroy ... G-3
Cheat Bridge ... E-6
Chester ... A-6
Chloe ... E-4
Cisco ... D-4
Clarksburg ... D-5
Clay ... E-4
Clendenin ... E-4
Cleveland ... D-5
Clifftop ... F-5
Crab Orchard ... G-4
Craigsville ... E-5
Creston ... D-4
Dailey ... D-6
Davis ... D-7
Dellslow ... C-6
Diana ... E-5
Dixie ... E-4
Dunbar ... E-4

Dunlow ... F-3
Droop ... F-6
Eccles ... G-4
Echo ... F-3
Edray ... E-6
Eleanor ... E-4
Elizabeth ... D-4
Elkins ... D-6
Elkview ... E-4
Elkwater ... E-6
Ellenboro ... D-5
Elton ... F-5
Etam ... D-7
Evans ... E-4
Fairmont ... C-6
Fayetteville ... F-4
Fellowsville ... D-6
Follansbee ... B-6
Forest Hill ... G-5
Fort Ashby ... C-8
Fort Gay ... F-3
Frankford ... F-5
Franklin ... E-7
Frost ... F-6
Gallipolis Ferry ... E-3
Galloway ... D-6
Gary ... G-4
Gauley Bridge ... F-5
Gilbert ... G-3
Gilmer ... D-5
Glenville ... D-5
Grafton ... C-6
Grantsville ... D-4
Hamlin ... F-3
Harper ... E-7
Harrisville ... D-5
Hastings ... C-5
Heaters ... E-5
Hico ... F-5
Hinton ... G-5
Hodgesville ... D-6
Hogsett ... E-3
Holden ... F-3
Huntington ... E-3
Hurricane ... E-3
Huttonsville ... E-6
Iaeger ... G-4
Intermont ... D-8
Inwood ... D-9
Jane Lew ... D-5
Jeffery ... F-4
Jesse ... G-4
Julian ... F-4
Junction ... D-8
Kenna ... E-4
Kenova ... E-3
Kermit ... F-3
Keyser ... C-8
Keystone ... G-4
Kiahsville ... F-3
Kingwood ... C-7
Larew ... C-7
Lavalette ... D-8
Lehew ... D-8
Leopold ... D-5
Lesage ... E-3
Lewisburg ... G-5
Liberty ... E-4
Lindside ... G-5
Littleton ... C-5
Lizemores ... E-5
Logan ... F-4
Looneyville ... E-4
Lost City ... D-8
Lost Creek ... D-6
Lost River ... D-8
Lumberport ... D-6
Maben ... G-4
Mace ... E-6
Madison ... F-4
Man ... G-4
Mannington ... C-6
Marlinton ... F-6
Marmet ... F-4
Martinsburg ... C-9
Mason ... D-3
Matewan ... G-3
Maysville ... D-7
McMechen ... B-5
Middlebourne ... C-5
Mill Point ... F-6
Mineralwells ... D-4
Moorefield ... D-8
Morgantown ... C-7
Moundsville ... B-5
Mountain ... C-5
Mt. Alto ... D-4
Mt. Gay ... F-3
Mt. Hope ... F-4
Mt. Storm ... D-7
Mt. Zion ... D-5
Mullens ... G-4
Needmore ... D-8
Nestorville ... D-6
New Cumberland ... A-5
New Martinsville ... C-5
Nimitz ... G-5
Nitro ... E-4
North Fork ... G-4
Norton ... D-6
Oak Flat ... E-7
Oak Hill ... F-5
Oceana ... G-4
Old Fields ... D-8
Orgas ... F-4

★ Denotes City only on Vicinity map. City not located on State map.

WEST VIRGINIA

Paden City C-5
Palestine D-4
Parkersburg D-4
Parsons D-7
Petersburg D-8
Peterstown G-5
Philippi D-6
Pickaway G-6
Pike D-5
Pineville G-4
Pipestem G-5
Pleasant Dale D-8
Point Pleasant D-3
Porterfield D-4
Prince F-5
Princeton G-5
Purgitsville D-8
Racine F-4
Rainelle F-5
Rand F-4
Ranger F-3
Ravenswood D-4
Reader C-5
Red Creek D-7
Reedy D-4
Renick F-5
Richwood F-5
Rio D-8
Ripley D-4
Riverton E-7
Robson F-5
Rock Camp G-5
Rock Cave E-6
Roderfield G-4
Romney D-8
Roncevert G-6
St. Albans F-4
St. Marys C-5
Salem D-6
Seneca Rocks D-7
Seth F-4
Shinnston D-6
Sistersville C-5
Slanesville C-8
Slate F-4
Smithers F-4
Smithfield C-5
Smithville D-5
Sophia G-4
South Charleston F-4
Spencer D-4
Springfield C-8
Stickney F-4
Summersville F-5
Sweetland F-3
Switzer G-3
Thomas D-7
Thornwood E-7
Troy D-5
Tunnelton D-7
Union G-5
Valley Bend E-6
Valley Head E-6
Van F-4
Vienna C-4
Walkersville D-6
Waneta E-6
War G-4
Washburn F-3
Wayne F-3
Webster Springs E-5
Weirton B-5
Welch G-4
Wellsburg B-5
W. Hamlin F-3
Weston D-6
Westover C-6
W. Union D-5
Wheeling B-5
White Sulphur Springs F-6
Whitesville F-4
Williamson G-3
Williamstown C-4
Wymer D-7

WISCONSIN
Pages 90-91

Abbotsford F-5
Adams H-5
Adell J-8
Algoma G-8
Alma G-2
Alma Center G-4
Almena F-2
Altoona G-3
Amery F-2
Aniwa F-6
Antigo F-6
Appleton G-7
Arcadia H-3
Argyle K-5
Arlington J-6
Ashland D-4
Ashwaubenon G-7
Athens F-5
Auburndale G-5
Augusta G-4
Avoca K-5
Baldwin F-2
Balsam Lake E-2
Bangor H-4
Baraboo J-5
Barneveld K-5
Barron F-3
Bay City G-2
Bayfield C-4
Bayside J-8
 Vicinity ..... Pg. 133, A-6
Beadstown J-4
Beaver Dam J-7
Belgium J-8
Belleville K-6
Belmont K-5
Beloit L-6
Benton K-5
Berlin H-6
Big Bend ..... ★
 Vicinity ..... Pg. 133, H-1
Birchwood E-3
Birnamwood F-6
Black Creek G-7
Black Earth K-5
Black River Falls G-4
Blair H-3
Blanchardville K-5
Bloomer F-3
Bloomington K-4
Bonduel G-7
Boscobel K-4
Boyceville F-2
Boyd F-4
Brandon J-7
Brillion H-8
Brodhead L-6
Brokaw F-6
Brookfield ..... ★
 Vicinity ..... Pg. 133, D-3
Brown Deer ..... ★
 Vicinity ..... Pg. 133, A-5
Browntown L-6
Bruce F-3
Buena Park ..... ★
 Vicinity ..... Pg. 133, K-1
Buffalo H-2
Burlington K-8
Butler ..... ★
 Vicinity ..... Pg. 133, C-3
Butternut D-5
Cable D-3
Caddy Vista ..... ★
 Vicinity ..... Pg. 133, J-6
Cadott F-3
Caledonia ..... ★
 Vicinity ..... Pg. 133, K-6
Calhoun ..... ★
 Vicinity ..... Pg. 133, E-3
Cambra J-6
Cambridge K-7
Cameron F-3
Camp Douglas H-5
Campbellsport J-8
Carrollville ..... ★
 Vicinity ..... Pg. 133, H-6
Cascade J-8
Casco G-8
Cashton J-4
Cassville K-4
Catawba E-4
Cazenovia J-5
Cecil G-7
Centuria E-1
Chetek F-3
Chilton H-8
Chippewa Falls F-3
Clayton F-2
Clear Lake F-2
Cleveland H-8
Clinton L-7
Clintonville G-7
Cochrane H-3
Colby G-5
Coleman F-8
Colfax F-3
Colgate ..... ★
 Vicinity ..... Pg. 133, A-1
Coloma H-6
Columbus J-7
Coon Valley J-4
Cornell F-4
Couderay E-3
Crandon E-7
Crivitz F-8
Cross Plains K-6
Cuba City L-4
Cudahy K-8
 Vicinity ..... Pg. 133, F-6
Cumberland E-2
Dane J-6
Darien L-7
Darlington K-5
De Pere G-8
De Soto J-4
DeForest J-6
Deerfield K-6
Delavan K-7
Denmark G-8
Dickeyville L-4
Dodgeville K-5
Dorchester F-5
Dousman K-7
Dresser F-1
Duplainville ..... ★
 Vicinity ..... Pg. 133, D-2
Durand G-2
Durham ..... ★
 Vicinity ..... Pg. 133, H-3
Eagle K-7
Eagle River E-6
East Troy K-7
Eastman K-4
Eau Claire G-3
Eden J-7
Edgar F-5
Edgerton K-6
Egg Harbor F-9
Elano F-6
Eleva G-3
Elk Mound G-3
Elkhart Lake H-8
Elkhorn K-7
Ellsworth G-2
Elm Grove ..... ★
 Vicinity ..... Pg. 133, D-3
Elmwood G-2
Elroy J-5
Embarrass G-7
Ephraim F-9
Ettrick H-3
Evansville K-6
Exeland E-3
Fairchild G-4
Fall Creek G-4
Fall River J-7
Fennimore K-4
Ferryville J-4
Fifield E-5
Florence E-7
Fond Du Lac H-7
Fontana L-7
Footville L-6
Forestville G-8
Fort Atkinson K-7
Fountain City H-3
Fox Lake J-7
Fox Point ..... ★
 Vicinity ..... Pg. 133, B-6
Francis Creek H-8
Franklin K-8
 Vicinity ..... Pg. 133, H-4
Franksville ..... ★
 Vicinity ..... Pg. 133, K-6
Frederick E-2
Fremont H-7
Friendship H-6
Fussville ..... ★
 Vicinity ..... Pg. 133, B-3
Galesville H-3
Gays Mills J-4
Genoa J-4
Genoa City L-8
Germantown J-8
 Vicinity ..... Pg. 133, A-3
Gillett G-8
Gilman F-4
Glen Flora E-4
Glendale ..... ★
 Vicinity ..... Pg. 133, B-6
Glenwood City F-2
Goerkes Corner ..... ★
 Vicinity ..... Pg. 133, D-2
Grafton J-8
Granton G-5
Grantsburg E-1
Granville ..... ★
 Vicinity ..... Pg. 133, A-4
Gratiot L-5
Green Bay G-8
Green Lake H-6
Greendale K-8
Greendale ..... ★
 Vicinity ..... Pg. 133, G-4
Greenfield ..... ★
 Vicinity ..... Pg. 133, F-5
Greenwood G-4
Gresham G-7
Hales Corners ..... ★
 Vicinity ..... Pg. 133, G-4
Hammond F-2
Hancock H-6
Hartford J-7
Hartland K-8
Haugen E-2
Hawkins E-4
Hayward E-3
Hazel Green L-4
Heafferd Jct. E-5
Highland K-5
Hilbert H-8
Hillsboro J-4
Holmen H-3
Horicon J-7
Hortonville G-7
Howard G-8
Howards Grove H-8
Hudson F-1
Hurley D-5
Husher ..... ★
 Vicinity ..... Pg. 133, J-6
Independence G-3
Ingram E-4
Iola G-6
Iron River C-3
Jackson J-8
Janesville K-6
Jefferson K-7
Johnson Creek K-7
Junction City G-5
Juneau J-7
Kaukauna H-8
Kendall H-5
Kennan E-5
Kenosha L-8
Keshena F-7
Kewaskum J-8
Kewaunee G-9
Kiel H-8
Kimberly H-8
Kingston J-6
Kneeland ..... ★
 Vicinity ..... Pg. 133, A-5
La Crosse H-3
La Farge J-4
Lac Du Flambeau D-5
Ladysmith E-3
Lake Delton J-5
Lake Geneva L-7
Lake Nebagamon D-3
Lancaster K-4
Lannon ..... ★
 Vicinity ..... Pg. 133, B-2
Lena K-5
Linden K-5
Little Chute G-7
Livingston K-4
Lodi J-6
Loganville J-5
Lomira J-7
Lone Rock J-5
Loyal G-4
Lublin F-4
Luck K-6
Luxemburg G-8
Madison K-6
Manawa G-7
Manitowish D-5
Manitowoc H-9
Marathon City F-5
Marcy ..... ★
 Vicinity ..... Pg. 133, C-2
Marinette F-8
Marion G-7
Markesan J-6
Marshall K-6
Marshfield G-5
Mason D-4
Mauston H-5
Mayville J-7
Mazomanie J-6
Medford F-4
Meeker ..... ★
 Vicinity ..... Pg. 133, A-2
Mellen D-4
Melrose H-4
Melvina H-4
Menasha H-7
Menomonie F-2
Menomonee Falls ..... ★
 Vicinity ..... Pg. 133, A-2
Menomonie G-2
Mequin ..... ★
Merrill F-5
Merrillan G-4
Middleton K-6
Milltown E-2
Milton K-7
Milwaukee K-8
 Vicinity ..... Pg. 133
Mineral Point K-5
Minong D-3
Mishicot H-8
Mondovi G-3
Monico E-6
Monona K-6
Monroe L-5
Montello H-6
Montfort K-5
Monticello K-6
Montreal D-4
Mosinee G-6
Mount Horeb K-6
Mount Sterling J-4
Mukwonago K-7
Muscoda K-4
Muskego K-8
 Vicinity ..... Pg. 133, G-2
Necedah H-5
Neenah H-7
Neillsville G-4
Nekoosa H-5
Nelson G-2
Nelsonville G-6
Neshkoro H-6
New Berlin K-8
 Vicinity ..... Pg. 133, E-2
New Glarus K-5
New Holstein H-8
New Lisbon H-5
New London G-7
New Richmond F-2
Niagara E-8
North Cape ..... ★
 Vicinity ..... Pg. 133, K-8
North Fond du Lac H-7
North Hudson F-1
Norwalk H-4
Oak Creek K-8
 Vicinity ..... Pg. 133, G-6
Oakwood ..... ★
 Vicinity ..... Pg. 133, H-6
Oconomowoc K-7
Oconto F-8
Oconto Falls G-8
Omro H-7
Onalaska H-3
Ontario J-4
Oostburg J-8
Orfordville K-6
Osceola F-1
Oshkosh H-7
Osseo G-3
Owen F-4
Oxford H-6
Paddock Lake L-8
Palmyra K-7
Pardeeville J-6
Park Falls E-4
Park Ridge G-6
Patch Grove K-4
Paynesville ..... ★
 Vicinity ..... Pg. 133, H-5
Pembine E-8
Pepin G-2
Peshtigo F-8
Pewaukee ..... ★
 Vicinity ..... Pg. 133, C-1
Phelps D-6
Phillips E-5
Pigeon Falls G-3
Pittsville G-5
Plain J-5
Plainfield H-6
Platteville K-4
Plover G-6
Plum City G-2
Plymouth H-8
Poplar C-3
Port Edwards H-5
Port Washington J-8
Portage K-6
Potosi K-4
Pound F-8
Prairie du Chien K-4
Prairie du Sac J-6
Prentice E-5
Prescott G-1
Princeton H-6
Prospect ..... ★
 Vicinity ..... Pg. 133, F-2
Pulaski G-7
Racine K-8
Radisson E-3
Randolph J-7
Rawson ..... ★
 Vicinity ..... Pg. 133
Raymond ..... ★
 Vicinity ..... Pg. 133, K-4
Redgranite H-6
Reedsburg J-5
Reedsville H-8
Rhinelander E-6
Rib Lake F-5
Rice Lake E-3
Richland Center J-5
Ridgeland F-2
Ridgeway K-5
Rio J-6
Ripon H-7
River Falls G-1
River Hills ..... ★
 Vicinity ..... Pg. 133, A-5
Riverside D-2
Roberts F-2
Rosendale H-7
Rosholt G-5
Rothschild G-5
Saint Croix Falls E-1
Saint Francis K-8
Saint Francis ..... ★
 Vicinity ..... Pg. 133, F-6
Saint Martins K-8
 Vicinity ..... Pg. 133, G-2
Sauk City J-5
Saukville J-8
Schofield F-6
Seymour G-7
Sharon L-7
Shawano G-7
Sheboygan H-9
Sheboygan Falls J-8
Sheldon F-3
Shell Lake E-2
Shiocton G-7
Shorewood ..... ★
 Vicinity ..... Pg. 133, C-7
Shullsburg L-5
Siren G-1
Sister Bay F-9
Soldiers Grove J-4
Solon Springs D-3
Somerset F-1
South Milwaukee K-8
 Vicinity ..... Pg. 133, G-6
Sparta H-4
Spencer G-4
Spooner E-3
Spring Green J-5
Spring Valley F-2
Stanley F-4
Stevens Point G-6
Stockbridge H-7
Stockholm G-2
Stoddard J-4
Stoughton K-6
Stratford G-5
Strum G-3
Sturgeon Bay F-8
Sturtevant K-8
Sun Prairie J-6
Superior C-2
Suring F-7
Sussex ..... ★
 Vicinity ..... Pg. 133, B-1
Tabor ..... ★
 Vicinity ..... Pg. 133, J-7
Taylors Falls E-1
Tennyson K-4
Tess Corners ..... ★
 Vicinity ..... Pg. 133, G-3
Theresa J-7
Thompsonville ..... ★
 Vicinity ..... Pg. 133, K-5
Thorp F-4
Tichigan ..... ★
 Vicinity ..... Pg. 133, J-1
Tigerton G-7
Tomah H-4
Tomahawk E-6
Tony F-4
Trempealeau H-3
Turtle Lake F-2
Two Rivers H-9
Union Center J-5
Union Church ..... ★
 Vicinity ..... Pg. 133, J-4
Union Grove K-8
Unity G-5
Valders H-8
Vernon ..... ★
 Vicinity ..... Pg. 133, G-1
Verona K-6
Vesper G-5
Village of Superior C-2
Viroqua J-4
Walworth L-7
Washburn C-3
Waterford K-7
 Vicinity ..... Pg. 133, K-1
Waterloo K-6
Watertown J-7
Waukesha K-7
 Vicinity ..... Pg. 133, E-1
Waunakee ..... ★
 Vicinity ..... Pg. 133, F-2
Waupaca G-7
Waupun J-7
Wausau F-6
Wausukee F-8
Wauwatosa K-8
 Vicinity ..... Pg. 133, D-4
Webster E-2
West Allis ..... ★
 Vicinity ..... Pg. 133, K-4
West Bend J-8
West Granville ..... ★
 Vicinity ..... Pg. 133, B-5
West Milwaukee ..... ★
 Vicinity ..... Pg. 133, E-5
Westby J-4
Westfield H-6
Weyauwega G-6
White Lake F-7
Whitefish Bay K-8
 Vicinity ..... Pg. 133, C-6
Whitehall G-3
Whitelaw H-8
Whitewater K-7
Whiting G-6
Wild Rose H-6
Willow Creek ..... ★
 Vicinity ..... Pg. 133, A-2
Wind Pt. K-8
Winneconne H-7
Winter E-4
Wisconsin Dells J-6
Wisconsin Rapids G-5
Withee F-4
Wittenberg G-6
Wonewoc J-5
Woodruff E-6
Wrightstown G-8
Wyeville H-5
Wyocena J-6
Yuba J-4

WYOMING
Pages 92-93

Acme B-8
Afton F-3
Aladdin B-12
Albany J-9
Albin H-12
Alcova F-9
Alpne Jct. E-3
Alva B-11
Arapahoe F-6
Arlington H-9
Arminto E-8
Arvada B-9
Atlantic City G-6
Auburn F-3
Baggs J-7
Bairoil G-8
Banner B-8
Bar Nunn F-9
Barnum D-8
Basin C-7
Beckton B-8
Bedford F-3
Beulah B-12
Big Horn B-8
Big Piney G-4
Big Sandy F-5
Big Trails D-8
Bill E-10
Bitter Creek H-6
Bondurant E-4
Border G-3
Bosler H-10
Boulder F-5
Boxelder F-10
Buffalo C-8
Burgess Jct. B-7
Burlington C-6
Burns J-12
Burntfork J-4
Burris E-5
Byron B-7
Calpet G-4
Canyon Jct. B-4
Carpenter J-12
Carter J-3
Casper F-9
Centennial J-9
Cheyenne J-11
Chugwater H-11
Clareton D-11
Clark B-5
Clearmont B-9
Cody C-5
Cokeville G-3
Colony B-12
Cora F-4
Cowley B-6
Creston Jct. H-7
Crowheart E-5
Daniel F-4
Dayton B-8
Deaver B-6
Devil's Tower Jct. B-11
Diamondville H-3
Dixon J-7
Douglas F-10
Dubois E-5
East Thermopolis D-7
Eden H-5
Edgerton E-9
Egbert J-12
Elk Basin B-6
Elk Mountain H-9
Elkol H-3
Elmo H-9
Emblem C-6
Encampment J-9
Ethete E-6
Etna F-3
Evanston J-3
Evansville F-9
Fairview F-3
Farson G-5
Federal J-11
Fort Bridger J-4
Fort Laramie G-11
Fort Washakie F-5
Four Corners C-12
Frannie B-6
Freedom F-3
Frontier H-4
Garland B-6
Gillette C-10
Glendo F-11
Glenrock F-10
Granger H-4
Grass Creek D-6
Green River H-5
Greybull C-7
Grover F-3
Guernsey G-11
Hamilton Dome D-6
Hampshire D-11
Hanna H-9
Hartville G-11
Hawk Springs H-12
Hiland E-8
Hillsdale J-12
Hobock Jct. E-3
Horse Creek J-11
Hudson F-6
Hulett B-11
Huntley G-12
Hyattville C-8
Iron Mountain H-11
Jackson E-3
Jay Em G-12
Jeffrey City G-7
Jenny Lake D-3
Kaycee D-8
Keeline F-11
Kelly E-3
Kemmerer H-3
Kinnear E-5
Kirby D-7
La Barge G-4
La Grange H-12
Lake Jct. B-4
Lamont G-8
Lance Creek E-11
Lander F-6
Laramie J-10
Leiter B-9
Lightning Flat B-11
Linch D-9
Lingle G-12
Little America J-4
Lonetree J-4
Lost Cabin E-8
Lost Springs F-11
Lovell B-6
Lucerne D-7
Lusk F-12
Lyman J-4
Lysite E-7
Madison Jct. B-3
Mammoth Springs Jct. B-3
Manderson C-7
Manville F-11
Marbleton F-4
Mayoworth D-8
McFadden H-10
McKinnon K-4
Medicine Bow H-9
Meeteese C-6
Merna F-4
Midwest E-9
Millburne J-4
Mills F-9
Moneta E-7
Moorcroft C-11
Moose D-3
Moran Jct. D-4
Morrisey D-11
Morton E-6
Mountain Home J-10
Mountain View J-4
Mule Cr. Jct. E-12
Natrona E-9
New Haven B-11
Newcastle D-12
Node F-12
Norris Jct. B-3
Old Faithful C-3
Opal H-4
Orin F-11
Orpha F-10
Osage D-12
Oshoto B-11
Otto C-7
Parkman B-8
Pavillion E-6
Piedmont J-4
Pine Bluffs J-12
Pine Tree Jct. D-10
Pinedale F-5
Pitchfork C-6
Point of Rocks H-6
Powder River F-8
Powell B-6
Quealy J-5
Ralston B-6
Ranchester B-8
Rawlins H-8
Recluse B-10
Red Desert H-7
Redbird E-12
Reliance H-6
Reno Jct. D-10
Riverside J-9
Riverton F-7
Robertson J-4
Rochelle D-11
Rock River H-10
Rock Springs H-5
Rocky Point B-11
Rozet C-10
Sage H-3
Saint Stephens F-6
Saratoga J-9
Savageton D-10
Savery J-8
Shawnee F-11
Shell C-7
Sheridan B-8
Shirley Basin G-9
Shoshoni E-7
Sinclair H-8
Slater H-11
Smoot F-3
South Pass City G-6
Spotted Horse B-10
Story C-8
Sundance C-12
Sunrise G-11
Superior H-6
Sussex D-9
Table Rock H-7
Ten Sleep D-8
Teton Village D-3
Thayne F-3
Thermopolis D-6
Tie Siding J-10
Torrington G-12
Tower Jct. B-4
Turnerville F-3
Ucross C-9
Upton C-11
Urie J-4
Valley C-5
Van Tassell F-12
Veteran G-12
Walcott H-9
Waltman E-8
Wamsutter H-7
West Thumb Jct. C-3
Weston B-10
Wheatland G-11
Wilson E-3
Woods Landing J-10
Worland D-7
Wright D-10
Yoder H-12

★ Denotes City only on Vicinity map. City not located on State map.